AMSCO®

ADVANCED PLACEMENT EDITION

WORLD HISTORY:

MODERN [1200–PRESENT]

Senior Reviewers

Phil Cox
AP® World History Table Leader
Broad Run High School
Ashburn, Virginia

David L. Drzonek
AP® World History Teacher
Carl Sandburg High School
Orland Park, Illinois

Charles Hart
AP® World History Exam Table Leader
Westmont High School
Westmont, Illinois

John Maunu
AP® World History Exam Table Leader
Cranbrook/Kingswood High School
Bloomfield Hills, Michigan

Writers and Reviewers

Jody Janis
AP® European History Teacher
J. Frank Dobie High School
Houston, Texas

David Brian Lasher
AP® World History Exam Reader
Northwest Pennsylvania Collegiate
    Academy
Erie, Pennsylvania

Amie La Porte-Lewis
AP® World History Exam Table Leader
Holy Innocents' Episcopal School
Atlanta, Georgia

Kevin Lewis
AP® World History Exam Table Leader
Holy Innocents' Episcopal School
Atlanta, Georgia

Jamie Oleson
AP® World History Teacher
Rogers High School
Spokane, Washington

James Sabathne
AP® World History Teacher and Former
    Chair of the AP® U.S. History
    Test Development Committee
Hononegah Community High School
Rockton, Illinois

Thomas J. Sakole
AP® World History Exam Question and
    Exam Leader
Riverside High School
Leesburg, Virginia

Clara Webb
AP® European History Exam Table
    Leader
Boston Latin School
Boston, Massachusetts

AMSCO®

ADVANCED PLACEMENT® EDITION

WORLD HISTORY:
MODERN [1200–PRESENT]

PERFECTION LEARNING®

Advanced Placement® and AP® are trademarks registered
and/or owned by the College Board, which was not involved
in the production of, and does not endorse, this product.

© 2022 Perfection Learning®

Please visit our website at:
www.perfectionlearning.com

When ordering this book, please specify:
Softcover: ISBN 978-1-6636-7440-1 or **T887501**
eBook: ISBN 978-1-6636-7441-8 or **T8875D**

All rights reserved. No part of this book may be reproduced, stored in a retrieval
system, or transmitted in any form or by any means, electronic, mechanical,
photocopying, recording, or otherwise, without the prior permission of the
publisher. For information regarding permissions, write to:
Permissions Department, Perfection Learning,
2680 Berkshire Parkway, Des Moines, Iowa 50325.

16 17 18 19 20 21 22 23   MS   29 28 27 26 25 24

Printed in the United States of America

Contents

PERIOD 1: c. 1200 to c. 1450

PERIOD 2: c. 1450 to c. 1750

PERIOD 3: c. 1750 to c. 1900

PERIOD 4: c. 1900 to Present

Introduction

Advanced Placement® courses can be challenging and demanding and you already have a lot of pressures in high school. So why take an AP® course like this one in world history? A growing number of students are enrolling in AP® classes because they realize the many benefits they provide, including:

- They are a great preparation for college. AP® courses require independent work, like research and analysis, and you have to cover a lot of material in a short time. Taking college level courses can help ease the transition from high school to college.

- They strengthen your college application. College admissions officers value how AP® courses show that you are ready for college level work. They indicate that you are serious about education and are able to handle a challenge.

- They can increase your chance of getting scholarship aid. Nearly one-third of colleges consider AP® work when deciding on who will get academic merit assistance.

- They save time and money. Getting college credit for classes will enable you to graduate sooner. This saves not only on tuition, but on room and board, and living expenses.

- They are associated with greater college success. Students who take AP® courses and exams have a higher likelihood than other students of academic achievement and completing college on time.

- They provide greater flexibility in college. With basic coursework handled through AP® credit, you will be free to explore elective studies, study abroad and still graduate on time, and add variety to your academic plan.

Advanced Placement® classes are a good choice whatever your academic goals are–getting into college, saving time and money, and succeeding in and enjoying your college career. The placement and credits offered will vary from college to college. The College Board's website provides a comprehensive list of colleges and universities that accept AP® examinations and the credits they award for passing scores. The rewards of taking on the challenges of an AP® program go beyond the scores and placement. They include the development of lifelong reading, reasoning, and writing skills, as well as an increased enjoyment of history.

This introduction will help you understand the structure, content organization, and question types of the AP® World History: Modern exam.

Overview of the AP® World History Exam

This textbook was created to help you learn world history at the level assessed on the AP® World History: Modern exam. The exam emphasizes the historical thinking skills used by historians such as analyzing primary and secondary sources, making connections between ideas, and developing historical arguments. It asks students to apply three reasoning processes: explaining comparisons, explaining causation, and explaining continuity and change. The AP® World History: Modern exam is 3 hours and 15 minutes long. The details of the exam, including exam weighting and timing, are outlined below:

Section	Question Type	Number of Questions	Exam Weighting	Timing
I	**Part A** **Multiple-Choice Questions**	55	40%	55 minutes
	Part B **Short-Answer Questions** • Question 1: Secondary source(s) • Question 2: Primary source *Students select one of the following:* • Question 3: No stimulus • Question 4: No stimulus	3	20%	40 minutes
II	**Free-Response Questions**	2		
	Document-Based Question • Question 1		25%	60 minutes (includes 15-minute reading period)
	Long Essay Question *Students select one of the following:* • Question 2 • Question 3 • Question 4		15%	40 minutes

Source: Adapted from AP® World History: Modern Course and Exam Description

AP® Scoring

Each of these exam components will be explained in this introduction. AP® exams score student performance on a five-point scale:

- 5: Extremely well qualified
- 4: Well-qualified performance
- 3: Qualified
- 2: Possibly qualified
- 1: No recommendation

An AP® score of 3 or higher is usually considered evidence of mastery of course content similar to that demonstrated in a college-level introductory course in the same subject area. However, the requirements of introductory courses may vary from college to college. Many schools require a 4 or a 5.

The AP® exams are built differently than typical classroom tests. For example, the developers of the AP® exams want to generate a wider distribution of scores. They also want higher reliability, which means a higher likelihood that test takers repeating the same exam will receive the same scores. In addition, AP® exams are scored differently. The cutoff for a "qualified," or level 3, score varies from year to year depending on how well a group of college students who take the test do on it.

The writers of the AP® exam also design it to be more difficult. If you take a practice exam before you have fully prepared for the test, don't be surprised if you have difficulty with many of the questions. More importantly, don't be discouraged. AP® World History: Modern is challenging. But like many challenges, it can be mastered by breaking it down into manageable steps.

How This Book Can Help

The goal of this textbook is to provide you with the essential content and instructional materials based on the *AP® World History: Modern Course and Exam Description* (released Fall 2023) needed to develop the knowledge and the historical reasoning and writing skills needed for success on the exam. You can find these in the following parts of the book:

- Introduction This section introduces the thinking skills and reasoning processes, six course themes, and nine units of the course. A step-by-step skill development guide provides instruction for answering (1) the multiple-choice questions, (2) the short-answer questions, (3) the document-based essay question, and (4) the long essay question.

- Concise History The nine units, divided into 72 topics of essential historical content and accessible explanation of events, are the heart of the book. Each unit begins with an overview that sets the context for the events in the unit and a list of the learning objectives covered in each topic.

- Maps and Graphics Maps, charts, graphs, cartoons, photographs, and other visual materials are also integrated into the text to help students practice analytical skills.

- Historical Perspectives Each unit includes a section that introduces significant historical issues and conflicting interpretations.

- Key Terms by Themes To assist reviewing, each topic ends with a list of key terms organized by theme.

- Multiple-Choice Questions Each topic contains one set of three multiple-choice questions to assess your historical knowledge and skills using a variety of sources.

- Short-Answer Questions Each topic contains two short-answer questions to provide practice writing succinct responses.

- Document-Based Questions Each unit includes one DBQ for practice.

- Long Essay Questions Each unit contains long essay questions based on each of the reasoning processes.

- Practice Examination Following the final unit, the book includes a complete practice examination.

- Index. The index is included to help locate key terms for review.

A separate Answer Key is available for teachers and other authorized users of the book and can be accessed through the publisher's website.

The Study of AP® World History: Modern

Historians attempt to give meaning to the past by collecting historical evidence and then explaining how this information is connected. They interpret and organize a wide variety of evidence from primary sources and secondary texts to understand the past. AP® World History: Modern should develop a student's ability to think like a historian: to analyze and use evidence, and to deal with probing questions about events, individuals, developments, and processes from 1200 to the present. Often there is no one "answer" for historical questions any more than one historical source can provide a complete answer for a question. Rather, AP® teachers and readers are looking for the student's ability to think about history and to support ideas with evidence.

AP® candidates should appreciate how both participants in history and historians differ among themselves in their interpretations of critical questions in world history. Each unit of this book includes a Historical Perspectives feature to introduce some of the issues raised and debated by historians. The AP® World History: Modern exam does not require an advanced knowledge of historiography—the study of ways historians have constructed their accounts of the past—which some refer to as "the history of history." Nevertheless, prior knowledge of the richness of historical thought can add depth to your analysis of historical questions.

Students planning to take the AP® World History: Modern exam also need to become familiar with and then practice the development of 1) historical thinking skills, 2) the reasoning processes to apply when engaging in historical study, 3) thematic analysis, and 4) the concepts and understandings of the nine units that provide the organization of the course content. These four course components are explained below for orientation and future reference.

Don't become overwhelmed with this introduction, or try to comprehend all the finer points of taking the AP® exam in the first few days or weeks of studying. Mastery of these skills and understanding takes time and is an ongoing part of the study of AP® history. This introduction will become more helpful as a reference after you have studied some historical content and have begun to tackle actual assignments.

The Historical Thinking Skills and Reasoning Processes

Advanced Placement® history courses encourage students to become "apprentice historians." The College Board, which creates the AP® exams, has identified six historical thinking skills and three historical reasoning processes for this course. Every question on the exam will require you to apply one or more of these skills or processes. Questions and features at the end of each topic and unit provide frequent opportunities to use them.

Historical Thinking Skills

Throughout the AP® World History: Modern course, students develop the complex skills that historians exhibit, and benefit from multiple opportunities to acquire these skills. These six skills are:

1. Identify and explain **historical developments and processes.** This involves, based on the historical evidence, identifying the characteristics and traits of a historical concept, development, or process. Using specific historical evidence, it requires explaining how and why a historical concept, development, or process emerged.

2. Analyze **sourcing and situation** of primary and secondary sources. This requires identifying the point of view, purpose, historical situation, or audience of a historical source and describing its significance and limitations.

3. Analyze **claims and evidence** in primary and secondary sources. This involves identifying what a source is trying to prove and the evidence used to support the argument, comparing the arguments of at least two sources, and explaining how the evidence affects the argument.

4. Analyze the **context** of historical events, developments, or processes. This entails identifying and explaining how a specific historical development or process fits within a historical context.

5. Using historical reasoning processes (comparison, causation, continuity and change), analyze patterns and **connections** between and among historical developments and processes. This skill allows students to connect all concepts by identifying patterns among historical developments and processes and explaining how one historical development or process relates to another one.

6. Develop an **argument**. This requires: making a historically defensible claim; supporting an argument with evidence; using historical reasoning to explain relationships within pieces of evidence; and corroborating, qualifying or modifying an argument.

Historical Reasoning Processes

Historical reasoning processes are taught in AP® World History: Modern and tested on the exam. These are the basic cognitive methods that historians use to understand the past and connect with the historical thinking skills. They include:

1. **Comparison** This skill is the ability to describe, compare, contrast, and evaluate two or more historical events or developments in the same or different eras or periods, or in the same or different locations. It requires an ability to identify, compare, contrast, and evaluate a given historical event or development from multiple perspectives.

2. **Causation** This skill is the ability to identify, analyze, and evaluate the relationships among many historical events and developments as both causes and effects. Not all causes and effects are equally important. A key task of a historian is to determine which causes and effects are primary, and which are secondary. Showing persuasive evidence of causation is difficult. Many events are simply correlated, which means they occur at the same time or one occurs right after the other, but there is no persuasive evidence that one caused the other.

3. **Continuity and Change over Time** This skill is the ability to recognize, analyze, and evaluate the dynamics of history over periods of time of varying lengths, often investigating important patterns that emerge. The study of themes in history (explained later in this introduction) is often the tool of choice to understand continuity and change over time.

Course Themes

Each AP® World History: Modern exam question is also related to one or more of six course themes. The strong focus on these six themes and related concepts will help you think about the main ideas and deepen your understanding of world history. They help identify trends and processes that have developed throughout centuries in different parts of the world:

1. **Humans and the Environment** The environment shapes human societies, and as populations grow and change, these populations in turn shape their environments.

2. **Cultural Developments and Interactions** The development of ideas, beliefs, and religions illustrates how groups in society view themselves, and the interactions of societies and their beliefs often have political, social, and cultural implications.

3. **Governance** A variety of internal and external factors contribute to state formation, expansion, and decline. Governments maintain order through a variety of administrative institutions, policies, and procedures, and governments obtain, retain, and exercise power in different ways and for different purposes.

4. **Economic Systems** As societies develop, they affect and are affected by the ways that they produce, exchange, and consume goods and services.

5. **Social Interactions and Organization** The process by which societies group their members, and the norms that govern the interactions between these groups and between individuals, influence political, economic, and cultural institutions and organizations.

6. **Technology and Innovation** Human adaptation and innovation have resulted in increased efficiency, comfort, and security, and technological advances have shaped human development and interactions with both intended and unintended consequences.

Source: Adapted from AP® World History: Modern Course and Exam Description

Understanding and applying the themes will enable you to make connections across units (explained below) and to think about broad historical ideas and trends.

Course Units

The AP® World History: Modern course is divided into nine units that are arranged in a sequence frequently used in college texts. Chronological periods are covered in two or three specific units although the dates are not intended to be limiting. Events, processes, and developments may begin before, or continue after, the dates assigned to each unit. Each unit will include examining the topics using historical thinking skills and reasoning processes. The units are further broken down into topics. The nine historical units are:

- The Global Tapestry (c. 1200 to c. 1450) This unit's topics address developments in East Asia, Dar al-Islam, South and Southeast Asia, and Europe, and state building in the Americas, as well as comparisons of these various developments.

- Networks of Exchange (c. 1200 to c. 1450) This unit's topics address important trade and cultural interchange developments including the Silk Roads, the Mongol Empire, and the Indian Ocean and trans-Saharan trade. The unit discusses the cultural and environmental consequences of these exchanges and suggests economic comparisons of the various networks.

- Land-Based Empires (c. 1450 to c. 1750) This unit describes and compares the expansion, administration and belief systems of various land-based empires.

- Transoceanic Interconnections (c. 1450 to c. 1750) This unit includes: the technological innovations of that time; the causes and events connected to exploration in that period; the trade of natural resources, populations, technology, and diseases between the Americas, Europe, and Africa after Columbus' explorations; and the establishment, maintenance and development of maritime empires. It addresses challenges to state power and changes in social hierarchies and focuses on a discussion of continuity and change during this period.

- Revolutions (c. 1750 to c. 1900) This unit first deals with the Enlightenment, nationalism, and revolutions during this period. It then focuses on the Industrial Revolution: its beginnings, spread, and the associated technologies. The unit further addresses the role of governments, economic developments, reactions to the industrial economy, and societal changes in the age of industrialization. Finally, it concentrates on examining continuity and change during this period.

- Consequences of Industrialization (c. 1750 to c. 1900) This unit addresses the rationales for imperialism and describes the state expansion at that time, as well as the indigenous populations' response to it. Global economic development and imperialism are topics, and the causes and effects of migration are discussed. This unit emphasizes causation as an essential reasoning process in historical analysis.

- Global Conflict (c. 1900 to the Present) This unit examines the global power shifts after 1900 and the causes and conduct of World War I. It explores the economy between the two world wars, the tensions following World War I, and the causes and conduct of World War II. The unit also discusses the mass atrocities after 1900 and examines causation in global conflict.

- Cold War and Decolonization (c. 1900 to the Present) This unit begins with the antecedents of the Cold War and decolonization. It discusses the period of the Cold War, its effects, and its end. It addresses the spread of communism and decolonization, including resistance to established power structures and newly independent states. It finally focuses on causation in this period.

- Globalization (c. 1900 to the Present) This unit examines advances and limitations of technology after 1900. It considers economics in the global age as well as the calls for reform. Globalized culture and institutions are addressed and the resistance to globalization is reviewed. The final topic emphasizes continuity and change in the era of globalization.

The following table specifies the weight given to each unit in the AP® exam.

Unit	Chronological Period	Exam Weighting
Unit 1: The Global Tapestry	c. 1200 to c. 1450	8–10%
Unit 2: Networks of Exchange	c. 1200 to c. 1450	12–15%
Unit 3: Land-Based Empires	c. 1450 to c. 1750	12–15%
Unit 4: Transoceanic Interconnections	c. 1450 to c. 1750	12–15%
Unit 5: Revolutions	c. 1750 to c. 1900	12–15%
Unit 6: Consequences of Industrialization	c. 1750 to c. 1900	12–15%
Unit 7: Global Conflict	c. 1900 to the present	8–10%
Unit 8: Cold War and Decolonization	c. 1900 to the present	8–10%
Unit 9: Globalization	c. 1900 to the present	8–10%

Source: Adapted from AP® World History: Modern Course and Exam Description

Answering the AP® Exam Questions

History, like any field of study, is a combination of subject matter and methodology. The history thinking skills, reasoning processes, and themes are methods or tools to explore the subject matter of history. One cannot practice these skills without knowledge of the historical content and understanding of specific historical evidence.

The following section provides suggestions for development of another set of skills useful for answering the questions on the AP® exam. Again, the "mastery" of these skills, particularly writing answers to AP® questions, takes practice. This section will suggest how to develop the skills related to each different kind of question on the exam:

- multiple-choice questions
- short-answer questions
- document-based questions
- long essay questions

The AP® exam assesses six historical thinking skills.

Historical Thinking Skill	Multiple-Choice Questions	Free-Response Questions
Skill 1: Developments and Processes	Multiple-choice questions assess students' ability to identify and explain historical developments and processes.	The short-answer questions, document-based question, and long essay question assess students' ability to identify and explain historical developments and processes.
Skill 2: Sourcing and Situation	Multiple-choice questions assess students' ability to analyze sourcing and situation of primary and secondary sources. Students will need to identify and explain a source's point of view, purpose, historical situation and audience, including its significance. Additionally, students will need to explain how the sourcing and situation might limit the use(s) of a source.	Short-answer questions 1 and/or 2 assess students' ability to analyze the sourcing or situation in primary or secondary sources. The document-based question assesses students' ability to analyze how the point of view, purpose, historical situation, and/or audience is relevant to an argument.
Skill 3: Claims and Evidence in Sources	Multiple-choice questions assess students' ability to analyze arguments in primary and secondary sources, including identifying and describing claims and evidence used. Additionally, students will need to compare arguments and explain how claims or evidence support, modify, or refute a source's argument.	Short-answer questions 1 and/or 2 assess students' ability to analyze arguments in primary or secondary sources. The document-based question also provides opportunities for students to analyze arguments in primary sources.
Skill 4: Contextualization	Multiple-choice questions assess students' ability to identify and describe a historical context for a specific historical development or process as well as explain how a specific development or process is situated within a broader historical context.	The document-based question and long essay question assess students' ability to describe a broader historical context relevant to the topic of the question. One or two of the short-answer questions may also assess this skill.
Skill 5: Making Connections	Multiple-choice questions assess students' ability to analyze patterns and connections between and among historical developments and processes using historical reasoning (e.g., comparison, causation, continuity and change).	The document-based question, long essay question, and one or more of the short-answer questions all assess this skill.
Skill 6: Argumentation	No multiple-choice questions explicitly assess the argumentation skill.	The document-based question and long essay question assess argumentation.

Source: AP® World History: Modern Course and Exam Description

Section I: Part A—Multiple-Choice Questions (MCQs)

The College Board asks 55 multiple-choice questions on the AP® World History: Modern exam, and students have 55 minutes to complete this section. Questions will be related to the analysis of a stimulus—a primary or secondary source, such as a passage, image, map, or table. Each question will have one best answer and three distracters. The questions will emphasize the student's ability to analyze the source and use the historical reasoning skill the question requires. This textbook provides preparation for the multiple-choice questions section of the exam through items at the end of each topic and on the Practice Exam at the end of the book. The MCQs in this book are similar in form and purpose to those appearing on the AP® exam but are also designed to review the content and understanding of the topic. A plan of action for answering multiple choice questions consists of several steps:

- Analyzing the Stimulus On the AP® exam, multiple-choice questions will be introduced with a stimulus. When analyzing a stimulus, ask yourself basic questions to spark your thinking: Who? What? When? Where? and Why? Beyond these questions, one of the most important questions to ask is, "What is the point of view of the author, artist, or speaker?" The multiple-choice questions about an excerpt will test your understanding of it. In addition, the questions will focus on one or more historical thinking skills.

- Making a Choice You need to read the stem (the question or statement before the choices of possible answers) and all four choices carefully before you choose your answer. More than one choice may appear to be correct at first, but only one will be the best answer. If you are confident which answer is best, eliminate answers you recognize as incorrect. Choices that include words that reflect absolute positions, such as always or never are seldom correct, since historical evidence can rarely support such clarity. Make judgments about the significance of a variety of causes and effects. Since the exam format does not deduct for incorrect answers, you get no penalty for guessing wrong. So you should answer every question. Obviously, though, the process of first eliminating a wrong answer or two before guessing increases your chances of choosing the correct answer.

- Budgeting Your Time The exam allows 55 minutes to answer the 55 questions. Fifty-five minutes does not allow enough time to spend 2 or 3 minutes on difficult questions. For questions involving a passage, chart, or picture, read the question first. If you find a question is hard, make a guess and then come back to it later if you have time.

Recommended Activities Practicing sample multiple-choice questions is important before the exam, if for no reason other than to reduce the number of surprises about the format of the questions. However, for many students, the review of content through multiple-choice questions is not the most productive way to prepare for the exam. The purpose of the chapter content in this text is to provide a useful and meaningful review of the essential concepts and evidence needed for the exam. By reviewing the essential facts in the historical content, you will better recall and understand connections between events, which is extremely important for applying the historical reasoning skills.

Section I: Part B—Short-Answer Questions (SAQs)

The AP® World History: Modern exam will include four SAQs. No thesis is required in the SAQ answers. You will have 40 minutes to answer three of them. Each question consists of three parts, labeled A, B, and C.

- Short-answer question 1 is required and includes a secondary source stimulus. The topic of the question will include historical developments or processes between the years 1200 and 2001.

- Short-answer question 2 is required and includes a primary source stimulus. The topic of the question will include historical developments or processes between the years 1200 and 2001.

- Students may select either short-answer question 3 or 4, neither of which includes a stimulus. Short-answer question 3 will focus on historical developments or processes between the years 1200 and 1750. Short-answer question 4 will focus on historical developments or processes between the years 1750 and 2001.

Section II: Free Response Questions— Document-Based Question (DBQ)

The exam includes one document-based question (DBQ) that includes seven documents. The topic of the DBQ will include historical developments or processes between the years 1450 and 2001. The answer should do the following:

- Respond to the prompt with a historically defensible thesis or claim that establishes a line of reasoning.

- Describe a broader historical context relevant to the prompt.

- Use the provided documents to support an argument in response to the prompt.

- Use historical evidence beyond the documents relevant to an argument about the prompt.

- For at least two documents, explain how or why the document's point of view, purpose, historical situation, and/or audience is relevant to an argument.

- Demonstrate a complex understanding of the historical developments through the effective use of evidence that makes an argument addressing the question.

Source: AP® World History: Modern Course and Exam Description

In short, you should state a clear thesis and provide support for it from the documents. To receive a top score, you will need to refer to at least six of the documents in your analysis. To strengthen the probability of earning the maximum point value for this question, however, use all seven documents. In addition, you should analyze one or more of these elements of three documents:

- the creator's point of view
- the creator's purpose
- the historical situation when the document was produced
- the intended audience for the document

Some teachers refer to this analysis of the elements as "sourcing" the document. Earning credit for sourcing a document requires more than a simple statement such as "The intended audience is the elite class." You will also need to state the significance of this analysis. In other words, give a reason or further explanation of the significance for the point of view, purpose, historical situation, or intended audience. To determine significance, ask yourself, "What is the creator's point of view?" "Why did the creator produce the document?" "In what historical situation was the document created?" "What audience was the creator addressing?" The answers to these questions are often overlapping.

Besides using evidence stated in the documents, you should include outside knowledge in your response. This consists of additional examples, details, and analysis that provide context or clarify what is in the documents or that provide new information that supports your thesis. Answering a DBQ builds on the skills for writing responses to the essay questions. (These are discussed in more detail in the following section on the long essay question.) The same skills apply here:

- Write a thesis statement that addresses all parts of the question.
- Provide historical context for your argument.
- Build argumentation supported by relevant specific evidence.
- Use the historical thinking skill targeted in the question.
- Use evidence in a compelling way.

The most important difference between a DBQ response and a long essay is that your DBQ response should refer to specific sources to support arguments. A common mistake writers make in answering a DBQ is to write little more than a descriptive list of the documents. The order of the documents in the DBQ should not control the organization of the essay. Rather, group the documents based upon how they support your thesis. Analyze the documents for evidence they provide, and integrate them into an organized and persuasive essay.

In a strong essay, a writer groups pieces of evidence from the documents that relate to each other. However, grouping requires more than simply placing related evidence within the same paragraph. It also requires seeing commonalities and contradictions in the evidence, and explaining how they both fit your argument. Words and phrases such as *similarly, in addition*, and *as well as* alert the reader that you see a common element among the documents. Phrases such as *in contrast to* or *this is different from* alert the reader that you see contradictory evidence in the documents.

Use the practice DBQs to develop your historical reasoning skills as well as the writing skills needed for answering the DBQ on the exam. Here are some tips for writing an effective DBQ:

1. Use the 15-minute reading period to make marginal notes on the documents. Underline key parts of the prompt to help keep you on track. Before writing, formulate a thesis that addresses all parts of the question.

2. Keep references to the documents brief. Because the exam readers know the content of the documents, you do not need to quote them. A reference to the document's author or title is enough. Many writers simply cite the document number in parentheses, such as (Doc. 1). Readers like this system as well because it is simple and clear.

3. Use all of the documents. However, recognize that each document represents a point of view, and some might contain information that is not accurate.

4. Address contradictory evidence. Your thesis should be complex enough to account for evidence that does not support your argument, and you should demonstrate that you understand other points of view and the context in which documents were created. Demonstrate your judgment about the sources based on your knowledge of the historical period.

Recommended Activities As a prewriting activity for the DBQs, work with a small group of classmates to read and discuss a contemporary primary source document and two historical ones. For each, discuss the author's point of view, intended audience, purpose, and historical context. Following is a practice scoring guide for DBQs based on the College Board's grading rubric. (Check apcentral.collegeboard.com for the full rubric and any updates.) Use this guide to evaluate your work and to internalize the criteria for writing a strong DBQ essay.

Scoring Guide for a Document-Based Question Answer

A. Thesis/Claim: 0–1 Point

❑ 1 point for a historically defensible thesis/claim that establishes a line of reasoning to address the question and does not merely restate it. The thesis must be at least one sentence and located in one place, either in the introduction or in the conclusion.

B. Contextualization: 0–1 Point

❑ 1 point to describe the broader historical context of the question, such as developments either before, during, or after its time frame. Describing the context requires more than a mere phrase or reference.

C. Evidence: 0–3 Points

Evidence from the Documents: 0–2 Points

❑ 1 point for accurately describing the content of three documents that address the question.

OR (Either the 1 point above or the 2 points below, but not both.)

❑ 2 points for accurately using the content of four documents to support the arguments used in response to the question. Using the documents requires more than simply quoting them.

Evidence Beyond the Documents: 0–1 Point

❑ 1 point for using at least one additional piece of specific historical evidence beyond those found in the documents that is relevant to the arguments for the question. The evidence must be different from evidence used for the contextualization point and more than a mere phrase.

D. Analysis and Reasoning: 0–2 Points (Unlike the LEQ scoring, both points can be gained)

❑ 1 point for using at least two documents to explain how or why the document's point of view, purpose, historical situation, and/or audience is relevant to an argument used to address the question.

❑ 1 point for demonstrating a complex understanding of the historical developments by analyzing the multiple variables in the evidence, such as causes or effects, similarities or differences, continuities or changes, and connections across geographic areas or across periods. Additionally, this point can be earned by using seven documents to support an argument, sourcing four documents, or using evidence to demonstrate a sophisticated understanding of different perspectives.

Source: AP® World History: Modern Course and Exam Description

Section II: Free Response Questions
Long Essay Questions (LEQs)

In forty minutes, test takers will answer one of three questions with a long essay. All three options focus on the same reasoning process, but on historical developments and processes in different time periods. The first period is from 1200 to 1750, the second from 1450 to 1900 and the third from 1750 to 2001.

Before you begin to write, take a few minutes to identify key points and plan the structure of your essay. Your essay responses will be evaluated on the argument you present. It is important to provide a clear thesis and support it with evidence.

Development of Essay Writing Skills

Begin developing your writing skills as soon as the course starts. Rather than simply writing and rewriting complete essays, break down the skills needed to write an effective AP® history essay into sequential steps and work on one of them at a time. Following are basic steps in writing an essay:

- Analyze the question.
- Organize the evidence.
- Take a position and express it in a thesis and introductory paragraph.
- Write the supporting paragraphs and conclusion.
- Evaluate the essay.

1. **Analyze the Question** Some students rush to start writing and fail to grasp the question fully. Before writing, ask yourself two questions:
   - What is the topic?
   - What is the historical reasoning skill?

Read over the question or prompt two or more times. What are the key words or phrases in the question? Underline them. They could be verbs such as *evaluate, analyze, explain, support,* or *refute.* All questions have one thing in common: They demand the use of historical reasoning skills and analysis of the evidence. An essay answer will not receive full credit by simply reporting information: You need to demonstrate that you can use the targeted historical reasoning skill.

An essay that fails to deal with all parts of the question will receive a lower score than one that addresses the entire question. The few seconds you take to identify the topic and key reasoning process will help you avoid the mistake of writing a clear, information-rich essay that receives little or no credit because you answered a question that was not asked.

Recommended Activity As an initial skill-building activity, analyze essay questions provided throughout this book. Underline the key words that indicate what the writer should do, and circle the words that indicate the specific parts or aspects of the content that need to be addressed.

2. **Organize the Evidence** Directions for the AP® World History: Modern exam advise students to spend some time planning before starting to answer the essay question. This advice emphasizes how critical it is to first identify what you know about the question and then organize your information. A recommended practice is to spend five minutes to create a brief outline, table, or other graphic organizer summarizing what you know about the question.

Recommended Activity Practice identifying the type of evidence you will need to answer questions by creating an outline, table, Venn diagram, or other graphic organizer for a provided sample essay question.

3. **State Your Thesis in the Introductory Paragraph** After you organize the evidence that you know, you can write a thesis statement that you can support. A strong thesis, or argument, is an essential part of every long essay answer. Writers usually state the thesis in the first paragraph and they often restate it in the final paragraph.

A thesis must be more than a restatement of the question. A thesis requires taking a position on the question. In other words, it must be evaluative. Many students have difficulty taking a position necessary to build a strong argument. Sometimes they are afraid of making a mistake or taking a position they think the readers will disagree with. But think about the nature of history. History does not offer the certitude of mathematics or the physical sciences. Disagreement over the interpretation of historical evidence develops because of the limitations of the evidence available and the differing perspectives of both participants and historians. AP® readers are looking not for the "right answer" but for a writer's ability to interpret the evidence and use historical support for that interpretation. If you think that you can write an essay without making some judgment that results in a thesis statement, you have not understood the question.

Recommended Activity Work with one or two partners. Each of you should write a prompt that might appear on a test based on a current event in the news. Exchange prompts. Then write a thesis statement in response to your partner's prompt. Compare and discuss your thesis statements using these guide questions:

- Does the thesis take a position?
- Does the thesis offer an interpretation of the question?
- Does the thesis help organize ideas for an essay?

The main point of the first paragraph is to state clearly a thesis that addresses the question. Readers will look for a clear thesis that sets the organization for the rest of the essay. An effective introductory paragraph may also provide the context of the question and a preview of the main arguments that will be developed in the subsequent paragraphs. However, this additional information should not distract from the thesis statement.

One classic model for making an argument is the five-paragraph essay. It consists of a one-paragraph introduction, three paragraphs of support, and a one-paragraph conclusion that ties back to the introduction. This model shows the importance of the introductory paragraph in shaping the full essay, including the arguments to be developed. However, the total number of paragraphs in your essay is for you to determine. Your introduction and your conclusion might each require more than one paragraph, and you are likely to need more than three paragraphs of support.

Recommended Activity Practice writing introductory paragraphs for the sample essay questions. Next, follow up the introductory paragraph with an outline of the supporting paragraphs. For each paragraph, list historical evidence that you will link to the thesis. The exercise of writing an introductory paragraph and an outline of your supporting paragraphs helps in two ways.

- It reinforces the connection of the main points in the introduction to the supporting paragraphs.
- It requires you to think in terms of historical evidence before you start writing a complete essay.

4. **Write the Supporting Paragraphs and Conclusion** The number and lengths of the paragraphs forming the body of the essay will vary depending on the thesis, the main points of your argument, and the amount of historical evidence you present. To receive the highest score, you must also explain how specific historical evidence is linked to the thesis. Each essay also will have a targeted historical reasoning skill that you should use to analyze the historical development or process you identified in your thesis.

The list that follows shows the main focus of an essay based on key words in the prompt.

- Compare: Provide a description or explanation of similarities and/or differences.

- Describe: Provide the relevant characteristics of a specified topic.

- Evaluate: Judge or determine the significance or importance of information, or the quality or accuracy of a claim.

- Explain: Provide information about how or why a relationship, process, pattern, position, situation, or outcome occurs, using evidence and/or reasoning. Explaining "how" typically requires analyzing the relationship, process, pattern, position, situation, or outcome, whereas explaining "why" typically requires analysis of motivations or reasons for the relationship, process, pattern, position, situation, or outcome.

- Identify: Indicate or provide information about a specified topic, without elaboration or explanation.

- Support an Argument: Provide specific examples and explain how they support a claim.

Source: AP® World History: Modern Course and Exam Description

Besides your ability to address the targeted reasoning process, your essay will be assessed on how well you develop your argument. Readers will consider how well you use specific historical evidence, recognize the historical context, and include evidence from outside the theme and time period of the question prompt. Your goal is not to fill a specific number of pages but to write an insightful, persuasive, and well-supported answer. Many students fail to achieve the full potential of their essay because they simply list a few generalities or a "laundry list" of facts, and they do not answer the full question.

Keep in mind that the readers of your essay are not looking for a retelling of history, or "stories." They will be grading you on your ability to craft an analytical essay that supports an argument with specific evidence. A short yet concise essay in which every word has a purpose is better than an essay bloated with fillers, flowery language, and interesting stories.

Your conclusion should restate the thesis. In addition, it should answer the larger question of "So what?" That is, the conclusion should provide the context and explain why the question is relevant in a broader understanding of history.

General Writing Advice Here are some tips to keep in mind as you start practicing the writing of history essays for the exam.

- Write in the third person. Avoid using first-person pronouns (I, we). Write your essay in the third person (it, they, she, etc.).

- Write in the past tense. Use past tense verbs, except when referring to sources that currently exist (e.g., the document implies).

- Use the active voice. Readers prefer the active voice ("The Mongols conquered China.") over the passive voice ("China was conquered by the Mongols.") because it states cause and effect more clearly.

- Use precise words. Use words that clearly identify persons, factors, and judgments. Avoid vague verbs such as felt. Use stronger verbs instead such as insisted, demanded, or supported. Also, avoid vague references, such as they and others, unless you are clearly referring to people already identified. Use specifics, such as Louis XVI of France. Use verbs that communicate judgment and analysis, such as reveal, exemplify, demonstrate, imply, and symbolize.

- Explain key terms. The majority of questions will deal with specific terms, and an essential part of your analysis should be an explanation of these terms.

- Anticipate counterarguments. Consider arguments against your thesis to show that you are aware of opposing views. The strongest essays confront conflicting evidence by explaining why it does not undercut the thesis. The statement of counterarguments is known as the concession or the conciliatory paragraph. Writers often present it directly following the introduction.

- Remain objective. Avoid opinionated rhetoric. The AP® test is not the place to argue that one group was the "good guys," while another was the "bad guys." And do not use slang terms such as "bad guys"!

- Communicate your organization. Each paragraph in your essay should develop a main point that is clearly stated in the topic sentence. It is also good practice to provide a few words or a phrase of transition to connect one paragraph to another. Each paragraph should also include a sentence that links the ideas in the paragraph to the thesis statement.

- Return to the thesis. Writers often restate their thesis in the final paragraph in a fresh and interesting manner or explain its significance. The conclusion should not try to summarize all the data or introduce new evidence. If you are running out of time, but have written a well-organized essay with a clear thesis that is supported with evidence, your conclusion can be very short. As noted earlier, including your thesis in the first and the last paragraph helps you make sure you have stated it clearly.

Recommended Activity Your first effort to write an AP® World History: Modern essay will be a more positive experience if it is an untimed assignment. After gaining confidence in writing the essay, you should try your hand at a timed test similar to that of the AP® exam (40 minutes for the essay). The purpose of such practice is to become familiar with the time constraints of the exam and to learn ways of improving the clarity as well as the efficiency of your writing and to gain insight into the type of information needed. The feedback from these practice tests—whether from teachers, peers, or self-evaluation—is essential for making progress.

5. **Evaluate Your Essay** Peer evaluation, as well as self-evaluation, can also help you internalize the elements of an effective essay and learn ways to improve. Breaking down the process into manageable steps is one key for improvement. The use of the essay-evaluation techniques can help students better understand the characteristics of an excellent essay.

Recommended Activity The following activity provides a set of questions about how effectively an essay achieves the elements that the AP® readers look for in their grading:

1. **Introductory Paragraph** Underline the thesis and circle the structural elements identified in the introduction. How effectively does the introductory paragraph prepare the reader for the rest of the essay? How might you improve the introductory paragraph?

2. **Thesis** Is the thesis clear? Does it take a position and address all parts of the question?

3. **Analysis** Does the body of the essay provide analysis of the question? Does the body reflect the argument and controlling ideas stated in the introductory paragraph? Does the body acknowledge opposing points of view? How could the analysis be improved?

4. **Evidence** Is the thesis supported clearly with substantial, relevant information? Is the evidence clearly connected to the stated thesis through strong paragraph topic sentences? What significant additional information or evidence could have been used for support?

5. **Errors** What minor or major errors in fact or analysis does the essay display?

6. **Presentation** How well organized and persuasive is the essay? Do the supporting paragraphs and their topic sentences address all parts of the essay prompt and stated thesis? Do paragraph composition, sentence structure, word choice, and spelling add to or detract from the essay? Identify areas that need improvement.

Recommended Activity Evaluation by a teacher and self-evaluation of essay work may be initially less threatening than peer evaluation, but once a level of confidence is established, peer evaluation can help you become a better writer and is often the most useful form of feedback.

This scoring guide for the long essay question is based on the College Board's grading rubric. (Check apcentral.collegeboard.com for the full rubric and any updates.) Use the guide to evaluate your work and internalize the characteristics of a strong long essay.

Scoring Guide for a Long Essay Question Answer

A. Thesis/Claim: 0–1 Point

❏ 1 point for a historically defensible thesis/claim that establishes a line of reasoning to address the question and not merely restate it. The thesis must be at least one sentence and located in one place, either in the introduction or in the conclusion.

B. Contextualization: 0–1 Point

❏ 1 point to describe the broader historical context of the question, such as developments either before, during, or after its time frame. Describing the context requires more than a mere phrase or reference.

C. Evidence: 0–2 Points

❏ 1 point for providing two specific pieces of evidence relevant to the question.

OR (Either the 1 point above or the 2 points below, but not both.)

❏ 2 points for for supporting an argument using two specific pieces of eveidence relevant to the question.

D. Analysis and Reasoning: 0–2 Points

❏ 1 point for using historical reasoning to frame or structure the arguments that address the question, such as causation, comparison, or continuity and change over time. Reasoning may be uneven or not as complex as needed to gain 2 points.

OR (Either the 1 point above or the 2 points below, but not both.)

❏ 2 points for using using historical reasoning to demonstrate a complex understanding that uses at least four pieces of relevant evidence to support a nuanced argument or to effectively use evidence to demostrate a thorough understanding of a different perspective relevant to the prompt.

Source: AP® World History: Modern Course and Exam Description

Review Schedule

Plan how you will prepare to take the AP® World History exam. Set a schedule for your review of each unit. You might spread your review over a long or a short amount of time. Many students find that study groups are helpful. The following is a sample of a review schedule using this text. It assumes the review will take place over six weeks:

- Week 1: Review writing skills
- Week 2: Period 1, (Units 1–2)
- Week 3: Period 2, (Units 3–4)
- Week 4: Period 3, (Units 5–6)
- Week 5: Period 4, (Units 7–9)
- Week 6: Complete and review the Practice Exam

Staying with a schedule requires discipline. A study group that chooses a specific time and place to meet and sets specific objectives for each meeting can reinforce the discipline of all its members. Some individuals may find it more productive to create a review schedule for themselves. If this review text has been used in conjunction with a history course, your familiarity with the essential content and skills developed in this book should make it an even more convenient and efficient review tool.

PROLOGUE: History before 1200 C.E.

Part 1: Human Development to c. 600 B.C.E.

The First Migrations

Modern humans first appeared in East Africa between 200,000 B.C.E. and 100,000 B.C.E. (Before the Common Era, sometimes referred to as B.C.). They survived by hunting animals and foraging for seeds and edible plants. Living in small groups, usually no more than a few dozen people, they did not have permanent homes. As they moved about in search of food, they slowly adapted to new environments, developed genetic and cultural differences, learned how to control fire and make stone tools, and created artistic drawings and paintings. They developed a system of religious beliefs called animism, a reverence for deities associated with features of nature, such as animals or specific mountains or rivers. These societies were fairly egalitarian, but they showed early signs of **patriarchy**, domination by males.

Sometime between 100,000 and 60,000 years ago, and perhaps due to the end of the last major ice age, people's movements in search of food took them beyond East Africa. They began populating the rest of the globe. By 10,000 B.C.E., humans lived on every continent except Antarctica.

MIGRATION OUT OF AFRICA

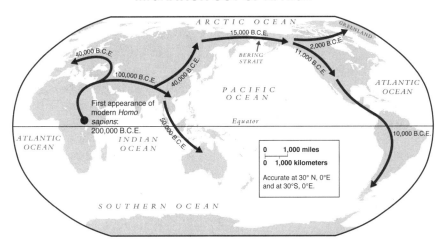

The Agricultural Revolution

Around 10,000 years ago, or about 8000 B.C.E., the climate was warming from an Ice Age. As it did, humans began to plant crops and raise animals for food. This change, called the **Agricultural Revolution**, began in the Middle East. Because of this development, people began to produce a surplus of food. For the first time in human history, one part of the population produced enough food to feed everyone. This allowed part of the population to specialize in non-food producing activities. This specialization change transformed every aspect of human life, causing innovations and trends that have existed ever since:

- The population grew. People lived in larger settlements that eventually developed into cities.
- People became highly skilled at one job. Artisans made tools and weapons. Merchants engaged in trade. Priests conducted rituals.
- People developed new technology. They learned how to improve irrigation systems, make use of the wheel in transportation, and replace stone with metals such as bronze and iron for making tools and art.
- People created more extensive governments and taxation. The desire to keep records about trade and taxes led to the invention of writing.
- Competition for resources and the accumulation of wealth increased group conflicts. However, the development of government provided a more peaceful way to settle conflicts between individuals.
- People became more sharply divided into social classes by wealth and occupation. In general, the status of women declined.

The First Civilizations

Trends that began to emerge after the Agricultural Revolution led to the first civilizations, large societies with cities and a powerful state. Most were in river valleys, places with fresh water and fertile land.

Mesopotamia The world's first civilization was in Mesopotamia, a region around the Tigris and Euphrates rivers in what is today Iraq. Several cultures emerged in this region, many based on city-states. A **city-state** is an independent state made up of a city and its surrounding territory. All city-states were highly patriarchal, built monumental architecture such as religious temples called ziggurats, and engaged in long-distance trade. The people were polytheistic, believing in many gods.

Sumer was a city-state along the southernmost region of ancient Mesopotamia. As taxes and trade became more complex, the Sumerians invented cuneiform, the first written language in history. They used cuneiform to record the first written laws.

Egypt In the Nile River valley, Egypt prospered. Though it shared many traits with Mesopotamia, Egypt was highly centralized under one ruler, called a pharaoh. The Egyptians developed their own writing system (hieroglyphics) and a complex system of mathematics. They built monumental architecture (pyramids) that demonstrated the pharaoh's power. Egyptian women were allowed to own property, and they were recognized as legally equal to men in court. These rights gave women a higher social standing than their counterparts in other patriarchal civilizations.

Indus Archaeological remains show the sophistication of ancient civilizations along the Indus River in South Asia. Cities such as Harappa and Mohenjo-Daro engaged in long-distance trade with Mesopotamia, practiced polytheism, developed technology such as indoor plumbing, and planned the layout of urban areas. However, no one has deciphered their language, so less is known about them than about other early civilizations.

China Along the Huang He River in northern China, a highly patriarchal and centralized system developed. One of its distinctive features was the special honor that its people gave to their ancestors.

Non-River Valley Civilizations Two early civilizations in the Americas did not develop in river valleys. The Olmec in Mesoamerica and the Chavin in the Andes were complex societies that participated in extensive trade.

Source: Getty Images

Source: Getty Images

Monumental architecture such as pyramids in Egypt (upper) and ziggurats in Mesopotamia (lower) reflected the power of early governments to organize workers to build large structures.

Hinduism and Judaism

At the same time that cities were growing, people began developing new ideas about religion. In animism, most deities were identified with specific places. Over time, people developed more abstract beliefs in which deities were not fixed in location. As people moved, they could take their deities with them. In some places, belief in many gods (polytheism) was replaced with a belief in just one supreme deity, monotheism.

Hinduism The belief now called **Hinduism** is sometimes categorized as polytheistic and sometimes as monotheistic. The origins of Hinduism go back at least 3,500 years. People called Aryans from north of the Himalaya Mountains migrated south to what is now Pakistan and India. They spoke an Indo-European language, and they brought with them scriptures called the Vedas and a belief that many deities existed. However, over time, people came to regard all deities as the expression of one supreme deity.

The Vedas taught that the soul of a person is reborn, or reincarnated, many times. Eventually, a soul would spiritually advance enough to become liberated from this cycle of death and rebirth. The Vedas taught that people should organize society into sharply defined classes, called castes. The caste system prohibited social mobility. While the caste system kept society stratified, society was also unified.

Zoroastrianism A clear example of an early form of monotheism is Zoroastrianism. This belief system developed in Persia. Followers of this faith focus on human free will and the eternal battle between the forces of good and evil.

Judaism The most influential example of monotheism is **Judaism**. Its earliest adherents were known as Hebrews or Israelites, but they have long been called Jews. Judaism developed in and around what is now the state of Israel. The Jewish people trace their history to the teachings of Abraham, who lived about 4,000 years ago.

Jews believe that they have entered into a covenant, or mutual promise, with their God, whom they call YHWH (Yahweh), Elohim, or Adonai. In return for their devotion, Yahweh would consider them his chosen people. Judaism was further developed with the codification of Hebrew Scriptures, sometimes called the Old Testament.

Like Judaism, two other faiths—Christianity and Islam—are also monotheistic religions that looked back to Abraham as an important figure. Christianity and Islam will be discussed later in this Prologue.

Part 2: The Classical Era, c. 600 B.C.E. to c. 600 C.E.

Several great empires that arose between 600 B.C.E. and 600 C.E. became the core foundations of later civilizations in their region:

- western Eurasia: the Persian, Greek, Roman and Byzantine empires
- southern Asia: the Mauryan and Gupta empires
- eastern Asia: the Qin and Han dynasties
- Mesoamerica: the Mayan Empire

These empires provided political and economic security for their people. Goods and ideas flowed along land routes such as the ones in Eurasia known as the **Silk Roads** and maritime routes in the Mediterranean Sea and Indian Ocean. These trade routes fostered the development of such great cities as Rome (Italy), Constantinople (Turkey), Damascus (Syria), Pataliputra (India), and Chang'an (China).

THE SPREAD OF BUDDHISM

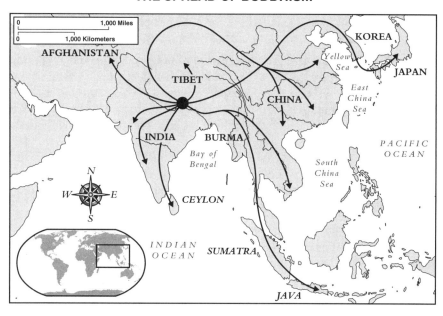

Buddhism and Developments in South Asia

While intense spirituality and distinct social organization have provided continuity in South Asian history, strong political centralization has not. The region was unified under a single government only twice during the Classical Period. The most influential development in South Asia was the development of the religion of Buddhism.

Beginning of Buddhism The founder of **Buddhism** was Siddhartha Gautama. Born into a wealthy Hindu family around 530 B.C.E., he became sharply aware of all the suffering people endured. To understand why people suffered, he left his wealthy family and pursued a life of poverty and meditation. According to Buddhist traditions, Siddhartha had been meditating for several days underneath a bodhi tree when he finally understood the cause of suffering and how to end it. He called himself the Buddha or "enlightened one," and sought to teach others what he had come to understand.

Buddhist doctrines became summarized in the Four Noble Truths, which sought to eliminate desire and suffering by following the Eightfold Path. This path requires an individual to meditate, reflect, and refrain from excessive earthly pleasures. The goal is, over time, to achieve enlightenment and the peaceful bliss known as nirvana, which would end the cycle of reincarnation.

The Spread of Buddhism Buddhism provided an alternative to the Vedic beliefs that were the foundation of Hinduism. Because Buddhism rejected the caste system, it became popular with members of the lower caste. It spread quickly throughout India and across Asia. Those spreading it included missionaries and merchants along the Silk Roads and around the Indian Ocean.

Unlike Hinduism and Judaism, which remained the faiths of particular groups of people in particular places, Buddhism was a universalizing religion, one that actively sought converts among all people. Buddhism is also a monastic faith, one that develops monastery communities for men and women.

The Mauryan Empire The first period of unity in South Asia was under the **Mauryan Empire** (322 B.C.E.–187 B.C.E.) It reached its high point during the rule of Ashoka. He promoted prosperity by creating an efficient tax system and by building roads that connected commercial centers. Ashoka spread knowledge of the law by inscribing his edicts on pillars throughout the empire.

Ashoka is one of the few powerful rulers in history who converted from one faith—Hinduism—to another. He became a Buddhist. His conversion helped spread the faith throughout India. After Ashoka, the Mauryan Empire soon declined in power, resulting in political decentralization.

The Gupta Empire The second period of unity in South Asia was under the **Gupta Empire**. It ruled from c. 320 C.E. to c. 550 C.E. (C.E. stands for Common Era, sometimes called A.D.; c. stands for *circa* and means approximately). This period is referred to as the Golden Age of India. Under a centralized government based in Pataliputra, a city in northwestern India, intellectual and cultural life flourished. In public hospitals, physicians made advances in medicine, such as using inoculations to prevent disease. Mathematicians developed a numbering system that combined a small number of symbols, 0 through 9, and the idea of place value. The system was so efficient that it is used throughout most of the world today.

The social structure in the Gupta era was patriarchal. Men held most positions of power in public life. To unify people, the Gupta strongly supported Hinduism. Hinduism is the most common religion in India today.

Confucianism and Developments in East Asia

Central China was united under the Zhou Dynasty (1076 B.C.E.–256 B.C.E.). However, as the dynasty weakened, China suffered a time of instability and decentralization referred to as the Warring States period.

Mandate of Heaven One legacy of the Zhou Dynasty in China was in how people thought about government. This was the concept of a **Mandate of Heaven,** the idea that "heaven," or some universal force, provided the justification for an emperor and his family to rule China. If the ruler was corrupt or ineffective, "heaven" would show its displeasure in the form of natural disasters. These disasters, such as drought or famine, were a sign to the Chinese people that the ruler had lost the Mandate of Heaven. Several major peasant uprisings in China were a direct result in this belief.

Confucianism During the Warring States period, around 551 B.C.E., the philosopher K'ung Fu-tzu, whose westernized name is **Confucius**, was born. He lived around the same time as the Buddha in India. The teachings of Confucius, written down by his followers in the *Analects*, describe how people should behave in everyday life. Unlike the teachings of Hinduism and Judaism, the *Analects* do not focus on any deity. Rather, Confucius focused on education, benevolence, virtue, respect for those with authority (especially the emperor), and a patriarchal social structure. He emphasized filial piety, the duty of people to honor their ancestors. The teachings of Confucius affected Chinese beliefs and values more than any other philosophy.

Daoism A second response to the chaos of the Warring States period was Daoism. While Confucianism focused on how people could live in harmony with one another, **Daoism** focused on how people could live in harmony with nature. The practices of Daoism emphasized internal reflection more than external behavior. Daoism would be influential throughout Chinese history.

The Qin and Han Dynasties China regained stability when the **Qin Dynasty** (221 B.C.E.–207 B.C.E.) and **Han Dynasty** (206 B.C.E.–220 C.E.) established centralized control. The Qin standardized Chinese script, established a uniform system of weights and measures, and built canals and roads. Together, these changes provided the foundation for increased trade and prosperity.

Building on the accomplishments of the Qin, the Han Dynasty became a Golden Age of Chinese history. Under the Han, China was more peaceful and its population grew. Chinese science and technology prospered, producing such developments as the magnetic compass, paper, and the sternpost rudder. Under Han regulation, trade extended from Chang'an, the capital of the empire, west to the Mediterranean Sea. Most of the trade was in luxury items such as spices, gems, precious metals, tea, and, most famously, silk.

The Han transformed China's government by creating a **civil service exam**. It required students to analyze Confucian teachings. Those who scored well received prestigious jobs in the government bureaucracy. This system produced a government of well-educated individuals and allowed for some social mobility.

Civilizations of Western Eurasia and Christianity

In western Eurasia between 600 B.C.E. and 600 C.E., strong civilizations developed in Persia, Greece, and Rome. Trade, war, and the flow of ideas connected these civilizations to one another. Each civilization prospered through a combination of trade and military strength.

Persia Around 559 B.C.E., a large empire developed in Persia (modern-day Iran) under the leadership of Cyrus the Great. The **Persian Empire** included most of the lands from the Aegean Sea in the west to the border of India in the east. The empire also became known as the Achaemenid Empire.

With a strong centralized government, efficient bureaucracy, and network of roads, the Persian empire promoted trade, prosperity, and stability. The vast empire was ethnically and religiously diverse, which the government recognized by practicing religious toleration.

Greece While Persia was a vast but united empire, Greece was divided into approximately 1,000 city-states. The numerous islands and mountainous terrain made unifying the Grecian region under one leader very difficult.

One cultural trait shared by Greeks was religion. Unlike the monotheistic Hebrews who worshipped a single all-powerful God, the Greeks believed in many deities and each possessed human frailties. These frailties help explain why Greeks developed a feeling that they controlled their own destiny.

Two of the largest city-states, Athens and Sparta, reflected the great variety among Greece's many city-states.

- Spartans organized their society around a powerful military. Women, the elderly, and enslaved people all filled roles that allowed free men to train as soldiers and fight when needed.

- Athenians made impressive advances in architecture, literature, theater, and philosophy. Many of these came during its Golden Age in the late 400s B.C.E. Athens also developed the concept of **democracy**, a system of government in which a large part of the population runs the government. Athens allowed free adult males the ability to participate directly in making political decisions.

In the 300s B.C.E., the army of Alexander the Great spread Greek culture into Egypt, across Persia, and east to India. This region became known as the Hellenistic world.

Rome According to legend, Rome was founded in 753 B.C.E. Roman culture borrowed heavily from the Greeks. The Romans incorporated the Greek gods into their pantheon of deities, relied on slavery, and made advances in government that continue to have lasting influence on governments today. Romans developed the practice of a representative government and of the judicial concept "innocent until proven guilty." To protect individual rights, the Romans publicly displayed written laws known as the Twelve Tables. Spreading awareness of laws provided a check on abuses of government power, a concept that would be built into numerous constitutions in the future.

Like Greece, Rome had a patriarchal society. However, compared to Greek women, Roman women gained more rights, including the right to own and inherit property and the right to initiate divorce proceedings.

While the Greek city-states remained small, Rome expanded outward in all directions, turning the Mediterranean Sea into "a Roman lake." At the peak of its power, the Roman Empire ruled territory from Scotland to northern Africa to the Middle East. In the large size of its territory, Rome was more like Persia. Both Rome and Persia were land-based empires under a strong central government. Both fostered trade and prosperity with well-maintained roads and strong militaries to protect travelers. Rome was also famous for other publicly funded projects, such as aqueducts, which were systems to transport water to cities, and large stadiums for public entertainment.

Despite Rome's wealth and power, it faced many challenges. Roman leaders over-extended the Roman military, were often corrupt, and failed to deal with devastating epidemics caused by smallpox and the bubonic plague. Gradually, trade and urban populations declined. As a result, Roman lands suffered economically. Rome's decline was made worse by invasions from groups such as the Huns, Ostrogoths, Visigoths, and Vandals. By 476 C.E., the empire was so weak that a non-Roman became emperor for the first time in more than a thousand years.

The Development of Christianity Rome's most enduring legacy was not in its military or its engineering achievements. It was in religion. Rome generally tolerated all faiths as long as subjects agreed to accept the divine nature of the emperor. People with polytheistic beliefs could do this easily.

THE ROMAN EMPIRE

However, monotheists could not. In particular, Jews living the Middle East refused to recognize any deity but their own. Roman persecution of Jews living in the Middle East contributed to the **diaspora,** or spreading, of Jews to lands throughout northern Africa and Europe as they looked for places to worship freely.

One leader who emerged from the Jewish community was Jesus. For his teachings, he was executed by the Romans. Since the followers of his teachings considered him the Christ, or savior of humanity sent by God, they became known as Christians. Despite persecution by the Romans, Jesus's disciples continued to spread his teachings. By the end of the 1st century C.E., Christians were practicing their faith throughout the empire.

This new faith was particularly attractive to the poor because it taught that people could have a better life after death if they believed in Jesus. Despite continued persecution, **Christianity** grew stronger. In the 4th century, under the emperor Constantine, Christianity became legal and was accepted as the official religion of the empire.

Constantine's endorsement of Christianity accelerated its growth. Like Buddhism, Christianity was a universalizing religion, meaning it actively sought converts and it was easily adaptable to areas outside its place of origin. It also offered monastic lifestyles for men (monks) and women (nuns) to devote their lives to practicing the faith. This new monotheistic faith would have far-reaching impact on future civilizations.

Byzantine By the middle of the 4th century, the eastern half of the Roman Empire had become wealthier and politically more powerful than the western half. For this reason, in 330, Emperor Constantine moved the capital of the empire eastward to Byzantium and renamed the city Constantinople (Istanbul today). In 395, the **Roman Empire** was divided into two distinct entities. Rome became the capital in the west, and Constantinople became the capital in the east.

Constantinople quickly became a political and economic hub. Geography aided its rise to prominence as rivers from the north flowed into the nearby Mediterranean and Black seas. As an **entrepôt**, or coastal trading center, Constantinople prospered as raw goods arrived from northern Europe, cereals came from Egypt, and precious spices and finished products came from the east.

At its height, the **Byzantine Empire** extended throughout the eastern half of the Mediterranean world. The reign of Justinian the Great (527–565) included great accomplishments. One was the construction of a magnificent church called Hagia Sophia (537). Another was the creation of the Justinian Code. This consolidation of Roman law would serve as the foundation of legal knowledge in Europe into the 19th century. Though constantly threatened by foreign incursion, the Byzantine Empire would survive for another 900 years.

Source: Getty Images w
Hagia Sophia was originally built as a Christian church. After Constantinople was conquered by the Ottomam Empire in 1453, it became a mosque. Today it is a museum.

Early American Civilizations

Afro-Eurasian civilizations developed in isolation from American civilizations during the classical era. Two of the most important were in Mesoamerica, the region that is now Mexico and Central America.

Teotihuacan One of the most important civilizations in the Americas was based in the city of **Teotihuacan**, located near modern-day Mexico City. It was a multicultural urban area that prospered through regional trade. By the 6th century C.E., its population of 125,000 made it one of the largest cities in the world. Teotihuacan featured streets laid out on a grid and monumental religious temples dedicated to the gods of the sun and moon. The city was abandoned by 650, but the "city of the gods" as it was called, would later influence other powerful civilization such as the Aztecs.

The Mayans South of Teotihuacan lived the **Mayans**. They were the most influential classical civilization in the Americas. The Mayans can be traced as far back as 1500 B.C.E. They reached their height of population and wealth between 250 C.E. and 900 C.E. The Mayans developed the most complex written language in the Americas before contact with people from Europe. Mayan priests created a very accurate calendar, a sign that they studied and understood the movement of Earth through space. Mayans understood the importance of the concept of zero, something people in the Mediterranean world had not grasped in this period.

Comparisons in the Classical Age

The empires that emerged between 600 B.C.E. and 600 C.E. shared several traits in economics and politics. In general, increased trade, technological innovation, and centralized government worked together to make the lives of people longer, safer, and more comfortable. In general, the empires also shared similar reasons for their decline.

Early Trade Networks As technological developments made trade easier, strong and stable governments provided the wealth and security to foster and sponsor trade. The Eurasian exchange networks utilized the strength of the Roman and Han innovations, such as stirrups that made riding horses easier and networks of places to rest and eat that made long journey travel more dependable.

Other key technologies included the improvements in sail design and ship hulls that enabled ships to maneuver in less than favorable wind conditions. The knowledge of monsoon winds facilitated trade along the entrepôts in the Indian Ocean. The improvements to the camel saddle made caravan trade profitable and possible across the Sahara.

The Mediterranean Sea lanes continued to facilitate cultural exchange and goods between the Phoenicians, Greeks, Romans, and people of North Africa. Long-distance trade was only beginning to hit its stride. These developments ushered in the first Golden Age of the Silk Roads.

Decline of Classical Empires By 600 C.E., many of the great classical empires were losing or had lost their unity and political power. As a result, people faced growing problems that they could not agree on how to address. Each unsolved problem then made peace and prosperity more precarious:

- challenges collecting taxes weakened government
- declines in trade decreased access to foreign goods and markets
- spread of disease reduced urban populations
- increases in the gap between the rich and poor created social conflict
- lack of broad support for leadership made solving problems harder
- attacks by outside groups led to a need for more spending on defense

In some areas, the spread of a common religion helped keep society unified even as a government failed. In later centuries, this unity would help new empires arise. For example, in Europe, the Roman Empire broke apart in the 5th century, but Christianity held society together. Confucianism filled a similar role in China, while Hinduism and Buddhism did the same in South Asia.

Government in the Classical Period, c. 600 B.C.E. to c. 600 C.E.

Civilization	Form	Important Individuals and Government Bodies	Characteristics	Role of Religion
Mauryan and Gupta (c. 320 B.C.E.– c. 550 C.E.)	Centralized empire	• Ashoka	Developed a sophisticated bureaucracy	The Gupta tolerated religious diversity, but Hindus dominated
Qin/Han (221 B.C.E.–220 C.E.)	Centralized empire	• Qin Shi Huangdi • Han Wudi	Used a civil service exam to create a merit-based bureaucracy	The Han supported Confucianism
Persian (c. 550 B.C.E.– c. 330 B.C.E.)	Centralized empire	• Darius • Xerxes	Organized empire into regional provinces	State was religiously tolerant
Greek (c. 550 B.C.E.–336 B.C.E.)	Decentralized city-states	• Pericles • Assembly of Citizens	Created a direct democracy in Athens for free adult males	Religion was separate from government but influential
Roman (c. 509 B.C.E.– c. 476 C.E.)	Centralized republic and then empire	• Julius Caesar • Ceasar Augustus • Senate	Allowed citizens to elect senators	Religion was separate from government but influential
Byzantine (c. 330 C.E.–1453 C.E.)	Centralized empire	• Justinian	Established laws known as the Justinian Code	The government appointed religious leaders
Mayan (c. 250 C.E.– c. 900 C.E.)	Decentralized city-states	•None are well-known	Considered emperors as descended from a deity	A theocracy with powerful priests

Part 3: Postclassical Civilizations, c. 600–c. 1200

In many parts of the world, the decline of classical civilizations was marked by a century or more of declines in trade, intellectual innovation, and social stability. However, new centralized states that promoted peace and prosperity emerged to replace them. Throughout Afro-Eurasia, trade intensified after 600 as networks of exchange widened and became more profitable. The Silk Roads, the **Indian Ocean trade networks**, and the **trans-Saharan trade routes** were brimming with items such as porcelain, ivory, teakwood, spices, and silk. These networks of exchange also provided ways for technology and ideas to move from one culture to another. More and more regions became familiar with the compass, the astrolabe, new forms of credit, paper money, and new religious beliefs.

However, all of this exchange came with a high price. Deadly diseases also spread along these same pathways.

Afro-Eurasia and the Americas remained separate, but people in Mesoamerica and the Andes Mountains experienced similar developments. The growth of more centralized states in each region also promoted trade and the spread of ideas.

The Spread of Islam

At the beginning of the 7th century, the people of the Middle East were a mixture of animists, Zoroastrians, Jews, Christians, and others. A merchant named Muhammad living on the Arabian Peninsula believed that he had received revelations from God. These revelations were later recorded in the Quran, the sacred scriptures of the religion of **Islam**. Those who followed the teachings in the Quran became known as Muslims. They believed that Muhammad was last in a line of great prophets that included Abraham, Moses, and Jesus.

The Teachings of Islam The core principles of the Quran became known as the Five Pillars of Islam: a belief in one god called Allah, ritual prayer, almsgiving, fasting, and making a pilgrimage to Mecca. They evolved a law code based on the Quran, called *sharia*, to regulate Muslim religious and civic behavior. Unlike the laws of the Romans, sharia made no distinction between religious and civil law.

Sunnis and Shi'as Through Muhammad's leadership, Islam quickly unified and brought peace to the warring tribes of the Arabian Peninsula. However, Islam experienced a crisis upon the death of Muhammad in 632. He had made no provision for a successor. People fell into two warring camps over who should become the political leader, called the caliph, of the Islamic community. This rift, which continues today, created a divide between the two major branches of Islam: Sunni and Shi'a. Sunni Muslims felt that the caliph could be selected from among all leaders in the Islamic community.

Shi'a Muslims felt that the caliph should be a blood relative of Muhammad. Today, Sunnis form the majority of Muslims in the world. Shi'a Muslims are strongest in Iran and Iraq.

Expansion of Islam Despite this early division among Muslims, Islam spread rapidly. In less than a century, Islam had united southern Spain, North Africa, the Middle East, and parts of India. This area became known as the House of Islam, or **Dar al-Islam**.

The Abbasids The most influential rulers in Dar al-Islam were those of the **Abbasid Caliphate** (750–1258). Under them, Islamic culture experienced a golden age. A stable government allowed trade to once again prosper. The Abbasids helped China, then under the Tang Dynasty, reestablish a booming trade along the Silk Roads. They also facilitated the growth of trans-Saharan trade to West Africa and were major participants in the diffusion of ideas and goods throughout the Indian Ocean.

Islamic society, particularly in the capital in Baghdad, thrived under the Abbasids. The empire became a center of learning where people made advances in medicine, built astronomical observatories, developed algebra, improved the astrolabe, and preserved Greek and Roman texts. The government practiced a degree of religious toleration. Non-Muslims could keep their faith by paying an additional tax called the *jizya*.

The Abbasids ended female infanticide and strengthened the marriage and property rights of women. The Abbasids continued to support the veiling of women and the right of a man to take up to four wives.

THE SPREAD OF ISLAM, 622-750

China

After the Han Dynasty declined in the 3rd century, China suffered three centuries of turmoil and disunity. However, after that, China experienced several centuries of growth.

Sui Dynasty China's period of troubles was ended by the short-lived **Sui Dynasty** (581–618). By reconstituting a centralized government, the Sui provided the foundation on which China again became prosperous. The dynasty's most dramatic accomplishment was the construction of the Grand Canal. Stretching over 1,000 miles, it connected the agricultural south to the population centers in the north. Besides fostering economic growth, the Grand Canal helped unify the varied ethnic and cultural groups of China.

Tang Dynasty Building on the accomplishments of the Sui, the **Tang Dynasty** (618–907) extended China's boundaries north into Mongolia, west into Central Asia, and south into Vietnam. China's population grew significantly under the Tang. Learning to grow a fast-ripening variety of rice allowed peasants to produce more calories per acre, so the land could support more people.

The Tang expanded the civil service exam and the empire's bureaucracy, which developed into an ongoing feature of the Chinese government. Under the Tang, the Chinese invented gunpowder and developed paper money, which facilitated trade. Political stability and steady demand for China's silk, porcelain, and other goods ushered in a second golden age of the Silk Roads.

SUI AND TANG CHINA

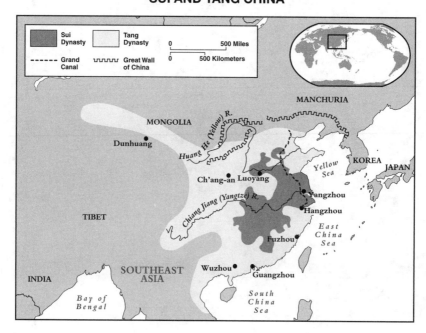

The Chinese had long viewed their country as the "Middle Kingdom," possibly because they believed they were at the center of cultural advances in the world. Based on this viewpoint, they developed the tributary system, the idea that surrounding kingdoms should make payment, or tribute, to the Chinese and officially submit to their rule in exchange for trading privileges.

The strength of the Tang eventually declined. A combination of internal peasant uprisings and invasions from the west and north led to the downfall of the dynasty.

Song Dynasty After the Tang collapsed, a new dynasty, the **Song Dynasty** (960–1279), was able to restore order. Under the Song, China continued its golden age. Chinese meritocracy allowed for more upward mobility than any other hiring system of its time. China became the leading manufacturer in the world, producing iron, steel, silk, and porcelain, and it had the largest cities in the world. Neo-Confucianism, a melding of Confucian, Buddhist, and Daoist philosophies that had begun under the Tang, became popular. It was during this time that paper money and the magnetic compass was exported from East Asia to other parts of the world.

Japan

Between about 800 and 1200, Japan had its own golden age of achievements in painting and literature. Though influenced by China, Japan always had a separate and distinctive culture. However, by the end of this period, powerful clans of land-owning nobles were eroding the emperor's power. As government became more decentralized, warfare between these clans increased. A strong political and social hierarchy developed over the control of land and included hierarchical obligations. At the top was the **shogun**, a military general, followed by powerful landlords called **daimyos**. Each daimyo had a force of warriors called samurais who pledged loyalty to serve him. Below the samurai were the peasants, followed by merchants.

Culturally, Japan's official religion was **Shinto**, a set of beliefs centered on the veneration of ancestors and nature spirits. However, missionaries from China and Korea brought Buddhism to the country, and it became popular at this time. Many Japanese adopted Buddhism yet keep their Shinto beliefs.

Africa

In most of sub-Saharan Africa between 600 and 1200, people often lived in small self-governing chiefdoms in which many people were related. These kin-based communities often cooperated with one another and sometimes formed larger political units. While cultures were as diverse as the geography of the continent, similarities existed. Some similarities resulted from the migrations of Bantu-speaking people out of a region in west central Africa between c. 1000 B.C.E. and c. 1500 C.E. These migrating people spread a language, farming techniques, and knowledge of how to work with iron.

By 1000 C.E., complex agricultural practices such as irrigation and the allocation of land for people to cultivate demanded the development of more complex forms of government. With a stronger government came more control over production and distribution of surplus products. This government regulation, combined with the introduction of the camel and use of the camel saddle, led to long-distance trade across the Sahara. Muslim merchants greatly increased trade, which benefited the kingdom of **Ghana** (c. 700–c. 1240). The trans-Saharan trade route allowed Ghana to become very wealthy. The rulers of Ghana protected these trade routes and taxed the gold and salt that continually entered or exited their trading centers.

The development of trade also affected the religion of the people of West Africa. As Muslim merchants from North Africa traded in the region, they spread Islam. The region became part of Dar al-Islam. The legacy of this period can be seen today in the large number of Muslims in some countries. In Nigeria, about 50 percent of the population identifies as Muslim. In Mali, over 90 percent do.

On the east coast of Africa, merchants linked into the Indian Ocean trading network. Through it, Africans and people from the Middle East, South Asia, and Southeast Asia were all connected. African merchants exported gold, ivory, and enslaved people. They imported porcelain, silk, and spices.

While governments were generally small and local in most of Africa, outside of West Africa, one large kingdom arose in the southeast part of the continent, **Great Zimbabwe**. It dominated the region between the 12th and 15th centuries. The reasons Great Zimbabwe declined are not clear, though one reason was probably the reduced output of gold mines in the region.

South Asia and Southeast Asia

After the fall of the Gupta empire in 550, South Asia was riddled by disunity and fighting. Despite this decentralization, Hinduism and the caste system kept southern India unified and relatively stable. Northern India, however, suffered a series of invasions and weak confederations. One of those invasions brought Islam to the region in 711.

Despite a period of divisions and conflict, South Asian trade flourished. As people better understood the pattern of the **monsoon winds**, India's location made it the hub of Indian Ocean trade. Silks and porcelain from East Asia, spices from southeast Asia, horses from the Middle East, and enslaved people and ivory from Africa were all traded in India.

Religion and trade dominated South Asia's influence on Southeast Asia. Buddhists and Hindus used trade networks to spread their religions' teachings. Islam also significantly influenced Southeast Asia at this time. Muslim merchants, though often not consciously missionaries, spread their faith by settling in new regions with their families. Islam soon became the dominant religion in the Spice Islands and the Malay peninsula.

Source: Getty Images.

The Temple of Borobudur was built around 800 C.E. on the island of Java in Indonesia. With its statue of Buddha and its Hindu-style temples, it shows the interaction of the two religions.

Europe

The Postclassical period saw a dramatic shift in Europe. The Eastern Roman Empire, based in Constantinople, flourished. In contrast, the decline of the Western Roman Empire left a power vacuum in the rest of the continent. Invasions of people from Northern Europe, known as the Vikings, brought another group of people into the cultural exchanges. Central and western Europe devolved into thousands of duchies and fiefdoms. As a result of the lack of strong central governments, Europe could not provide the protection and stability merchants desired. It did not benefit from long distance Afro-Eurasian trade as much as other regions did.

Just as Hinduism provided cultural unity to a politically divided South Asia, Christianity became the one unifying force in central and western Europe. In 800, the pope demonstrated his power and authority by bestowing on the French king, Charlemagne, the title of "Emperor of the Romans." However, European Christian unity would not endure. In 1054, it split into two branches, the **Roman Catholic Church** in the west and the **Orthodox Church** in the east.

In 1095, the Roman Catholic pope called for a Holy Crusade to free Jerusalem and the lands around it from Islamic control. The early crusaders had some limited success. But after two centuries of trying, the crusades failed to seize power. However, they had a large impact culturally. The Crusades made Europeans more aware of the achievements of the Middle East and the rest of Asia. This awareness was one factor in stimulating Europe to become more interested in intellectual and technological advances.

The Americas

By the year 900, the Mayan golden age in Mesoamerica was ending. A combination of environmental degradation, drought, and warfare caused Mayans to abandon many of their cities. However, some Mayan cities, such as Chichen Itza, continued to be inhabited.

Two other large civilizations developed in the Western Hemisphere during this time. One was the **Mississippian** civilization, near present-day St. Louis. It flourished between the 8th century and the 16th century. Its city of Cahokia was a major trade hub with a population larger than that of London.

The other was the **Toltecs** civilization, which emerged in the 10th century in Mesoamerica. The Toltecs adopted many Mayan practices, including a religion that was both polytheistic and animistic. The Toltecs had a major influence on a later empire in the region, the Aztecs.

Source: Herb Roe, www.chromesun.com

A diorama at the Cahokia Historic Site n Collinsville, Illinois, shows a number of scenes from the Mississippian culture, including this figure of a flintknapper—someone who shapes the sharp edges of a flint tool.

The World in 1200

By 1200, much of the world had recovered from the decline of the classical civilizations. In many regions, new states were emerging that were promoting trade and the transfer of ideas among regions:

- Africa, Europe, and Asia were connected through Indian Ocean trade, the Silk Roads, and trans-Saharan trade routes.

- The Byzantine Empire and various Islamic empires provided some stability in the region from Eastern Europe through the Middle East to South Asia.

- China and Dar al-Islam continued to be leading centers of learning and innovation.

- Western Europe and Japan had decentralized systems of government that featured powerful land-owning nobles.

- Africa largely remained stateless, except for some regions in West Africa and East Africa that were part of Dar al-Islam.

- Afro-Eurasia, America, and Oceania were developing in isolation from each other.

In 1200, people in Africa and Eurasia might have predicted that in the next three centuries, the regions of the world would remain on their paths. China would grow wealthier, Islamic states would become stronger, and Europe would continue to learn from other regions. However, few could have guessed that in the 13th century a little-known group of nomads from Central Asia would upend life in Eurasia. Then, in 1492, a voyage by a European would reshape the lives of people around the world.

Source: Library of Congress Prints and Photographs Division

Columbus arrives in the Americas, L. Prang and Co.,1893

KEY TERMS BY THEME

CULTURE: Religion
Hinduism
Judaism
Buddhism
Confucius
Daoism
Christianity
Islam
Dar al-Islam
Shinto
Roman Catholic Church
Orthodox Church

SOCIETY: Patterns
patriarchy
civil service exam
diaspora
entrepôt
shogun
daimyos

ENVIRONMENT: Food and Trade
Agricultural Revolution
monsoon winds

CULTURE: Americas
Teotihaucan
Mayans
Mississippian
Toltecs

ECONOMY: Trade
Silk Roads
Indian Ocean trade routes
trans-Saharan trade routes

GOVERNMENT: Classical
city-state
Mauryan Empire
Gupta Empire
Mandate of Heaven
Qin
Han
Persian Empire
Greece
Roman Empire
Byzantine Empire

GOVERNMENT: Postclassical
Abbasid Caliphate
Sui Dynasty
Tang Dynasty
Song Dynasty
Ghana
Great Zimbabwe

REFLECT ON THE PROLOGUE

1. **Comparison** In what ways are Judaism, Islam, and Christianity alike?

2. **Comparison** Describe the difference between centralized and decentralized civilizations and give an example of each.

3. **Causation** Name at least three causes for the decline of Classical civilizations.

4. **Causation** Explain how trade networks caused Islam and Buddhism to spread.

5. **Continuity** Identify a continuity that kept southern India unified despite disruptions after the fall of the Gupta Empire.

6. **Change** Identify one new historical development after 600 C.E.

UNIT I: The Global Tapestry from c. 1200 to c. 1450

Understand the Context

Between 1200 and 1450, several large empires emerged around the world. Some were modified revivals of earlier empires in their region. Others represented new developments. All were shaped by the context of regional trade, which had been increasing since around 600.

The Revival of Large Empires Between 1200 and 1450, the wealthiest and most innovative empire in the world was the Song Dynasty in China. It was the latest in a series of states that had ruled a unified and prosperous China. Similarly, in Mesoamerica, the rise of the Aztec was influenced by an earlier empire under the Mayans. Two other centers of great intellectual achievement, Baghdad and Spain, reflected the emphasis on learning in the Islamic world.

However, in parts of Africa and Southeast Asia, the growth of regional trade produced larger and more complex states than had previously existed in those regions. Trade across the Sahara resulted in the West African empires of Ghana and Mali. Trade in the Indian Ocean provided the context for large states in Zimbabwe in East Africa and various states in India and Southeast Asia.

Unity in Central Eurasia Shaping the context for events throughout Eurasia between 1200 and 1450 was the remarkable emergence of the Mongols. A group of nomads from Central Asia, the Mongols conquered lands from central Europe to the Pacific Ocean, creating the largest land empire in human history. The conquest came with great devastation. However, the unity of so much territory under the rule of one group allowed trade to flourish once again across Eurasia, with new ideas and technology spreading easily. These developments set the stage for the intensifying global interactions that helped define the period after 1450.

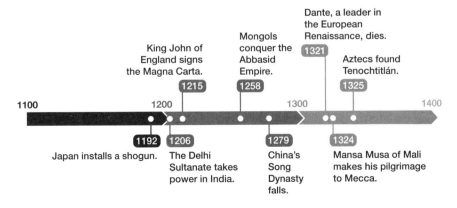

Dante, a leader in the European Renaissance, dies. **1321**

King John of England signs the Magna Carta. **1215**

Mongols conquer the Abbasid Empire. **1258**

Aztecs found Tenochtitlán. **1325**

1100   1200   1300   1400

1192 Japan installs a shogun.

1206 The Delhi Sultanate takes power in India.

1279 China's Song Dynasty falls.

1324 Mansa Musa of Mali makes his pilgrimage to Mecca.

Topics and Learning Objectives

Topic 1.1: Developments in East Asia pages 3–14

A: Explain the systems of government employed by Chinese dynasties and how they developed over time.

B: Explain the effects of Chinese cultural traditions on East Asia over time.

C: Explain the effects of innovation on the Chinese economy over time.

Topic 1.2: Developments in Dar al-Islam pages 15–22

D: Explain how systems of belief and their practices affected society in the period from c. 1200 to c. 1450.

E: Explain the causes and effects of the rise of Islamic states over time.

F: Explain the effects of intellectual innovation in Dar al-Islam.

Topic 1.3: Developments in South and Southeast Asia
pages 23–32

G: Explain how the various belief systems and practices of South and Southeast Asia affected society over time.

H: Explain how and why various states of South and Southeast Asia developed and maintained power over time.

Topic 1.4: Developments in the Americas pages 33–42

I: Explain how and why states in the Americas developed and changed over time.

Topic 1.5: Developments in Africa pages 43–52

J: Explain how and why states in Africa developed and changed over time.

Topic 1.6: Developments in Europe pages 53–64

K: Explain how the beliefs and practices of the predominant religions in Europe affected European society.

L: Explain the causes and consequences of political decentralization in Europe from c. 1200 to c. 1450.

M: Explain the effects of agriculture on social organization in Europe from c. 1200 to c. 1450.

Topic 1.7: Comparison in the Period from c. 1200 to c. 1450 pages 65–68

N: Explain the similarities and differences in the processes of state formation from c. 1200 to c. 1450.

1.1

Developments in East Asia

*From now on, our ordinances will be properly enforced
and the morality of our people will be restored.*

—Ming Dynasty "Prohibition Ordinance" (1368–1644)

Essential Question: How did developments in China and the rest of East
Asia between c. 1200 and c. 1450 reflect continuity,
innovation, and diversity?

The Song Dynasty in China (960–1279) was the leading example of diversity and innovation in Afro-Eurasia and the Americas during the 13th century. China enjoyed great wealth, political stability, and fine artistic and intellectual achievements. Neo-Confucian teachings, illustrated in the above quotation, supported the government and shaped social classes and the family system. In addition, China developed the greatest manufacturing capability in the world. However, the spread of Confucianism and Buddhism might be the most enduring testimony to Chinese influence.

Government Developments in the Song Dynasty

The **Song Dynasty** replaced the Tang in 960 and ruled for more than three centuries. They lost control of northern lands to invading pastoralists from Manchuria who set up the Jin Empire. Although the Song ruled a smaller region than the Tang, their reign was prosperous and under them the arts flourished.

Bureaucracy China's strength was partially the result of its **imperial bureaucracy**, a vast organization in which appointed officials carried out the empire's policies. The bureaucracy had been a feature of Chinese government since the Qin dynasty (221 B.C.E.–207 B.C.E.). It represented a continuity across centuries and dynasties. Under the Song, China's bureaucracy expanded. Early in the dynasty, this strengthened the dynasty.

Meritocracy and the Civil Service Exam One of Emperor Song Taizu's great achievements was that he expanded the educational opportunities to young men of the lower economic classes so they could score well on the civil service exams. By scoring well, a young man could obtain a highly desired job in the bureaucracy. These exams were based on knowledge of Confucian texts. Because officials obtained their positions by demonstrating their merit on these exams, China's bureaucratic system was known as a **meritocracy**. Though

SONG AND JIN EMPIRES

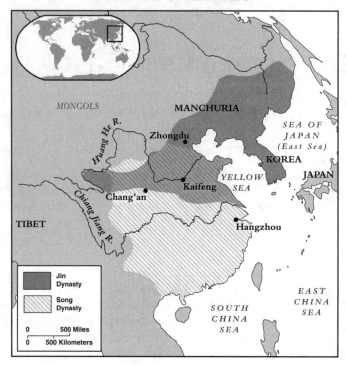

the poor were vastly underrepresented in the bureaucracy, the Chinese system allowed for more upward mobility than any other hiring system of its time.

However, by the end of the Song, the bureaucracy had grown so large that it contributed to the empire's weakness. By creating so many jobs and by paying these officials so handsomely, the Song increased the costs of government to the point that they began drying up China's surplus wealth.

Economic Developments in Postclassical China

The flourishing Tang Dynasty had successfully promoted agricultural development, improved roads and canals, encouraged foreign trade, and spread technology. These accomplishments led to rapid prosperity and population growth during the Song Dynasty. The **Grand Canal** was an inexpensive and efficient internal waterway transportation system that extended over 30,000 miles. Expanding the canal enabled China, under the Song Dynasty, to become the most populous trading area in the world.

Gunpowder Although gunpowder had been invented in China in previous dynasties, innovators in the Song Dynasty made the first guns. Over centuries, the technology of making gunpowder and guns spread from China to all parts of Eurasia via traders on the Silk Roads.

Agricultural Productivity Some time before the 11th century, **Champa rice**, a fast-ripening and drought-resistant strain of rice from the Champa

Kingdom in present-day Vietnam, greatly expanded agricultural production in China. This rice and other strains developed through experimentation allowed farming to spread to lands where once rice could not grow, such as lowlands, riverbanks, and hills. In some areas, it also allowed farmers to grow two crops of rice per year, a summer crop and a winter crop.

Innovative methods of production contributed to agricultural success. For example, Chinese farmers put manure (both human and animal) on the fields to enrich the soil. They built elaborate irrigation systems using ditches, water wheels, pumps, and terraces to increase productivity. New heavy plows pulled by water buffalo or oxen allowed previously unusable land to be cultivated.

The combination of these changes in agriculture produced an abundance of food. As a result, China's population grew quickly. In the three centuries of Song Dynasty rule, China's population increased from around 25 percent of the total world population to nearly 40 percent.

Manufacturing and Trade Industrial production soared, as did China's population. China's discovery of "black earth"—coal—in the 4th century B.C.E. enabled it to produce greater amounts of cast iron goods. Though massive use of coal to power machines wouldn't happened until the 18th century, China did have the greatest manufacturing capability in the world. The Chinese later learned how to take the carbon out of cast iron and began to manufacture steel. They used steel to make or reinforce bridges, gates, and ship anchors. They also used steel to make religious items, such as pagodas and Buddhist figurines. Steel also strengthened the agricultural equipment, contributing to the abundance of food production as well.

Under the Song—and earlier than in Western Europe—China experienced **proto-industrialization**, a set of economic changes in which people in rural areas made more goods than they could sell. Unlike later industrialization, which featured large-scale production in factories using complex machinery, proto-industrialization relied more on home-based or community-based production using simple equipment. For example, **artisans**, or skilled craftworkers, produced steel and other products in widely dispersed smelting facilities under the supervision of the imperial government. Artisans also manufactured porcelain and silk that reached consumers through expanding trade networks, especially by sea. Porcelain was highly desired because it was light-weight yet strong. Further, it was light-colored, so it could be easily painted with elaborate designs.

The Chinese used the compass in maritime navigation, and they redesigned their ships to carry more cargo. China's ability to print paper navigation charts made seafaring possible in open waters, out of sight of land, and sailors became less reliant on the sky for direction.

China became the world's most commercialized society. Its economy changed from local consumption to market production, with porcelains, textiles, and tea the chief exports. The Grand Canal supported a vibrant internal trade while advances in naval technology allowed China to control trade in the South China Sea. The military power of the Tang and Song enabled them to protect traders from bandits.

Taxes The Song also promoted the growth of a commercial economy by changing how they built public projects, such as roads and irrigation canals. Instead of requiring that people labor on these projects, the government paid people to work on them. This change increased the amount of money in circulation, promoting economic growth.

Tributes Another source of income for the government came from the tributary system, an arrangement in which other states had to pay money or provide goods to honor the Chinese emperor. This system cemented China's economic and political power over several foreign countries, but it also created stability and stimulated trade for all parties involved. The origins of the system existed in the Han Dynasty. By the time of the Song Dynasty, Japan, Korea, and kingdoms throughout southeast Asia were tributary states. The emperor expected representatives from tributary states to demonstrate their respect by performing a *kowtow,* a ritual in which anyone greeting the Chinese emperor must bow his or her head until it reached the floor. The Chinese sent out tremendous fleets led by Zheng He to demonstrate the power of the emperor and to receive tribute. (Zheng He's voyages are described in more detail in Topic 2.3.)

Social Structures in China

Through most of Chinese history, the majority of people lived in rural areas. However, urban areas grew in prominence in this productive period. At the height of the Song Dynasty, China was the most urbanized land in the world, boasting several cities containing more than 100,000 people. The largest cities, Chang'an (an ancient capital), Hangzhou (at the southern end of the Grand Canal), and the port city of Guangzhou were cosmopolitan metropolises— active centers of commerce with many entertainment options to offer.

China's Class Structure Though urbanization represented a significant development in China, life in rural areas grew more complex as well. The bureaucratic expansion created an entirely new social class, the **scholar gentry**. They soon outnumbered the aristocracy, which was comprised of landowners who inherited their wealth. The scholar gentry were educated in Confucian philosophy and became the most influential social class in China.

Three other classes ranked below the scholar gentry: farmers, artisans, and merchants. The low status of merchants reflected Confucian respect for hard work and creating value. The tasks of merchants did not require physical strength or endurance, and they simply exchanged goods without growing or making anything new.

Lower rungs of Chinese society included peasants who worked for wealthy landowners, often to pay off debts, and the urban poor. The Song government provided aid to the poor and established public hospitals where people could receive free care.

Role of Women Confucian traditions included both respect for women and the expectation that they would defer to men. This patriarchal pattern strengthened during the Tang and Song dynasties. One distinctive constraint on women's activities in China was the practice of **foot binding**, which became common among aristocratic families during the Song Dynasty. From a very young age, girls had their feet wrapped so tightly that the bones did not grow naturally. A bound foot signified social status, something suitors particularly desired. It also restricted women's ability to move and hence to participate in the public sphere. Foot binding was finally banned in 1912.

Intellectual and Cultural Developments

During the Tang and Song eras, China enjoyed affluence, a well-educated populace, and extensive contact with foreign nations. As a result, intellectual pursuits (technology, literature, and visual arts) thrived.

Paper and Printing The Chinese had invented paper as early as the 2nd century C.E., and they developed a system of printing in the 7th century. They were the first culture to use **woodblock printing**. A Buddhist scripture produced in the 7th century is thought to be the world's first woodblock printed work. (For information on the Gutenberg press, a related technology, see Topic 1.6.) In the Song era, printed booklets on how to farm efficiently were distributed throughout rice-growing regions.

CHINESE WOODBLOCK PRINTING

Source: Thinkstock

With the development of woodblock printing in China, people could make multiple copies of art or written texts without laboriously copying each by hand.

Reading and Poetry The development of paper and printing expanded the availability of books. Though most peasants were illiterate, China's privileged classes had increased access to literature. Confucian scholars not only consumed literature at a tremendous rate, they were also the major producers of literature throughout the era. The Tang and Song dynasties' emphasis on schooling created generations of well-rounded scholar-bureaucrats. Later, Europeans with such diverse skills would be called "Renaissance men."

Religious Diversity in China

Buddhism had come to China from its birthplace in India via the Silk Roads. Its presence is evident during the anarchic period between the later Han and the Sui dynasties. However, its popularity became widespread during the Tang Dynasty. The 7th century Buddhist monk Xuanzang helped build Buddhism's popularity in China.

Buddhism and Daoism Three forms of Buddhism from India came to shape Asia, each developing a different emphasis:

- **Theravada Buddhism** focused on personal spiritual growth through silent meditation and self-discipline. It became strongest in Southeast Asia.
- **Mahayana Buddhism** focused on spiritual growth for all beings and on service. It became strongest in China and Korea.
- **Tibetan Buddhism** focused on chanting. It became strongest in Tibet.

All three include a belief in the Four Noble Truths, which stress the idea that personal suffering can be alleviated by eliminating cravings or desires and by following Buddhist precepts. All three also embrace the Eight-Fold Path, the precepts (including right speech, right livelihood, right effort, and right mindfulness) that can lead to enlightenment or nirvana.

Monks introduced Buddhism to the Chinese by relating its beliefs to Daoist principles. For example, Buddhism's idea of dharma became translated as dao ("the way"). Eventually, Buddhist doctrines combined with elements of Daoist traditions to create the **syncretic**, or fused, faith **Chan Buddhism**, also known as **Zen Buddhism**. Like Daoism, Zen Buddhism emphasized direct experience and meditation as opposed to formal learning based on studying scripture. Because of its fusion with Chinese beliefs, Buddhism became very popular in China. Monasteries—buildings where monks lived together—appeared in most major cities.

The presence of these monasteries became a problem for the Tang bureaucracy. Many leaders of the Tang Dynasty, which considered itself the "Middle Kingdom," had trouble accepting that a foreign religion would have such prominence in society. Buddhism's popularity, which drew individuals away from China's native religions, made Daoists and Confucians jealous. Despite monasteries' closures and land seizures, however, Chan Buddhism remained popular among ordinary Chinese citizens.

Buddhism and Neo-Confucianism The Song Dynasty was somewhat more friendly towards Buddhism, but it did not go out of its way to promote the religion. It preferred to emphasize China's native traditions, such as Confucianism. However, Buddhism had a strong presence and many Confucians began to adopt its ideals into their daily lives. The development of printing had made Buddhist scriptures widely available to the Confucian scholar gentry. The Song Dynasty benefited from the Confucian idea of **filial piety**, the duty of family members to subordinate their desires to those of the male head of the family and to the ruler. The emphasis on respect for one's elders helped the Song maintain their rule in China.

Neo-Confucianism evolved in China between 770 and 840. It was a syncretic system, combining rational thought with the more abstract ideas of Daoism and Buddhism. This new incarnation of Confucianism emphasized ethics rather than the mysteries of God and nature. It became immensely popular in the countries in China's orbit, including Japan, Korea, and Vietnam.

Comparing Japan, Korea, and Vietnam

An important dynamic in the histories of Japan, Korea, and Vietnam was each country's relationship with China. When China was unified, its political strength, economic wealth, religious traditions, intellectual advances, and technological innovations made the world's most powerful realm. Its smaller neighbors benefited from being so close to China but faced a challenge of maintaining their own distinctive cultures. Each had to confront the issue of sinification, or the assimilation of Chinese traditions and practices.

Japan

Since Japan was separated from China by a sea rather than land, it had more ability to control its interactions with China than Korea or Vietnam could. The impact of Chinese culture appeared in many aspects of life:

- Japan's Prince Shotoku Taishi (574–622) promoted Buddhism and Confucianism along with Japan's traditional Shinto religion. During this era, Japan learned how to do woodblock printing from China.

- During the **Heian period** (794–1185) Japan emulated Chinese traditions in politics, art, and literature.

- However, Japanese writers also moved in new directions. For example, in the 11th century, a Japanese writer composed the world's first novel, *The Tale of Genji*. It is the story of a Japanese prince and his life at court, particularly his many romances.

Feudalism For hundreds of years, Japan had been a feudal society without a centralized government. Landowning aristocrats, the *daimyo*, battled for control of land, while the majority of people worked as rice farmers.

Japanese feudalism was similar to European feudalism, which is described in Topic 1.6. Both featured very little social mobility, and both systems were built upon hereditary hierarchies. In Japan, peasants, known as serfs, were born into lives of economic dependency, while samurai were born into their roles as protectors and daimyo were born into lives of privilege. In Europe, the three groups were serfs, knights, and nobles.

What distinguishes Japanese feudalism from that of Europe was that the daimyo enjoyed much more power than the nobility in Europe did. The daimyo ruled over vast stretches of land and, in reality, were more powerful than either the emperor or the shogun. By contrast, Europe's hierarchy placed the monarch above the nobility. Though there were periods when authority of the monarch waned and power was distributed among nobility, the main centralized power structure of European feudalism would not change until the Modern Industrial Era.

In Europe, the ideal knight held to the code of chivalry, with duty to countrymen, duty to God, and duty to women, the last expressed through courtly love and the virtues of gentleness and graciousness. In Japan, the code was known as *bushido* and stressed frugality, loyalty, the martial arts, and honor unto death.

Japan also differed from China in how it was governed. China was ruled by an emperor who oversaw a large civilian bureaucracy. For much of its history, China had a central government strong enough to promote trade and peace. In contrast, when the Heian court declined, a powerful land-owning family, the Minamoto clan, took charge. In 1192, the Minamoto installed a shogun, or military ruler, to reign. Though Japan still had an emperor, he had little power. For the following four centuries, Japan suffered from regional rivalries among aristocrats. Not until the 17th century would shoguns create a strong central government that could unify the country. (Connect: In a paragraph, explain how Buddhism and Confucianism influenced the development of Chinese governments in the period from 1200 to 1450. See Prologue.)

Korea

Korea's location gave it a very direct relationship with China. The countries share a land boundary, and China extends to both the north and south of Korea.

Similarity to China Through its tributary relationship, Korea and China were in close contact. Thus, Korea emulated many aspects of China's politics and culture. It centralized its government in the style of the Chinese. Culturally, Koreans adopted both Confucian and Buddhist beliefs. The educated elite studied Confucian classics, while Buddhist doctrine attracted the peasant masses. Koreans adopted the Chinese writing system, which proved to be very awkward. The Chinese and Korean languages remained structurally very different. In the 15th century, Korea developed its own writing system.

Powerful Aristocracy One important difference between Korea and China was that the landed aristocracy were more powerful in Korea than in

China. As a result, the Korean elite were able to prevent certain Chinese reforms from ever being implemented. For example, though there was a Korean civil service examination, it was not open to peasants. Thus, there was no truly merit-based system for entering the bureaucracy.

Vietnam

Like Japan and Korea, Vietnam traded with and learned from China. For example, Vietnam adapted the Chinese writing system and architectural styles. However, Vietnam had a more adversarial relationship with China. At times, the Vietnamese launched violent rebellions against Chinese influence.

Gender and Social Structure Vietnamese culture differed from Chinese culture in several ways, which explains the strong resistance to Chinese power. For example, Vietnamese women enjoyed greater independence in their married lives than did Chinese women in the Confucian tradition. While the Chinese lived in extended families, the Vietnamese preferred **nuclear families** (just a wife, husband, and their children). Vietnamese villages operated independently of a national government; political centralization was nonexistent.

Although Vietnam adopted a merit-based bureaucracy of educated men, the Vietnamese system did not function like the Chinese scholar-bureaucracy. Instead of loyalty to the emperor, scholar-officials in Vietnam owed more allegiance to the village peasants. In fact, Vietnamese scholar-officials often led revolts against the government if they deemed it too oppressive. Vietnamese women resented their inferior status under the Chinese. In particularly, they rejected the customs of foot binding and **polygyny**, the practice of having more than one wife at the same time. In spite of Vietnamese efforts to maintain the purity of their own culture, sinification did occur.

Military Conflict with China As the Tang Dynasty began to crumble in the 8th century, Vietnamese rebels pushed out China's occupying army. In their battles against the Chinese, they showed a strong capacity for guerilla warfare, perhaps due to their deep knowledge of their own land.

KEY TERMS BY THEME

ECONOMICS: China	**GOVERNMENT: China**	Tibetan Buddhism
Champa rice	Song Dynasty	syncretic
proto-industrialization	imperial bureaucracy	Chan (Zen) Buddhism
artisans	meritocracy	Neo-Confucianism
SOCIETY: China	**TECHNOLOGY: China**	**GOVERNMENT: Japan**
scholar gentry	woodblock printing	Heian period
filial piety	**CULTURE: China**	**CULTURE: Vietnam**
ENVIRONMENT: China	foot binding	nuclear families
Grand Canal	Buddhism	polygyny
	Theravada Buddhism	
	Mahayana Buddhism	

MULTIPLE-CHOICE QUESTIONS

Questions 1 to 3 refer to the passage below.

"[Hangzhou, China, has] ten principal markets. . . . [They] are all squares of half a mile to the side, and along their front passes the main street, which is 40 paces in width, and runs straight from end to end of the city, crossing many bridges of easy and commodious [convenient] approach. . . . So also parallel to this great street, but at the back of the market places, there runs a very large canal, on the bank of which towards the squares are built great houses of stone, in which the merchants from India and other foreign parts store their wares, to be handy for the markets. In each of the squares is held a market three days in the week, frequented by 40,000 or 50,000 persons."

Marco Polo, The Travels of Marco Polo, c. 1300

1. Based on the passage, which of the statements concerning the trading city of Hangzhou is most accurate?
   (A) Foreigners were not welcome in Chinese trading cities, because they were considered barbarians and had nothing of value to trade.
   (B) Many of the people coming to trade in cities in China were Europeans traveling along the Silk Roads.
   (C) Hangzhou was a vital trading city because it had foreign merchants and was also accessible by the Grand Canal for internal trade.
   (D) Chinese imperial governments limited the number of markets in Hangzhou to just a few centrally-located areas of the city.

2. What development, which began before the passage above was written, allowed Europeans to obtain the products of East Asia?
   (A) Chinese dynasties, such as the Tang and the Song, grew stronger, so long-distance trade could be conducted with less risk.
   (B) New maritime technology allowed for ocean-going ships to travel safely between Europe and Asia, going around southern Africa.
   (C) The Tang Dynasty expanded into the Middle East, so the trade routes between Europe and Africa were under one ruler.
   (D) With the defeat of the Islamic caliphates, Europeans were able to establish direct contact with the Tang and the Song dynasties.

3. What products would Indians and other non-Chinese merchants be most likely to purchase in a market such as the one described in the passage?
   (A) silk, porcelain, and tea
   (B) pepper, nutmeg, and cinnamon
   (C) cows, pigs, and oxen
   (D) rugs, parchment, and horses

1. **Use the passage below to answer all parts of the question that follows.**

"The Moral Nature

Being upright and modest, reserved and quiet, correct and dignified, sincere and honest: these constitute the moral nature of a woman. Being filial and respectful, humane and perspicacious [shrewd, wise], loving and warm, meek and gentle: these represent the complete development of the moral nature. The moral nature of being innate in our endowment, it becomes transformed and fulfilled through practice. It is not something that comes from the outside but is actually rooted in our very selves.

Cultivation of the Self

. . . Now if the self is not cultivated, then virtue will not be established. If one's virtue is not established, rarely can one be an influence for good in the family–how much less in the wider world. Therefore, the wife is one who follows her husband. The way of husband and wife is the principle of the strong and the weak. In the past, the reason why enlightened monarchs were careful about establishing marriage was that they valued the way of procreation and perpetuation. [The rise and fall of the state is intimately linked to the prosperity or decline of the family.]"

Empress Xu, Instructions for the Inner Quarters, c. 1420

(A) Identify ONE way in which Xu's argument was influenced by long-standing Asian cultural traditions.

(B) Explain ONE example of how cultures in Asia from 1200–1450 resisted the expectations for women as recommneded by Xu.

(C) Explain ONE historical situation from 1200–1450 in which states in Asia attempted to limit Chinese political power.

2. **Answer all parts of the question that follows.**

(A) Identify ONE response by Chinese political leaders to the growing influence of Buddhism during the period of 1200–1450.

(B) Describe ONE example of Chinese culture tradition that withstood the spread of Buddhism during the period 1200–1450.

(C) Explain ONE example of how the spread of Buddhism influenced Confucianism during the period 1200–1450.

THINK AS A HISTORIAN: CONTEXTUALIZE HISTORICAL DEVELOPMENTS

To contextualize is to look at an event, development, or process in history within the situation, or context, in which it occurs. After you place events in context, you begin to see themes and patterns emerge in history. Historians use these themes and patterns to understand the interactions of laws, institutions, culture, events, and people.

For example, one way to understand the Song Dynasty's success from 960 to 1279 is to place its political, social, and economic development in the context of what came before and after it. In the context of what came before, the imperial bureaucracy represents a political continuity, since the bureaucratic system had been in place in earlier dynasties as well. However, its modification under the Song to allow more upward mobility represents a change. Similarly, considering the Song imperial bureaucracy in the economic context of what came after, you might gain insights into causation. That is, the cost of supporting the bureaucracy drained China of its wealth, which in turn helped create problems that led to the decline of the Song Dynasty. Contextualizing also promotes understanding of comparisons among different cultures and time periods.

Explain how the passage below provides context for the spread of Buddhism in China in light of other developments of the time.

In 629, a Chinese Buddhist monk named Xuanzang left China to go on a pilgrimage to India, the birthplace of Buddhism. He traveled west on the Silk Roads to Central Asia, then south and east to India, which he reached in 630. Along the way and in India he met many Buddhist monks and visited Buddhist shrines. In order to gain more insight into Buddhism, he studied for years in Buddhist monasteries and at Nalanda University in Bilar, India—a famous center of Buddhist knowledge. After 17 years away, Xuanzang finally returned to China, where people greeted him as a celebrity. He brought back many Buddhist texts, which he spent the rest of his life translating into Chinese. These writings were highly instrumental in the growth of Buddhist scholarship in China.

REFLECT ON THE TOPIC ESSENTIAL QUESTION

1. In one to three paragraphs, explain how developments in China and other parts of East Asia between c. 1200 and c. 1450 reflect continuity, innovation, and diversity.

1.2

Developments in Dar al-Islam

Allah will admit those who embrace the true faith and do good works
to gardens watered by running streams.

—The Quran, Chapter 47

Essential Question: In the period from c. 1200 to c. 1450, how did Islamic states arise, and how did major religious systems shape society?

After the death of **Muhammad** in 632, Islam spread rapidly outward from Arabia. Through military actions and the activities of merchants and missionaries, Islam's reach extended from India to Spain. As the quotation suggests, many Islamic leaders showed tolerance to Christians, Jews, and others who believed in a single god and did good works. Under the Abbasid Empire, scholars traveled from far away to Baghdad to study at a renowned center of learning known as the **House of Wisdom**. The Islamic community helped transfer knowledge throughout Afro-Eurasia. When the Abbasids declined, they were replaced by other Islamic states.

Invasions and Shifts in Trade Routes

In the 1100s and 1200s, the Abbasid Empire confronted many challenges. Like the Chinese, they had conflicts with nomadic groups in Central Asia. Unlike the Chinese, they also confronted European invaders.

Egyptian Mamluks Arabs often purchased enslaved people, or **Mamluks**, who were frequently ethnic Turks from Central Asia, to serve as soldiers and later as bureaucrats. Because of their roles, Mamluks had more opportunities for advancement than did most enslaved people. In Egypt, Mamluks seized control of the government, establishing the **Mamluk Sultanate** (1250–1517). They prospered by facilitating trade in cotton and sugar between the Islamic world and Europe. However, when the Portuguese and other Europeans developed new sea routes for trade, the Mamluks declined in power.

Seljuk Turks Another challenge to the Abbasids came from the Central Asian **Seljuk Turks**, who were also Muslims. Starting in the 11th century, they began conquering parts of the Middle East, eventually extending their power almost as far east as Western China. The Seljuk leader called himself **sultan**, thereby reducing the role of the highest-ranking Abbasid from caliph to chief Sunni religious authority.

Crusaders The Abbasids allowed Christians to travel easily to and from their holy sites in and around Jerusalem. However, the Seljuk Turks limited this travel. European Christians organized groups of soldiers, called **Crusaders**, to reopen access. (See Topic 1.6.)

Mongols The fourth group to attack the Abbasid Empire were among the most famous conquerors in history—the **Mongols**. (See Topic 2.2.) Like many Mamluks and the Seljuk Turks, they came from Central Asia. The Mongols conquered the remaining Abbasid Empire in 1258 and ended the Seljuk rule. They continued to push westward but were stopped in Egypt by the Mamluks.

Economic Competition Since the 8th century, the Abbasids had been an important link connecting Asia, Europe, and North Africa. Goods and ideas flowed from one region to another on trade routes controlled by the Abbasids. Many went through **Baghdad**. However, trade patterns slowly shifted to routes farther north. As Baghdad lost its traditional place at the center of trade, it lost wealth and population. It could not afford to keep its canals repaired. Farmers could not provide enough food for the urban population. Slowly, the infrastructure that had made Baghdad a great city fell into decay.

Cultural and Social Life

Over time, the Islamic world fragmented politically. Many of these new states adopted Abbasid practices, but they were distinct ethnically. The **Abbasid Caliphate** was led by Arabs and Persians, but the later Islamic states were shaped by Turkic peoples who descended from people in Central Asia. For example, the Mamluks in North Africa, the Seljuks in the Middle East, and the Delhi Sultanate in South Asia were all at least partially Turkic. By the 16th century, three large Islamic states had their roots in Turkic cultures—the Ottoman Empire in Turkey, the Safavid Empire in Persia, and the Mughal Empire in India. (See Topic 3.1.)

However, these Islamic states continued to form a cultural region. Trade spread new goods and fresh ideas. The common use of shariah created similar legal systems. Great universities in Baghdad, Iraq; Córdoba, Spain; Cairo, Egypt; and Bukhara in Central Asia created centers for sharing intellectual innovations.

Cultural Continuities Islamic scholars followed the advice of the prophet Muhammad: "Go in quest of knowledge even unto China." By learning from many cultures, they carried on the work of earlier thinkers:

- They translated Greek literary classics into Arabic, saving the works of Aristotle and other Greek thinkers from oblivion.

- They studied mathematics texts from India and transferred the knowledge to Europeans.

- They adopted techniques for paper-making from China. Through them, Europeans learned to make paper.

Cultural Innovations In addition to building on the intellectual achievements of other cultures, scholars during the "golden age" in Baghdad made their own achievements. **Nasir al-Din al-Tusi** (1201–1274) was one of the most celebrated Islamic scholars. He contributed to astronomy, law, logic, ethics, mathematics, philosophy, and medicine. An observatory built under his direction was the most advanced in the world and produced the most accurate astronomical charts. He studied the relationship between the lengths of the sides of a triangle and the angles. This laid the groundwork for making trigonometry a separate subject. Medical advances and hospital care improved in cities such as Cairo, while doctors and pharmacists studied for examinations for licenses that would allow them to practice.

Ibn Khaldun (1332–1406) was well known for his historical accounts and is widely acknowledged as a founder of the fields of historiography (the study of the methods of historians) and sociology.

Sufi poet and mystic **'A'ishah al-Ba'uniyyah** (1460–1507) may be the most prolific female Muslim writer before the 20th century. Her best-known work, a long poem honoring Muhammad called "Clear Inspiration, on Praise of the Trusted One," refers to many previous poets, reflecting her broad learning. Many of her works describe her journey toward mystical illumination.

'A'ishah's poetry reflects a contrast between most Muslims and Sufis. Unlike Muslims who focused on intellectual pursuits, such as the study of the Quran, **Sufis** emphasized introspection to grasp truths that they believed could not be understood through learning. Sufism may have begun as a mystical response to the perceived love of luxury by the early Umayyad Caliphate.

Sufi missionaries played an important role in the spread of Islam. They tended to adapt to local cultures and traditions, sometimes interweaving local religious elements into Islam, and in this way they won many converts.

Commerce, Class, and Diversity Helping to power the golden age of natural and moral philosophy and the arts was commerce. Islamic society viewed merchants as more prestigious than did other societies in Europe and Asia at the time. Muhammad himself had been a merchant, as had his first wife. With the revival of trade on Silk Roads, merchants could grow rich from their dealings across the Indian Ocean and Central Asia. They were esteemed as long as they maintained fair dealings and gave to charity in accord with the pillars of the Islamic faith. Some merchants were even sent out as missionaries.

In the non-Arab areas of Islamic expansion, control by Islamic caliphs led to discrimination against non-Arabs, though rarely to open persecution. This discrimination gradually faded in the 9th century. The caliph's soldiers were forbidden to own territory they had conquered. The presence of a permanent military force that kept order but did not own property allowed life for most of the inhabitants of the countryside to remain virtually unchanged. However, people paid tribute to Islamic caliphs rather than to Byzantine rulers.

Slavery Islam prohibited Muslims from enslaving other Muslims or monotheists such as Jews, Christians, and Zoroastrians. (See Prologue.) However, it permitted enslaving others. Muslims often imported enslaved people from Africa, Kievan Rus (present-day Belarus, Russia, and Ukraine), and Central Asia, but the institution of hereditary slavery had not developed. Many enslaved people converted to Islam, after which their owners freed them.

Enslaved women might find themselves serving as concubines to Islamic men who already had wed their allotment of four wives. They were allowed more independence—for example, to go to markets and to run errands—than the legal wives. Only enslaved women were permitted to dance or perform musically before unrelated men. This opportunity to earn money sometimes enabled females in slavery to accumulate enough to buy their freedom.

Free Women in Islam

Some practices now associated with Islam were common cultural customs in Central Asia and the Byzantine Empire before the time of Muhammad. For example, women often covered their heads and faces. This practice solidified under Islam, with most women observing *hijab,* a term that can refer either to the practice of dressing modestly or to a specific type of covering. Men often wore head coverings, from turbans to skull caps. While women could study and read, they were not to do so in the company of men not related to them.

Muhammad's Policies Muhammad raised the status of women in several ways. He treated his wives with love and devotion. He insisted that dowries, the payments prospective husbands made to secure brides, be paid to the future wife rather than to her father. He forbade female infanticide, the killing of newborn girls. Muhammad's first wife was educated and owned her own business, which set a pattern for the recognition of women's abilities.

The Status of Women Overall, Islamic women enjoyed a higher status than Christian or Jewish women. Islamic women were allowed to inherit property and retain ownership after marriage. They could remarry if widowed, and they could receive a cash settlement if divorced. Under some conditions, a wife could initiate divorce. Moreover, women could practice birth control. Islamic women who testified in a court under shariah (see Topic 3.3) were to be protected from retaliation, but their testimony was worth only half that of a man. One gap in the historical record is written evidence of how women viewed their position in society: most of the records created before 1450 were written by men.

The rise of towns and cities in Islamic-ruled areas resulted in new limitations on women's rights, just as it did in other cultures. The new status of women might best be symbolized by the veil and the harem, a dwelling set aside for wives, concubines, and the children of these women. (Connect: In a paragraph, compare the status of women in Chinese society to the status of women in Islamic society in the period c. 1200 to c. 1450.)

Islamic Rule in Spain

While the Umayyads ruled only briefly in the Middle East, they kept power longer in Spain. In 711, after Muslim forces had defeated Byzantine armies across North Africa, they successfully invaded Spain from the south. They designated Córdoba as their capital for Spain.

Battle of Tours The Islamic military was turned back in 732 when it lost the Battle of Tours against Frankish forces. This defeat, rare for Islamic armies during the 700s, marked the limit of rapid Islamic expansion into Western Europe. Most of the continent remained Christian, but Muslims ruled Spain for the next seven centuries.

Prosperity Under Islam Like the Abbasids in Baghdad, the Umayyad rulers in Córdoba created a climate of toleration, with Muslims, Christians, and Jews coexisting peacefully. They also promoted trade, allowing Chinese and Southeast Asian products to enter into Spain and thus into the rest of Europe. Many of the goods in this trade traveled aboard ships called dhows. These ships, first developed in India or China, had long, thin hulls that made them excellent for carrying goods, though less useful for conducting warfare.

Cultural and Scholarly Transfers The Islamic state in Spain, known as al-Andalus, became a center of learning. Córdoba had the largest library in the world at the time. Among the famous scholars from Spain was Ibn Rushd, known in Europe as Averroes (12th century). He wrote influential works on law, secular philosophy, and the natural sciences.

The Muslims, Christians, and Jews living in al-Andalus—all "people of the book" as Muslims regarded them—not only tolerated one another but also influenced one another. For example, Ibn Rushd's commentaries on Aristotle influenced the Jewish philosopher Maimonides (c. 1135–c. 1204). Maimonides developed a synthesis of Aristotle's reasoning and biblical interpretation. He, in turn, influenced Christian philosophers, including St. Thomas Aquinas (1225–1274). Islamic scholarship and scientific innovations, along with the knowledge transferred from India and China, laid the groundwork for the Renaissance and Scientific Revolution in Europe. For example, making paper, a technology developed in China and taught to Europeans by Muslims, was vital to spreading ideas in Europe.

KEY TERMS BY THEME

GOVERNMENT: Empires	CULTURE: Religion	CULTURE: Golden Age
Mamluk Sultanate	Mamluks	House of Wisdom
Seljuk Turks	Muhammad	Baghdad
sultan	Crusaders	Nasir al-Din al-Tusi
Mongols	Sufis	'A'ishah al-Ba'uniyyah
Abbasid Caliphate		

Questions 1 to 3 refer to the passage below.

"In the name of God the Merciful and the Compassionate: This is the safe-conduct accorded by the servant of God Umar, the Commander of the Faithful, to the people of [Jerusalem]. He accords them safe-conduct for their persons, their property, their churches, their crosses, their sound and their sick, and the rest of their worship. . . . No constraint shall be exercised against them in religion nor shall any harm be done to any among them. . . .

The people of [Jerusalem] must pay the jizya [required tax on non-Muslims] in the same way as the people of other cities. They must expel the Romans [Byzantine soldiers and officials] and the brigands from the city. Those who leave shall have safe-conduct for their persons and property until they reach safety.

Those of the people of [Jerusalem] who wish to remove their persons and effects and depart with the Romans [Byzantines] and abandon their churches and their crosses shall have safe-conduct for their persons, their churches, and their crosses, until they reach safety."

Muhammad ibn Jarir al-Tabari, History of the Prophets and Kings, "Peace Terms with Jerusalem, 636 C.E.," 10th century

1. Which trait of Islamic rule described in this passage was also evident in Islamic rule in al-Andalus?

    (A) The persecution of other religions by Islamic leaders

    (B) The toleration of other religions by Muslims in conquered territory

    (C) The conflict between Romans and Byzantines over territory

    (D) The desire to improve relations with the Romans in Jerusalem

2. What viewpoint led Umar to this trait of Islamic rule?

    (A) He did not actively seek converts to his faith.

    (B) He believed Christians and Jews were only a small a threat to his faith.

    (C) He was more concerned with political than religious issues.

    (D) He considered Christians and Jews to be "People of the Book."

3. Which development resulted from a change in Umar's policy toward Jerusalem by the Seljuks?

    (A) The beginning of the Crusades by European Christians

    (B) A shift in trade patterns

    (C) An increase in the power of the Byzantine Empire

    (D) A decrease in taxes paid by Jerusalem residents

1. Use the passage below to answer all parts of the question that follows.

"I paid a visit to the tomb of John the son of Zechariah [a figure in the Christian Bible]—God's blessing on both of them!—in the village of Sebastea in the province of Nablus [a region in the Middle East near the Jordan River]. After saying my prayers, I came out into the square that was bounded on one side by the Holy Precinct [a place of worship]. I found a half-closed gate, opened it and entered a church. Inside were about ten old men, their bare heads as white as combed cotton. They were facing east, and wore on their chests [wooden sticks] ending in crossbars turned up like the rear of a saddle. They took their oath on this sign and gave hospitality to those who needed it. The sight of their piety touched my heart, but at the same time it displeased and saddened me, for I had never seen such zeal and devotion among the Muslims.

For some time I brooded on this experience, until one day, as Mu'in ad-Din and I were passing . . . he said to me: 'I want to dismount here and visit the Old Men [people who practice severe self-discipline].'

'Certainly,' I replied, and we dismounted and went into a long building set at an angle to the road. For the moment I thought there was no one there. Then I saw about a hundred prayer mats, and on each a sufi, his face expressing peaceful serenity, and his body humble devotion. This was a reassuring sight, and I gave thanks to Almighty God that there were among the Muslims men of even more zealous devotion than those Christian priests. Before this I had never seen sufis in their monastery, and was ignorant of the way they lived."

> A Muslim describing Christians in the 12th century, quoted in
> Francesco Gabrieli, *Arab Historians of the Crusades,* 1969

(A) Identify ONE way that religious syncretism appeared in Dar al-Islam in the period 1200–1450.

(B) Explain ONE way in which the behavior of the Sufis demonstrates a difference within the practice of Islam in the period 1200–1450.

(C) Explain ONE outcome of Christians and Muslims living in close proximity in the period 1200–1450.

2. Answer all parts of the question that follows.

(A) Identify ONE way the status of women under Islam differed from the status of women in China during the period 1200–1450.

(B) Explain ONE way in which the Umayyad rulers in Córdoba were successful during the period 1200–1450.

(C) Explain ONE reason why Umayyad leaders were to keep power in Spain during the period 1200–1450.

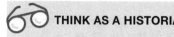 **THINK AS A HISTORIAN:** IDENTIFY HISTORICAL CONCEPTS, DEVELOPMENTS, AND PROCESSES

Unit 1 is called "The Global Tapestry" to suggest that world history is a complex interweaving of different threads from different parts of the world at different times. However, to fully appreciate the whole, historians try to unravel the tapestry thread by thread to see just how each fits in. As they do, they use such *historical concepts* as change, continuity, perspective, cause and effect, significance, and empathy. Applying these concepts, they come to understand *historical developments*—patterns of changes or growth over time. To see these patterns, they look at subjects in historical context—how did they start out, and what did they become over time? Historians also try to understand the *historical processes* that made certain developments possible, such as migration, industrialization, conquest, and state building.

Practice identifying historical concepts, developments, and processes by completing the activities below.

1. Read the paragraph labeled **Economic Competition** on page 14. Explain the historical concept of cause and effect and how it applies to the decline of Baghdad.

2. Explain the historical concept of continuities and how Muhammad's advice to "go in quest of knowledge even unto China" resulted in historical continuities. (See page 16.)

3. Explain the historical process of knowledge transfers that began with the Jews, Muslims, and Christians living in al-Andalus and laid the groundwork for the Scientific Revolution and Renaissance in Europe. (See page 19.)

REFLECT ON THE TOPIC ESSENTIAL QUESTION

1. In one to three paragraphs, explain how Islamic states arose and how major religious systems shaped society in the periods between c. 1200 and c. 1450.

1.3

Developments in South and Southeast Asia

What the books taught me, I've practised.
What they didn't teach me, I've taught myself.
I've gone into the forest and wrestled with the lion.
I didn't get this far by teaching one thing and doing another.

—Lal Ded (1320–1392)

Essential Question: How did various beliefs and practices in South and Southeast Asia affect society and the development of states?

The poetry of Lal Ded, known as Mother Lalla, illustrates a major cross-interaction between religious traditions that shaped the history of South and Southeast Asia. She was born in Kashmir, a region of northern India. While a Hindu, her emphasis on experience appealed to many Muslims, particularly Sufis. The interaction of Hindus and Muslims, though sometimes violent, created dynamic developments in religious thought, politics, economics, art, and architecture. Despite the strong Islamic presence in the region, local Hindu kingdoms continued to play a major role in India's decentralized political landscape. A third religion, Buddhism, also had a strong presence in the area, particularly in the Sinhala dynasties in present-day Sri Lanka and the great kingdoms of Southeast Asia.

Political Structures in South Asia

South Asia was only occasionally united as a single state in its history. After the Gupta Dynasty that had dominated South Asia collapsed in 550, ending the so-called Golden Age or Classical Era of Indian history, disunity returned to the region for most of the next 1,000 years. Northern and southern India developed separate political structures. However, Hinduism provided some cultural unity throughout the region. Many people combined their own local faith tradition with adherence to the same scriptures and core beliefs respected throughout the region.

Political Structures in Southern India Southern India was more stable than northern India. The first kingdom, the Chola Dynasty, reigned over southern India for more than 400 years (850–1267). During the 11th century, the dynasty extended its rule to Ceylon, the large island just south of India. (Today it is known as Sri Lanka.)

The second kingdom, the **Vijayanagara Empire** (1336–1646) took its name from the word for "the victorious city." It began with the arrival of two brothers, Harihara and Bukka, from the Delhi Sultanate in north-central India. They were sent to the area because the Delhi Sultanate wished to extend its rule to southern India. These brothers had been born as Hindus and converted to Islam for the sake of upward mobility. When they left the region controlled by the Delhi Sultanate, they once again embraced the religion of their birth and established their own Hindu kingdom. The Vijayanagar Empire existed from the mid-1300s until the mid-1500s, when a group of Muslim kingdoms overthrew it.

Political Structures in Northern India Northern India experienced a great deal more upheaval than did southern India. After the fall of the Gupta Empire (see Prologue), the **Rajput kingdoms** gradually formed in northern India and present-day Pakistan. These were Hindu kingdoms led by leaders of numerous clans who were often at war with one another. Because of the competition among clans, no centralized government arose, once again demonstrating the diversity and the regionalism of South Asia. The lack of a centralized power left the kingdoms vulnerable to Muslim attacks.

While the Himalayas protected India from invasions from the north and east, mountain passes in the northwest allowed invasions by Muslim armies. Each attack disrupted a region that had been mostly Hindu and Buddhist. Over time, the Islamic presence in the region grew:

- In the 8th century, Islamic armies invaded what is today Pakistan. However, they brought little change to everyday life. Located on the eastern fringes of the Dar al-Islam, the region was isolated from the center of the culture. In addition, the Rajput princes skillfully wielded their power to limit the Muslim conquerors' influence.

- In the 11th century, Islamic forces plundered northern India's Hindu temples and Buddhist shrines for their riches. In addition, they erected mosques on Hindu and Buddhist holy sites—much to the anger of followers of those faiths.

In the early 13th century, Islamic forces managed to conquer the city of Delhi and much of the northern portion of South Asia. Bringing Islam into India, the **Delhi Sultanate** reigned for 300 years, from the 13th through the 16th centuries. The interaction of Islam and Hinduism in northern India dominated the political history of the era. While some Hindus converted to Islam, others resented Muslims and considered them foreigners. One factor contributing to this resentment was that the Delhi Sultanate imposed a tax, called the jizya, on all non-Muslim subjects of the empire.

Throughout its reign, the Delhi Sultanate never organized an efficient bureaucracy in the style of the Chinese. For this reason, sultans had difficulty imposing their policies in a land as vast and diverse as India. Despite the strong

Islamic presence in the region, local kingdoms continued to play a major role in India's decentralized political landscape.

The sultans wanted to extend their rule southward. Before they succeeded, though, they became focused on defending themselves from an onslaught by the Mongol army from the northwest. The Delhi Sultanate prevented the Mongols themselves from conquering South Asia. However, in 1526, the sultans lost power to a new empire, the Mughals, whose leaders did trace their ancestry to the Mongols.

Religion in South Asia

Religion always held a dominant place in South Asian history. Before the arrival of Islam, most South Asians practiced Hinduism, while a smaller number identified themselves as Buddhists. South Asians encountered a starkly different religion when Islam arrived.

- Hindus pray to many gods, while Islam is strictly monotheistic.

- Hindu temples and artwork are replete with pictures of deities, while Muslims disapprove of any visual representation of Allah.

- Hinduism was associated with a hierarchical caste system, while Islam has always called for the equality of all believers.

- Hindus recognize several sacred texts, while Muslims look to only the Quran for spiritual guidance.

The Arrival of Islam The relationship between Hindus and Muslims shaped the history of South Asia beginning in the 7th century, and it continues to shape regional culture and politics today. Islam initially entered India forcefully yet eventually took on a more peaceful approach. But while Islam was a universalizing religion, one that wanted to **proselytize**, or actively seek converts, Muslim rulers found early in their reign that forcing their Hindu and Buddhist subjects to convert was not successful. Thus, most converts came to Islam voluntarily. Many Muslim merchants in the Indian Ocean trade moved to Indian port cities and married. Their wives often ended up converting to their husband's religion.

With its emphasis on the equality of all believers, Islam also attracted low-caste Hindus who hoped that conversion would improve their social status. In this sense, Islam in India was like Christianity in the Roman Empire. Both appealed to the people who suffered the most under the existing social structure.

The largest numbers of converts to Islam, however, were Buddhists. Corruption among the monks and raids on monasteries by early Muslim conquerors left the Buddhist religion disorganized. The spread of Islam helped make Buddhism a minority religion in its place of birth. (Connect: Make an outline comparing the spread of Islam in South Asia to the spread of Buddhism in China. See Topic 1.1.)

Social Structures in South Asia

The arrival of Islam did little to alter the basic structure of society in South Asia. India's caste system is its strongest historical continuity. While obviously inequitable, it lent stability to a politically decentralized land. The caste system was flexible and able to accommodate newcomers. Muslim merchants and migrants, even though they were not Hindu, found a place for themselves within the caste hierarchy based on their occupation. These subcastes based on occupation operated like workers' guilds, soon becoming absorbed into the social fabric of Indian society. Connect: Write a paragraph comparing the caste system in South Asia to the social structures in China in the period from 1200 to 1450. See Topic 1.1.)

At the same time, most of those who tried to escape the grip of the caste system failed. The low-caste Hindus who converted to Islam as a way to improve their social status usually did not achieve that goal. Individuals required more education and opportunities for better jobs, not just a new religion, to help them escape their low status in life.

As Islam spread, Muslims varied how they applied its core teachings, depending on their culture before converting. For example, Islam did not alter gender relations greatly. In South Asia, women in the Hindu tradition were confined to a separate social sphere, and Islamic women received similar treatment. In Southeast Asia, women enjoyed more independence before the arrival of Islam. This pattern continued as people became Muslims. Thus, converts in South and Southeast Asia found ways to accommodate a new faith, but most people did not reject their traditions in the process.

Cultural Interactions in South Asia

People in South Asia and the Middle East shared their intellectual and cultural achievements with each other. For example, Arab astronomers and mathematicians added to the body of knowledge begun by their Indian counterparts. Indian developments in algebra and geometry were translated into Arabic, and spread throughout Dar al-Islam. One result of this movement of ideas was that the numeral system referred to in the West as "Arabic numerals," actually originated in India.

In India itself, sultans erected buildings melding the intricate artistic details of Hindu art with the geometric patterns preferred by Islamic architecture. The city of Delhi is filled with examples of Islamic architecture built during the Delhi Sultanate. One famous example, the **Qutub Minar**, stands in the southern part of the city. Rulers from the Delhi Sultanate built an elaborate mosque on top of a Hindu temple and used materials for the mosque from nearby Hindu and other religious shrines. Towering over the mosque is the Qutub Minar itself, a gigantic leaning tower, the tallest structure in India today. Historians debate the reason for its construction; one obvious function is its presence as a symbol of Islamic influence and, at one time, dominance of northern India.

An entirely new language developed among Muslims of South Asia: **Urdu**. Urdu melded the grammatical pattern of Hindi (the language of Northern Indians), and with the vocabulary of Arabic and some elements of Farsi (the language of Persians). Today, Urdu is the official language of Pakistan.

The Bhakti Movement Beginning in the 12th century, some Hindus began to draw upon traditional teachings about the importance of emotion in their spiritual life. Rather than emphasize studying texts or performing rituals, they focused on developing a strong attachment to a particular deity. This development, known as the **Bhakti Movement**, started in southern India. It was especially appealing to many believers because it did not discriminate against women or people of low social status. For example, one of the most famous figures of the Bhakti Movement would be a female, the poet Mira Bai, who lived in the 16th century.

Though the bhaktis were Hindus, they were similar in some ways to Sufi Muslims. Both groups were mystical movements, ones that emphasized inner reflection in order to achieve a direct personal relationship with a deity. Because they placed less emphasis on strict adherence to traditional rituals and beliefs, bhaktis and Sufis each appealed to people outside their traditions. Just as the Sufis helped spread Islam, the Bhaktis helped spread Hinduism.

Source: Thinkstock

Religious structures in India often demonstrate syncretism in architecture. Qutub Minar combines towers common in Hindu temples with domes common in Islamic mosques.

Southeast Asia

Like China, South Asia strongly influenced its neighbors, particularly the lands of Southeast Asia—today's Indonesia, Malaysia, Cambodia, Thailand, Laos, and Vietnam. Indian merchants had contact with these Southeast Asian lands as early as 500 B.C.E. The merchants sold gold, silver, metal goods, and textiles in the region and brought back its fine spices. Trade voyages introduced the Indian religions of Hinduism and Buddhism to Southeast Asia. Much of the region became and remains today mostly Buddhist. The region, like Southwest Asia, was strategically significant. Whoever controlled this region could influence the valuable trade between South Asia and East Asia.

Sea-Based Kingdoms Because Southeast Asia was so important, several kingdoms emerged there. Two were particularly long-lasting:

- The **Srivijaya Empire** (670–1025) was primarily a Buddhist kingdom based on Sumatra. It built up its navy and prospered by charging fees for ships traveling between India and China. As a religious center of the region, Srivijaya dominated for centuries but it was weakened by the expansion of other powers, one of them being the Majapahit Kingdom.

- The **Majapahit Kingdom** (1293–1520) based on Java had 98 tributaries at its height. Like Srivijaya, Majapahit sustained its power by controlling sea routes. Unlike Srivijaya, Majapahit was a Hindu kingdom (but with strong Buddhist influences). The empire began a slow decline after the deaths of several key leaders and as Islamic influence began to grow in the region.

Land-Based Kingdoms Other kingdoms in Southeast Asia drew power from their control over land. The **Sinhala dynasties** in Sri Lanka had their roots in the arrival of early immigrants, most likely merchants, from north India. Buddhists arrived in the 3rd century B.C.E. and the island became a center of Buddhist study. Monasteries and nunneries flourished. Both men and women found a life of contemplation and simple living attractive.

Buddhism was so deeply embedded that Buddhist priests often served as advisors to the monarchs. The government of one of the kingdoms oversaw the construction of a network of reservoirs and canals to create an excellent irrigation system, which contributed to economic growth. However, attacks by invaders from India and conflicts between the monarchy and the priests ultimately weakened the kingdoms.

The **Khmer Empire**, also known as the Angkor Kingdom (802–1431), was situated near the Mekong River and also did not depend on maritime prowess for its power. The kingdom's complex irrigation and drainage systems led to economic prosperity, making it one of the most prosperous kingdoms in Southeast Asia. Irrigation allowed farmers to harvest rice crops several times a year, and drainage systems reduced the impact of the heavy monsoon rains.

The Khmer capital was at Angkor Thom. The temples there showed the variety of Indian cultural influences on Southeast Asia. Hindu artwork and sculptures of deities abounded. But at some point the Khmer rulers became Buddhist. Starting in the 12th and 13th centuries, they added Buddhist sculptures and artwork to the temples without destroying any of the Hindu artwork.

During the same period and only one-half mile from Angkor Thom, rulers constructed the ornate and majestic Buddhist temple complex of Angkor Wat. In 1431, the Thais of the **Sukhothai Kingdom** invaded the area, forcing the Khmers out. Nevertheless, ruins of the magnificent structures in Angkor Thom and Angkor Wat still stand, testifying not only to the sophistication of Southeast Asian culture but also to the powerful influence of Indian culture on the region.

Source: Rajasthani Painting of Meerabai. https://en.wikiquote.org/wiki/Meera_Bai#/media/File:Meerabai.jpg.

The great temple complex at Angkor Wat, in both its architecture and its use, reflects the interaction between Hinduism and Buddhism in Southeast Asia.

Islam Islam's movement into the Indian Ocean region paralleled its expansion elsewhere. The first Southeast Asian Muslims were local merchants, who converted in the 700s, hoping to have better trading relations with the Islamic merchants who arrived on their shores. Islam was most popular in urban areas at the time. Islam spread to Sumatra, Java, and the Malay Peninsula. Today, Indonesia includes more Muslims than any other country.

Sufis Sufis also did missionary work in Southeast Asia. (See Topic 1.2.) Because of their tolerance for local faiths, people felt comfortable converting to Islam. They could be Muslims and still honor local deities.

KEY TERMS BY THEME

GOVERNMENT: South Asia
Vijayanagara Empire (Southern India)
Rajput kingdoms (North India)
Delhi Sultanate

GOVERNMENT: Southeast Asia
Srivijaya Empire (Sumatra)
Majahapit Kingdom (Java)
Sinhala dynasties (Sri Lanka)
Khmer Empire (Cambodia)
Sukhothai Kingdom (Thailand)

CULTURE: Religion
proselytize
Bhakti Movement

CULTURE: Blending
Qutub Minar
Urdu

MULTIPLE-CHOICE QUESTIONS

Questions 1 to 3 refer to the excerpt below.

"The Hindus believe that there is no country but theirs, no nation like theirs, no kings like theirs, no religion like theirs, no science like theirs. They are haughty, foolishly vain, self-conceited, and stolid. They are by nature [reluctant] in communicating that which they know, and they take the greatest possible care to withhold it from men of another caste among their own people, still much more, of course, from any foreigner. . . . Their haughtiness is such that, if you tell them of any science or scholar in Khorasan [a region in southwest Asia] and Persia, they will think you to be both an ignoramus and a liar. If they traveled and mixed with other nations, they would soon change their mind, for their ancestors were not as narrow-minded as the present generation is."

Al-Beruni, Muslim scholar at the court of Mahmud of Ghazni,
early 11th century

1. Which element of Al-Beruni's point of view does he express most clearly in this passage?

   (A) He was a monotheist writing about people he considered polytheists.

   (B) He was a non-Hindu who was writing about Hindus.

   (C) He belonged to a group that had been conquered by the people he was writing about.

   (D) He grew up in a region to the west of the region he was describing.

2. Which part of India's history most directly supports al-Beruni's claim about how the Hindu culture he observed differed from earlier culture in India?

   (A) The decreasing importance of the caste system

   (B) The policies on religion of Ashoka

   (C) The development of the Bhakti movement

   (D) The raids by Mahmud of Ghazni

3. The outcome of the Bhakti Movement was most closely related to which of the ideas expressed by Al-Beruni?

(A) Many Hindus in Southeast Asia converted to Islam.

(B) Muslims expelled nearly all Hindus from South Asia.

(C) Hindus were prohibited from traveling to countries with high Muslim populations.

(D) Hindus and Sufi Muslims found some agreement in religious beliefs.

SHORT-ANSWER QUESTIONS

1. Use the passage below to answer all parts of the question that follows.

" 'Moreover, you should not say this, since even fools know that wives should follow their husbands. For thus it is said:

- Moonlight goes with the moon, the lightning clings to the cloud, and women follow their husbands . . . .

- A woman who follows after her husband shall surely purify three families: her mother's, her father's, and that into which she was given in marriage. . . .

- What profit is there in the life of a wretched woman who has lost her husband? Her body is as useless as a banyan tree in a cemetery. . . .'

Thus speaking she fell at the king's feet, begging that a fire be provided for her. And when the king heard her words . . . he caused a pyre to be erected . . . and gave her leave . . . . and in his presence [she] entered the fire together with her husband's body."

Anonymous collection of stories about a semi-legendary king
in South Asia named Vikrama, assembled between the 11th
and 13th centuries

(A) Identify ONE way in which the status of women in South Asia was similar to the status of men in the same region in the 12th or 13th century.

(B) Explain ONE way in which the status of women in South Asia changed between 1200 and 1450.

(C) Explain ONE way in which Islam in India between 1200 and 1450 was like Christianity in the Roman Empire.

2. **Answer all parts of the question that follows.**

   (A) Identify ONE way in which political structures were similar between Southern India and Northern India in the period 1200–1450.

   (B) Explain ONE way in which two kingdoms in Southeast Asia differed in the period 1200–1450.

   (C) Explain ONE example of Islamic influence in South and Southeast Asia during the period 1200–1450.

 THINK AS A HISTORIAN: IDENTIFY CLAIMS

A claim is a statement asserted to be true. It differs from provable fact, such as "Baghdad was the largest city in the Abbasid Empire" or simple preference, such as "World history is more interesting than algebra." Instead, in modern scholarship, a claim expresses a viewpoint with which thoughtful people can reasonably disagree. It forms the basis of an *argument*—reasoning backed up with evidence.

A claim is often a somewhat general statement that reflects a judgment shaped by the point of view of the writer. In some historical texts with a clear bias, the claim may simply be the author's main idea, and it may be based more on opinion or overgeneralization than rigorous reasoning. In modern scholarship, however, claims should be grounded in facts and informed opinions. While claims are general, the evidence used to support them should be specific.

Reread the excerpt by the Muslim scholar Al-Beruni on page 30. Determine which sentence below best expresses his claim by looking for the most general statement. Then explain whether the claim is based on informed opinions or overgeneralizations.

1. [Hindus] are haughty, foolishly vain, self-conceited, and stolid.

2. The Hindus believe that there is no country but theirs, no nation like theirs, no kings like theirs, no religion like theirs, no science like theirs.

3. The present generation of Hindus is narrow-minded.

4. If you tell them of any science or scholar in Khorasan and Persia, they will think you to be both an ignoramus and a liar.

REFLECT ON THE CHAPTER ESSENTIAL QUESTION

1. In one to three paragraphs, explain how various beliefs and practices in South and Southeast Asia affected society and the development of states.

1.4

Developments in the Americas

I love the song of the mockingbird,
Bird of four hundred voices,
I love the color of jade
And the intoxicating scent of flowers,
But more than all I love my brother, man!

—Nezahualcoyotl (1402–1472), Aztec poet

Essential Question: What states developed in the Americas, and how did they change over time?

Following the decline of the Olmecs in Mesoamerica and the Chavin in the Andes, new civilizations, such as the Mayans, the Aztecs, and the Incas rose in the same regions. In addition, the first large-scale civilization in North America developed. As in Afro-Eurasia, several of these civilizations developed strong states, large urban centers, and complex belief systems. Current knowledge about these civilizations combines archaeological evidence, oral traditions, and writings by Europeans who came to the Americas after 1492. One poem recorded by the Spanish was the one above from an Aztec writer.

The Mississippian Culture

The first large-scale civilization in North America emerged in the 700s or 800s in what is now the eastern United States. Since it started in the Mississippi River Valley, it is known as the **Mississippian** culture. While other cultures built monumental buildings, Mississippians built enormous earthen mounds, some of which were as tall as 100 feet and covered an area the size of 12 football fields. The largest of these mounds is **Cahokia**, located in southern Illinois.

Government and Society The Mississippian society had a rigid class structure. A chief called the Great Sun ruled each large town. Below the Great Sun was an upper class of priests and nobles and a lower class of farmers, hunters, merchants, and artisans. At the bottom were enslaved people, who usually were prisoners of war. In general, women farmed and men hunted. The Mississippians had a **matrilineal society**, which means that social standing was determined by the woman's side of the family. For example, when the Great Sun died, the title passed not to his own son, but to a sister's son.

The Decline of Mississippian Civilization People abandoned Cahokia around 1450, and other large Mississippian cities by 1600. Historians disagree on why the Mississippian people moved. One theory posits that flooding or other weather extremes caused crop failures and the collapse of the agricultural economy needed to sustain the populations of the large cities. Another theory suggests that diseases introduced by the Europeans decimated the population.

Chaco and Mesa Verde

Soon after the rise of the Mississippian Civilization, various cultures emerged in what is now the southwestern United States. Living in a dry region, people developed ways to collect, transport, and store water efficiently. In addition, because of the climate, trees were small and scarce, so people had little wood to use to build homes. Two cultures became well-known for their innovations:

- The Chaco built large housing structures using stones and clay, some of which included hundreds of rooms.
- The people of Mesa Verde built multi-story homes into the sides of cliffs using bricks made of sandstone.

Both groups declined in the late 13th century as the climate became drier.

The Maya City-States

Mayan civilization reached its height between 250 and 900 C.E. Mayans stretched over the southern part of Mexico and much of what is now Belize, Honduras, and Guatemala. Most lived in or near one of the approximately 40 cities that ranged in size from 5,000 to 50,000 people. At its peak, as many as 2 million Mayans populated the region.

Mayan Government The main form of Mayan government was the **city-state**, each ruled by a king and consisting of a city and its surrounding territory. Most rulers were men. However, when no male heir was available or old enough to govern, Mayan women ruled. Wars between city-states were common. At times, city-states were overthrown. However, Mayans rarely fought to control territory. More often they fought to gain tribute—payments from the conquered to the conqueror—and captives to be used as **human sacrifices** during religious ceremonies.

Each Mayan king claimed to be descended from a god. The Mayans believed that when the king died, he would become one with his ancestor-god. The king directed the activities of the elite scribes and priests who administered the affairs of the state. Royal rule usually passed from father to son, but kings who lost the support of the people were sometimes overthrown. The common people were required to pay taxes, usually in the form of crops, and to provide labor to the government. City-states had no standing armies, so when war erupted, governments required citizens to provide military service. No central government ruled all Mayan lands, although often one city-state was the strongest in a region and would dominate its neighbors.

Mayan Religion, Science, and Technology The Mayans were innovative thinkers and inventors. For example, they incorporated the concept of zero into their number system, developed a complex writing system, and learned to make rubber out of liquid collected from rubber plants.

Mayan science and religion were linked through astronomy. Based on the calendar, priests decided when to celebrate religious ceremonies and whether to go to war. As a result, keeping an accurate calendar was very important. Although the Mayans had no telescopes, they made very precise observatories atop pyramids such as the one at Chichen Itza. Their observations enabled priests to design a calendar more accurate than any used in Europe at the time.

One task of priests, who could be either male or female, was to conduct ceremonies honoring many deities. Among the most important deities were those of the sun, rain, and corn. Mayans made offerings to the gods so prayers might be answered. War captives were sometimes killed as offerings. (Connect: Compare the political structures of the Mayans with the political structures of South Asia. See Topic 1.3.)

Source: Thinkstock

Mayan pyramids, with steps going up the side, were similar to Mesopotamian ziggurats. Similarly shaped architecture can be found from Spain and Algeria to China and Indonesia.

The Aztecs

The **Aztecs**, also known as the **Mexicas**, were originally hunter-gatherers who migrated to central Mexico from the north in the 1200s. In 1325, they founded their capital Tenochtitlán on the site of what is now Mexico City. Over the next 100 years, they conquered the surrounding peoples and created an empire that stretched from the Gulf of Mexico to the Pacific Ocean.

Capital City The Aztecs located Tenochtitlán on an island in the middle of a swampy lake in order to protect it from attacks. Tenochtitlán grew to almost 200,000 people, making it one of the largest cities in the world. To provide water for the city, they built a network of aqueducts. At the center of the city, the Aztecs built a pyramid that rose 150 feet into the air. This Great Pyramid and other pyramids, temples, and palaces were made of stone. On Lake Texcoco, the Aztecs built floating gardens called *chinampas* to increase the amount of space for food production. The Aztecs dug ditches to use lake water to irrigate their fields and to drain parts of the lake for more land.

Source: DEQ/G DAGLIORTI/ Granger, NYC

The construction of chinampas in Mesoamerica was one way people expanded the land on which to grow crops.

Government, Economy, and Society As the Aztecs conquered much of Mesoamerica, they developed a tribute system that insured their dominance. Conquered people were forced to pay tribute, surrender lands, and perform military service. Tribute included practical goods such as food, cloth, and firewood, as well as luxury items such as feathers, beads, and jewelry. The Aztecs allowed local rulers to stay in their positions to serve as tribute collectors. This allowed Aztec political dominance without direct administrative control. In exchange, the conquered people were extended Aztec protection.

To administer the empire, the Aztecs grouped city-states into provinces. They moved warriors and their families to each province's capital to make sure the province remained under Aztec control. In addition, an Aztec official was stationed in each capital to collect tribute from local officials.

Aztec government was a **theocracy**, which is rule by religious leaders. At the top was the emperor, known as the Great Speaker, who was the political ruler as well as a divine representative of the gods. Next in the social hierarchy were land-owning nobles, who also formed the majority of Aztec military leadership. Next in rank were scribes and healers, followed by craftspeople and traders. A special merchant class called *pochteca* traded in luxury goods. Below the traders were the peasants and soldiers. Aztec people could be enslaved as well, usually because they did not pay their debts or were being punished for crimes. Besides being used for labor, enslaved people were also offered up as sacrifices in religious ceremonies.

Religion The intricate and complex religion of the Aztecs was central to their society. They worshipped an ever-evolving pantheon of hundreds of deities, many of whom were considered to have both male and female aspects.

Worship among the Aztecs involved a great many rituals and feast days as well as human sacrifices. The Aztecs believed that the gods had sacrificed themselves in order to create the world—thus human sacrifice and blood-letting was a sort of repayment and atonement for human sin. Human sacrifice probably had a political component, in the sense that it demonstrated the great might of the Aztec Empire in dramatic fashion. The number of human sacrifices may never be known. Much of the information about Aztec society comes from Spanish invaders, who may have exaggerated the extent of human sacrifice in order to make the Aztecs seem more deserving of conquest.

Role of Women Women played an important role in the Aztec tribute system since they wove the valuable cloth that local rulers demanded as part of the regular tribute. As the demand for cloth tribute increased, an Aztec husband might obtain more than one wife in order to be able to pay the tribute. While most Aztec women worked in their homes, some became priestesses, midwives, healers, or merchants. A few noblewomen worked as scribes to female members of royal families. Therefore, at least these few women knew how to read and write.

The Decline of the Aztecs By the late 15th century, the Aztec Empire was in decline. The Aztecs' comparatively low level of technology—such as the lack of wheeled vehicles and pack animals—meant that agriculture was arduous and inefficient. The Aztecs' commitment to military victory and the constant desire for more human sacrifices induced the leadership to expand the empire beyond what it could reasonably govern. Finally, the extraction from conquered people of tribute and sacrifice victims inspired more resentment than loyalty. Because of this resentment, many tribes ruled by the Aztecs were ready to rebel if they thought they had an opportunity to succeed. This opportunity would come later, when Spaniards arrived in 1519.

The Inca

In 1438, a tribal leader who called himself **Pachacuti**, which means "transformer" or "shaker" of the earth, began conquering the tribes living near what is now Cuzco, Peru. His military victories, followed by those of his son, combined the small tribes into a full-fledged state, the **Incan Empire**. It extended from present-day Ecuador in the north to Chile in the south. By 1493, Pachacuti's grandson, Huayna Capac, ruled the empire. He focused on consolidating and managing the many lands conquered by his predecessors.

Government, Economy, and Society In order to rule the extensive territory efficiently, the Incan Empire was split into four provinces, each with its own governor and bureaucracy. Conquered leaders who demonstrated loyalty to the empire were rewarded. In contrast to the people living under the Aztecs, conquered people under the Inca did not have to pay tribute. Rather, they were subject to the **mit'a system**, mandatory public service. Men between the ages of 15 and 50 provided agricultural and other forms of labor, including the construction of roads.

Religion The name Inca means "people of the sun," and Inti, the sun god, was the most important of the Incan gods. Inca rulers were considered to be Inti's representative on the earth. As the center of two critical elements in Incan religion—honoring of the sun and royal ancestor veneration—the **Temple of the Sun** in Cuzco formed the core of Incan religion.

Royal ancestor veneration was a practice intended to extend the rule of a leader. Dead rulers were mummified and continued to "rule" as they had in life and were thought to retain ownership of their servants, possessions, and property. Thus, Incan rulers could not expect to inherit land or property upon assuming power. This practice was a partial motivator for the constant expansion of the empire.

Priests were consulted before important actions. To the Inca, the gods controlled all things, and priests could determine the gods' will by studying the arrangement of coca leaves in a dish or by watching the movement of a spider. Priests diagnosed illnesses, predicted the outcome of battles, solved crimes, and determined what sacrifices should be made to which god. Serious events such as famines, plagues, and defeat in war called for human sacrifices— although scholars do not believe that human sacrifice was practiced with the same frequency as it probably was with the Aztecs.

Inca religion included some **animism**—the belief that elements of the physical world could have supernatural powers. Called *huaca,* they could be large geographical features such as a river or a mountain peak. Or, they could be very small objects such as a stone, a plant, or a built object, such as a bridge.

Achievements In mathematics, the Inca developed the *quipu,* a system of knotted strings used to record numerical information for trade and engineering and for recording messages to be carried throughout the empire. In agriculture, the Inca developed sophisticated terrace systems for the cultivation of crops such as potatoes and maize. The terraces utilized a technique called *waru waru*, raised beds with channels that captured and redirected rain to avoid erosion during floods and that stored water to be used during dry periods.

The Inca were especially good builders of bridges and roads. Using captive labor, they constructed a massive roadway system called the **Carpa Nan**, with some 25,000 miles of roads used mainly by the government and military. In a mountainous region, bridges were particularly important.

Decline Upon the arrival of Spanish conquistador Francisco Pizarro in 1532, the Incan Empire was in the midst of a civil war of succession after the death of emperor Huayna Capac. Some scholars believe that the civil war weakened the Incan army, making it easier for Pizarro's forces to prevail. Others believe that other factors such as diseases introduced by the Europeans led to the decline. In 1533, the Spanish conquered the core of the empire, although outposts held out until 1572. Today, the Inca ruins at Machu Picchu are one of the most-visited sites in the world.

Continuities and Diversity

Historians have debated how closely Mesoamerican cultures are related to one another. Many argue that most are based on the Olmec civilization, since many later cultures adopted some of its features. For example, the Olmecs' feathered snake-god became fundamental in both the Mayan and Aztec religion. The subjects depicted on Olmec pottery have been found in pottery in other civilizations. The Olmecs' ritual sacrifices, pyramids, and ball courts were also continued in other cultures. Other historians argue that different cultures developed complex civilizations more or less independently.

Comparing Three American Civilizations			
	Maya	**Aztec**	**Inca**
Region	Mexico/Central America	Central Mexico	Andes in South America
Period	400–1517	1200–1521	1200–1533
Crops	• Corn • Beans • Squash	• Corn • Beans • Squash • Tomatoes	• Corn • Cotton • Potatoes
Trade	• Moderate	• Extensive	• Limited
Religion	• Polytheistic • Some human sacrifice	• Polytheistic • Some human sacrifice	• Polytheistic • Some human sacrifice
Government	• Organized city-states, each with a king • Wars for tribute	• Powerful king • Wars for captives • System of tribute	• Powerful king • Wars for conquest • Mit'a system
Technology and Thought	• Writing • Step pyramids • Accurate calendar	• Step pyramids • Chinampas • Accurate calendar	• Waru waru • Roads • Masonry
Reasons for Decline	• Drought • Deforestation	• European diseases • Subjects rebelled • Spanish attacks	• European diseases • Civil war • Spanish attacks

KEY TERMS BY THEME

CULTURE: North America
Mississippian
matrilineal society

TECHNOLOGY:
Mound-Building
Cahokia

CULTURE: Mayan
city-states

GOVERNMENT: Aztec
Mexica (Aztecs)
theocracy

RELIGION: Aztec
human sacrifice

GOVERNMENT: Inca
Pachacuti
Incan Empire
mit'a system

TECHNOLOGY: Inca
Carpa Nan

RELIGION: Inca
Temple of the Sun
animism

Questions 1 to 3 refer to the passage below.

"The Inka [Inca] ruled the greatest empire on earth. Bigger than Ming Dynasty China, bigger than Ivan the Great's expanding Russia, bigger than Songhay [Songhai] in the Sahel or powerful Great Zimbabwe in the East Africa tablelands, bigger than the cresting Ottoman Empire, bigger than the Triple Alliance (as the Aztec Empire is more precisely known), bigger by far than any European state, the Inka dominion extended over a staggering thirty-two degrees of latitude—as if a single power held sway from St. Petersburg to Cairo. The empire encompassed every imaginable type of terrain, from the rainforest of upper Amazonia to the deserts of the Peruvian coast and the twenty-thousand-foot peaks of the Andes in between. 'If imperial potential is judged in terms of environmental adaptability,' wrote the Oxford historian Felipe Fernandez-Armesto, 'the Inka [Inca] were the most impressive empire builders of their day.' "

Charles Mann, *1491: New Revelations of the Americas Before Columbus*, 2005

1. Why were the Inca able to achieve the accomplishment described in the passage?

    (A) They divided their empire into four provinces so it would be easier to govern.

    (B) They demanded heavy tribute from conquered groups living on the edges of their empire.

    (C) They routinely sent armies through the empire to collect tribute.

    (D) They forced conquered people to adopt the language of the Inca.

2. The Carpa Nan demonstrates the main point expressed by the writer in the excerpt because it

    (A) made living in the rainforest possible

    (B) provided a common system of written communication

    (C) provided irrigation for terraced farmlands

    (D) connected the parts of the empire

3. When the author of the passage describes the Incan civilization as the "greatest empire on earth," he means that it

    (A) constructed great buildings and other structures

    (B) conquered other empires, including the Aztecs

    (C) adapted successfully to diverse environments

    (D) were the wealthiest civilization in the world in 1491

SHORT-ANSWER QUESTIONS

1. Use the passage below to answer all parts of the question that follows.

"Unluckily, the accounts of Spanish authors concerning Maya mythology do not agree with the representations of the gods delineated [described precisely] in the codices. That the three codices have a mythology in common is certain. Again, great difficulty is found in comparing the deities of the codices with those represented by the carved and stucco bas-reliefs of the Maya region. It will thus be seen that very considerable difficulties beset the student in this mythological sphere. So few data have yet been collected regarding the Maya mythology that to dogmatize [represent as absolute truth] upon any subject connected with it would indeed be rash [impulsive]. But much has been accomplished in the past few decades, and evidence is slowly but surely accumulating from which sound conclusions can be drawn."

Lewis Spence, *The Myths of Mexico and Peru*, 1913

(A) Identify Spence's claim in the passage above.

(B) Explain ONE piece of evidence from an outside source that supports Spence's claim.

(C) Explain how Spence's argument affects understanding Mayan history.

2. Answer all parts of the question that follows.

(A) Identify ONE way in which culture from the Incan civilization is similar to the culture of the Aztec civilization.

(B) Explain ONE difference in how the Incas and the Aztecs maintained their empires.

(C) Explain ONE reason why the people living under Aztec rule wanted a change in rulers at the time the Europeans arrived.

Source: Library of Congress, Washington, D.C. (neg. no. LC-USZC4-743)

The image to the left is an illustration from a reproduction of the 16th century Codex Magliabecchi, a primary source. The artist is depicting an Aztecan sacrifice ritual that offers a human heart to the war god Huitzilopochtli.

Primary sources are those created during the historic period to which they refer. They are the first records of the subject being described and include firsthand or eyewitness reports. Secondary sources, in contrast, are those that analyze primary sources or other secondary sources to draw conclusions on a subject. Historians use both kinds of sources as evidence to support their arguments.

The Codex Magliabecchi from which the above illustration is taken is an ancient manuscript that offers historians a primary source with possible evidence about Aztec society. If you were developing an argument about the Aztec population's attitude toward human sacrifice, what evidence might you use from this illustration, and what argument might it support?

REFLECT ON THE TOPIC ESSENTIAL QUESTION

1. In one to three paragraphs, identify the states that developed in the Americas and explain how they changed over time.

1.5

Developments In Africa

After that the chief of the poets mounts the steps of the pempi [a raised platform on which the ruler sits] and lays his head on the sultan's lap, then climbs to the top of the pempi and lays his head first on the sultan's right shoulder and then on his left, speaking all the while in their tongue, and finally he comes down again. I was told that this practice is a very old custom amongst them, prior to the introduction of Islam, and that they have kept it up.

—Ibn Battuta, c. 1352

Essential Question: How and why did states develop in Africa and change over time?

Ibn Battuta's commentary on Mali society sheds light on the cultural forces at work in Sub-Saharan Africa during the 14th century. A scholar from Morocco on the northwest coast of Africa, he was well versed in Islamic law, also known as shariah. Islamic governments in Mogadishu (east Africa) and Delhi (India) sought his advice and welcomed him to their lands. Ibn Battuta's travelogue demonstrated how Islam's phenomenal growth increased connections among cultures of Asia, Africa, and southern Europe. As Ibn Battuta's account makes clear, African societies that had adopted Islam kept many of their traditions.

Some parts of Africa resisted Islam. To better defend themselves against attacks by Islamic forces, they built churches with labyrinths, reservoirs, and tunnels. Other parts of the continent, especially in the south, had little contact with Islam until later in history.

Political Structures in Inland Africa

The development of Sub-Saharan Africa was heavily shaped by the migrations of Bantu-speaking people outward from west-central Africa. By the year 1000, most of the region had adopted agriculture. With the sedentary nature of agriculture, people needed more complex political relationships to govern themselves. In contrast to most Asian or European societies, those in Sub-Saharan Africa did not centralize power under one leader or central government. Instead, communities formed **kin-based networks**, where families governed themselves. A male head of the network, a **chief**, mediated conflicts and dealt with neighboring groups. Groups of villages became districts, and a group of chiefs decided among themselves how to solve the district's problems.

EARLY STATE-BUILDING AND TRADE IN AFRICA

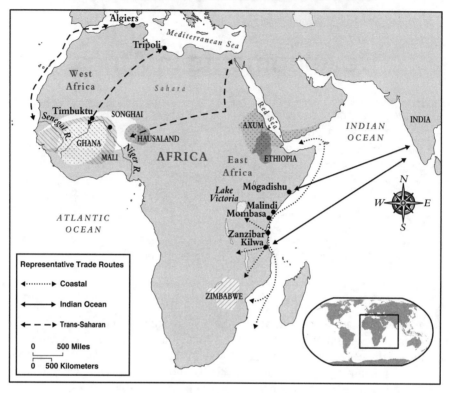

As populations grew, kin-based networks became more difficult to govern. Competition among neighbors increased, which in turn increased fighting among villages and districts. Survival for small kin-based communities became more challenging. Though many such communities continued to exist in Sub-Saharan Africa until the 19th century, larger kingdoms grew in prominence, particularly after 1000.

The Hausa Kingdoms Sometime before 1000, in what is now Nigeria, people of the Hausa ethnic group formed seven states, the **Hausa Kingdoms**. The states were loosely connected through kinship ties, though they too had no central authority. People established prospering city-states, each with a speciality. For example, several were situated in plains where cotton grew well.

Though the region lacked access to the sea, contact with people from outside the region was important. Many Hausa benefited from the thriving **trans-Saharan trade**, a network of trading routes across the great desert. A state on the western edge of the region specialized in military matters and defended the states against attack. Because the states lacked a central authority, however, they were frequently subject to domination from outside. In the 14th century, missionaries introduced Islam to the region. (Connect:

Write a paragraph contrasting the decentralized political systems of the peoples in inland Africa with those of the Inca. See Topic 1.4.)

Political Structures of West and East Africa

Kingdoms on both the western and eastern sides of Africa benefited from increased trade. The exchange of goods brought them wealth, political power, and cultural diversity. The spread of Islam added to the religious diversity of the continent, where animism and Christianity were already practiced. Four of these kingdoms were Ghana, Mali, Zimbabwe, and Ethiopia.

Ghana Nestled between the Sahara and the tropical rain forests of the West African coast, the kingdom of **Ghana** was not in the same location as the modern nation of Ghana. Historians believe that the kingdom had been founded during the 5th century, at least two centuries before the time of Muhammad, but Ghana reached its peak of influence from the 8th to the 11th centuries. Ghana's rulers sold gold and ivory to Muslim traders in exchange for salt, copper, cloth, and tools. From Ghana's capital city, Koumbi Saleh, the king ruled a centralized government aided by nobles and an army equipped with iron weapons.

Source: Daderot / Wikimedia Commons

Source: Thinkstock

The gold artifacts (upper) were part of the valuable trans-Saharan trade in West Africa. The modern photo of foods and spices (lower) shows the types of goods that have been popular in the Indian Ocean trade in East Africa since the 8th century C.E.

Mali By the 12th century, wars with neighboring societies had permanently weakened the Ghanaian state. In its place arose several new trading societies, the most powerful of which was **Mali**. You will read more about Mali in Topic 2.4. Most scholars believe that Mali's founding ruler, Sundiata, was a Muslim and used his connections with others of his faith to establish trade relationships with North African and Arab merchants. Sundiata cultivated a thriving gold trade in Mali. Under his steady leadership, Mali's wealth grew tremendously. His nephew, Mansa Musa, made a pilgrimage to Mecca where his lavish displays of gold left a lasting impression. (See Topic 2.4 for the later developments in West Africa, such as the growth of the city of Timbuktu and the Songhai Empire.)

Zimbabwe In East Africa, the architecture demonstrated the growing wealth of one kingdom. Though most houses had traditionally been constructed from wood, by the 9th century chiefs had begun to construct their "zimbabwes," the Bantu word for "dwellings," with stone. This word became the name of one of the most powerful of all the East African kingdoms between the 12th and 15th centuries—**Zimbabwe**. It was situated between the Zambezi and Limpopo rivers in modern-day Zimbabwe and Mozambique.

Zimbabwe built its prosperity on a mixture of agriculture, grazing, trade, and, above all, gold. Like Ghana and Mali on the other side of the continent, Zimbabwe had rich gold fields, and taxes on the transport of gold made the kingdom wealthy. While Ghana and Mali relied on land-based trade across the Sahara, Zimbabwe traded with the coastal city-states such as Mombasa, Kilwa, and Mogadishu. Through these ports, Zimbabwe was tied into the **Indian Ocean trade**, which connected East Africa, the Middle East, South Asia, and East Asia. In East Africa, traders blended Bantu and Arabic to develop a new language, **Swahili**. Today, Swahili is spoken by various groups in the African Great Lakes region as well as other parts of Southeast Africa.

The rise and decline of Zimbabwe was reflected in the defensive walls used to protect cities. By the end of the 13th century, a massive wall of stone, 30 feet tall by 15 feet thick, surrounded the capital city, which became known as the **Great Zimbabwe**. The stone wall was the first large one on the continent that people built without mortar. Inside the wall, most of the royal city's buildings were made of stone. In the late 15th century, nearly 20,000 people resided within the Great Zimbabwe. However, overgrazing so damaged the surrounding environment that residents of the bustling capital city abandoned it by the end of the 1400s. The wall still stands in the modern country of Zimbabwe.

Ethiopia Christianity had spread from its origins along the east coast of the Mediterranean Sea south into Egypt and beyond. In what is today **Ethiopia**, the kingdom of Axum developed. It prospered by trading goods obtained from India, Arabia, the Roman Empire, and the interior of Africa. Beginning in the 7th century, the spread of Islam made the region more diverse religiously.

In the 12th century, a new Christian-led kingdom in Ethiopia emerged. Its rulers, like those of other countries, expressed their power through architecture. They ordered the creation of 11 massive churches made entirely of rock.

Source: Thinkstock
This is one of the 11 Christian churches in Ethiopia built out of rock.

Carved rock structures had been a feature of Ethiopian religious architecture since the 2nd millennium B.C.E.

From the 12th through the 16th centuries, Ethiopia was an island of Christianity on the continent of Africa. Separated from both the Roman Catholic Church of western Europe and the Orthodox Church of eastern Europe, Ethiopian Christianity developed independently. People combined their traditional faith traditions, such as ancestor veneration and beliefs in spirits, with Christianity to create a distinct form of faith.

Social Structures of Sub-Saharan Africa

In Sub-Saharan Africa, strong central governments ruling over large territories were uncommon. Instead, Sub-Saharan Africa's small communities were organized around several structures: kinship, age, and gender. Kinship connections allowed people to identify first as members of a clan or family. Age was another significant social marker. An 18-year-old could do more hard labor than a 60-year-old, but younger people often relied on the advice of their elders. Thus, communities divided work according to age, creating age grades or age sets. Finally, gender had an influential role in social organization.

- Men dominated most activities that required a specialized skill. For example, leather tanners and blacksmiths were typically men.

- Women generally engaged in agriculture and food gathering. They also took the primary responsibilities for carrying out domestic chores and raising their family's children.

Slavery in Sub-Saharan Africa and Southwest Asia Slavery had a long history in Africa. Prisoners of war, debtors, and criminals were often enslaved. Most men and some women did agricultural work. Most women and some men served in households. In many kin-based societies, people could not own land privately, but they could own other people. Owning a large number of enslaved people increased one's social status. Slavery existed in many forms.

Comparing Three Forms of Slavery			
	Chattel	**Domestic**	**Debt Bondage**
Description	People were the legal property of the owner.	People served as cooks, cleaners, or other household workers.	People became enslaved, sometimes through mutual agreement, to repay a debt.
Examples	Common in the Americas, 16th century to 19th century	Common in Classical Greece and Rome, and in the Middle East	Common in East Africa before the 15th century and in European colonies in the Americas
Was enslavement permanent?	Yes	Often	Not in theory, but it often happened in practice
Were the children of enslaved people automatically enslaved?	Yes	Often	Children often inherited the debts of their parents
Did enslaved people have any rights?	No	Some: laws or customs might prevent a master from selling a person	Some: laws or customs might limit how severely a master could punish a person

A strong demand in the Middle East for enslaved workers resulted in an **Indian Ocean slave trade** between East Africa and the Middle East. This trade started several centuries before the Atlantic Ocean slave trade between West Africa and the Americas. In some places, it lasted into the 20th century.

The enslaved East Africans, known in Arabic as *zanj,* provided valuable labor on sugar plantations in Mesopotamia. However, between 869 and 883, they and many Arab workers mounted a series of revolts known as the **Zanj Rebellion**. About 15,000 enslaved people successfully captured the city of Basra and held it for ten years before being defeated. The large size and long length of time before it was defeated make the Zanj Rebellion one of the most successful slave revolts in history.

Cultural Life in Sub-Saharan Africa

Playing music, creating visual arts, and telling stories were and continue to be important aspects of cultures everywhere because they provided enjoyment and mark rituals such as weddings and funerals. In Africa, these activities carried additional significance. Because traditional African religions included ancestor veneration, song lyrics provided a means of communicating with the spirit world. African music usually had a distinctive rhythmic pattern, and vocals were interspersed with percussive elements such as handclaps, bells, pots, or gourds.

Visual arts also commonly served a religious purpose. For example, metalworkers created busts of past rulers so that ruling royalty could look to them for guidance. Artists in Benin, West Africa, were famous for their intricate sculptures in iron and bronze. In the late 19th century, the sophistication of these pieces of art would cause some Europeans to increase their respect for West African cultures.

Griots and Griottes Literature, as it existed in Sub-Saharan Africa, was oral. *Griots,* or storytellers, were the conduits of history for a community. Griots possessed encyclopedic knowledge of family lineages and the lives and deeds of great leaders. In general, griots were also adept at music, singing their stories and accompanying themselves on instruments, such as the drums and a 12-string harp called the kora.

The griots were both venerated and feared as they held both the power of language and of story. People said that a griot could sing your success or sing your downfall. By telling and retelling their stories and histories, the griots preserved a people's history and passed that history on from generation to generation. Kings often sought their counsel regarding political matters. When a griot died, it was as though a library had burned.

Just as men served as griots, women served as griottes. They would sing at special occasions, such as before a wedding. For example, the griotte would counsel the bride to not talk back if her mother-in-law abused her or reassure the bride that if things got too bad, she could return home. Griottes provided women with a sense of empowerment in a patriarchal society.

KEY TERMS BY THEME

SOCIETY: Sub-Saharan	TECHNOLOGY: Building	GOVERNMENT: West Africa
kin-based networks	Great Zimbabwe	Ghana
Swahili		Mali
Zanj Rebellion	GOVERNMENT: Kinship	
	chief	
ECONOMY: Trade	Hausa Kingdoms	GOVERNMENT: East Africa
trans-Saharan trade		Zimbabwe
Indian Ocean trade		Ethiopia
Indian Ocean slave trade		

Questions 1 to 3 refer to the image below.

Source: 2630ben / Thinkstock
The ruins of the wall at Great Zimbabwe.

1. One achievement represented by the structure in the image was that it was built

   (A) with techniques used by Arabs and the Portuguese

   (B) without mortar

   (C) without slave labor

   (D) away from any large settlement of people

2. What characteristic of cities around the world from 1200–1450 is reflected in this image?

   (A) Cities were reliant on walls for protection against attackers.

   (B) Cities were being founded in increasingly dry regions.

   (C) Cities were becoming less dependent on trade.

   (D) Cities were founded in open areas that were easier to defend.

3. One factor that contributed to the declines of both Great Zimbabwe and of the Mayans was

   (A) invasions by neighbors with iron weapons

   (B) contact with Europeans

   (C) environmental damage

   (D) ethnic conflicts within the community

1. Use the image below to answer all parts of the question that follows.

Source: Painting attributed to Abraham Cresques, 1375. Gallica Digital Library.

This painting of Mansa Musa shows him holding a gold coin and wearing a gold crown. Some of the buildings in the painting have domes that were characteristic of Middle Eastern architecture.

(A) Identify ONE way in which the painting shows a continuity in the sources of wealth of the kingdoms of Ghana and Mali.

(B) Explain ONE way in which the painting shows a connection between the Middle East and West Africa.

(C) Explain ONE way in which the painting shows the importance of Mansa Musa.

2. Answer all parts of the question that follows.

(A) Identify ONE way in which the political structures in inland Africa differed from those in East Africa in the period 1200–1450.

(B) Identify ONE way in which the political structures in West Africa were similar to those in East Africa in the period 1200–1450.

(C) Explain ONE way in which slavery affected relations among African states in the period 1200–1450.

THINK AS A HISTORIAN: EXPLAIN THE HISTORICAL CONCEPT
OF CONTINUITY

One of the historical concepts historians use to understand the past is *continuity*. Looking through the lens of continuity, historians can identify and explain—or make logically understandable—developments and processes that show endurance or continuation over time and space. For example, the influence of Islam has had an enduring effect on politics, economics, and culture within African societies.

Explain how the following statements apply the concept of continuity to historical developments and processes.

1. For more than 700 years, trans-Saharan trade brought considerable wealth to the societies of West Africa, particularly the kingdoms of Ghana and Mali.

2. Mansa Musa deepened Mali's connection to Islam after his 1324 pilgrimage to Mecca. Though many West Africans held onto their traditional beliefs, today 95 percent of people in Mali are Muslim.

3. Between the 12th and 15th centuries, Zimbabwe was the most powerful of all the East African kingdoms.

4. Sub-Saharan societies that had converted to Islam did not adopt all of its norms concerning gender.

5. Slavery was a long-standing tradition in Africa before Europeans arrived.

REFLECT ON THE TOPIC ESSENTIAL QUESTION

1. In one to three paragraphs, explain how and why states developed in Africa and changed over time.

1.6

Developments in Europe

I should not wish to be Aristotle if this were to separate me from Christ.
—Peter Abelard, Letter 17 to Heloise, 1141

> **Essential Question** How did the beliefs and practices of the predominant religions, agricultural practices, and political decentralization affect European society from c. 1200 to c. 1450?

As the Roman Empire declined in power in the 5th and 6th centuries, Western Europe entered the Middle Ages, sometimes called the medieval period. Throughout Europe, trade declined, intellectual life receded, and the united Roman state was replaced by smaller kingdoms that frequently fought one another for control of territory. In response, European kings, lords, and peasants worked out agreements to provide for common defense. Only the Roman Catholic Church remained powerful in most of Europe from Roman times to the 16th century.

However, between 1000 to 1450, learning and trade began to revive in Europe. This era is called the High Middle Ages. Like many scholars of this period, Peter Abelard studied classical thinkers such as Aristotle and sometimes criticized the Church, but he remained a faithful throughout his life.

Feudalism: Political and Social Systems

European civilization in the Middle Ages was characterized by a decentralized political organization based on a system of exchanges of land for loyalty known as **feudalism**. Lacking a strong government, people needed some protection from bandits, rival lords, and invaders such as the Vikings from northern Europe. The core of feudalism was a system of mutual obligations:

- A monarch, usually a king, granted tracts of land, called *fiefs,* to lords. In return, a lord became a king's *vassal*, a person who owed service to another person of higher status.

- Lords then provided land to knights. In return, knights became vassals of the lord, and pledged to fight for the lord or king.

- Lords also provided land and protection to peasants. In return, peasants were obligated to farm the lord's land and provide the lord with crops and livestock, and to obey the lord's orders.

Feudalism provided some security for peasants, equipment for warriors, and land to those who served a lord. Since the entire system was based on agriculture, wealth was measured in land rather than in cash.

The feudal system incorporated a *code of chivalry*—an unwritten set of rules for conduct focusing on honor, courtesy, and bravery—as a way to resolve disputes. Since women were to be protected, the code put them on a pedestal while not investing them with any significant additional importance. In practice, women did not have many rights. (Connect: Compare European feudalism and Japanese feudalism. See Topic 1.1.)

Manorial System Large fiefs or estates were also referred to as **manors**. The **manorial system** provided economic self-sufficiency and defense. The manor produced everything that people living on it required, limiting the need for trade or contact with outsiders. Many serfs spent their entire lives on a single manor, little aware of events in the rest of Europe.

Manor grounds were small villages that often included a church, a blacksmith shop, a mill, and wine presses. They included the homes of peasants known as **serfs**. Serfs, while not enslaved, were tied to the land. This meant they could not travel without permission from their lords. Nor could they marry without their lord's approval. In exchange for protection provided by the lord of the manor, they paid tribute in the form of crops, labor, or, in rare cases, coins. Children born to serfs also became serfs.

As both climate and technology slowly improved, the amount of arable or farmable land gradually increased. Agriculture became more efficient near the end of the Middle Ages. The **three-field system**, in which crops were rotated through three fields, came into use.

- One field was planted with wheat or rye, crops that provided food.
- A second field was planted with legumes such as peas, lentils, or beans. These made the soil more fertile by adding nitrogen to it.
- A third field was allowed to remain fallow, or unused, each year.

Technological developments included windmills and new types of plows. Heavier plows with wheels worked well in the dense soil north of the Alps, while lighter plows worked better in southern Europe. These changes promoted population growth.

Political Trends in the Later Middle Ages

In the later Middle Ages, monarchies grew more powerful at the expense of feudal lords by employing their own bureaucracy and a military. These employees worked directly for the king or queen. (In contrast, in modern countries such as the United States, bureaucrats and soldiers work for the country, not the chief executive.) The lands these monarchs collected under their control, particularly in England and France, were beginning to look like the modern countries of Europe.

EUROPE IN THE MIDDLE AGES

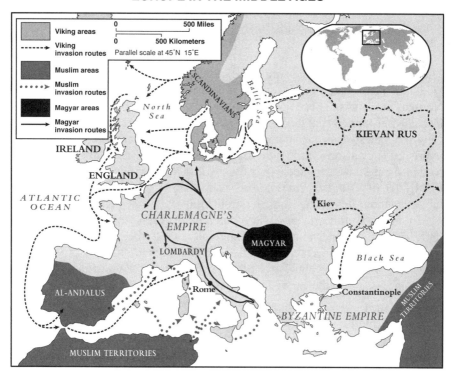

France King Philip II (ruled 1180–1223), was the first to develop a real bureaucracy. Yet it was not until Philip IV (ruled 1285–1314) that the first **Estates-General** met. The Estates-General was a body to advise the king that included representatives from each of the three legal classes, or **estates**, in France: the clergy, nobility, and commoners. Although the French kings consulted this Estates-General when necessary, they did not exact regular taxes from the upper two estates, the clergy and nobility. Consequently, the Estates-General had little power. The clergy and nobility felt little responsibility to protect a government that they were not financing, a problem that only continued to increase in France up to the eve of the French Revolution of 1789.

Holy Roman Empire The German king **Otto I** was crowned Holy Roman Emperor in 962, hearkening back to Charlemagne's designation as Emperor of the Romans. Otto's successors survived the power struggle with the papacy over the **lay investiture controversy** of the 11th and 12th centuries. This dispute was over whether a secular (non-religious) leader, rather than the pope, could invest bishops with the symbols of office. It was finally resolved in the Concordat of Worms of 1122, when the Church achieved autonomy from secular authorities. The Holy Roman Empire remained vibrant until it was virtually destroyed during the Thirty Years' War (1618–1648). It lingered on, but with little power. The Empire came to a formal end when the French leader Napoleon Bonaparte invaded central Europe in 1806.

Norman England The Normans were descendents of Vikings who settled in northwestern France, a region known as Normandy. In 1066, a Norman king, William the Conqueror, successfully invaded England. This gave him kingdoms on both sides of the English Channel. He presided over a tightly organized feudal system, using royal sheriffs as his administrative officials. The fusion of Normans and Anglo-Saxons created the modern English people.

Many English nobles objected to the power of William and the succeeding Norman monarchs. These nobles forced limits on that power. In 1215, they forced King John to sign the **Magna Carta**, which required the king to respect certain rights, such as the right to a jury trial before a noble could be sentenced to prison. They also won the right to be consulted on the issue of scutage (a tax paid on a knight who wanted to pay money instead of provide military service). Finally, the first **English Parliament** was formed in 1265. These developments increased the rights of the English nobility, but not of the general population.

In the first full parliamentary meeting in 1265, the House of Lords represented the nobles and Church hierarchy, while the House of Commons was made up of elected representatives of wealthy townspeople. Eventually, the power of these two legislative bodies in England became stronger than that of similar bodies on the European continent.

The Hundred Years' War Between 1337 and 1453, the rival monarchies of England and France fought a series of battles known as the Hundred Years' War. English archers armed with longbows (about six feet long) helped win several early victories. However, by the end of the conflict, the English retained only the port of Calais in France. Two other important results of the war were on how people saw themselves and how they fought.

- On each side, serving under a monarch fostered a sense of unity among soldiers who often spoke distinct languages or dialects. The war marked another step towards people identifying themselves as "English" or "French" rather than from a particular region.

- The war also demonstrated the spreading use of gunpowder weapons. Gunpowder had been invented by the Chinese and spread west by Mongols.

Christians versus Muslims In addition to conquering England, the Normans also conquered Sicily, taking control of that Mediterranean island from Muslims. Muslims had conquered Spain in the 8th century. From that time, Christians had wanted to reconquer it. This effort, called the *reconquista*, occurred over many centuries. It was finally completed in 1492.

Roman Catholic Church During the Middle Ages

In 1054, the Christian Church in Europe divided into two branches, a split called the **Great Schism**. The Roman Catholic Church continued to dominate most of Europe for another five centuries, while the Orthodox Church was powerful farther east, from Greece to Russia.

The Roman Catholic Church was the most powerful institution in a Europe divided into hundreds of small political states. Often Church staff were the only people in a community who knew how to read and write. If common people needed something written or read, they asked a Church official to do it. Most manors had a small church and a priest on the grounds. Christianity provided people a shared identity even as vernacular languages, ones spoken by the people in a region, emerged to replace Latin.

Education and Art The Church established the first universities in Europe. Because the Church led in the area of education, most philosophers, writers, and other thinkers of the Middle Ages were religious leaders. All artists worked for the Church. Most artwork focused on religious themes, which provided images to help illiterate serfs understand the Bible.

Church and State The Church held great power in the feudal system. If a lord displeased the Church, it could pressure the lord in various ways. For example, a local bishop might cancel religious services for his serfs. This angered the serfs, who would demand that the lord give in to the bishop.

Like the Roman Empire, the Roman Catholic Church had an extensive hierarchy of regional leaders. The regional religious leaders, called bishops, owed allegiance to the pope, the supreme bishop in Rome. The bishops also selected and supervised local priests.

Monasticism Although some Christian clergy withdrew to monasteries to meditate and pray, they remained part of the economies of Western Europe. The monasteries had the same economic functions of agriculture and protection as other manors. Women were permitted to become nuns and exerted their influence in the monasteries of the Catholic Church.

Reform Although clergy took vows of poverty and supported charities in their communities, the clergy also wielded considerable political influence, and some monasteries became quite wealthy. Wealth and political power led to corruption during the 13th and 14th centuries. Eventually, corruption, as well as theological disagreements, drove reformers such as Martin Luther to take stands that would shatter the unity of the Roman Catholic Church in the 16th century.

Christian Crusades

Just as Europeans fought to drive Muslims out of Sicily and Spain, they also sought to reclaim control of the Holy Land, the region of Palestine in the Middle East that contains sites of spiritual significance to Jews, Christians, and Muslims. European Christians had enjoyed access to these lands for centuries, even after they came under the control of Muslims.

Social and economic trends of the 11th century added to the pressure among Europeans to invade the Middle East. Rules of **primogeniture**, under which the eldest son in a family inherited the entire estate, left a generation of younger sons with little access to wealth and land. The landed nobles saw a military campaign as a way to divert the ambitions of these restless nobles as well as unemployed peasants, who often pillaged the lands of neighboring lords. Furthermore, merchants desired unfettered access to trade routes through the Middle East. The combination of these religious, social, and economic pressures resulted in the **Crusades**—a series of European military campaigns in the Middle East between 1095 and the 1200s.

Politics shaped the conduct of Crusades. Tensions between popes and kings strengthened the intention of the Roman Catholic Church to take control. The Church also used its spiritual authority to recruit believers. It granted relief from required acts of atonement and penance and even promised people they would reach heaven sooner if they joined a Crusade. Support came for the Orthodox branch of Christianity as well. Alarmed by news of the persecution of Christian pilgrims by Seljuk Turks, the Orthodox patriarch at Constantinople appealed to Pope Urban II to help retake the Holy Land from Islamic control.

The First Crusade Of the four major Crusades, only the first was a clear victory for Christendom. The European army conquered Jerusalem in July 1099. However, Muslim forces under Saladin regained control of Jerusalem in 1187. The Crusades did promote cultural exchange between Europe and the Middle East. The Middle East had a higher standard of living, and European Crusaders increased the demand for Middle Eastern goods. (Connect: Create a timeline tracing the spread of Islam up through the Crusades. See Topic 1.2.)

The Fourth Crusade During the fourth and last major Crusade (1202–1204), Venice, a wealthy city-state in northern Italy, had a contract to transport Crusaders to the Middle East, an area known as the Levant. However, Venice was not paid all of what was due, so the Venetians persuaded the Crusader debtors first to sack Zara, an Italian city, and then Constantinople, a major trade competitor of Venice. The Fourth Crusade never made it to the Holy Land. Eventually, Islamic forces prevailed in the Levant.

Economic and Social Change

The Crusades were just part of the changes occurring in Europe in the late Middle Ages. Local economic self-sufficiency in Europe gradually gave way to an interest in goods from other European areas and from far-flung ports.

Marco Polo In the late 13th century **Marco Polo**, an Italian native from Venice, visited the court of Kublai Khan in Dadu, modern-day Beijing. Polo's captivating descriptions of the customs of the people he met intrigued Europeans. For example, he described how Mongols had multiple marriages, drank mare's milk, burned black stones (coal) to heat their homes, and bathed frequently—often three times per week. Curiosity about Asia skyrocketed, stimulating interest in cartography, or mapmaking.

Social Change Growth in long-distance commerce changed the social pyramid of Western Europe. Economic success started to rival religious vocation or military service in winning status. This middle class, between the elite nobles and clergy and the mass of peasants, began to grow. Known as the **bourgeoisie**, or **burghers**, it included shopkeepers, merchants, craftspeople, and small landholders.

Urban Growth With renewed commerce came larger cities. The change to the three-field system and other advances in agriculture led to population growth in the late Middle Ages. This agricultural surplus encouraged the growth of towns and of markets that could operate more frequently than just on holidays. As the demand for more labor on the manors increased, the supply decreased. A series of severe plagues swept through Eurasia in the 14th century. In Europe, an outbreak of bubonic plague known as the Black Death killed as many as one-third of the population. The growing demand for labor and the deaths of so many people gave serfs more bargaining power with lords.

Urban growth was hampered after about 1300 by a five-century cooling of the climate known as the **Little Ice Age**. Lower temperatures reduced agricultural productivity, so people had less to trade and cities grew more slowly. The Little Ice Age led to an increase in disease and an increase in unemployment. These, in turn, created social unrest. The crime rate increased, and Jews, and other groups that already faced discrimination, were the victims of scapegoating—being blamed for something over which they had no control.

Jews During the Middle Ages, the small Jewish population in Christian Europe began to grow. Many Jews lived in Muslim areas in the Iberian Peninsula (present-day Spain and Portugal) and around the Mediterranean Sea when these areas were overtaken by European Christians. In time, Jews who could afford to moved northward in Europe. Some political leaders, particularly in Amsterdam and other commercial cities, welcomed them, since they brought valuable experience in business and trade.

The Roman Catholic Church also had a policy that Christians could not charge interest on loans to other Christians. However, Jews were not bound by this restriction. With few other economic opportunities, many northern European Jews became moneylenders. The resulting increase in the flow of money contributed to the economic growth of Europe.

However, anti-Jewish sentiment, or **antisemitism**, was widespread among Christians. They thought of Jews as outsiders and untrustworthy. Jews were expelled from England in 1290, France in 1394, Spain in 1492, and Portugal in 1497, as well as from various independent kingdoms and cities in northern and central Europe. Jews expelled from western and central Europe often moved to eastern Europe. While Jews had lived in this region since the 1st century, their numbers increased greatly because of the expulsions.

Muslims Like Jews, Muslims faced discrimination in Europe. In 1492, the Spanish king expelled the remaining Muslims in the kingdom who would not convert to Christianity. Many Muslims moved to southeastern Europe. In the 13th century, the Muslim Ottoman Empire expanded its reach from Turkey into the Balkan countries of present-day Albania, Kosovo, and Bosnia and Herzegovina. These countries developed large Muslim populations.

While Europe was predominantly Christian, and despite their persecution, both Jews and Muslims helped shape society. Unlike most people in Europe in the Middle Ages, Jews lived in urban areas, and they served as a bridge between Christians and the Muslims whose goods they desired in trade. Contacts with traders in Muslim caliphates opened up a world of trade and a world of ideas for Europeans who had long been self-sufficient and isolated under feudalism.

Gender Roles Women found their rights eroding as a wave of patriarchal thinking and writing accompanied the movement from an agricultural society to a more urban one. Even fewer women than men received an education, although women often managed manor accounts. One place where women had greater opportunities to display their skills in administration and leadership was in religious orders. Some women became artisans and members of guilds—associations of craftspeople and merchants—although not all had property rights. Women in Islamic societies tended to enjoy higher levels of equality, particularly in parts of Africa and Southeast Asia.

Renaissance

The expansion of trade, the growth of an agricultural surplus, and the rise of a middle class able to patronize artists sparked great creativity in Europe. The **Renaissance** was a period characterized by a revival of interest in classical Greek and Roman literature, art, culture, and civic virtue. Scholars recovered and studied decaying manuscripts that had been written many centuries earlier. Developed in 1439, Johannes Gutenberg's movable-type printing press initiated a revolution in print technology. The printing press allowed manuscripts to be mass-produced at relatively affordable costs. It fostered a growth in literacy and the rapid spread of ideas.

One characteristic of the Renaissance was the interest in **humanism**, the focus on individuals rather than God. Humanists sought education and reform. They began to write secular literature. Cultural changes in the Renaissance, such as the increased use of the vernacular language, propelled the rise of powerful monarchies, the centralization of governments, and the birth of nationalism. (Connect: List three elements of classical Greece and Rome revived by the Renaissance. See Prologue.)

Southern Renaissance In the regions of Italy and Spain, church patronage supported the Renaissance. For example, the writer Dante Alighieri (1265–1321) used a religious framework for *The Divine Comedy,* which features hell, purgatory, and heaven. Nevertheless, his fearlessness in criticizing corrupt religious officials and his willingness to use Italian vernacular instead of Latin reflected his independence from the Roman Catholic Church. Wealthy families, such as the Medicis of Florence, used their money to support painters, sculptors, and architects.

Northern Renaissance By 1400, the Renaissance spirit spread to northern Europe. While many Renaissance artists emphasized piety in their work, others emphasized human concerns. Geoffrey Chaucer, writing in *The Canterbury Tales* in the late 1300s, portrayed a microcosm of middle-class occupations in England, including several Church positions. His satirical writings portrayed monks who loved hunting and overly sentimental nuns. Like Dante a century earlier, Chaucer chose a vernacular, Middle English, for this work, although many of his other writings were in Latin.

LEADING CITIES DURING THE RENAISSANCE IN EUROPE

The Origins of Russia

During the late Middle Ages in Eastern Europe, extensive trade in furs, fish, and grain connected people from Scandinavia to the Mediterranean to Central Asia. The city-state at the center of this trade was Kievan Rus, based in what is today Kiev, Ukraine. Because it adopted the Orthodox Christianity, it maintained closer cultural relationships with Byzantium than with Roman Catholic Europe. In the 13th century, the Mongols overtook this region, so it developed even more separately from of the rest of Europe. (See Topic 2.2.)

The Mongols required local nobles to collect taxes for them. As these nobles grew wealthy in their role, they began to resist Mongol rule. In the late 15th century, under the leadership of a Moscow-based ruler known as Ivan the Great, the region became independent of the Mongols. This marked the beginning of the modern state of Russia.

KEY TERMS BY THEME

GOVERNMENT: England
Magna Carta
English Parliament

ECONOMY: Self-sufficiency
manors
manorial system

TECHNOLOGY: England
three-field system

SOCIETY: Hierarchies
feudalism
serfs
primogeniture
bourgeoisie
burghers

GOVERNMENT: France
Estates-General
estates

**GOVERNMENT: Holy
  Roman Empire**
Otto I

CULTURE: Ideas
Crusades
Marco Polo
Renaissance
humanism

CULTURE: Religion
lay investiture
  controversy
Great Schism
antisemitism

**ENVIRONMENT:
  Climate**
Little Ice Age

MULTIPLE-CHOICE QUESTIONS

Questions 1–3 refer to the chart below.

AVERAGE AIR TEMPERATURES IN EASTERN EUROPE, 850-1950

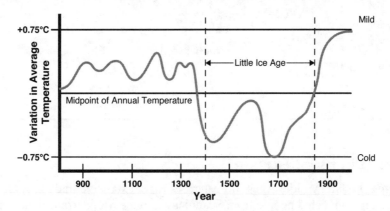

Source: Adapted from H.H. Lamb, "Climatic Fluctuations," H. Flohn, ed. *World Survey of Climatology*, vol. 2, General Climatology, (New York: Elsevier, 1969), p. 236.

1. Which trend followed the temperature pattern shown in the graph?

(A) The centralization of political power

(B) The rate of growth in the urban population

(C) The use of systems of coerced labor

(D) The spread of Christianity in Europe

2. Which statement accurately reflects an effect of the temperature pattern shown in the graph?

(A) The Little Ice Age caused shortages of food and reduced the amount of agricultural surplus available for trade.

(B) One result of the Little Ice Age was that Vikings from Scandinavia began raiding coasts along England and France.

(C) As climates in Spain cooled, Ferdinand and Isabella financed the voyages of Christopher Columbus in search of land for cash crops.

(D) As a result of the pollution from the growth of industry in Western Europe, temperatures began to rise as the ozone became depleted.

3. A historian would most likely use the chart to research which of the following developments in the period 1450–1750?

(A) The decline of Norse colonies in Greenland

(B) Native American transfer from dependence on agriculture to hunting

(C) European civil unrest and weakened economies

(D) A surge in witch trials on both sides of the Atlantic

SHORT-ANSWER QUESTIONS

1. Use the passage below to answer all parts of the question that follows.

"With these pieces of paper they can buy anything and pay for anything. And I can tell you that the papers that reckon as ten bezants [a quantity of money] do not weigh one. . . .There is no one who does not visit a bath-house at least three times a week and take a bath—in winter every day, if he can manage it. Every man of rank or means has his own bathroom in his house. . . .

Here too the inhabitants worship Mahomet [Muhammad] and are subject to the Great Khan. It has villages and towns in plenty. . . . There are rivers here in which are found stones called jasper and chalcedony [quartz crystals] in plenty. There is no lack of the means of life. Cotton is plentiful. The inhabitants live by trade and industry."

Marco Polo, *The Travels of Marco Polo*, c. 1300

(A) Identify ONE way in which the writings of Marco Polo affected European relationships with other regions.

(B) Explain ONE way in which Marco Polo's point of view fits into the context of intercultural interactions in the period 1200–1450.

(C) Explain how the passage by Marco Polo illustrates the limitations of intercultural knowledge and understanding.

2. **Answer all parts of the question that follows.**

   (A) Identify ONE way in which Russia was linked to Europe in the period 1200–1450.

   (B) Explain ONE historical situation in the period 1200–1450 that influenced the development of the Christian crusades.

   (C) Explain ONE way in which technological developments affected European manorial systems in the period 1200–1450.

 THINK AS A HISTORIAN: IDENTIFY HISTORICAL DEVELOPMENTS

Europe in c. 1200 was an area of decentralized feudal kingdoms with little contact with the world beyond the manor. Europe in c. 1450, in contrast, was a region of agricultural abundance, growing towns and cities, increasing trade with other parts of the world, growing commerce, and centralizing states.

For each of the following aspects of life in Europe, write a sentence identifying a development—an event or series of events that fit into a broader pattern—that contributed to the changes between c. 1200 and c. 1450. Review the chapter as needed.

1. Agriculture

2. Growth of towns and cities

3. Contact with other parts of the world

4. Social structures

5. Shift from decentralized toward central governments

REFLECT ON THE TOPIC ESSENTIAL QUESTION

---

1. In one to three paragraphs, explain how the beliefs and practices of the predominant religions, agricultural practices, and political decentralization affected European society from c. 1200 to c. 1450.

1.7

Comparison in the Period from c. 1200 to c. 1450

The world is divided into men who have wit and no religion and men who have religion and no wit.

—Ibn Sīnā (Avicenna) (980–1037), Persian philosopher and physician

Essential Question: In what ways was the process of state-building in various parts of the world between c. 1200 and c. 1450 similar and different?

Between c. 1200 and c. 1450, states in core areas of civilization grew larger while smaller states declined. In this way, much of the world followed the same trend of building more centralized, more powerful states. However, the process varied from place to place. In most of Asia, the military strength of the Mongols created the largest land-based empire in world history. In West Africa, the Middle East, and South Asia, the religion of Islam was a key part of state-building. In Europe, trade, both internal and with the more advanced civilizations of the Middle East, had greater impact.

State-Building and New Empires

As stronger, more centralized states rose, the influence of nomadic societies began to wane by the 15th century. During this period, new empires emerged and states around the world expanded.

- The Song Dynasty in China continued a long period of technological and cultural progress.

- The Abbasid Caliphate in the Middle East was fragmented by invaders and shifts in trade. Following it, new Muslim states arose in Africa, the Middle East, and Spain.

- In South and Southeast Asia, the Chola Kingdom and Vijayanagar Empire used trade to build strong states, while the Delhi Sultanate in northern India was more land-based.

- In Africa, the rulers of Mali created an empire that was bigger and more centrally administered than the Empire of Ghana that preceded it.

- In the Americas, the Aztecs formed a tributary empire in Mesoamerica that relied on a strong military. The Inca Empire in the Andean region used the elaborate mit'a system as a way to support state-building. In contrast, most of the Americas lacked centralized states.

- In Europe, feudal ties declined in importance as centralized states developed. This development was clearer in the Western European kingdoms of England and France than in Eastern Europe.

- Japan, unlike most states, became more decentralized and feudal.

The Role of Religion in State-Building

One similarity in much of the world was that religion was a vital part of state-building. To help unite a diverse population, empires and states often turned to religion to strengthen political control over their territory. One excellent example of how religion worked with state-building was in the Islamic world. Through the unifying power of shared beliefs and a use of the common language of Arabic, Islam provided the basis for the legitimacy of rulers from West Africa to Southeast Asia.

China and East Asia Other states also were strengthened by religion. In China, the Confucian belief system was closely tied to civil service. The Song Dynasty relied on Confucian scholars to run a powerful, enduring bureaucracy. No other state had such a well-established and extensive system for conducting government affairs across such a large territory. The ability to implement laws and carry out imperial edicts was a key part of state-building in China.

Neo-Confucianism (see Topic 1.1) spread to Korea and Japan, allowing rulers in these East Asian regions to justify and consolidate their political power as well. Similarly, rulers in South and Southeast Asia relied on Hinduism and Buddhism to aid them in strengthening their states.

Europe In Europe, the relationship between Roman Catholic Church and state-building was somewhat different than in most of Eurasia. At times, the Church was part of the state-building process. However, because European states were so weak for most of the Middle Ages, the Church had provided an alternative structure for organizing society. Then, between 1200 and 1450, as more powerful states emerged in France and the Holy Roman Empire, the Church sometimes became a rival power.

Diffusion of Religion The spread of major religions during this time period resulted in the influence of religion over wide areas. Islam, Buddhism, and Christianity all encouraged their followers to convert non-believers. Therefore, missionary activity was an important factor in the decline in the practice of local religions in places such as Sub-Saharan Africa, Southeast Asia, and East Asia. In South Asia, converts to Islam increased partly as a result of military invasions by Islamic armies from Central Asia. However, Hinduism remained the predominant religion in South Asia, setting the stage for intermittent periods of conflict and tolerance between followers of Islam and Hinduism on the sub-continent. Trade networks in the Indian Ocean, South China Sea, East and Central Asia, and across the Sahara Desert helped to spread religions as commercial activity increased.

State-Building Through Trade

Fueled by increased trade, cross-cultural exchanges of technology and innovation increased. Innovations in crop production, such as Champa rice that spread from Vietnam to China, helped the Song Dynasty feed and sustain a growing population. The resulting effect, a larger and more urban citizenry, supported the development of China's manufacturing capability—the largest in the world at the time. Porcelain, silk, steel, and iron production all increased during this time. Together, these changes built the Song into the strongest state in China since the time of the Han a millennium earlier.

Paper manufacturing, invented in China in the 2nd century B.C.E., made its way across Eurasia, reaching Europe around the 13th century. The resulting printed material led to increased literacy rates across Europe, the Middle East, and North Africa. The focus on intellectual thought and learning led to advances in mathematics and medicine, especially in Islamic centers of learning such as the House of Wisdom in Bagdad.

Europe benefited from exchanges with the Middle East, and through it with the rest of Asia. Not all contact between Europe and Asia was peaceful. Muslims had conquered Spain by force in the 8th century and Christian crusaders attempted to seize lands they considered holy in the Middle East beginning around 1100. The Mongols fostered the transfer of knowledge, but only after they carried out brutal conquests. All of these contacts with Asia contributed to state-building in Europe. Between 1200 and 1450, the process was small and slow, held back by the manorial system and serfdom, but it was noticeable. After 1450, state-building would increase in speed and significance in Europe.

The Impact of Nomadic Peoples

Nomadic peoples played a key role in the process of state building between 1200 and 1450. The Mongols, a pastoral people from the steppes of Central Asia, ruled over significant areas of Asia and Eastern Europe during the 13th century. (For more on the Mongols, see Topic 2.2.) The political stability resulting from Mongol dominance allowed trade across Eurasia to greatly expand. Cross-cultural interactions and transfers intensified and some of the first direct contacts between Europe and China since the classical period occurred, also facilitated by Mongol rule.

Similar to the Mongols, Turkish peoples, also from the Central Asian steppes, increased their dominance over large land-based empires in the eastern Mediterranean, Persia, and South Asia that lasted well past 1450. However, unlike the Mongols, who built their empire initially as a coordinated campaign by unified Mongol clans, different Turkish groups built separate empires.

The Seljuk and Ottoman Turks became dominant forces in the Mediterranean region while another Turkish group established an empire located in Persia and the surrounding territories.

The creation of these empires would be among the last major impacts of the interaction between settled and nomadic peoples. The role of nomads in commerce and cross-cultural exchange diminished as they were replaced by organized groups of merchants and trading companies.

Patriarchy and Religion

Social organization in most cultures remained patriarchal. However, cultures varied. While religion often reinforced the power of men, its record was mixed. For example, convent life for Christians in Europe and in Jainist and Buddhist religious communities in South Asia provided women with opportunities for learning and leadership. In contrast, in China, women lost some independence as the custom of foot binding became more common.

Four Types of State-Building, c. 1200–c. 1450		
Processes	Description	Examples
Emergence of New States	States arise in land once controlled by another empire	• Mamluk Empire (formerly Abbasid territory) • Seljuk Empire (formerly Abbasid territory) • Delhi Sultanate (formerly Gupta territory)
Revival of Former Empires	New leadership continues or rebuilds a previous empire with some innovations	• Song Dynasty (based on the Han Dynasty) • Mali Empire (based on the Ghana Kingdom) • Holy Roman Empire (based on the Roman Empire)
Synthesis of Different Traditions	A state adapts foreign ideas to local conditions	• Japan (Chinese and Japanese) • Delhi Sultanate (Islamic and Hindu) • Neo-Confucianism
Expansion in Scope	An existing state expands its influence through conquest, trade, or other means	• Aztecs in Mesoamerica • Incas in South America • City-states in East Africa • City-states in Southeast Asia

REFLECT ON THE ESSENTIAL QUESTION

1. **Comparison** Create a chart comparing continuities, innovations, and diversity in six regions covered in Unit 1.

2. In one to three paragraphs, explain the similarities and differences in the process of state-building in various parts of the world between c. 1200 and c. 1450.

UNIT 1 REVIEW

HISTORICAL PERSPECTIVES: WHO DEVELOPED GUNS?

The development of gunpowder and its use in guns revolutionized world history. However, historians presented various arguments to explain who was responsible for starting this revolution.

Chinese Claims and European Doubts While the Chinese long took credit for developing both gunpowder and guns, European historians were traditionally skeptical because they doubted the Chinese had the technological ability to make such advances. For example, Henry Hime, a British military officer, argued in his 1904 book, *Gunpowder and Ammunition: Their Origin and Progress,* that the Chinese "possessed little genius for mechanical or chemical inventions" so they had probably "obtained their first gunpowder and firearms from the West."

Fireworks European scholars gradually recognized Chinese contributions to the technologies that led to the development of guns. They first recognized that the Chinese had invented gunpowder and that knowledge of the explosive substance had been carried by traders and the Mongols to Europe in the 13th century. However, European historians continued to argue that the Chinese had used gunpowder only for fireworks, not for weaponry. Historian Jack Kelly, in a recent book about the history of gunpowder, noted that historians had not moved much beyond Hime's argument in their views of Chinese abilities. "The notion of China's benign relationship with gunpowder sprang in part from Western prejudices about the Chinese character. Some viewed the Chinese as amateurs who stumbled onto the secret of gunpowder but couldn't see its potential. Others saw them as pacifist sages who wisely turned away from its destructive possibilities."

Agreement The next step was for Europeans to acknowledge that the Chinese historians were correct, and that the Chinese had begun using gunpowder to make early forms of guns since the 10th century. British scholar Joseph Needham revolutionized Western attitudes toward China with his multivolume work *Science and Civilization in China.* Begun in 1954, it continued after Needham's death under other scholars and now includes more than 25 volumes. Needham called the development of gunpowder "no doubt the greatest of all Chinese military inventions." And he concluded that the Chinese had developed the first gun "before other peoples knew of the invention at all."

Develop an Argument: Evaluate the extent to which historical evidence supports one of the perspectives on the historical development and use of gunpowder. (Review outside sources as necessary.)

WRITE AS A HISTORIAN: CHECKLIST FOR A LONG ESSAY ANSWER

The long essay question will require you to develop an *argument*, which requires asserting a *defensible claim* and backing it up with *evidence*. (For more on arguments, claims, and evidence, see page xxxviii.) The process for developing your argument is described in the checklist below. (See also pages xxxiii-xxxviii.) Each stage of the process will be the focus of a writing activity at the end of units 3–8. These activities will help you apply to each stage the historical thinking skills you must demonstrate in your essay.

1. **Carefully read and analyze the task.** Read the question carefully. Within your argument, you will be asked to evaluate the extent to which subjects show similarity or difference, continuities or changes, or causation. (See page xxiii.) Look for key words defining the task. Note the geographic area(s) and time period(s) framing the task.

2. **Gather and organize the evidence you will need to complete the task.** Write down everything you know that is *directly* related to the topic. Include both broad ideas and specific incidents or events. Then review your information looking for patterns and connections. Also determine a way to organize the evidence to fulfill the task.

3. **Develop a thesis—a defensible claim—that lays out a line of reasoning.** (See page xxxiv.) You should be able to defend your claim using the evidence you collected and express your thesis in one or more sentences in the same location in your essay, typically in the introduction.

4. **Write an introductory paragraph.** Use the introduction to relate your thesis statement to a broader historical context. Explain how it fits into larger or divergent historical trends.

5. **Write the supporting paragraphs.** Use information you gathered in step 2 to support the argument expressed in your thesis statement with corroboration (support), modification (slight change), or qualification (limitation). Use transitional words to tie ideas together.

6. **Write the conclusion.** To unify your essay, return to the ideas in your introduction. Instead of restating your thesis statement, however, extend it to draw a nuanced conclusion that follows from your evidence.

7. **Reread and evaluate your essay.** Become familiar with the scoring rubric (see page xxxix). Check your essay to make sure you have included everything needed to earn the maximum number of points.

Application: Follow the steps above as you develop a long essay in response to a prompt on page 71.

For current free response question samples, visit: https://apcentral.collegeboard. org/courses/ap-world-history/exam

LONG ESSAY QUESTIONS

Directions: Write an essay in response to one of the prompts below. The suggested writing time for an essay is 40 minutes.

In your response, you should do the following:

- Respond to the prompt with a historically defensible thesis or claim that establishes a line of reasoning.
- Describe a broader historical context relevant to the prompt.
- Support an argument in response to the prompt using at least two pieces of specific and relevant evidence.
- Use historical reasoning (e.g., comparison, causation, continuity or change) to frame or structure an argument that addresses the prompt.
- Demonstrate a complex understanding of a historical development related to the prompt through sophisticated argumentation and/or effective use of evidence.

Source: *AP® World History Course and Exam Description*

1. By the 14th century, Islam, Hinduism, and Confucianism each included movements within them that placed greater emphasis on either emotion or reason.
   Develop an argument that evaluates the extent to which two religious or ethical systems of thought were similar or different up through the 15th century.

2. Because of its size, wealth, and cultural innovations, China had a significant influence on its East Asian neighbors in the years 1200 to 1450—whether those neighbors were friendly or hostile.
   Develop an argument that evaluates the extent to which Chinese cultural traditions led to political or social change in other East Asian societies in that time period.

3. Abundant natural resources and the rise of powerful centralized governments affected African states between the 12th and the 15th centuries.
   Develop an argument that evaluates the extent to which change or continuity over time occurred in the economics and politics during that time period in one African state.

4. Abundant natural resources and the rise of powerful centralized governments affected American states between the 12th and the 15th centuries.
   Develop an argument that evaluates the extent to which change or continuity over time occurred in the economics and politics during that time period in one American state.

DOCUMENT-BASED QUESTION

Directions: Question 1 is based on the accompanying documents. The documents have been edited for the purpose of this exercise. You are advised to spend 15 minutes planning and 45 minutes writing your answer.

1. Evaluate the extent to which contact among groups of people influenced cultural development in sub-Saharan Africa during the period c. 1200 to c. 1450.

In your response you should do the following:

- Respond to the prompt with a historically defensible thesis or claim that establishes a line of reasoning.
- Describe a broader historical context relevant to the prompt.
- Support an argument in response to the prompt using at least four documents.
- Use at least one additional piece of specific historical evidence (beyond that found in the documents) relevant to an argument about the prompt.
- For at least two documents, explain how or why the document's point of view, purpose, historical situation, and/or audience is relevant to an argument.
- Demonstrate a complex understanding of a historical development related to the prompt through a sophisticated argument and/or effective use of evidence.

Source: *AP® World History Course and Exam Description*

Document 1

Source: Account by an Egyptian official of the ruler of Mali, Mansa Musa during his royal visit to Cairo, Egypt, while on a pilgrimage to Mecca in the early 1300s.

This man [Mansa Musa] spread upon Cairo the flood of his generosity: there was no person, officer of the court, or holder of any office of the sultanate who did not receive a sum of gold from him.

I tried to persuade him [Mansa Musa] to go up to the Citadel to meet the sultan, but he refused persistently saying: "I came for the Pilgrimage and nothing else. I do not wish to mix anything else with my Pilgrimage." I realized that the audience was repugnant to him because he would be obliged to kiss the ground and the sultan's hand. I cajoled him and he made excuses but the sultan's protocol demanded that I should bring him into the royal presence, so I kept on at him until he agreed.

When we came in the sultan's presence we said to him: 'Kiss the ground!' but he refused outright saying: 'How may this be?'. . . Then he said: 'I make obeisance [a gesture of respect] to God who created me!' then he prostrated himself [lay flat on ground] and went forward to the sultan.

Document 2

Source: Description of the Kingdom of Mali by Ibn Battuta, Muslim scholar and explorer, mid-1300s.

Among the admirable qualities of these people, the following are to be noted:

1. The small number of acts of injustice one finds there; they are of all peoples those who most abhor [hate] injustice, the sultan pardons no one who is guilty of it.

2. The complete and general safety one enjoys throughout the land. The traveler has no more reason than the man who stays at home to fear brigands or thieves.

3. They make their prayers punctually. . . .

4. They zealously learn the Qu'ran by heart. Those children who are neglectful of this are put in chains until they have memorized the Qu'ran. On one festival day I visited the qadi [teacher] and saw children thus enchained and asked him "Will you not let them free?" He replied "Only when they know the Qu'ran by heart."

Document 3

Source: Description by a northern Nigerian artisan of the process used in coastal Benin to make a bronze sculpture, early 1400s.

In the name of Allah the Compassionate, the Merciful. This account will show how the Benin figures are made. This work is one to cause wonder.

This kind of work is done with clay, and wax, and red metal, and solder and lead, and fire. The clay figure is set in a fire. . . . Then it is placed in a hole to make a mold. The hole is cleaned out and molten metal poured in. . . . the outside cover of clay is broken off. Then you see a beautiful figure.

Document 4

Source: Summary of the reports of Arab merchants in West Africa in the 1300s by Ibn Khaldun, Arab historian, early 1400s.

Merchants penetrated the western part of the land of the Sudan and found among them no greater king than the king of Ghana. . . . the authority of the rulers of Ghana dwindled away and they were overcome by the Susu, a neighboring people of the Sudan, who subjugated and absorbed them.

Later the people of Mali outnumbered the peoples of the Sudan in their neighborhood and dominated the whole region. They vanquished the Susu and occupied all their possessions, both their ancient kingdom and that of Ghana as far as the ocean on the west [the Atlantic].

Document 5

Source: Muslim scholar Al-Sadi, account of the rule of Songhai king Sunni Ali after he conquered the Mali Empire, mid 1400s.

. . . the great oppressor and notorious evil-doer, Sunni 'Ali, he was a man of great strength and colossal energy, a tyrant, a miscreant, an aggressor, a despot, and a butcher who killed so many human beings that only God Most High could count them. He tyrannized the scholars and holy men, killing them, insulting them, and humiliating them. One of the characteristics of this wicked tyrant was to make a mockery of his (Islamic) religion.

Document 6

Source: Benin figure placed on the altar of a dead king, late 1400s.

Document 7

Source: Leo Africanus, historian, recounting in *History and Description of Africa* (1526) a visit to Timbuktu in the Kingdom of Songhai, late 1400s.

Here there are many shops of artisans and merchants, [who sell] European cloth. The inhabitants . . . are exceedingly rich, since the present king married both of his daughters to rich merchants. Here are many wells, containing sweet water. Whenever the Niger River overflows, they carry the water into town by means of sluices [a device used to control the water flow]. This region yields great quantities of grain, cattle, milk, and butter . . . When I was there, I saw one camel-load of salt sold for eighty ducats.

The rich king of Timbuktu has many plates and scepters of gold, some of which weigh 1,300 pounds, and he keeps a magnificent and well-furnished court. . . . Here are great numbers of religious teachers, judges, scholars and learned persons, who are bountifully maintained at the king's expense.

UNIT 2: Networks of Exchange from c. 1200 to c. 1450

Understand the Context

Between 1200 and 1450, economic activity along existing trade routes increased in volume and scope. Technological and commercial innovations, imperial expansion, and demand for luxury goods were key factors in the ongoing expansion of trade. Growing trade networks accelerated cultural, biological, and technological diffusion across Afro-Eurasia.

Factors that Expanded Trade Between 1200 and 1450, the rise of powerful states and empires played a critical role in increasing the volume and geographical reach of existing trade networks. The Mongol Empire promoted trade along the Silk Roads, creating a vast commercial network across Eurasia. Trade routes across the Sahara and in the Indian Ocean added both West Africa and East Africa to this network. Improvements to previously existing commercial practices, including forms of credit, facilitated larger networks of exchange. Driving this growth in trade was a growing demand for luxury goods, such as silk and porcelain from China and gold from Africa.

Consequences of Trade In the context of this growing trade, powerful new trading cities emerged scattered across Africa and Eurasia. Trade provided the setting for significant cross-cultural exchanges. As merchants and other travelers moved from place to place, they introduced religious beliefs such as Islam and developments in technology such as paper making and gunpowder to new communities. Against the backdrop of this transfer of ideas and things, came also the rapid spread of deadly diseases, most notably the bubonic plague.

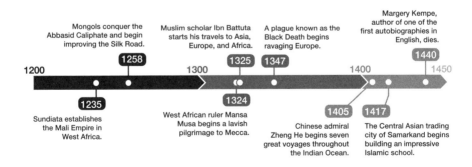

Mongols conquer the Abbasid Caliphate and begin improving the Silk Road. **1258**

Muslim scholar Ibn Battuta starts his travels to Asia, Europe, and Africa. **1325**

A plague known as the Black Death begins ravaging Europe. **1347**

Margery Kempe, author of one of the first autobiographies in English, dies. **1440**

1200   1300   1400   1450

Sundiata establishes the Mali Empire in West Africa. **1235**

West African ruler Mansa Musa begins a lavish pilgrimage to Mecca. **1324**

Chinese admiral Zheng He begins seven great voyages throughout the Indian Ocean. **1405**

The Central Asian trading city of Samarkand begins building an impressive Islamic school. **1417**

Topic and Learning Objectives

Topic 2.1: The Silk Roads pages 77–84

A: Explain the causes and effects of growth of networks of exchange after 1200.

Topic 2.2: The Mongol Empire and the Modern World
pages 85–94

B: Explain the process of state building and decline in Eurasia over time.

C: Explain how the expansion of empires influenced trade and communication over time.

D: Explain the significance of the Mongol Empire in larger patterns of continuity and change.

Topic 2.3: Exchange in the Indian Ocean pages 95–102

E: Explain the causes of the growth of networks of exchange after 1200.

F: Explain the effects of the growth of networks of exchange after 1200.

G: Explain the role of environmental factors in the development of networks of exchange in the period from c. 1200 to c. 1450.

Topic 2.4: Trans-Saharan Trade Route pages 103–110

H: Explain the causes and effects of the growth of trans-Saharan trade.

I: Explain how the expansion of empires influenced trade and communication over time.

Topic 2.5: Cultural Consequences of Connectivity pages 111–120

J: Explain the intellectual and cultural effects of the various networks of exchange in Afro-Eurasia from c. 1200 to c. 1450.

Topic 2.6: Environmental Consequences of Connectivity
pages 121–126

K: Explain the environmental effects of the various networks of exchange in Afro-Eurasia from c. 1200 to c. 1450.

Topic 2.7: Comparison of Economic Exchange pages 127–133

L: Explain the similarities and differences among the various networks of exchange in the period from c. 1200 to c. 1450.

2.1

The Silk Roads

And don't forget that if you treat the custom-house officers with respect,
and make them something of a present in goods or money, as well as their
clerks and dragomen, they will behave with great civility, and always be ready
to appraise your wares below their real value.

—Italian merchant Francesco Balducci Peglotti (1471)

Essential Question: What were the causes and effects of the growth
of networks of exchange after 1200?

More than 1,300 years after the first accounts of travel on the Silk Roads, these fabled routes that had fallen into disuse had revived by the 8th and 9th centuries. As described by merchant Peglotti, the land route of the Silk Roads was vibrant and essential to interregional trade in the 14th and 15th centuries.

Demand for luxury goods increased in Europe and Africa. Chinese, Persian, and Indian artisans and merchants expanded their production of textiles and porcelains for export. Caravans made travel safer and more practical, and the Chinese developed a system using paper money to manage increasing trade. Interregional trade on the Silk Roads flourished.

Causes of the Growth of Exchange Networks

The Crusades helped pave the way to expanding networks of exchange, as lords and their armies of knights brought back fabrics and spices from the East. Despite the inroads on the Byzantine Empire by the Ottoman Turks, the Silk Roads trade routes remained in operation, as did sea routes across the Mediterranean Sea and the Indian Ocean. China was still eager for Europe's gold and silver, and Europe was growing more eager than ever for silk, tea, and rhubarb. Global trade increased. Although Europeans had not yet found a route around the Cape of Good Hope at the southern tip of Africa, they had been making overland trips across Europe for many centuries.

Rise of New Empires After the collapse of classical civilizations such as the Roman and Han empires, the first golden age of the Silk Roads came to an end, and activity declined dramatically. However, by the 8th and 9th centuries, Arab merchants from the Abbasid Empire revived the land route of the Silk Roads as well as sea routes in the Indian Ocean. Tang China had much to offer the newly revived global trade network, including the compass, paper, and gunpowder. China exported porcelain, tea, and silk. From other parts of Asia, China imported cotton, precious stones, pomegranates, dates, horses, and grapes. These luxury goods appealed to the upper class of Chinese society, whose members reveled in their country's newfound affluence. This period marked the second golden age of the Silk Roads.

No other cause, however, had as significant an impact on the expansion of trade as did the rise of the **Mongol Empire**. Mongols conquered the Abbasid Caliphate in 1258, and in the 14th century China came under their control as well. Parts of the Silk Roads that were under the authority of different rulers were, for the first time, unified in a system under the control of an authority that respected merchants and enforced laws. The Mongols improved roads and punished bandits, both of which increased the safety of travel on the Silk Roads. New trade channels were also established between Asia, the Middle East, Africa, and Europe. Those who survived the conquests by the Mongols and their descendants benefited from the reinvigoration of trade routes that had not been heavily used since the days of the Roman and Han Empires. (You will read more about the Mongols in Topic 2.2.)

Improvements in Transportation Technologies Another cause for the expansion of exchange networks was the improvement of transportation. Travelers on the overland Silk Roads learned that traveling with others in caravans was safer than traveling alone. They also learned how to design saddles for camels that greatly increased the weight of the load the animals could carry.

Centuries earlier, China had made advances in naval technology that allowed it to control sea-based trade routes in the South China Sea. During the Han Dynasty, Chinese scientists developed the **magnetic compass** and improved the **rudder**, both of which helped aid navigation and ship control along the seas. The Chinese **junk**, also developed in the Han Dynasty, was a boat similar to the Southwest Asian dhow. It had multiple sails and was as long as 400 feet—at least triple the size of the typical Western European ship of its time. The hull of a junk was divided into compartments. The walls making these divisions strengthened the ship for rough voyages at sea and made sinking less likely.

Effects of the Growth of Exchange Networks

Two significant effects of the expansion and stability of the Silk Roads were the series of oases that developed along the routes, including thriving cities, and commercial innovations that greatly helped to manage the increasing trade.

Cities and Oases Long stretches of the overland Silk Roads passed through inhospitable terrain—hot arid lands where water was scarce. Cities along the routes that were watered by rivers became thriving centers of trade. For example, the city of **Kashgar** is located at the western edge of China where northern and southern routes of the Silk Roads crossed, leading to destinations in Central Asia, India, Pakistan, and Persia. It sits where the Taklamakan Desert meets the Tian Shan Mountains and is watered by the Kashgar River, which has made the lands along it fertile for crops such as wheat, rice, fruits, and cotton. Travelers on the Silk Roads depended on Kashgar for its abundance of water and food. Artisans in Kashgar produced textiles, rugs, leather goods, and pottery. Its food and handicrafts were sold in a bustling market. At the crossroads of both ideas and goods, the once primarily Buddhist city also became a center of Islamic scholarship.

Similarly, **Samarkand,** in present-day Uzbekistan in the Zeravshan River valley, was a stopping point on the Silk Roads between China and the Mediterranean. Samarkand was a center of cultural exchange as much as it was a center for trading goods. Archaeological remains show the presence of diverse religions, including Christianity, Buddhism, Zoroastrianism, and Islam. Like Kashgar, Samarkand was known for its artisans as well as its centers of Islamic learning and magnificently decorated mosques.

SILK ROADS, C. 1200

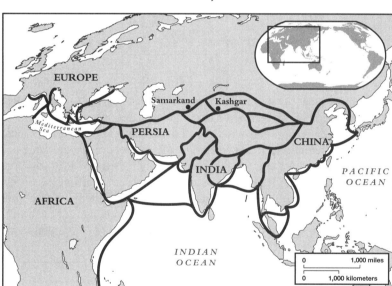

Caravanserai Large flourishing trading cities such as Kashgar and Samarkand, however, were not the only oases along the arid Silk Roads. Once the routes of the Silk Roads became stabilized, inns known as **caravanserai** sprang up, often about 100 miles apart. That distance is how far camels could travel before they needed water. At the caravanserai, travelers could rest both themselves and their animals and sometimes trade their animals for fresh ones. The word *caravanserai* derives from the Persian words for caravan and palace.

Commercial Innovations To manage the increasing trade, China developed new financial systems. China had long been a **money economy**—using money rather than bartering with such commodities as cowrie shells or

Source: Wikimedia Commons
Credit: Photo by Babak Gholizadeh

The entrances to caravanserais were large enough to allow animals as well as people to enter. Inside the enclosure, there were stalls for animals as well as chambers for people. This caravanserai is in Iran.

salt. However, the copper coins they used became too unwieldy to transport for everyday transactions, so the government developed a system of credit known as **flying cash**. This allowed a merchant to deposit **paper money** under his name in one location and withdraw the same amount at another location. Locations for exchanging flying cash became the model for the banks of the modern era, including the **banking houses** established in European cities in the 1300s. At a banking house, a person could present a **bill of exchange**—a document stating the holder was legally promised payment of a set amount on a set date—and receive that amount of money in exchange. Each of these innovations encouraged and supported trade by providing convenience and the stability of institutions.

The Crusades awakened Europeans' interest in luxury goods from Asia. To acquire them, they organized the trade of European resources. In the 13th century, cities in northern Germany and Scandinavia formed a commercial alliance called the **Hanseatic League**. Controlling trade in the North Sea and the Baltic Sea, member cities of the league, such as Lubeck, Hamburg, and Riga, were able to drive out pirates and monopolize trade in goods such as timber, grain, leather, and salted fish. League ships would leave the Baltic and North Seas. They would round the Atlantic Coast of Western Europe, proceeding to the ports of the Mediterranean. There, they might pick up valuable goods from Arab caravans. The league lasted until the mid-17th century, when national governments became strong enough to protect their merchants.(Connect: Write a paragraph analyzing the effects in Asia of European interest in Asian goods. See Topic 1.1.)

Innovations in Commerce, 500 B.C.E. to 1603 C.E.			
Financial Instrument	**Description**	**Origin Date**	**Early Location**
Coin	Minted precious metals (silver, bronze, gold) with own inherent value	c. 500 B.C.E.	Lydia, Turkey
Caravanserai	Inns along trade routes where travelers could trade, rest, and replenish	c. 500 B.C.E.	Persian Empire
Paper Money	Currency in paper form	c. 800 C.E.	China
Hanseatic League	First common market and confederation of merchant guilds	1296 C.E.	Germany
Banking House	Precursor to modern banking	c. 200 B.C.E.	China
Bill of Exchange	A written order without interest that binds one party to pay a fixed sum to another party at a predetermined date in the future	c. 700 C.E.	China

Increase in Demand The growing demand for luxury goods from Afro-Eurasia, China, Persia, and India led to a corresponding increase in the supply of those goods through expanded production. Craftworkers expanded their production of such goods as silk and other textiles and porcelains for export. Increased demand also led to the expansion of iron and steel manufactured in China, motivating its proto-industrialization. (See Topic 1.1.)

KEY TERMS BY THEME

TECHNOLOGY: Sea Trade
magnetic compass
rudder
junk

GOVERNMENT: New
  Empires
Mongol Empire

CULTURE: Trade
  Cities
Kashgar
Samarkand

ECONOMICS: Innovations
caravanserai
money economy
flying cash
paper money
banking houses
bill of exchange
Hanseatic League

MULTIPLE-CHOICE QUESTIONS

Questions 1 to 3 refer to the passage below.

"The road you travel from Tana to Cathay [China] is perfectly safe, whether by day or by night, according to what the merchants say who have used it. . . . Cathay is a province which contained a multitude of cities and towns. Among others there is one in particular, that is to say the capital city, to which is great resort of merchants, and in which there is a vast amount of trade; and this city is called Cambalec. And the said city hath a circuit of one hundred miles, and is all full of people and houses and of dwellers in the said city."

Francesco Pegolotti, The Merchant's Handbook, c. 1471

1. Which statement about China and trade does this passage best support?
   (A) Trade between Europe and Cathay was greatly enhanced by the security established by the Mongol and Ming Empires.
   (B) Merchants rarely traveled between Tana and Cathay because the road was very dangerous.
   (C) Cambalec was an important trading hub, but it was not a large city.
   (D) The author felt the risks of trade with China outweighed the rewards.

2. Which development was the turning point that led to the expansion of trade between Asia and Europe?
   (A) The formation of the Silk Roads by Marco Polo allowed goods from Asia to be imported into Europe for the first time.
   (B) The conquests by Mongols, which led to improved trade routes and reduced trading costs.
   (C) The invention of silk cloth during the early Mongol rule allowed the Mongols to trade for pottery, wool, and other European goods.
   (D) The invention of paper money by Venetian bankers helped to facilitate trade between Europe and Asia.

3. Which objects or ideas was the author most likely writing about that represented continuity or change in Chinese trade?
   (A) Silver, gems, and gold went from Europe to China; wool, horses, and the ideas of Islam went from China to Europe
   (B) Silk, paper, and Christianity went from Europe to China; gunpowder, silver, and Buddhism went from China to Europe
   (C) Silver, gems, and gold went from Europe to China; silk, paper, and gunpowder went from China to Europe
   (D) Paper and Christianity went from Europe to China; silk, gunpowder, horses, and wool went from China to Europe

1. **Use the passage below to answer all parts of the question that follows.**

   "Throughout the city there are fine roadways with open spaces well laid out: and round these are seen many great buildings and houses, each with its main doorway facing the square. Such are the caravanserais [inns]: and within are constructed separate apartments and shops with offices that are planned for various uses. Leaving these caravanserais you pass into the market streets where goods of all kinds are sold: such as silk stuffs and cotton cloths, crapes [crepes, a type of silk or wool fabric], taffetas [a fine silk fabric], raw silk and jewelry: for in these shops wares of every kind may be found. There is indeed an immense concourse of merchants and merchandise here . . . . Now the dress the women wear in the streets is that they go covered in a white sheet, and they wear over their faces a black mask of horse-hair, and thus they are concealed completely so that none may know them. Throughout Tabriz [a city in what is now northwestern Iran] many fine buildings may be seen, the Mosques more especially these being most beautifully adorned with tiles in blue and gold. . . ."

   > Excerpt from Ruy González de Clavijo's account of his Silk
   > Roads travels as an ambassador to Tamerlane by King
   > Henry III in Spain between 1402 and 1406

   (A) Identify ONE aspect of social structure in Tabriz that demonstrated continuity with earlier periods in history.

   (B) Explain Clavijo's attitude toward the society and culture at Tabriz.

   (C) Explain how caravanserais affected interregional trade in luxury goods during the period 1200–1450.

2. **Answer all parts of the question that follows.**

   (A) Identify ONE example of cultures spreading between the East and West.

   (B) Explain ONE example of commercial practices that affected Silk Roads trade during the period 1200–1450.

   (C) Explain ONE example of money economies that affected Silk Roads trade during the period 1200–1450.

THINK AS A HISTORIAN: IDENTIFY AND DESCRIBE CONTEXT

When you contextualize a historical development or process, you place it within a larger historical perspective—a "bigger picture." Sometimes to get this perspective you look at the causes of a development or process. For example, the historical development of intercultural connections was possible in the Classical Era because of the interregional trade along the Silk Roads. In the "bigger picture," these intercultural connections bridged the East and the West and began the foundations of a global community.

Identify and describe a context, or "bigger picture," by looking for a cause of each of the following developments during the Song Dynasty.

1. China developed new financial systems in response to increasing trade with Arab merchants from the Abbasid Empire.

2. Russia was able to exchange goods and services with other cultures farther west.

3. The demand for exported silks and Chinese porcelain in Europe and India grew as the Indian Ocean trade grew.

4. Thriving cities developed in Asia.

5. Guns and gunpowder spread from China to all parts of Eurasia.

REFLECT ON THE TOPIC ESSENTIAL QUESTION

1. In one to three paragraphs, explain the causes and effects of the growth of networks of exchange after 1200.

The Mongol Empire and the Modern World

Swarming like locusts over the face of the earth, they [the Mongols] have brought terrible devastation to the eastern parts [of Europe], laying it waste with fire and carnage. After having passed through the land of the Saracens [Muslims], they have razed cities, cut down forests, overthrown fortresses, pulled up vines, destroyed gardens, killed townspeople and peasants.

—Matthew Paris, from the *Chronica Majora* (1240)

Essential Question: How did Eurasian empires grow over time, and how did their expansion influence trade and communication?

The **Mongols** of Central Asia marched across much of Eurasia throughout the 13th century, leaving destruction and chaos in their wake. The reputation of the Mongols for slaughter spread even farther than their actual conquest. Matthew Paris had no firsthand knowledge of the Mongols as he wrote from the safe vantage point of a Benedictine abbey in England. Like Paris, most writers of the time focused on Mongol atrocities. However, in their quest for blood and treasure, the Mongols also sparked a period of interregional connection and exchange at a level that the world had not experienced in a thousand years.

The Mongols and Their Surroundings

In the 12th century, the Mongols were multiple clans of pastoral nomads who herded goats and sheep and who were also hunter-foragers, north of the **Gobi Desert** in East Asia. Life on the arid Asian steppes was harsh, and it shaped the Mongol culture.

The Mongols expected everyone, male and female, to become skilled horse riders, and they highly valued courage in hunting and warfare. They were surrounded by other tribes—the Tatars, the Naimans, the Merkits, and the powerful Jurchen in northern China. The Mongols coveted the relative wealth of tribes and kingdoms that were located closer to the Silk Roads and had easier access to luxury goods such as silk clothing and gold jewelry.

Genghis Khan

The Mongol leader Temujin, born in 1162, spent the early decades of his life creating a series of tribal alliances and defeating neighboring groups one by one. He formed key friendships and married his oldest son to the daughter of a neighboring **khan**, or king. Temujin was intensely focused on building power. With this focus, he sometimes appointed talented nonfamily members to positions over family members. He was often also ruthless. For example, he killed his own stepbrother. He considered personal loyalty the best way to run his growing kingdom. In 1206, Temujin gathered the Mongol chieftains at a meeting called a **kuriltai** where he was elected khan of the Mongolian Kingdom. He took the name **Genghis Khan**, or "ruler of all."

Temujin, better known as Genghis Khan. 14th century, National Palace Museum

The Beginning of Conquest In 1210, Genghis Khan and his troops headed east and attacked the powerful Jin Empire, which had been established by the Jurchens a century earlier and now ruled Manchuria, Inner Mongolia, and northern China. Its capital was the city of Zhongdu, present-day Beijing. Genghis Khan earned his reputation as a terrifying warrior during this campaign; anyone who resisted him was brutally killed in retribution. Sometimes the Mongols wiped out the civilian populations of entire towns after defeating their armies. Stories of Khan's brutality spread in advance of his new westward campaigns, inducing some leaders to surrender before an attack. In 1219, Khan conquered both the Central Asian Kara Khitai Empire and the Islamic Khwarazm Empire farther west. By 1227, Genghis Khan's **khanate**, or kingdom, reached from the North China Sea to eastern Persia. (Connect: Write a paragraph comparing the reign of Genghis Khan to the reign of Sundiata. See Topic 1.5.)

Genghis Khan at War Khan's empire would not have been possible without the skilled and fearsome soldiers under his command. Mongolian soldiers were strong riders and proficient with the short bow. They were also highly disciplined, and Khan developed an efficient command structure. To help with communication between units, a messenger force was created whose members rode for days without stopping, even sleeping on their horses while continuing to ride. With the help of Genghis Khan, the Mongolian armies developed special units that mapped the terrain so that they were prepared against attacks and knew which way to go to attack their enemies. Their military strategies extended to surprise and craft. For instance, Mongol forces frequently deployed a band of warriors smaller than that of their enemy, retreating in feigned defeat; usually, enemy forces pursued the retreating Mongols, who then amassed larger forces to confuse and outflank the enemy.

When coming upon an enemy settlement, Genghis Khan sent a small group ahead to ask for surrender. If the enemy refused, he killed all the aristocrats. Craftworkers, miners, and others with skills, such as the ability to read and write, were recruited for the Mongol Empire. Others were used as laborers for tasks such as carrying looted goods back to the Mongol capital or as fodder in the front lines of battles.

Mongols quickly incorporated into their military the weapons and technology of the peoples they conquered. For example, when they conquered parts of China and Persia, they exploited the expertise of captured engineers who knew how to produce improved **siege weapons**, such as portable towers used to attack walled fortifications and catapults that hurled stones or other objects. To keep contact with the far reaches of the empire, Genghis Khan created a type of pony express, except instead of carrying written letters riders carried oral messages.

Genghis Khan at Peace Those who expected Genghis Khan to govern the way he made war were surprised. The period of Eurasian history between the 13th and 14th centuries is often called the **Pax Mongolica**, or Mongolian peace. Genghis Khan established the capital of his empire at Karakorum, near the center of what is now the modern country of Mongolia. In constructing the city and establishing his government, he consulted with scholars and engineers of Chinese and Islamic traditions. Genghis Khan may have been responsible for more new bridges than any other ruler in history. The social policies of Genghis Khan were liberal for the day. For example, he instituted a policy of religious tolerance throughout the empire, which was unusual in the 13th century. Freed from years of warfare, Genghis Khan's soldiers took charge of protecting the Silk Roads, making them safe for trade and ushering in the third golden age of the Silk Roads. New trade channels were also established between Asia, the Middle East, Africa, and Europe. Those who survived the conquests by the Mongols and their descendants benefited from the reinvigoration of trade routes that had not been heavily used since the days of the Roman and Han Empires. (Connect: List the similarities and differences in religious policies between the Pax Mongolica and the Romans. See Prologue.)

Genghis Khan's effort to unify his empire included directing a scribe captured in 1204 to adapt the **Uyghur alphabet** to represent Mongol. Although the effort to establish one system throughout the empire failed, the alphabet is still used in Mongolia today.

Mongolian Empire Expands

Three of Genghis Khan's grandsons set up their own khanates, further expanding the empire into Asia and Europe. With each conquest, the empire expanded, with new people absorbed into its economy and networks of exchange.

Batu and the Golden Horde In 1236, **Batu**, the son of Khan's oldest son, led a Mongolian army of 100,000 soldiers into Russia, which at the time was a loose network of city-states and principalities. Batu's army, which came to be known as the **Golden Horde**, marched westward, conquering the small Russian kingdoms and forcing them to pay tributes. In 1240, the capital city of Kiev was looted and destroyed.

MONGOL EMPIRES IN THE 13TH CENTURY

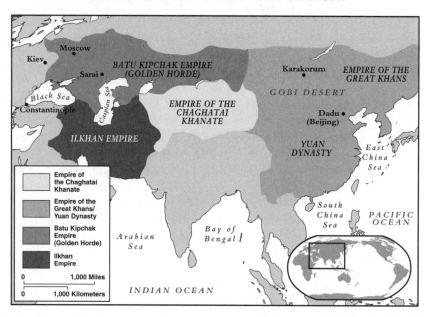

The Golden Horde continued pushing westward. An initial period of sympathy for the Mongols, based on religious toleration and promotion of trade, evaporated when Western Europe saw the Golden Horde conquer a Christian region, Russia. In 1241, Batu led the Golden Horde into a successful military encounter with Polish, German, and French knights under the leadership of King Henry of Silesia. Soon afterward, Batu defeated a force of Hungarian knights. He next set his sights on Italy and Austria, but fate intervened. Back in Karakorum, Ogodei Khan, the Great Khan's successor, had died. Batu called off the attacks and returned home to attend the funeral and to see to issues of succession. By the time Batu returned to Europe, he had apparently lost interest in conquering Western Europe.

The Mongols ruled northern Russia by working through existing Russian rulers, who sent regular tributes. The Mongols chose this form of indirect rule because they did not want to live in the forests. The rulers of the city-state of **Moscow** began collecting additional tributes, which they set aside to develop an army to resist the Mongols, and began building an anti-Mongol coalition among the Russian city-states. This coalition, under Moscow's leadership, rose up against the Golden Horde and defeated it in 1380 at the Battle of Kulikovo. After this battle, Mongol influence began to decline. By the mid-16th century, Russia had defeated all of the descendant khans of the Mongols except the Crimean Tatars, who were not defeated until the late 18th century. (Connect: Create a five-event timeline tracing the history of Russia from the Mongols to the development of the modern state. See Topics 1.6 and 2.1.)

The Mongols had long-lasting impact on Russia. As elsewhere, Russia suffered widespread devastation and death from the Mongol attacks. But once the destruction by the Golden Horde was over, Russia began to recover. The invasions prompted Russian princes to improve their military organization and to accept the value of more centralized leadership of the region. In addition, three centuries of Mongol rule severed Russia's ties with much of Western Europe. As a result, Russia developed a more distinctly Russian culture than it had before, and resistance to the Mongols created the foundation for the modern Russian state.

Hulegu and the Islamic Heartlands While Batu led the western armies, **Hulegu**, another grandson of Genghis Khan, took charge of the southwest region. In 1258, Hulegu led the Mongols into the Abbasid territories, where they destroyed the city of Baghdad and killed the caliph, along with perhaps 200,000 residents of the city. Hulegu's Mongolian armies continued to push west, threatening more of the Middle East. In 1260, however, they were defeated as a result of a temporary alliance between the Muslim Mamluks, under their military leader Baibars, and Christian Crusaders in Palestine. Both religious groups viewed the Mongols as a serious threat.

At the time of this defeat, Hulegu's kingdom, called the **Il-khanate**, in Central Asia stretched from Byzantium to the Oxus River, which is now called the Amu Darya. Mongols ruled this kingdom, but Persians served as ministers and provincial and local officials. The Mongols found that this arrangement resulted in maximum tax collection.

Eventually, Hulegu and most of the other Mongols living in the Il-khanate converted to Islam. Before this conversion, the Mongols had tolerated all religions in Persia. After the conversion, however, Mongols supported massacres of Jews and Christians.

Kublai Khan and the Yuan Dynasty Meanwhile, in the eastern part of the Mongolian Empire, a grandson of Genghis Khan, **Kublai Khan**, set his sights on China, which was then ruled by the Song Dynasty. China was a more formidable opponent than those faced by the other khans, and Kublai's armies spent the years from 1235 to 1271 attempting to conquer China. In 1260, Kublai assumed the title of Great Khan, and eleven years later finally defeated the Chinese. Adhering closer to Chinese tradition, rather than enforcing Mongolian practices of leadership and control, Kublai Khan established the **Yuan Dynasty**.

He rebuilt the capital at Zhongdu, which had been destroyed by the Mongols in 1215, calling it Dadu. Kublai Khan proved to be skilled at governing a large, diverse territory. Like his grandfather, he instituted a policy of religious tolerance, which inspired loyalty in formerly oppressed groups such as Buddhists and Daoists, who were out of favor in China at the time. His policies were also tolerant toward Muslims, Jews, and Christians. With these and other reforms and the protection of the Mongolian armies, most Chinese initially enjoyed the rule of the Great Khan; he brought prosperity to China because of cultural exchanges and improved trade with other countries, including European ones.

Mongol women led more independent lives than women in other societies of the time. In their nomadic culture, women tended flocks of sheep and goats in addition to raising children and providing meals for the family. Since they rode horses as Mongol men did, the women wore the same kind of leather trousers. Mongol women could remarry after being widowed and could initiate divorces.

Mongols Lose Power Despite Kublai Khan's adoption of many Chinese customs, Mongolian leaders eventually alienated many Chinese. They hired foreigners for the government rather than native-born Chinese. By promoting Buddhists and Daoists and dismantling the civil service exam system, the Mongols distressed the Chinese scholar-gentry class who were often Confucians. Although the official policy was one of tolerance, the Mongolians tended to remain separate from the Chinese and prohibited non-Mongols from speaking Mongolian.

Just as Batu had reached the limit of Mongol expansion to the west, the Mongolian rulers of China failed to expand beyond China. Starting in 1274, the Yuan Dynasty tried and failed to conquer Japan, Indochina, Burma, and the island of Java. These defeats suggested to the already disenchanted Chinese population that the Mongols were not as fearsome as they once had been. In the 1350s, the secret **White Lotus Society** began quietly organizing to put an end to the Yuan Dynasty. In 1368, **Zhu Yuanzhang**, a Buddhist monk from a poor peasant family, led a revolt that overthrew the Yuan Dynasty and founded the **Ming Dynasty** (1368–1644).

The Mongols' defeat in China paralleled a general decline in their power elsewhere, and the empire began to shrink. The Golden Horde had lost its territory by about 1369, while Central Asian territories were conquered by Tamerlane, also known as Timur the Lame, at around the same time.

(Connect: Describe what the Mongols desired in each of their conquests. See Topic 2.1.)

The Long-Term Impact of the Mongolian Invasions

The Mongolian invasions played a key role in history in many ways, positive and negative.

- Mongols conquered a larger area than the Romans, and their bloody reputation was usually well-earned. Their empire was the largest continuous land empire in history.

- During the period known as the Pax Mongolica (c. 1250–c. 1350), Mongols revitalized interregional trade between Asia, the Middle East, Africa, and Europe. The Mongols built a system of roads and continued to maintain and guard the trade routes.

- Interregional cultural exchange occurred as well. Islamic scientific knowledge made its way to China, and paper from China made possible the revolution in communication powered by the Gutenberg printing press (see Topic 1.6). The Mongols transferred Greco-Islamic medical knowledge and the Arabic numbering system to Western Europe.

- The Mongol conquests helped to transmit the fleas that carried the **bubonic plague**, termed the Black Death, from southern China to Central Asia, and from there to Southeast Asia and Europe. It followed familiar paths of trade and military conquest.

- The Mongols ruled successfully due to their understanding of centralized power, a capacity that would transfer in many cases to the occupied civilizations. The Mongols devised and used a single international law for all their conquered territories. Thus, after the Mongols declined in power, the kingdoms and states of Europe, Asia, and Southeast Asia continued or copied the process of centralizing power.

- Mongol fighting techniques led to the end of Western Europe's use of knights in armor. The heavily clad knights could not react in time to the Mongols' use of speed and surprise.

- The era of the walled city in Europe also came to an end, as walls proved useless against the Mongols' siege technology. Some consider the **cannon** a Mongol invention, cobbled together using Chinese gunpowder, Muslim flamethrowers, and European bell-casting techniques.

KEY TERMS BY THEME

GOVERNMENT: Northern China and Central Asia
Mongols
khan
kuriltai
Genghis Khan
khanate
Pax Mongolica

GOVERNMENT: Russia and Western Europe
Batu
Golden Horde
Moscow

GOVERNMENT: Islamic Heartlands
Hulegu
Il-khanate

GOVERNMENT: China
Kublai Khan
Yuan Dynasty
Zhu Yuanzhang
Ming Dynasty

ENVIRONMENT: Asia
Gobi Desert

TECHNOLOGY: Warfare
siege weapons
cannon

CULTURE: Writing
Uyghur alphabet

SOCIETY: Revolt
White Lotus Society

SOCIETY: Disease
bubonic plague

Questions 1 to 3 refer to the passage below.

"The [Russian] Duke who had spoken before gave a short account of all that had taken place since the death of [Genghis Khan], and the partition of his vast dominions. And then the younger Duke, Wsewolodovics, took up the tale.

'Lord King!' he began, 'these Mongols don't carry on warfare in an honorable, chivalrous way. They fight only to destroy, they are bloodthirsty, merciless; their only object is to plunder, slay, murder, and burn, not even to make any use of what lands they conquer. They are like a swarm of locusts. They stay till everything is eaten up, till all are plundered, and what they can't carry off, that they kill, or reduce to ashes. They are utterly faithless; their words and promises are not in the least to be trusted, and those who do make friends with them are the first upon whom they wreak their vengeance if anything goes wrong. We are telling you no fairy tales! We know to our own cost what they are, we tell you what we have seen with our own eyes. And let me tell you this, my lord king, their lust of conquest and devastation knows *no bounds*! If it is our turn today, it will be yours tomorrow! And, therefore, while we seek a refuge in your land, we at the same time warn you to be prepared! For the storm is coming, and may sweep across your frontiers sooner than you think.'"

> Baron Nicholas Jósika (1796–1865), *'Neath the Hoof of the Tartar, or*
> *The Scourge of God*, 1904

1. What did the Russian duke think motivated the Mongols?

   (A) The Mongols were interested primarily in seizing wealth rather than in controlling Russian territory.

   (B) The Mongols choose their tactics in warfare because those tacitces were used in fairy tales.

   (C) The Mongols believed they could fool foes with rumors of atrocities.

   (D) The Mongols wanted to be thought of as honorable warriors.

2. The most valid counterargument to the description of the Mongols by the Russian duke was that the Mongols

   (A) had little interest in wealth so they took only what they needed to survive from people they conquered

   (B) appreciated architecture and art and hence rarely destroyed cities

   (C) had no reason to invade other areas west of Russia

   (D) established political institutions and peace in the territories they conquered

3. How would the Mongols use the Russian duke's description to their advantage if they chose to invade Hungary?

(A) to frighten the Hungarians into surrendering

(B) to persuade Hungarians to fight against other Christian kingdoms

(C) to cause the Hungarians to convert to Islam

(D) to attract Hungarian knights who admired their style of warfare

SHORT-ANSWER QUESTIONS

1. Use the passage below to answer all parts of the question that follows.

"And the Monarch of the World, the Hatim of the Age, [Mengü] Qa'an [Khan] passed away, Güyük, his eldest son had not returned from the campaign against the Qifchaq, and therefore in accordance with precedent the dispatch of orders and the assembling of the people took place at the door of the . . . palace of his wife, Möge Khatun. . . . But since Törengene Khatun was the mother of his eldest sons and was moreover shrewder and more sagacious than Möge Khatun, she [Törengene Khatun] sent messages to the princes, i.e. the brothers and nephews of the Qa'an . . . and said that until a Khan was appointed by agreement someone would have to be ruler and leader in order that the business of the state might not be neglected nor the affairs of the commonwealth thrown into confusion; in order, too, that the army and the court might be kept under control and the interests of the people protected. . . . therefore, until a quriltai [an assembly of Mongol nobles] was held, it was she [Törengene Khatun] that should direct the affairs of the state, and the old ministers should remain in the service of the Court, so that the old and new yasas [political structure or order] might not be changed from what was the law."

Ala-ad Din Ata-Malik Juvaini, a Persian scholar from the
13th century, The History of the Conqueror

(A) Identify ONE way in which Mongol leadership continued unchanged under Törengene Khatun.

(B) Explain ONE reason Mongol nobles accepted a woman's leadership.

(C) Explain ONE way in which the status of women in Islamic society in the 13th century differed from the status of women in Mongol culture during the 13th century.

2. **Answer all parts of the question that follows.**

   (A) Identify ONE example of a pattern of Mongolian expansion in the period 1200–1450.

   (B) Explain ONE way in which Mongol political structures changed when they ruled China.

   (C) Explain ONE example of a connection between Mongolian and Chinese political structures in the period 1200–1450.

 THINK AS A HISTORIAN: IDENTIFY CONNECTIONS BETWEEN HISTORICAL DEVELOPMENTS

Making connections helps historians see developments not as isolated happenings but rather as pieces of a larger pattern. For example, examining the exchange of goods between c. 1200 and c. 1450 takes on much more meaning when it is connected with the exchange of ideas, knowledge, technology, and religion. The impact of trade on states that participated in the Silk Roads exchanges from c. 1200 to c. 1450 went far beyond just the goods that changed hands.

Explain the connection between the development described in each statement and the overall development of the Mongol Empire from 1210 to 1369.

   1. The Mongols' bloody reputation spread farther than their conquest.

   2. The Mongols incorporated the weapons and technology of the people they conquered into their military.

   3. Kublai Khan instituted a policy of religious tolerance.

   4. The Mongols restored interregional trade among Asia, the Middle East, Africa, and Europe.

   5. The Black Death moved throughout Southeast Asia and Europe with the Mongol conquests.

REFLECT ON THE TOPIC ESSENTIAL QUESTION

1. In one to three paragraphs, explain how Eurasian empires grew over time and how their expansion influenced trade and communication.

2.3

Exchange in the Indian Ocean

Seek ye knowledge, even to China.

—Hadith (9th century)

Essential Question: What were the causes and effects of the growth of networks of exchange after 1200, and how did environmental knowledge support that expansion?

The saying from the Hadith, traditionally attributed to the prophet Muhammad, provides guidance to Muslims, encouraging them to travel and learn. Following this advice, it is understandable that Dar al-Islam—literally the House of Islam, or Muslim world—might be called the world's first global empire. It connected societies from North Africa to South Asia.

Even before missionaries and imperial armies spread Islam around the world, Muslim merchants paved the way by travelling to non-Muslim lands in search of trading partners. In fact, Arab merchants had been traveling to South Asia for centuries before Islam began expanding. Muslim merchants' connections to Dar al-Islam interacted with developments in sailing technology and environmental knowledge to transform the Indian Ocean into an economic hot spot during the Postclassical Era.

Causes of Expanded Exchange in the Indian Ocean

South Asia, with its location in the center of the Indian Ocean, benefited enormously from the trade in the **Indian Ocean Basin**. (Connect: Write a paragraph comparing the Islamic global empire with the Mongolian Empire. See Topic 2.2.) Although some of the causes of expanded trade in the Indian Ocean Basin were the same as those of expanded overland routes, some related specifically to ocean travel and knowledge.

Spread of Islam Although the Indian Ocean trade had existed as early as 200 B.C.E., the expansion of Islam connected more cities than ever before. Trading partners existed in East Africa, East and Southeast Asia, and South Asia. Muslim Persians and Arabs were the dominant seafarers and were instrumental in transporting goods to port cities across the Indian Ocean. Cities on the west coast of India, such as **Calicut** and Cambay, became thriving centers of trade due to interactions with merchants from East Africa and Southwest Asia.

Calicut, especially, became a bustling port city for merchants in search of spices from southern India. Foreign merchants from Arabia and China met in Calicut to exchange goods from the West and the East, respectively. Local rulers welcomed the presence of Muslim and Chinese merchants, as it brought the city wealth and prominence in the Indian Ocean Basin.

Increased Demand for Specialized Products As the Indian Ocean trade grew, so did the demand for specialized products. Every region involved in trade had something special to offer its trading partners.

- India became known for the high quality of its fabrics, particularly cotton. In addition, merchants traveled to India in search of meticulously woven carpets as well as high-carbon steel (used for knives and swords), tanned leather, and artisan-crafted stonework. Merchants also sought pepper from India's southern coastal cities.

- Modern-day Malaysia and Indonesia became known as the **Spice Islands** because of the fragrant nutmeg, cinnamon, cloves, and cardamom they exported.

- Enslaved people, ivory, and gold came from the Swahili coastal cities of Mombasa, Mogadishu, and Sofala.

- China exported silks, and Chinese porcelain became coveted worldwide, which is why people in the West still refer to their fancier dishes as "fine china."

- From Southwest Asia came horses, figs, and dates.

Trade in enslaved people also played a role in exchanges in the Indian Ocean. While most Africans who were enslaved and transported to the Americas after 1500 came from west and central Africa, there had been a long-running slave trade in the eastern part of the continent. By routes over land or in the Indian Ocean, enslaved people from eastern Africa were sold to buyers in northern Africa, the Middle East, and India. Many were transported to the islands off the southeast coast of Africa, such as Madagascar. The trade reached its peak in the 18th and 19th centuries.

Enslaved people taken in the Indian Ocean trade suffered fates different from those who were taken across the Atlantic. Those in the Indian Ocean trade were more likely to provide forced labor in seaports in the shipping industry and as household servants. Some worked as sailors or even soldiers. Living in towns or cities, they had more opportunity to develop communities and to work alongside free laborers than did enslaved people taken to the Americas. Enslaved people who ended up in Islamic communities had certain rights, such as the right to marry. As a result of the **Indian Ocean slave trade**, African words, musical styles, and customs can be found in Oman, India, and elsewhere.

Environmental Knowledge Knowledge of **monsoon winds** was essential for trading in the Indian Ocean. In the winter months, winds originated from the northeast, while in the spring and summer, they blew from the southwest. Thus, merchants had to time their voyages carefully, often remaining in port cities for months at a time, depending on when favorable winds would come their way.

Advances in Maritime Technology Travelers needed ships capable of navigating the Indian Ocean's winds. Arab sailors used sailing technology to aid their travel. It is debatable whether Arab sailors invented the triangular **lateen sails** that they used, but the sails were popular because sailors found that the triangular shape could easily catch winds coming from many different directions. Chinese sailors during the classical period had invented the **stern rudder**, which gave their ships more stability and made them easier to maneuver. The small wooden dhows used by Arab and Indian sailors dominated the seas during the Postclassical Era. Trade facilitated the rapid spread of sailing technology across the many lands bordering the Indian Ocean in this period. (See Topic 4.1 for later Chinese maritime technology, such as the magnetic compass and improved rudder.) The **astrolabe**, improved by Muslim navigators in the 12th century, allowed sailors to determine how far north or south they were from the equator.

Growth of States The trading networks in the Indian Ocean fostered the growth of states to help institutionalize the revenue from trade. One Muslim city-state, **Malacca**, also spelled **Melaka**, became wealthy by building a navy and by imposing fees on ships that passed through the Strait of Malacca, a narrow inlet that many ship captains used to travel between ports in India and ports in China. The Sultan of Malacca became so powerful in the 1400s that he expanded the state into Sumatra and the southern Malay Peninsula. As in city-states in East Africa, Italy, and the Americas, Malacca's prosperity was based on trade rather than agriculture or mining or manufacturing.

The sultanate ended when the Portuguese invaded the city in 1511. The Portuguese hoped that by conquering the key city on the Strait of Malacca, they could control the trade that flowed through it between Europe, India, and China. They were successful enough to generate great wealth for their empire. However, they were less successful than they had hoped. Their conquest touched off conflicts among the other states in the region and caused traders to diversify their routes and the ports they used.

Effects of Expanded Exchange in the Indian Ocean

Some of the very factors that caused expansion of exchange networks in the Indian Ocean also, in time, became effects.

Diasporic Communities Without the arrival of merchants in distant lands, trade could not have expanded. As a natural result of waiting for favorable winds for travel, these merchants interacted with the surrounding cultures and peoples of the region. In fact, many Arab and East African merchants stayed in western Indian port cities permanently because they married women they met there. Arab and Persian merchants settled in East Africa. Thus, these merchants from Dar al-Islam were the first to bring Islam to southern Asia, not through missionary work or conquest, but through intermarriage. Their children would generally be raised within Muslim traditions.

Settlements of people away from their homeland are known as a **diaspora**. In these communities, settlers introduced their own cultural traditions into the indigenous cultures. Those cultures, in turn, influenced the culture of the merchants. Diasporas arose through trade in many parts of the world.

Merchants in Diasporic Communities		
Merchant Community	Region(s)	Products
Muslim	China, Indian Ocean Basin, Europe	Silk, paper, porcelain, spices, gems, woods, gold, salt, amber, furs
Chinese	Southeast Asia, Africa	Cotton, tea, silk, metals, opium, salt
Sogdian (in Samarkand)	Main caravan merchants along Silk Roads, China	Silk, gold, wine, linens
Jewish	China, India, Europe	Glass beads, linens, dyes, spices
Malay	Sri Lanka	Nutmeg, pepper, cloves

Source: Iranica Online. "Sogdian Trade," http://www.iranicaonline.org/articles/sogdian-trade

Response to Increased Demand In a similar way, increased demand for products caused trade to expand. At the same time, however, it resulted in several effects with long-lasting impact. For example, to meet rising demand, producers needed to find ways to become more efficient—to grow more crops, to make more textiles, to manufacture more iron. In some places, the role of the state increased even more to oversee these efforts at efficiency and to raise money through customs—taxes on imported goods—and fees for the use of seaports. The western Indian Rajput kingdom of **Gujarat,** for example, became the go-between for trade between the East and West. The revenue from customs in Gujarat was many times more than the entire worth of some European states.

Swahili City-States The Indian Ocean trade also created thriving city-states along the east coast of Africa, sometimes known as the Swahili city-states. "Swahili," which literally means "coasters," referred to the inhabitants of bustling commercial centers, such as Kilwa, Mombasa (in modern Kenya), and Zanzibar (in modern Tanzania). The traders of the Zanj Coast, as it was known in Arabic, sold ivory, gold, and enslaved people to their Arab trading partners, as well as more exotic goods such as tortoise shells, peacock feathers, and rhinoceros horns. In exchange, the "Zanj" cities acquired Chinese porcelain, Indian cotton, and manufactured ironwork. Trade was so vigorous with East Asia that Chinese porcelain remains a common find among the ruins of Swahili cities.

Trade brought considerable wealth to the cities on the East African coast. Architectural ruins in Kilwa suggest the wealth and grandeur that once existed there. For example, most buildings had traditionally been constructed of mud and clay. However, at the Indian Ocean trade's height, many mosques and wealthy merchants' homes were made of stone or coral.

Significant Cultural Transfers The transfer of knowledge, culture, technology, commerce, and religion intensified as a result of thriving trade in the Indian Ocean Basin. The voyages of the Muslim admiral **Zheng He** (1371–1433) reflect this transfer, as well as the conflicts it sometimes generated. In 1405, the Ming emperor Yongle sent Zheng He on the first of seven great voyages. Zheng traveled to Indonesia, Ceylon, and other coastal areas on the Indian Ocean, to Arabia, and to the east coast of Africa as well as to the Cape of Good Hope. The main purposes of the voyages were to display the might of the Ming Dynasty to the rest of the world and to receive tribute from the people he encountered. Zheng's fleet was impressive: At its height, his fleet included more than 300 ships that carried 28,000 people.

THE VOYAGES OF ZHENG HE, 1405–1433

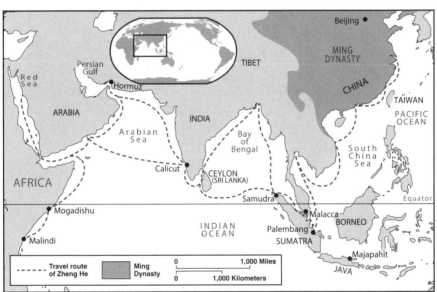

The expeditions won prestige for the Chinese government and opened up new markets for Chinese goods. Zheng He and his crew returned to China with exotic treasures, such as the first giraffe the Chinese had ever seen. They also brought back a new understanding of the world beyond China's borders. The voyages inspired some to immigrate to ports in Southeast Asia and elsewhere.

Zheng He's voyages stirred controversy, though. Confucianism promoted a stable, agrarian lifestyle, and scholars worried that greater interaction and trade with foreign cultures threatened China's social order. Some critics simply looked down upon other cultures, deeming them barbaric and vastly inferior to Chinese culture. Some thought the voyages were too expensive.

Emperor Yongle's successor, his son Zhu Gaozhi, ended Zheng He's travels, and he also discouraged all Chinese from sailing away from China. To emphasize his point, he made building a ship with more than two masts a punishable offense. Zheng's voyages did have one positive short-term result:

They put a stop to pirate activities off the coast of China and in Southeast Asia. However, after China stopped sending armed merchant ships into the ocean, the pirate activities resumed, especially on the China Sea.

KEY TERMS BY THEME

GOVERNMENT: States
Malacca (Melaka)
Gujarat
Swahili city-states

ECONOMY: Trade
Calicut
Spice Islands

ENVIRONMENT: Ocean
Indian Ocean Basin
monsoon winds

TECHNOLOGY: Sailing
lateen sails
stern rudder
astrolabe

CULTURE: Disruptions and Transfers
Indian Ocean slave trade
diaspora
Zheng He

MULTIPLE-CHOICE QUESTIONS

Questions 1 to 3 refer to the map below.

WINTER WIND PATTERNS

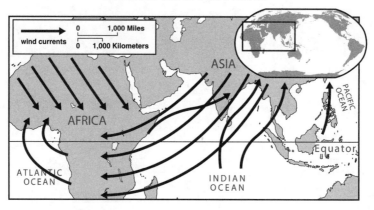

1. The map helps explain why South Asian merchants preferred to travel
   (A) to Africa in the winter months
   (B) to Southeast Asia in the winter months
   (C) to China in the summer months
   (D) to the Middle East in the summer months

2. Since merchants were often delayed in foreign ports for lengthy periods of time, they frequently
   (A) became involved in local political affairs
   (B) married wives who often converted to their religion
   (C) lost their connection to the culture of their homeland
   (D) settled in the foreign port and converted to the local faith

3. The coastal cities of Mombasa, Sofala, and Mogadishu often exported

(A) silks and porcelain.

(B) cotton and steel.

(C) horses, figs, and dates.

(D) enslaved people, ivory, and gold.

SHORT-ANSWER QUESTIONS

1. Use the passage below to answer all parts of the question that follows.

"Merchants boast that their wisdom and ability are such as to give them a free hand in affairs. They believe that they know all the possible transformations in the universe and therefore can calculate all the changes in the human world, and that the rise and fall of prices are under their command. These merchants do not know how insignificant their wisdom and ability really are . . . . If farmers do not work, there will be an insufficiency of food; if craftsmen do not work, there will be an insufficiency of tools; if merchants do not work, circulation of the three necessities will be cut off, which will cause food and materials to be insufficient . . . . As to the foreigners in the Southeast, their goods are useful to us just as ours are to them. To use what one has to exchange for what one does not have is what trade is all about . . . . Foreigners are recalcitrant [uncooperative] and their greed knows no bounds."

Chang Han, Ming official, the 15th century

(A) Identify ONE way the ideas of Chang Han provided the political context for Zhu Gaozhi's decision on Zheng He's voyages.

(B) Explain ONE way the ideas of Chang Han provided the economic context for Zhu Gaozhi's decision on Zheng He's voyages.

(C) Explain ONE way the ideas of Chang Han reflect a traditional Chinese view of China's relationship with other cultures.

2. Answer all parts of the question that follows.

(A) Identify ONE cause of expanded trade in the Indian Ocean Basin in the period 1200–1450.

(B) Explain ONE effect of expanded trade in the Indian Ocean Basin in the period 1200–1450.

(C) Explain the relationship between the expansion of maritime trade in the Indian Ocean Basin 1200–1450 and the expansion of trade over the land routes of the Silk Roads.

THINK AS A HISTORIAN: APPROACHES TO MAKING HISTORICAL CONNECTIONS

Making historical connections requires the use of three reasoning processes: comparison, causation, and/or continuity and change. Following are questions you can ask yourself to make historical connections using these processes. The answers to these questions will reveal connections.

- Comparison: What topic, idea, or event in history is like another topic, idea, or event? How is one topic, idea, or event like and/or unlike another? *Possible answer and connection:* The expansion of sea routes for trade is like the expansion of the land-based Silk Roads for trade. They are alike in that they both extended global interconnections and depended on new technologies.

- Causation: What caused something to happen? *Possible answer and connection:* China's withdrawal from sailing to distant lands caused a return of piracy in the China Sea.

- Continuity and change: In what ways is something a continuation of what came before it? In what ways did something differ from what preceded it? *Possible answer and connection:* Trade in the Indian Ocean had periods in which it flourished before the spread of Islam, and flourishing trade continued after the spread of Islam. Some changes after the spread of Islam were the high regard afforded Muslim merchants and the expansion of trade routes.

Make three historical connections between what you read about in this topic and what you learned in previous topics, or even what you know about other times in history, including the present. Ask yourself the above questions to discover the connections. Write them down and share them with your classmates.

REFLECT ON THE TOPIC ESSENTIAL QUESTION

1. In one to three paragraphs, explain the causes and effects of the growth of networks of exchange after 1200 and the way environmental knowledge supported that expansion.

Trans-Saharan Trade Routes

From Timbuktu I sailed down the Nile [Niger] on a small boat, hollowed out of a single piece of wood...I went on . . . to Gawgaw [Gaogao], which is a large city on the Nile [Niger]... The buying and selling of its inhabitants is done with cowry-shells, and the same is the case at Malli [the city of Mali]. I stayed there about a month, and then set out in the direction of Tagadda by land with a large caravan of merchants from Ghadamas.

—Ibn Battuta (1304–1353)

Essential Question: What were the causes and effects of trans-Saharan trade, and how did the growth of empires influence trade and communication?

While the East African Coast had been fairly well populated for many centuries before the arrival of Islam, few societies had inhabited the **Sahara Desert** because its arid climate made it nearly impossible to farm. Though nomadic communities did conduct some trade across the Sahara, the volume of trade increased with the arrival of Muslim merchants in the 7th and 8th centuries. When empires such as Mali took over the area in the early 1200s, commerce expanded dramatically. As illustrated in the commentaries of Ibn Battuta, a Muslim scholar and explorer of the 14th century, merchants and traders used caravans to facilitate commerce. Africans traded gold, ivory, hides, and enslaved people for Arab and Berber salt, cloth, paper, and horses.

Trans-Saharan Trade

The Sahara Desert is immense, occupying 3.6 million square miles—about the same size as China. Of that vast expanse of sand and rock, only about 800 square miles are **oases**—places where human settlement is possible because water from deep underground is brought to the surface, making land fertile. In some oases, the water comes from underground naturally. In others, humans have dug wells to access the water.

Camels, Saddles, and Trade Muslim merchants from Southwest Asia traveled across the Sahara on camels. Native to the Islamic heartland (Arabia), camels began to appear in North Africa in the 3rd century B.C.E. Accustomed to the harsh, dry climate of the **Arabian Desert**, camels adapted well to living in the Sahara. Compared to horses, camels can consume a large quantity of water at one time (over 50 gallons in three minutes) and not need more water for a long time. They began to replace horses and donkeys after 300 C.E.

As use of the camel spread, people developed as many as 15 types of **camel saddles** for different purposes. South Arabians developed a saddle in which the rider sits in back of the hump, which makes riding easier because the rider can hold onto the hair of the hump. Northern Arabians developed a saddle for sitting on top of the hump, putting them high in the air, which gave them greater visibility in battles. Being near the animal's head gave the rider the best possible control over the camel.

However, the saddle that had the greatest impact on trade was one the Somalis in Eastern Africa developed. They were semi-nomadic and needed to carry their possessions with them, so they designed a saddle for carrying loads up to 600 pounds. Without the development of this type of saddle, camels could not have been used to carry heavy loads of goods in trade.

Comparing Pack Animals			
Animal	**Location**	**Benefits**	**Drawbacks**
Camel	Northern Africa and Sub-Saharan West Africa	• Able to travel long distances • Can eat thorny plants and drink salty water found in deserts • Has long eyelashes that protect against desert winds • Only animal that can cross deserts • Does not spook easily • Can carry up to 600 pounds	• Requires high level of salt to stay healthy • Can be very aggressive and even vengeful • Cannot be controlled with a bit • Cannot be boarded in a stall
Ox	Eurasia and the Americas	• Has high level of stamina • Can pull heaviest loads • Unlikely to stray or be stolen • Can survive on local grazing • Tolerates various climates and diets	• Moves slowly compared to other pack animals • Requires more water and food than other pack animals
Horse	Worldwide	• Can run at high speeds • Can be controlled with a bit • Can be used in battle • Can adapt to most climates and terrains	• Requires grain to keep fit • Spooks easily • Can be stolen easily • Strays easily • Less sure-footed than other pack animals • Cannot tolerate high heat
Llama	Americas	• Maintains traction in mountains • Has calm disposition • Requires little water • Adapts well to cold and mountainous climates	• Cannot pull heavy loads • Can carry less than other pack animals • Cannot tolerate high heat

The caravans that crossed the Sahara often had thousands of camels laden not only with goods to trade but also with enough provisions, including fresh water, to last until the travelers could reach the next oasis. The people leading the caravans generally walked the entire way. The map on page 44 shows some of the main trade routes across the Sahara. There were seven north-south trade routes and two east-west routes. These put the people in Sub-Saharan Africa in touch with an expanding number of cultures and trading partners.

By the end of the 8th century C.E., the **trans-Saharan trade** had become famous throughout Europe and Asia. Gold was the most precious commodity traded. West African merchants acquired the metal from the waters of the Senegal River, near modern-day Senegal and Mauritania. Foreign traders came to West Africa seeking not only gold but also ivory and enslaved people. In exchange, they brought salt, textiles, and horses. For more than 700 years, trans-Saharan trade brought considerable wealth to the societies of West Africa, particularly the kingdoms of Ghana and Mali. They also brought Islam, which spread into Sub-Saharan Africa as a result. (Connect: Compare the impact of trade across the Sahara and throughout the Andes. See Topic 1.4.)

Source: Wikimedia Commons (NASA)
Satellite image of the expansive Sahara

West African Empire Expansion

By the 12th century, wars with neighboring societies had permanently weakened the Ghanaian state. (See Topic 1.5.) In its place arose several new trading societies, the most powerful of which was **Mali**. North African traders had introduced Islam to Mali in the 9th century.

Mali's Riches The government of Mali profited from the gold trade, but it also taxed nearly all other trade entering West Africa. In that way, it became even more prosperous than Ghana had been. Most of Mali's residents were farmers who cultivated sorghum and rice. However, the great cities of **Timbuktu** and Gao accumulated the most wealth and developed into centers of Muslim life in the region. Timbuktu in particular became a world-renowned center of Islamic learning. By the 1500s, books created and sold in Timbuktu brought prices higher than most other goods.

Expanding Role of States The growth in trade and wealth gave rise to the need to administer and maintain it. For example, rulers needed to establish a currency whose value was widely understood. In Mali, the currency was cowrie shells, cotton cloth, gold, glass beads, and salt. Rulers also needed to protect both the trade routes and the areas where their currencies were made or harvested or their other trade resources were produced. Sometimes empires expanded their reach to take over resource-rich areas. They did so with military forces well provisioned with horses and iron weapons bought with the tax revenue. With each expansion, more people were drawn into the empire's economy and trade networks, bringing more people in touch with distant cultures.

Mali's founding ruler, **Sundiata**, became the subject of legend. His father had ruled over a small society in West Africa in what today is Guinea. When his father died, rival groups invaded, killing most of the royal family and capturing the throne. They did not bother to kill Sundiata because the young prince was crippled and was not considered a threat. In spite of his injury, he learned to fight and became so feared as a warrior that his enemies forced him into exile. His time in exile only strengthened him and his allies. In 1235, Sundiata, "the Lion Prince," returned to the kingdom of his birth, defeated his enemies, and reclaimed the throne for himself.

Sundiata's story made him beloved within his kingdom, but he was also an astute and capable ruler. Most scholars believe he was a Muslim and used his connections with others of his faith to establish trade relationships with North African and Arab merchants. Sundiata cultivated a thriving gold trade in Mali. Under his steady leadership, Mali's wealth grew tremendously.

Mansa Musa In the 14th century, Sundiata's grand-nephew, **Mansa Musa**, brought more fame to the region. However, Mansa Musa was better known for his religious leadership than for his political or economic acumen. A devout Muslim, Mansa Musa began a pilgrimage in 1324 to **Mecca**, Islam's holiest city. His journey, however, was unlike that of any ordinary pilgrim. Mali's prosperity allowed him to take an extraordinarily extravagant caravan to Arabia, consisting of 100 camels, thousands of enslaved people and soldiers, and gold to distribute to all of the people who hosted him along his journey. His pilgrimage displayed Mali's wealth to the outside world.

Mansa Musa's visit to Mecca deepened his devotion to Islam. Upon his return, he established religious schools in Timbuktu, built mosques in Muslim trading cities, and sponsored those who wanted to continue their religious studies elsewhere. Though most West Africans continued to hold onto their traditional beliefs, Mansa Musa's reign deepened the support for Islam in Mali.

However, in fewer than 100 years after Mansa Musa's death, the Mali kingdom was declining. By the late 1400s, the **Songhai Kingdom** had taken its place as the powerhouse in West Africa. Following processes like those Mali had gone through, Songhai became larger and richer than Mali. In spite of Mali's fall, Mansa Musa's efforts to strengthen Islam in West Africa succeeded: The religion has a prominent place in the region today.

Empires in Western Eurasia and Africa in the 13th Century				
	Mali	**Al-Andalus**	**Byzantine Empire**	**Kievan Rus**
Location	West Africa	Spain	Middle East	Russia
Peak Years	1200s to 1400s	711 to 1492	330 to 1453	900s to 1200s
Major City	Timbuktu	Cordoba	Constantinople	Kiev
Key Figures	• Sundiata: founder who built a strong trade network • Mansa Musa: political and religious leader	• Ibn Rushd: Islamic legal scholar and philosopher • Maimonides: Jewish scholar of ethics	• Justinian: ruler responsible for the *Body of Civil Law* • Heraclius: shifted focus to the East	• Vladimir I: converted to Christianity in 989 • Yaroslav I: codified the legal system
Legacy	• Connected West and North Africa through trade • Spread Islam in West Africa	• Created vibrant, tolerant society • Preserved classical Greek learning	• Fostered trade between Asia, Europe, and Africa • Carried on Roman legacy	• Developed first large civilization in Russia • Spread Christianity eastward

KEY TERMS BY THEME

GOVERNMENT: Sub-Saharan
Mali
Sundiata
Mansa Musa
Songhai Kingdom

CULTURE: Islam
Timbuktu
Mecca

ECONOMICS: Trade
trans-Saharan trade

ENVIRONMENT: Africa
Sahara Desert
oases

ENVIRONMENT: Southwest Asia
Arabian Desert

TECHNOLOGY: Pack animals
camel saddles

Questions 1 to 3 refer to the chart below.

Camel Saddles		
Region	**Location of Rider**	**Advantage**
South Arabia	Behind the hump	Makes riding easiest
North Arabia	On top of the hump	Gives the rider the best visibility
North Africa	In front of the hump	Provides the rider the best control
East Africa	Not designed for a rider	Carries the largest load

1. Which was the most important impact of the improvements in saddles in assisting the spread of Islam in Africa?

   (A) They allowed younger people to ride camels.

   (B) They increased the demand for camels.

   (C) They contributed to increased trans-Saharan trade.

   (D) They strengthened Islamic armies.

2. The information on camel saddles is an example of how

   (A) people adapted technology based on their needs

   (B) differences in camels suited them for different tasks

   (C) innovation results from outside influences

   (D) climate variations influenced the relationship between people and animals

3. Where was the saddle developed that had the greatest impact on trade throughout the Middle East and Africa?

   (A) Along the Mediterranean coast

   (B) Near the Islamic centers of Timbuktu and Gao

   (C) In countries of the Sahara

   (D) On East African trade routes

1. **Use the passages below to answer all parts of the question that follows.**

"Between the 11th and the 17th centuries West Africa was the leading supplier of gold to the international economy. African gold contributed to the functioning of the domestic economy in Europe . . . . And it contributed to the wealth of the great states of the Western Sudan."

Anthony G. Hopkins, *An Economic History of West Africa*,
1973

"Copper mined in Mali came to be a crucial element in trade patterns. It could be exchanged with the peoples to the south who controlled the sources of gold. Kola nuts, animal skins, slaves, grain, meat, and even dairy products were also transported by trading networks."

J. Rotondo-McCord, 1998

(A) Identify ONE example of transportation technology that led to growth in interregional trade during the period 1200–1450.

(B) Explain ONE way in which Mali's wealth contributed to the expansion of its government during the period 1200–1450.

(C) Explain ONE way in which a resource from Mali was used in Sub-Saharan trade during the period 1200–1450.

2. **Answer all parts of the question that follows.**

(A) Identify ONE economic impact Muslim traders had on Sub-Saharan Africa.

(B) Identify ONE cultural influence Muslim traders had on Sub-Saharan Africa.

(C) Explain ONE similarity between trans-Saharan trade and trade on the Silk Roads in Asia.

THINK AS A HISTORIAN: IDENTIFY HISTORICAL PROCESSES BY
ASKING "HOW"

One way to identify historical processes is to ask the question, "How?"
How did Islam spread? How did trade grow between Southwest Asia
and Sub-Saharan Africa? How did small clan-based kingdoms become
empires? In each of these questions, you can substitute the words "By
what process" in the place of "How." Identifying processes—how
things came to be what they are—can give you a basis for understanding
different times and different places in history. For example, if you
know the process China followed in its proto-industrialization, you can
determine what stages of the process in other industrializing regions
may be the same or different.

*Which of the following identifies a historical process? Explain your
answers. Your explanation is as important as your answer.*

1. The government of Mali's power grew as it taxed nearly all trade
   entering West Africa.

2. Trans-Saharan trade followed seven north-south and two east-
   west routes.

3. In East Africa, a large variety of imports and exports overlapped.

4. Mansa Musa's reign deepened the support for Islam in Mali.

REFLECT ON THE TOPIC ESSENTIAL QUESTION

1. In one to three paragraphs, explain the causes and effects of trans-
   Saharan trade and how the growth of empires influenced trade and
   communication.

2.5

Cultural Consequences of Connectivity

I have not told half of what I saw, for I knew I would not be believed.

—Marco Polo (1245–1324)

Essential Question: What were the intellectual and cultural effects of the trade networks from c. 1200 to c. 1450?

Whether by caravan through the Sahara or Gobi deserts or by junk or dhow on the China Sea or Indian Ocean, goods, people, and ideas traveled with relative freedom through the networks of exchange in Afro-Eurasia in the years between c. 1200 and c. 1450. One reason for this free exchange was the stability of the Mongol Empire and the protection it offered merchants and travelers. The empire reached well past former boundaries, incorporating new people, goods, and ideas within its authority. Technological developments, such as gunpowder and paper from China, were diffused by trade. Literary and artistic interactions and cultural exchanges were documented by travelers such as Marco Polo and Ibn Battuta, who told of the wonders they saw and the extraordinary people they met. The known world became a larger place.

Religious, Cultural, and Technological Effects of Interaction

The diffusion of different religions between c. 1200 and c. 1450 had varying effects. In some cases, the arrival of a new religion served to unify people and provide justification for a kingdom's leadership. It often also influenced the literary and artistic culture of areas to which it spread, where themes, subjects, and styles were inspired by the spreading religion. In other places, it either fused or coexisted with the native religions. The interactions resulting from increased trade also led to technological innovations that helped shape the era.

Influence of Buddhism on East Asian Culture Buddhism came to China from its birthplace in India via the Silk Roads, and the 7th-century Buddhist monk Xuanzang helped make it popular. Monks related Buddhism to familiar Daoist principles, and in time Buddhist doctrines fused with elements of Daoist traditions to create the syncretic faith Chan Buddhism, also known as Zen Buddhism. Although some leaders in China did not want China's native religions diminished as a result of the spread of Buddhism, Chan Buddhism remained popular among ordinary Chinese citizens. Under the Song Dynasty (960–1279), many Confucians among the scholar gentry began to adopt its ideals into their daily lives. The development of printing had made Buddhist scriptures widely available to the Confucian scholar gentry. Buddhist writers also influenced Chinese literature by writing in the vernacular rather than the formal language of Confucian scholars, a practice that became widespread.

Source: Nezu Art Museum, Tokyo

Detail of dusk over fisher's village, from the handscroll "Eight Views of Xiaoxiang" by Chan Buddhist painter Mu-ch'i, c. 1250, Nezu Art Museum. Mu-ch'i is credited with starting the "sketch style" of painting that uses the fewest lines possible to suggest a subject. His work was very influential in East Asian art.

Japan and Korea, countries in China's orbit, also adopted Buddhism, along with Confucianism. In Korea, the educated elite studied Confucian classics, while Buddhist doctrine attracted the peasants. Neo-Confucianism was another syncretic faith that originated in China, first appearing in the Tang Dynasty but developing further in the Song Dynasty. Neo-Confucianism fused rational thought with the abstract ideas of Daoism and Buddhism and became widespread in Japan and Vietnam. It also became Korea's official state ideology.

Spread of Hinduism and Buddhism   Through trade, the Indian religions of Hinduism and Buddhism made their way to Southeast Asia as well. The sea-based Srivijaya Empire on Sumatra was a Hindu kingdom, while the later Majapahit Kingdom on Java was Buddhist. The South Asian land-based Sinhala dynasties in Sri Lanka became centers of Buddhist study with many monasteries. Buddhism's influence was so strong under the Sinhala dynasties that Buddhist priests often advised monarchs on matters of government. (See Topic 1.3.)

The Khmer Empire in present-day Cambodia, also known as the Angkor Kingdom, was the most successful kingdom in Southeast Asia. The royal monuments at Angkor Thom are evidence of both Hindu and Buddhist cultural influences on Southeast Asia. Hindu artwork and sculptures of Hindu gods adorned the city. Later, when Khmer rulers had become Buddhist, they added Buddhist sculptures and artwork onto buildings while keeping the Hindu artwork.

Spread of Islam   Through merchants, missionaries, and conquests, Islam spread over a wide swath of Africa, South Asia, and Southeast Asia. The chart below summarizes some of the cultural influences of that expansion.

Cultural Influences of Islam in Afro-Eurasia	
Region	**Influences**
Africa	• **Swahili** language is a blend of Bantu and Arabic and is still widely spoken today.
	• Timbuktu became a center of Islamic learning.
	• Leaders of African states deepened Islamic ties through pilgrimages to Mecca.
South Asia	• Before Islam, Hinduism and Buddhism were popular.
	• After Islam arrived, Buddhists converted more readily than Hindus because they were disillusioned by the corruption among Buddhist priests.
	• With its emphasis on equality, Islam also attracted lower-caste Hindus.
	• Architecture blended Hindu designs with Islamic patterns.
	• **Urdu** language had influences from Sanskrit-based Hindi, as well as from Arabic and Farsi, a Persian language.
	• Bhakti poets and missionaries sought links between Hinduism and Islam.
Southeast Asia	• Muslim rulers on Java combined Mughal Indian features, local traditions, and Chinese-Buddhist and Confucian traits.
	• Traditional Javanese stories, puppetry, and poetry absorbed Muslim characters and techniques.

Scientific and Technological Innovations   Along with religion, science and technology traveled the trade routes. Islamic scholars translated Greek literary classics into Arabic, saving the works of Aristotle and other Greek thinkers from oblivion. Scholars also brought back mathematics texts from

India and techniques for papermaking from China. They studied medicine from ancient Greeks, Mesopotamians, and Egyptians, making advances in hospital care, including surgery. (See Topic 1.2.)

Improvements in agricultural efficiency, such as the use of Champa rice, spread from India to Vietnam and China. With a reliable food supply, the population grew, as did cities and industries, such as the production of porcelain, silk, steel, and iron. Papermaking reached Europe from China in the 13th century and along with printing technology helped lead to a rise in literacy.

Seafaring technology improved with **lateen sails**, the **stern rudder**, the **astrolabe**, and the **magnetic compass** as Chinese, Indian, and Southwest Asians expanded their knowledge of astronomy and other aspects of the natural world. Production of gunpowder and guns spread from China and influenced warfare as well.

Thanks, in part, to the writing of Marco Polo, historians have a good picture of the city of **Hangzhou** in China. It shows how trade supported urbanization. Hangzhou was large—it was home to about one million people—but other Chinese cities were larger. Chang'an had about two million people. However, Hangzhou was the center of culture in southern China, the home of poets such as Lu Yu and Xin Qiji, and other writers and artists. Located at the southern end of the Grand Canal, it was also a center of trade. Like other important cities of the era, such as Novgorod in Russia, Timbuktu in Africa, and Calicut in India, the city grew and prospered as its merchants exchanged goods. This trade brought diversity to Hangzhou, including a thriving community of Arabs.

Other cities on the trade routes that grew and thrived included **Samarkand** and **Kashgar.** (See Topic 2.1.) They were both known as centers of Islamic scholarship, bustling markets, and sources for fresh water and plentiful food for merchants traveling the Silk Roads.

Factors Contributing to Growth of Cities
• Political stability and decline of invasions
• Safe and reliable transportation
• Rise of commerce
• Plentiful labor supply
• Increased agricultural output

Declining Cities Kashgar, however, declined after a series of conquests by nomadic invaders and in 1389–90 was ravaged by Tamerlane. (See Topic 2.2.) Another once-thriving city, the heavily walled **Constantinople** in present-day Turkey, also suffered a series of traumatic setbacks. Mutinous Crusader armies weakened Constantinople after an attack in the Fourth Crusade in 1204 (see Topic 1.6), and in 1346 and 1349, the bubonic plague killed about half of the people in Constantinople. After a 53-day seige, the city finally fell to the Ottomans in 1453, an event some historians believe marks the end of the High Middle Ages. (Connect: Describe the relationship between urban growth in Europe and later urban decline. See Topic 1.6.)

Factors Contributing to Decline of Cities
• Political instability and invasions • Disease • Decline of agricultural productivity

Effects of the Crusades Knowledge of the world beyond Western Europe increased as Crusaders encountered both the Byzantine and Islamic cultures. The encounters also increased demand in Europe for newfound wares from the East. In opening up to global trade, however, Western Europeans also opened themselves to disease. The plague, referred to as the **Black Death**, was introduced to Europe by way of trading routes. A major epidemic broke out between 1347 and 1351. Additional outbreaks occurred over the succeeding decades. As many as 25 million people in Europe may have died from the plague. With drastically reduced populations, economic activity declined in Europe. In particular, a shortage of people to work on the land had lasting effects on the feudal system. Also, exposure to new ideas from Byzantium and the Muslim world would contribute to the Renaissance and the subsequent rise of secularism.

Travelers' Tales

As exchange networks intensified and literacy spread as a result of paper and printing technology, an increasing number of travelers within Afro-Eurasia wrote about their journeys for eager readers.

Source: Hangzhou City Gate, China (1906), Public Domain

The pagoda behind the gate is a common Buddhist building design in China.

Marco Polo In the late 13th century, **Marco Polo**, an Italian native from Venice, visited the court of Kublai Khan. (See Topic 2.2.) Chinese cities impressed Polo. After Polo returned to Italy in 1295, he wrote a book about his travels. However, many Europeans refused to believe his descriptions of China's size, wealth, and wonders. Only when other Europeans followed Polo's route to China did people widely accept that China was prosperous and innovative. Polo's captivating descriptions of the customs of the people he met intrigued Europeans. Polo wrote extensively about the high levels of urbanization he saw in the 13th century. Polo's point of view as a merchant kept him focused on trade-related matters.

> They use paper money as currency. The men as well as the women are fair-skinned and handsome. Most of them always dress themselves in silk, as a result of the vast quantities of that material produced in Hangzhou, exclusive of what the merchants import from other provinces.

Ibn Battuta He was just 21 years old, **Ibn Battuta** (1304–1353), a Muslim scholar from Morocco, set out to see the world he read about.

> I set out alone, having neither fellow-traveller in whose companionship I might find cheer, nor caravan whose part I might join, but swayed by an overmastering impulse within me and a desire long-cherished in my bosom to visit these illustrious sanctuaries.

Over 30 years, Ibn Battuta traveled through Central Asia, Southeast Asia, South Asia, China, Spain, North Africa, and Mali, mainly to Muslim lands. After telling his tales to the Sultan of Morocco, Battuta was told to "dictate an account of the cities which he had seen in his travel, and of the interesting events which had clung to his memory, and that he should speak of those whom he had met of the rulers of countries, of their distinguished men of learning, and of their pious saints." His book *A Gift to Those Who Contemplate the Wonders of Cities and the Marvels of Traveling* provides a wealth of detail about the places he visited and their cultures. Unlike Polo, Battuta had the point of view of a Muslim devoted to his faith. His journey was in large part to learn as much as he could about Islam and its people and accomplishments.

Margery Kempe English mystic **Margery Kempe** (c. 1373–c. 1440), whose *The Book of Margery Kempe* was one of the earliest autobiographies in English, if not the first, could neither read nor write. She dictated her book to scribes who wrote down her descriptions of her pilgrimages to Jerusalem, Rome, Germany, and Spain. She does relate details of her travel experiences, such as being so overcome by the sight of Jerusalem as she approached it that she nearly fell off her donkey. However, her book is also significant because it is a firsthand account of a middle-class medieval woman's life. Kempe conveys both the intense spiritual visions and feelings of her mystical experiences and the trials of everyday life for a woman with 14 children.

KEY TERMS BY THEME

ENVIRONMENT: Disease
Black Death

CULTURE: Travel Writers
Marco Polo
Ibn Battuta
Margery Kempe

CULTURE: Language
Swahili
Urdu

TECHNOLOGY: Nautical
    Improvements
lateen sails
stern rudder
astrolabe
magnetic compass

SOCIETY: Cities
Hangzhou
Samarkand
Kashgar
Constantinople

MULTIPLE-CHOICE QUESTIONS

Questions 1 to 3 refer to the passage below.

"Ibn Battuta traveled primarily in Muslim-ruled lands, the Dar al-Islam [House or Abode of Islam], while the Christian Polo, son of a European merchant, lived and worked in countries whose cultures and religions were foreign to him. This difference makes a comparison of their works most interesting. Marco Polo's knowledge of four Asian languages as well as Italian allowed him to communicate with foreigners and even work as an administrator for the Chinese emperor. Yet, in all his travels, he remained culturally an 'outsider' to the peoples he met, and this fact enhanced his power of observation and stimulated his natural curiosity. By contrast, Ibn Battuta usually traveled as an 'insider' and his hosts accepted him as a respected Muslim jurist [qadi] and student of Islamic mysticism [Sufism]. Traveling to more than sixty Muslim courts, where he met rulers and their officials, Ibn Battuta was able to judge the behavior of his hosts in light of the Muslim scripture, the Koran, and the precepts of Islamic law. For him, the difference between their native cultures and his own North Arabic culture was a secondary importance."

Marco Polo and Ibn Battuta: The Merchant and the Pilgrim, 1994

1. Which of the following would have been most likely to "set the stage" for Marco Polo to have been able to travel to the lands that he did?

   (A) The Pax Mongolica

   (B) The voyages of Vasco da Gama

   (C) The conquests of the Umayyad Dynasty

   (D) The development of the printing press

2. Which of the following were most responsible for influencing the point of view of the travelers mentioned in the passage?

(A) Religion and economics

(B) Military and technology

(C) Social hierarchy and governance

(D) Religion and philosophy

3. Which of the following statements most accurately describes the difference in the worlds in which Polo and Ibn Battuta traveled?

(A) Polo traveled to areas that shared his language and religion while Ibn Battuta traveled to areas that did not.

(B) Polo traveled primarily to areas that were less prosperous than where he grew up while Ibn Battuta traveled primarily to areas that were more prosperous than where he grew up.

(C) Polo traveled to regions very different from Europe while Ibn Battuta traveled mostly within the Islamic world.

(D) Polo traveled to regions that Europe was closely connected to while Ibn Battuta traveled to regions that were not closely connected to his home region.

Source: Wikimedia Commons

Place where Battuta visited

1. Use the passage below to answer all parts of the question that follows.

"The borrowing and lending necessary for most of the crusaders stimulated credit formation and the development of credit institutions and instruments. Indeed, the money economy as a whole must have been stimulated by these great enterprises which took so much money. The transformation of gold and silver altar ornaments into coin for crusaders may have helped to heighten the inflation that occurred during the Crusades, especially in the later 12th century. The sale of land to finance most assuredly helped to make the market in real estate which was bringing about a new social order in the age of the Crusades. The principal beneficiaries of all these financial transactions were the bourgeoisie, who loaned the money, bought the land, sold the provisions, furnished the transportation, and generally benefited from the financial activity of the crusaders."

Fred Cazel, "Financing the Crusades," 1989 .

(A) Identify Cazel's point of view of the Crusades from the passage.

(B) Explain Cazel's argument about the economic situation that resulted from the Crusades.

(C) Explain ONE way in which the 12th-century economy affected the Crusades.

2. Answer all parts of the question that follows.

(A) Identify ONE way in which the diffusion of Buddhism to Southeast Asia was evident during the period 1200–1450.

(B) Explain ONE way in which the arrival of Islam influenced African culture during the period 1200–1450.

(C) Explain the perspective of ONE travel writer in the period 1200–1450.

THINK AS A HISTORIAN: SOURCING AND SITUATION IN PRIMARY SOURCES

Historical evidence comes from many sources, including such primary sources as ruins and eyewitness accounts in diaries and letters as well as secondary sources created later based on information from primary sources and other secondary sources. While they all might be "truthful," each has a perspective, or point of view, that might color the interpretation of events and experiences. To evaluate historical evidence, identify a source's point of view, purpose, historical situation, and/or audience. Ask the following questions:

- Who created this evidence?
- What might be unique about his or her point of view?
- For what purpose was the source created?
- For whom and in what situation was it created?
- How did people use it at the time?

The answers to these questions will help you determine what strengths and limitations a source may have in interpreting history.

Reread the excerpt from Marco Polo and Ibn Battuta: The Merchant and the Pilgrim *on page 117. Then answer each of the questions above for both Marco Polo's reports and those of Ibn Battuta as described by the writer. Identify a possible strength and possible limitation in each report for representing an accurate picture of historical conditions.*

REFLECT ON THE TOPIC ESSENTIAL QUESTION

1. In one to three paragraphs, explain the intellectual and cultural effects of the trade networks from c. 1200 to c. 1450.

2.6

Environmental Consequences of Connectivity

Dead bodies filled every corner.

—Giovanni Boccaccio (1313–1375)

Essential Question: What were some of the environmental effects of trade in Afro-Eurasia from c. 1200 to c. 1450?

Although trade networks enabled the spread of novel agricultural products, such as the introduction of certain citrus fruits to the Mediterranean basin, the most dramatic environmental consequence of increased commerce was not food, but rather disease. Bubonic plague, or "Black Death," swept from Central Asia; struck in China, India, Persia, and Egypt; and arrived in Europe in 1347. The epidemic is estimated to have killed from 75 to 200 million people in Eurasia and peaked in Europe from 1347 to 1351. Boccaccio, whose famous work *The Decameron* was inspired by living through the plague, described the horrors he saw.

Agricultural Effects of Exchange Networks

Along with luxury goods, spices, textiles, and religions, merchants in some places introduced crops where they had not grown before. The new crops often had an impact on land use and population growth and distribution. In some areas, people found ways to sustain abundant production; in others, overuse of the land led to environmental degradation.

Migration of Crops Few crops had as significant an impact as the quick-ripening **Champa rice**, which was introduced to the Champa states by Vietnam, a Hindu state, and then offered to the Chinese as tribute. Because of the Hindu influence on Champa in present-day central Vietnam, some scholars believe Champa rice may have originated in India. It was drought-resistant, flood-resistant, and capable of yielding two crops a year. It was widely distributed in China to meet the needs of the growing population and in turn contributed to the population growth.

It also had an impact on land use. Through terraced farming in the uplands and paddies in the lowlands, Champa rice was grown in many parts of China where once land was thought unusable for growing rice. Nonetheless, as the population of China grew, people tended to migrate southward to the original rice growing region, contributing to the growth of cities.

Indonesian seafarers traveling across the Indian Ocean had introduced **bananas** to Sub-Saharan Africa. The nutrition-rich food led to a spike in population. Many Indonesians settled on the island of Madagascar. Bananas allowed the Bantu-speaking peoples (see Prologue) with their metallurgy skills and farming techniques to migrate to places where yams—a traditional food source—did not easily grow. To grow bananas, farmers increased land for cultivation, which enriched diets and led to population growth.

As caliphs conquered lands beyond the Arabian Peninsula, they spread Islam, the Arabic language, and the cultivation of cotton, **sugar**, and **citrus crops**. New foods were also available at the markets along the trade routes. The markets of Samarkand, for example, introduced new fruits and vegetables, as well as rice and citrus products from Southwest Asia, to Europe. Europeans' demand for sugar would become so high that it became a key factor in the massive use of enslaved people in the Americas in the 1500s and after. (Connect: Compare the techniques used by Chinese farmers to raise food products with the techniques of Indonesian or Vietnamese farmers. See Topic 1.1.)

Source: Library of Congress, Prints and Photographs Division

This photo was taken in 1911 of a vendor in the central Asian city of Samarkand. In the valleys in this region, people have long grown melons, grapes, apples, citrus fruits, pomegranates, apricots, peaches, and other fruits. These products were then widely distributed by merchants who traveled on the Silk Roads.

Environmental Degradation Increases in population put pressure on resources. For example, **overgrazing** outside of Great Zimbabwe was so severe that people had to abandon the city in the late 1400s. (See Topic 1.5.) In feudal Europe, overuse of farm land and **deforestation** led to **soil erosion**, reducing agricultural production. The Little Ice Age (c. 1300–c. 1800) also contributed to a decrease in agricultural products. Environmental degradation was a factor in the decline of the Mayans in the Americas as well.

Spread of Epidemics through Exchange Networks

While scholars in Dar al-Islam and India were developing advances in medical understanding and treatment, no knowledge at the time could have prevented the spread of deadly infectious diseases that accompanied trade. The Mongol conquests helped to transmit the fleas that carried the **bubonic plague**, termed the Black Death, from southern China to Central Asia, and from there to Southeast Asia and Europe. Some historians believe the caravanserai that housed people and animals together may have contributed to the spread of the disease, since the animals likely carried infected fleas.

The Black Death had a tremendous impact on Europe, killing one-third of the population there in a few years. With fewer workers, agricultural production continued its decline. However, the reduced number of workers led to a new relationship between workers and those they worked for: each person's labor became more valuable, so workers could demand higher wages. This shift helped lay the groundwork for the economic changes that developed as feudalism declined.

The Black Death led to similar loss of life in other areas, including North Africa, China, and Central Asia. About 25 million Chinese and other Asians died between 1332 and 1347. South Asia and Sub-Saharan Africa were spared because there were few trading ports in those regions.

KEY TERMS BY THEME		
ENVIRONMENT: Crop Diffusion Champa rice bananas sugar citrus crops	**ENVIRONMENT: Degradation** overgrazing deforestation soil erosion	**ENVIRONMENT: Disease** bubonic plague

Questions 1 to 3 refer to the map below.

SPREAD OF THE BLACK DEATH IN EUROPE, 1346–1353

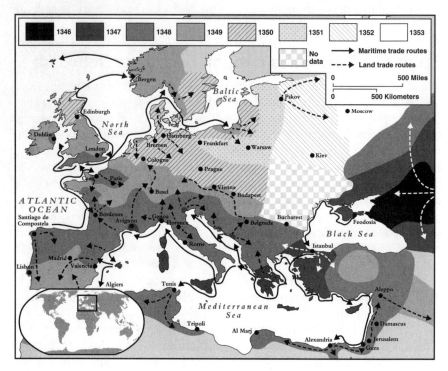

1. Which explanation for the cause of the rapid spread of the Black Death is best supported by this map?

   (A) The migrations of Central Asians into eastern Europe

   (B) The spread of rodents through trade

   (C) Pollution caused by growing concentrations of people in cities

   (D) Poverty among Europeans resulting from feudalism

2. One significant long-term impact of the Black Death was

   (A) the end of the Indian Ocean as a viable trade network

   (B) the decline of the feudal system in Europe

   (C) the increased use of camels in the Silk Roads trade

   (D) the rise of the Ottoman Turks

3. Which of the following statements does the map support most clearly?

(A) Muscovy traded extensively with Western Europe.

(B) Africa never experienced the Black Death.

(C) The Black Death entered Western Europe through the Mediterranean Sea.

(D) The strain of the Black Death that moved along the Indian Ocean was not fatal.

SHORT-ANSWER QUESTIONS

1. Use the passages below to answer all parts of the question that follows.

- Moroccan historian Ibn Khaldun wrote about the black plague outbreak this way: "Civilization both in the East and the West was visited by a destructive plague which devastated nations and caused populations to vanish. It swallowed up many of the good things of civilization and wiped them out. . . . Civilization decreased with the decrease of mankind. Cities and buildings were laid waste, roads and way signs were obliterated, settlements and mansions became empty, dynasties and tribes grew weak. The entire inhabited world changed."

- In *The Travels of Ibn Battuta*, the great traveler noted that as of 1345, "the number that died daily in Damascus [Syria] had been two thousand," but the people were able to defeat the plague through prayer.

- An Italian lawyer, Gabriele de Mussis, recorded: "The whole army was affected by a disease which overran the Tartars [Mongols] and killed thousands upon thousands every day." He [charges] that the Mongol leader "ordered corpses to be placed in catapults and lobbed into the city in hopes that the intolerable stench would kill everyone inside."

- A French churchman, Gilles li Muisis, notes that a "calamitous disease befell the Tartar army, and the mortality was so great and widespread that scarcely one in twenty of them remained alive." However, he depicts the Mongol survivors as surprised when the Christians in Kaffa also came down with the disease.

Kallie Szczepanski, "How the Black Death Started in Asia,"
Thought Co., 2020

(A) Identify ONE pattern the excerpts show about the Black Death.

(B) Explain ONE way the Black Death spread during the period 1200–1450.

(C) Compare ONE report of the plague's impact on the environment during the period 1200–1450 from an outside source to one of the reports in the above passage.

2. **Answer all parts of the question that follows.**

   (A) Identify ONE example of an agricultural advancement that developed during the period 1200–1450.

   (B) Explain ONE way in which exchange networks affected agriculture during the period 1200–1450.

   (C) Explain ONE way in which trade affected the environment during the period 1200–1450.

 THINK AS A HISTORIAN: MAKING CONNECTIONS BY ANALYZING CAUSATION

One way to make connections across cultures and eras is to analyze cycles of cause and effect. For example, improved agricultural production often leads to increased population. Increased population, in turn, requires even more agricultural production. Efforts to fulfill agricultural and other needs associated with increased population, in turn, may lead to pressure on resources, including environmental degradation, and the population may decline as a result or be vulnerable to disease or conquest. However, with the next improvement in agriculture or another economic advancement, the population may grow again, and so the cycle continues. Recognizing this somewhat predictable cycle of cause and effect can help you make connections by seeing it in action in different geographic areas at different times in history.

Describe a similar cycle of cause and effect related to increased demand for goods rather than for food. Then, analyze cause-and-effect connections between cultures that were involved in transregional exchange networks from c. 1200 to c. 1450.

REFLECT ON THE TOPIC ESSENTIAL QUESTION

1. In one to three paragraphs, explain some of the environmental effects of trade in Afro-Eurasia from c. 1200 to c. 1450.

2.7

Comparison of Economic Exchange

Wealthy merchants bring in big cargoes, which they unload and unhesitatingly send into the markets without thinking in the meantime of any security, or checking the account, or keeping watch over the goods.

—Abdu Razzak, "Description of Calicut," 1442

Essential Question: What were the similarities and differences among the various networks of exchange in the period from c. 1200 to c. 1450?

Calicut was known as the "City of Spices," a market city where merchants traded their goods for pepper and cinnamon from India and a variety of goods from other areas as well. In some ways, such as its ability to provide security and the diversity of people who patronized the markets, Calicut was like other big trading cities along the well-traveled trade routes. In other ways, such as the type of currency it used and how the polity, or governmental unit, made money on trade, it differed from trading cities elsewhere. The similarities and differences among trading cities were also reflected in the larger trading networks.

Similarities Among Networks of Exchange

Several major trading networks connected people in Africa, Europe, and Asia in the years between c. 1200 and c. 1450:

- the Silk Roads through the Gobi Desert and mountain passes in China and Central Asia to Southwest Asia and Europe, on which merchants tended to specialize in luxury goods

- the monsoon-dependent trade routes in the Indian Ocean linking East Asia with Southeast Asia, South Asia, and Southwest Asia, on which merchants exchanged goods too heavy to transport by land

- the trans-Saharan trade routes from North Africa and the Mediterranean Basin across the desert to West and East Africa, on which merchants traded salt from North Africa with gold from the kingdoms south of the desert

While each exchange network had its unique characteristics, all were similar in their origins, purpose, and effects.

Origins Interregional trade began well before the common era as agrarian cultures consolidated into stable settlements. The trade that flourished between c. 1200 and c. 1450 built on the routes these early traders—and conquerors—first traced. As kingdoms and empires expanded, so did the trade routes they controlled and traveled.

The Postclassical trading networks also needed the stability of established states to grow and expand. Stable kingdoms, caliphates, city-states, or empires assured merchants that the routes and the merchants themselves would be protected—which is why the wealthy merchants in Calicut could walk away from their cargoes knowing they would not be stolen. Stable polities also supported the technological upgrades that made trade more profitable—nautical equipment such as the magnetic compass and lateen sail, high-yielding strains of crops, and saddles to allow for the carriage of heavy loads of goods.

Purpose The trading networks shared an overall economic purpose: to exchange what people were able to grow or produce for what they wanted, needed, or could use to trade for other items. In other words, their purpose was primarily economic. However, as you have read, people exchanged much more than just products. Diplomats and missionaries also traveled the trade routes, negotiating alliances and proselytizing for converts. Together, merchants, diplomats, and missionaries exchanged ways of life as well as economic goods.

Effects All the exchange networks also experienced similar effects. Because of the very nature of a network—which can be described as a fabric of cords crossing at regular distances, knotted for strength at the crossings—the trade routes all gave rise to trading cities, the "knots" that held the network together.

Routes	Trading Cities
Silk Roads	Chang'an (present-day China), Samarkand (present-day Uzbekistan), Aleppo (present-day Syria), Mosul (present-day Iraq)
Indian Ocean	Malacca (present-day Malaysia), Calicut (present-day India), Hormuz (present-day Iran), Mombasa (present-day Kenya), Alexandria (present-day Egypt)
Trans-Saharan	Gao, Timbuktu (both present-day Mali), Marrakesh (present-day Morocco), Cairo (present-day Egypt)

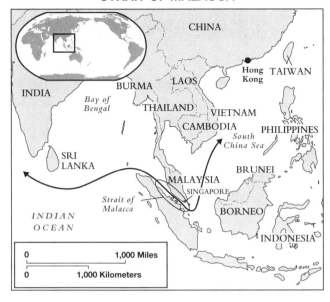

STRAIT OF MALACCA

The shortest route from East Asia to Southwest Asia on the Indian Ocean trade route was through the Strait of Malacca.

The growth of trading cities gave rise to another effect of the trade networks: centralization. Malacca, for example, grew wealthy from the fees levied on ships and cargoes passing through the Strait of Malacca. To prevent piracy, Malacca used its wealth in part to develop a strong navy—an endeavor that required centralized planning. Trading cities along each of the trade routes underwent similar developments, using their wealth to keep the routes and the cities safe.

Another aspect of trade in the cities that encouraged centralization was the desire for a standardized currency. Widely accepted currencies sped up transactions and enabled merchants to measure the value of products.

Many trading cities also became known as centers of learning. This is the Ulugh Beg Madrasa (Islamic religious school) that was built in Samarkand between 1417 and 1422.

Source: La madrasa Oulough Begh du Registan (Samarcande, Ouzbékistan)
Author: Jean-Pierre Dalbéra from Paris, France

Differences Among Networks of Exchange

Despite their similarities, the networks of exchange were different in some ways, especially in the goods they exchanged, the nature of the routes and transportation, the technologies they inspired, and the religions they spread.

Routes	Goods	Transportation	Religions
Silk Roads	**East to West:** • Silk • Tea • Spices • Dyes • Porcelain • Rice • Paper • Gunpowder **West to East:** • Horses • Saddles • Fruit • Domestic animals • Honey • Textiles	• Horses • Camels **Technologies** • Saddles • Caravanserai	• Buddhism from South Asia to East and Southeast Asia • Neo-Confucianism from China to Korea, Japan, and Vietnam • Islam from Southwest Asia to South Asia
Indian Ocean (and Mediterranean Basin)	**From East Africa:** • Gold • Ivory • Quartz • Animal skins **From Southwest Asia:** • Citrus • Fruits • Dates • Books **From Southern India:** • Textiles • Peppers • Pearls	• Dhows • Junks **Technologies** • Stern rudder • Lateen sail • Astrolabe • Magnetic compass	• Buddhism from South Asia to East and Southeast Asia • Neo-Confucianism from China to Korea, Japan, and Vietnam • Islam from South Asia to Southeast Asia • Christianity from Mediterranean Basin
Trans-Saharan	**North to South:** • Horses • Books • Salt **South to North:** • Gold • Ivory • Cloth • Enslaved people	• Caravans of camels for carrying goods • People walked **Technology** • Saddles to increase load bearing	• Islam from Southwest Asia and North Africa to Sub-Saharan Africa

The trading networks also had unique currencies and commercial practices. For example, at one time silk was not only a commodity but also a currency. In places in Southeast Asia, tin ingots were used as a currency standard. West African states used cowrie shells as currency.

In time, however, states shifted to a money economy based on gold and other metal coins. To make commerce less bulky, the Chinese invented "flying cash" (see Topic 2.1) and established the precursors of banks, including the practice of extending credit.

Fanam coins from the Eastern Gupta Dynasty in Kalinga (1078–1434)
Source: Wikimedia Common   **Credit:** Sujit Kumar

Social Implications of Networks of Exchange

The rising demand for luxury goods spurred efforts to make production more efficient than it had been. China went through a period of proto-industrialization as it sought to meet the demand for iron, steel, and porcelain. (See Topic 1.1.) New business practices, such as partnerships for sharing the risk of investment, began to emerge.

The production of goods such as textiles and porcelain in China and spices in South and Southeast Asia increased to meet demands. As the amount of goods increased, the volume of trade on maritime trade routes began to supersede that of the overland trade routes. Larger ships were needed as well as improved navigational knowledge and technology.

Labor The demand for labor rose along with the growing demand for products. The forms of labor from earlier periods continued—free peasant farmers, craft workers or artisans in cottage industries, people forced to work to pay off debts, and people forced into labor through enslavement. Trade in enslaved people was common along the Indian Ocean and trans-Saharan routes.

Large-scale projects—irrigation canals, military defenses, great buildings—called for the work of thousands of organized laborers. Kinship ties often played a role in coordinating these large-scale projects. In the *Narrative of Domingo Paes* (1520–1522), a Portuguese traveler described the work of completing a giant reservoir in the Vijayanagara Empire in South India:

"In the tank I saw so many people at work that there must have been fifteen or twenty thousand men, looking like ants, so that you could not see the ground on which they walked, so many there were; this tank the king portioned out amongst his captains, each of whom had the duty of seeing that the people placed under him did their work, and that the tank was finished and brought to completion."

Social and Gender Structures The typical social structures during the period between 1200 and 1450 were still defined by class or caste, and societies, with rare exceptions, remained patriarchies. There were, however, areas where women exercised more power and influence. For example, even though the vast Mongol Empire was a patriarchy, Mongol women had somewhat more freedom than women in most other parts of Afro-Eurasia. Mongol women moved about freely and refused the burka from the West and foot binding from the East. Women were also often top advisors to the great khan.

In Europe, women worked as farmers and artisans, and they had their own guilds. In Southeast Asia, women were skilled in the practices of the marketplace, operating and controlling marketplaces as representatives of powerful families. Outside of these limited areas, however, women within other major regions still experienced far fewer opportunities and freedoms than men in virtually all aspects of life.

Environmental Processes The interconnections that spurred so much vibrant economic and cultural exchange also led to a steep population decline as merchants, diplomats, and missionaries transferred the bubonic plague and other infectious diseases along the trade routes. The plague, named the Black Death, contributed to the decline of once-great cities, such as Constantinople. Most believe that at least a third of Europe's population died during this period. China experienced outbreaks in the 1330s and 1350s, causing tens of millions of deaths.

Changes in trade networks led to cultural diffusion and the development of educational centers in cities such as Canton, Samarkand, Timbuktu, Cairo, and Venice. Political instability and increased agriculture strained the environment. For example, soil erosion from deforestation, or overgrazing, forced growing populations to migrate to other areas.

1. **Comparison** Prepare a graphic showing the similarities and differences between interregional trade in 1200 and interregional trade in 1450.

2. In one to three paragraphs, explain the similarities and differences among the various networks of exchange in the period from c. 1200 to c. 1450.

Source: Gallica Digital Library

Caravan on the Silk Road, painting by Abraham Cresques, 1375

UNIT 2 REVIEW

 HISTORICAL PERSPECTIVES: HOW BRUTAL WAS GENGHIS KHAN?

Was Genghis Khan a brutal destroyer who murdered millions, or was he a great unifier who promoted prosperity by unifying most of Eurasia?

The Destroyer Many historians emphasize that Khan was a bloodthirsty tyrant. Military historian Steven R. Ward writes that "Overall, the Mongol violence and depredations killed up to three-fourths of the population of the Iranian Plateau." Total deaths attributed to the Mongols during his rule and the rule of his descendants are in the tens of millions. Stories of his massacres of innocent people and of using unarmed civilians to protect his own soldiers show him to have had little regard for human life.

The Empire Builder Other historians focus on Khan's role as a great leader. Mongolian scholars, proud of their countryman, argue that charges of brutality have been exaggerated. As historians from Europe and the United States focused more on trade and toleration, they saw benefits of the Mongol rule, often referring to *Pax Mongolica*. Genghis Khan forged a united China and established a system of Eurasian trade that renewed the links between China and Europe that had lapsed. Further, the Mongols were open to ideas and tolerant of different religions. Khan believed in a meritocracy, and he established one writing system across his empire. His rule opened the way for new systems of laws, for trade, and for cultural expansion.

A Man of Energy One Persian historian takes a position broad enough that everyone can agree with: "Genghis was possessed of great energy, discernment, genius, and understanding, awe-inspiring, a butcher, just, resolute, an over-thrower of enemies, intrepid, sanguinary, and cruel."

Develop an Argument: Evaluate the extent to which historical evidence supports one of the perspectives of Genghis Khan.

WRITE AS A HISTORIAN: HISTORICAL THINKING SKILLS AND LONG ESSAYS

Writing answers to long essay questions requires using historical thinking skills. Different stages of the process call for using different historical thinking skills. Study the chart below.

Stages in the Writing Process	Historical Thinking Skills
Analyze the question by identifying the exact task and the geographic and chronological framework.	Identify, describe, and explain a historical concept, development, or process. (See pages 22 and 64.)
Gather and organize the evidence you will need to complete the task.	Identify, describe, and explain patterns or connections among historical concepts, developments, and processes. (See pages 94 and 102.) These patterns and connections provide the key to organizing your evidence. Make sure your organization supports the task in the prompt. (See pages 183 and 266.)
Develop a thesis that lays out a line of reasoning.	Make a historically defensible claim related directly to the task and your evidence as the basis for your argument. Use historical reasoning (comparison, continuity and change, or causation) to frame your argument. (See pages 358 and 444.)
Write an introductory paragraph.	Identify and describe a broader historical context for your argument, and explain how the development or process you are examining is situated within that context. (See page 444.)
Write the supporting paragraphs.	Support an argument using specific and relevant evidence, explaining how the evidence ties to the argument. Explain relationships among various pieces of evidence. (See page 537.)
Write the conclusion.	Reinforce and extend relevant and insightful connections within and across periods as you tie together your complex argument. (See page 624.)
Reread and evaluate your essay.	Be sure it demonstrates a complex understanding of the question and uses historical evidence to corroborate, qualify, or modify an argument. (See pages 624 and 714.)

Application: Find the scoring rubric and sample essays for World History on the College Board website. Work in a small group to prepare a presentation explaining how to earn the most possible points on a long essay question. Share your presentation with the rest of the class.

For current free-response question samples, visit: https://apcentral.colleg-eboard.org/courses/ap-world-history/exam

LONG ESSAY QUESTIONS

Directions: Write essay responses to 1, 2, and EITHER 3 or 4. The suggested writing time for each essay is 40 minutes.

1. Some historians consider the Mongols' military success and vast commercial empire in the 13th century as the beginning of the early modern era.
   Develop an argument that evaluates the extent to which the Mongol Empire was significant in larger patterns of continuity or change between 1200 and 1450.

2. Goods and ideas flowed through African and Eurasian trade networks in the period from 1200 to 1450.
   Develop an argument that evaluates the extent to which the various networks of exchange in that time and place were similar or different.

3. Weather patterns, foods, and disease affected exchange networks in Eurasia and Africa in the period from 1200 to 1450.
   Develop an argument that evaluates the extent to which various networks of exchange in Afro-Eurasia during that time affected the environment.

4. Although the primary purpose of most African and Eurasian trading networks between 1200 and 1450 was economic, ideas and art also traveled through them.
   Develop an argument that evaluates the extent to which trading networks in these regions between 1200 and 1450 affected the diffusion of cultural traditions.

In each response you should do the following:

- Respond to the prompt with a historically defensible thesis or claim that establishes a line of reasoning.
- Describe a broader historical context relevant to the prompt.
- Support an argument in response to the prompt using at least two pieces of specific and relevant evidence.
- Use historical reasoning (e.g., comparison, causation, continuity or change) to frame or structure an argument that addresses the prompt.
- Demonstrate a complex understanding of a historical development related to the prompt through sophisticated argumentation and/or effective use of evidence.

Source: *AP® World History Course and Exam Description*

DOCUMENT-BASED QUESTION

Directions: Question 1 is based on the accompanying documents. The documents have been edited for the purpose of this exercise. You are advised to spend 15 minutes planning and 45 minutes writing your answer.

1. Evaluate the extent to which women were influential within the gender structures of Afro-Eurasian societies, during the period c. 1200 to c. 1450.

In your response you should do the following:

- Respond to the prompt with a historically defensible thesis or claim that establishes a line of reasoning.
- Describe a broader historical context relevant to the prompt.
- Support an argument in response to the prompt using at least four documents.
- Use at least one additional piece of specific historical evidence (beyond that found in the documents) relevant to an argument about the prompt.
- For at least two documents, explain how or why the document's point of view, purpose, historical situation, and/or audience is relevant to an argument.
- Demonstrate a complex understanding of a historical development related to the prompt through a sophisticated argument and/or effective use of evidence.

Source: *AP® World History Course and Exam Description*

Document 1

Source: Ala ad-Din Juvaini, Persian historian, writing about the daughter-in-law of Genghis Khan, Sorqotani Beki [also Sorqoqtani or Sorghaghtani], in *The History of the World-Conqueror*, c. 1200.

After the death of Sorqotani Beki's husband, the new Khan [Mongol ruler] commanded that as long as he lived, affairs of state should be administered in accordance to the council of Sorqotani Beki and her sons that the army and the people, great and small, should be under the control of her command.

Her hand was ever open in great generosity and gift giving. Although she was a follower of the religion of Jesus, she would bestow alms and presents also upon *imams* [Muslim prayer leader] and *shaikhs* [tribal chiefs] and strove also to revive the sacred observances of the faith of Mohammed. And as the token and proof of this statement she gave a significant amount of money that a *madrasa* [Islamic college] might be built in Bokhara [Uzbekistan, central Asia].

Document 2

Source: Painting by Japanese artist Shitomi Kangetsu in the late 1700s, of Tomoe Gozen, a female samurai (warrior) known for her bravery, archery skills, and horsemanship during the Genpei War in Japan, c. 1200.

Document 3

Source: Excerpt from the chronicles of Minhaji Siraj Juzjani, Persian Historian, on the reign of Sultan Raziyya bint Iltutmish, the first woman to ascend to the throne and lead the army of the Delhi Sultanate in Northern India, c. 1250.

Sultan Raziyya—may she rest in peace—was a great sovereign, wise, just, and beneficent, the patron of the learned, a dispenser of justice, the cherisher of her subjects, and of warlike skills. She was endowed with all the admirable attributes and qualities required of kings.

But as she did not attain the destiny,* in her birth as a woman, of being valued among men, of what advantage were all these excellent qualifications unto her?

Raziyya was removed from power by her half-brother after four years.

Document 4

Source: Ibn Battuta, Muslim scholar and explorer, excerpt from his memoirs, *Rihla* (*My Travels*), on his journey to the court of Mansa Musa, sultan of Mali (sub-Saharan Africa), c. 1350.

The condition of these people is strange and their manners unfamiliar. None of them derives his genealogy [family ancestry] from his father but, on the contrary, from his maternal uncle. A man does not pass on inheritance except to the sons of his sister to the exclusion of his own sons.

With regard to their women, they are not modest in the presence of men, they do not veil themselves despite their perseverance in prayers. He who wishes to marry among them can marry, but the women do not travel with the husband, and if one of them wanted to do that, she would be prevented by her family. The women there have friends and companions amongst men outside the prohibited degrees of marriage [i.e. other than brothers, fathers, etc.]

Likewise, for the men, there are companions from amongst women outside the prohibited degrees. One of them would enter his house to find his wife with her companion and would disapprove of that conduct.

Document 5

Source: Christine de Pizan, Italian poet and author at the court of King Charles VI of France, *The Book of the City of Ladies*, c. 1400.

Just the sight of this book [by 13th century religious leader and poet Matheolus, which negatively portrayed women], even though it was of no authority, made me wonder how it happened that so many different men—and learned men among them—have been and are so inclined to express both in speaking and in their treatises and writings so many wicked insults about women and their behavior. Not only one or two . . . but, more generally, from the treatises of all philosophers and poets and from all the orators—it would take too long to mention their names—it seems that they all speak from one and the same mouth.

Thinking deeply about these matters, I began to examine my character and conduct as a natural woman and, similarly, I considered other women whose company I frequently kept—princesses, great ladies, women of the middle and lower classes—who had graciously told me of their most private and intimate thoughts, hoping that I could judge impartially and in good conscience whether the testimony of so many notable men could be true. To the best of my knowledge, no matter how long I confronted or dissected the problem, I could not see or realize how their claims could be true when compared to the natural behavior and character of women.

Document 6

Source: Empress Xu, third wife of the Ming Emperor, Yongle, *Instructions for the Inner Quarters*, c. 1400.

Being upright and modest, reserved and quiet, correct and dignified, sincere and honest: these constitute the moral nature of a woman. Being filial [loyal to family as is due of a son or daughter], and respectful, humane and perspicacious [insightful], loving and warm, meek and gentle: these represent the complete development of the moral nature.

Upright women in the past ordered their feelings and nature based on moral principle, kept control over the workings of their mind, and honored the Way [Confucianism and family loyalty] and its virtue. Therefore, they were able to complement their husbands in fulfilling the teachings of the Way.

If one's virtue is not established, rarely can one be an influence for good in the family—how much less in the wider world? Therefore, the wife is one who follows her husband. The way of husband and wife is the principle of the strong and the weak. . . . The prosperity or decline of the family and the rise and fall of the state are intimately linked to this.

Document 7

Source: Joan of Arc, also called "The Maid" was a young French girl who felt herself to be called by God to help the French resist the English in the Hundred Years War, *Letter to the King of England*, c. 1450.

King of England, give account to the King of Heaven of your royal blood. Return the keys of all the good cities which you have seized. The Maid is sent by God to reclaim the royal blood, and is fully prepared to make peace, if you will give her satisfaction; that is, you must render justice, and pay back all you have taken.

King of England, if you do not do these things, I am the commander of the military; and in whatever place I shall find your men in France, I will make them flee the country, whether they wish to or not; and if they will not obey, the Maid will have them all killed. She comes sent by the King of Heaven, body for body, to take you out of France, and the Maid promises and certifies to you that if you do not leave France, she and her troops will raise a mighty outcry as has not been heard in France in a thousand years.

UNIT 3: Land-Based Empires from c. 1450 to c. 1750

Understand the Context

Great land-based empires existed before 1450 and after 1750. However, between these years, several of history's greatest land-based empires reached their peak of wealth and influence. Among these were the Songhai in West Africa; the Safavids based in Persia; the Mughals in northern India; the Ottomans in the Middle East, Eastern Europe, and Northern Africa; and the Manchus in eastern Asia. They were multiethnic states that had direct political control over large regions and overland trade routes.

Expansion Since these empires measured their power in land, they frequently warred against neighbors over territory. The Manchus, who established the Qing Dynasty in China in 1644, were very successful in this. By 1911, they had tripled the amount of land they controlled.

Centralization Land-based empires in this period prospered by consolidating their power in a central government. They employed bureaucratic elites to enforce laws and military professionals to provide defense. To pay for the bureaucrats and soldiers, they collected tributes from weaker states and taxes from their citizens. To demonstrate their wealth and power, they constructed great palaces, religious buildings, and shrines.

Belief Systems Land-based empires were often closely tied with particular religious faiths. As a result, political and religious conflicts were intertwined. In Europe, Roman Catholics and Protestants fought wars in which millions of people died. In Asia, the Safavids, who were Shi'a Muslims, and the Mughals, who were Sunni Muslims, were often at war.

After 1750 Many land-based empires began declining in power in the 18th century. The increasing importance of ethnic identities for individuals, ocean routes for trade, and economic relationships among businesses undermined the unity and influence that land-based empires initially developed.

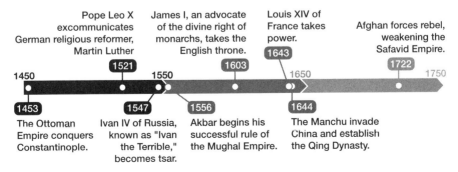

Pope Leo X excommunicates German religious reformer, Martin Luther — **1521**

James I, an advocate of the divine right of monarchs, takes the English throne. — **1603**

Louis XIV of France takes power. **1643**

Afghan forces rebel, weakening the Safavid Empire. **1722**

1450 · · **1550** · · · **1650** · **1750**

1453 The Ottoman Empire conquers Constantinople.

1547 Ivan IV of Russia, known as "Ivan the Terrible," becomes tsar.

1556 Akbar begins his successful rule of the Mughal Empire.

1644 The Manchu invade China and establish the Qing Dynasty.

Topics and Learning Objectives

Topic 3.1: European, East Asian, and Gunpowder Empires Expand pages 143–154

A: Explain how and why various land-based empires developed and expanded from 1450 to 1750.

Topic 3.2: Empires: Administration pages 155–166

B: Explain how rulers used a variety of methods to legitimize and consolidate their power in land-based empires from 1450 to 1750.

Topic 3.3: Empires: Belief Systems pages 167–176

C: Explain continuity and change within the various belief systems during the period from 1450 to 1750.

Topic 3.4: Comparison in Land-Based Empires pages 177–181

D: Compare the methods by which various empires increased their influence from 1450 to 1750.

3.1

European, East Asian, and Gunpowder Empires Expand

What men call sovereignty is a worldly strife and constant war;
Worship of God is the highest throne, the happiest of all estates.

—Suleiman the Magnificent (1494–1566)

Essential Question: How did certain land-based empires develop and expand in the period from 1450–1750?

From its origins in China, gunpowder spread via the trade routes and became a powerful source of change between 1450 and 1750. The term **Gunpowder Empires** refers to large, multiethnic states in Southwest, Central, and South Asia that relied on firearms to conquer and control territories. In addition to Russia, the Gunpowder Empires included three in which Islam was strong: the Ottoman, the Safavid, and the Mughal Empires. Suleiman the Magnificent, quoted above, ruled the Ottoman Empire at its height. Although he declared religious worship the happiest of all practices, he also personally led Ottoman armies in conquering Christian strongholds in Belgrade, Rhodes, and Hungary in Southeastern Europe. The Gunpowder Empire societies tended to be militaristic, yet all three left splendid artistic and architectural legacies, created in part to reflect the legitimacy of their rulers.

The Qing Empire of China also expanded, and although it experienced several invasions, it also prospered during long periods of stability. Europe's expansion involved an even wider exchange network than that which spread gunpowder: transoceanic connections with the Americas. (You will read more about this path to empire expansion in Unit 4.)

Armed trade was common in expanding empires during this period. The different empires traded with one another. However, they kept troops and armaments at the ready in case another empire questioned their right to trade. This type of exchange differed from the free markets of later eras.

Europe

The year 1450 has traditionally signified the ending of the medieval period and the beginning of the early modern period. The mid-1400s saw the end of a wave of plagues, the conclusion of the Hundred Years' War between

France and England (see Topic 1.6), and the invention of the **Gutenberg printing press** followed by an increase in literacy. After the slow political and economic development of the Middle Ages, several countries in Europe were becoming powerful, wealthy nations. New monarchies began to launch overseas explorations and establish colonies around the world.

The nature of the new monarchies in Europe in the 1500s was the result of the desire of certain leaders to centralize power by controlling taxes, the army, and many aspects of religion. These new monarchs included the Tudors in England, the Valois in France, and Queen Isabella and King Ferdinand in Spain. In each area, bureaucracies increased and the power of the middle class grew at the expense of lords and the churches. For example, the new monarchies moved to curb the private armies of the nobility.

Russia

Western Europeans were long unsure what to think of Russia: Was Russia more European in its outlook and character, or was it more Asian? Russia was in a pivotal position for trade. It was able to exchange goods and services with other cultures farther east and west. However, Russia remained tightly linked to Europe. Its capital—whether Kiev, St. Petersburg, or Moscow—was located in Europe. Although a product of Mongol influence from Central Asia to the east, Russia was also a product of Europe as a result of Viking invasions and trading.

When **Ivan IV** (ruled 1547–1584), called Ivan the Terrible, was crowned tsar in 1547, he immediately set about to expand the Russian border eastward, first by taking control of the khanates of Kazan, Astrakhan, and Siberia held by the descendants of the Golden Horde, the Mongolian conquerors. This expansion came to rely more and more upon the use of gunpowder.

Control of the Volga Wanting to expand east to control the fur trade, Ivan IV allowed the Stroganovs, major Russian landowners, to hire bands of fierce peasant warriors known as Cossacks to fight the local tribes and the Siberian khan. The Stroganovs' forces were successful, gaining control of the Volga

EXPANSION OF RUSSIA

1462–1505	1506–1584
1585–1725	1726–1796

0   1,000 Miles
0   1,000 Kilometers

River, which flows into the Caspian Sea. Possessing this outlet to the sea, Moscow could trade directly with Persia and the Ottoman Empire without having to deal with the strong forces of the Crimean Tartars.

To the Pacific Russia continued moving east into Siberia after the reign of Ivan IV. Fur traders and militias defeated one indigenous tribe after another. Missionaries followed, converting many to the Eastern Orthodox faith, although the local shamans, or religious leaders, continued to have influence. By 1639, the Russians had advanced east as far as the Pacific Ocean. Explorations and fur trading expeditions continued across the Pacific to Alaska (1741) and down the coast of North America to California (1814).

East Asia

China's Yuan Dynasty, founded by Mongol invader Kublai Khan in 1271, was overthrown by the **Ming Dynasty** in 1368 after less than a century in power. Ming rulers managed to stabilize the East Asian region for nearly 300 years. During the Ming era, the Portuguese and other Europeans arrived, aiming to encroach on the Asian trade network. Then, in 1644, the powerful **Manchu** from neighboring Manchuria seized power and established the **Qing Dynasty**, which ruled until 1911. During both of these dynasties, Japan and Korea experienced parallel developments but with unique aspects.

The Ming Dynasty also expanded the size of China, conquering lands in Mongolia and Central Asia. It did not hold them for long, however. In the 1440s, Mongol armies defeated Ming forces and even took the Ming emperor prisoner. In reaction to renewed Mongol power, China's leaders looked to the Great Wall of China for protection. The Wall had not been maintained under Mongol rule, but under the Ming Dynasty it was restored and expanded to help keep out invaders from the north. (Connect: Create a chart comparing the Ming and Yuan Dynasties. See Topic 2.2.)

Emperor Kangxi One of China's longest-reigning emperors, **Kangxi** (ruled 1661–1722) presided over a period of stability and expansion during the Qing Dynasty in China. Kangxi sent forces into Taiwan, Mongolia, and Central Asia, incorporating those areas into the empire. China also imposed a protectorate over Tibet, the mountainous land north of India, a policy reflected in China's control of the region today.

Emperor Qianlong Another important Qing ruler was **Emperor Qianlong** (ruled 1736–1796), a poet, who was also knowledgeable in art and calligraphy. At the beginning of his reign, the country was well administered and government tax collections were at an all-time high. Qianlong initiated military campaigns in lands west of China, which led to the annexation of Xinjiang accompanied by the mass killings of the local population. Even today, parts of Xinjiang remain troubled. The local Muslim population, called Uighurs, has never fully become incorporated into the rest of Chinese culture.

Qianlong also sent armies into Tibet to install the Dalai Lama on the throne there. A campaign against the Nepalese was successful, forcing them to submit to Chinese rule. However, campaigns against Burma and Vietnam were unsuccessful and costly, resulting in the emptying of the empire's treasury.

Conflicts with the West Needing funds, the Qing Dynasty sold limited trading privileges to the European powers but confined them to Guangzhou (also known as Canton). The British were not satisfied with these limited privileges, so they asked for more trading rights in 1793. Emperor Qianlong responded with a letter to King George III stating that the Chinese had no need for British manufactured goods. During the later part of Qianlong's reign, the traditionally efficient Chinese bureaucracy became corrupt, levying high taxes on the people. In response to these high taxes and a desire to restore the Ming Dynasty, a group of peasants organized the White Lotus Rebellion (1796–1804). The Qing government suppressed the uprising brutally, killing around 100,000 peasants.

Rise of the Islamic Gunpowder Empires

The warrior leaders of the Ottoman, Safavid, and Mughal Empires shared many traits besides being Muslims:

- They descended from Turkic nomads who once lived in Central Asia.
- They spoke a Turkic language.
- They took advantage of power vacuums left by the breakup of Mongol khanates.
- They relied on gunpowder weapons, such as artillery and cannons.

The initial success of the Gunpowder Empires was a result of their own military might along with the weakness and corruption of the regimes that they replaced. As European nations fought among themselves rather than uniting to topple the new powers growing in the east, the Gunpowder Empires further expanded.

The Rule of Tamerlane The invasion of Central Asia and the Middle East by **Tamerlane** (Timur the Lame, a Mongol-Turkic ruler of the late 14th century) set the stage for the rise of the Turkic empires. Leading an army partly composed of nomadic invaders from the broad steppes of Eurasia, Tamerlane moved out from the trading city of Samarkand (in modern-day Uzbekistan) to make ruthless conquests in Persia (modern-day Iran) and India. The Eurasian steppes were also the birthplace of the **ghazi ideal**—a model for warrior life that blended the cooperative values of nomadic culture with the willingness to serve as a holy fighter for Islam. According to some historians, the ghazi ideal served as the model for warriors who participated in the rise of the Gunpowder Empires, and it was a model that fit Tamerlane well.

Some historians believe that Tamerlane's violent takeover of areas of Central Asia included the massacre of some 100,000 Hindus before the gates of Delhi in India. The pattern of conquest was marked by violence that resulted in new dynasties: the Ottomans, the Safavids, and the Mughals. Nonetheless, Tamerlane's rule in Samarkand encouraged learning and the arts—a trend also typical of these later empires. For example, Tamerlane championed literature, and he himself corresponded with European rulers and wrote his own memoirs. Buildings still standing in the city of Samarkand are lasting reminders of his interest in architecture and decorative arts.

While the empire he created largely fell apart (except for the area that his descendant Babur would take over to create India's Mughal Dynasty), Tamerlane's invasions were a testament to the significance of gunpowder. He used it to build a government dependent upon his military and the use of heavy artillery. He also used it to protect land routes on the Silk Roads. However, he failed to leave an effective political structure in many of the areas he conquered. Without effective government, the expenses of the wars eventually ravaged the empire's economy.

Tamerlane's rule casts light on two major forces that had battled each other continually from the late 10th century to the 14th century—Mongols from the northeast versus Islamic forces from Arabia and the areas around the Mediterranean Sea. These forces would clash continuously with the rise and fall of the three Asian Gunpowder Empires that are the focus of the rest of this chapter.

The Ottoman Empire

By the 15th century, the Ottoman Empire was already becoming a major power. Extending into modern-day Turkey as well as to the Balkan areas of Europe and parts of North Africa and Southwest Asia, the **Ottoman Empire** was the largest and most enduring of the great Islamic empires of this period. Founded by the Osman Dynasty in the 1300s, the empire lasted until its defeat in 1918 by the Allies in World War I. Thus a single dynasty controlled the empire for more than 600 years.

Mehmed II Called the Conqueror, Mehmed II (ruled 1451–1481) firmly established the empire's capital after his forces besieged Constantinople (once the center of the Byzantine Empire) in 1453. Despite its triple fortifications, the city fell as its walls crumbled under the bombardment of Ottoman cannons. The Ottomans used a 26-foot bronze cannon and several other cannons from 15 to 22 feet in length. Under Mehmed II's rule, the city—its name changed to Istanbul—prospered because of its location. A nexus for trade, the city controlled the Bosporus Strait, the only waterway linking the Aegean Sea with the Black Sea.

The armies of Mehmed II next seized lands around the western edge of the Black Sea. Then they moved into the Balkans in Southeast Europe. To counter the power of Venice, an expanding state on the Adriatic Sea with a robust maritime trade, Mehmed strengthened the Ottoman navy and attacked various areas of Italy. Although he did not conquer Venice, he forced the city to pay him a yearly tax. In the early 16th century, the Ottomans added to their empire lands in present-day Syria, Israel, Egypt, and Algeria. When the Mamluk Dynasty's power declined, Istanbul became a center of Islam. (For more on the Mamluk Empire, see Topic 1.2.)

Suleiman I The Ottoman Empire reached its peak under **Suleiman I** (ruled 1520–1566). His armies overran Hungary in 1526 and, by 1529, were hammering at the gates of Vienna, the main city in Austria. Their attempt to take Vienna failed twice, but the ability of the Ottomans to send troops so far into Christian Europe caused great fear there.

In 1522, Suleiman's navy captured the island of Rhodes (now part of Greece) in the eastern Mediterranean, which had long been a stronghold of Christian knights. In the 1550s, the Ottoman navy took control of Tripoli in North Africa. The Ottoman Empire would experience a transformation as the state adapted to new internal and external pressures. A period of reform would follow by the 18th century. Challenges in defending Ottoman territory against foreign invasion and occupation led to the Ottoman defeat and dissolution by 1922.

The Safavids

The Safavid dynasty had its origin in the Safavid order of Sufism, established in the northern Azerbaijan region (Iran). An early Safavid military hero named **Ismail** conquered most of Persia and pushed into Iraq. Although only 14 or 15 years old, he soon conquered all of Iran and was proclaimed **shah** (equivalent to king or emperor) in 1501.

The **Safavid Empire** had two problems. First, despite being on the Arabian Sea (part of the Indian Ocean), the empire did not have a real navy. Second, the Safavids lacked natural defenses. Nevertheless, the Safavids rose to power in the 1500s due to their land-based military might and strong leadership.

Called Abbas the Great, **Shah Abbas I** (ruled 1588–1629) presided over the Safavid Empire at its height. His troops included soldiers—often Christian boys pressed into service—from as far northwest as Georgia in Russia. Abbas imported weaponry from Europe and also relied on Europeans to advise his troops about this newly acquired military technology. Slowly, the shahs came to control religion as well as politics. Using Shi'a Islam as a unifying force, Shah Ismail built a power base that supported his rule and denied legitimacy to any Sunni. This strict adherence to Shi'a Islam caused frequent hostilities with the Ottoman Empire, a stronghold of Sunni Islam. In 1541, Safavid forces were stopped by the Ottomans at Tabriz, a city in Persia that became part of the border between Sunni and Shi'a societies. The hostility between the two groups lives on in present-day Iraq and Iran.

Conflicts between Ottomans and Safavids were not entirely religious, however. Another conflict arose over control of overland trade routes. The Ottomans used trade embargoes, official bans on trade, consistently against the Safavid silk traders as a way to assert dominance over their eastern rival.

Women in the Safavid Empire Women are rarely mentioned in local Safavid histories; however, Safavid women were permitted to participate in their societies. While Safavid women were still veiled and restricted in their movements, as was traditional in the region, they had access to rights provided by Islamic law for inheritance and, in extreme cases, divorce.

Mughal India

In the 1520s, Babur, a descendant of Tamerlane (see Topic 2.2), founded a 300-year dynasty during a time when India was in disarray. He completed conquests in northern India and, under the new Mughal name, formed a central government similar to that of Suleiman in Turkey. **Akbar**, Babur's grandson, achieved grand religious and political goals.

The **Mughal Empire** under Akbar was one of the richest and best-governed states in the world. Overseas trade flourished during the relatively peaceful period; Arab traders conducted most of the commerce. Traded goods included textiles, tropical foods, spices, and precious stones, all of which were often exchanged for gold and silver. Trade within the borders of the empire was carried on by merchant castes. Members of the merchant castes were allowed to participate in banking and the production of handicrafts.

Castes, or *jatis*, are strict social groupings designated at birth. The caste system divides Hindu people into four categories: Brahmins, Kshatriyas, Vaishyas, and the Shudras. Outside of the system are the achhoots, or the Dalits, the untouchables. The Indian caste system is the basis of educational and vocational opportunities for Indian society.

Mughal India flourished from Babur's time through the early 18th century. Magnificent architectural accomplishments are remaining testaments to the wealth and sophistication of the Mughal empire.

Decline of the Gunpowder Empires

The Ottoman, Safavid, and Mughal Empires declined as Western Europe grew in strength economically and militarily—particularly in terms of sea power. Unlike these three Islamic empires, Russia modernized and reorganized its army, modeling it after the armies of England, France, and the Netherlands. The Islamic empires did not modernize and, as a result, Russia remained powerful enough to survive as an independent nation-state, while the other Gunpowder Empires fell.

Decline of the Ottoman Empire In 1571, after Suleiman's death, a European force made up mostly of Spaniards and Venetians defeated the Ottomans in a great naval conflict known as the Battle of Lepanto. After the reign of Suleiman, the Ottomans fell victim to weak sultans and strong European neighbors. In time, the empire became known as the Sick Man of Europe. Successors to Suleiman were often held hostage to "harem politics," the efforts of wives and concubines of the sultan to promote their own children

THREE ISLAMIC EMPIRES IN THE SIXTEENTH CENTURY

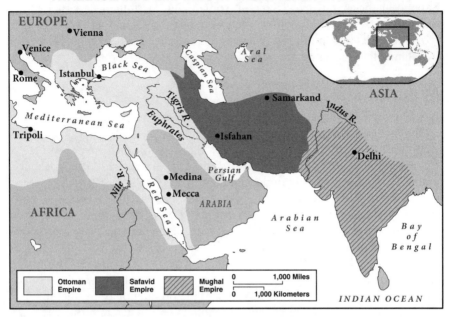

as likely heirs to the throne. In this way, some women became powerful behind the scenes. The failed Siege of Vienna in 1683 marked a turning point in Ottoman domination in Eastern Europe. British and French involvement in the Ottoman territories, Greece's independence in 1821, and the Russian expansion in the 19th century further weakened the Ottoman Empire.

Safavid Decline The ineffectual leaders who followed Shah Abbas combined lavish lifestyles and military spending with falling revenues, resulting in a weakened economy. In 1722, Safavid forces were not able to quell a rebellion by the heavily oppressed Sunni Pashtuns in present-day Afghanistan. The Afghan forces went on to sack Isfahan, and their leader, Mahmud, declared himself Shah of Persia. While the Safavid Dynasty remained nominally in control, the resulting chaos was an impediment to centralization and tax collection. Taking advantage of the weakened Safavids, the Ottomans and the Russians were able to seize territories. The Safavid Dynasty declined rapidly until it was replaced by the Zand Dynasty in 1760.

Mughal Decline Shah Jahan's son and successor, Aurangzeb (ruled 1658–1707), inherited an empire weakened by corruption and the failure to keep up with the military innovations of external enemies. Nevertheless, Aurangzeb hoped to increase the size of the empire and bring all of India under Muslim rule. Additionally, he wanted to rid the empire of its Hindu influences.

In expanding the empire to the south, he drained the empire's treasury and was unable to put down peasant uprisings. Some of these uprisings were sparked by Aurangzeb's insistence on an austere and pious Islamic lifestyle and an intolerance of minority religions—Sikhs, Hindus, and others. His policies led to frequent conflicts and rebellions.

There were revolts as well among the Hindu and Islamic princes. The empire grew increasingly unstable after his death, which allowed the British and French to gain more and more economic power in India. The British would take political power away from the Mughals in the 19th century.

KEY TERMS BY THEME

GOVERNMENT: China
Ming Dynasty
Manchu
Qing Dynasty
Kangxi
Emperor Qianlong

TECHNOLOGY: Literacy
Gutenberg printing press

GOVERNMENT: Turkic
Gunpowder Empires
Ottoman Empire
shah
Safavid Empire
Mughal Empire

SOCIETY: Turkic
ghazi ideal
castes

GOVERNMENT: Leaders
Ivan IV (Russia)
Tamerlane
Suleiman I (Ottoman
 Empire)
Ismail (Safavid Empire)
Shah Abbas I (Safavid
 Empire)
Akbar (Mughal Empire)

Source: Wikimedia Commons
Author: shakko

This statue was made after Tamerlane was exhumed in 1941. It represents accurate facial reconstruction based on his skull. Examination of his skeleton also revealed that he was indeed "lame"—he kept his right knee bent all the time. He also had a withered right arm. Tamerlane's invasion of Central Asia and the Middle East set the stage for the rise of the Turkic empires.

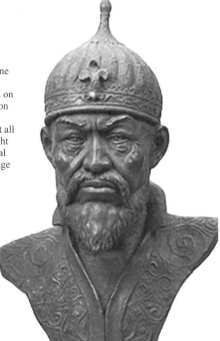

Questions 1 to 3 refer to the passage below.

"Throughout the sixteenth century, the Safavi [Safavid] empire remained a profoundly disturbing force in the Moslem [Muslim] world, dedicated to the defense and propagation of Shi'a doctrines at home and abroad. This policy implied a normal state of hostility with the Ottoman empire, punctuated only briefly by periods of peace. By the seventeenth century, however, when the Safavi empire reached its apogee [peak] under Shah Abbas the Great (1587–1629), the fanaticism of the Shi'a revolution had faded, at least in court circles; and a lasting peace with the Ottomans was concluded in 1639."

William H. McNeill, *The Rise of the West*, 1963

1. Which would be the most useful source of evidence to support McNeill's contention that "the Safavi [Safavid] empire remained a profoundly disturbing force in the Moslem [Muslim] world"?

   (A) A private diary written by an Ottoman government official

   (B) A biography written in 2018 by an anti-Shi'a leader

   (C) A Hollywood movie script about Shah Abbas I

   (D) A campaign speech by Iran's current leader on his country's history

2. Today, Iran and Turkey are often political rivals. This passage suggests that this rivalry is based on historical conflicts over

   (A) democracy and political extremism

   (B) control of the cities of Medina and Mecca

   (C) the role of leaders such as the shah and emperor

   (D) how to practice Islam correctly

3. What brought an end to the "normal state of hostility" between the Safavids and Ottomans mentioned in the passage?

   (A) Safavid fervor for its brand of Islam slowly declined until the two empires stopped fighting.

   (B) The constant fighting increased the respect of the empires for each other, which eventually led to peace between them.

   (C) Both sides united to fight against European Christian forces that threatened them.

   (D) The Ottomans slowly weakened until the Safavids no longer saw them as a threat.

1. Use the passage below to answer all parts of the question that follows.

"[H]aving on one occasion asked my father [Akbar] the reason why he had forbidden any one to prevent or interfere with the building of these haunts of idolatry [Hindu temples], his reply was. . . : 'I find myself a powerful monarch, the shadow of God upon earth. I have seen that he bestows the blessings of his gracious providence upon all his creatures without distinction. Ill [badly] should I discharge the duties of my exalted station, were I to withhold my compassion and indulgence from any of those entrusted to my charge. With all of the human race, with all of God's creatures, I am at peace: why then should I permit myself, under any consideration, to be the cause of molestation or aggression to any one? Besides, are not five parts in six of mankind either Hindus or aliens to the faith; and were I to be governed by motives of the kind suggested in your inquiry, what alternative do I have but to put them all to death! I have thought it therefore my wisest plan to let these men alone.' "

Jahangir, Mughal emperor from 1605 to 1627, *Memoirs*

(A) Identify ONE example of Akbar's display of religious tolerance.

(B) Explain ONE way in which Akbar's response to religious diversity compared to the practices of the Mongols during the 13th century.

(C) Explain ONE way in which Akbar's practice of tolerance was different from the religious tolerance of the Safavids.

2. Answer all parts of the question that follows.

(A) Identify ONE way in which technological advances affected the expansion of the land-based empires.

(B) Explain ONE reason the Gunpowder Empires rose during the period 1450–1750.

(C) Explain ONE way in which the cultures of the Gunpowder Empires differed from one another.

THINK AS A HISTORIAN: EXPLAIN THE HISTORICAL CONCEPT
OF EMPIRE

In this topic, you read about the expansion of empires between 1450 and 1750, especially in Russia, China, and Southwest, Central, and South Asia. Although it may seem obvious what an empire is, historians have thought carefully about the *concept* of an empire. A concept is a general, abstract idea often formed from specific instances.

For example, Paul James and Tom Nairn, editors of *Globalization and Violence*, conceptualize "empire" this way:

> "As a general phenomenon, empires extend relations of power across territorial spaces over which they have no prior or given legal sovereignty, and where, in one or more of the domains of economics, politics, and culture, they gain some measure of extensive hegemony over those spaces for the purpose of extracting or accruing value."

Steven Howe, in his book *Empire*, argues that an empire typically also has diverse ethnic, national, cultural, and religious elements under its power.

If you combine these conceptualizations and then break them down into their component parts, you would likely come up with these features of empires:

- extension of power over spaces in which they have no previous or legal control
- exertion of major control of economic, political, or cultural aspects of subjects
- extraction or accumulation of value as a result of domination
- control of diverse ethnic, national, cultural, and religious elements

Choose two of the following empires, and explain how well they fit with the concepts of empire outlined above.

1. Qing Dynasty   **3.** Safavid Empire

2. Ottoman Empire   **4.** Mughal Empire

REFLECT ON THE TOPIC ESSENTIAL QUESTION

1. In one to three paragraphs, explain how certain land-based empires developed and expanded in the period from 1450–1750.

Empires: Administrations

The state of monarchy is the supremest thing upon earth:
for kings are not only God's lieutenants upon earth, and sit upon
God's throne, but even by God himself they are called gods.

—King James I (1566–1625)

Essential Question: How did rulers in land-based empires legitimize and consolidate their power from 1450 to 1750?

By the end of the 16th century, centralization of power by controlling taxes, the army, and some aspects of religion coalesced into a system of government that led to a powerful monarch in England and absolute monarchy in France. In other states, different methods were used to solidify authority: building temples, as with the Inca; paying the military elite a salary, as with the samurai in Japan; and forcibly establishing a captive governmental bureaucracy, as with the Ottoman devshirme system.

Rulers of empires in the years 1450 to 1750 developed methods for assuring they maintained control of all the regions of their empires. Some of the successful methods included using bureaucratic elites to oversee sections of the empire and developing a professional military.

Centralizing Control in Europe

England's King James I believed in the **divine right of kings**, a common claim from the Middle Ages that the right to rule was given to a king by God. Under this belief, a king was a political and religious authority. As seen in the quote above, James believed himself outside of the law and any earthly authority and saw any challenge toward him as a challenge to God.

England's Gentry Officials In England, the Tudors (ruled 1485–1603) relied on **justices of the peace,** officials selected by the landed gentry to "swear that as Justices of the Peace . . . in all articles in the King's Commission to you directed, ye shall do equal right to the poor and to the rich after your cunning wit, and power, and after the laws and customs of the realm and statutes thereof made," according to their oath of office. In other words, their job was to maintain peace in the counties of England, even settling some legal matters, and to carry out the monarch's laws. The number and responsibilities of the justices of the peace increased through the years of Tudor rule, and they became among the most important and powerful groups in the kingdom. Under Tudor rule, the power of feudal lords weakened. Many seats in the House of Commons in Parliament were occupied by justices of the peace. The justices of the peace as well as the Parliament, which had been established in 1265, gave legitimacy to the monarch's claim to authority.

Parliament also checked the monarch's powers. In 1689, England's rulers William and Mary signed the **English Bill of Rights**, which assured individual civil liberties. For example, legal process was required before someone could be arrested and detained. The Bill of Rights also guaranteed protection against tyranny of the monarchy by requiring the agreement of Parliament on matters of taxation and raising an army.

Absolutism in France In contrast to developments in England, the French government became more **absolute**—directed by one source of power, the king, with complete authority—in the 17th and 18th centuries. Henry IV (ruled 1589–1610) of the House of Valois listened to his advisor Jean Bodin, who advocated the divine right of the monarchy. Building on these ideas, Louis XIII (ruled 1610–1643) and his minister **Cardinal Richelieu** moved to even greater centralization of the government and development of the system of intendants. These **intendants** were royal officials—bureaucratic elites— sent out to the provinces to execute the orders of the central government. The intendants themselves were sometimes called **tax farmers** because they oversaw the collection of various taxes in support of the royal governments.

The Sun King, **Louis XIV** (ruled 1643–1715), espoused a theory of divine right and was a virtual dictator. His aims were twofold, just as those of Richelieu had been: He wanted to hold absolute power and expand French borders. Louis declared that he was the state: "L'etat, c'est moi." He combined the lawmaking and the justice system in his own person—he was absolute. He kept nobles close to him in his palace at **Versailles**, making it difficult for them to act independently or plot against him. Louis and his successors' refusal to share power eventually weakened the French government.

Kangxi and Louis XIV		
Emperor Kangxi	**Both**	**King Louis XIV**
• Ruled Qing Dynasty China for 61 years • Encouraged introduction of Western education • Opened ports to foreign trade • Extended control over Tibet	• Became ruler during childhood • Spoke multiple languages • Supported the arts • Promoted study of sciences • Loved landscape gardens • Ruled during golden age of their empire	• Ruled France for 72 years • Known as the Sun King or Louis the Great • Built palace at Versailles • Extended France's eastern borders • Known as a symbol of absolute monarchy

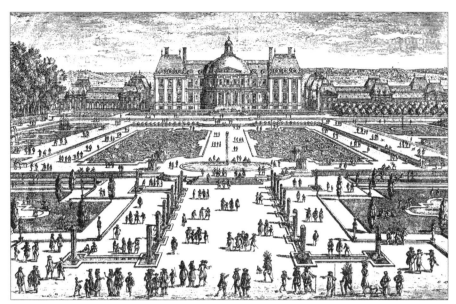

Source: Getty Images

Every aspect of the Palace at Versailles was built to glorify King Louis XIV, including more than 700 rooms, 60 staircases, and gardens that cover more than 30,000 acres and are decorated with 400 sculptures and 1,400 fountains. The Sun King moved the French government to Versailles in 1682.

Reigning in Control of the Russian Empire

Social hierarchy in Moscow was almost static—much as it had been in Kievan Russia earlier. The noble landowning class, the **boyars**, stood at the top of the social pyramid. Below them were the merchants. Last and most numerous were the peasants, who would gradually sink more and more deeply into debt and, as a result, into **serfdom**. Serfs were peasants who received a plot of land and protection from a noble. In return, the serfs were bound to that land and had little personal freedom. Transfers of land ownership to another noble included control over the serfs on that land.

The Efforts of Ivan IV The boyar class experienced tensions with the rulers similar to the tensions between nobles and rulers in Western Europe. Boyars of Novgorod had opposed the expansionist policies of **Ivan IV**, so Ivan punished them after his forces defeated Novgorod. Ivan IV confiscated the lands of his boyar opponents and forced them and their families to move to Moscow. Like Louis XIV, he wanted to keep an eye on the nobility.

To further control the boyars, Ivan established a paramilitary force loyal to him called the *oprichnina*. Dressed in black and traveling quickly on horseback, the members showed fierce loyalty to Ivan. They were drawn from lower-level bureaucrats and merchants to assure their loyalty to Ivan rather than to the boyars. The oprichnina's methods would be reflected later in the development of the Russian secret police. (Connect: Create a table comparing Ivan IV and Sundiata. See Topic 2.4.)

Peter the Great The **Romanov Dynasty** took control of Russia in 1613 after a period of turmoil following Ivan's death in 1584. Under the autocratic control of the Romanovs, three main groups in Russia had conflicting desires and agendas: the Church, bent on conserving traditional values and beliefs; the boyars, desiring to gain and hold power; and members of the tsar's royal family. The rise to power of **Peter I**, also known as Peter the Great (ruled 1682–1725), illustrates these conflicting ambitions. First, to gain full control of the throne, Peter had to defeat his half-sister Sophia and her supporters, a boyar-led elite military corps called the Streltsy. He consolidated power by forcing Sophia into a convent. Later, the Streltsy rebelled against Peter's reign, so he temporarily disbanded them and then integrated them into Russia's regular army.

Peter the Great was known as the Defender of Orthodoxy, participating closely in ecclesiastical [church] affairs. However, Peter would eventually lose the support of the Russian clergy over his reforms. Later in his reign, Peter reorganized the Russian government by creating provinces (first 8 and later 50 administrative divisions). Provincial officials received a salary, replacing the old system of local officials "feeding off the land" (getting money through bribes, fees, and taxes). Another government reform was the creation of a senate, a council to advise government officials when Peter was away.

Centralizing Control in the Ottoman Empire

To ensure their control over large areas, the Ottoman sultans used a selection system called **devshirme** to staff their military and their government. This system began in the late 14th century and expanded in the 15th and 16th centuries. Through this system, Christian boys who were subjects of the empire were recruited by force to serve in the Ottoman government. Boys ages 8 to 20 were taken each year from conquered Christian lands in Europe.

The system of devshirme developed from an earlier system of slavery in the Ottoman Empire. In both systems, enslaved people were considered tribute owed to the empire after conquest, which was typically one-fifth of the conquered land's wealth. Since Islamic law prohibited enslavement of "people of the book"—Muslims and Jews—Christian boys were forcibly removed from their families, especially from Balkan territories.

The Christian boys were taught various skills in politics, the arts, and the military and received a very high level of education. The most famous group, called **Janissaries**, formed elite forces in the Ottoman army. Other boys were groomed to become administrators of the newly conquered territories; some were scribes, tax collectors, and even diplomats. They were indoctrinated to be fiercely loyal to the sultan—some served as bodyguards. In some ways, becoming a Janissary provided a path of upward mobility in the Ottoman Empire, even though the Janissaries continued to be called "slaves of the state." Some parents even wanted their sons to be recruited into the service.

Centralizing Control in East and South Asia

Following the collapse of the Mongol-led Yuan Dynasty, the Ming ruled in China from 1368–1644. The Ming Dynasty in China wanted to erase the influence of Mongol rulers of the Yuan Dynasty. To help accomplish this goal, the Ming brought back the traditional civil service exam, improved education by establishing a national school system, and reestablished the bureaucracy, which had fallen into disuse under the Mongols. (See Topic 2.2.) During the Qing Dynasty, in the later part of Qianlong's reign, the traditionally efficient Chinese bureaucracy became corrupt, levying high taxes on the people. The Qing government used harsh military control to put down a rebellion against these developments and maintain its authority.

Consolidating Power in Japan Military leaders called shoguns ruled Japan in the emperor's name from the 12th to the 15th centuries. Yet conflict between landholding aristocrats called **daimyo** left Japan in disarray. Each daimyo had an army of warriors (known as samurai); ambition to conquer more territory; and power to rule his fiefdoms as he saw fit. The samurai were salaried, paid first in rice and later in gold, which gave them significant economic power. Finally, just as gunpowder weapons enabled the rise of new empires in Turkey, Persia, and India, gunpowder weapons helped a series of three powerful daimyo to gradually unify Japan. (Connect: Write a paragraph connecting shogun rule with the rule of the daimyo. See Topic 1.1.)

The first of these powerful daimyo was Oda Nobunaga. Armed with muskets purchased from Portuguese traders, Nobunaga and his samurai took over Kyoto in 1568. He then began to extend his power, forcing daimyo in the lands around Kyoto to submit. Nobunaga had unified about one-third of what is today Japan when he was assassinated in 1582.

Nobunaga's successor, Toyotomi Hideyoshi, continued expanding the territory until most of what we now know as Japan was under his control. After his death in 1598, the center of power shifted to the city of **Edo** (Tokyo), controlled by the daimyo **Tokugawa Ieyasu** (ruled 1600–1616), who was declared shogun in 1603. His successors would continue to rule Japan into the mid-19th century, in an era known as the **Period of Great Peace.**

The **Tokugawa shogunate** set about reorganizing the governance of Japan in order to centralize control over what was essentially a feudal system. Japan was divided into 250 hans, or territories, each of which was controlled by a daimyo who had his own army and was fairly independent. However, the Tokugawa government required that daimyo maintain residences both in their home territory and also in the capital; if the daimyo himself was visiting his home territory, his family had to stay in Tokyo, essentially as hostages. This kept the daimyo under the control of the shogunate, reducing them to landlords who managed the hans, rather than independent leaders.

Consolidating Mughal Power in South Asia Ruling from 1556 to 1605, **Akbar** proved to be the most capable of the Mughal rulers. For the first 40 years of his rule, he defeated Hindu armies and extended his empire southward and westward. From his capital in **Delhi**, Akbar established an efficient government and a system of fairly administered laws. For example, all his people had the right to appeal to him for final judgment in any lawsuit. As Akbar's fame spread, capable men from many parts of Central Asia came to serve him. They helped Akbar create a strong, centralized government and an effective civil service. Paid government officials called **zamindars** were in charge of specific duties, such as taxation, construction, and the water supply.

Later, they were given grants of land rather than salaries but were permitted to keep a portion of the taxes paid by local peasants, who contributed one-third of their produce to the government. The system worked well under Akbar. Under the rulers who came after him, though, the zamindars began to keep more of the taxes that they collected. With this money, they built personal armies of soldiers and civilians loyal to them.

Legitimizing Power through Religion and Art

European governments sought to legitimize the authority of the monarch through the idea of the divine right of monarchy. (For more information about the divine right of monarchy, see Topic 3.3.) They also built impressive structures, such as the Palace of Versailles in France, to demonstrate their power and glory. Governments in other parts of the world followed similar patterns to consolidate and legitimize their authority. (See Topic 1.4 for links among religion, grand temples and pyramids, human sacrifice, and political power in the Mexica and Incan cultures.)

Peter and St. Petersburg When Peter the Great seized lands on the Baltic Sea from Sweden, the conquest gave Russia its own warm-water port on the Baltic—St. Petersburg. Peter moved the Russian capital from Moscow to St. Petersburg so he could keep watch on the boyars there, who were doing their required state service by working in his government.

The new city became a testament to Peter's determination to have his own capital. Architects laid out streets in a rectangular grid, unlike the irregular pattern of Moscow and other cities. Peasants and Swedish prisoners of war were forced to work, draining marshes and building streets and government structures. In the mid-18th century, workers built the famous Winter Palace. It was designed in a European rather than a Byzantine style to show Peter's admiration of Europe and its rulers.

Askia the Great of Songhai Askia Mohammad I, or **Askia the Great**, came to power in 1493. He claimed his predecessor, Sunni Ali, was not a faithful Muslim. Like Mansa Musa of Mali, Askia the Great promoted Islam throughout his kingdom and made an elaborate pilgrimage to Mecca. Under his leadership, Songhai became the largest kingdom in its day in West Africa. Askia made Islam Songhai's official religion in an attempt to unite his empire. In addition to legitimizing his rule through promoting Islam, he also supported an efficient bureaucracy to bring the empire together.

Shah Jahan Mughal India produced a number of magnificent architectural accomplishments, including the **Taj Mahal**, built by **Shah Jahan** (ruled 1628–1658) as a tomb for his wife. Mughal rulers also beautified Delhi and had forts built. The craftspeople and builders of Mughal India combined the arts of Islam (calligraphy, illumination of manuscripts, and ceramics) with local arts to create magnificent, airy structures with decorative geometric designs. All these accomplishments showed the power of the rulers.

Ottoman Architectural and Artistic Achievements Tremendous changes in government and religion took place in Ottoman territory. However, the arts, the culture, and the economy showed continuities, though they now legitimized the rule of the Ottomans. Constantinople, renamed Istanbul, remained the western end of the overland Silk Roads, and the Grand Bazaar there continued to be full of foreign imports. Coffeehouses, although banned by Islamic law, continued to do a thriving business throughout the towns of the empire.

Source: Thinkstock

Source: Thinkstock

Source: Thinkstock

The Islamic Gunpowder Empires built monumental architecture with spiritual significance. The Ottomans built the Suleymaniye Mosque in Istanbul (top). The Safavids built the Mosque of Isfahan (lower left). The Mughals built the Taj Mahal, a mausoleum, in Agra. (lower right).

Istanbul grew more beautiful and expanded across both sides of the Strait of Bosporus. One famous landmark is the royal residence of the sultans, *Topkapi Palace*. Mehmed II (lived 1432–1481) began construction on this landmark. Suleiman I (lived 1494–1566) ordered many mosques, forts, and other great buildings constructed in the cities under his control. For example, he ordered the construction in Istanbul of the magnificent Suleymaniye Mosque.

Istanbul remained a center of arts and learning. Poets and scholars from across Asia met in coffeehouses and gardens. They discussed works by Aristotle and other Greek writers, as well as the works of many Arabic scholars. Cultural contributions of the Ottomans included the restoration of some of the glorious buildings of Constantinople, most notably the cathedral of Saint Sophia (which the Ottomans turned into a grand mosque). From the time of Mehmed II, who established a workshop for their production, Ottoman miniature paintings and illuminated manuscripts became famous.

French Architecture The spacious and elegant palace at **Versailles** became a political instrument. Louis XIV entertained the nobles there and kept them from conducting business elsewhere, such as fomenting rebellion in their home provinces. Louis XIV's grand buildings at Versailles helped legitimize his power. The palace at Versailles, for example, could accommodate hundreds of guests. During the rule of Louis XIV, some 1,000 employees worked in the palace or on the grounds.

Financing Empires

As in other matters of building and maintaining empires, different methods of raising money worked—or fell short—in different empires. In all of the world's empires, raising money to fund the goals of imperial expansion and extend state power was a key endeavor.

Taxation in Russia Peter established new industries owned by the state, especially shipyards in St. Petersburg and iron mines in the Ural Mountains. He also encouraged private industries such as metallurgy [technology of metal products], woodwork, gunpowder, leather, paper, and mining. He brought in Western European naval engineers to build ships according to Western models.

When industrialization failed to bring in the revenue Peter needed for his military ventures, he raised taxes and began to compel workers to work in the shipyards—a sort of urban extension of serfdom. In 1718, the tax on land in Russia was replaced by a tax on heads (individuals), and peasants became more oppressed than ever.

Ottoman and Mughal Taxation To finance an economy backed by a powerful military, the Ottomans levied taxes on the peasants and used **tax farming** to collect it. The tax farmers—local officials and private tax collectors distant from the central government—grew wealthy and corrupt from skimming money from the taxes in their areas, as some of the zamindars did in the Mughal Empire. Agricultural villages continued to be burdened with the upkeep of officers and troops. This burden of taxes and the military would eventually contribute to the economic decline of the empire.

Tax Collection in the Ming Dynasty In Ming China as well as in the Ottoman Empire, tax collection was the responsibility of private citizens, in this case wealthy families, each seeing to the collection of land taxes in their area of the countryside. Land taxes made up the bulk of the taxes collected, and the rates tended to be low. Taxes were collected in the form of grains and, later, silver. Some grains were stored in local facilities. Others were sent on the Grand Canal to military locations. The state also collected taxes on salt, wine, and other goods. For many years, the vaults stored a surplus of grains. However, after about 1580, wars, extravagant imperial spending, and the repression of rebellions left the dynasty in bankruptcy.

Tributes Empires, including China, also collected **tributes** from other states as a way to demand recognition of their power and authority. Typically as a form of wealth, tributes were given as a sign of respect, submission, or allegiance. For example, Korea was a tributary state for China. The Mexica had extensive tributary arrangements from the people they conquered, although most Aztec citizens, merchants, and artisans paid taxes. An Aztec official was stationed in each capital to collect tributes from local officials.

The Songhai Empire also had tributary states. Askia the Great assigned governors and officials to preside over tributary states in the Niger Valley. As long as local officials obeyed Songhai policies, they could rule their districts.

KEY TERMS BY THEME

GOVERNMENT: Europe
divine right of kings

GOVERNMENT: England
justices of the peace
English Bill of Rights

GOVERNMENT: France
absolute
Cardinal Richelieu
intendants
Louis XIV

GOVERNMENT: Russia
Ivan IV
Romanov Dynasty
Peter I

GOVERNMENT: Ottoman Empire
devshirme
Janissaries

GOVERNMENT: Japan
daimyo
Edo
Tokugawa Ieyasu
Period of Great Peace
Tokugawa shogunate

GOVERNMENT: Songhai
Askia the Great

GOVERNMENT: Mughal Empire
Akbar
Delhi
Shah Jahan

ECONOMY: France
tax farmers

ECONOMY: Ottoman Empire
tax farming

ECONOMY: China
tributes

ECONOMY: Mughal Empire
zamindars

CULTURE: Mughal Empire
Taj Mahal

CULTURE: France
Versailles

SOCIETY: Russia
boyars
serfdom

MULTIPLE-CHOICE QUESTIONS

Questions 1 to 3 refer to the passage below.

"Demonized as an enemy of the faith by the Muslim narrative sources, yet lionized as a warrior hero in the oral tradition, Sunni Ali, who reigned from 1464 to 1492, is one of the most controversial figures of the African Middle Ages. . . . Relying on a swift and mobile cavalry force as well as on naval control of the Niger River, Sunni Ali had conquered the agriculturally rich central Niger or 'inland delta,' including the wealthy and scholarly cities of Timbuktu and Jenne, by the 1470s. . . . He was well aware that a vast empire could not be held together by military conquests alone, but need[ed] an effective and efficient administrative structure as well. Indeed, the organization of Songhay [Songhai] government which was developed to a great degree under Sunni Ali differed substantially from previous Sudanic patterns of empire. These had been based more on alliances and relationships with tributary states than on the high degree of centralization characteristic of Songhay [Songhai]."

> J. Rotondo-McCord, "Kingdoms of the Medieval Sudan," Xavier University,
> http://webusers.xula.edu/jrotondo/Kingdoms/Songhay/SunniAli01.html

1. The Songhai Empire was like Japan under the Tokugawa shogunate because the Songhai
   (A) created a strong central government
   (B) expanded its territory by creating distant colonies
   (C) was ruled by a Muslim
   (D) was the first empire in its region to trade gold extensively

2. The Songhai Empire under Sunni Ali was different from the empire under Askia the Great because
   (A) Sunni Ali made a pilgrimage to Mecca
   (B) Askia used religion to legitimize his control
   (C) Sunni Ali made Songhai the largest kingdom in West Africa
   (D) Askia used zamindars to collect taxes

3. How did Askia the Great challenge Sunni Ali's legitimacy?
   (A) He claimed Sunni Ali was a weak military commander.
   (B) He questioned Sunni Ali's faithfulness to the principles of Islam.
   (C) He established strong tributary ties that had more allegiances to him than to Sunni Ali.
   (D) He reformed taxation policies throughout the kingdom.

1. **Use the passage below to answer all parts of the question that follows.**

"Farmers of all provinces are strictly forbidden to have in their possession any swords, short swords, bows, spears, firearms, or other types of weapons. If unnecessary implements of war are kept, the collection of annual rent *(nengu)* may become more difficult, and without provocation uprisings can [occur]. . . . The heads of the provinces, samurai who receive a grant of land, and deputies must collect all the weapons described above and submit them to Hideyoshi's government. . . . If farmers possess only agricultural implements and devote themselves exclusively to cultivating the fields, they and their descendants will prosper. This compassionate concern for the well-being of the farms is the reason for the issuance of this edict, and such concern is the foundation for the peace and security of the country and the joy and happiness of all the people."

> Toyotomi Hideyoshi, Imperial Regent of Japan, edicts issued
> in 1588

(A) Identify ONE technological advance that allowed Hideyoshi and other shoguns to enforce such edicts over farmers.

(B) Explain ONE way in which Hideyoshi's goals were similar to those of Louis XIV.

(C) Explain ONE interpretation historians could develop of Hideyoshi's ideas about the Japanese economy from this piece of evidence.

2. **Answer all parts of the question that follows.**

(A) Identify ONE way in which political structures of Europeans differed from those of the Ottomans in the period 1450–1750.

(B) Explain ONE way in which political structures of the Aztecs were similar to those in China in the period 1450–1750.

(C) Explain ONE reason that the Mughal leaders constructed impressive buildings for worship and as memorials during the period of 1450–1750.

THINK AS A HISTORIAN: CONTEXTUALIZING ACROSS CULTURES

One way historians contextualize is by examining what came before and what came after an event or development within a culture (see page 14). Contextualization is also useful across cultures. To contextualize a specific development across cultures, ask: In what other cultures were there similar developments? In what ways were those developments similar to the specific development in the culture under study? In what ways were those developments different from the specific development in the culture under study? As you answer these questions, think about origins, purposes, and outcomes.

Consider the development of the devshirme system. Within the context of global slavery between 1450 and 1750, how was devshirme like or unlike slavery elsewhere, and why? Complete a chart like the one below to contextualize devshirme in a broader setting. Then draw a conclusion about the devshirme system.

Region/Culture	Origins	Purposes	Outcomes
Ottomans	Tribute from conquered people	Educated and trained for administrative and military service and paid a salary	Became influential members of society and first standing army
Americas			
China			
Africa			

REFLECT ON THE TOPIC ESSENTIAL QUESTION

1. In one to three paragraphs, explain how rulers in land-based empires legitimized and consolidated their power from 1450 to 1750.

3.3

Empires: Belief Systems

Paris is well worth a Mass.

–Henry of Navarre, King of France (ruled 1589–1610)

Essential Question: How did different belief systems endure or change during the period from 1450–1750?

Religion, a key factor in the expansion of empires, was a divisive force as much as it was a unifying one. Christianity remained a dominant force in Europe, but its split into several factions during the 16th and 17th centuries led to significant historical changes. French King Henry IV, often known as Henry of Navarre, converted to Catholicism in 1593 for the sake of solidifying his power and ensuring peace, as the quote above suggests. His action demonstrates the willingness of monarchs to approach ruling with practicality rather than theology. Henry IV also sanctioned religious toleration of the Huguenots (French Calvinists).

Islam, too, experienced a split, and political rivalries between the Ottoman and Safavid empires deepened the breach between the Sunni and Shi'a branches of the religion. At the same time, Sikhism provided a way to combine Hindu and Sufi Muslim beliefs.

Protestant Reformation

The Roman Catholic Church faced many challenges in the European shift from feudalism to centralized governments. International in organization and influence and boasting a large bureaucracy of its own, the Church was subject to corruption. Efforts to curb corruption resulted in numerous Church councils and reform movements. However, efforts at reform were unsuccessful.

Theological disagreements began to surface as well. John Wycliffe and the Lollards (advocates of Catholic doctrine reforms and Wycliffe followers) in England in the late 14th century argued that priests were unnecessary for salvation. Wycliffe was vilified for translating parts of the Bible into the English vernacular to make it available to the mass of believers, who neither read nor understood Latin. In the early 14th century, Hussites, followers of Jan Hus in Bohemia, were declared heretics for beliefs similar to Wycliffe's. Hus himself was burned at the stake. Huldrych Zwingli campaigned in Geneva for a religion that would follow the exact teachings of the scriptures and discard customs that had evolved later. For example, he opposed the requirement for celibacy of the clergy because he argued that the rule was imposed long after the scriptures were written.

The power of the Church suffered during the so-called Babylonian Captivity (1309–1377), when the papacy was located in France rather than in Rome. The Captivity gave French rulers greater influence over the Church, even the ability to decide who should be pope. Newly centralizing rulers who coveted Church lands and authority began confiscating wealthy Catholic monasteries and sometimes established their own churches. In the eyes of believers, the Church suffered further when it failed to stop the Black Death. (Connect: Write a paragraph connecting the Reformation with the problems of the medieval Church. See Topic 1.6.)

Lutheranism A monk named **Martin Luther** in Wittenberg, a German city in the Holy Roman Empire (800–1806), concluded that several traditional Church practices violated biblical teachings. He objected to the sale of **indulgences**, which granted a person absolution from the punishments for sin, and to **simony**, the selling of church offices. As a result, Luther defiantly challenged the Church by nailing his charges, the *95 Theses*, to a church door. Luther advocated for the theological stance of "sola fide," faith alone, for the basis of salvation for the Christian believer.

The Church reacted harshly. It, and the local political ruler, needed the money these practices generated. Luther persisted. In January 1521, Pope Leo X excommunicated Luther. Several German political leaders saw an opportunity to free themselves from the power of the pope. They sided with Luther. Soon, what had begun as a minor academic debate became a major split in the Roman Catholic Church and the Holy Roman Empire.

Luther was not a political or social revolutionary. (When German peasants rebelled, he did not support them.) But his theological ideas had social impact on the clergy as well as on women. Luther taught that women could have direct access to God just as men could. Luther's emphasis promoted women's literacy. He believed that women had significant roles in the family, particularly teaching their children to read the Bible. However, Protestants generally did not organize convents. As a result, Protestant women did not have the opportunity to become leaders in a vital institution the way Roman Catholic women did.

Calvinism The French theologian **John Calvin** broke with the Catholic Church around 1530. In 1536, he authored *The Institutes of the Christian Religion* and helped reform the religious community in Geneva, Switzerland. The **elect**, those **predestined** to go to heaven, ran the community, which was based on plain living, simple church buildings, and governance by the elders of the church. Calvin's followers in France were called Huguenots. Other offshoots of Calvinism included the Reformed Church of Scotland, led by John Knox, and the **Puritans** in England and later in Boston, who wanted to purify the Church of England of Catholic remnants. Historian and sociologist Max Weber pointed out that an important socioeconomic impact of Calvinism is contained in the phrase "Protestant work ethic." Calvinists were encouraged to work hard and reinvest their profits; prosperity ostensibly showed that God favored their obedience and hard work. Prosperity also indicated their position among the elect. Calvinists viewed their work ethic as righteous living that elevated them to positions of secular leadership. Together, the various reform efforts are known as the **Protestant Reformation**.

DOMINANT FAITHS IN WESTERN EUROPE IN 1560

Anglicanism The last of the three major figures of the Reformation was England's King **Henry VIII** (ruled 1509–1547). Henry wanted a male heir to succeed him. After his wife gave birth to several daughters, Henry asked the pope to annul his marriage so he could marry another woman, **Anne Boleyn**. But the pope refused out of worry over the reaction of **Charles V**, the powerful emperor of the Holy Roman Empire. Henry, with the approval of the English Parliament, set himself up as head of the new Church of England, or **Anglican Church**—one that would be free of control by the pope in Rome.

The Orthodox Church and Reforms in Russia

Charles V had revitalized the concept of the universal monarchy and spent most of his reign defending the integrity of the Holy Roman Empire from the Protestant Reformation. Like Charles V, Peter the Great of Russia asserted his authority as he moved against the Orthodox Church. The Church had long been the force unifying the Russian people and the tsars, who claimed to rule by divine right. Peter confirmed his power over the Church by abolishing the position of patriarch, the head of the Church, and incorporating the Church into the government. In place of the patriarch, he established the **Holy Synod**, composed of clergymen overseen by a secular official who answered to the tsar. Peter raised the minimum age for men to become eligible to be monks to 50, preferring that the young serve first as soldiers. Peter's reforms were not welcomed by many peasants and Old Believers, a sect that opposed earlier reforms.

Counter-Reformation or Catholic Reformation

The Roman Catholic Church, all-powerful in Europe since the fall of Rome, did not sit quietly by and let the Reformation groups take over. Instead, it embarked on a vigorous **Counter-Reformation** to fight against the Protestant attacks. A three-pronged strategy yielded such gains for the Church that it remains the largest Christian denomination in the world:

- The Church increased the use of the **Inquisition**, which had been established in the late 12th century to root out and punish nonbelievers. The Inquisition sometimes allowed the use of torture to achieve its ends.

- The **Jesuits**, or Society of Jesus, a religious order founded in 1540 by Ignatius of Loyola, also opposed the spread of Protestantism. The Jesuits undertook missionary activity throughout the Spanish Empire as well as in Japan and India.

- The **Council of Trent** (1545–1563) corrected some of the worst of the Church's abuses and concentrated on reaffirming the rituals such as marriage and other sacraments improving the education of priests. The Council also published the *Index of Prohibited Books*, a list of writings that the Church banned, including Protestant copies of the Bible and the writings of Copernicus.

The Counter-Reformation was successful in that Catholicism remained predominant in the areas of Western Europe near the Mediterranean Sea. Moreover, later colonies of the European powers often followed the lead of the home country in religion. Therefore, most of the people in the Spanish, Portuguese, and French colonies became Catholic.

Charles V abdicated as ruler of the Holy Roman Empire in 1555, discouraged by his inability to stop the spread of Lutheranism. He left Spain to his son **Philip II** and the Holy Roman Empire to his brother Ferdinand. Philip II took the Catholic crusade to the Netherlands and ruled its 17 provinces from 1556 to 1581. He later tried to conquer and convert England. In 1588, his **Spanish Armada** was defeated by English naval power.

Wars of Religion

Europe's religious divisions led to frequent wars. In 1546 and 1547, the forces of Charles V fought the German Lutheran Schmalkaldic League. Conflict between Lutherans and the Holy Roman Empire resulted in the 1555 **Peace of Augsburg**, which allowed each German state to choose whether its ruler would be Catholic or Lutheran. As a result, churches and inhabitants were forced to practice the state religion. People who refused could move to another state where their preferred religion was practiced.

France In France, Catholics and Huguenots fought for nearly half a century. Then, in 1593, King Henry IV, who had been raised as a Protestant, tried to unify the country by becoming a Catholic, reportedly saying that "Paris is well worth a Mass." Five years later, in another step to bring peace, Henry issued the **Edict of Nantes**, which allowed the Huguenots to practice their faith. The edict provided religious toleration in France for the next 87 years. In 1685, Louis XIV of France issued the Revocation of the Edict of Nantes. As a result, France experienced social and economic effects. For example, many skilled craftsmen left France, taking knowledge of important industry techniques and styles with them.

Thirty Years' War The final great religious conflict between Catholics and Protestants in Europe culminated in the **Thirty Years' War** (1618–1648), which led to economic catastrophe for most of the continent. The Thirty Years' War was initially the result of religious conflict within the Holy Roman Empire; it gradually developed into a more general conflict involving European powers. Much of the destruction was caused by troops who were allowed to loot as part of their compensation. The war resulted in widespread famine, starvation, and disease.

The war culminated in the **Peace of Westphalia**, which allowed each area of the Holy Roman Empire to select one of three religious options: Roman Catholicism, Lutheranism, or Calvinism. After this settlement, France, Spain, and Italy were predominantly Catholic. Northern Europe was either Lutheran or Calvinist. England was Protestant with a state church.

Allowing rulers of various areas of the Holy Roman Empire to choose a denomination had important political effects. It gave the countries and duchies much more autonomy than they previously had. Consequently, the states of Prussia (now part of Germany) and Austria began to assert themselves, although they still formally belonged to the Holy Roman Empire. Prussia, after suffering tremendous destruction during the Thirty Years' War, developed a strong military to protect itself. The Prussian military tradition would become a key factor in European politics into the 20th century.

Islamic Religious Schisms

As in the Holy Roman Empire, religion and the state were closely tied in Islamic empires. Islam continued to be an enduring belief system, spreading its sphere of influence despite factions that developed within it.

Ottoman, Safavid, and Mughal Empires, 1450–1750			
	Ottoman Empire	**Safavid Empire**	**Mughal Empire**
Religion	• Mostly Sunni with some measure of tolerance under Suleiman • Less tolerance under later rulers	• Mostly Shi'a • No tolerance; Ismail I made conversion mandatory for Sunni population	• Tolerance under Akbar, but his blend of Islam and Hinduism did not prove popular • Less tolerance under later rulers

Ottoman Empire Until 1453, much of the area had been controlled by the Byzantine Empire and followed the Eastern Orthodox religion. After the siege of Constantinople, the area became Ottoman and the dominant religion became Islam. A sultan replaced the emperor, and the Byzantine Empire's Justinian Law was replaced by **shariah**. This is a strict Islamic legal system that deals with all aspects of life, such as criminal justice, marital laws, and issues of inheritance.

The Safavids Using Shi'a Islam as a unifying force, Shah Ismail built a power base that supported his rule and denied legitimacy to any Sunni. This strict adherence to Shi'a Islam caused frequent hostilities within the Ottoman Empire.

Mughal Toleration and Prosperity Akbar tolerated all religions. He gave money or land to Hindus and Muslims. He also gave money for a Catholic church in Goa, on India's southwest coast. He provided land grants for the relatively new religion of **Sikhism**, which developed from Hinduism and may have been influenced by the Islamic mysticism known as Sufism. (See Topics 1.2 and 1.3.) Sikhism, a monotheistic faith that recognized the rights of other faiths to exist, became the fifth most popular religion in the world by the 21st century. Akbar tried to ease tensions between Hindus and Muslims. He gave Hindus positions in his government—zamindars of high and low positions could be Hindu—and married Hindu wives. He exempted Hindus from poll taxes paid by non-Muslims in the empire. Because he enjoyed religious discussions, Akbar invited Catholic priests to Delhi to explain Christianity to him.

Regarded as one of the world's outstanding rulers, Akbar encouraged learning, art, architecture, and literature. He tried (and failed) to prohibit child marriages and sati, the ritual in which widows killed themselves by jumping on the funeral pyres of their husbands. He died in 1605 without successfully converting his Hindu and Islamic subjects to the religion called Din-i Ilahi, or "divine faith," which he had promoted to reconcile Hinduism and Islam.

Religious Schisms Through History			
Religion and Region	**Schism**	**Leaders**	**Nature of Dispute**
Buddhism in India	Theravada and Mahayana (approximately 300 B.C.E. to 100 C.E.)	• Four councils held after the Buddha's death	Disagreement between emphasis on personal meditation (Theravada) and public rituals and compassion (Mahayana)
Islam in Middle East	Sunni and Shi'a (632 C.E.)	• Abu Bakr • Ali	Disagreement over the rightful successor to Muhammad as leader of the Islamic community
Christianity in Europe and Byzantine Empire	Roman Catholics and Orthodox (1054 C.E.)	• Pope Leo IX • Patriarch of Constantinople, Michael Cerularius	Disagreement over the role of faith, issues of salvation. Disagreement over the authority of the pope and differences in rituals
Christianity in Europe	Roman Catholics and Protestants (1517 C.E.)	• Martin Luther • John Calvin • King Henry VIII	Disagreements over the role of faith, the role of the clergy and the pope, and how to interpret the Bible

Scientific Revolution

In the early 1600s, scientific thinking gained popularity in northern Europe as trends in Renaissance ideas, curiosity, investigation, and discovery spread. In a period of religious schisms, scientific thought represented a very different kind of thinking—one based on reason rather than on faith—that would set in motion a monumental historical change. In 1620, English scientist and philosopher Francis Bacon developed an early scientific method called **empiricism**, which insisted upon the collection of data to back up a hypothesis. Bacon challenged traditional ideas that had been accepted for centuries and replace them with ones that could be demonstrated with evidence.

Scientific thinking advanced through the correspondence of leading scholars with one another, even during the religious wars, and by the establishment of a Royal Academy of Science in France and England. Sir Isaac Newton, combining Galileo's laws of terrestrial motion and Johannes Kepler's laws of planetary motion, published a work on gravitational force called *Principia* (1687). The ideas in *Principia* influenced science and mathematics and helped lead to a new vision of the world. Many intellectuals thought that science showed that the world was ordered and rational and that natural laws applied to the rational and orderly progress of governments and society. This thinking is a key to the Enlightenment. (See Topic 5.1.)

KEY TERMS BY THEME

GOVERNMENT: Europe
Henry VIII
Anne Boleyn
Charles V
Philip II
Spanish Armada
Peace of Augsburg
Edict of Nantes
Thirty Years' War
Peace of Westphalia

CULTURE: Catholicism
indulgences
simony

Holy Synod
Counter-Reformation
Inquisition
Jesuits
Council of Trent

CULTURE: Protestantism
Martin Luther
95 Theses
John Calvin
elect
predestined

Puritans
Protestant Reformation
Anglican Church

CULTURE: Islam
shariah
Sikhism

CULTURE: Science
empiricism

MULTIPLE-CHOICE QUESTIONS

Questions 1 to 3 refer to the passage below.

"He is very valiant and has a great liking for warfare and weapons of war, which he has constantly in his hands: we have been eye-witnesses of this because, whenever we were with him, he was adjusting his [swords], testing his [muskets], etc . . . This is the great experience, which he has obtained of warfare over so many years, that he makes it in person and from the first has made him a fine soldier and very skilled, and his men so dexterous that they are little behind our men in Europe. He has introduced into his militia the use of and esteem for [muskets], in which they are very practiced. Therefore it is that his realm has been so much extended on all sides. . . . All the above mentioned soldiers, who will total some 100,000, receive pay for the whole year."

> Father Simon, a European Roman Catholic priest, in a report
> to the pope on meeting the Safavid Shah Abbas I, 1588

1. Which claim about Father Simon's purpose for meeting Shah Abbas I is best supported by the above passage?

    (A) Simon was impressed by the new technology used by the Safavids.

    (B) Simon wanted the pope to know of the Safavids' military power.

    (C) Simon hoped the pope would sell new weapons to the Safavids.

    (D) Simon thought the Safavids could teach Europeans about how to organize a military.

2. Which most strongly contributed to the historical development reflected in Father Simon's description of the Safavid military structure?

(A) Safavid intolerance for the Sunni population

(B) Mughal support for Sikhism

(C) Ottoman development of shariah

(D) The Thirty Years' War

3. This source supports the claim that the Safavids were similar to the Ottomans and the Mughals in that all three

(A) used gunpowder weapons

(B) practiced identical religious beliefs

(C) threatened to attack regions of Europe

(D) were ahead of the Europeans in military power

SHORT-ANSWER QUESTIONS

1. Use the passage below to answer all parts of the question that follows.

"Let no one think that this Commandment entirely forbids the arts of painting, engraving, or sculpture. The Scriptures inform us that God Himself commanded to be made images of Cherubim [a category of angel], and also the brazen serpent. The interpretation, therefore, at which we must arrive, is that images are prohibited only inasmuch as they are used as deities to receive adoration, and so to injure the true worship of God. . . .

He [the pastor] will also inform the unlettered . . . of the use of images, that they are intended to instruct in the history of the Old and New Testaments, and to revive from time to time their memory; that thus, moved by the contemplation of heavenly things, we may be the more ardently inflamed to adore and love God Himself. He should, also, point out that the images of the Saints are placed in churches, not only to be honored, but also that they may admonish us by their examples to imitate their lives and virtues."

Council of Trent: Catechism for Parish Priests, 1566

(A) Identify ONE way in which the passage reflects a response to the Protestant Reformation during the period 1450 to 1750.

(B) Explain ONE way in which the passage reflects how the centralization of states impacted the role of religion during the period 1450 to 1750.

(C) Explain ONE way in which the passage reflects how the challenges to the Roman Catholic Church were similar to the religious challenges in the Gunpowder Empires between 1450 and 1750.

2. Answer all parts of the question that follows.

(A) Identify ONE way in which the Protestant Reformation and the Scientific Revolution were similar in the period 1450–1750.

(B) Explain ONE way in which Renaissance ideals influenced European states' policies in the period 1450–1750.

(C) Explain ONE way in which Renaissance ideals influenced the Protestant Reformation in the period 1450–1750.

 THINK AS A HISTORIAN: EXPLAIN POINT OF VIEW IN A SOURCE

While historians try to describe the past fairly, their nationality, ethnicity, gender, and other characteristics can shape their values. In turn, these values shape how they see the past. An interpretation of history is a historian's view of why events happened and why they were significant.

In each pair of statements, which one more clearly represents a point of view of the past that might reflect the values of the writer? Explain the point of view of the choice you identify.

1. Protestant Reformation

a. "Paris is well worth a Mass," King Henry IV wrote in the 16th century, shedding light on how he and other monarchs of his time were willing to bargain and compromise, ruling with practicality rather than theology.

b. A Roman Catholic monk, Martin Luther, presented a set of objections to various Church practices, a document known as the *95 Theses*, to Church leaders in Wittenberg, Germany, on October 31, 1517.

2. Religion and Toleration

a. The final great religious war was the Thirty Years' War (1618–1648), which involved the Netherlands, Denmark, Sweden, France, and Spain.

b. "The humanist project for changing the world was soon caught up in a 'theological road-rage' of grimly competing religious orthodoxies. The liberation symbolized by 1517 took effect in the savage suppression of the Peasants' Revolt, and in the relentless oppression of radicals by Protestants and Catholics alike, culminating in the evisceration of Europe in the Thirty Years' War." —Fleur Houston

---

REFLECT ON THE TOPIC ESSENTIAL QUESTION

1. In one to three paragraphs, explain how different belief systems endured or changed during the period from 1450–1750.

Comparison in Land-Based Empires

Foreigners appreciate only military power. . . . Thus,
they submit to us wholeheartedly and do not dare to despise
China once we display our hunting techniques to them.

—Quinlong, Emperor of China,1735

Essential Question: By what methods did empires increase their societal and cultural influence from c. 1450–c. 1750?

Building and maintaining large land-based empires is a major theme in the period c. 1450–c. 1750. These empires grew as they incorporated lands they conquered. Their rulers implemented policies to solidify or legitimize their rule over a diverse population. However, the conquered often did not totally assimilate to the life and culture of their conquerors. In some cases the conquered influenced the conquerors, helping to shape a blended culture. The interconnection of hemispheres also led to blended cultures.

Source: Wikimedia Commons

As part of its conquest of present-day Hungary, the Ottoman Empire under Suleiman I besieged the Habsburg-controlled city of Esztergom in 1543 with the help of French artillery. The figure at the far left is a Janissary. Suleiman is on horseback.

Not all empires were able to maintain their authority. For example, the Gunpowder Empires declined, unable to compete with European trading companies, especially the British, and unable to resolve conflicts of heirs motivated by harem politics (see Topic 3.1). Other factors in the decline included weak or corrupt leadership and failure to keep up with developments in military and naval technology. The expensive armies each empire needed to maintain control placed harsh financial burdens on the peasants and villages in the form of taxes and other obligations. Religious conflicts also divided and weakened the Gunpowder Empires.

A deep religious schism divided Muslims and Hindus in Mughal India, just as a schism divided Sunni Ottomans and Shi'a Safavids and set the stage for conflict between the present-day countries of Iraq and Iran. (Connect: Write a paragraph comparing the decline of Mughal India with the decline of the Mongol Empire. See Topic 2.1.)

Military Might

The armies of these land-based empires were well trained, well organized, well equipped, and well led. Empires in Eurasia all relied on gunpowder weapons, including large cannons, in support of more traditional cavalry and infantry units. In the Americas, the fierceness of both the Aztec and Incan warriors allowed them to intimidate and conquer neighboring territories.

Soldiers In some cases, the rulers of land-based empires developed an elite group of soldiers to use in solidifying their control over their territories. For instance, both the Ottoman sultan and Safavid shah used enslaved soldiers to offset the power of troops who had more loyalty to their tribe or local governor than to the sultan or shah. The Janissaries in the Ottoman Empire helped to preserve the power of the Ottoman sultan and the Ghulams helped to protect the Safavid shah from rival clans. Both the Janissaries and the Ghulams were often recruited from minority religious or ethnic groups found within the empires. The Janissaries were often enslaved people taken from Christian areas of the Ottoman Empire, while the Ghulams came from the Georgian, Armenian, or Circassian populations within the Safavid Empire. The system of taking people as part of a "blood" tax (in the Ottoman Empire this was known as devshirme) or tribute was not limited to the Ottomans or Safavids. Aztecs also required enslaved people or prisoners as part of the tribute offered by conquered states.

Warfare These strong militaries did not prevent conflict among the land-based empires. The Ottoman Empire and Safavid Empire went to war over the territorial claims each had at its border. However, religion also played a role as an underlying cause of this conflict. The Ottoman Empire was a predominantly Sunni Muslim state, while the Safavids were mainly Shi'a. Each believed the other to practice a heretical type of Islam and was willing to go to war over this split. Religion was not as important a factor in the conflict between the Safavids and the Mughals as it was in the Ottoman-Safavid War. Instead, control over resources and trade routes in present-day Afghanistan was at the core of the war between these two land-based empires.

Two Muslim powers conflicted when Morocco invaded the Songhai Empire in 1591. Moroccan forces sacked the capital of Gao and ended the empire. However, Morocco was unable to hold onto all the Songhai territory.

Centralized Bureaucracy

Controlling a large area with such diverse populations required land-based empires to establish an organized and centralized bureaucracy. Recruiting bureaucratic elites took several forms. In the Ming and Manchu dynasties of China, the civil service examination system was used to assess the abilities of the members of the scholar-gentry who wished to enter government service. In the Ottoman Empire, the devshirme system provided the sultan with a ready-made pool of civil servants strictly loyal to him, while in the Safavid Empire, the shah would enlist a class of bureaucrats from the Persian population of the empire, known as "the men of the pen."

Ottoman, Safavid, and Mughal Empires, 1450–1750			
	Ottoman Empire	Safavid Empire	Mughal Empire
Taxes	• Taxes on non-Muslims • Taxes on peasants	• Taxation policies used to encourage adherence to Shi'a Islam	• Taxes on unbelievers were abolished by Akbar but reinstated later • Taxes on peasants
Military	• Warriors (often trained Janissaries) were granted villages to provide for their subsistence • The military functioned as a dual authority with central government • Strong navy	• Warriors were the Qizilbash, Turcoman militants who helped establish the empire • Leaders made the military independent of central government • No significant navy	• Warriors were granted villages to provide their upkeep • Officials known as zamindars made the military independent of central government • Small navy

In the Songhai Empire, the *mansa*, a Mandika word meaning "sultan," employed bureaucrats from the scholarly class educated in the schools, or madrasas, of Timbuktu. While the Incas did not use a dedicated scholarly class to rule their empire as the Ming and Manchus did, they did organize their empire into a federal system of provinces headed by nobles loyal to the emperor. Further, these nobles oversaw a very organized political structure that was divided on the basis of a decimal system.

Despite its many similarities to other land empires, the Aztec Empire was less centralized and bureaucratic than the other land empires. The Aztec created a tributary empire and had little to no direct control over the territory within the region of Mesoamerica. It kept control over this region through force, fear, and intimidation rather than through a centralized bureaucracy.

Source: Wikimedia Commons

A portrayal of Aztec warriors from the Florentine Codex, written between 1540 and 1549.

Taxation Some form of taxation or revenue collection was necessary to support the bureaucracy and military of the land-based empires of this period. Taxation took many forms in these empires:

- **Mughal zamindar tax collection:** Mughal emperors appointed tax officers or zamindars to collect taxes from the peasant class based on land and production.

- **Ottoman tax farming:** Rather than employing government tax collectors, the Ottoman sultans appointed "tax farmers" to pay an annual fixed sum of money for an area to the central government and then recoup the outlay by collecting money or salable goods from the residents of the area. Many Janissaries were paid their salaries in this manner by collecting more money than they paid out to the central government.

- **Aztec tribute lists:** As the Aztecs (or Mexica) formed a tributary empire, the main source of revenue that supported the Aztec noble class and military came from yearly offerings or tributes from the surrounding areas. The lists included whichever local product was made or valued but could also include a demand for people, many of whom became human sacrifices in Aztec religious rituals.

- **Ming collection of "hard currency:"** The Ming Empire, like its predecessors, issued paper currency as a means to facilitate trade and tax collection; however the use of paper money led to rampant counterfeiting and hyperinflation. The Ming then ordered that all taxes should be paid in the form of rice, and later silver coins, known as "hard currency."

Striving for Legitimacy

While the diversity of the populations of the land-based empires was beneficial to the economic and political strength of the empires, ruling over populations that included many ethnicities, religions, and tribal ties was challenging. Therefore many rulers turned to other than political means to unite their subjects in their loyalty to the state. Rulers used religion, art, and monumental architecture to legitimize their rule. Akbar attempted a syncretic approach to religion in the Mughal Empire, but he had little success in that area.

Sources of Legitimacy	Examples
Religion	• Rulers in Islamic empires used references to the title "caliph," or successor to the Prophet.
	• European monarchs claim to "divine right" that gave the monarch the mandate to rule by the Christian God.
	• Conversion to Islam of Songhai rulers and noble class provides a religious and legal structure to the empire.
	• Aztec (Mexica) use human sacrifice in religious rituals.
Art	• Portraits of the Qing emperors and other high officials
	• Miniature paintings in the Ottoman Empire
	• Financial support of artists by European rulers
Monumental Architecture	• Mausolea, such as the Taj Mahal and mosques in the Mughal Empire
	• European palaces, such as the Palace of Versailles in France and El Escorial in Spain

REFLECT ON THE ESSENTIAL QUESTION

1. **Comparison** Create a chart comparing the effects of transoceanic connections in the Eastern and Western Hemispheres. Include the impact on trade, on relations with other empires, and on culture.

2. In one to three paragraphs, explain the methods empires used to increase their societal and cultural influence from c. 1450 to c. 1750.

UNIT 3 REVIEW

HISTORICAL PERSPECTIVES: WHY DID THE ISLAMIC GUNPOWDER
EMPIRES RISE AND DECLINE?

The term "Gunpowder Empires" was coined by Marshall G. S. Hodgson in the 1970s to refer to the large land empires of Southwestern and South Asia that flourished the from 1450 to 1750 (*The Venture of Islam: The Gunpowder Empires and Modern Times*). The term is often used to describe the Ottomans, Safavids, and Mughals.

Trade and the Rise of Empires Kenneth Pomeranz and Steven Topik, in their 2005 book *The World That Trade Created*, described the empires as part of the growing global economy. These authors, taking economic and social perspectives, used coffee as one example of the international character of consumer goods: "Coffee's role in sociability and prestige in Europe was enhanced by the arrival of emissaries of the Ottoman sultan in France and Austria in 1665–1666, who poured the exotic liquor for their aristocratic European guests during extravagant soirees."

Reasons for Decline Historians have given various reasons for their declines, but most fall into three categories: (1) ineffectiveness; (2) intolerance of minorities; and (3) failure to modernize. One reviewer summarized historian Vladimir Minorsky's reasons for the decline of the Safavid Empire:

a. decline of theocratic ideology

b. opposition between old and new elements in the military class

c. disturbance in equilibrium among the service classes, which lost interest in the cause they were supporting

d. the "shadow government" represented by the harem

e. degeneration of the dynasty as a result of its insular nature

Military Weakness William McNeill pointed out that rulers and military administrators did not try to keep up with "subsequent European innovations in military and naval matters, leaving them woefully exposed to attack." McNeill noted that the Ottomans' guns were able to defeat their Islamic rivals, the Safavids, because "until about 1600, the Ottoman army remained technically and in every way in the very forefront of military proficiency." Nevertheless, after the time of Suleiman, leaders did not themselves lead soldiers in battle, and military discipline declined just as efficiency and technology began to lag behind Western Europe.

Tolerance and Intolerance Amy Chua, *Day of Empire: How Hyperpowers Rise to Global Dominance—and Why They Fall*, suggested a different reason for the eventual failure of the Gunpowder Empires. Her thesis was that intolerance ultimately became an obstacle to retaining great power. She suggested that empires were successful in holding their power when they were at their most religiously and ethnically tolerant. This thesis can help explain why the Ottoman Empire, with its relative tolerance, outlived the more intolerant Safavid and Mughal Empires.

Develop an Argument: Evaluate the extent to which historical evidence supports one of the perspectives on the rise and decline of the Gunpowder Empires.

As you have read, the first stage in writing a long essay is to carefully read and analyze the question so you know exactly what the framework is for your response. (See page 183.) In addition to surface-level analysis of the terms of the question, you also apply the historical thinking skill of analyzing historical developments and processes for a deeper understanding of the question.

Suppose, for example, you choose to answer the following long essay question: "Develop an argument that evaluates the extent to which religion created unity or conflict between 1450 and 1750 in Europe and in South Asia." For a surface level analysis, you could complete a chart like the one below.

Key Terms and Framework	
Key Terms	Argument, evaluate, extent, role of religion, unity, and conflict
Framework	*Geographic Areas:* Europe and South Asia *Time Period:* 1450–1750
Reasoning Process	Comparison

For a deeper analysis of the question, use the thinking skill of analyzing historical developments and processes. Ask questions such as the following to arrive at a deeper understanding of the question.

Questions for Deeper Analysis
What is the role of religion in the development of unity?
What is the role of religion in the development of conflict?
How did religion develop unity in Europe?
How did religion develop conflict in Europe?
How did religion develop unity in South Asia?
How did religion develop conflict in South Asia?
What other developments between 1450 and 1750 were taking place in Europe that are relevant to the role of religion?
What other developments between 1450 and 1750 were taking place in South Asia that are relevant to the role of religion?

In the next stage of writing, these questions will help you focus the evidence you gather to answer the question.

Application: Suppose you choose to answer the following long essay question: "Develop an argument that evaluates the extent to which continuity or change occurred in the participation of China in the expanding global trade networks from 1450 to 1750." Complete a Key Terms and Framework chart for the question to understand the basic requirements of the task. Then create a Questions for Deeper Analysis chart to help you develop a more complex understanding of the question.

For current free response question samples, visit: https://apcentral.collegeboard. org/courses/ap-world-history/exam

LONG ESSAY QUESTIONS

Directions: Write an essay in response to one of the prompts below. The suggested writing time for an essay is 40 minutes.

In your response, you should do the following:

- Respond to the prompt with a historically defensible thesis or claim that establishes a line of reasoning.
- Describe a broader historical context relevant to the prompt.
- Support an argument in response to the prompt using at least two pieces of specific and relevant evidence.
- Use historical reasoning (e.g., comparison, causation, continuity or change) to frame or structure an argument that addresses the prompt.
- Demonstrate a complex understanding of a historical development related to the prompt through sophisticated argumentation and/or effective use of evidence.

Source: *AP® World History Course and Exam Description*

1. In Africa and Eurasia from 1450–1750, various forms of Islam and Christianity were key factors in the expansion of empires.

   Develop an argument that evaluates the extent to which the various belief systems showed continuity or change over time during the period from 1450–1750.

2. Rulers of empires in Africa and Eurasia from 1450–1750 developed new methods of governing to solidify their authority over their citizens.

   Develop an argument that evaluates the extent to which changes in government caused the consolidation of power in empires in the period 1450–1750.

3. New technology, including gunpowder weapons, shaped empires throughout southern and southwestern Asia from 1450–1750.

   Develop an argument that evaluates the extent to which various land-based empires in southern and southwestern Asia developed in similar ways from 1450–1750.

4. New technology, including gunpowder weapons, shaped empires in Russia and China from 1450–1750.

   Develop an argument that evaluates the extent to which various land-based empires in Russia and China developed in similar ways from 1450–1750.

DOCUMENT-BASED QUESTION

Directions: Question 1 is based on the accompanying documents. The documents have been edited for the purpose of this exercise. You are advised to spend 15 minutes planning and 45 minutes writing your answer.

1. Evaluate the extent to which rulers in Eurasia succeeded in consolidating power within their states, during the period c. 1450 to c. 1750.

In your response, you should do the following:

- Respond to the prompt with a historically defensible thesis or claim that establishes a line of reasoning.
- Describe a broader historical context relevant to the prompt.
- Support an argument in response to the prompt using at least four documents.
- Use at least one additional piece of specific historical evidence (beyond that found in the documents) relevant to an argument about the prompt.
- For at least two documents, explain how or why the document's point of view, purpose, historical situation, and/or audience is relevant to an argument.
- Demonstrate a complex understanding of a historical development related to the prompt through a sophisticated argument and/or effective use of evidence.

Source: *AP® World History Course and Exam Description*

Document 1

Source: Account from the Tun Bu village gazetteer (a village record updated periodically), Tun Bu village, southern China, c. 1450.

The responsibility of the tax captains in the early Ming Dynasty was very important.

When they visited local villages, they were accorded a courteous reception. When the village leaders came to see the tax captains, they did not dare sit and remained standing. From each township the Ming dynasty chose one tax captain who was then responsible for the payment of all the grain and silver taxes of that local area.

A tax captain's home was furnished with an official table and chair, and bamboo sticks and other implements of punishment were also kept at hand. A tax captain was allowed to order an arrest with a warrant written in red ink and to set deadlines for the payment of taxes. When the time limit was up, the tax captain would call in the responsible village leader and force them to pay.

Document 2

Source: Italian writer, Niccolo Machiavelli, *The Prince*, excerpt on Ottoman Sultan, Suleyman the Magnificent, 1513.

The entire monarchy of the [Ottoman] Turks is governed by one ruler, the Sultan, the others are his servants; and, dividing his kingdom into sanjaks [subprovinces], he sends there different administrators, and shifts and changes them as he chooses. But the King of France is placed in the midst of an ancient body of lords [administrators], acknowledged by their own subjects, and beloved by them; they have their own prerogatives [power], nor can the king take these away except at his peril.

Therefore, he who considers both of these states will recognize great difficulties in seizing the state of the Turk but, once it is conquered, great ease in holding it. The causes of the difficulties in seizing the kingdom of the Turks are that the usurper [conqueror] cannot be called in by the princes of the kingdom, nor can he hope to be assisted in his designs by the revolt of those whom the ruler (Sultan) has around him. This arises from the reasons given above; for his ministers and administrators, being all slaves and bondmen, can only be corrupted with great difficulty, and one can expect little advantage from them when they have been corrupted, as they cannot carry the people with them, for the reasons assigned.

Document 3

Source: Tokugawa Shogun (king), Toyotomi Hideyoshi, *The Edicts of Toyotomi Hideyoshi*, excerpt from *Collection of Swords*, 1588.

1. Farmers of all provinces are strictly forbidden to have in their possession any swords, short swords, spears, firearms, or other types of weapons. If unnecessary implements of war are kept, the collection of annual rent may become more difficult, and without prompting uprisings can occur. Therefore, those who perpetrate improper acts against samurai [warriors] who receive a grant of land must be brought to trial and punished. Therefore, the heads of the provinces, and samurai who receive a grant of land, and deputies must collect all the weapons described above and submit them to Hideyoshi's government.

2. The swords and short swords collected in the above manner will not be wasted. They will be used as nails and bolts in the construction of the Great Image of Buddha. In this way the farmers will benefit not only in this life but also in the lives to come.

3. If farmers possess only agriculture implements and devote themselves exclusively to cultivating the fields, they and their descendants will prosper. This compassionate concern for the well-being of the farms is the reason for the issuance of this edict, and such concern is the foundation for the peace and security of the country and the joy . . . of all the people.

Document 4

Source: Ernest Lissner, Russian painter, *Salt Riot in Moscow*, 1938.

Credit: Wikimedia Commons

Painted in 1938, the image depicts the violent riots in 1648 by artisans and serfs against Czar Alexei I's government over the implementation of a universal tax on salt. The uprising led to the government making several changes in response to serfs' demands. However, the changes unintentionally institutionalized serfdom for centuries.

Document 5

Source: Dr. François Bernier, French traveler to Egypt and the Ottoman Empire, and employee of the Mughal emperor, account of his experiences, 1668.

The king [of India], as proprietor of the all the land in India, gives a certain quantity of land to military men, as an equivalent for their pay. . . . Similar land grants are made to governors, in lieu of their salary, and also for the support of their troops, on condition that they pay a certain sum annually to the king out of any surplus revenue that the land may yield. . . .

The persons this put in possession of the land, whether as soldiers, governors, or farmers, have an authority almost absolute over the peasantry, and nearly as much over the artisans and merchants of the towns and villages within their district; and nothing can be imagined more cruel and oppressive than the manner in which it is exercised. . . .

The peasant cannot avoid asking himself this question: "Why should I toil for a tyrant who may come tomorrow and lay his greedy hands upon all I possess?" The soldiers, governors, and farmers, on their part reason in this manner "why should the neglected state of this land create uneasiness in our minds? And why should we expend our money and time to render it fruitful?"

Document 6

Source: Saint Simon, Duke at the court of French King, Louis XIV, *Memoirs 1691-1709*, published 1829.

Louis XIV wished to reign by himself. His jealousy on this point became weakness. He reigned, indeed, in little things; the great he could never reach: even in the former, too, he was often led by others.

The superior ability of his early ministers and his early generals soon wearied him. He liked nobody to be in any way superior to him. Thus he chose his ministers, not for their knowledge, but for their ignorance; not for their capacity, but for their lack of it. He liked to lead them, as he said; liked to teach them even the most trifling things. It was the same with his generals. He took credit to himself for instructing them; wished it to be thought that from his cabinet he commanded and directed all his armies.

This vanity, this unmeasured and unreasonable love of admiration, was his ruin. His ministers, his generals, his mistresses, his courtiers, soon perceived his weakness. They praised him with emulation and spoiled him. Praises, or to say truth, flattery, pleased him to such an extent, that the coarsest was well received, the vilest even better relished. It was the sole means by which you could approach him.

Document 7

Source: Jean Rousset de Missy, French Protestant writer, *Life of Peter the Great*, 1730.

The tsar labored at the reform of fashions, or, more properly speaking, of dress. Until that time the Russians had always worn long beards, which they cherished and preserved with much care, allowing them to hang down on their bosoms, without even cutting the moustache. With these long beards they wore the hair very short . . . The tsar, in order to reform that custom, ordered that gentleman, merchants, and other subjects, except priests and peasants, should each pay a tax of one hundred rubles a year if they wished to keep their beards; the commoners had to pay one kopek each. Officials were stationed at the gates of the towns to collect that tax, which the Russians regarded as an enormous sin on the part of the tsar and as a thing which tended to the abolition of their religion.

These insinuations, which came from the priests, occasioned the publication of many pamphlets in Moscow, where for that reason alone the tsar was regarded as a tyrant and a pagan; and there were many old Russians who, after having their beards shaved off, saved them preciously, in order to have them placed in their coffins, fearing that they would not be allowed to enter heaven without their beards. As for the young men, they followed the new custom with the more readiness as it made them appear more agreeable to the fair sex.

UNIT 4: Transoceanic Interconnections from c. 1450 to c. 1750

Understand the Context

The voyage by Christopher Columbus in 1492 that connected the Eastern and Western hemispheres led to the first global trade networks. They provided the framework for historical events for the following centuries.

Establishment of Maritime Empires Between 1450 and 1750, European states, starting with the Portuguese and Spanish, sought a transoceanic route to Asia. Europeans established trading post empires in the Indian Ocean that inadvertently brought them into contact with the Americas.

Global Exchanges Trans-Atlantic trade linked the Americas, Europe, and Africa for the first time. European colonists who wanted sugar and other crops to sell in the global market developed plantations in the Americas. Their desire for laborers fueled the trade in enslaved Africans. Trans-Pacific trade flourished as well. Silver mined in Latin America was the major commodity.

Over time, the transfer of crops, animals, and disease between the Eastern and Western hemispheres, known as the Columbian Exchange, altered life everywhere. The introduction of potatoes, corn, and tomatoes to Europe led to population growth. The introduction of deadly pathogens, such as small pox and measles, devastated the populations of the Americas.

Change and Continuity Within the context of increasing European influence, regional commerce and established states in Afro-Eurasia continued to flourish. The Mughal, Ottoman, and Qing Empires expanded, creating ethnically diverse states. Across the globe, peasant and artisan labor intensified as the demand for goods and food increased. These developments set the stage for the revolutions that defined the period after 1750.

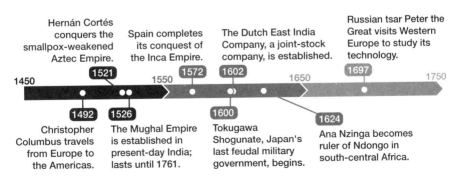

Hernán Cortés conquers the smallpox-weakened Aztec Empire. **1521**

Spain completes its conquest of the Inca Empire. **1572**

The Dutch East India Company, a joint-stock company, is established. **1602**

Russian tsar Peter the Great visits Western Europe to study its technology. **1697**

1450 — 1550 — 1650 — 1750

1492 Christopher Columbus travels from Europe to the Americas.

1526 The Mughal Empire is established in present-day India; lasts until 1761.

1600 Tokugawa Shogunate, Japan's last feudal military government, begins.

1624 Ana Nzinga becomes ruler of Ndongo in south-central Africa.

Topics and Learning Objectives

Topic 4.1: Technological Innovations pages 191–198

A: Explain how cross-cultural interactions resulted in the diffusion of technology and facilitated changes in patterns of trade and travel from 1450 to 1750.

Topic 4.2: Exploration: Causes and Events pages 199–208

B: Describe the role of states in the expansion of maritime exploration from 1450 to 1750.

C: Explain the economic causes and effects of maritime exploration by the various European states.

Topic 4.3: Colombian Exchange pages 209–217

D: Explain the causes of the Columbian Exchange and its effects on the Eastern and Western Hemispheres.

Topic 4.4: Maritime Empires are Established pages 218–231

E: Explain the process of state building and expansion among various empires and states in the period from 1450 to 1750.

F: Explain the continuities and changes in economic systems and labor systems from 1450 to 1750.

G: Explain changes and continuities in systems of slavery in the period from 1450 to 1750.

Topic 4.5: Maritime Empires are Maintained and Developed pages 232–242

H: Explain how rulers employed economic strategies to consolidate and maintain power throughout the period from 1450 to 1750.

I: Explain the continuities and changes in networks of exchange from 1450 to 1750.

J: Explain how political, economic, and cultural factors affected society from 1450 to 1750.

K: Explain the similarities and differences in how various belief systems affected societies from 1450 to 1750.

Topic 4.6: Internal and External Challenges to State Power pages 243–250

L: Explain the effects of the development of state power from 1450 to 1750.

Topic 4.7: Changing Social Hierarchies pages 251–260

M: Explain how social categories, roles and practices have been maintained or have changed over time.

Topic 4.8: Continuity and Change from 1450 to 1750
pages 261–264

N: Explain how economic developments from 1450 to 1750 affected social structures over time.

4.1

Technological Innovations

The sailors, moreover, as they sail over the sea, when in cloudy weather they can no longer profit by the light of the sun, or when the world is wrapped up in the darkness of the shades of night, and they are ignorant to what point of the compass their ship's course is directed, they touch the magnet with a needle, which (the needle) is whirled round in a circle until, when its motion ceases, its point looks direct to the north.

—Alexander Neckham (1157-1217)

Essential Question: How did cross-cultural interactions spread technology and facilitate changes in trade and travel from 1450 to 1750?

Although land-based empires were important during this period, various inventions allowed Europeans to venture long distances on the ocean. The magnetic compass, originally created in China for fortune telling, helped steer a ship in the right direction, as described by Alexander Neckham. The astrolabe, improved by Muslim navigators in the 12th century, let sailors find out how far north or south they were from the equator. The caravel, a small, three-masted sailing ship developed by the Portuguese in the 15th century, allowed sailors to survive storms at sea better than earlier-designed ships. **Cartography**, or mapmaking, and knowledge of current and wind patterns also improved navigation.

Demographic pressures pushed Europeans into exploration and trade. As the population grew, not all workers in Europe could find work or even food. Not all sons of the wealthy could own land because **primogeniture laws** gave all of each estate to the eldest son. In the early 17th century, religious minorities searched for a place to settle where people were tolerant of their dissent. All of these groups, as well as those just longing for adventure and glory, were eager to settle in new areas. Those who left their homelands in search of work, food, land, tolerance, and adventure were part of a global shift in demographics.

Developments of Transoceanic Travel and Trade

Europe was never totally isolated from East and South Asia. The Indian Ocean trade routes had long brought silk, spices, and tea to the Mediterranean by way of the Red Sea. Islamic traders had long known of land routes from China to the cities of Baghdad and Constantinople and from there to Rome. Then, in the 16th century, more and more Europeans became active in the Indian Ocean, with hopes of finding wealth and new converts as their twin motives. However, Europeans faced competition from Middle Eastern traders based in kingdoms such as Oman. For example, the Portuguese set up forts in Oman but were repeatedly challenged by attempts to remove them. The **Omani-European rivalry** was one reason for Christopher Columbus's search for a new route to India.

The voyages by Columbus connected people across the Atlantic Ocean. European traders became go-betweens linking Afro-Eurasia and the Americas.

- From the Americas, they purchased sugar, tobacco, and rum.
- From Africa, they purchased enslaved people.
- From Asia, they purchased silk, spices, and rhubarb.

This extensive trade transformed Spain, Portugal, Great Britain, France, and Holland into **maritime empires**, ones based on sea travel.

Much of this trade was carried out by men. However, in Southeast Asia, Europeans conducted most of their business with women, who traditionally handled markets and money-changing services in those cultures.

Classical, Islamic, and Asian Technology

Western European countries such as Portugal, Spain, and England were developing their naval technology. They were aware of traditions of sailing that went back to the classical Greeks, such as using the stars to navigate. They combined this knowledge with new ideas developed by Islamic and Asian sailors and scholars, which they learned about because of the cross-cultural interactions resulting from trade networks. Al-Andalus, in what is now Spain, was a place where Islamic ideas diffused into Europe.

The leading European figure in this development was Portuguese ruler Prince Henry the Navigator. While he never sailed far enough out to sea to lose sight of land, he strongly supported exploration. He financed expeditions along Africa's Atlantic Coast and around the Cape of Good Hope. With his backing, Portugal explored African coastal communities and kingdoms before other European powers.

Advances in Ideas As scholars gathered knowledge, they improved the safety of sailing on the ocean. For example, Newton's discovery of gravitation increased knowledge of the tides. As a result, sailors could reliably predict when the depth of water near a shore would be decreasing, thereby exposing dangerous rocks. As people kept increasingly accurate records on the direction and intensity of winds, sailors could sail with greater confidence.

Improvements in cartography also improved navigation. An **astronomical chart** is any map of the stars and galaxies. Mariners relied on these maps to guide ships' direction, especially before the introduction of the compass, using the skies to help them determine their location. Ancient astronomers in Babylonia and Mesopotamia had created star charts as early as the 2nd millennium B.C.E. Charts by Chinese astronomers date back to the 5th century B.C.E. Charts were also used widely by classical Greek astronomers. Using telescopes to help create astronomical charts began in 1609, and the practice was widely used to map the stars by the end of the 17th century. Astronomers typically divided the charts into grids to help locate specific constellations and astronomical objects.

Advances in Equipment Several developments in the equipment used on ships made sailing safer and faster than ever. Ships moved adroitly, aided by a new type of rudder, another idea imported from China. The astrolabe, improved by Muslim navigators in the 12th century, allowed sailors to determine how far north or south they were from the equator.

The compass is the primary direction-finding device used in navigation. It works either with magnets or a gyroscope, which is a wheel or disk mounted to spin rapidly around an axis in various directions. Other compasses determine the location of the sun or a specific star. The magnetic compass, originally invented in China, allowed sailors to steer a ship in the right direction. This type of compass works as Earth itself acts as an enormous bar magnet. Earth's magnetic field is almost parallel to the north-south axis of the globe, which means that freely moving magnets, such as those in a compass, take on the same orientation.

The lateen sail, or a ship sail in the shape of a triangle, was a pivotal piece of technology. Used by Arab sailors and in the Indian Ocean, it significantly affected medieval navigation and trade. The ancient square sails that preceded the lateen allowed sailing only in a single direction and had to be used with the wind. The lateen, however, could catch the wind on either side of the ship, allowing it to travel in different directions. When used with the square sail, the lateen allowed sailors to travel successfully into large bodies of water, including oceans, for the first time, thus expanding trade routes.

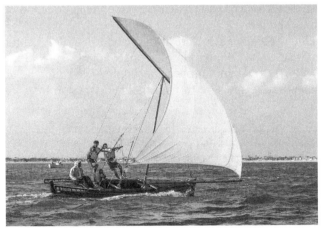

Source: Getty Images

Lateen sails are still used on modern sailboats.

New types of ships also improved trade. By adjusting the ratio of length to width of a ship, adding or reducing the number of masts, and using different types of sails, builders could adapt ships to improve their efficiency. (Connect: Compare the technological advances of the Mongols and Chinese of the 12th and 13th centuries with those in the chart below. See Topic 2.1.)

Three Types of Ships					
Ship	Typical Length	Sails and Masts	Purpose	Primary Users	Centuries of Peak Use
Carrack	150 feet	Square and lateen on 3-4 masts	Trade	Portugal	14th to 17th
Caravel	75 feet	Lateen sails on 2 or 3 masts	Long voyages at great speed	Portuguese and Spanish	15th to 17th
Fluyt	80 feet	Square on 2 or 3 masts	Trade	Dutch	16th to 17th

Long-Term Results The long-term result of combining navigational techniques invented in Europe with those from other areas of the world was a rapid expansion of exploration and global trade. About the only part of the Afro-Eurasia world not affected by the rapid increase in global trade was Polynesia, since it was far removed from trading routes.

The introduction of gunpowder, another Chinese invention, aided Europeans in their conquests abroad. Soon enough, however, sea pirates also used the new technology, particularly the Dutch pirates known as Sea Beggars.

In North Africa and in the trading cities along Africa's east coast, Islam spread rapidly as a result of the growth of the Abbasid Empire, centered in Baghdad, and the activities of Muslim merchants. Interactions among various cultures inside and outside of Africa brought extensive trade and new technology to the continent.

Navigational techniques continued to spread throughout the 17th century. Russia's Tsar Peter the Great visited Western Europe in 1697 to observe military and naval technology. His interest in European technology led him to hire technicians from Germany and elsewhere to help build Russia's military and naval power.

KEY TERMS BY THEME

ECONOMICS: Europe	**TECHNOLOGY:** Navigation	**GOVERNMENT:** Europe
primogeniture laws	cartography	maritime empires
Omani-European rivalry	astronomical chart	

Questions 1 to 3 refer to the image below.

Source: Musée national de la Marine, Paris, France. Wikimedia Commons.

This model of a caravel shows some of the innovations that made ocean travel easier.

1. The specific technological innovation depicted here that improved deep water navigation was the

   (A) compass

   (B) upper deck oars

   (C) astrolabe

   (D) lateen sails

2. The technological innovation depicted in the above image was first used in

(A) the Black Sea

(B) the East African coastal city of Kilwa

(C) Constantinople

(D) the Indian Ocean

3. The European leader who made the greatest use of this new technology was

(A) Prince Henry

(B) Henry VIII

(C) Mehmed the Great

(D) Pope Urban II

SHORT-ANSWER QUESTIONS

1. Use the passages below to answer all parts of the question that follows.

"After the year 1500 there was no pepper to be had at Calicut that was not dyed red with blood."

Voltaire, 1756

"Gunpowder weapons were not new. The Chinese invented gunpowder and they made the first true guns in the tenth century, primarily for defensive purposes. The Mongols improved these Chinese weapons into a more effective offensive force, to blow open city gates. By 1241, these weapons had reached Europe. Early modern Europeans, Turks, Mughals, and Chinese owed their strength in part to improvements in gunpowder weaponry. Combined with better military organization and seagoing capability, advanced weaponry inevitably affected political and social systems.

As they spread throughout Eurasia and North Africa, gunpowder weapons changed warfare. Europeans learned how to make particularly deadly weapons, improving the technology in part because they had easier access to metals."

Craig A. Lockard, *Societies, Networks, and Transitions: A Global History, Volume II: Since 1450* (2010)

(A) Identify ONE way in which the passage from Lockard reflects technological developments that influenced social structures in the period 1450–1750.

(B) Explain ONE way the words of Voltaire reflect technological developments that influenced political structures in the period 1450–1750.

(C) Explain ONE historical situation in the period 1450–1750, other than the ones illustrated in the passages, in which states in Asia or Africa had an impact on the development of European states.

2. **Answer all parts of the question that follows.**

(A) Identify ONE economic motivation for understanding wind patterns.

(B) Identify ONE political motivation for developing navigational technology.

(C) Explain ONE way in which state interactions in the period 1450–1750 had an impact on different cultures.

Source: Pierre5018/Wikimedia Commons
A French astrolabe made in 1603

THINK AS A HISTORIAN: IDENTIFY AND DESCRIBE A HISTORICAL CONTEXT

Suppose the topic you have just read was the only topic you have read so far. What would you make of it? Without a context, it would be hard to appreciate fully. Chances are, though, that you have read some topics before this one, so you do have a context in which to situate this information. To understand context, first simply identify it—in this case, an era of the expansion of trade and empires. Then, to understand the context as fully as possible, describe it. In this case, you might describe the context as one of ambitious rulers eager to stake out territory for both trade and political control, centralizing political states, religious differences so strong that they led to warfare, and an interest in humanism and the natural world. Finally, among all the descriptors you thought of, narrow the context down to the most relevant. For example, if you are trying to contextualize humanism, you would focus on the context of philosophy and ideas rather than that of expanding trade.

In three or four sentences, identify and describe a historical context for each of the following.

1. The magnetic compass
2. The introduction of gunpowder
3. The invention of the printing press
4. Knowledge of monsoon winds

REFLECT ON THE TOPIC ESSENTIAL QUESTION

1. In one to three paragraphs, explain how cross-cultural interactions spread technology and facilitated changes in trade and travel from 1450 to 1750.

Exploration: Causes and Events

*You can never cross the ocean unless you have
the courage to lose sight of the shore.*

—Christopher Columbus (1451-1506)

Essential Question: What were the causes and effects of the state-
sponsored expansion of maritime exploration?

Thanks in part to improved navigation techniques, Italian cities with ports
on the Mediterranean had a monopoly on European trade with Asia. By
controlling access to the trade routes, the Italians controlled prices of Asian
imports to Europe, driving Spain and Portugal, and later France, England, and
the Netherlands, into the search for new routes to Asia. Explorers hoped to find
riches overseas, especially gold and silver. In addition to these economic and
political reasons, explorers were interested in converting others to Christianity.
Also, technological breakthroughs in sailing and navigation made bold new
voyages possible.

Christopher Columbus, quoted above and credited with "discovering the
New World," was fortunate in 1492 to gain the support of the Spanish monarchs,
Queen Isabella and King Ferdinand, for his voyages across the Atlantic. His
journeys helped increase the interest in discovery, and the English, French, and
Dutch supported later exploration.

The Role of States in Maritime Exploration

European states were seeking ways to expand their authority and control of
resources in the era of empire-building. Conquests brought new wealth to
states through the collection of taxes and through new trading opportunities.
In time it also brought great material wealth, especially in silver, to European
states. Rivalries among European states stoked efforts to expand before
another power might claim a territory. Religion was also a motivating force
for exploration and expansion. Many Europeans believed that it was their
Christian duty to seek out people in other lands to convert them.

For all these reasons, states were centrally involved in maritime exploration.
Voyages such as those Columbus undertook were expensive, and without the
financial support of a state, they would most likely have been too expensive

for explorers and even most merchants to be able to afford. Since religion was tightly woven into the government of most European states, preserving and spreading a state's religion became another reason for state involvement.

Also, in the 17th century, Europeans generally measured the wealth of a country in how much gold and silver it had accumulated. For this reason, countries set policies designed to sell as many goods as they could to other countries—in order to maximize the amount of gold and silver coming into the country—and to buy as few as possible from other countries—to minimize the flow of precious metals out of the country. This theory, known as **mercantilism**, required heavy government involvement.

Expansion of European Maritime Exploration

In no nation were the interests of the state and the interest of explorers as closely tied as they were in Portugal, which led the way in European exploration as it had in maritime innovations. (See Topic 2.3.)

Portuguese in Africa and India The small kingdom of Portugal, bounded on the east by the Spanish kingdoms of Castile and Aragon, could expand only overseas. Three people led its exploration:

- **Prince Henry the Navigator** (1394–1460) became the first European monarch to sponsor seafaring expeditions, to search for an all-water route to the east as well as for African gold. Under him, Portugal began importing enslaved Africans by sea, replacing the overland slave trade.

- **Bartholomew Diaz** sailed around the southern tip of Africa, the Cape of Good Hope, in 1488, into waters his crew did not know. Diaz feared a mutiny if he continued pushing eastward, so he returned home.

- **Vasco Da Gama** sailed farther east than Diaz, landing in India in 1498. There he claimed territory as part of Portugal's empire. The Portuguese ports in India were a key step in expanding Portugal's trade in the Indian Ocean and with points farther east.

Portuguese in Southeast and East Asia Early in the 16th century, the ruthless Portuguese admiral Afonso de Albuquerque won a short but bloody battle with Arab traders and set up a factory at Malacca in present-day Indonesia. He had previously served as governor of Portuguese India (1509–1515), sending strings of Indians' ears home to Portugal as evidence of his conquests.

China's exploration of the outside world came to an end after Zheng He's final voyage in the 1430s. (See Topic 2.3.) However, less than a century later, in 1514, the outside world arrived on China's doorstep in the form of Portuguese traders. At that time, Portugal's superior ships and weapons were unmatched among the Europeans. As a result of this advantage, the Portuguese had already won control of both the African and Indian coasts. They had won a decisive victory over a Turkish-Egyptian-Venetian fleet at Diu, India, in 1509.

Initial Portuguese visits had little impact on Chinese society. But the traders were followed by Roman Catholic missionaries, mainly Franciscans and Dominicans, who worked to gain converts among the Chinese people.

The Jesuits soon followed and tried to win over the Chinese court elite. Scientific and technical knowledge were the keys to success at the court. Jesuit missionaries in Macau, such as Matteo Ricci (an Italian, arrived 1582) and Adam Schall von Bell (a German, arrived 1619), impressed the Chinese with their learning. However, they failed to win many converts among the hostile scholar-gentry, who considered them barbaric.

Trading Post Empire To ensure control of trade, the Portuguese had constructed a series of forts stretching from Hormuz on the Persian Gulf (built in 1507) to Goa in western India (built in 1510) to Malacca on the Malay Peninsula (built in 1511). The aims of the fort construction were to establish a monopoly (complete control over a market) over the spice trade in the area and to license all vessels trading between Malacca and Hormuz. The forts gave Portugal a global **trading post empire**, one based on small outposts, rather than control of large territories. The Portuguese also restricted Indian Ocean trade to those who were willing to buy permits.

Portuguese Vulnerability The Portuguese succeeded in global trade for several decades, but Portugal was a small nation, lacking the workers and the ships necessary for the enforcement of a large trade empire. Many Portuguese merchants ignored their government and traded independently. Corruption among government officials also hampered the trading empire. By the 17th century, Dutch and English rivals were challenging the Portuguese in East Asia, including islands that are today part of Malaysia and Indonesia.

The Dutch captured Malacca and built a fort at Batavia in Java in 1620. From Batavia, the Dutch attempted to monopolize the spice trade. As a result, the English focused on India, pushing the Portuguese out of South Asia.

In the early 16th century, the Portuguese also travelled to Japan to trade, followed by Christian missionaries in 1549. They formed large Catholic settlements until the 1600s, when Japanese rulers outlawed Catholicism and expelled the missionaries.

Spanish in the Philippines Portuguese explorers such as Vasco da Gama were the first Western Europeans to reach the Indian Ocean by sea by going around the southern tip of Africa. Spanish ships, however, became the first to circumnavigate the globe when the government sponsored the voyage of **Ferdinand Magellan**. He died on the voyage in the Philippine Islands in 1522, but one of the ships in his fleet made it around the world, proving that the earth could be circumnavigated.

Spain annexed the Philippines in 1521 when Magellan's fleet arrived there. The Spanish returned in 1565 and started a long campaign to conquer the Filipinos, who put up fierce resistance. **Manila** became a Spanish commercial center in the area, attracting Chinese merchants and others. Because of the Portuguese and Spanish occupations, many Filipinos became Christians.

The Lure of Riches

Columbus and other European explorers sought a new route to Asia and hoped to find gold, silver, and other valuable resources. The Spanish found so little of value in their first two decades of contact that they considered stopping further exploration. The English, after sponsoring voyages in the 1490s, made little attempt to explore or settle for almost a century.

However, European interest in the Americas was rekindled when the Spanish came into contact with the two major empires in the region, the Aztecs in Mesoamerica and the Incas in South America. These empires had the gold and silver that made exploration, conquest, and settlement profitable. In addition, Europeans soon realized that, by using enslaved Native Americans and later enslaved Africans, they could grow wealthy by raising sugar, tobacco, and other valuable crops.

Trade Across the Pacific China was a particularly enthusiastic consumer of this silver from the Western Hemisphere. Silver, for example, made its way from what is now Mexico across the Pacific Ocean to East Asia in heavily armed Spanish ships known as **galleons** that made stops in the Philippines. At the trading post in Manila, Europeans exchanged silver for luxury goods such as silk and spices, and even for gold bullion. The impressive Manila galleons allowed the silver trade to flourish. Indeed, the Chinese government soon began using silver as its main form of currency. By the early 17th century, silver had become a dominant force in the global economic system.

SPAIN'S GOLD AND SILVER IMPORTS FROM THE AMERICAS, 1503–1660

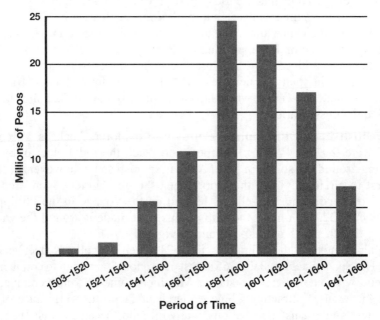

Source: Earl J. Hamilton "Imports of American Gold and Silver into Spain, 1503–1660." *The Quarterly Journal of Economics.* 1929.

Spain's rivals in Europe also explored and claimed regions in the Americas. French, English, and Dutch explorers all looked for a **northwest passage**—a route through or around North America that would lead to East Asia and the precious trade in spices and luxury goods.

French Exploration In the 1500s and 1600s, the French government sponsored expeditions in search of a northwest passage. In 1535, for example, French explorer **Jacques Cartier** sailed from the Atlantic Ocean into the St. Lawrence River at today's northern U.S. border. He did not find a new route to Asia, but he did claim part of what is now Canada for France. Eventually, explorers such as Cartier and **Samuel de Champlain** (explored 1609–1616) realized there were valuable goods and rich resources available in the Americas, so there was no need to go beyond to Asia.

Like the Spanish, the French hoped to find gold. Instead, they found a land rich in furs and other natural resources. In 1608, they established a town and trading post that they named **Quebec**. French traders and priests spread across the continent. The traders searched for furs; the priests wanted to convert Native Americans to Christianity. The missionaries sometimes set up schools among the indigenous peoples. In the 1680s, a French trader known as La Salle explored the Great Lakes and followed the Mississippi River south to its mouth at the Gulf of Mexico. He claimed this vast region for France.

Unlike the Spanish—or the English who were colonizing the East Coast of what is now the United States—the French rarely settled permanently. Instead of demanding land, they traded for the furs trapped by Native Americans. For this reason, the French had better relations with natives than did the Spanish or English colonists and their settlements also grew more slowly. For example, by 1754, the European population of **New France**, the French colony in North America, was only 70,000. The English colonies included one million Europeans.

English Exploration In 1497, the English king sent an explorer named **John Cabot** to America to look for a northwest passage. Cabot claimed lands from Newfoundland south to the Chesapeake Bay. The English, however, did not have enough sea power to defend themselves against Spanish naval forces—although English pirates called "sea dogs" sometimes attacked Spanish ships. Then in 1588, the English surprisingly defeated and destroyed all but one third of the Spanish Armada. With that victory, England declared itself a major naval power and began competing for lands and resources in the Americas.

At about the same time the French were founding Quebec, the English were establishing a colony in a land called Virginia. In 1607, about one hundred English colonists traveled approximately 60 miles inland from the coast, where they built a settlement, **Jamestown**, on the James River. Both the settlement and the river were named for the ruling English monarch, James I. Jamestown was England's first successful colony in the Americas, and one of the earliest colonies in what would become the United States. The first colonies in the present-day United States were Spanish settlements in Florida and New Mexico.

Comparing Transoceanic Voyages, c. 1300–c. 1800				
Sponsoring Empire	Explorer	Key Voyages	Purpose	Impact
China	Zheng He	• India • Middle East • Africa	To open up trade networks with India, Arabia, and Africa and to spread Chinese culture	China decided not to continue exploring
England	John Cabot	• North America	To find a sea route to the East going west from Europe	Claimed land in Canada for Britain and established a shorter, more northerly route across the Atlantic than Columbus's route.
Portugal	Vasco da Gama	• West coast of Africa • India	To open a sea route from Europe to India and China	Portugal expanded trade and cultural exchange between India and Europe
Spain	Christopher Columbus	• Caribbean islands • Central America	To find a sea route to India and China going west from Europe	Spain led the European exploration and colonization of the Americas
Spain	Ferdinand Magellan	• South America • Philippines	To demonstrate that Europeans could reach Asia by sailing west	Spain established links between the Americas and Asia across the Pacific Ocean

Dutch Exploration In 1609, the Dutch sent **Henry Hudson** to explore the East Coast of North America. Among other feats, he sailed up what became known as the Hudson River to see if it led to Asia. He was disappointed in finding no northwest passage. He and other explorers would continue to search for such a route. Though it would travel through a chilly region, it offered the possibility of being only half the distance of a route that went around South America.

Though Hudson did not find a northwest passage, his explorations proved valuable to the Dutch. Based on his voyage, the Dutch claimed the Hudson River Valley and the island of Manhattan. On the tip of this island, they settled a community called **New Amsterdam**, which today is known as New York City. Like many port towns, New Amsterdam prospered because it was located where a major river flowed into the ocean.

New Amsterdam became an important node in the Dutch transatlantic trade network. Dutch merchants bought furs from trappers who lived and worked in the forest lands as far north as Canada. They purchased crops from lands to the south, particularly tobacco from Virginia planters. They sent these goods and others to the Netherlands in exchange for manufactured goods that they could sell throughout colonial North America (Connect: Explain how one of the European explorers in Topic 4.2 compares to Marco Polo. See Topic 2.5.)

KEY TERMS BY THEME

ECONOMICS: Europe	**GOVERNMENT:**	**GOVERNMENT:** Colonies
mercantilism	Exploration	Quebec
trading post empire	Christopher Columbus	New France
Manila	Bartholomew Diaz	Jamestown
	Vasco Da Gama	New Amsterdam
GOVERNMENT: Portugal	Ferdinand Magellan	
Prince Henry the Navigator	northwest passage	
	Jacques Cartier	
TECHNOLOGY: Maritime	Samuel de Champlain	
galleons	John Cabot	
	Henry Hudson	

MULTIPLE-CHOICE QUESTIONS

Questions 1 to 3 refer to the passage below.

"When the Portuguese go from Macao, the most southern port city in China, to Japan, they carry much white silk, gold, perfume, and porcelain and they bring from Japan nothing but silver. They have a great ship that goes to Japan every year, and brings back more than 600,000 coins' worth of Japanese silver. The Portuguese use this Japanese silver to their great advantage in China. The Portuguese bring from China gold, perfume, silk, copper, porcelain, and many other luxury goods."

Ralph Fitch, a British merchant, in an account
of his travels to the East Indies, 1599

1. Which conclusion about the Portuguese is best supported by the passage above?
   (A) They manufactured luxury goods that they could sell in China.
   (B) They made great profits transporting goods between Asian countries.
   (C) They primarily wanted to accumulate silver.
   (D) They preferred to trade with China rather than Japan.

2. Which statement best describes the point of view of the source, Ralph Fitch?
   (A) He was ridiculing the Portuguese for working so hard for so little profit.
   (B) He was embarrassed that the Portuguese were taking advantage of the Chinese and Japanese.
   (C) He was hoping to make profits just as the Portuguese were doing.
   (D) He was criticizing the Portuguese for being so focused on acquiring wealth.

3. Which statement best explains why Portugal established a trading post empire?
   (A) It had a large navy and was able to conquer nearby lands.
   (B) It was a landlocked country and could not expand except by sea.
   (C) It had a small population and navy so controlling large territories was not possible.
   (D) It had fallen behind other European powers in development of navigational technology.

1. **Use the chart below to answer all parts of the questions that follow.**

European Voyages in Search of a Water Route to Asia			
Empire	**Explorer and Year**	**Region**	**Impact**
Spain	Christopher Columbus, 1492	Caribbean Sea	Spain took the lead in colonizing America
England	John Cabot, 1497	Canada	England claimed Canada
Portugal	Pedro Cabral, 1500	Brazil	Portugal strengthened its claim on Brazil
France	Jacques Cartier, 1535	St. Lawrence River	France claimed Canada
Holland	Henry Hudson, 1609	New York	Holland founded New Amsterdam

(A) Identify ONE technological improvement in the period 1450–1750 that originated outside of Europe yet helped Europeans in their voyages of discovery.

(B) Explain how ONE explorer listed in the chart affected the empire that sponsored him beyond the impact identified in the last column.

(C) Explain how ONE explorer listed in the chart affected the indigenous population of the Americas.

2. **Answer all parts of the question that follows.**

(A) Identify ONE social similarity between the Spanish and French settlements in the Americas in the period 1450–1750.

(B) Explain ONE political or economic difference between the English and French settlements in the Americas in the period 1450–1750.

(C) Explain ONE political or economic difference between the Dutch and French settlements in the Americas in the period 1450–1750.

THINK AS A HISTORIAN: MAKE CONNECTIONS BY RELATING
HISTORICAL DEVELOPMENTS

Historians of exploration might well focus a specialized study on the search for a northwest passage—on the details of each effort to find one and the outcome of the exploration. In a similar way, economic historians might well focus a specialized study on the expansion of trade networks as a global economy began to develop. However, to appreciate the interconnections of historical developments, historians would relate the exploratory and the economic developments, looking for ways in which developments in one field of study influenced developments in the other field. For example, the explorers failed in their mission to find a northwest passage, but they found instead that there were goods to trade on the land they traveled through, and they explored new territories that proved rich with trading possibilities. These findings, in turn, led to the desire for more exploration that would lead to new participants in the global trade network.

In a sentence or two, relate each of the following economic developments to another historical development in a different field of study, such as military history or social history.

1. Mercantilism

2. Trading post empire

3. Increased tax revenue

REFLECT ON THE TOPIC ESSENTIAL QUESTION

1. In one to three paragraphs, explain the causes and effects of the state sponsored expansion of maritime exploration.

4.3

Columbian Exchange

We are crushed to the ground; we lie in ruins.
There is nothing but grief and suffering in Mexico and Tlatelolco,
where once we saw beauty and valor.

—from "Flowers and Songs of Sorrow," anonymous
Aztec poet, (c. 1521–1540)

Essential Question: What were the causes of the Columbian Exchange and its effects on the Eastern and Western Hemispheres?

As the excerpt from the poem above suggests, initial contact and the subsequent conquest and colonization of the Americas proved disastrous for the native peoples. Overpowered by superior weapons and decimated by disease, many native populations declined, dissipated, or were forced to submit to new rulers and a new religion.

Although European conquest seriously damaged entire native societies and their ways of life, eventually new ways of life developed out of the interaction of three broad traditions of culture: indigenous American, European, and African. In the process, the Eastern and Western Hemispheres became linked in a new way, sharing disease, foods, and animals. For the role Christopher Columbus played in establishing the link, these interactions became known as the **Columbian Exchange**.

The Columbian Exchange had far-reaching effects beyond dramatic changes in population and biodiversity. It also contributed to a changing global economy, sometimes with unintended consequences. For example, Spain successfully mined silver in the Americas. However, this silver sparked inflation in Spain, which contributed to the downfall of the Spanish Empire.

Diseases and Population Catastrophe

Until the arrival of Columbus, the peoples of the Western and Eastern Hemispheres had been almost completely isolated from each other. For that reason, the indigenous people of the Americas had no exposure—and therefore no immunity—to the germs and diseases brought by Europeans. Although European horses, gunpowder, and metal weapons helped conquer indigenous Americans, disease was responsible for the majority of deaths.

Spanish soldiers, called **conquistadores**, such as Francisco Pizarro and

Hernán Cortés, brought **smallpox** with them. Smallpox pathogens are spread through the respiratory system. When Europeans, who were largely immune after millennia of exposure in Afro-Eurasia, had face-to-face contact with indigenous populations, they infected these populations with the deadly disease.

As colonists began to settle in the Americas, so did insects, rats, and other disease-carrying animals. Measles, influenza, and malaria, in addition to smallpox, also killed many native peoples of the Americas.

The indigenous population of the Americas fell by more than 50 percent through disease alone in less than a century. Some American lands lost up to 90 percent of their original populations. It was one of the greatest population disasters in human history.

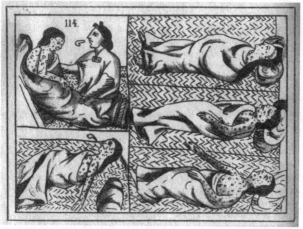

Source: Wikimedia Commons

Deadly diseases such as smallpox that came from Europe spread rapidly in the Americas.

Animals and Foods

Germ and disease transmissions were only one part of the Columbian Exchange. Another major component of the exchange was the sharing of new crops and livestock in both directions. Before the exchange began around 1500, Mesoamerican peoples consumed very little meat. Although contemporary Mexican food sold in the United States is reliant on pork, beef, and cheese, the indigenous people of Mexico knew nothing of pigs or cows until Europeans introduced them. These animals, along with Mediterranean foods such as wheat and grapes, were introduced to the Western Hemisphere and eventually became staples of the American diet.

Another domesticated animal the Europeans brought to the Americas, the **horse**, transformed the culture of the American Indians living in the Plains region. With the arrival of the horse, Indians could hunt buffalo on horseback so efficiently—and over a larger region—that they had a surplus of food. That efficiency gave them more time for other pursuits, such as art and spirituality. However, competition and even armed conflict among tribes increased, with those having the most horses having the most power.

At the same time, European explorers took back Mesoamerican **maize** (corn), potatoes, tomatoes, beans, peppers, and **cacao** to their home countries, where people started to grow them. Potatoes became so popular in Europe that they are often thought of as being native to certain regions, such as Ireland. The introduction of these vegetable crops caused tremendous population growth in Europe in the 16th and 17th centuries.

Cash Crops and Forced Labor

People themselves also became part of the exchange. The coerced arrival of enslaved Africans to the Americas brought biological and demographic changes. For example, Africans brought **okra** and **rice** with them to the Americas. Tobacco and cacao produced on American plantations with forced labor were sold to consumers in Europe, Africa, and the Middle East.

Even though slave traders kidnapped millions of Africans from their homelands, populations actually grew in Africa during the 16th and 17th centuries. That population growth happened because of the nutritious foods that were introduced to the continent. Yams and manioc, for example, were brought to Africa from Brazil.

The Lure of Sugar While Spain and Spanish America profited from silver, the Portuguese empire focused its endeavors on agriculture. Brazil, the center of the Portuguese-American empire, with its tropical climate and vast tracts of land, was perfect for **sugarcane** cultivation. As disease had decimated the indigenous population, however, there were not enough laborers available to do the cultivation. Moreover, many of the people who were forced to labor in the sugar fields escaped to the uncharted Brazilian jungle. In response, the Portuguese began to import enslaved people from Africa, especially from the Kongo Kingdom and cities on the Swahili coast.

Slavery Sugar's profitability in European markets dramatically increased the number of Africans captured and sold through the **transatlantic slave trade**. Sugar cultivation in Brazil demanded the constant importation of African labor. African laborers were so numerous in Brazil that their descendants became the majority population of the region. Slave importers sold more than 90 percent of enslaved Africans to the Caribbean and South America. Only about 6 percent went to British North America. Until the mid-1800s, more Africans than Europeans went to the Americas.

Enslaved people often died from backbreaking working conditions, poor nutrition, lack of adequate shelter, and tropical heat and the diseases that accompanied such heat. Sugar plantations processed so much sugar that they were referred to as **engenhos**, which means "engines" in Portuguese. Because of the engenhos' horrible working conditions, plantation owners lost from 5 to 10 percent of their labor force per year. Slavery is discussed in more detail in the Topic 4.4.

Growing Cash Crops The Spanish noticed Portugal's success with plantation agriculture and returned to the Caribbean to pursue **cash crop** cultivation, such as sugar and tobacco. Cash crops are grown for sale rather than subsistence. Soon, sugar eclipsed silver as the main moneymaker for the European empires. (Connect: Write a paragraph comparing the economic practices of Spain in the Americas and Portugal in South, Southwest, and Southeast Asia. See Topic 4.2.)

African Presence in the Americas

African cultures were not completely lost once captives arrived in the Americas. In fact, during the **African Diaspora** (dispersion of Africans out of Africa), enslaved Africans retained some aspects of their cultures.

Languages With a few exceptions, Africans were not able to transplant their languages to the Americas. The captives were forced away from their communities, and they soon found themselves on ships among captives from all across West Africa (and, on some slave ships, from across East Africa as well).

Since captives were taken from myriad African cultural groups, most did not share a common language. Understandably, they found it difficult, if not impossible, to communicate en route. Because of their linguistic isolation on the ships and in the Americas, most Africans lost their languages after a generation. In spite of this forced isolation from their cultures, West Africans managed to combine European colonizers' languages (English, Spanish, French, or Portuguese, for example) with parts of their West African languages and grammatical patterns to create new languages known broadly as **creole**.

Because the Caribbean islands had a larger concentration of enslaved Africans than did North America, creole languages dominate there even today. In the United States, which had a smaller percentage of Africans in comparison to the total population, few examples of creole languages exist. One notable exception is the Gullah or Geechee language of coastal South Carolina and Georgia, in places where enslaved people once composed 75 percent of the population.

Music Africans brought their music with them. The syncopated rhythms and percussion they used influenced later styles. These include gospel, blues, jazz, rock and roll, hip-hop, rap, samba, reggae, and country music.

One reason many African descendants maintained their musical traditions was because enslaved Africans in America used them as a means of survival. They sang tunes from home to help them endure long workdays as well as to communicate with other Africans, such as when planning an escape. They blended European Christian music with their own religious songs, known today as Negro spirituals—essential elements of American folk music history. Enslaved people also invented the banjo, which is very similar to stringed instruments found in West Africa.

Food In addition to rice and okra, Africans brought their knowledge of how to prepare these foods. The dish known as **gumbo**, popular in the southern United States, has roots in African cooking. With influences on language, music, food, and much more, African culture has had a profound and lasting impact on life in the Americas.

Columbian Exchange: Eastern Hemisphere to Western Hemisphere		
Type of Exchange	Examples	Effects on the Western Hemisphere
Crops	• Sugar • Wheat • Barley • Okra • Rice • Oranges * Grapes • Lettuce • Coffee	• Deforestation to make way for sugar, wheat, barley, okra, rice, and other crops • Soil depletion from growing the same crops repeatedly on the same land
Animals	• Horses • Oxen • Pigs • Cattle • Sheep • Goats • Mosquitoes • Rats • Chickens	• Overgrazing by cattle, sheep, and goats • Soil erosion because of overgrazing • Spread of diseases from mosquitoes, rats, and livestock
People	• Europeans • Africans	• Racial diversity • Chattel slavery • Social structures based on race and ethnicity
Diseases	• Smallpox • Measles • Typhus • Bubonic plague • Influenza	• Spread of disease • Millions of deaths among Native American populations
Technology and Ideas	• Alphabetic writing • Firearms	• Improved communication • New methods for hunting and warfare

Columbian Exchange: Western Hemisphere to Eastern Hemisphere		
Type of Exchange	Examples	Effects on the Eastern Hemisphere
Crops	• Potatoes • Maize • Manioc • Tobacco • Cacao • Peanuts	• Better nutrition • Increase in population • Greater wealth
Animals	• Turkeys • Llamas • Alpacas • Guinea pigs	• More diverse diet • New types of textiles
Diseases	• Syphilis	• Increased health risks
People	• Native Americans	• Ethnic diversity
Technology and Ideas	• Rubber • Quinine	• Rubber was first used as an eraser • Quinine provided a treatment for malaria

Environmental and Demographic Impact

Contact between Afro-Eurasia and the Americas brought dramatic changes to both. Most changes resulted from the Columbian Exchange. In addition, though, Europeans used agricultural land more intensively than did American Indians. For example, colonists cut down trees to clear areas for planting crops, and they created large fields that they cultivated year after year. As a result, deforestation and soil depletion became problems in the Americas. In addition, Europeans often lived in more densely populated communities than did American Indians. This increased the strain on water resources and created more concentrated areas of pollution.

KEY TERMS BY THEME

ENVIRONMENT: Disease
smallpox

ENVIRONMENT: Animals
horse

GOVERNMENT: Empire
conquistadores

ENVIRONMENT: Foods
maize
cacao
okra
rice
sugarcane

CULTURE: African
creole
gumbo

ECONOMY: Exchanges
Columbian Exchange
transatlantic slave trade
engenhos
cash crop

SOCIETY: Population
African Diaspora

Questions 1 to 3 refer to the passage below.

"And so at the rumor of the rich deposits of mercury . . . in the years 1570 and 1571, they started the construction of the town of Huancavelica de Oropesa in a pleasant valley at the foot of the range. It contains 400 Spanish residents, as well as many temporary shops of dealers in merchandise and groceries, heads of trading houses, and transients, for the town has a lively commerce. . . . Up on the range there are 3,000 or 4,000 Indians working in the mine. . . . The ore was very rich black flint . . . and when they have filled their little sacks, the poor fellows, loaded down with ore, climb up those ladders or rigging, some like masts and others like cables, and so trying and distressing that a man empty-handed can hardly get up them."

Antonio Vazquez de Espinosa, *Compendium and Description*
of the West Indies, 1622

1. The excerpt implies that Espinosa felt

   (A) sympathy for those working in the mine

   (B) loyalty to the Spanish government

   (C) concern for the souls of the indigenous population

   (D) interest primarily in making profits from the mine

2. The conditions faced by the Indian laborers described in the passage were most similar to those of

   (A) enslaved Africans in North America

   (B) bureaucrats serving in Song China

   (C) guild members in European cities

   (D) merchants involved in the trans-Saharan trade

3. What impact did the products of mines described in the passage, along with metals extracted from other mines, have on Spain and the rest of the world?

   (A) It enabled the Spanish navy to defeat the English navy in 1588.

   (B) It resulted in inflation and a worldwide devaluation of silver.

   (C) It caused gold to become the new form of worldwide currency.

   (D) It allowed many South Americans to move to Europe.

1. **Use the passages below to answer all parts of the question that follows.**

"On the evening of October 11, 1492. . . . The two worlds [Old and New world], which God had cast asunder, were reunited, and the two worlds, which were so very different, began on that day to become alike. That trend toward biological homogeneity is one of the most important aspects of the history of life on this planet since the retreat of the continental glaciers."

Alfred W. Crosby Jr., The Colombian Exchange: Biological
and Cultural Consequences of 1492 (1972)

"Maize was the most important grain of the American Indians in 1491, and it is one of the most important grain sources in the world right now. It is a standard crop of people not only throughout the Americas, but also southern Europe. It is a staple for the Chinese. It is a staple in Indonesia, throughout large areas of Africa. If suddenly American Indian crops would not grow in all of the world, it would be an ecological tragedy. It would be the slaughter of a very large portion of the human race."

Alfred W. Crosby Jr., Smithsonian.com, October 4, 2011

(A) Identify Crosby's argument about the interactions that occurred between the Americas and Europe/Africa in the period 1450–1750.

(B) Explain ONE way in which the biological impact referred to in the passage differed from other encounters between the Americas and Europe/Africa in the period 1450–1750.

(C) Explain ONE historical situation in the period 1450–1750, other than the one illustrated in the passage, in which states experienced environmental impact.

2. **Answer all parts of the question that follows.**

(A) Identify ONE way in which disease transformed the Americas, Africa, and Europe in the period 1450–1750.

(B) Explain ONE way in which commodities affected economies in the Americas, Africa, and Europe in the period 1450–1750.

(C) Explain ONE way in which European practices affected the environment in the Americas in the period 1450–1750.

THINK AS A HISTORIAN: IDENTIFY EVIDENCE IN AN ARGUMENT

Historians develop arguments to explain and interpret the past. They develop claims—statements that express the assertions they make—and they support their claims with evidence.

Reread the second passage by Alfred W. Crosby Jr. in question 1 on the previous page. Then answer these questions.

1. What claim(s) does Crosby make in this passage?

2. Identify five pieces of evidence Crosby uses to back up his claims.

REFLECT ON THE TOPIC ESSENTIAL QUESTION

1. In one to three paragraphs, explain the causes of the Columbian Exchange and its effects on the Eastern and Western Hemispheres.

Source: Getty Images

Maize is one of the most important grain sources in the world today.

Maritime Empires Link Regions

You grow your peanuts
And plenty millet
The king sets a hand on everything
And says it is not yours anymore!
In the deepest of your sleep
The king beats his drum
And says wake up!
You are not free anymore –

—Anonymous West African griot (storyteller) song

Essential Question: How were the empires of European states established between 1450 to 1750, and what economic and labor systems fueled them?

European nations, driven largely by political, religious, and economic rivalries, established new maritime empires and administered trading posts in Asia and Africa and colonies in the Americas. Asian trade frequently exchanged silver and gold for luxury goods such as silk and spices, while newly developed colonial economies in the Americas often depended on agriculture.

American plantations relied on existing labor systems and also introduced new labor systems. Among these were **indentured servitude**, arrangements through which servants contracted to work for a specified period of years in exchange for passage. Another was **chattel slavery**, a system in which individuals were considered as property to be bought and sold. The appalling shock of free people being seized and enslaved is captured in the griot (storyteller) song of the West African Wolof people. The growth of the plantation economy increased the demand for enslaved Africans in the Americas, leading to significant demographic, social, and cultural changes.

State-Building and Empire Expansion

The explorations of European states (see Topic 4.2) were the foundation of maritime empires. States claimed lands and established the basis of an empire in the areas they explored.

Trading Posts in Africa and Asia

Certain regions of East and West Africa were the targets of European conquest during the late 15th century. Portuguese ruler Prince Henry the Navigator was keenly interested in navigational technology. (See Topic 4.2.) He financed expeditions along Africa's Atlantic Coast and around the Cape of Good Hope, exploring African coastal communities before other European powers.

With the cooperation of local rulers, first Portuguese and then other European traders set up trading posts along Africa's coasts. Some local rulers traded enslaved people to the Europeans in exchange for gunpowder and cannons, giving those coastal governments a military advantage when battling neighboring villages. Some African city-states grew wealthy by selling enslaved Africans to Europeans. In particular, the Kingdom of Dahomey grew stronger because it raided other villages to enslave people, and sold them to European merchants.

African States In central West Africa, Portuguese explorers, traders, and missionaries made inroads into the Kongo and Benin kingdoms. Artwork from these societies bears signs of European as well as African cultural influences. As early as the 16th century, Benin artisans incorporated images of the European "intruder" into their carvings and sculptures. Yet the expansion of maritime trading networks supported the growth of some African states, including the **Asante Empire** and the **Kingdom of the Kongo**. Their participation in trade led to an increase in their influence.

In 1498, Portuguese explorer Vasco da Gama (see Topic 4.1) invaded the Swahili city-states of East Africa, most of which were thriving commercial centers in the Indian Ocean trade. The Portuguese took over trade in Kilwa, Mombasa, and other city-states by sending heavily armed ships and building fortresses. This takeover threw the region into a devastating decline.

Japan Just as European states were expanding their trade networks, Japan was sharply restricting its networks. Japan had tolerated the first Portuguese and Dutch traders and missionaries in the mid-16th century. Thousands of Japanese converted to Christianity. Some Christians, intolerant of other faiths, destroyed Buddhist shrines. In response, in 1587, the Japanese government banned Christian worship services. Over the next 40 years, Japan took additional steps to persecute Christians and limit foreign influences. By the 1630s, the government had expelled nearly all foreigners, banned most foreign books, and prohibited Japanese people from traveling abroad.

For more than two centuries, Japan was partially isolated from the rest of the world. They allowed some Dutch merchants to live on a small island in Nagasaki harbor, in almost total seclusion. In addition, Japan continued some trade with the Chinese, mostly carried out by regional lords who were far from the capital city with easy access by sea to Korea, Taiwan, and Okinawa. The Japanese thought that they were through with the "uncouth" Europeans. However, Europeans and Americans would return in the mid-19th century.

China After the voyages of Zheng He in the 15th century, the **Ming**

Dynasty tried to limit outside influence on China by restricting trade. The Ming prohibited private foreign trade, destroyed some dockyards, limited the size of ships that could be built, and began reconstructing the Great Wall. These changes were part of a broader pattern of conservatism under the Ming to undo the influence of the Mongol Yuan Dynasty that ruled China before them. For example, the Ming reemphasized the importance of Confucianism and reinvigorated the traditional exam system. Many of the limits on trade were eventually reversed, and China resumed its important role in global trade.

European Rivalries on Five Continents

European rivalries fueled by political, economic, and religious motives shaped the expansion of empires. Several powers established trading posts in India:

- The British East India Company had begun a commercial relationship with the Mughal Empire in the 17th century.
- Portugal controlled a coastal trading post in the southwestern state of Goa.
- France controlled Pondicherry, a city in the southeastern state of Tamil Nadu.

During the mid-18th century, France and Great Britain, along with their respective allies, competed for power on five continents in the Seven Years' War. Britain's victory in that war in 1763 drove the French out of India. The Portuguese remained in India until driven out in the mid-20th century.

British in India At first, British trading posts in India were typical of those established by Europeans in India and elsewhere. The East India Company (EIC) established small forts on the coasts that focused solely on making a profit through trade. Limited by the power of India's Mughal Empire, the EIC posts controlled very little territory.

However, the EIC then began to expand. It took advantage of the tensions between Muslims and Hindus in India and began to increase its political power through treaties with local rulers. With the help of European-trained Indian private forces called sepoys, the East India Company moved inland, spreading its influence. Ultimately, Britain intervened in India politically and militarily to such an extent that it controlled much of the subcontinent.

The British Global Network The British also set up trading posts in West Africa, where the Asante Empire limited their impact. Trading posts in Africa, India, and elsewhere paved the way for globalization. Each post became a node, an intersection of multiple points serving as a trade center for goods from many parts of the world.

Europeans in the Americas

Before the arrival of Europeans in the late 15th century, the **Aztec Empire** in Mexico and the **Inca Empire** in South America each included 10 million to 15 million people. However, the spread of European diseases caused their populations to plummet. Both empires collapsed quickly when attacked by Spanish forces.

In Mexico, helped by groups that the Aztecs had conquered, Cortés's forces overthrew the Aztec by 1521 and established the colony of **New Spain**. The Spaniards melted down the Aztecs' treasures and sent the gold back home. They destroyed Tenochtitlán and built their own capital, **Mexico City**, on its ruins.

In the Andes of South America, **Francisco Pizarro** and his crew attacked the Inca and captured their ruler, **Atahualpa**. Pizarro offered to release Atahualpa if the Inca would fill a large room with gold. The Inca complied. However, in 1533 the Spanish killed Atahualpa anyway. By 1572, the Spaniards had completed their conquest of the Inca Empire.

Spain Versus Portugal In the **Treaty of Tordesillas** of 1494, Spain and Portugal divided the Americas between them. Spain reserved all lands to the west of a meridian that went through eastern South America. Portugal reserved all lands east of this line. This arrangement put Brazil under Portugal's rule, while Spain claimed the rest of the Americas.

SPANISH AND PORTUGUESE COLONIES, C. 1600

In addition to establishing colonies in Mesoamerica and South America, Spain explored other parts of North America north of present-day Mexico. The explorer Pedro Menéndez de Avilés established a fort in St. Augustine on the east coast of Florida in 1565, which became the oldest continuous settlement in what later became the United States. Spain would not be able to control all of North America, however, because the French, British, and Dutch later made claims and settlements there.

France Versus Britain France and Britain continued to vie for dominance in North America. As British settlers moved into former Dutch territory in upper New York, they began to form ties with the powerful Iroquois, who had been in conflict with the French over trade issues for decades. The British hoped that the Iroquois could frustrate French trade interests. Over time, the Iroquois began to realize that the British posed more of a threat than the French. In a shift of alliances, the Iroquois and French signed a peace treaty known as the Great Peace of Montreal in 1701. In the same war in which Britain drove France out of India, the British drove France out of Canada as well. The North American portion of this war is sometimes called the French and Indian War.

FRENCH, ENGLISH, AND DUTCH COLONIES, C. 1650

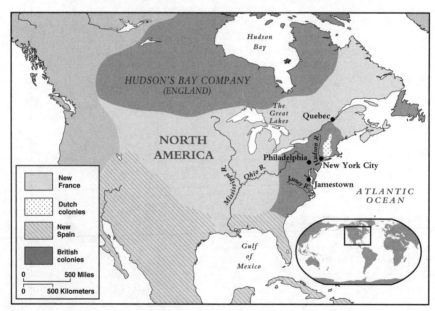

Continuity and Change in Economic Systems

Although the intensification of trade and the increasing influence of Europeans brought some disruption to the Indian Ocean trading networks, on the whole, the system absorbed the changes and continued its familiar ways of doing business. Merchants in the Indian Ocean networks were used to paying taxes and fees to states controlling sea lanes and ports and operated often through religious and ethnic ties. They did not use arms to protect their trade, and if the fees in one trading center became too high, they were free to move elsewhere.

Europeans in the Indian Ocean Trade The Portuguese, however, arrived with superior naval forces, religious zeal, and a determination to profit from the increasingly diverse products being traded, both from Asia to Europe and also within Asia. In addition to porcelain and silk from China, cloth from Gujarati weavers in western India, agricultural goods from Java, and spices from many places created an abundant market for trade and profit. In contrast to the ethnic and religious trading ties developed over hundreds of years, the Portuguese used their military superiority to take control of trade, creating a string of armed trading posts along the trade routes of the Indian Ocean. In 1509, for example, the Portuguese had a decisive victory in the Battle of Diu in the Arabian Sea over the combined forces of Gujaratis, the Mamluks of Egypt, and the Zamorin of Calicut with the support of Venice, Portugal's European competitor.

Despite the differences between the traditional trading networks and those controlled by European powers, merchants in the Indian Ocean trade networks continued as before in many ways—paying for the right to use certain ports or passageways and developing trade links through traditional networks.

Spain and Gold in the Americas The Western European search for profit began with Columbus. On his first voyage, he was convinced that gold was plentiful on **Hispaniola**, the name he gave the island now occupied by Haiti and the Dominican Republic. But gold was sparse in the Caribbean. Desiring to return home with something valuable, Columbus and his crew kidnapped Tainos, indigenous peoples, and took them, enslaved, to Spain.

In the early 1500s, the Spanish established a system called the **encomienda** to gain access to gold and other resources of the Americas. **Encomenderos**, or landowners, compelled indigenous people to work for them in exchange for food and shelter, as landowners required of serfs in Europe's manorial system. This **coercive labor system** was notorious for its brutality.

The Spanish crown often granted land to **conquistadores** as a reward for their efforts. The **hacienda system** arose when landowners developed agriculture on their lands—wheat, fruit, vegetables, and sugar. They used coerced labor to work the fields. Most conquistadores were men and many had children with native women. This made the Spanish colonies unlike British colonies.

Silver While gold did not yield riches for Spanish conquistadores, the discovery of **silver** in Mexico and Peru revived economic fortunes—for both individual explorers and Spain. The use of mercury to separate silver from its ore increased the profitability of silver mining. By the end of the 16th century, the cities of Zacatecas, in Mexico, and especially Potosí, in the Andes Mountains in modern-day Bolivia, became thriving centers of silver mining.

For this industry to flourish, Spanish prospectors needed labor. The indigenous populations would do all but the most dangerous work in the mines. In response, Spanish authorities in Peru transformed the traditional

Incan **mit'a system** of labor obligation, in which young men were required to devote a certain amount of labor to public works projects, into a coerced labor system. Villages were compelled to send a percentage of their male population to do the dangerous work in the mines for a paltry wage.

Silver and Mercantilism The silver trade not only made individual Spanish prospectors wealthy, it also strengthened the Spanish economy. European powers at the time were adopting **mercantilism**, an economic system that increased government control of the economy through high tariffs and the establishment of **colonies**, claimed lands settled by immigrants from the home country. In the case of Spain, the main purpose of the colonies in the Americas was to supply as much gold and silver as possible.

Another way to increase national wealth, according to the mercantilist system, was for a colonizing country to export more than it imported. A percentage of overseas silver production went directly to the Spanish crown. The empire used this wealth to build up the military and establish foreign trade.

Continuity and Change in Labor Systems

Different regions and different economies used different labor systems.

Types of Labor in the Early Modern Period			
Laborer	**Location**	**Type of Work**	**Freedoms/Limits**
Enslaved	• Americas • Africa	• Domestic labor • Agricultural labor	• Considered property • Had few or no rights
Serf	• Europe • Asia	• Subsistence farming • Most of the yield belonged to the lord	• Attached to the land: not free to move at will • Had little or no legal protection
Indentured Servant	• All regions	• Domestic labor • Field work	• Employer paid for transport to a new location • Individual worked without pay for up to seven years
Free Peasant	• Europe • Asia	• Farming • Craft labor (blacksmithing, weaving, etc.)	• Worked on their own land • Sometimes owned a business • Paid taxes to the lord • Paid tithes to the church
Nomad	• Europe • Asia • Africa	• Animal breeding • Pastoralism • Herding	• Did not own land permanently • Used land temporarily • Had freedom to move
Guild Member	• Europe	• Skilled craft labor • Workers organized to set standards for quality and price	• Started as an apprentice • Could eventually work independently

During this era, Europeans sought sources of inexpensive labor in the Americas. Western European countries such as Portugal, Spain, and England were developing their naval technology, but Portugal was ahead of the others. In West Africa during the latter part of the 1400s, Portuguese trading fleets arrived in the Kingdom of the Kongo seeking enslaved people. Initially they took the enslaved Africans back to Europe to work as domestic servants.

Slavery existed in Africa—including the extensive enslavement of women as household workers—well before Europeans sought labor for their investments in the Americas. For example, in many societies, the entire community shared the land. In order to establish positions of wealth and power, individuals not only showcased the property they owned, but also showcased the enslaved people they owned.

Europeans were also not the first foreigners to seek out African labor. Arab merchants during the Postclassical Era (600–1450) often bought enslaved people during their travels to the Swahili Coast of East Africa. However, it was the Atlantic slave trade that wreaked the most havoc on African societies. (Connect: Compose a graphic organizer comparing slavery during Sub-Saharan Africa's early colonial period with slavery from 600 to 1450. See Topic 2.3.)

Why Africans? Several factors converged to make Africa a target for slave raids by Europeans after 1450. Slavery in Latin America and the Caribbean began toward the end of the 16th century, when European conquistadores sought fortunes in gold, silver, and sugar. Land was plentiful, but labor to make the land profitable was scarce.

Europeans initially forced indigenous people to do the hard labor of mining and farming, but European diseases wiped out large portions of these coerced laborers. The enslaved indigenous people who survived often escaped bondage because, compared to Europeans, they were more familiar with the territory, had social networks that could protect them, and could easily camouflage themselves within the native population. Repeated efforts to enslave Native Americans failed, although other efforts to coerce labor did have some success.

Labor for Plantations In North America, plantation owners recruited European indentured servants who would come to work, mostly to grow tobacco, for a specified period in exchange for passage, room, and board. However, most of these people were not used to the backbreaking agricultural working conditions and the climate of the Americas. In addition, indentured servants were required to work for only about seven years. If they survived their indenture, they became free laborers. Thus, landowners did not think of indigenous captives and European indentured servants as ideal workers.

Transport of Enslaved Africans to the Americas Capturing Africans for slavery was invariably violent. When African leaders along the coast realized that their kingdoms could economically benefit from the slave trade, they invaded neighboring societies in a quest for enslaved people to take back to the coast. At times, African rulers were also willing to hand over individuals from the lower rungs of their own societies, such as prisoners of war, servants, or criminals.

However, King Afonso of Kongo understood that slave raids were not easily controllable. Though he had initially allowed slave trading in his kingdom, he had no intention of giving up his society's elite to slavery, nor did he want Kongo to be depopulated. King Afonso also saw that his authority was undermined because his subjects were able to trade enslaved people for European goods without his involvement. Before the Europeans came, he had been able to control all trade in his domain.

Source: Wikimedia Commons, Public Domain
Enslaved people being transported in Africa, 19th century engraving

The Horrors of the Journey Captive Africans, swept away from their families, were taken to holding pens in West Africa known as barracoons, or "slave castles." The modern country of Ghana has preserved these "Points of No Return," where thousands upon thousands of Africans saw their homeland for the last time. Today, people can visit one such holding prison—the so-called House of Slaves on Ile de Gorée (Gorée Island), on the coast of Senegal.

From these holding pens, slave traders next crammed their captives into the dank cargo section of a ship, providing them little water, food, or even room for movement. The grueling journey across the Atlantic was known as the **Middle Passage**, because it was the middle part of the captives' journey. Many captured Africans attempted rebellions at sea, but most uprisings were crushed.

During the journey to the Americas, which usually took about six weeks, up to half of a ship's captives might die. Over the hundreds of years of the Atlantic slave trade, from the early 1500s to the mid-19th century, 10 to 15 percent of all African captives perished before reaching the Americas. (Connect: Write an outline of the effects of the Atlantic slave trade on Africa. See Topic 4.3.)

Destination of Enslaved Africans by Colonial Region	
Destination	**Percentage**
Portuguese Colonies	39%
British West Indian Colonies	18%
Spanish Colonies	18%
French Colonies	14%
British Mainland Colonies	6%
Dutch West Indian Colonies	2%
Other	3%

Source: Stephen D. Behrendt et al. Africana: The Encyclopedia of the African and African American Experience.

Demographic, Social, and Cultural Changes The growth of the planation economy and the expansion of slavery in the Americas led to significant changes that affected not only countless individual lives but also broad patterns of history. The physical migration of captives had significant impact on the demographics of both their African homes and the countries of their captivity. The exportation of enslaved people that was required to keep the population continuing in the country of captivity caused a century-long decline in population in African home countries.

In addition to physical migration, slavery resulted in a migration of status, from free person to enslaved, setting up social classes that remain influential in post-slavery countries. Further, it disrupted family organization, since families were often separated, and more men than women were taken captive. Polygyny (having more than one wife) became more common. With people treated as commodities, as chattel slavery, social and family groupings were determined more by supply and demand than by the familial bonds of kinship.

Each region in which slavery was introduced was affected in a unique way. However, in all of them, people with African roots helped shape and enrich the language and culture of the societies into which they were brought. The mixing of ethnic groups resulted in new groups of multiracial people, such as mestizos and mulattos.

The Indian Ocean Slave Trade While most Africans who were enslaved and transported to the Americas came from west and central Africa, there was a long-running slave trade in the eastern part of the continent. By routes overland or in the Indian Ocean, enslaved East Africans were sold to buyers in northern Africa, the Middle East, and India. Many were transported to the islands off the southeast coast of Africa, such as Madagascar. The trade reached its peak in the 18th and 19th centuries.

Enslaved people taken in the Indian Ocean trade suffered different fates from those taken across the Atlantic. People from the Indian Ocean region were more likely to work in seaports as laborers in the shipping industry and as household servants. Some worked as sailors or even soldiers. Living in towns or cities, they had some opportunity to develop communities and to work alongside free laborers. Those who ended up in Islamic communities had certain rights, such as the right to marry. As a result of the Indian Ocean slave trade, African words, musical styles, and customs can be found in Oman, India, and elsewhere.

KEY TERMS BY THEME

GOVERNMENT: African States
Asante Empire
Kingdom of the Kongo

GOVERNMENT: East Asian States
Ming Dynasty

GOVERNMENT: Americas
Aztec Empire
Inca Empire
New Spain
Mexico City
Francisco Pizarro
Atahualpa
Treaty of Tordesillas
Hispaniola
conquistadores

ECONOMY: Products
silver

ECONOMY: Economic Systems
mercantilism
colonies

ECONOMY: Labor Systems
indentured servitude
chattel slavery
encomienda
encomenderos
coercive labor system
hacienda system
mit'a system
Middle Passage

Questions 1 to 3 refer to the image below.

Source: Oil on canvas. 1760. Juan Patricio Morlete Ruiz (1713-1772) Gift of the 2011 Collectors Committee / LACMA

A Spanish colonist, an American Indian woman, and their child

1. One difference between Spanish and British colonies reflected in this painting is that in Spanish colonies men were more likely to
   (A) be a farmer
   (B) be married to a woman much younger than himself
   (C) have a child with a Native woman
   (D) have accumulated considerable wealth

2. In which region is this painting most likely set?
   (A) Hudson Bay
   (B) Gulf of Mexico
   (C) James River
   (D) Great Lakes

3. Which of the following best describes the cultural exchange represented in the painting?

(A) The man has adopted aspects of the culture of the woman.

(B) The child is dressed in native-style clothing.

(C) The plants are mostly of European origin.

(D) The woman has adopted aspects of the culture of the man.

SHORT-ANSWER QUESTIONS

1. **Use the passage below to answer all parts of the question that follows.**

"The widespread use of slavery was a systematic Spanish adaptation on the north Mexican frontier wherever nomadic Indians were encountered. Almost at the very moment that the New Laws (1542) made slavery illegal in Mesoamerican Mexico, the Mixtón War (1541-1542) in Nueva Galicia provided the initial reason for retaining the practice legally on the frontier for generations. The discovery of silver at Zacatecas sealed the fate of Spanish-Indian relations not only on the Gran Chichimeca, but throughout most of the North. The inevitable resistance by hunter-gatherers to Spanish domination, the shortage of labor, and the semiautonomous political power wielded by provincial and local authorities insured the survival of slavery and encomienda in northern New Spain into the eighteenth century."

> José Cuello, *The Persistence of Indian Slavery and Encomienda in the Northeast of Colonial Mexico, 1577–1723,* (1988)

(A) Identify Cuello's argument in the passage.

(B) Explain ONE way in which the treatment of enslaved people in Mexico was different from the treatment of people taken in the Indian Ocean trade in the period 1450–1750.

(C) Explain ONE historical situation in the period 1450–1750, other than the one illustrated in the passage, in which European states transformed the lives of colonized states.

2. **Answer all parts of the question that follows.**

(A) Identify ONE economic impact that the mit'a system had on Europe in the period 1450–1750.

(B) Explain ONE similarity between the trade in the Indian Ocean networks before the arrival of the Portuguese and the trade after their arrival in the period 1450–1750.

(C) Explain ONE difference between the economic development of Portugal and the economic development of China in the period 1450–1750.

THINK AS A HISTORIAN: PURPOSE AND AUDIENCE IN PRIMARY SOURCES

One way to determine the accuracy of historical sources is to identify their purpose. However, their stated purpose is not necessarily their real purpose. Identifying their intended audience can help pin down the purpose of sources.

Spanish historian, reformer, and later Dominican Friar Bartolomé de las Casas (c. 1484–1566) wrote what he referred to as eyewitness accounts of the suffering the Spaniards inflicted on the indigenous people. The following passage is from *A Brief Account of the Destruction of the Indies* published in Seville in 1552. Las Casas had used his observations to help pass the so-called New Laws in 1542, which outlawed forcing indigenous people into slavery and attempted to ban the system of encomienda.

> "In the Year 1509, the Spaniards sailed to the Islands of St. John and Jamaica . . . with the same purpose and design they proposed to themselves in the Isle of Hispaniola, perpetrating innumerable Robberies and Villanies as before; whereunto they added unheard of Cruelties . . . . and Finally by afflicting and harassing them with un-exampled Oppressions and torments in the Mines, they spoiled and unpeopled this Contrey [country] of these Innocents. These two Isles containing six hundred thousand at least, though at this day there are scarce two hundred men to be found in either of them, the remainder perishing without the knowledge of Christian Faith or Sacrament."

Answer the following questions to help understand how the intended audience can reveal an author's purpose.

1. For what audience did Las Casas write these accounts? What does that audience suggest about his purpose for writing?

2. Suppose these accounts had been written by a visitor from a competing European power eager to remove the Spanish from the Americas and take over the land for itself. What might be that author's audience and purpose?

3. Read the Historical Perspectives on the brutality of the Spanish on page 265. Then in a sentence or two explain the role of identifying purpose and audience in determining the accuracy of a historical source, referring to specific examples from that page.

REFLECT ON THE TOPIC ESSENTIAL QUESTION

1. In one to three paragraphs, explain how the empires of European states were established between 1450 to 1750 and what economic and labor systems fueled them.

4.5

Maritime Empires Develop

All of the residents of these United Provinces [the Netherlands] shall be allowed to participate in [the Dutch East India] Company and to do so with as little or as great an amount of money as they choose.

—Charter, Dutch East India Company, 1602

Essential Question: What economic strategies did maritime empires use to increase their power, and how did the developing empires affect political, economic, religious, and cultural dynamics?

M aritime (sea-based) empires transformed commerce from local, small-scale trading, mostly based on barter, to large-scale international trade using gold and silver. These empires employed new economic models, such as joint-stock companies, through which investors financed trade by buying shares in corporations such as the East India Company, supporting increased trade in Asia. New ocean trade routes were opened, aiding the rise of this extended global economy. The Atlantic trading system involved the movement of labor—including enslaved people—and the mixing of African, American, and European cultures and peoples, with all groups contributing to a cultural synthesis. Silver, sugar, and slavery were the keys to the development of these mercantilist empires.

Economic Strategies

In the 17th century, Europeans generally measured the wealth of a country in how much gold and silver it had in its coffers. To achieve this wealth, countries used economic strategies designed to sell as many goods as they could to other countries in order to obtain maximum amounts of gold and silver. To keep their wealth, countries would also spend as little of their precious metals as possible on goods from other countries.

The accumulation of **capital**, material wealth available to produce more wealth, in Western Europe grew as entrepreneurs entered long-distance markets. Capital changed hands from entrepreneurs to laborers, putting laborers in a better position to become consumers—and even investors, as the above quote suggests. Despite restrictions by the Church, lending money at high rates of interest became commonplace. Actual wealth also increased with gold and silver from the Western Hemisphere.

Commercial Revolution

The transformation to a trade-based economy using gold and silver is known as the **Commercial Revolution**. The Commercial Revolution affected all regions of the world and resulted from four key factors: the development of European overseas colonies; the opening of new ocean trade routes; population growth; and inflation, caused partly by the pressure of the increasing population and partly by the increased amount of gold and silver that was mined and put in circulation. The high rate of inflation, or general rise in prices, in the 16th and early 17th century is called the **Price Revolution**.

Aiding the rise of this extended global economy was the formation of **joint-stock companies**, owned by investors who bought stock or shares in them. People invested capital in such companies and shared both the profits and the risks of exploration and trading ventures. Offering **limited liability**, the principle that an investor was not responsible for a company's debts or other liabilities beyond the amount of an investment, made investing safer.

The developing European middle class had capital to invest from successful businesses in their home countries. They also had money with which to purchase imported luxuries. The Dutch, English, and French all developed joint-stock companies in the 17th century, including the British **East India Company** in 1600 and the **Dutch East India Company** in 1602. In Spain and Portugal, however, the government did most of the investing itself through grants to certain explorers. Joint-stock companies were a driving force behind the development of maritime empires as they allowed continued exploration as well as ventures to colonize and develop the resources of distant lands with limited risk to investors.

Commerce and Finance The Dutch were long the commercial middlemen of Europe, having set up and maintained trade routes to Latin America, North America, South Africa, and Indonesia. Dutch ships were faster and lighter than those of their rivals for most of the 17th century, giving them an early trade advantage. The Dutch East India Company was also highly successful as a joint-stock company. It made enormous profits in the Spice Islands and Southeast Asia.

Source: Wikimedia Commons

The Dutch ship *Vryburg* on Chinese export porcelain, 1756

Pioneers in finance, the Dutch had a stock exchange as early as 1602. By 1609, the Bank of Amsterdam traded currency internationally. The Dutch standard of living was the highest in Europe as such goods as diamonds, linen, pottery, and tulip bulbs passed through the hands of Dutch traders.

France and England were not so fortunate. Early in the 18th century, both fell victim to speculative financial schemes. Known as financial bubbles, the schemes were based on the sale of shares to investors who were promised a certain return on their investment. After a frenzy of buying that drove up the price of shares, the bubble burst and investors lost huge amounts of money, sending many into bankruptcy and inflicting wide damage to the economy.

Triangular Trade The Europeans' desire for enslaved workers in the Americas coupled with Portugal's "discovery" of West Africa meant that Africa became the source for new labor. Enslaved Africans became part of a complex Atlantic trading system known as the **triangular trade**, because voyages often had three segments. A ship might carry European manufactured goods such as firearms to West Africa, and from there transport enslaved Africans to the Americas, and then load up with sugar or tobacco to take to Europe. Sugar was the most profitable good from the Americas. By the 1700s, Caribbean sugar production and rum (made from sugar) were financing fortunes in Britain, and to a lesser extent, in France and the Netherlands.

TRIANGULAR TRADE

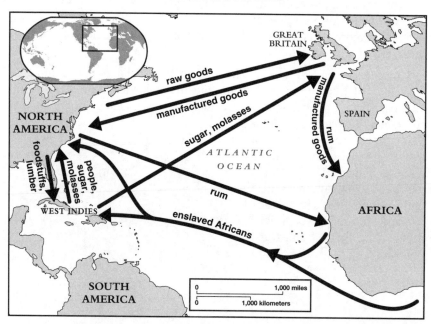

Rivalries for the Indian Ocean Trade

After Europeans stumbled on the Americas, trade over the Atlantic Ocean became significant. However, states continued to vie for control of trade routes on the Indian Ocean as well. The Portuguese soundly defeated a combined Muslim and Venetian force in a naval battle in the Arabian Sea in 1509 (see Topic 4.4) over controlling trade. They met a different fate, though, when they tried to conquer Moroccan forces in a battle on land in 1578.

Its coffers depleted after the victory, Morocco looked inland to capture the riches of the Songhai Kingdom, despite the prohibition of waging war on another Muslim state. With thousands of soldiers, camels, and horses, as well as eight cannons and other firearms, Moroccan forces traveled months to reach Songhai. In 1590, in a battle near Gao, the Songhai—despite their greater number of fighters—were overcome by the force of firearms. The empire crumbled. The Spanish and Portuguese soon overtook much of this territory.

Change and Continuities in Trade Networks

The trading networks involved a new global circulation of goods, wealth, and labor. Silver from the Spanish colonies in the Americas flowed to Asia, where Asians were eager to exchange their goods—silks, porcelain, steel products—for silver. Asian goods were eagerly purchased in the Atlantic markets.

New Monopolies One way these patterns of trade were maintained was through **monopolies** chartered by European rulers. Monopolies granted certain merchants—usually through a joint-stock company—or the government itself the exclusive right to trade. For example, the Spanish government established a monopoly first over all the domestic tobacco grown and then over all the tobacco grown in its American colonies. The profits from this monopoly greatly enriched the Spanish government. The income from tobacco in Spain made up about one-third of total revenues.

Ongoing Regional Markets At the same time, traditional regional markets continued to flourish in Afro-Eurasia. However, improved shipping offered merchants the opportunity to increase their volume of products. The increasing output of peasant and artisan labor—wool and linen from Western Europe, cotton from India, and silk from China—exchanged hands in port cities with global connections.

Effects of the Atlantic Slave Trade

The Atlantic slave trade greatly weakened several West African kingdoms, such as Kongo. The loss of so many people slowed population growth. Trade competition led to violence among their societies, but also made African slave-raiding kingdoms economically dependent on goods from Europe. Such societies were slow to develop more complex economies in which they produced their own goods. Thus, the slave trade set the stage for European conquest and imperialism of the late 19th century. (See Topic 6.2.)

Economically, African societies that conducted slave raids, such as the **Dahomey** and the **Oyo**, became richer from selling their captives to Europeans. This trade also had political effects, because when a society such as the Dahomey exchanged enslaved people for guns, its raiders easily took advantage of rival societies that had no firearms. Without firearms, neighboring groups could not fight off slave raids, so raiding societies became even richer and more fortified with firearms. Intergroup warfare thus became more common and bloodier as a result of the slave trade.

Slavery and Gender Those most affected by the slave trade were the peoples and civilizations of West Africa in present-day Ghana and Benin, from which most Africans were kidnapped or sold. Gender distributions in those regions became severely imbalanced, because more than two-thirds of those taken were males. The resulting predominance of women prompted a rise in **polygyny** (the taking of more than one wife) and forced women to assume duties that had traditionally been men's jobs.

Impact of New Foods While the Atlantic trading system weakened Africa in many ways, it also ultimately spurred population growth through an improved diet. The Columbian Exchange introduced new crops to the continent, such as the American crops maize, peanuts, and manioc (also known as yucca or cassava), which became staples in the African diet.

Political and Cultural Changes for Indigenous Peoples

Earlier land-based empires, such as those of the Romans, Muslims, and Mongols, all grappled with how to deal with conquered people's traditions and cultures. These empires either allowed traditions to exist or they tried to graft their ways onto those of their subjects. European empires in the Americas stood in stark contrast to these land-based empires. The Spanish and Portuguese empires managed to erase the basic social structures and many of the cultural traditions of the indigenous Americans within a century of when the first European explorers arrived. Europeans' actions nearly depopulated the Americas.

Political Changes: Colonial Administration Indigenous political structures in Latin America were soon replaced by Spanish and Portuguese colonial administrations. Spanish royalty appointed **viceroys** to act as administrators and representatives of the Spanish crown. To keep these viceroys from operating independently of the crown, Spain established **audiencias**, or royal courts, to which Spanish settlers could appeal viceroys' decisions or policies. Slow transportation and communication networks between Europe and the Americas, however, made it difficult for the Spanish crown to exercise direct control over New Spain. As a result, the Spanish throne did not focus on colonial affairs in the Western Hemisphere.

Cultural Changes The indigenous peoples of the Americas lost a great deal of their culture and history at the hands of conquerors. Conquistadors, such as Cortés in Mexico, ordered the burning of native books, which were thought to be unholy. Thus, very few original accounts written in Nahuatl, the language of the Aztec, exist today.

The scarcity of firsthand accounts from indigenous peoples has shaped how historians view this period. For example, because the Spanish burned nearly all Aztec documents, most of the information about the Aztec comes from documents that were written by Spanish conquistadores and priests after the conquest. The authors' biases and lack of familiarity with Nahuatl limits the value of these sources. However, some sources are considered reliable. For example, in 1545, a Spanish priest named Bernardino de Sahagún began compiling the Florentine Codex, one of the most widely cited sources about Aztec life before conquest. (A codex is a type of book.)

Spanish and Portuguese conquerors transplanted their own languages and religion into the Americas. The remnants of this cultural interaction are present today. Although indigenous languages thrive in certain regions—in Guatemala and in the mountains of Mexico, for example—Spanish predominates through much of Latin America, and Brazilians overwhelmingly speak Portuguese.

By 1750, those born in America of Spanish origin, or **creoles**, enjoyed political dominance in New Spain. They soon began clamoring for independence from the Spanish throne. (Connect: Create a two-column chart comparing the influence of Spanish and Portuguese maritime empires on native populations from the 16th and 17th centuries. See Topic 4.4.)

Effects of Belief Systems

The increase and intensity of newly established global connections between hemispheres extended the reach of existing religions. In some areas, the new connections contributed to the development of syncretic belief systems and practices. In other areas, the connections contributed to religious conflicts.

Syncretic Belief Systems in the Americas

African religions in the Americas provide powerful examples of religious **syncretism,** or the combining of different religious beliefs and practices. Africans melded aspects of Christianity, usually Roman Catholicism, with their West African religious traditions, such as drumming, dancing, and a belief in spirits that could take over and act through a person:

- **Santería** means "the way of the saints." Originally an African faith, it became popular in Cuba and then traveled throughout Latin America and to North America.

- **Vodun** means "spirit" or "deity." This belief system originated with African peoples of Dahomey, Kongo, and Yoruba who were enslaved and living in Saint-Domingue, which is now Haiti.

- **Candomblé** means "dance to honor the gods." It is a combination of Yoruba, Fon, and Bantu beliefs from different parts of Africa. It developed in Brazil.

Enslaved Africans in the United States also laid the roots for the African American church, a hybrid of Christianity and African spiritual traditions that remains one of the oldest and most stable institutions in African American communities.

Islam About 1 in 10 of the enslaved Africans practiced Islam. While some of the men who sailed with Columbus may have been Muslims, these enslaved Africans became the first significant presence of Islam in the Americas.

Religion in Latin America Several Catholic religious orders in Europe, such as the Dominicans, Jesuits, and Franciscans, sent missionaries to Latin America to convert people to Christianity. The missionaries were so successful that today most Latin Americans are Roman Catholic Christians. In recent decades, Protestant denominations have begun to gain members.

Numerous examples of religious syncretism originated in the Spanish colonies. Catholic saints' days that coincided with days honored by indigenous people were especially celebrated. In Mexico, a cult developed around the dark-complexioned **Virgin of Guadalupe**, who was revered for her ability to perform miracles.

Global Interactions and Religious Conflicts

Syncretic religions also developed in Afro-Eurasia as global interactions intensified. Sufism, for example, with its focus on personal salvation, helped spread Islam and may have influenced Sikhism, which blended Muslim and Hindu belief systems. The Mughal leader Akbar (see Topic 3.2) tried to mediate conflicts between Muslims and Hindus under his control.

Religion also played a role in conflicts as global interactions increased. The split between Sunni and Shi'a Muslims worsened conflicts between the Ottoman and Safavid empires. (See Topic 3.1.) The split between Catholicism and Protestantism, and between official state religions such as Anglicanism and other Protestant sects, helped drive the settlement of North America as people sought freedom to worship as they saw fit.

KEY TERMS BY THEME

ECONOMY: Strategies	CULTURE: Blending	GOVERNMENT: Latin America
capital	syncretism	viceroys
Commercial Revolution	polygyny	audiencias
Price Revolution	creoles	
joint-stock companies	Santéria	SOCIETY: Slave Trade
limited liability	Vodun	Dahomey
East India Company	Candomblé	Oyo
Dutch East India Company	Virgin of Guadalupe	
triangular trade		
monopolies		

Questions 1 to 3 refer to the map below.

THE AFRICAN SLAVE TRADE, 1500–1900

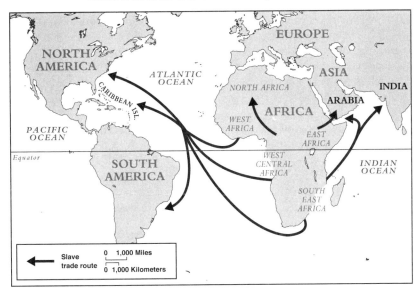

1. Of the movements shown on the map, the largest resulted from a high demand for labor to grow

   (A) sugar

   (B) cotton

   (C) rubber

   (D) tea

2. This map best supports the claim that between 1500 and 1800 Africa's population was becoming

   (A) too large in 1500 to be supported by the technology of that time

   (B) too small in 1800 to enable the slave trade to continue

   (C) more diverse as immigrants replaced people who had been enslaved

   (D) smaller than it would have without the slave trade

3. The movements shown on the map were part of a global trend between 1500 and 1800 of

   (A) greater contact among people of different ethnic backgrounds

   (B) greater separation among people living in different continents

   (C) states becoming smaller and more homogenous

   (D) states becoming larger but more homogenous

1. **Use the passage below to answer all parts of the question that follows.**

"Vodou [Vodun] as we know it in Haiti and the Haitian diaspora today is the result of the pressures of many different cultures and ethnicities of people being uprooted from Africa and imported to Hispanola [the island that includes Haiti] during the African slave trade. Under slavery, African culture and religion was suppressed, lineages were fragmented, and people pooled their religious knowledge and out of this fragmentation became culturally unified. In addition to combining the spirits of many different African and Indian nations, pieces of Roman Catholic liturgy have been incorporated to replace lost prayers or elements; in addition images of Catholic saints are used to represent various spirits or 'mistè' ('mysteries,' actually the preferred term in Haiti), and many saints themselves are honored in Vodou in their own right. This syncretism allows Vodou to encompass the African, the Indian, and the European ancestors in a whole and complete way."

Haitian Consulate, "Haitian Vodou," 2012

(A) Identify ONE way that Vodou is an example of religious syncretism.

(B) Explain ONE way that Christianity in Latin America demonstrated religious syncretism.

(C) Explain ONE specific example of religious syncretism other than Vodou that resulted from the Atlantic slave trade.

2. **Answer all parts of the question that follows.**

(A) Identify ONE way in which mercantilism affected economies in Africa and Asia in the period 1450–1750.

(B) Explain ONE way in which the development of a global economy affected societal structures in European states between 1450–1750.

(C) Explain ONE way in which the Commercial Revolution transformed global economies in the period 1450–1750.

THINK AS A HISTORIAN: IDENTIFY A CLAIM IN A NON-TEXT
SOURCE

While most of the primary sources describing the conquest of Central and South America were written by Spaniards, a few pictorial manuscripts, such as the Florentine Codex and Kingsborogh Codex (or Codex *Tepetlaoztoc*, named for the region in Mexico where it was produced), relate events from the Aztec point of view. Images as well as text-based sources can assert a *claim,* a statement or position asserted to be true.

Which of the following best represents the claim in the picture below from the Codex *Tepetlaoztoc*?

1. Spaniards worked the indigenous people too hard.

2. The indigenous people were not prepared to do the physical labor necessary.

3. Spaniards treated the indigenous people with cruelty.

4. The indigenous people were obedient and did what they were told to do.

1. In one to three paragraphs, explain the economic strategies maritime empires used to increase their power and the effect of the developing empires on political, economic, religious, and cultural dynamics.

Source: Wikimedia Commons

Portrait of the Virgin of Guadalupe, patron saint of New Spain, by Josefus De Ribera Argomanis

4.6

Internal and External Challenges to State Power

The English made them drunk and then cheated them in Bargains.

—John Easton, *A Narrative of the Causes Which Led to Philip's Indian War,* 1858

Essential Question: How did the development of state power result in external and internal challenges in the period between 1450 and 1750?

In the 16th and 17th centuries, powers around the globe sought stronger governments and larger empires abroad. As governments grew stronger and empires developed, a variety of groups resisted state expansion through social, political, and economic challenges to state power. Some of these revolts occurred in the home of the empire as citizens fought overreaching governments. Other disturbances took place within colonies where indigenous peoples stood against foreign control.

Resistance to Portugal in Africa

By the 17th century, the Dutch and the English had pushed the Portuguese out of South Asia. (See Topic 1.3.) The Portuguese looked to Africa, where it had carried out slave raids since the 15th century, to build a colony. In 1624, **Ana Nzinga** became ruler of **Ndongo** in south-central Africa (present-day Angola). In addition to the slave raids by Portugal, other African peoples were attacking Ndongo. In exchange for protection from neighboring powers and an end to Portugal's raids, Nzinga became an ally of Portugal. Nzinga was baptized as Christian, with the governor of the Portuguese colony as her godfather. However, the alliance broke down. Nzinga and her people fled west, taking over the state of **Matamba**. She then incited a rebellion in Ndongo, allied with the Dutch, and offered freedom in Matamba to enslaved Africans. Nzinga ruled for decades, building Matamba into an economically strong state.

Source: Schomburg Center for Research in Black Culture, Photographs and Prints Division, The New York Public Library

Lithograph of Ana Nzinga, queen of Matamba, by François Villain (1800)

Local Resistance in Russia

In contrast to the Portuguese empire, pressures on state power came from within Russia, not outside of it. While conditions had improved for serfs (see Topic 1.6) in Western Europe by the 14th century, the same was not true for the serfs in Russia. Wars during the 14th and 15th centuries weakened the central government and increased the power of the nobility.

As demand for grain increased, nobles imposed harsh conditions on serfs. But Russian serfs had long been oppressed. First the Mongols and later the Russian princes collected heavy tribute and taxes (for services such as protection or to support the government's army) from the peasants. As a result, the peasants' debts increased, and over time more peasants lost their lands and were forced into serfdom.

Serfdom, Power, and Control The practice of serfdom benefitted the government because it kept the peasants under control, regulated by the nobility. Serfdom also benefitted the landowners because it provided free labor. Although townspeople were also controlled and not permitted to move their businesses freely to other cities, the serfs were practically enslaved, their labor bought and sold along with the lands of their owners.

As Russian territory expanded west to the Baltic and east to Siberia, the institution of serfdom expanded with it. An agricultural state, Russia kept serfs tied to the land long after the practice had ended, practically if not legally, in Western Europe. For example, Elizabeth I freed the last remaining serfs in England in 1574. In contrast, a law of 1649 chained Russian serfs to the lands where they were born and ensured their service to their landlords, who could buy and sell them and administer punishments. The village communes, called **mirs,** also controlled even the small landholders among the peasants.

Cossacks and Peasant Rebellions Southwest of Moscow, near the **Black Sea**, peasants who were skilled fighters lived on the grassy, treeless **steppes**. Many were runaway serfs who lived in small groups, influenced by the ways of the neighboring nomadic descendants of the Mongols. These fierce Cossack warriors were sometimes at odds with the central, autocratic government of the tsars. However, these fiercely independent warriors could also be hired as mercenaries to defend "Mother Russia" against Swedish, Tartar, and Ottoman forces. The Cossacks were thus important in Russia's expansion to the Ural Mountains and farther east into Siberia.

A Cossack known as **Yemelyan Pugachev** began a peasant rebellion against Catherine the Great in 1774 for giving the nobility power over the serfs on their lands in exchange for political loyalty, leaving the peasants without ties or recourse to the state. Falsely claiming to be Catherine's murdered husband, Peter III, Pugachev gathered a following of discontented peasants, people from different ethnic groups, and fellow Cossacks. At one point, these groups controlled the territory between the Volga River and the Urals. Within a year, though, the Russian army captured Pugachev and the Russian government executed him. The **Pugachev Rebellion** caused Catherine to increase her oppression of the peasants in return for the support of the nobles to help her avoid future revolts.

Rebellion in South Asia

In the 16th and 17th centuries, the Mughal empire controlled much of what is now India and Pakistan. (See Topic 3.1.) The Mughals centralized government and spread Persian art and culture as well as Islam. However, much of the population remained Hindu. The Maratha—a Hindu warrior group—fought the Mughals in a series of battles from 1680–1707. They created the Hindu **Maratha Empire.** It lasted until 1818, effectively ending the Mughal rule of India.

Revolts in the Spanish Empire

Spain also experienced rebellions within its territories. The **Pueblo Revolt** took place in 1680 against the Spanish in what is now New Mexico. The Pueblo and Apache, two indigenous groups, fought colonizers who were trying to force religious conversions. The indigenous people killed about 400 Spaniards, drove the rest out of the area, and destroyed churches. The Spanish reconquered the area in 1692.

Civil Unrest in France

In 1643, four-year-old Louis XIV inherited the French crown. Until Louis came of age, his mother Anne and chief minister Cardinal Jules Mazarin ruled in his place. Mazarin pushed for increased taxes to pay for recent wars. Nobles and judicial bodies (called Parlements) refused to pay the tax, forcing the burden to fall on the bourgeoisie. In 1648, a mob in Paris used children's slings (frondes) to destroy property of government officials in response to the taxes. The violence intensified and the royal family fled the capital. With most of the military committed to fighting Spain, the French government was forced to make concessions and a tenuous peace was reached with the Paris Parlement.

The peace was short-lived. The increasingly unpopular Mazarin had several rebellion leaders arrested in 1650, plunging the country back into chaos. Fighting continued between various factions attempting to establish control and unseat Mazarin. Pressure from numerous groups forced Mazarin to briefly flee again until the government was finally able to end the civil disturbance, that came to be known as the Fronde, and restore order in 1653.

Young Louis XIV watched these events unfold and as a result came to distrust nobility. When Mazarin died in 1661, Louis chose not to appoint another chief minister and moved toward absolute rule. (See Topic 3.2.)

Struggles for Power in England and Its Colonies

Although Spain colonized much of the Caribbean, England's power there grew stronger. England defeated Spanish colonists and took control of much of Jamaica in 1655. Enslaved people in the Caribbean and former Spanish territories in the Americas fought to gain freedom in what were known as **Maroon wars** (1728–1740 and 1795–1796).

Maroons were descendants of Africas who had escaped slavery in Jamaica. They escaped their owners and formed independent settlements. **Queen Nanny**, herself had escaped slavery, united all the maroons of the island. Jamaicans later recognized her as a national hero.

Slave revolts were common in the Americas, especially in those locations where enslaved Africans outnumbered free Europeans. The first recorded slave revolt in what is now the United States was the **Gloucester County Rebellion** in Virginia in 1663. In this rebellion, enslaved Africans and white indentured servants conspired together to demand their freedom from the governor. Authorities found out about the plot and arrested the conspirators.

English colonists used underhanded tactics (such as that described in the quote at the beginning of the topic) in their continuing pressure to control Native American lands resulting in **Metacom's War** (1675–1678), also called King Philip's War. This conflict was the final major effort of the indigenous people to drive the British from New England. The war spread throughout New England and resulted in the destruction of 12 towns. Some Native American groups, including the **Mohegan** and **Pequot**, sided with the English. Although Native American peoples continued to live in the region, the war ended with the subjugation of the **Wampanoag** people to the English colonists.

Struggles for power took place within England as well. In 1685, **James II** became king. James was Catholic, and his anti-Protestant measures enraged many English people. A group of nobles invited **William of Orange**, who was James's nephew and son-in-law, to invade England with an army and become the new king. He agreed, landing in England in 1688. James fled to France. In 1689, William and his wife **Mary II** (James's daughter) began their joint rule of England. Both William and Mary were Protestant, and the English throne remained in Protestant hands after that.

English people called this revolt the **Glorious Revolution** or the Bloodless Revolution. It strengthened the power of Parliament, which passed a law forbidding Catholics to rule England. That revolution took place without much violence, but religious tensions continued in England and throughout much of the world. (Connect: Create a graphic organizer of the rebellions that were beginning to challenge growing European empires.)

Internal and External Challenges to State Powers	
State	**Internal/External Challenge**
Portugal	• Dutch and English pushed Portugal out of South Asia (external) • Rebellion in Ndongo allied with Dutch (external)
France	• Fronde civil disturbances against royal power (internal)
Russia	• Cossack rebellion (internal) • Pugachev rebellion (internal)
South Asia	• Hindu Marathas ended Mughal rule (internal)
Spanish Empire	• Pueblo and Apache groups rebelled in present-day New Mexico (internal to the colonies)
British Empire	• Maroon wars (internal to the colonies) • Gloucester County Rebellion (internal to the colonies) • Metacom's War (internal to the colonies) • Glorious Revolution (internal)

KEY TERMS BY THEME

ENVIRONMENT: Locations
Ndongo
Matamba
Black Sea
steppe
Maratha Empire

CULTURE: Social Organizations
mirs

GOVERNMENT: Leaders and Rebels
Ana Nzinga
Yemelyan Pugachev
Queen Nanny
James II
William of Orange
Mary II

SOCIETY: Native American Peoples
Mohegan
Pequot
Wampanoag

SOCIETY: Revolts
Fronde
Metacom's War
Pugachev Rebellion
Pueblo Revolt
Maroon wars
Gloucester County Rebellion
Glorious Revolution

MULTIPLE-CHOICE QUESTIONS

Questions 1 to 3 refer to the passages below.

"This small Christian clan stranded in a tiny corner of the earth, surrounded by half-savage Mohammedan tribes and by soldiers, considers itself highly advanced, acknowledges none but Cossacks as human beings, and despises everybody else. The Cossack spends most of his time in the cordon [i.e., frontier fort], in [military] action, or in hunting and fishing."

Leo Tolstoy, The Cossacks: A Tale of 1852, published in 1863

"That night he stayed at home and dreamed, of the [American] West. His memory, coupled with what he had heard and idealized by his imagination, conjured dim visions of what he had once known and forgotten; of a land where men and conditions harked back to the raw foundations of civilization."

B. M. Bower, The Lure of the Dim Trails, 1907

1. One similarity between Cossacks and American cowboys was that both
   (A) lived on the frontier of an expanding country
   (B) were criminals forced into exile by their government
   (C) often formed alliances with the native inhabitants of their region
   (D) represented the spread of urban society

2. Why would Tsar Ivan IV (Ivan the Terrible) use Cossacks to expand the Russian empire into Siberia?
   (A) They lived in a harsh climate and could withstand the Siberian winters.
   (B) They lived near Muslims and therefore could negotiate with Siberian Muslims.
   (C) They had a tradition of being fierce warriors.
   (D) They were Ukrainian and would defend Ivan from rebellions by Siberian Russians.

3. The conflict between the Cossacks and Catherine the Great known as the Pugachev Rebellion was most similar to
   (A) the Mongol conquests because it was a fight over control of wealth
   (B) the English Civil War because it was a fight between a monarch and a legislature
   (C) the Thirty Years' War because it was a fight dominated by religious beliefs
   (D) the conflicts in Japan during the Heian period in which feudal lords controlled the lives of the serfs

1. **Use the passage below to answer all parts of the question that follows.**

"The Pueblo Revolt of 1680 was one of the most significant events in New Mexico history. But 1680 was not the first time New Mexico's Pueblos had attempted to rebel against the Spanish government. Beginning with the Acoma Revolt of 1599, Spanish intolerance of Pueblo religious practices and a persistent abuse of Pueblo labor had prompted several revolts against the Spanish in the seventeenth century. These uprisings, however, were discovered and ruthlessly crushed before they could grow into broader action. . . .

The Spanish remained at El Paso until 1692. For a while it appeared that the revolt had indeed succeeded. Popay and the other Pueblo leaders began a systematic eradication of all signs of Christianity and Spanish material culture. Everyone was to bathe in a ritual which washed away any trace of baptism, and Christian marriages were invalidated until reconfirmed by native tradition. . . .

But it was easier to order the eradication of all vestiges of the Spanish presence than to accomplish it. Many items of material culture which had been introduced by the Spanish—iron tools, sheep, cattle, and fruit trees, for example—had become an integral part of Pueblo life. A few individuals, deeply influenced by the teachings of the Franciscans, rescued and hid the sacred objects of their adopted religion to await the eventual return of the Spanish friars."

Robert Torrez, Former New Mexico State Historian

(A) Identify ONE way in which the Pueblo Revolts were similar to the battles between the Marathas and the Mughals.

(B) Identify ONE way in which the Pueblo Revolts differed from the Cossack Revolts.

(C) Compare Torrez's view of the long-term impact of Spanish rule in New Mexico with the long-term impact of Metacom's War.

2. **Answer all parts of the question that follows.**

(A) Identify ONE example of how social structures affected a state's ability to maintain order in settlements in the period 1450–1750.

(B) Identify ONE example of how economic structures affected a state's ability to maintain order in settlements in the period 1450–1750.

(C) Explain ONE historical situation in the period 1450–1750 in which state power was challenged by internal pressures.

THINK AS A HISTORIAN: SITUATE HISTORICAL DEVELOPMENTS IN CONTEXT

Understanding the internal and external challenges to state power from 1450 to 1750 requires understanding the broader context in which they developed. This understanding should go beyond simple identification, such as "The context in which internal and external challenges to state power took place was the widespread expansion of empires." Instead, work to *explain* how or why the context specifically relates to the internal and external challenges to state power. That is, ask, "What specifically about the context sheds light on the challenges?" To answer that question, complete the following activities.

First, review the four features of the historical concept of empire outlined on the last page of Topic 3.1. For each bullet point, explain in a sentence or two how that context relates to the internal or external challenges to state power you read about in this topic.

Next, copy the timeline on page 189 on separate paper, leaving plenty of room between dates. Then review this topic, adding into the timeline the rebellions, revolts, and wars that arose as challenges to state power. By situating these developments in a chronological context, you may discover additional explanations.

REFLECT ON THE TOPIC ESSENTIAL QUESTION

1. In one to three paragraphs, explain how the development of state power resulted in external and internal challenges in the period between 1450 and 1750.

Source: Wikimedia Commons
William of Orange and his English wife

4.7

Changing Social Hierarchies

We . . . order the said Jews and Jewesses of our kingdoms to depart and never to return or come back to them or to any of them.

—Ferdinand and Isabella, Edict of the Expulsion of the Jews, 1492

Essential Question: How were social categories, roles, and practices maintained or changed from 1450 to 1750?

$\mathbf{A}$s societies faced rebellions from outside and within, social hierarchies began to develop and transform. In Europe, the treatment of Jews showed that majorities treated non-majority ethnic groups in different ways. Jews had been expelled from England (1290), France (1394), and, as stated above, Spain (1492). The Ottoman Empire, however, provided a safe haven for Jews fleeing discrimination in Europe.

Throughout the world, civilizations developed distinctive social hierarchies. Different groups—including royalty, nobility, landowners, scholars, and soldiers—sought power and influence. In some societies, merchants and artisans began to form a middle class. And peasants, serfs, poor people, and enslaved people often struggled to stay alive.

Many states created policies that discriminated against some groups based on religion, ethnicity, or social class. For example, Huguenots—French Protestants in the predominantly Catholic country—suffered great persecution, and many fled to other European countries or to colonies. States also supported the formation of elite classes, including the boyars in Russia and the nobility in Europe. These elites both supported ruling power and challenged it.

Social Classes and Minorities in Gunpowder Empires

Tension between the military elite and absolutist rulers existed in three Islamic empires: the Ottoman (Turkey), the Safavids (Iran), and the Mughals (India). They are called *gunpowder empires* because they succeeded militarily by using guns and cannons when they first became widely available. (See Topic 3.1.)

Ottoman Society The Ottoman social system was built around a warrior aristocracy that soon began to compete for positions in the bureaucracy with the ulama, who were scholars and experts in Islamic law. Within the military, the Janissaries gained power and prestige. (See Topic 3.2.) Ultimately, the Janissaries tried to mount coups against the sultans.

As sultans became increasingly ineffective and incapable, strong advisors called *viziers* gained influential positions in government, where they spoke for the sultan. However, the sultan still had considerable powers. These included **timar,** a system in which the sultan granted land or tax revenues to those he favored. The sultan also used timar to reward soldiers and keep them loyal.

Treatment of Religious Minorities One reason for the success of the Ottoman Empire was its relative tolerance toward Jews and Christians. After the Spanish monarch exiled Jews from his kingdom in 1492, Sultan **Mehmed II** invited them to settle in Istanbul. Many did. Some Jews became court physicians and diplomats. Others contributed to the literary community and might have brought the printing press to the Ottoman Empire. While they were allowed to worship, they did not have full equality:

- They were permitted to live only in specified areas of the cities.

- They paid a tax called a jizya that was required of all non-Muslims in the empire.

- They could not hold top positions in the empire, which were reserved for Muslims.

Religious Toleration in the Mughal Empire The Mughal Empire in what is now India began in 1526. Probably its greatest emperor was **Akbar the Great** (ruled 1556–1605), remembered for his military successes and his administrative achievements. To help keep his huge, fractious empire together, Akbar, like Ottoman rulers, was tolerant of all religions. He ended the jizya tax. He gave grants of land and money to Hindus and Muslims, provided funds to build a Catholic church, and supported Sikhism. (For more on Akbar's religious toleration, see Topic 3.3.)

Women in the Ottoman Empire Women also played social and political roles at court. Many wives and concubines of the sultan tried to promote their own children as likely heirs to the throne. This practice led to "harem politics," a reference to the **harem**, a residence where a powerful man's wives and concubines lived.

One woman, **Roxelana**, became unusually powerful in the Ottoman Empire. When she was a young girl, Crimean raiders stole Roxelana from her home in Eastern Europe and sold her into slavery in the Ottoman Empire. She was forced to convert to Islam and entered the harem of Suleiman the Magnificent, sultan of the empire. Suleiman was notable for his military and administrative skill. Suleiman married Roxelana, which was highly unusual. She went from being enslaved to commissioning ambitious public works projects.

Roxelana's son succeeded Suleiman. During the son's reign, viziers complained about a "sultanate of the women." They believed members of the harem had too much influence on politics. Roxelana's rise showed that it was possible—though rare—for people at this time to attain a different social class.

Other Social Classes Merchants and artisans formed a small middle class in the empire. Below the middle class were the peasants, who were usually poor—particularly because they had to pay tribute to the government to help support the Ottoman armies. Below the peasants were the enslaved. They came from many areas as the Ottoman armies penetrated Central and Eastern Europe, capturing prisoners of war in Ukraine and elsewhere. **Barbary pirates**, those who plied the seas near North Africa along the Barbary Coast (named for the Berbers who lived there) captured other Europeans in the Mediterranean and then sold them to the sultan or other high-ranking officials. Some people were **impressed**, or forced into service, in the navy as enslaved galley workers. As many as one million people were impressed between the 16th and 19th centuries.

Source: Titian, *La Sultana Rossa*, c. 1550. John and Mable Ringling Museum of Art. Wikimedia Commons

Roxelana became famous for her power as an Ottoman leader.

Manchu Power and Conflicts in the Qing Dynasty

China's **Qing Dynasty** lasted from 1644 until 1912. Under this dynasty, the **Manchu** people from Manchuria ruled over the majority Han Chinese and other ethnic groups. Like the Mongols some 400 years earlier, the Manchu were ethnically and culturally distinct from the people they ruled. However, they were less tolerant than the Mongol leaders, and they resolved to make their culture dominant in China.

Like the Mongols, the Qing put their own people in the top positions of government. Also like the Mongols, the Qing maintained continuity with some traditional Chinese practices. For example, they maintained the Chinese civil service exams and bureaucracy. They recruited Han Chinese to work under or alongside Manchus. In time, some—but not all—Chinese came to accept the Qing Dynasty as legitimate rulers of China.

Conflicts with the Han The Han ethnicity in China experienced Qing intolerance most severely. Although non-official Han civilians were allowed to wear Hanfu, or traditional Han clothing, all men were required to wear their hair in **queues**, the braided pigtail style of the Manchu. This policy was a test of loyalty for the Manchu, but it was also a humiliating reminder of the way Qing authority challenged traditional Confucian values. A man who refused to wear his hair in a queue could be executed.

The Qing used Han Chinese defectors to carry out massacres against Han who refused to assimilate to Qing practices. These defectors played a massive role in the Qing conquest of China. Han Chinese General **Li Chengdong**, for example, orchestrated three separate massacres in the city of Jaiding within one month. By the end of those four weeks, there was hardly a person left alive in the city. Later, Han Chinese defector **Liu Liangzuo** massacred the entire population of Jiangyin, killing between 74,000 and 100,000 people.

European Hierarchies

Like states in South and East Asia, European states also had a social hierarchy. In Europe the top level was royalty—members of a royal family. The aristocracy or **nobility** was the next highest level. Nobles were usually wealthy landowners. Nearly every state in Europe had laws that recognized a class of nobles and granted them special privileges. The nobility made up a small minority of the population but owned most of the land. They maintained their power through a system in which lands and titles passed down from one generation to the next through a system of inheritance.

The Nobility Makes Gains In the Netherlands and England, the nobility held power and took an active part in the government. Dutch landowners provided the stable support for local provincial government. In England, large landowners controlled Parliament. However, the landowners had to contend with radical religious sects and the middle class, which were two growing segments of the social order.

The Nobility Faces Losses Nobles struggled for power with royalty, the emerging middle class of merchants and skilled workers, the priestly class, and the common people. A failed uprising in France in the mid-1600s convinced **Louis XIV** that he must keep power from the common people and the nobility. The nobility also faced criticism from writers and thinkers of the time. The English statesman Thomas More wrote this about the nobility: "Living in idleness and luxury without doing society any good no longer satisfies them; they have to do positive evil."

Power of Royalty over Nobility Gunpowder, cannons, and other technological advances allowed rulers to destroy nobles' fortresses and seize their lands. Many rulers believed they deserved absolute power. Louis XIV is famous for saying, "I am the state." However, Frederick of Prussia saw things differently. He declared, "I am the first servant of the state." (Connect: Trace the changes in social hierarchy from feudal Europe to the 17th century. See Topic 1.6.)

Growing Acceptance of Jews Jews began to have a larger role in many countries starting in the 17th century. Their expulsion from Spain, by Ferdinand and Isabella, was particularly significant because so many Jews lived there. Many resettled in areas around the Mediterranean Sea, in northern Africa or the Middle East. Since the Hebrew word for Spain is *Sepharad,* Jews who trace their heritage back to Spain became known as **Sephardic Jews**. In contrast, Jews from central and eastern Europe became known as **Ashkenazi Jews**. Jewish scholars once used the term Ashkenazi to refer to Germany.

Under the influence of the scientific revolution and the Enlightenment, prejudices against Jews declined somewhat. Jews began to move more freely in Europe. They became particularly important in banking and commerce. The Netherlands was especially tolerant of religious dissent, and the Jewish minority faced less discrimination there than in most of Europe. Many Jews hoped the centuries of discrimination they had confronted were over.

Russian Social Classes

Moscow's social hierarchy continued that of Kievan Rus in the 11th century. The noble landowning class, the **boyars**, topped the social pyramid. Below them were the merchants. Last and most numerous were the peasants, who gradually sank into debt and lost more freedom. **Serfs** were the lowest group among peasants. Since they received a plot of land and protection from a noble, serfs were bound to that land and had little personal freedom. If the noble sold their land, control of the serfs went with it. Though not technically enslaved, serfs led very hard lives.

The boyar class experienced tensions with the rulers similar to the tensions between nobles and rulers in Western Europe. Boyars of Novgorod opposed the expansionist policies of **Ivan IV**, known as "Ivan the Terrible" for murdering his own son, among other crimes. After Ivan's forces defeated Novgorod, Ivan confiscated the lands of his boyar opponents. He forced them and their families to move to Moscow, where he could keep them under surveillance.

Political and Economic Elites in the Americas

Social structures in the Americas changed drastically during this period because of the arrival of Europeans, the importation of African slave labor, and outbreaks of disease that killed tens of millions. The combination of European settlers, imported Africans, and the conquered indigenous populations led to the development of a new social hierarchy based on race and ancestry. Skin color became a signifier of power and status in many parts of the Americas and, in fact, in all European colonies. Racial and ethnic background defined social status in a formal way in the Spanish and Portuguese empires in the Western Hemisphere for centuries following the Europeans' arrival.

The Casta System in Latin America At the top of the social pyramid in Latin America stood the **peninsulares**, those who were born on the Iberian peninsula. Next down the pyramid were the **criollos**, those of European ancestry who were born in the Americas. Below these two groups were the **castas**, people of mixed-race ancestry. At the top of this group were **mestizos**, those of mixed European and indigenous ancestry, followed by **mulattoes**, those of mixed European and African ancestry, and **zambos**, those of mixed indigenous and African ancestry. Indigenous peoples and enslaved Africans made up the bottom of the hierarchy.

People were assigned to their levels at baptism and could not move up except by intermarriage. People in the bottom layers of the hierarchy had to pay higher taxes and tributes, even though they could often least afford them.

Source: English Wikipedia

To show the importance of the casta system, the Spanish had paintings made delineating the groups within it. This painting shows a zambo, a person with one black parent and one indigenous parent.

KEY TERMS BY THEME

GOVERNMENT: Power and Authority
Mehmed II
Akbar the Great
Roxelana
Qing Dynasty
Manchu
Li Chengdong
Liu Liangzuo
Louis XIV
Ivan IV

SOCIETY: Ottoman Empire
timar
harem

SOCIETY: Russia
boyar

SOCIETY: Europe
nobility
serf

SOCIETY: Latin America
peninsulares
criollo
castas
mestizos
mulattos
zambos

ECONOMY: Piracy
Barbary pirates
impressed

CULTURE: Religion and Ethnicity
queues
Sephardic Jew
Ashkenazi Jew

MULTIPLE-CHOICE QUESTIONS

Questions 1 to 3 refer to the passage below.

"Learned men of various kinds and from every country, as well as adherents of many different religions and creeds, assembled at his court and were admitted to converse with him. Night and day people did nothing but inquire and investigate…His Majesty collected opinions of every one, especially of those who were not Mohammedans [Muslim]…and collected everything which people can find in books, with a talent of selection peculiar to him and a spirit of inquiry opposed to every Islamitic principle. Thus…as the result of all the influences which were brought to bear upon him, there grew…the conviction in his heart that there were sensible men in all religions and abstemious thinkers and men endowed with miraculous powers among all nations."

Badā'ūnī's History – section on the Mughal emperor, Akbar

1. Based on the passage and what you have read in this unit, what were Akbar's policies toward religion?
   - (A) Akbar favored strict Islamic practice and sometimes persecuted Catholics.
   - (B) Akbar focused almost exclusively on the relatively new religious teachings of the Sikhs.
   - (C) Akbar showed tolerance of and interest in a variety of religions.
   - (D) Akbar was not interested in religion, pursuing philosophy instead.

2. In the above passage, what is the author's attitude toward Akbar's behavior?
   - (A) He disapproves of Akbar's lack of adherence to Islamic practice.
   - (B) He is impressed by Akbar's curiosity and open-mindedness.
   - (C) He wants to participate in the religious discussions in Akbar's court.
   - (D) He believes Islamic thought has too much influence over Akbar.

3. Which of the following had policies on religion that most resembled those of Akbar?
   - (A) Spain under Ferdinand and Isabella
   - (B) Qing dynasty
   - (C) Ottoman Empire under Mehmed II
   - (D) England under Edward I

1. **Use the passage below to answer all parts of the question that follows.**

"Nowadays, some 185 years after most of the Latin American nations obtained their independence, none of the Latin governments consider race to be an issue. All of these governments are firmly convinced that the racial caste system of colonial times has totally disappeared. This firmly held conviction is, however, not shared by academics and ordinary citizens who have noticed the distinct racial stratification of the Latin American societies. For these dissenters, the prevailing racial economic hierarchy and the easily uncovered attitudes that consider the dark-skinned unattractive and inferior clearly indicate that the racial caste system continues to operate.

Today's racial caste system is, of course, not nearly as rigid as it was in colonial times. But the fact that it has survived 185 years of social, economic, and political advances implies that this system is deeply embedded in the Latin societies. Hence, it must have relevant social, economic, and political effects."

Rutilio Martinez and Vish Iyer, Latin America's Racial Caste
System: Salient Marketing Implications (2008)

(A) Identify ONE way in which the casta system changed European economies in the period 1450–1750.

(B) Explain the authors' argument in the passage about the racial caste system.

(C) Explain ONE historical situation in the period 1450–1750, other than the one illustrated in the passage, in which imperial states adopted policies that limited the political power and influence of groups of people.

2. **Answer all parts of the question that follows.**

(A) Identify ONE way in which challenges to an elite class affected political or economic structures in the period 1450–1750.

(B) Explain ONE way in which social structures in 1450–1750 in the Americas compares to the social structures in China during the Qing dynasty.

(C) Explain ONE way in which policies of monarchs and leaders withstood challenges in the period 1450–1750.

Evidence in an argument can serve a variety of purposes. Its most common purpose is to support the claim at the heart of an argument. Specific facts or examples that demonstrate the truth of a more general assertion in the thesis fulfill this purpose. Evidence can also modify a claim by providing facts, examples, or reasoning that show that parts of the claim are true but that other parts are not. Evidence can also refute, or disprove, a claim. Evidence that serves this purpose provides facts, examples, or reasoning that support an alternative or opposing claim.

Consider the claim (in bold type below) in this argument: When King Ferdinand expelled the Jews from Spain in 1492, he provided for a three-month period for them to ready themselves for departure. The King promised that the state would "take and receive them under our Security, protection, and royal safeguard" and "that during the said time, no one shall harm them, nor injure them, no wrong shall be done to them against justice." **Although the King's promises sound respectful of the Jews' rights to safety, the very act of expulsion marked them as inferior and exposed them to relentless harms.**

The statements below are from an account written by an Italian Jew in 1495 (Internet Jewish History Source Book). For each statement, determine whether it could best be used to support, modify, or refute the claim above.

1. "When the edict of expulsion became known. . . . vessels came from Genoa to the Spanish harbors to carry away the Jews. The crews of these vessels. . . acted maliciously and meanly toward the Jews, robbed them, and delivered some of them to the famous pirate of that time who was called the Corsair of Genoa. To those who escaped and arrived at Genoa the people of the city showed themselves merciless, and oppressed and robbed them, and the cruelty of their wicked hearts went so far that they took the infants from the mothers. . . . ."

2. "One hundred and twenty thousand [Jews] went to Portugal, according to a compact which a prominent man. . . had made with the King of Portugal [who] allowed them to stay in his country six months. . . . [A]fter the six months had elapsed he made slaves of all [who] remained in his country, and banished seven hundred children to a remote island to settle it, and all of them died."

3. "Many ships with Jews, especially from Sicily, went to the city of Naples on the coast. The King of this country was friendly to the Jews, received them all, and was merciful towards them, and he helped them with money. The Jews that were at Naples supplied them with food . . . and sent around to the other parts of

Italy to collect money to sustain them. . . . [But] all this was not enough. Some of them died by famine, others sold their children to Christians to sustain their life. Finally, a plague broke out among them, spread to Naples, and very many of them died, so that the living wearied of burying the dead."

REFLECT ON THE TOPIC ESSENTIAL QUESTION

1. In one to three paragraphs, explain how social categories, roles, and practices were maintained or changed from 1450 to 1750.

Source: Royal Spanish Academy

The Mexican Castes, oil painting by Ignacio Maria Barreda, 1777

Continuity and Change from c. 1450 to c. 1750

The seams of [the world] were closing, drawn together by the sailmaker's needle.

—Alfred Crosby, historian who identified the Columbian Exchange, 1986

Essential Question: How did economic developments from 1450 to 1750 affect social structures over time?

By 1750, most of the world was integrated within a system of economic, political, and cultural connections. Better technology enabled the Eastern and Western hemispheres to connect. Meanwhile, Western European maritime powers created trading empires in the Indian Ocean trading network and in the Americas. Religions and other cultural practices continued to spread as a result of these interactions, but they also were transformed as new or syncretic forms developed. Coercive labor systems continued to exist in this newly connected world. However, new forms developed as new economic systems sought to exploit natural resources and to generate wealth for Western European nations.

Transoceanic Travel and Trade

The most significant change to the global economy in this period was the integration of the Western Hemisphere into the global trading network. This change resulted from Western European states wanting to find a sea route to Asia. They borrowed and developed technology that made ocean travel easier:

- astronomical charts
- astrolabe
- compass
- magnetic compass
- lateen sail
- carrack
- caravel
- fluyt

The result was the Columbian Exchange: a biological exchange of crops, animals, people, and diseases between the Eastern and Western Hemisphere. The Columbian Exchange had wide-ranging effects on both hemispheres.

The Atlantic System The Columbian Exchange also caused the development of a transoceanic trading network called the Atlantic System. The Atlantic System was made up of the regions of Western Europe, Western Africa, and the Americas and involved the movement of goods and people among those regions. Columbian Exchange forever changed who grew what foods where and how they grew them. It also unleashed deadly diseases on populations that had no immunity to them. In addition, it led to massive migrations, many of them forced, and new social structures.

As people migrated or were forced to migrate within the Atlantic System, cultural changes occurred. For instance, religion spread and often created syncretic belief systems and practices.

EMPIRES IN 1750

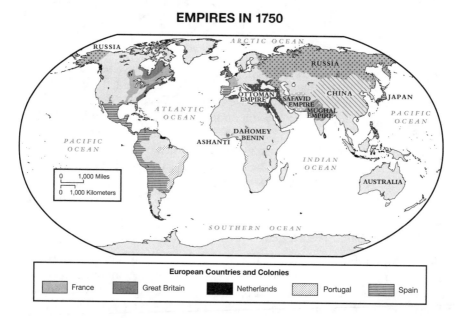

European Countries and Colonies

France Great Britain Netherlands Portugal Spain

Economic Changes

European transoceanic voyages resulted in the integration of the Western Hemisphere within the global trading network. This integration had profound effects on the global economy. Maritime trading empires emerged, led by the Portuguese and followed by the Dutch and the English. As a result, Europeans established trading ports and cities along the coasts of Africa and the Indian Ocean. This brought Europeans into contact—and often into conflict—with existing merchant networks.

One consequence of this contact and conflict was that Europeans came to dominate global trade at the expense of Arab, Indian, and Chinese merchants.

Europeans, then, made considerable profits from transporting the goods from one region to another. (Connect: Identify the differences between the Atlantic System and trade on the Indian Ocean. See Topic 2.3.)

Colonies in the Americas In contrast to the trading empires in the Indian Ocean, Spain created an empire in the Americas. Soon Portugal, England, France, and the Netherlands established colonies there. The discovery of large deposits of silver in Spain's colonies helped further integrate Europeans into the global economy. Asian markets and merchants, especially in China, desired silver. Shipments of silver to Asia from the Americas became a regular feature of the global trade network and helped finance the increasing volume of trade between Asia and Europe. Some experts estimate that the amount of silver in the global economy tripled in the 16th century.

Mercantilism and Capitalism European rulers soon came to see the benefits of encouraging the expansion of trade, as the wealth that could be amassed was considerable. To ensure they participated in wealth accumulation from trade, many European monarchs devised mercantilist economic policies that would provide the ruler with a steady stream of income. While expanded international trade continued to be an important goal of European monarchs, mercantilism eventually gave way to capitalism as the predominant economic system in the new global economy. Investors formed joint-stock companies, also called chartered companies, so they could share the risks and rewards of global trading opportunities.

Effects of the New Global Economy

The new global flow of goods and profits produced some significant benefits. The flow of wealth into Europe helped to expand the middle class and provided the capital that would lead to the Industrial Revolution. However, the huge amounts of gold and silver flowing into Spain and China from the Americas also produced negative economic effects. In particular, the increase in the quantity of money in circulation caused inflation.

Source: Rijksmuseum Amsterdam. Wikimedia Commons

Rembrandt's *The Syndics of the Amsterdam Drapers' Guild,* 1662. This shows a group of Dutch officials evaluating a carpet from Persia.

As a result of the activities of European merchants, regional markets in Europe, Africa, and Asia continued to prosper. Funding for the arts increased as merchants and governments used their rising profits and revenue to sponsor artists and authors. Some rulers used their sponsorship of the arts to produce art and architecture that helped to legitimize their rule. Other art symbolized the growing importance of global trade.

Demand for Labor Intensifies

The new global economy also brought about significant disruptions. The Columbian Exchange and the Atlantic System caused a demographic shift in Africa as the Atlantic slave trade intensified. Slavers captured and sold millions of African men. These African men ended up on American plantations, producing cash crops that included sugar, cotton, and tobacco. As a result, some African communities experienced a gender imbalance. Africa's population declined because of the Atlantic slave trade. Eventually, the population increased as people grew new crops, such as manioc.

Traditional forced labor systems, such as serfdom, continued in areas of Afro-Eurasia. However, other coerced labor systems developed in the Americas as a result of the Columbian Exchange and the Atlantic System, in addition to the chattel slavery of the Atlantic slave trade. Many European settlers first arrived in the Americas as indentured servants, contracted to work for a period of time before they were free to pursue other jobs or occupations. The encomienda and hacienda systems, as well as the adoption of the Inca mit'a system, are examples of other coerced labor systems in the Spanish American colonies.

New Social Structures As Europeans, Africans, and Native Americans coexisted in the new American colonies, the social structures of the Americas changed. New social systems appeared that were based on racial or ethnic identity. This division led to a rigid and hierarchial society, with white Europeans or Americans of European descent possessing the majority of wealth and political power. A new subculture appeared that consisted of people who were of mixed European and African heritage. Societal conflicts eventually led to revolutions.

REFLECT ON THE ESSENTIAL QUESTION

1. **Continuity and Change** Identify four historical developments in the period from c. 1450–c. 1750. Rank them according to how significant they were in either 1) maintaining continuity or 2) bringing about change. Explain your rankings in a paragraph.

2. In one to three paragraphs, explain how economic developments from c. 1450 to c. 1750 affected social structures over time.

UNIT 4 REVIEW

HISTORICAL PERSPECTIVES: HOW HARSH WERE THE SPANISH?

After the first voyage of Christopher Columbus, Spanish conquistadors created a vast colonial empire in the Americas. In 1552, the Dominican friar Bartolomé de Las Casas described the greed, ruthlessness, and cruelty that Spanish officials inflicted on native populations. Ever since, historians have debated the accuracy of his observations.

Origins of the Black Legend Writing in 1914, Spanish historian Julián Juderías labeled this belief in the evils of Spanish rule as the Black Legend. He argued that during the 16th and 17th centuries, other Europeans were jealous of Spanish wealth and power. As a result, they were prepared to believe the worst about Spain's rule. Juderías suggested that historians focused so much on cruelty that they ignored the positive achievements of Spanish colonialism.

Debating the Black Legend Besides jealousy, another factor affecting how historians viewed Spain was religion. During the centuries of struggle between Protestants and Catholics, the Black Legend fit with the negative views many Protestants had toward Catholics. In the United States, where Protestants dominated the writing of history in the 19th century, acceptance of the Black Legend was common.

In the first half of the 20th century, many Spanish historians shared the perspective of Juderías. Their works reflected the intense national pride that many Spaniards felt about their past. In defending Spanish colonization, they developed what their critics called a White Legend to counter the Black Legend.

Emphasis on Reform One American historian active in the debate over Spanish colonization was Lewis Hanke. He argued against the Black Legend by trying to show that Las Casas was just one of many Spanish reformers. Through the efforts of these reformers, Hanke argued, the Spanish empire was "one of the greatest attempts the world has seen to make Christian precepts [rules] prevail in the relations between peoples."

Defenders of the Black Legend thought Hanke had exaggerated the strength of Las Casas and the reformers, thereby making the Spanish look better than they were. Others emphasized that despite any attempts at reform, what actually happened was extraordinarily harsh.

The Global Context In recent years, historians taking a more global approach to history have compared colonial empires more systematically than did previous historians. While they have noted differences among Europeans in the Americas, they have found widespread examples of brutality. Whether the Spanish were any worse than other Europeans remains hard to determine.

Develop an Argument: Evaluate the extent to which historical evidence supports one of the perspectives on Spanish colonization.

After analyzing the task and developing questions you need to answer to complete it (see page 183), the next step in writing a long essay is to gather and organize your evidence. *Gathering evidence* relies on recall—how much you remember from your reading and other studies. *Organizing evidence* requires the skills of seeing patterns and connections and using historical reasoning.

Suppose you are answering this long essay question: "Develop an argument that evaluates the extent to which continuity or change over time characterized the participation of China in the expanding global trade networks from 1450 to 1750." Gather the evidence by writing down everything you know about China's role in global trade networks between 1450 and 1750. (Answer the questions you developed in the application activity on page 183.) Your essay might include the following:

- Emperor Kangxi relaxed the limits on foreigners, opening Chinese ports to European merchants and missionaries.

- China exported silk, porcelain, spice, and tea and imported little.

- Confucian philosophy preferred farmers who produced food over merchants who transferred food from one person to another.

- Confucian philosophers respected the Jesuits.

- China regarded its culture as superior to those of other countries.

- With the Silk Roads and Indian Ocean trade networks pouring gold and silver into China for their goods, the Chinese felt wealthy and in no need of foreign commodities.

After writing everything you can remember, organize your evidence. Review your notes, looking for patterns related to the task. Which pieces of evidence represent a continuity? Which represent a change? Make a simple chart to place the evidence in the correct category. Then evaluate the extent to which change outweighed continuity or vice versa.

Application: On a separate sheet of paper, expand on the evidence you recall about China's participation in global trade networks between 1450 and 1750 by adding notes to the above list. Then make a chart like the one below. Place each piece of evidence in the appropriate column.

Continuities	Changes

For current free response question samples, visit: https://apcentral. collegeboard.org/courses/ap-world-history/exam

LONG ESSAY QUESTIONS

Directions: Write an essay in response to one of the prompts below. The suggested writing time for an essay is 40 minutes.

In your response, you should do the following:

- Respond to the prompt with a historically defensible thesis or claim that establishes a line of reasoning.
- Describe a broader historical context relevant to the prompt.
- Support an argument in response to the prompt using at least two pieces of specific and relevant evidence.
- Use historical reasoning (e.g., comparison, causation, continuity or change) to frame or structure an argument that addresses the prompt.
- Demonstrate a complex understanding of a historical development related to the prompt through sophisticated argumentation and/or effective use of evidence.

Source: *AP® World History Course and Exam Description*

1. In the period from 1450 to 1750, trans-Atlantic trade brought new inventions and ideas to societies in the Eastern and Western hemispheres.

   Develop an argument that evaluates the extent to which cross-cultural interactions resulted in the diffusion of technology and helped cause changes in patterns of trade and travel during that era.

2. Strong central governments, mercantilism, and trading enslaved people all shaped Europeans' transoceanic explorations from 1450 to 1750.

   Develop an argument that evaluates the extent to which economic systems and labor systems showed continuities or changes over time during that period.

3. The Columbian Exchange brought riches to Europe from 1450 to 1750, but it also brought misery to the Americas and Africa.

   Develop an argument that evaluates the extent to which the systems of slavery in that era showed changes or continuities over time.

4. A desire to convert others, the development of syncretic belief systems, and religious conflicts changed the Americas, Africa, and Eurasia from 1450 to 1750.

   Develop an argument that evaluates the extent to which the effect on societies of various belief systems was similar or different during that time period.

DOCUMENT-BASED QUESTION

Directions: Question 1 is based on the accompanying documents. The documents have been edited for the purpose of this exercise. You are advised to spend 15 minutes planning and 45 minutes writing your answer.

1. Evaluate the extent to which rivalries between states, during the period c. 1450 to c. 1750, were caused by economic disputes.

In your response, you should do the following:

- Respond to the prompt with a historically defensible thesis or claim that establishes a line of reasoning.
- Describe a broader historical context relevant to the prompt.
- Support an argument in response to the prompt using at least four documents.
- Use at least one additional piece of specific historical evidence (beyond that found in the documents) relevant to an argument about the prompt.
- For at least two documents, explain how or why the document's point of view, purpose, historical situation, and/or audience is relevant to an argument.
- Demonstrate a complex understanding of a historical development related to the prompt through a sophisticated argument and/or effective use of evidence.

Source: *AP® World History Course and Exam Description*

Document 1

> **Source:** Hernando Cortes, Spanish conqueror of the Aztec Empire (Mexico) writing to the Spanish king and Holy Roman Emperor Charles V to describe his conquest of the Aztecs, "Second Letter to Charles V," 1520.
>
> This great city of Tenochtitlan [capital of Aztec Empire] is built on the salt lake . . . [and] is as large as Seville [large Spanish city] . . . The city has many squares in which are situated markets . . . One square is surrounded by arcades and has more than sixty thousand people daily, engaged in buying and selling . . .
>
> I came to teach them that they were to adore but one God and that they must turn from their idols and their abominable rites they had practiced until then, for these were lies and deceptions of the devil . . . I likewise came to teach them that Your Majesty, by the will of Divine Providence, rules the world, and that they also must submit themselves to the imperial yoke, and do all that we who are Your Majesty's ministers here might order them.

Document 2

Source: Draft declaration from the government of Elizabeth I, Queen of England, upon the Spanish Armada's attempted invasion of England, 1588.

[the Spanish are] certainly known in favor of the Pope, whom they make their God on the earth . . .

to deny their [British subjects] allegiance to her Majesty [Elizabeth] their sovereign natural Lady and Queen, and to change and subvert the happy state of the realm [kingdom], and to make the same subject to the Pope's will, and the Crown to be translated to such a foreign potentate [ruler] as he shall thereto name to usurp [seize power] the same . . .

for so by therein writing they do directly pronounce the intentions of the Pope to be, in procuring [obtaining control] of the King of Spain, and other rulers vasselled [in service] to the Pope . . .

to invade this realm, and to gain the Crown and the realm with the wealth thereof to therein devours, which cannot be imagined to be done without a full tyrannical conquest of the same, by depriving of her Majesty, and by slaughter of all such her subjects of all degrees both noble and others, as shall for their conscience towards Almighty God, persist in the true profession of Christian Religion [Protestantism]. . .

and for their allegiance towards her Majesty . . . her subjects: shall risk their lives, both in defense of her Majesty's person, and to the maintenance of this Crown, Kingdom Country, and people, in the Kingly honor, and ancient liberty wherein it hath remained and been inhabited with kings and people of mean English blood, more than this five hundred years.

Document 3

Source: Abd al-Aziz al-Fishtali, Moroccan writer and official chronicler and poet of the Sultan of Morocco Ahmad al-Mansur, describing communications between al-Mansur and Songhai leader Askia Ishaq II about the Songhai paying a salt tax, 1621.

[Sultan al-Mansur] did not exchange correspondence with him [Ishaq] until he had asked his *ulama* [Islamic scholars] for a legal opinion of it. . . . So they gave him a legal opinion . . . that the control of the [salt] mines belongs unconditionally and solely to the Sultan (al-Mansur), and that it was not for anyone to have any authority in this matter except by permission of the sultan or his deputies. And al-Mansur sent those *fatwas* [Islamic rulings] along with the letter directed to him with the messenger.

[Upon receiving no response from Ishaq, the Sultan met with] his commanders . . . and the notables of his kingdom and . . . the men of judgment to ask their advice on an invasion [of Songhai]. Those who were present fell silent and did not ask anything. So he said to them "Are you silent in approval of my opinion or is there a difference between your view of the situation and mine?" [They responded] your answer was effective and its correctness inspired us so that there is no longer anything for anyone to say. There is truth in the saying "The minds of kings are the kings of minds."

Document 4

Source: Friedrich Schiller, German historian in the late 1700s, excerpt from his book, *The Thirty Years War (1618-1648).*

Religion alone could have rendered possible all that was accomplished, but it was far from being the sole motive of the war [between German states and European kingdoms]. Had not private advantages and state interests been closely connected with it, vain and powerless would have been the arguments of theologians; and the cry of the people would never have met with princes so willing to support their cause, nor the new doctrines have found such numerous, brave, and persevering champions. . . .

Princes fought in self-defense or for aggrandizement [to increase their own power], while religious enthusiasm recruited their armies, and opened to them the treasures of their subjects. Of the multitude who flocked to their standards [fought for them], such as were not lured by the hope of plunder [stolen riches], imagined they were fighting for the truth, while in fact they were shedding their blood for the personal power of their princes.

Document 5

> **Source:** Don Alonzo del Campo y Espinosa, Spanish General, letter to Henry Morgan, English privateer,* 1669.
>
> Having, through our friends and neighbors, received news that you have had the boldness to commit hostilities in the territories and cities owing obedience to His Catholic Majesty, the king of Spain my master, I have come to this place, according to my bounden duty, and have built up again that fortress which you took from a set of faint-hearts and from which you flung down the guns, that I may prevent your escape from this lake and do you all the injury my duty requires.
>
> Nevertheless, if you will surrender with humility all which you have taken (a considerable amount of goods and five thousand pieces of eight), including all the slaves and other prisoners, I will have the clemency to let you pass, that you may return to your own country.
>
> Should you stubbornly resist these honorable conditions which I propose, I shall send for ships from Caracas [the capital of Spain's Empire in Venezuela], in which I shall embark my troops with orders to destroy you utterly and put every man to the sword. This is my final resolution: take heed, and be not ungrateful for my kindness. I have with me valiant soldiers, yearning to be allowed to revenge unrighteous acts you have committed against the Spanish nation in America.
>
> *Privateers were sea captains who were given permission by the English government to raid Spanish ports and ships to acquire gold and other goods.

Document 6

> **Source:** *The Gentleman's Magazine*, a newly founded monthly magazine in London, England, article by Edward Cave, 1731.
>
> The Rebecca [British trading ship], Capt. Jenkins, was taken [boarded] in her passage from Jamaica, by a Spanish Guarde Costa [coast guard vessel], who put her people to the torture; part of which was, that they hang'd up the Capt. three times, once with the Cabin-boy at his feet; they then cut off one of his Ears, took away his candles and instruments, and detain'd him a whole day. Being then dismissed, the Captain bore away [sailed] for the Havana, which the Spaniards perceiving stood after her, and declared, that if she did not immediately go for the Gulf, they would set the Ship on fire; to which they were forced to submit, and after many Hardships and Perils arrived in the River Thames [in London], June 11. The Captain has since been at Court and laid his case before his Majesty.

Document 7

Source: *England's Glory*, etching by William Rayner commissioned by the British Parliament, depicts the Battle of Suvali 1612, off the coast of Gujarat (western India in the Arabian Sea), 1739.

The text underneath describes a victory of four English East India Company ships over four Portuguese ships. This small naval battle marked the end of the Portuguese trade monopoly with India, and the beginning of the rise of the East India Trading Company presence in India.

UNIT 5: Revolutions from c. 1750 to c. 1900

Understand the Context

Between 1750 and 1900, people continued becoming more integrated into a global trade network. New technology, from machinery for spinning thread to locomotives to telegraphs to steel mills, fostered closer integration. The increased use of machinery in producing goods, a shift known as the Industrial Revolution, caused manufacturing output to skyrocket. It began in Great Britain and affected all of the world by 2000. The Industrial Revolution set the stage for dramatic changes in international relations, politics, and demography.

Foreign Power As global trade increased, industrializing countries protected the access of their businesses to resources for manufacturing and to markets for selling goods by establishing control over overseas lands. However, these lands often rebelled against foreign domination. Among the first to rebel were the United States and Haiti in the 18th century.

A New Type of Country Industrialization provided the background for reorganizing states. Before the 1800s, most people lived in large multiethnic empires or small homogenous kingdoms. After 1800, people increasingly lived in nation-states, a country in which everyone shared the same culture, and everyone who shared a culture lived in the same country. Breaking up empires and combining kingdoms to create nation-states frequently led to war.

Movements of People Industrialization was also the context for massive human migrations. As demand for labor shifted, millions moved in search of work. For example, many Europeans voluntarily resettled in the Americas and Australia. South Asians were coerced into taking jobs in southern Africa. Millions of Africans were enslaved and taken forcibly to the Americas. These movements diversified communities across the world.

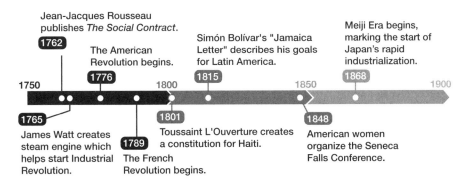

Jean-Jacques Rousseau publishes *The Social Contract*.
1762

The American Revolution begins.
1776

Simón Bolívar's "Jamaica Letter" describes his goals for Latin America.
1815

Meiji Era begins, marking the start of Japan's rapid industrialization.
1868

1750   1800   1850   1900

James Watt creates steam engine which helps start Industrial Revolution.
1765

The French Revolution begins.
1789

Toussaint L'Ouverture creates a constitution for Haiti.
1801

American women organize the Seneca Falls Conference.
1848

Topics and Learning Objectives

5.1

The Enlightenment

Except our own thoughts, there is nothing absolutely in our power.
—René Descartes (1596–1650)

Essential Question: How did the Enlightenment shape the intellectual and ideological thinking that affected reform and revolution after 1750?

As empires expanded and trade routes led to more interactions, intellectuals in the 17th and 18th centuries such as Descartes began to emphasize reason over tradition and individualism over community values. These shifts were called the **Enlightenment.** The ideals of this movement, such as individualism, freedom, and self-determination, challenged the roles of monarchs and church leaders and planted the seeds of revolution in the United States, France, and around the world.

An Age of New Ideas

Growing out of the Scientific Revolution and the humanism of the Renaissance, Enlightenment thought was optimistic. Many writers believed that applying reason to natural laws would result in progress. While not denying the existence of God, they emphasized human accomplishments in understanding the natural world. Such beliefs led to the conclusion that natural laws governed the social and political spheres as well. While traditional religion did not disappear, it became less pervasive.

New ideas emerged about how to improve society. Schools of thought including *socialism* and *liberalism* arose, giving rise to the period being called "the Age of Isms." Opposing socialism and liberalism were the currents of *conservatism*, particularly popular among the European ruling class. (All of these "isms" are defined later in this topic.)

The clash between new ideas and old political structures led to revolutions that often had two aims: independence from imperial powers and constitutional representation. The breakup of empires and the emergence of new forms of government often followed. These developed out of the concept of **nationalism**, a feeling of intense loyalty to others who share one's language and culture. The idea that people who share a culture should also live in an independent nation-state threatened to destroy all of Europe's multiethnic empires.

New Ideas and Their Roots

In the 17th century, Francis Bacon emphasized empirical methods of scientific inquiry. **Empiricism** is the belief that knowledge comes from sensed experience, from what you observe through your experience, including through experiments. Rather than relying on reasoning about principles provided by tradition or religion, Bacon based his conclusions on his observation of natural data.

Hobbes and Locke In the same century, philosophers Thomas Hobbes (author of *Leviathan*, 1651) and **John Locke** (author of *Two Treatises of Government,* 1690) viewed political life as the result of a **social contract**. Hobbes argued that people's natural state was to live in a bleak world in which life was "nasty, brutish, and short." However, by agreeing to a social contract, they gave up some rights to a strong central government in return for law and order.

Locke, on the other hand, argued that the social contract implied the right, even the responsibility, of citizens to revolt against unjust government. Locke thought that people had natural rights to life, liberty, and the pursuit of property. Another of Locke's influential ideas is found in *An Essay Concerning Human Understanding* (1690), in which he proposed that a child was born with a mind like a "blank slate" (**tabula rasa**) waiting to be filled with knowledge. In a world in which most people believed that an individual's intelligence, personality, and fate were heavily determined by their ancestry, Locke's emphasis on environment and education in shaping people was radical.

The Philosophes In the 18th century, a new group of thinkers and writers who came to be called the **philosophes** explored social, political, and economic theories in new ways. In doing so, they popularized concepts that they felt followed rationally upon those of the scientific thinkers of the 17th century. Taking their name from the French word *philosophe* ("philosopher"), these writers included Thomas Jefferson and Benjamin Franklin from America, Adam Smith from Scotland, and several French thinkers

Of particular importance to writers of the new constitutions in France and America in the 18th and 19th centuries were the ideas of **Baron Montesquieu**. His famous work *The Spirit of Laws* (1748) praised the British government's use of checks on power because it had a Parliament. Montesquieu thus influenced the American system, which adopted his ideas by separating its executive branch (the president) from its legislative branch (Congress) and both from its third branch (the federal judiciary).

Francois-Marie Arouet, pen name **Voltaire**, is perhaps best known for his social satire *Candide* (1762). He was famous during his lifetime for his wit and for his advocacy of civil liberties. Exiled for three years due to a conflict with a member of the French aristocracy, Voltaire lived in England long enough to develop an appreciation for its constitutional monarchy and a regard for civil rights. He brought these ideas back to France, where he campaigned for religious liberty and judicial reform. His correspondence with heads of state (such as Catherine the Great of Russia and Frederick the Great of Prussia) and his extensive writings, including articles in Diderot's *Encyclopedia,* are still quoted today. His idea of religious liberty influenced the U.S. Constitution.

A contemporary of Voltaire was the writer **Jean-Jacques Rousseau**, who expanded on the idea of the social contract as it had passed down through the work of Hobbes and Locke. One of Rousseau's early works was *Emile, or On Education* (1762) in which he laid out his ideas on child-rearing and education. A later work, *The Social Contract* (1762), presented the concept of the General Will of a population and the obligation of a sovereign to carry out that General Will. An optimist who believed that society could improve, Rousseau inspired many revolutionaries of the late 18th century.

Adam Smith One of the most influential thinkers of the Enlightenment was **Adam Smith**. In his book ***The Wealth of Nations*** (1776), Smith responded to mercantilism by calling for freer trade. While Smith did support some government regulations and saw the benefits of taxes, he generally advocated for **laissez-faire,** a French phrase for "leave alone." This approach meant that governments should reduce their intervention in economic decisions. Smith believed that if businesses and consumers were allowed to make choices in their own interests, the "invisible hand" of the market would guide them to make choices beneficial for society. His ideas provided a foundation for **capitalism,** an economic system in which the means of production, such as factories and natural resources, are privately owned and are operated for profit. (Connect: Create a chart or Venn diagram that compares and contrasts mercantilism and the free market. See Topics 4.4 and 4.5.)

Source: Getty Images

Adam Smith was one of the first modern economists.

Deism The Enlightenment's emphasis on reason led some thinkers to reexamine the relationship of humans to God. Some adopted **Deism**, the belief that a divinity simply set natural laws in motion. Deists compared the divinity to a watchmaker who makes a watch but does not interfere in its day-to-day workings. Deists believed these laws could be best understood through scientific inquiry rather than study of the Bible. Despite their unorthodox ideas, many Deists viewed regular church attendance as an important social obligation and a way people received moral guidance.

Thomas Paine, never one to shrink from conflict, was militant in his defense of Deism in the book *The Age of Reason* (1794). Paine's previous work, *Common Sense* (1776), made him popular in America for advocating liberty from Britain, but his anti-church writings damaged much of his popularity.

European Intellectual Life, 1250–1789		
Period	**Representative Thinkers**	**Characteristics**
Medieval Scholasticism	• St. Thomas Aquinas (1225–1274)	• Used reason to defend faith • Argued through writing and debating • Relied heavily on Aristotle • Used little experimentation
Renaissance Humanism	• Erasmus (1466–1536) • Mirandola (1463–1494)	• Wrote practical books, such as Machiavelli's *The Prince* • Emphasized human achievements • Focused on secularism and the individual
Scientific Revolution and Enlightenment	• Francis Bacon (1561–1626) • Isaac Newton (1642–1727) • Thomas Hobbes (1588–1679) • John Locke (1632–1704) • French philosophes	• Emphasized use of empirical data • Believed in natural rights, progress, and reason • Wanted new constitutions • Supported religious toleration • Wrote for the reading public

The Age of New Ideas Continues

In Europe and America, Enlightenment thinkers reacted to the social ills caused by increasing urbanization and industrialization. Poverty in the cities increased. Poor workers lived in slums without proper sanitation and without political representation. Various writers proposed solutions to the observable problems. Some wanted more government regulations and programs, and many Christians called for greater private charity. But some conservatives blamed the poor themselves and called on them to change. **Conservatism** is a belief in traditional institutions, favoring reliance on practical experience over ideological theories, such as that of human perfectability.

Utopian Socialism The economic and political theory of **socialism** refers to a system of public or direct worker ownership of the means of production such as the mills to make cloth or the machinery and land needed to mine coal. Various branches of socialism developed in the 19th century, providing alternative visions of the social and economic future. Those who felt that society could be channeled in positive directions by setting up ideal communities were often called **utopian socialists**:

- **Henri de Saint-Simon,** of France, believed that scientists and engineers, working together with businesses, could operate clean, efficient, beautiful places to work that produced things useful to society. He also advocated for public works that would provide employment. He proposed building the Suez Canal in Egypt, a project that the French government later undertook and which opened in 1869.

- **Charles Fourier** identified some 810 passions that, when encouraged, would make work more enjoyable and workers less tired. Like other utopian socialists, Fourier believed that a fundamental principle of utopia was harmonious living in communities rather than the class struggle that was basic to the thinking of Karl Marx.

- **Robert Owen** was born in Great Britain. He established intentional communities—small societies governed by the principles of utopian socialism—in New Lanark, Scotland, and New Harmony, Indiana. He believed in education for children who worked, communal ownership of property, and community rules to govern work, education, and leisure time.

In the later 19th century, socialist groups such as the **Fabian Society** formed in England. The Fabians were gradual socialists: they favored reforming society by parliamentary means. Writers H. G. Wells, Virginia Woolf, and George Bernard Shaw were prominent Fabians. By the mid-20th century, socialist principles would influence most of Western Europe.

Classical Liberalism Others advocated **classical liberalism**, a belief in natural rights, constitutional government, laissez-faire economics, and reduced spending on armies and established churches. Most classical liberals were professionals, writers, or academics. In Britain they pursued changes in Parliament to reflect changing population patterns so that new industrial cities would have equal parliamentary representation. Classical liberals backed the Reform Bills of 1832, 1867, and 1884, all of which broadened male suffrage.

Feminism This period saw the emergence of the movement for women's rights and equality based on Enlightenment ideas. The French writer Olympe de Gouges fought for these rights in the era of the French Revolution. In 1789, France had adopted the "Declaration of the Rights of Man and of the (Male) Citizen," a pioneering document in the history of human rights. In 1791, de Gouges published a "Declaration of the Rights of Woman and of the (Female) Citizen," to point out that women's rights had not been addressed.

In 1792 in England, the pioneering writer **Mary Wollstonecraft** published *A Vindication of the Rights of Women.* In it, she argued that females should receive the same education as males. Universal education, she argued, would prepare women to participate in political and professional society, enabling them to support themselves rather than relying on men. Wollstonecraft's ultimate goal was for women to gain the same rights and abilities as men through the application of reason. Women won the full right to vote in 1928.

Source: Library of Congress

Mary Wollstonecraft,
engraving by James
Heath, c. 1797 after the
painting by John Opie

In 1848 in Seneca Falls, New York, activists gathered to promote women's rights and suffrage (the ability to vote). In the convention's "Declaration of Sentiments," organizers Lucretia Mott and Elizabeth Cady Stanton declared, "All men and women are created equal." They demanded women deserved the right to vote and hold office, hold property and manage their own incomes, and be the legal guardians of their children. The Seneca Falls Convention was a landmark in the history of the women's rights movement.

Abolitionism Reform movements to provide rights and equality extended to freedom for enslaved people and the end of serfdom. **Abolitionism**, the movement to end the Atlantic slave trade and free all enslaved people, gained followers in the 18th century. Slave trading was banned earlier than slavery itself. The first states to ban the slave trade were with Denmark in 1803, Great Britain in 1807, and the United States in 1808. In most countries, the slave system depended on a steady supply of new enslaved people in order to function. As a result, as soon as the slave trade stopped, slavery began to decline. In most parts of the Americas, slavery was abolished within 30 years of the end of the slave trade. The United States was the rare country where numbers increased after the importation of enslaved people ended. The last country in the Americas to end slavery was Brazil, in 1888.

The End of Serfdom Serfdom in Europe had been declining as the economy changed from agrarian to industrial. Peasant revolts pushed leaders toward reform. Queen Elizabeth I abolished serfdom in 1574. The French government abolished all feudal rights of the nobility in 1789. Alexander II of Russia abolished serfdom in 1861. The Russian emancipation of 23 million serfs was the largest single emancipation of people in bondage in human history.

Zionism Yet another "ism" in the late 19th century was the emergence of **Zionism**—the desire of Jews to reestablish an independent homeland where their ancestors had lived in the Middle East. After centuries of battling **anti-Semitism**, hostility toward Jews, and pogroms—violent attacks against Jewish communities—many European Jews had concluded that living in peace and security was not a realistic hope. To be safe, Jews needed to control their own land. Leading the movement was an Austro-Hungarian Jew, **Theodor Herzl**.

Support for Zionism increased after a scandal in France known as the **Dreyfus Affair**. In 1894, Alfred Dreyfus, a military officer who was Jewish, was convicted of treason against the French government. However, the conviction had been based on forged documents by people promoting anti-Semitism. Dreyfus was ultimately pardoned after time in prison, but the case illustrated how widespread anti-Semitism was in France, one of the countries where Jews seemed least oppressed.

Zionists faced many obstacles. The land they wanted was controlled by the Ottoman Empire, and Palestinian Arabs were already living in the region. Both the Ottomans and the Palestinians were predominantly Muslim, which added a religious aspect to the conflict. However, the Zionist movement grew in strength until 1948, when the modern country of Israel was founded.

KEY TERMS BY THEME

GOVERNMENT: Reforms	CULTURE: Isms	ECONOMY: Reforms
John Locke	Enlightenment	Adam Smith
social contract	nationalism	*The Wealth of Nations*
tabula rasa	empiricism	laissez-faire
philosophes	deism	capitalism
Baron Montesquieu	Thomas Paine	socialism
Voltaire	conservatism	utopian socialists
Jean-Jacques Rousseau	classical liberalism	Henri de Saint-Simon
	feminism	Charles Fourier
	Mary Wollstonecraft	Robert Owen
	abolitionism	Fabian Society
	Zionism	
	anti-Semitism	
	Theodor Herzl	
	Dreyfus Affair	

Questions 1 to 3 refer to the passage below.

"Who made man the exclusive judge, if women partake with him the gift of reason? In this style, argue tyrants of every denomination, from the weak king to the weak father of a family; they are all eager to crush reason; yet always assert that they usurp its throne only to be useful. Do you not act a similar part, when you force all women, by denying them civil and political rights, to remain immured [confined against their will] in their families groping in the dark? For surely, sir, you will not assert that a duty can be binding which is not founded on reason? . . .

Let there be, then, no coercion established in society, and the common law of gravity prevailing, the sexes will fall into their proper places. And now, that more equitable laws are forming your citizens, marriage may become more sacred, your young may choose wives from motives of affection, and your maidens allow love to root out vanity."

> Mary Wollstonecraft, *A Vindication of the Rights of Women*
> (dedicatory letter to Talleyrand of France), 1792

1. Wollstonecraft's main goal in this passage is to
   (A) secure inheritance rights for surviving wives
   (B) secure female equality with males
   (C) allow men and women to marry based on love
   (D) encourage Britain to support the bourgeoisie in the French Revolution

2. Which of the following writers would LEAST likely support the goals of Mary Wollstonecraft?
   (A) A conservative
   (B) A utopian socialist
   (C) A classical liberal
   (D) A Marxist

3. What part of the excerpt is connected most closely to the ideals of the Enlightenment?
   (A) Its reference to equality in marriage
   (B) Its mention of equitable laws
   (C) Its appeal to reason
   (D) Its rejection of tyrants

1. **Use the passage below to answer all parts of the question that follows.**

"I wish I knew what mighty things were fabricating. If a form of government is to be established here, what one will be assumed? Will it be left to our Assemblies to choose one? And will not many men have many minds? And shall we not run into dissensions among ourselves? I am more and more convinced that man is a dangerous creature; and that power, whether vested in many or a few, is ever grasping. . . . How shall we be governed so as to retain our liberties? . . . Who shall frame these laws? Who will give them force and energy? . . . When I consider these things, and the prejudices of people in favor of ancient customs and regulations, I feel anxious for the fate of our monarchy or democracy, or whatever is to take place."

Abigail Adams, letter to her husband John, November 1775

(A) Identify ONE way in which the passage reflects one philosophical debate in the late 18th or early 19th centuries.

(B) Explain ONE way in which the ideas of Adams support or reject the ideas of Thomas Hobbes.

(C) Explain ONE way in which the ideas of Adams support or reject the ideas of John Locke.

2. **Answer all parts of the question that follows.**

(A) Identify ONE way in which the ideas of the Renaissance impacted the ideas of the Enlightenment.

(B) Explain ONE way in which Enlightenment thinkers in Britain and America were similar in the period 1750–1900.

(C) Explain ONE way in which Enlightenment thinkers in Britain and America differed in the period 1750–1900.

 THINK AS A HISTORIAN: DESCRIBE AN ARGUMENT

The Enlightenment was a time of lively debate and argument centered on the human capacity to reason—a key aspect of argument itself. Arguments can use reason in a variety of ways. For example, deductive reasoning, sometimes called "top-down reasoning," builds an argument from a general proposition (All men are mortal) to a more specific premise (Socrates is a man) and finally to a conclusion that must be true if the other premises are true (Therefore, Socrates is mortal). Inductive, or "bottom up" reasoning, in contrast, uses specific facts to form an uncertain generalization (Chicago has never received snow on any day in August, so it's likely that no future August day will see snow). Arguments can also use reasoning by analogy, a form of inductive reasoning, to assert that two things known to be alike in some ways are likely similar in other unknown ways (Human mammals experience a wide range of emotions, so it is likely nonhuman mammals experience a similar range). Most arguments use several different kinds of reasoning to develop their ideas fully. Knowing how to describe the structure of an argument and the types of reasoning can help you evaluate the strength of its conclusions.

Read the following excerpt from a report on public education by French government official and former bishop M. Talleyrand-Péri-gord presented in 1791 to the National Assembly of France. Then read the excerpt from the dedicatory letter for Mary Wollstonecraft's A Vindication of the Rights of Women *that responds to Talleyrand's position. Describe the argument and types of reasoning in each excerpt, and give reasons for your description.*

"Let us bring up women, not to aspire to advantages which the Constitution denies them, but to know and appreciate those which it guarantees them . . . Men are destined to live on the stage of the world. A public education suits them. . . . The paternal home is better for the education of women; they have less need to learn to deal with the interests of others, than to accustom themselves to a calm and secluded life."—Talleyrand

"Contending for the rights of women, my main argument is built on this simple principle, that if she be not prepared by education to become the companion of man, she will stop the progress of knowledge . . . . If children are to be educated to understand the true principle of patriotism, their mother must be a patriot; and the love of mankind, from which an orderly train of virtues spring, can only be produced by considering the moral and civil interest of mankind; but the education and situation of woman, at present, shuts her out from such investigations. . . .[I] earnestly wish to see woman placed in a station in which she would advance, instead of retarding, the progress of those glorious principles that give a substance to morality. My opinion, indeed, respecting the rights and duties of woman, seems to flow so naturally from these simple principles, that I think it scarcely possible, but that some of the enlarged minds who formed your admirable constitution, will coincide with me."—Mary Wollstonecraft (1792)

REFLECT ON THE TOPIC ESSENTIAL QUESTION

1. In one to three paragraphs, explain how the Enlightenment shaped the ideological and intellectual thinking that affected reform and revolution in the period after 1750.

5.2

Nationalism and Revolutions

Every nation gets the government it deserves.

—Joseph de Maistre (1753–1821)

Essential Question: What were the causes and effects of the various revolutions in the period from 1750 to 1900, including influences of the Enlightenment and emerging nationalism?

The age of new ideas led to political and philosophical conflicts. Like the English statesman Edmund Burke, the French thinker Joseph de Maistre was a conservative who went against the tide of Enlightenment thinking. In the view of conservative thinkers such as Burke and Maistre, revolutions were bloody, disruptive, and unlikely to yield positive results. However, try as conservatives might to quell revolutionary change, the desire of common people for constitutional government and democratic practices erupted in revolutions throughout the 19th century. And many nations did, indeed, get a new form of government that responded to the new wave of thinking with its key ideals: progress, reason, and natural law.

The American Revolution

The ideals that inspired the American Revolution had their roots in European Enlightenment philosophy. The economic ideas of the physiocrats also played a part in the American Revolution, providing a defense of free market ideas in opposition to English mercantilism. Additionally, the American colonists had become increasingly independent politically. Colonial legislatures were making decisions usually made by Parliament. Moreover, great distances separated the colonists from Parliament and the king in London. With economic and political desires for independence grew a new social spirit.

Declaration of Independence On July 4, 1776, the **Declaration of Independence** expressed the philosophy behind the colonists' fight against British rule. In the document, Thomas Jefferson picked up the phrase "unalienable rights" from John Locke. For Jefferson, these rights were to life, liberty, and the pursuit of happiness. In the war that followed, the colonists triumphed in 1783 with crucial help from Britain's long-time enemy, France.

The New Zealand Wars

New Zealand had been occupied by Polynesian people, the Maori, since at least the mid-1200s. In the period between their arrival and the arrival of Europeans the Maori developed a rich culture. The people were divided into individual tribes, or *iwi*, who sometimes engaged in warfare. After colonization by the British, made official by annexation of New Zealand in 1840, English control over Maori affairs increased, as did pressure for their land. These issues resulted in a series of wars between the Maori and British collectively known as the New Zealand Wars. Though the Maori tribes fought together, developing a sense of Maori nationalism, by 1872, the British had won.

The French Revolution

In France in the 1780s, revolutionary ideals took on their own spin, summarized in the slogan ***liberté, égalité, et fraternité*** (liberty, equality, and fraternity). These ideas, which struck many people as radical, were popularized throughout Europe in the writings of the **philosophes**.

Economic Woes However, awditional causes led to the French Revolution. France had long spent more than it was taking in, partly to finance a series of wars. Among this spending was the economic aid that France supplied the Americans in their revolution. To address its financial situation, the French government called a meeting of the Estates-General in spring 1789. Three sectors of society, or estates, made up the Estates-General: the clergy (religious officials), the nobility, and the commoners. However, inequality in voting caused the commoners (who made up 97 percent of French society) to break away and form a new body, the National Assembly.

The Revolution Begins In the early days of the French Revolution, moderates such as Marquis de Lafayette seemed to be on the point of establishing a constitutional monarchy. The National Assembly began meeting in Paris, but then the King threatened to arrest the leaders. Angry crowds rioted in Paris and elsewhere in France. On July 14, 1789, a crowd in Paris stormed the **Bastille**, a former prison that symbolized the abuses of the monarchy and the corrupt aristocracy. In the French countryside, peasants rose up against nobles, even burning some manor houses. Some royal officials fled France. The king was forced to accept a new government with a National Assembly in charge.

The date July 14, 1789, became French Independence Day. The most permanent changes were enacted early in the Revolution—the abolition of feudalism and the adoption of the **Declaration of the Rights of Man**, a statement declaring basic human rights. Louis XVI and the nobility refused to accept the limited monarchy, which led to dissatisfaction among radical groups such as the Jacobins and inspired the establishment of the First French Republic in 1792. The **Reign of Terror**, a period during which the government executed thousands of opponents of the revolution, including the king and queen, sprang from the Jacobins. After a period of turmoil and war, the brilliant general Napoleon Bonaparte became emperor of France in 1804.

The Haitian Revolution

At the end of the 18th century, revolutionary forces were also at work in the rich French sugar and coffee colony of **Haiti** on the western third of the island of St. Domingue, also known as Hispaniola. Enslaved Africans began the rebellion by killing their masters and burning their homes. They were soon joined by **Maroons,** individuals who had already escaped slavery in Haiti. The examples of the recent American and French revolutions led formerly enslaved **Toussaint L'Ouverture** to join the revolts in 1791 and then to lead a general rebellion against slavery. Besides being well-read in Enlightenment thought, L'Ouverture proved to be a capable general. His army of enslaved Africans and Maroons established an independent government and played the French, Spanish, and British against each other.

Haiti In 1801, after taking control of the territory that would become the independent country of Haiti, L'Ouverture produced a constitution that granted equality and citizenship to all residents. He also declared himself governor for life. Haiti next enacted land reform: plantations were divided up, with the lands being distributed among formerly enslaved and free black people.

L'Ouverture worked with the French but they betrayed and imprisoned him. He died in France in 1803. But he had cemented the abolition of slavery in Haiti, which he set on the road to independence from France.

In 1804, L'Ouverture's successor, Jean-Jacques Dessalines, orchestrated a Haitian declaration of permanent independence. Thus, Haiti became the first country in Latin America to win its independence and the first black-led country in the Western Hemisphere. It was also the only country to become permanently independent as a result of a slave uprising.

Comparing the Haitian and French Revolutions Both the Haitian and French revolutions grew out of the Enlightenment's insistence that men had natural rights as citizens, and that legal restraints were limiting the freedom of people by forcing them into various estates (social classes). However, in the case of the Haitians, the restraints were more severe—the rebellion was led by people who had no rights at all.

Source: Wikimedia Commons
Toussaint L'Ouverture

Creole Revolutions in Latin America

On the Latin American mainland, revolutionary ideals were taken up by **creoles**. Born of European ancestry in the Americas, the creoles were well educated and aware of the ideas behind the revolutions in North America and France. They considered themselves superior to the **mestizos**, who were born of European and Indian parents. Colonists who were born in Spain or Portugal, known as **peninsulares**, felt superior to everyone. At the bottom of the social ladder were the enslaved Africans the indigenous population, and **mulattoes**, those of African and either European or indigenous ancestry. (Some of these social distinctions remain today.)

There were many reasons for discontent in the colonies, each of which encouraged some people to desire independence from Spain:

- Many creoles were wealthy owners of estates, mines, or businesses. They opposed Spain's mercantilism, which required colonists to buy manufactured goods only from Spain and sell products only to Spain.

- Creoles wanted more political power. They resented that Spain tended to give important government jobs in the colonies to peninsulares.

- Mestizos wanted political power and a share of the wealth of the colonies. Many had jobs in the towns or worked in the mines or on the estates of the peninsulares and creoles.

The Bolívar Revolutions In many parts of South America, the desire for independence from Spain grew among the creole class. Fearing the masses, the creoles refused the support of mestizos, indigenous people, and mulattos (people of mixed African and European heritage). The creoles had seen the result in Haiti of a slave uprising as well as the excesses of the French Revolution during the Reign of Terror. Some creoles, such as **Simón Bolívar**, continued to push for Enlightenment ideals in Latin America. He promoted independence of areas that became Venezuela, Colombia, Ecuador, and Peru.

Bolívar was born in Venezuela in 1783 to a family whose ancestors had been village aristocrats in Spain. The family had grown very wealthy in Venezuela, and Bolívar had access to this wealth for his revolutionary causes. After considerable military success in Latin America fighting the Spanish, his forces achieved the formation of a large area that he called Gran Colombia. He hoped it would become a federation similar to the United States, one based on Enlightenment ideals. He described himself as a liberal who believed in a free market and the abolition of slavery. Bolívar's goals and concerns for Latin America are outlined in his "Jamaica Letter" (1815): "Generous souls always interest themselves in the fate of a people who strive to recover the rights to which the Creator and Nature have entitled them, and one must be wedded to error and passion not to harbor this noble sentiment."

The new nations of Latin America suffered from the long wars of independence. Armies loyal to their generals led to the rise of the caudillos— strong, local leaders with regional power bases. These men intervened in national politics to make or break governments. Sometimes the caudillos defended the interests of the regional elites and sometimes of the indigenous population and the peasants, but in general they disregarded representative forms of government and the rule of law.

Results of the Creole Revolutions Although the constitutions of the newly independent countries in Latin America legally ended slavery and some social distinctions, governments were often conservative. The first constitution of Peru, for example, forbade voting by those who could not read or write in Spanish, which effectively denied most indigenous people the vote until the constitution was changed in 1860. The creoles formed powerful and conservative upper class, as they had before the wars of colonial independence.

Women gained little from the revolutions in Latin America. They were still unable to vote or enter into contracts. Most women received little education until late in the nineteenth century, and most remained submissive to men. One notable exception was Manuela Sáenz (1797–1856), who was the lover of Simón Bolívar. She actively participated in fighting alongside Bolívar, for example, in 1822 in a battle near Quito, Ecuador. An excellent rider as well as courageous fighter, she rose to the rank of colonel. On one occasion, she saved Bolívar's life, for which she received the nickname "Liberator of the Liberator." (Connect: In a brief paragraph or outline, trace the connections between creole elites and revolutions in Latin America. See Topic 4.5)

Later Challenges to Spanish Colonialism Spain's grip on parts of its empire lasted throughout the 19th century. In the Caribbean, Puerto Rico and Cuba were among its final colonial holdings. Both islands saw uprisings against Spanish rule beginning in the year 1868.

While many individuals and organizations contributed to the spirit of revolution in Puerto Rico, the role of **Lola Rodríguez de Tió** was unique. A recognized poet during an era of little educational opportunity for women, Rodríguez de Tió became famous for her eloquent critiques of Spain's exploitive rule over Puerto Rico. Her home became a meeting place for political thinkers and revolutionaries. At such meetings, she began to read lyrics to a revolutionary song, "La Boriqueña," which encouraged her fellow Puerto Ricans, "Awake from your sleep, for it's time to fight!"

The 1868 uprising forced Rodríguez de Tió into exile in Venezuela. She was allowed to return in 1885, but her critical writings again ended in exile— this time in Cuba. Once there, she wrote and worked for Cuban independence, earning her exile from there, too, to New York. She returned to Cuba in 1899 and spent her remaining years as a campaigner for social justice there.

Revolt in the Philippines

The Philippines, too, remained a Spanish colony throughout the 19th century. Educational opportunities, even for well-to-do Filipinos, were limited and controlled by religious authorities. As a result, many young men (often creoles and mestizos) from wealthy families traveled to Europe, especially Madrid and Barcelona, to attend universities. An atmosphere of nationalist fervor and republicanism, inspired by Enlightenment thinking, existed in 1880s Europe, and these Filipino students embraced it.

José Rizal became the most prominent of these young agitators, all of whom contributed to magazines, pamphlets, and other publications advocating for greater autonomy for the Philippines. Called the **Propaganda Movement**, it did not call for revolution or independence. But Spanish authorities viewed its members with suspicion. Rizal's arrest in 1892 and execution in 1896 shocked Filipinos and helped spur the first nationalist movement with the organization and strength to truly challenge Spanish rule. A serious military upheaval, the Philippine Revolution, began in 1896.

Nationalism and Unification in Europe

As nationalism spread beyond Europe, people often created an identity under one government where none had existed before. Nationalism increased in France and in other areas of Europe and in the Americas. More than in the past, people felt a common bond with others who spoke their language, shared their history, and followed their customs. Nationalism thrived in France and beyond its borders in areas conquered by Napoleon, particularly those in the Germanic areas of the declining Holy Roman Empire. Nationalism was a unifying force that not only threatened large empires, but it also drove efforts to unite people who shared a culture into one political state.

Italian Unification Count di Cavour, the prime minister of Piedmont-Sardinia, led the drive to unite the entire **Italian Peninsula** under the only native dynasty, the House of Savoy. At the time, the region was divided among a patchwork of kingdoms and city-states, and most people spoke regional languages rather than Italian. Cavour himself spoke French better than he spoke Italian. Like other classical liberals, he believed in natural rights, progress, and constitutional monarchy. But he also believed in the practical politics of reality, which came to be called **realpolitik**. Thus, he did not hesitate to advance the cause of Italian unity through manipulation. In 1858, he maneuvered Napoleon III of France into a war with Austria, hoping to weaken Austrian influence on the Italian Peninsula. Napoleon III backed out of the war after winning two important battles, partly because he feared the wrath of the Pope, who did not want his Papal States to be controlled by a central Italian government.

Nevertheless, it was too late to stop the revolutionary fervor, and soon several areas voted by plebiscite, or popular referendum, to join Piedmont (the Kingdom of Sardinia). To aid the unification effort, Cavour adopted the radical romantic revolutionary philosophy of **Giuseppe Mazzini**, who had been agitating for Italian resurgence (**Risorgimento**) since early in the nineteenth century. Cavour also allied with the Red Shirts military force led by **Giuseppe Garibaldi**, which was fighting farther south in the Kingdom of Naples.

German Unification In Germany, nationalist movements had already strengthened as a result of opposition to French occupation of German states under Napoleon Bonaparte. Following the Congress of Vienna, which settled the Napoleonic Wars in 1815, revolutions occurred in a number of European states, including Prussia and Austria. The revolutions of 1848 were the result of both nationalism (especially a desire for independence) and liberalism (a desire for representation under constitutions that recognized civil liberties).

Prussian leader **Otto von Bismarck**, who like Cavour favored realpolitik, used nationalist feelings to engineer three wars to bring about German unification. Bismarck manipulated Austria into participating in two wars, the first with Prussia against Denmark (1864) and the second between Prussia and Austria (Seven Weeks' War of 1866). After winning both wars, Bismarck manipulated France into declaring war against Prussia. His armies beat the French soundly in the Franco-Prussian War (1870). In each of these three wars, Prussia gained territory. In 1871, Bismarck founded the new German Empire, made up of many territories gained from the wars, including Alsace-Lorraine, an area long part of France on the border between France and the new Germany.

Global Consequences By 1871, two new powers, Italy and Germany, were on the international stage in an environment of competing alliances. Balance of power would be achieved briefly through these alliances, but extreme nationalism would lead to World War I.

Unification did not solve all Italian troubles. Poverty in Italy, more in the south than in the north, led to considerable emigration in the late nineteenth century—particularly to the United States and to Argentina, where the constitution of 1853 specifically encouraged **immigration**, the movement of people into the country from other countries.

WARS OF UNIFICATION IN EUROPE

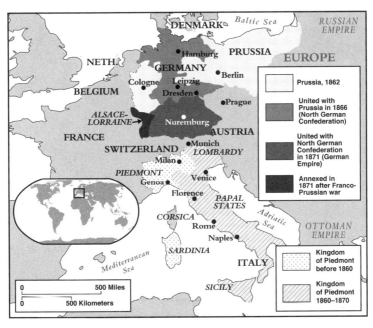

Balkan Nationalism The Ottoman Empire had been the dominant force in southeastern Europe for centuries. But for many reasons, the 17th century saw the beginning of its long, slow decline. A failed attempt to conquer Vienna in 1683 signaled the beginning of successful efforts by Austria and Russia to roll back Ottoman dominance in the Balkans. It was largely due to the increasing involvement and contact with Western European ideas and powers that Balkan nationalism developed.

In Greece, which by 1800 had been under Ottoman control for more than 350 years, increased contact with Western ideas meant exposure to Enlightenment principles. It also meant exposure to the reverence with which Greece and its ancient culture were viewed across Europe. Together, these developments helped reawaken Greek cultural pride and stoke the fires of Greek nationalism. A protracted civil war against Ottoman forces brought some success. However, it took the intervention of a British, French, and Russian fleet, which destroyed an Ottoman fleet in 1827, to help assure Greek independence.

Events in other Balkan regions, such as Serbia, Bulgaria, and Romania, followed a similar, but by no means identical, course. The waning of Ottoman control led to greater freedom and an influx of new ideas, including nationalism. People began to rally around important cultural markers, such as language, folk traditions, shared history, and religion. Later, outside powers, such as Russia or Austria, aided in achieving independence.

Source: Wikimedia Commons

This painting by Panagiotis Zografos shows the Ottoman seige of the Acropolis. Aided by British, French, and Russian forces, the Greeks won their independence by 1832.

Ottoman Nationalism The 1870s and 1880s saw the development in the Ottoman state of **Ottomanism**—a movement that aimed to create a more modern, unified state. Officials sought to do this by minimizing the ethnic, linguistic, and religious differences across the empire. Taking control of local schools and mandating a standard curriculum was a major part of this drive. But the effects of nationalism were not limited to Balkan territories and Ottoman officials. Ethnic and religious groups within the Ottoman Empire had nationalist urges of their own, and they viewed Ottomanism with suspicion. Ironically, this attempt to create a more unified state actually served to highlight and intensify subject people's feelings of difference and promote their desire for independence.

The Future of Nationalism While nationalism continues to shape how people view themselves and their political allegiances, some signs suggest that nationalism might be starting to decline. In Europe, many countries have agreed to use the same currency, to allow people to travel freely across borders, and to coordinate public policies. These changes might reflect a shift away from nationalism and toward a larger political grouping. Like city-states and empires, nations might someday give way to other forms of political organization.

KEY TERMS BY THEME

GOVERNMENT: American Revolution
Declaration of Independence

GOVERNMENT: French Revolution
philosophes
Declaration of the Rights of Man
Reign of Terror

CULTURE: France
liberté, égalité, et fraternité

GOVERNMENT: Haitian Revolution
Haiti
Toussaint L'Ouverture

GOVERNMENT: Bolivar Revolutions
Simón Bolívar

GOVERNMENT: Puerto Rico
Lola Rodríguez de Tió

GOVERNMENT: Philippines
Propaganda Movement

GOVERNMENT: Italian Unification
realpolitik
Giuseppe Mazzini
Risorgimento
Giuseppe Garibaldi

CULTURE: Italy
immigration

GOVERNMENT: German Unification
Otto Von Bismarck

GOVERNMENT: Balkans
Ottomanism

SOCIETY: Classes
Maroons
mestizos
peninsulares
mulattoes

SOCIETY: Europe
Bastille
Italian Peninsula

MULTIPLE-CHOICE QUESTIONS

Questions 1 to 3 refer to the table below.

Revolution	One Major Cause	Two Major Results
American Revolution	Opposition to taxation without representation	• Established independence • Created a written constitution
French Revolution	Opposition to the growing concentration of wealth	• Overthrew monarchy • Ended feudalism and serfdom
Haitian Revolution	Opposition to slavery	• Led to end of slavery • Redistributed land to free blacks and freed men and women
Creole Revolutions	Opposition to European control	• Established several independent countries • Led to social conflicts

1. How were the Creole Revolutions not like the American, French, and Haitian Revolutions?

   (A) The Creole Revolutions were mostly against Spain.

   (B) The Creole Revolutions united all social classes.

   (C) The Creole Revolutions occurred more quickly.

   (D) The Creole Revolutions were the only ones that succeeded.

2. Which revolution most directly addressed the unequal distribution of economic opportunity and resources?

   (A) American

   (B) Haitian

   (C) French

   (D) Creole

3. Which generalization applies to all the revolutions listed in the table?

   (A) All resulted in newly independent countries.

   (B) All advocated racial equality.

   (C) All were reversed within a generation of their completion.

   (D) All were inspired by Enlightenment ideals.

1. **Use the passage below to answer all parts of the question that follows.**

   "We are not European; we are not Indian; we are but a mixed species of aborigines and Spaniards. Americans by birth and Europeans by law, we find ourselves engaged in a dual conflict: we are disputing with the natives for titles of ownership, and at the same time we are struggling to maintain ourselves in the country that gave us birth against the opposition of the invaders."

   Simón Bolívar, speech to the Council of Angostura, 1819

   (A) Identify who was Bolívar's intended audience.

   (B) Explain ONE way in which the ideas of Bolívar support or reject the Enlightenment.

   (C) Explain ONE example of a long-term impact of Bolívar's actions.

2. **Answer all parts of the question that follows.**

   (A) Identify ONE example of why nationalism thrived in the period 1750–1900.

   (B) Explain ONE way in which nationalist movements in Italy and Germany were similar in the period 1750–1900.

   (C) Explain ONE way in which ideas of revolutions in the Americas differed in the period 1750–1900.

 THINK AS A HISTORIAN: COMPARE ARGUMENTS

Arguments rest on claims—main ideas with which people can reasonably disagree. Comparing the arguments or main ideas of two sources on the same subject can help you put arguments in perspective and evaluate the strength of their claims.

Read the following two passages from different sides of the argument on declaring American independence. Then answer the questions that follow.

"I know the name of liberty is dear to . . . us; but have we not enjoyed liberty even under the English monarchy? Shall we . . . renounce that to go and seek it in I know not what form of republic, which will soon change into a licentious anarchy and popular tyranny? In the human body the head only sustains and governs all the members, directing them . . . to the same object, which is self-preservation and happiness; so the head of the body politic, that is the king, in concert with the Parliament, can alone maintain the union of the members of this Empire . . . and prevent civil war by obviating all the evils produced by variety of opinions and diversity of interests."

—John Dickinson, Continental Congress, July 1, 1776

"The history of the present King of Great Britain is a history of repeated injuries and usurpations. . . . He has refused his Assent to Laws, the most wholesome and necessary for the public good. . . . He has called together legislative bodies at places unusual, uncomfortable, and distant. . . . He has dissolved Representative Houses repeatedly, for opposing with manly firmness his invasions on the rights of the people. . . . He has plundered our seas, ravaged our Coasts, burnt our towns, and destroyed the lives of our people. . . . [For these reasons], these United Colonies are, and of Right ought to be Free and Independent States. . . . And for the support of this Declaration, with a firm reliance on the protection of divine Providence, we mutually pledge to each other our Lives, our Fortunes and our sacred Honor."

—Declaration of Independence, July 4, 1776

1. What is John Dickinson's view about separating from the British monarch?

2. Describe the structure of Dickinson's argument. (See Topic 5.1, Think as a Historian.)

3. What is the main idea or claim of the passage from the Declaration of Independence?

4. In what ways does the passage from the Declaration of Independence draw on the ideas of Locke and other Enlightenment thinkers?

5. Explain the deductive reasoning behind the passage from the Declaration of Independence.

REFLECT ON THE TOPIC ESSENTIAL QUESTION

1. In one to three paragraphs, explain the causes and effects of the various revolutions in the period from 1750 to 1900, including influences of the Enlightenment and emerging nationalism.

5.3

Industrial Revolution Begins

One man draws out the wire, another straightens it, a third cuts it,
a fourth points it, a fifth grinds it at the top for receiving the
head; . . . and the important business of making a pin is, in
this manner, divided into about eighteen distinct operations.

—Adam Smith, *Wealth of Nations* (1776)

Essential Question: What factors contributed to and characterized
industrialization in the period from 1750 to 1900?

In addition to new ideas, new technologies were reshaping societies. These technologies led to a dramatic change in society and economies. This change was so dramatic that it is called the **Industrial Revolution.** The rigid structure of early factory work described by Adam Smith, Scottish economist and philosopher, is one of the most enduring images of the Industrial Revolution. **Industrialization,** the increased mechanization of production, and the social changes that accompanied this shift, had their roots in several influences. Among these were the Columbian Exchange and rise of maritime trading empires, increased agricultural productivity, and greater individual accumulation of capital. As the Industrial Revolution spread from Great Britain to Europe and North America, and then to the world, it reshaped society, increasing world population, shifting people from farm to city, and expanding the production and consumption of goods.

Agricultural Improvements

Just before the Industrial Revolution, in the early 1700s, an **agricultural revolution** resulted in increased productivity. **Crop rotation** (rotating different crops in and out of a field each year) and the **seed drill** (a device that efficiently places seeds in a designated spot in the ground) both increased food production. Also, the introduction of the potato from South America contributed more calories to people's diets. As nations industrialized, their populations grew because more food was available to more people. And because of improved medical care, infant mortality rates declined and people lived longer. With these demographic changes, more people were available to work in factories and to provide a market for manufactured goods.

Preindustrial Societies

During the early 18th century, most British families lived in rural areas, grew most of their food, and made most of their clothes. For centuries, wool and flax had been raised domestically, and people spun fabrics they needed.

However, one result of the commercial revolution and the establishment of maritime empires (see Topic 4.5) was that Indian cotton became available in Britain, and before long it was in high demand. Wool and flax could not be produced quickly enough or in a large enough quantity to compete with cotton imports. To compete with Indian cotton, investors in Britain began to build their nation's own cotton cloth industry. Using imported raw cotton produced by slave labor in the Americas, the British developed the **cottage industry** system, also known as the putting-out system, in which merchants provided raw cotton to women who spun it into finished cloth in their own homes.

Home spinning was hard work and pay was low, but cottage industries gave women weavers some independence. While working in their own homes, they were also close to children. But cottage industry production was slow. Investors demanded faster production, spurring the development of technologies and machinery that turned out cloth in more efficient ways.

Growth of Technology

By the mid-eighteenth century, the **spinning jenny** and the **water frame** reduced the time needed to spin yarn and weave cloth. The spinning jenny, invented by **James Hargreaves** in the 1760s, allowed a weaver to spin more than one thread at a time. The water frame, patented by **Richard Arkwright** in 1769, used waterpower to drive the spinning wheel. The water frame was more efficient than a single person's labor, and this mechanization doomed the household textile cottage industry, as textile production was moved to factories big enough to house these bulky machines. Arkwright was thus considered the father of the **factory system**.

Interchangeable Parts In 1798, inventor **Eli Whitney** created a system of **interchangeable parts** for manufacturing firearms for the U.S. military. In Whitney's system, if a particular component of a machine were to break, the broken component could easily be replaced with a new, identical part. Entrepreneurs adapted this method of making firearms to the manufacture of other products. The system of interchangeable parts was a pivotal contribution to industrial technology.

Whitney's system directly led to the **division of labor.** Factory owners no longer had to rely on skilled laborers to craft every component of a product. Instead, with **specialization of labor,** each worker could focus on one type of task. For example, one worker might cast a part, and then another worker would install the part on the finished product. In the early 20th century, Henry Ford expanded the concept of the division of labor, developing the moving **assembly line** to manufacture his Model T automobiles. (Connect: Compare the technological improvements of Islamic and Asian states with those in the Western world during the Industrial Revolution. See Topic 4.1.)

THE GROWTH OF BRITISH CITIES, C. 1800

Britain's Industrial Advantages

Britain had many environmental and geographic advantages that made it a leader in industrialization. Located on the Atlantic Ocean with its many **seaways**, the country was well placed to import **raw materials** and export finished goods.

Mineral Resources Britain also had the geographic luck of being located atop immense coal deposits. Coal was vital to industrialization because when burned it could power the steam engine. The burning of this fossil fuel, an energy source derived from plant and animal remains, was also essential in the process of separating iron from its ore. Iron production (and later steel production) allowed the building of larger bridges, taller buildings, and stronger ships. Coal mining became the major industry of northern and western Britain, including South Wales, Yorkshire, and Lancashire. When the United States industrialized, coal-mining areas developed in West Virginia, Pennsylvania, and Kentucky.

Resources from the Colonies As a colonizing power, Britain also had access to resources available in its colonies, including timber for ships. Largely because of the wealth they accumulated during the trans-Atlantic slave trade, enough British capitalists had excess **capital** (money available to invest in businesses). Without this capital, private entrepreneurs could not have created new commercial ventures.

Abundant Rivers Britain, the northeastern United States, and other regions also had a natural network of rivers supplemented by publicly funded canals and harbors. These water routes made transport of raw materials and finished products inexpensive.

Strong Fleets Britain also had the world's strongest fleet of ships, including naval ships for defense and commercial ships for trade. These ships brought agricultural products to Britain to be used to make finished products for consumers.

Protection of Private Property A vital factor that aided industrialization in Britain was the legal protection of private property. Entrepreneurs needed the assurance that the business they created and built up would not be taken away, either by other businesspeople or by the government. Not all nations offered these legal guarantees.

Growing Population and Urbanization The increases in agricultural production caused two shifts in society. As farmers grew more food, they could support more people. As they grew it more efficiently, society needed a smaller percentage of the population working in agriculture.

This growing population in rural areas did not remain there. Migration was sometimes the best of bad options. English towns had traditionally allowed farmers to cultivate land or tend sheep on government property known as "the commons." However, this custom ended with the **enclosure movement** as the government fenced off the commons to give exclusive use of it to people who paid for the privilege or who purchased the land. Many farmers became landless and destitute. The enclosure movement was thus instrumental in a wave of demographic change—forcing small farmers to move from rural areas to urban areas such as **Manchester** and **Liverpool.** The people who moved then became the workforce for the new and growing industries.

KEY TERMS BY THEME

TECHNOLOGY: Textiles	ECONOMY: Manufacturing	ENVIRONMENT: Britain
spinning jenny	Industrial Revolution	seaways
water frame	industrialization	raw materials
James Hargreaves	cottage industry	Manchester
Richard Arkwright	Eli Whitney	Liverpool
factory system	interchangeable parts	
TECHNOLOGY:	division of labor	
Agriculture	specialization of labor	
agricultural revolution	assembly line	
crop rotation	capital	
seed drill	enclosure movement	

Questions 1 to 3 refer to the chart below.

Urban Population in England, 1801–1901		
Year	Manchester	Liverpool
1801	328,609	85,627
1821	526,230	137,880
1841	860,413	271,824
1861	1,313,550	392,481
1881	1,866,649	649,613
1901	2,357,150	Not available

1. Which of the following changes best explains one of the main causes of the trend shown in the chart?

   (A) Increased use of cottage industries in Great Britain

   (B) Increased migration from rural to urban areas in Great Britain

   (C) Increased British demand for imports of coal

   (D) Increased British demand for imports from India and China

2. Which of the following changes explains one of the main effects of the trend shown in the chart?

   (A) Increased supply of workers for factory jobs

   (B) Increased protection for private property

   (C) Decreased support for the British fleet

   (D) Decreased reliance on the specialization of labor

3. Which was the most important part of the context in which the change shown in the chart was occurring?

   (A) The Enlightnment was influencing how Europeans thought about religion and individual rights.

   (B) The idea of nationalism was spreading from country to country throughout Europe.

   (C) The rise of maritime empires increased demand for British-made goods in other regions of the world.

   (D) The shifts in political forces created conflicts among European governments.

1. **Use the passage below to answer all parts of the question that follows.**

"The advances which gave this great economic change the name Industrial Revolution occurred in Great Britain, yet it would be contrary to the facts to regard the mechanization of industrial processes as strictly an English experience. . . . England was the leading innovator of methods for rendering raw materials more useful to man, but it by no means had a monopoly of inventions. A Frenchman, Antoine Lavoisier, discovered the chemical nature of combustion. . . . An American, Eli Whitney, invented the cotton gin. And a German, Justus von Liebig, determined the chief chemical components of plants and thus laid the basis for a chemical fertilizer industry."

> Shepard B. Clough, "The Industrial Revolution in England,"
> *Columbia History of the World*, 1972

(A) Identify ONE historical situation other than the one illustrated in the passage that also demonstrate how an economic development in history was more than the experience of a single country.

(B) Explain ONE historical situation other than the one illustrated in the passage that challenges Clough's view that the Industrial Revolution was more than "strictly an English experience."

(C) Explain how the time in which Clough was writing might have influenced his viewpoint toward the Industrial Revolution.

2. **Answer all parts of the question that follows.**

(A) Identify ONE way that natural environments contributed to the growth of the Industrial Revolution.

(B) Explain ONE way in which the development of the factory system affected economic structures in 1750–1900.

(C) Explain ONE way in which population growth affected the development of technology in the period 1750–1900.

THINK AS A HISTORIAN: EXPLAIN THE PROCESS OF
INDUSTRIALIZATION

Some processes move along in a linear way: water has to be heated up and reach a temperature of 212 degrees before it boils and changes state from liquid to gas. (First one thing happens, then another thing happens, and then another thing happens.) Not all processes are linear, however. The process of industrialization—the transformation of a mainly agrarian society to a mainly mechanized and urban society—is the result of many different factors that may not fall neatly into a linear progression.

Group the following factors related to industrialization into logical categories. Each can appear in more than one category. Then explain the role of each factor and category in the process of industrialization.

1. urbanization

2. accumulation and investment of capital

3. increased agricultural efficiency

4. technological improvements or breakthroughs

5. natural resources

6. stability of government

7. increased population

8. consumers

9. transportation

REFLECT ON THE TOPIC ESSENTIAL QUESTION

1. In one to three paragraphs, explain what factors contributed to and characterized industrialization in the period from 1750 to 1900.

5.4

Industrialization Spreads

No exertions of the masters or workmen could have answered the demands of trade without the introduction of spinning machines.

—John Aikin, *A Description of the Country . . . Around Manchester*, 1795

Essential Question: How did different types and locations of production develop and change over time?

Although the Industrial Revolution began in Britain, it soon spread elsewhere. The British cottage industry system for the production of cotton, in which merchants provided raw cotton to be spun into cloth in workers' homes, was supplanted by the industrialization of cotton manufacture in factories. Cotton became an increasingly valuable commodity in the world economy as industrialized Britain, with higher productivity, was able to replace Indian and Middle Eastern goods. After Britain industrialized, Belgium and then France and Germany followed, and eventually Russia and Japan became industrialized. These countries possessed many of the characteristics that allowed Britain to industrialize, including capital, natural resources, and water transportation.

Spread of Industrialization

After Britain industrialized, Belgium, and then France and Germany followed. Like Britain, these countries possessed capital, natural resources, and water transportation. The United States, Japan, and Russia also transformed as industrialization spread.

France and Germany Despite some favorable factors for industrialization, France had sparsely populated urban centers, which limited the amount of labor available for factories. Also, the French Revolution (1789–1799) and subsequent wars involving France and its neighbors consumed both the attention and the capital of France's elites. These factors delayed the Industrial Revolution in France.

Germany was politically fragmented into numerous small states, which delayed its industrialization. However, once Germany unified in 1871, it quickly became a leading producer of steel and coal.

The United States The United States began its industrial revolution in the 19th century. By 1900, the United States was a leading industrial force in the world. **Human capital** (the workforce) was a key factor in U.S. success. Political upheaval and widespread poverty brought a large number of immigrants to the United States from Europe and East Asia. These immigrants, as well as migrants from rural areas in the United States, provided the labor force to work in the factories.

Agricultural Products for Trade in the Nineteenth Century		
Product	Producers	Users (Finished Products)
Wheat	Russia, Britain	Britain (food)
Rubber	Brazilian Amazon	Britain (tires, footwear, fabrics)
Palm Oil	West Africa, Indonesia	Britain (cooking oil, soap)
Sugar	Caribbean Islands, Brazil	Britain (refined sugar)
Cattle and Hogs	United States, Ireland, Argentina	Britain, United States (meat)
Cotton	United States	Britain (textiles)

Russia Russia also began to industrialize, focusing particularly on railroads and exports. By 1900, Russia had more than 36,000 miles of railroad connecting its commercial and industrial areas. The **Trans-Siberian Railroad** stretched from Moscow to the Pacific Ocean, allowing Russia to trade easily with countries in East Asia, such as China and Japan. The Russian coal, iron, and steel industries developed with the railroad, mostly in the 1890s. By 1900, Russia had become the fourth largest producer of steel in the world. However, the economy remained overwhelmingly agricultural until after the Communists seized power in 1917.

Japan The first country in Asia to industrialize was the one that had the least contact with Europe since the 17th century: Japan. In the mid-19th century, Japan went through a process of defensive modernization. That is, it consciously adapted technology and institutions developed in Europe and the United States in order protect its traditional culture. By learning from the West, Japan built up its military and economic strength so it could maintain its own domestic traditions. In the last four decades of the 19th century, Japan emerged as a leading world power. For more details on Japan, see Topic 5.6.

Shifts in Manufacturing

While Middle Eastern and Asian countries continued to produce manufactured goods, these regions' share in global manufacturing declined.

Shipbuilding in India and Southeast Asia Shipbuilding initially saw a resurgence in India at the end of the 17th century, largely due to the political alliances formed between India and western countries. However, Indian shipbuilding ultimately suffered as a result of British officials' mismanagement of resources and ineffective leadership during the period of British colonization in the late 17th and 18th centuries. In 1830, Britain designated ships of the British East India Company as the Indian Navy. The Indian Navy was disbanded by 1863, however, when Britain's Royal Navy took complete control of the Indian Ocean.

Iron Works in India British colonial rule in India also affected the country's mineral production. During the period of **company rule**—British East India Company control over parts of the Indian subcontinent from 1757 to 1858—steep British tariffs led to the decline of India's ability to mine and work metals. The British also began to close mines completely, especially after the Rebellion of 1857, because they perceived that the mines were being used to extract lead for ammunition.

The ongoing fear of another uprising led to the Arms Act of 1878, which restricted not only access to minerals, but also to the subsequent production of firearms. British colonizers limited India's ability to mine and work metals in areas such as the mineral-rich state of Rajasthan. By the early 19th century, most of the mines in Rajasthan were abandoned and the mining industry was extinct.

Even though British colonial rule ended in 1948, mining and metalworking remained practically nonexistent in India until the early 20th century. Lack of technological innovation after so many years of abandoned mines led to a relatively crude, labor-intensive method of mining, which created the false impression that India's mineral resources were inaccessible. (Connect: Identify the similarities in how Britain treated its colonies in South Asia and its colonies in the Americas. See Topic 4.8.)

Textile Production in India and Egypt India and Egypt were both among the first to engage in the production and trade of textiles. Just as it stifled the production of ships and iron, British colonization also affected textile production in India. As the textile industry flourished in India, it undermined the British textile mills in Britain, specifically in Lancaster. The owners of the Lancaster textile mills pressured the British government in India to impose an "equalizing" five percent tax on all textiles produced at the more than 80 mills operating in Bombay, thus undermining their profitability.

Egypt's textile industry, too, experienced difficulties as a result of Europe's worldwide economic reach. In the 18th century, Egypt exported carpets, silks, and other textiles to Europe. By the mid-19th century, however, the huge growth in European textile production had changed matters. Egypt had lost not only its export market in textiles, but much of its domestic market as well.

KEY TERMS BY THEME	
ECONOMY: Railroads Trans-Siberian Railroad	**ECONOMY:** Manufacturing human capital company rule

Questions 1 to 3 refer to the passage below.

"The economic relations of Russia with western Europe are fully comparable to the relations of colonial countries with their metropolises. The latter consider their colonies as advantageous markets in which they can freely sell the products of their labor and of their industry and from which they can draw with a powerful hand the raw materials necessary for them. This is the basis of the economic power of the governments of western Europe, and chiefly for that end do they guard their existing colonies or acquire new ones. Russia was, and to a considerable extent still is, such a hospitable colony for all industrially developed states, generously providing them with the cheap products of her soil and buying dearly the products of their labor.

But there is a radical difference between Russia and a colony: Russia is an independent and strong power. She has the right and the strength not to want to be the eternal handmaiden of states which are more developed economically. She should know the price of her raw materials and of the natural riches hidden in the womb of her abundant territories, and she is conscious of the great, not yet fully displayed, capacity for work among her people. She is proud of her great might, by which she jealously guards not only the political but also the economic independence of her empire. She wants to be a metropolis herself. On the basis of the people's labor, liberated from the bonds of serfdom, there began to grow our own national economy, which bids fair to become a reliable counterweight to the domination of foreign industry."

Sergei Witte, Russian finance minister, secret report to Tsar
Nicholas II on industrialization, 1899

1. In the above passage, what policy is the Russian Minister of Finance urging?

    (A) Maintaining current political and commercial relationships

    (B) Supporting independent Russian industrial development

    (C) Relying on foreign industry for economic growth

    (D) Using military strength to prevent foreign industrial domination

2. What shift in economic focus did the emancipation of the serfs foster?

    (A) It created a pool of laborers who could more easily move to cities and work in industry.

    (B) It increased the power of nobles who could then travel more widely and bring new ideas to Russia.

    (C) It encouraged population growth, which increased tax revenues.

    (D) It established a new consumer base that could afford to purchase imported manufactured goods.

3. What was a critical strategy in the industrialization of Russia?

   (A) building an infrastructure of canals

   (B) controlling the settlement of Siberia

   (C) expanding the national railroad network

   (D) developing a free trade policy

SHORT-ANSWER QUESTIONS

1. Use the passage below to answer all parts of the question that follows.

"By this oath we set up as our aim the establishment of the national weal on a broad basis and framing of a constitution and laws.

1. Deliberative assemblies shall be widely established and all matters decided by public discussion.

2. All classes, high and low, shall unite in vigorously carrying out the administration of affairs of state.

3. The common people, no less than the civil and military officials, shall each be allowed to pursue his own calling so that there may be no discontent.

4. Evil customs of the past shall be broken off and everything based upon the just laws of Nature.

5. Knowledge shall be sought throughout the world so as to strengthen the foundations of imperial rule."

The Charter Oath of the Meiji Restoration, 1868

   (A) Identify ONE way in which the Charter Oath affected the development of Japan's industrialization.

   (B) Explain ONE way in which the passage reflects change in Japanese political or social structures in the period 1750–1900.

   (C) Explain ONE historical situation in the period 1750–1900, other than the one illustrated in the passage, that led to changes in Japan.

2. Answer all parts of the question that follows.

   (A) Identify ONE way in which revolution affected industrialization in France and the United States.

   (B) Explain ONE way in which industrialization affected Japan and Britain differently in the period 1750–1900.

   (C) Explain ONE way in which political policies and cultural traditions influenced the Asian or Middle Eastern share in global manufacturing.

THINK AS A HISTORIAN: CONNECT IMPERIALISM AND INDUSTRIALIZATION

Think about the historical development of imperialism and the process of industrialization. Could one have existed without the other? Did they develop on separate paths or is their development intertwined?

To understand if or how the two are related, begin by reviewing the paragraphs you wrote for the Think as a Historian activity for Topic 5.3. Then write new paragraphs explaining any relationships you find between imperialism and industrialization.

REFLECT ON THE TOPIC ESSENTIAL QUESTION

1. In one to three paragraphs, explain how different production methods and locations developed and changed over time.

Source: Wikimedia Commons

A painting of the Trans Siberian Railway, c. 1913

5.5

Technology in the Industrial Age

*Railroad iron is a magician's rod, in its power
to evoke the sleeping energies of land and water.*

—Ralph Waldo Emerson (1803–1882)

Essential Question: How did technology shape economic production
during the period from 1750 to 1900?

As the Industrial Revolution spread, it became increasingly important
economically. Although he later came to be troubled by the role of technology,
Ralph Waldo Emerson initially saw the innovations of the industrial age
as a delightful way to mold nature in the service of humankind. The steam
engine and then the internal combustion engine, powering railroads, ships, and
factories, increased access to resources and increased the distribution of goods
those resources helped produce.

The next technological wave, known as the second industrial revolution,
came in the late 19th and early 20th centuries and involved chemicals, steel,
precision machinery, and electronics. Electrification lit the streets, and the
telephone and radio made world-wide, instantaneous communication a reality.

The Coal Revolution

The new machinery of the Industrial Revolution benefitted from a new power
source, one more mobile than the streams that had powered the first factories
with their water power. The version of the **steam engine** made by **James Watt**
in 1765 provided an inexpensive way to harness **coal** power to create steam,
which in turn generated energy for machinery in textile factories. Within 50
years, steam was producing power for steam powered trains.

Water Transportation Steamships revolutionized sailing. The use of
coal made energy production mobile and dependable. Instead of being fixed in
one place as a river was, coal-powered steam engines could be built anywhere
and could be used on ships and trains. Further, unlike the wind, engines could
be turned on by people when needed and turned off when not. As a result,
ocean-going ships and boats on lakes were no longer dependent on winds for
power. On rivers, steam-powered ships were able to travel quickly upstream
on rivers, up to five miles per hour, instead of having to sail up or be towed by

people and animals along the shore. Over time, steam-powered ships replaced sailing ships in worldwide travel. As a result, **coaling stations**, especially at critical points on trade routes, such as Cape Colony in South Africa and various islands in the Pacific, became important refueling points.

Source: Hunter Wood, 1819/Wikimedia Commons
The *SS Savannah* was the first steam-powered ship to cross the Atlantic Ocean (1819).

Iron In addition to powering steam engines, coal made possible the mass production of iron. Throughout the 1700s and into the early 1800s, improved processes helped iron producers increase outputs. One of these was the introduction of coke, a refined form of coal that made possible the use of much larger iron producing furnaces. Cast iron was strong but brittle, making it difficult to stretch and shape. But in 1794, Englishman Henry Cort patented the process for making the less strong but much more workable wrought iron. Each was a valuable component in transportation and industry, but greater improvements were still to come.

A Second Industrial Revolution

The United States, Great Britain, and Germany were key players in what is known as the **second industrial revolution**, which occurred in the late 19th and early 20th centuries. The innovations of the first industrial revolution were in textiles, steam power, and iron. The developments of the second industrial revolution were in **steel**, chemicals, precision machinery, and electronics.

Steel Production The mass production of steel, an alloy of iron and carbon, became possible with the introduction of the Bessemer Process in

1856. This process involved blasting the molten metal with air as a means of removing impurities as well as helping keep the metal from solidifying. Over the years, Bessemer's innovation was refined and improved, allowing steel to become the strong and versatile backbone of the industrial society.

Oil In the mid-1800s, the first commercial oil wells were drilled, tapping into a vast new resource of energy. Petroleum, like coal, is a fossil fuel, an energy source derived from plant and animal remains. At first, the most important product from petroleum was kerosene, which was used for lighting and heaters. In 1847, inventors developed chemical techniques to extract kerosene from petroleum.

These techniques led to other developments, such as precision machinery and the internal combustion engine, which in turn led to automobile and airplane technologies. When automobiles were introduced in the early 1900s, gasoline as fuel became a more important product from petroleum than kerosene.

Electricity The harnessing of electrical power had to wait for the development of an effective electrical generator. In 1882 in London, the first public power station began production. Electrification led to street lighting and electric street trains in the 1890s.

Communications The development of electricity and electronics over the years helped lead to important developments in communication technology. Inventors had been working with the idea of transmitting sound by electrical means since the early 19th century. Finally, a patent for the telephone was issued to **Alexander Graham Bell** in 1876. Early phone systems were notoriously low in quality, but Thomas Edison's 1886 design of a refined voice transmitter made telephone use more practical.

Radio developed after the experiments of Italian physicist **Gugliemo Marconi**. In 1901, he was able to send and receive a radio signal across the Atlantic Ocean. After further refinements and inventions, radio become a form of popular mass media with an impact unlike any previously seen.

Global Trade and Migration

Railroads, steamships, and a new invention called the telegraph made exploration, development, and communication possible. The telegraph allowed immediate communication. The construction of railroads, including the **Transcontinental Railroad** that connected the Atlantic and Pacific oceans when it was completed in 1869, facilitated U.S. industrial growth. Like the canals, the railroads were heavily subsidized by public funds. The vast natural resources of the United States (timber, coal, iron, and **oil**, for example) and the ability to transport them efficiently contributed to the development of the United States as an industrial nation.

Source: U.S. Post Office.
The first transcontinental railroad was completed in 1869 in Utah.

The desire for **capital**, money available to invest in a business, was a driving force domestically and abroad. Products of industrialization, such as the railroad, steamship, and the telegraph, directly linked farmers, miners, manufacturers, customers, and investors globally for the first time in history.

With the development of the railroad and steamships, such countries as Great Britain, Germany, and the United States intensified industrialization, increasing the need for resources. Industrialized countries sought to protect their access to resources and markets by establishing colonies.

Whereas earlier trade and migration often centered on coastal cities, railroads, steamships, and the telegraph also opened up to exploration and development the interior regions around the globe. Access to these areas increased trade and migration. (Connect: Write a paragraph describing how the Silk Roads set the stage for the industrial developments of the 1800s. See Topic 2.1.)

KEY TERMS BY THEME		

ENVIRONMENT: Resources
coal
coaling stations
 	
TECHNOLOGY:
  Transportation and
  Communication
Alexander Graham Bell
Gugliemo Marconi
Transcontinental Railroad
	ECONOMY: Industry
	steam engine
	James Watt
	steel
	oil
	capital
		SOCIETY:
		second industrial
		  revolution

Questions 1 to 3 refer to the image below.

Source: Library of Congress

A girl working in a textile factory in the Industrial Revolution

1. Which statement provides the best context for interpreting this photo?

   (A) Machines used in factories during the Industrial Revolution were similar to the ones used in cottage industries.

   (B) One effect of the industrialization was that girls and boys worked side by side rather than in separate jobs.

   (C) As the Bessemer Process improved, textile machines became faster and more sophisticated.

   (D) The Industrial Revolution led to a division of labor that meant employees began to do highly specialized work.

2. For textile production as seen in the photo, which of the following relationships would have existed between an industrialized country and colony during the Second Industrial Revolution?

   (A) The colony would have provided resources for the industrialized country to make textiles

   (B) The colony would have sold finished textiles to the industrialized country.

   (C) The industrialized country would have sent its resources to the colony to be made into finished textiles.

   (D) The industrialized country would have located its textile-manufacturing headquarters in the colony.

3. The photo can best be used to demonstrate which of the following long-term effects of the Industrial Age?

(A) The growth in international trade

(B) The problem of water pollution

(C) The expansion of the work force

(D) The increase in the population

SHORT-ANSWER QUESTIONS

1. Use the image below to answer all parts of the question that follows.

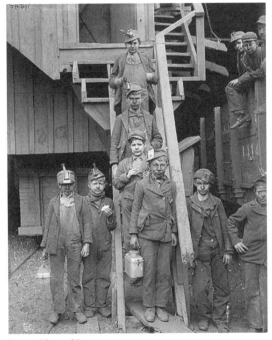

Source: Library of Congress
Breaker boys, Woodward Coal Mines, Kingston, Pa.

(A) Identify ONE technological development in the period 1750–1900 represented in the image.

(B) Explain ONE way the image above reflects changes in workplaces in the period 1750–1900.

(C) Explain ONE way new business practices affected workers like these in the period 1750–1900.

2. **Answer all parts of the question that follows.**

   (A) Identify ONE way technology affected communication in the period 1750–1900.

   (B) Explain ONE way in which the development of machines made the discovery of new resources possible in the period 1750–1900.

   (C) Explain ONE way that the Industrial Revolution affected global interactions in the period 1750–1900.

 THINK AS AN HISTORIAN: EXPLAIN THE EFFECTS OF THE DEVELOPMENT OF ELECTRICITY

Tracing the impact of a development requires recognizing causes and effects. For example, the development of harnessing electrical power caused far-reaching effects that continue to shape the modern world.

On separate paper, make a chart like the one below to explain and give examples of the specific effects of the development of electricity.

Specific Effects of Development of Electrical Power	
On creation of new industries	
On ease of daily life	
On communication	
On transportation	
On the environment	
On global connections	

REFLECT ON THE TOPIC ESSENTIAL QUESTION

---

1. In one to three paragraphs, explain how technology shaped economic production during the period from 1750–1900.

5.6

Industrialization: Government's Role

It is our purpose to select from the various institutions prevailing among enlightened nations such as are best suited to our present conditions, and adapt them in gradual reforms and improvements of our policy and customs so as to be upon an equality with them.

— Emperor Meiji, letter to President Ulysses Grant, 1871

Essential Question: What economic strategies did different states and empires adopt, and what were the causes and effects of those strategies?

As Western domination and technology spread, they met with varying degrees of acceptance in different nations. Each country experienced competing pressures between preservation of traditional values and modernization. Egypt early adopted policies that encouraged the use of industrialized innovations, such as the steam engine, to boost textile productivity. To compete with modernized countries and maintain its independence, Japan changed several of its institutions to reflect more Western practices.

Others, such as China, were less willing to accept European influences (and products) and suffered because of economic and political expansion by Western nations. China's weakened government and population was unable to promote industrialization effectively. (See Topic 6.5.)

Ottoman Industrialization

The Ottoman Empire, although bordering Europe, had not adopted Western technology or Enlightenment ideas. Moreover, rampant corruption led to rapid decline, and ethnic nationalism among the empire's diverse population led to widespread unrest. The empire earned the nickname "the sick man of Europe." The declining empire was eventually dismantled after World War I into the Republic of Turkey and several small independent countries. However, as the empire was weakening throughout the 17th and 18th centuries, not all the territory of the empire experienced similar struggles.

The Rise of Muhammad Ali One part of the Ottoman Empire where the sultan ruled in name but had little power was Egypt. In fact, the **Mamluks**, formerly enslaved Turks who formed a military class, had ruled there for some

600 years. In 1801, the sultan sent an Ottoman army to retake Egypt. In the conflict with the Mamluks, an Albanian Ottoman officer, **Muhammad Ali**, rose to prominence, and local leaders selected him to be the new governor of Egypt. The sultan lacked the power to do anything but agree.

Because of his power, Ali was able to act somewhat independently of the sultan. He joined the sultan's military campaigns when it benefited him, and also undertook several campaigns without the sultan's permission, including in the Sudan and Syria. He also began his own reforms in Egypt. He began by making over the country's military on a European model. He also established schools, sent military officers to be educated in France, and started an official newspaper—the first in the Islamic world.

Source: Wikimedia Commons.
Jean-François Portaels, portrait of Muhammad Ali, 1847

As part of his reform of the Egyptian economy, Ali taxed the peasants at such a high rate that they were forced to give up their lands to the state. The government could then control the valuable cotton production and make money on the export of cotton and other agricultural products. Secularizing religious lands put more agricultural produce in the hands of the government, resulting in large profits during the period of the Napoleonic wars (1799–1815), when prices for wheat were high in Europe.

Muhammad Ali also pushed Egypt to industrialize. He had textile factories built to compete with those of the French and British. In Cairo, he had factories built to produce armaments. In Alexandria, he set up facilities to build ships so that Egypt could have its own navy. The city of Cairo had dozens of small shops turning out locks, bolts of cloth, and other parts for uniforms and weaponry. Ali is called the first great modern ruler of Egypt partly because of his vision of state-sponsored industrialization.

Japan and the Meiji Restoration

Japan sought to maintain its cultural and territorial integrity in the face of Western challenges. Emperor Meiji resisted pressure from the West by using its innovations to strengthen Japan. Japan's transition to a modern, industrialized country took less than half a century to accomplish. No other country made such a rapid change.

A Challenge to Isolation Between 1600 and 1854, Japan had very little contact with the rest of the world. However, the rising imperial powers in the world were not content to let Japan keep to itself. The great powers of Europe, such as Great Britain, the Netherlands, and Russia, all wanted to sell goods in Japan. Further, in the age of coal-powered ships, trading states wanted to be able to refuel in Japan as they sailed to China and other parts of East Asia.

Japan Confronts Foreigners In 1853, a naval squad led by **Commodore Matthew Perry** in 1853 sailed into Yedo and Tokyo Bay, asking for trade privileges. The next year, Perry returned with even more ships, demanding that the Japanese engage in trade with the United States. Faced with the power of the U.S. warships, the Japanese gave in to U.S. demands. Soon they yielded to similar demands by other foreign states.

The arrival of Perry, and the threat he posed, caused Japanese leaders to realize the danger they and their culture were in. They had seen how even a large, traditionally powerful country such as China had been humiliated by Westerners. They had watched as the British had gone to war to force the Chinese to accept opium imports. While some Japanese argued that the country could defend itself, many reformers feared it could not. They argued that the country should adopt enough Western technology and methods so it could protect its traditional culture. To accomplish this goal, they overthrew the shogun and restored power to the emperor in 1868, an event know as the **Meiji Restoration.**

Reforms by the Meiji State Japan systematically visited Europe and the United States and invited experts to Japan in order to study Western institutions. Then, Japan adopted reforms based on what it admired:

- It formally abolished feudalism in 1868 by the **Charter Oath**.
- It established a constitutional monarchy based on the Prussian model in which the emperor ruled through a subordinate political leader.
- It established equality before the law and abolished cruel punishments.
- It reorganized the military based on the Prussian army, building a new navy and instituting conscription.
- It created a new school system that expanded educational opportunities, particularly in technical fields.
- It built railroads and roads.
- It subsidized industrialization, particularly in the key industries of tca, silk, weaponry, shipbuilding, and a rice wine called sake.

The government financed all of these reforms with a high agricultural tax. The taxes proved a good investment because they stimulated rapid economic growth. The government's ability to collect increased taxes also provided revenue for the bureaucracy, now centered in Tokyo.

However, in replicating the methods of Western countries, the Japanese also replicated some of industrial society's problems. For example, accounts of abuse and exploitation of female Japanese mill workers are similar to the experiences that British female mill workers had recorded decades earlier. (Connect: Write a brief paragraph comparing Japan's industrialization with developments in the West. See Topic 5.3.)

CHINA AND JAPAN IN THE 19TH CENTURY

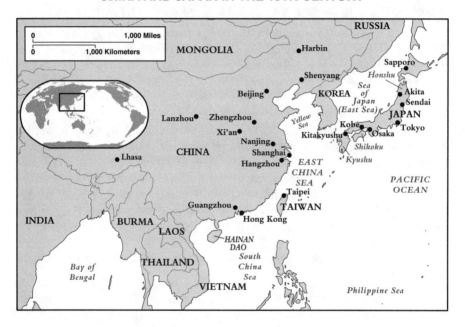

The Role of Private Investments While the relationship between industry and centralized government was key to modernization in Japan, private investment from overseas also became important. Once new industries were flourishing, they were sometimes sold to **zaibatsu**, powerful Japanese family business organizations like the conglomerates in the United States. The prospect of attracting investors encouraged innovation in technology. For example, a carpenter founded a company in 1906 called Toyoda Loom Works that made an **automatic loom**. The company prospered, modified its name, and grew into today's Toyota Motor Company.

Year	Coal Production (metric tons)	Steamships (total number)	Railroads (miles)
1872	----	----	18
1873	----	26	----
1875	600,000	----	----
1885	1,200,000	----	----
1887	----	----	640
1894	----	169	2,100
1895	5,000,000	----	----
1904	----	797	4,700
1913	21,300,000	1,514	----
1914	----	----	7,100

Table title: Japan's Economic Transformation, 1872–1914

Source: Thayer Watkins, "Meiji Restoration/Revolution," sjsu.edu. (data not available for all categories for all years)

KEY TERMS BY THEME

GOVERNMENT: Ottoman
Mamluks
Muhammad Ali

ECONOMY: Japan
Commodore Matthew Perry
zaibatsu

TECHNOLOGY: Japan
automatic loom

GOVERNMENT: Japan
Meiji Restoration
Charter Oath

Questions 1 to 3 refer to the passage below.

"Generally speaking, the strength or weakness of a country is dependent on the wealth or poverty of its people, and the people's wealth or poverty derives from the amount of available products. The diligence of the people is a major factor in determining the amount of products available, but in the final analysis, it can all be traced to the guidance and encouragement given by the government and its officials. . . . Your subject respectfully recommends that a clear-cut plan be established . . . to determine the priorities under which industries may be encouraged. . . . If the people are adequately wealthy, it follows naturally that the country will become strong and wealthy. . . . If so, it will not be difficult for us to compete effectively against major powers."

Okubo Toshimichi, "On the Role of the State in
Industrialization," 1874

1. The main idea of this passage is that the government of Japan should

   (A) persuade people in Japan to work more diligently

   (B) create a plan to encourage foreign investment in Japanese industry

   (C) avoid influencing private economic decisions

   (D) encourage industrialization to enable Japan to compete economically

2. Which possible government policy would most directly support the goal stated by the writer?

   (A) Reforming the Japanese educational system to increase training of workers and managers

   (B) Improving the Japanese agricultural system to feed the foreign residents brought into Japan to work in the industrial factories

   (C) Providing subsidies to the poor so they would not rebel

   (D) Passing laws that would encourage people to remain on farms

3. Which list of events related to the topic of the excerpt is in the correct chronological order?

   (A) Perry's ships arrive in Tokyo Bay, the Meiji Restoration, the Shogunate collapses, Japan industrializes

   (B) Japan industrializes, the Meiji Restoration, the collapse of the Shogunate, Perry's ships arrive in Tokyo Bay

   (C) Perry's ships arrive in Tokyo Bay, the Shogunate collapses, the Meiji Restoration, Japan industrializes

   (D) The Shogunate collapses, Perry's ships arrive in Tokyo Bay, the Meiji Restoration, Japan industrializes

1. **Use the passage below to answer all parts of the question that follows.**

   "It was cotton production, especially, that characterized the beginnings of Egypt's integration into the global capitalist system. Cotton was an important part of the British Industrial Revolution, as textile mills in Lancashire and elsewhere came to symbolize the changes that occurred as a society transitioned from a feudal mode of production to a capitalist one. Egypt's initial role in this chain of developments was to supply cotton to British textile mills, especially when the American Civil War cut off supplies of cotton from the southern United States (Beckert, 2004, p. 1405).

   . . . Many of the major changes in Egyptian agriculture, and in rural Egyptian society more broadly, can be traced to the development of the global capitalist system. As the British promoted cotton cultivation in Egypt, large estates took over land that had supplied the means of subsistence for peasants under pre-capitalist modes of production. The result was that 'the great majority of the peasantry was by the end of the nineteenth century either landless or land-poor, while a new class of large landowners—an agrarian bourgeoisie—had emerged' (Beinin and Lockman, 1987, p. 8). This agrarian bourgeoisie assumed much of the power in rural Egypt, yet the influx of foreign capital during this development of agricultural production in Egypt meant that the foreigners who controlled the capital also held much of the power over Egypt as a whole."

   Peter Bent, *Agrarian Change and Industrialization in Egypt* (2015)

   (A) Identify ONE way in which cotton production changed the economic or social structure of Egypt in the period 1750–1900.

   (B) Explain ONE way the passage reflects a difference between the political or economic policies of Egypt and China in the period 1750–1900.

   (C) Explain ONE historical situation in the period 1750–1900, other than the one illustrated in the passage, in which states in Asia or Africa adopted Western policies that affected traditional economic structures.

2. **Answer all parts of the question that follows.**

   (A) Identify ONE institution that both the Ottoman Empire and Japan modernized to be more like Western countries.

   (B) Explain ONE historical situation that supports the argument that modernization brought more problems than benefits to people in the Ottoman Empire and Japan.

   (C) Explain ONE historical situation that challenges the argument that modernization brought more problems than benefits to people in the Ottoman Empire and Japan.

THINK AS A HISTORIAN: IDENTIFY DIFFERING PATTERNS
OF INDUSTRIALIZATION

As historians make connections between cultures and eras, they look for not only consistent patterns but also for divergent ones. For instance, the pattern in France and Germany was consistent: these countries realized their need to follow Britain's charge towards industrializing production in order to strengthen their economic presence. This trend towards industrializing reveals their interest in gaining a global economic presence, perhaps even economic dominance. The states you read about in this topic, however, did not follow that pattern.

Review the information in this topic and identify a pattern of industrializing shared by the Ottomans and Japanese. In a few paragraphs, identify the pattern and explain how it differed from that of European states both socially and economically.

REFLECT ON THE TOPIC ESSENTIAL QUESTION

1. In one to three paragraphs, describe the economic strategies that different states and empires adopted and explain the causes and effects of those strategies.

5.7

Economic Developments and Innovations

Man is an animal that makes bargains: no other animal does this
- no dog exchanges bones with another.

—Adam Smith (1723–1790)

Essential Question: How did the development of economic systems,
ideologies, and institutions contribute to change
between 1750 and 1900?

Industrialization and modernization led to new philosophies and business structures. In the *Wealth of Nations* (1776), Adam Smith, arguing that humans are naturally transactional, provided a foundational text in support of capitalism and the establishment of private entrepreneurship and shaped the economics and politics of the industrial age and the centuries to follow. Mercantilism, a system of economic protectionism, was replaced by a laissez-faire ("leave alone" in French) policy that promoted minimal governmental involvement in commerce and encouraged countries to reduce tariffs on trade.

These economic ideas were reflected in, and supported by, emerging transnational institutions, including banks such as the Hong Kong and Shanghai Banking Corporation (HSBC) and manufacturers such as Unilever. As trade increased, so did the availability, affordability, and variety of consumer goods.

Effects on Business Organization

New ways of organizing businesses arose during the Industrial Revolution. Some manufacturers formed giant **corporations** in order to minimize risk. A corporation is a business chartered by a government as a legal entity owned by **stockholders** (individuals who buy partial ownership directly from the company when it is formed or later through a **stock market**). Stockholders might receive sums of money, known as dividends, from a corporation when it makes a profit. If a corporation experiences a loss or goes bankrupt, the stockholders are not liable for the losses. The most that stockholders can lose is what they paid for the stock in the first place.

Markets with One Seller Some corporations became so powerful that they could form a **monopoly**, control of a specific business and elimination of all competition. For example, Alfred Krupp of Essen, Germany, ran a gigantic company that used the **Bessemer process**, a more efficient way to produce steel, gaining a monopoly in the German steel industry. In the United States, John D. Rockefeller created a monopoly in the oil industry.

Companies Working Across Boundaries British-born **Cecil Rhodes**, founder of De Beers Diamonds, was an especially enthusiastic investor in a railroad project that was to stretch from Cape Town, in modern-day South Africa, to Cairo, Egypt. Connecting all of the British-held colonies with a transportation network could make governance easier and aid in conducting a war, if necessary. The project was never completed because Britain never gained control over all the land on which such a railroad was to be built. The overwhelming majority of railway workers in Africa were natives who were paid far lower wages than their European counterparts. Thus, railroad technology was a means of extracting as many resources as possible from subject lands while paying colonial laborers as little as possible.

De Beers was one of many **transnational** companies—those that operated across national boundaries—that emerged in the 19th century. For example, the **Hong Kong and Shanghai Banking Corporation**, a British-owned bank opened in its colony of Hong Kong in 1865, focused on finance, corporate investments, and global banking. The **Unilever Corporation**, a British and Dutch venture, focused on household goods—most famously, soap. By 1890 it had soap factories in Australia, Switzerland, the United States, and beyond. Unilever sourced the palm oil for its soaps first from British West Africa and later the Belgian Congo, where it operated huge plantations. Because these companies were transnational, they gained wealth and influence on a scale rarely approached before. (Connect: Defend or refute the claim— Mercantilism was necessary for the eventual growth of transnational companies. See Topic 4.4.)

Corporations A sole proprietorship is a business owned by a single person, and a partnership is a small group of people who make all business decisions. A corporation differs from these two other major forms of business ownership in that a corporation is a more flexible structure for large-scale economic activity. It replaced the traditional system of a single entrepreneur engaging in high-risk business endeavors with a system of larger companies, collectively engaging in lower-risk efforts. By spreading risk, investments became much safer and more attractive.

Four Features of a Corporation	
Feature	**Description**
Limited Liability	Capital suppliers are not subject to losses greater than the amount of their investment.
Transferability of Shares	Voting rights in the enterprise may be transferred easily from one investor to another.
Juridical Personality	The corporation itself acts as a "person" and may therefore sue and be sued, may make contracts, and may hold property.
Indefinite Duration	The life of the corporation may extend beyond the participation of any of its incorporators.

Despite critics' charges that corporations undermined individual responsibility, they became a common form of business organization. They eventually dominated many areas of business, from banking to manufacturing to providing services. With their growth, corporations gained great economic and political power. For example, the decision by a corporation about where to build a new factory could create thousands of new jobs for a community.

Banking and Finance Another way to reduce risk was through insurance, especially marine insurance. Lloyd's of London, with beginnings in a coffee house where merchants and sailors went for the most reliable shipping news, helped establish the insurance industry. The number of banks rose as merchants and entrepreneurs looked for a reliable place to deposit money and to borrow it when needed to build a factory or hire workers for a new enterprise.

Effect on Mass Culture

A culture of **consumerism** as well as of leisure developed among the working and middle classes of society in Great Britain, and for some people, living standards rose. Consumption needed to keep up with production, so producers began to advertise heavily, particularly to the middle class whose members had some disposable income, money that can be spent on nonessential goods.

Leisure activities such as biking and boating became popular during the late 1800s. In the 1880s, the penny-farthing bicycle (below left) was replaced by the newer safety bicycle (below right). The older style featured one large wheel and one small one. This allowed riders to travel fast, but the danger of falling over was high. The newer style, by using a chain connecting different sized gears on the wheels, could go the same speed, but with less risk.

BICYCLING.

Fig. 5.—MOUNTING.

Source: Getty Images

Companies encouraged their workers to participate in athletics, because they believed that sports rewarded virtues such as self-discipline and playing by the rules. The sales of athletic equipment also generated business for those who made everything from soccer balls to sports stadiums.

Perhaps because workers spent most of their waking hours in a bleak industrial environment, material goods and leisure entertainment became important escapes. In Europe, soccer (known there as football), became popular, while baseball dominated sports in the United States. Particular sports developed along class lines: tennis and golf in England, for example, were played by the upper classes, while certain types of rugby were played only by the lower classes.

The commercialization of the demand for public culture was also seen in the construction of music halls and public parks, particularly during the second half of the 19th century. Both the halls and the parks were built to accommodate a wide range of social classes. One aim of this mingling of classes was for the lower classes to see more civilized, rational behavior so that they would be encouraged to emulate it. The manner in which one class may have ultimately influenced the other is difficult to quantify, yet the enduring presence of such public mingling places remains intact.

KEY TERMS BY THEME

ECONOMY: Structures
corporations
stockholders
stock market
monopoly
Cecil Rhodes
transnational

ECONOMY: Businesses
Hong Kong and Shanghai
   Banking Corporation
Unilever Corporation

CULTURE: Population
consumerism

TECHNOLOGY: Industry
Bessemer process

Questions 1 to 3 refer to the passage below.

"It [creating a monopoly in the oil industry] was forced upon us. We had to do it in self-defense. The oil business was in confusion and daily growing worse. Someone had to make a stand. . . . This movement was the origin of the whole system of economic administration. It has revolutionized the way of doing business all over the world. The time was ripe for it. It had to come, though all we saw at the moment was the need to save ourselves from wasteful conditions. . . . The day of combination is here to stay. Individualism is gone, never to return."

John D. Rockefeller, interview, 1880

1. Which individual would most likely have agreed with the views expressed by Rockefeller on business combinations?

   (A) James Hargreaves

   (B) James Watt

   (C) Gugliemo Marconi

   (D) Cecil Rhodes

2. Which statement summarizes an important difference between Rockefeller and Enlightenment thinkers?

   (A) The perspective that an action could be "forced upon us" by others

   (B) The desire to end traditional practices that led to "wasteful conditions"

   (C) The conclusion that an innovation could have impact "all over the world"

   (D) The belief that "individualism is gone."

3. Which example provides support for the claims made by Rockefeller?

   (A) The Krupp steel industry in Germany.

   (B) The decline of the Ottoman Empire

   (C) The rise of cottage industries

   (D) The support for the American Declaration of Independence

1. **Use the passage below to answer all parts of the question that follows.**

"It is especially difficult to explain why consumers chose to use the increasing incomes which they had at their disposal for consumption rather than for saving or investment. Some historians suggest that consumption increased because consumers shared an almost instinctive desire to enjoy a higher standard of living and improve their material and psychological well-being. Others believe that consumers consumed in order to emulate those around them; as Perkin suggests, 'If consumer demand was the key to the Industrial Revolution, social emulation was the key to consumer demand. By the eighteenth century nearly everyone in England and the Scottish Lowlands received a money income, and nearly everyone was prepared to spend a large part of it in *keeping up with the Joneses*.' Other historians maintain that consumers were manipulated by the machinations of advertisers and other commercial interests. According to Royle, 'The lubricant to make the consumer society of the late twentieth century function smoothly was advertising, which was made all the easier with the advent of television.' "

John Benson, *Consumption and the Consumer Revolution*, 1996

(A) Identify ONE way in which ideas from the period 1750–1900 contributed to the development of the consumer.

(B) Explain ONE way in which industrialization influenced the consumer revolution in the period 1750–1900.

(C) Explain ONE way in which capitalism influenced supply and demand in the period 1750–1900.

2. **Answer all parts of the question that follows.**

(A) Identify ONE development that promoted business growth in the period 1750–1900.

(B) Explain ONE way in which free-trade policies affected a cultural structure in the period 1750–1900.

(C) Explain ONE way in which Western European countries changed a previous economic system in the period 1750–1900.

THINK AS A HISTORIAN: EXPLAIN RELATIONSHIPS BETWEEN
DEVELOPMENTS

Using reasoning processes of comparison, causation, and/or continuity and change, historians can explore and explain relationships between different historical developments. For example, they can explain the relationship between the historical development of state-building and the historical development of global trading networks by asking such questions as:

- How were these developments the same, and how were they different?

- What caused each development, and what were the effects? Did one development cause the other?

- What degree of change did the development bring about? In other words, to what extent was continuity preserved or disrupted?

Two developments during the period 1750 to 1900 have earned the term "revolution." These are the Agricultural Revolution in Britain and the Industrial Revolution. Answer the questions above about each revolution to explain the relationships between them. Prepare one or more graphics showing your analysis.

REFLECT ON THE TOPIC ESSENTIAL QUESTION

1. In one to three paragraphs, explain how the development of economic systems, ideologies, and institutions contributed to change in the period from 1750 to 1900.

5.8

Reactions to the Industrial Economy

For a second's sunlight, men must fight like tigers.
For the privilege of seeing the color of their children's eyes by
the light of the sun, fathers must fight like beasts in the jungle.

— Mary Harris "Mother" Jones (1837-1930)

Essential Question: What conditions led to calls for change in industrial societies, and what were the effects of those efforts?

The harsh conditions of industrial life provoked resistance and calls for reform. "Mother" Jones, a labor organizer, described the severe deprivations of the coal miners working underground all day, and other activists told of the horrors of factory work. Philosophers such as John Stuart Mill sought to address this growing inhumanity of the industrial era through social reforms Others, such as the utopian socialists, argued for completely changing a system they considered to be basically flawed. Workers formed trade unions to advocate for higher pay and safer working conditions. Various ideologies and political movements emerged, some promoting alternative visions of society.

The Ottoman Empire in the Mediterranean Basin, China, and Japan also instituted reforms to promote industrialization. In response, in each, faced reactions against the results of economic change.

Labor Unions

Dangerous and unsanitary working conditions, low wages, and long hours were common in factory work in the 19th century. A committee of Britain's Parliament released a study called the Sadler Report in 1833. The report described these conditions. It made many people in Britain, particularly in Parliament, aware of the need for reforms.

Workers also responded to low pay and harsh conditions. They began to form **labor unions**—organizations of workers that advocated for the right to bargain with employers and put the resulting agreements in a contract. For most of the 19th century, unions in Great Britain had to organize in secret because the government treated them as enemies of trade. However, by the 20th century, unions became more acceptable and membership increased.

Unions improved workers' lives by winning minimum wage laws, limits on the number of hours worked, overtime pay, and the establishment of a five-day work week.

Voting Rights Unions sparked a larger movement for empowerment among the working class. In 1832, 1867, and 1884, the British parliament passed reform bills to expand the pool of men who could vote, thereby giving more representation to British cities. The acts reduced property ownership qualifications as a requirement for voting. These reforms laid the foundation for expansion of the franchise (right to vote) to all men in 1918. British women would not gain equal suffrage (voting rights) until 1928.

Child Labor Along with unions, social activists and reformers hoped to improve the living conditions of the least powerful in society. Reformers' achievements especially benefited children. A law in 1843 declared that children under the age of 10 were banned from working in the coal mines. In 1881, education became mandatory for British children between the ages of 5 and 10. This focus on education, as opposed to work for monetary gain, permanently redefined the role of children in urban society.

The Intellectual Reaction

As trade and production became increasingly global, the ideas of early economists such as Adam Smith (see Topic 5.1) were taken in new directions. While Smith wrote in an age of individual entrepreneurs and small businesses, people of the 19th century witnessed the rise of large-scale transnational businesses. This shift caused people to think about society in new ways. For example, utopian socialists tried to create new communities to demonstrate alternatives to capitalism.

John Stuart Mill Some economists, clergy, and intellectuals criticized laissez-faire capitalism as inhumane to workers. One of these was a British philosopher, **John Stuart Mill** (1806–1873). He championed legal reforms to allow labor unions, limit child labor, and ensure safe working conditions in factories. While his ideas were controversial in his time, many of them eventually become widely adopted in industrial societies.

Mill's philosophy was called **utilitarianism.** Rather than state a set of timeless moral rules, as many religions or ethicists did, utilitarianism sought "the greatest good for the greatest number of people." Unlike utopian socialists, who wanted to replace capitalism, utilitarians wanted to address the growing problems they saw with it. They viewed themselves as moderate, rational advocates of gradual reform.

Karl Marx

While most reformers wanted to fix what they considered problems with capitalism, some people wanted more extensive changes. **Karl Marx** (1818–1883) was a German scholar and writer who argued for socialism. Unlike utopian socialists, whom he scorned because he thought they wanted to escape problems rather than confront them, he wanted to look at how the world actually operated. He called his approach to economics "scientific socialism."

In 1848, Karl Marx and his wealthy supporter **Friedrich Engels** published a pamphlet (now called the **Communist Manifesto**) that summarized their critique of capitalism. According to Marx, capitalism was an advance on feudalism because it produced tremendous wealth, but that it also produced needless poverty and misery. This contradiction between wealth and poverty occurred because capitalism divided society into two basic classes.

- The **proletariat** was essentially the working class, working in factories and mines, often for little compensation.

- The **bourgeoisie** included the middle class and investors who owned machinery and factories where workers produced goods.

Marx said that market competition drove the bourgeoisie to exploit the proletariat for the sake of higher profits. Because the bourgeoisie owned the **means of production**, such as machines, factories, mines, and land, they received most of the wealth produced. The proletariat, who did the physical and dangerous work, received very little, just enough to survive. Marx exhorted the proletariat to recognize their shared interest as a class and take control of the means of production and share the wealth they created fairly.

For Marx, socialism would replace capitalism. It, then, would later be replaced by a final stage of economic development, **communism**, in which all class distinctions would end. (Connect: Create a chart comparing utopian and Marxist thought. See Topic 5.1.)

Ottoman Response to Industrialization

In the 19th century, the Ottoman Empire was no longer at the peak of its political power. However, it maintained some economic power. Sultan **Mahmud II** (ruled 1808–1839) reformed the Ottoman system. In 1826, he abolished the corps of Janissaries, which had opposed him, and developed a new artillery unit trained by Europeans. When the Istanbul Janissaries revolted, he had them massacred. The abolition of the feudal system in 1831 marked the final defeat of the Janissaries' power. Military officers were no longer able to collect taxes directly from the populace for their salaries. Instead, tax collections went directly to the central government, which paid military personnel, thus ensuring their loyalty.

Mahmud's reforms also included building roads and setting up a postal service. To fight the power of popular religious charities, he set up a government directory of charities. To operate the central administration of government, Mahmud II created European-style ministries.

Reorganization Reforms after Mahmud (during the years 1839–1876) are called **Tanzimat** (reorganization) and include the following changes:

- The sultans in this period worked to root out long-standing and widespread corruption in the central government.

- Education had long been under the control of the ulama, the educated class of Muslim scholars. Now the sultans created a secular system of primary and secondary schools. Secular colleges were also gradually set up, one for each special purpose: military, engineering, translation, civil service, and so on.

- The sultans codified Ottoman laws and created new ones, including a commercial code (1850) and a penal code (1858). These codes made it easier for foreigners to do business in the empire.

- In 1856, the sultan issued an edict known as the **Hatt-i Humayun** (Ottoman Reform Edict) that updated the legal system, declaring equality for all men in education, government appointments, and justice regardless of religion or ethnicity. The new legal system also regulated the **millets**, which were separate legal courts established by different religious communities, each using its own set of religious laws. Christians in the Balkans protested the new regulations because they felt that their autonomy was being threatened. Muslims, on the other hand, protested the reforms because they conflicted with traditional values and practice.

Although not achieving religious equality, the Tanzimat reforms continued to have wide effects in areas such as the military and education. These effects continued even when succeeding sultans blocked other reforms.

Ottoman Economy and Society The reforms under Mahmud II and the Tanzimat occurred during a period of economic change in Turkey. After the Napoleonic wars ended in 1815, prices for food and other crops declined in the Ottoman Empire. However, a global economy was in place, built partially on the flow of wealth into the Mediterranean from European colonial expansion in the Americas. Ottoman workers were increasingly paid in cash rather than in goods. Financial enterprises such as banking increased. These economic changes occurred along with the slow spread of industrialization. The growth of industry affected men and women differently. For example, most new industrial jobs went to men.

Legal reforms also benefited men more than women. Traditionally, under shariah, women had been allowed to hold money, to gain from inheritance, and to receive some education. The reforms of Mahmud II made the law more secular, and ended the right of women to distribute their property or cash through trusts to family members.

Although women had indirect control of their property, the new nonreligious courts ended even these limited rights. Many reforms had no effect on women. Since women were excluded from the army, the professions, higher education, and commerce, reforms in these areas did not affect them directly. The Tanzimat reforms of 1839 did not even mention women.

Opposition to Reform When Sultan Abdulhamid took power in 1876, he supported the efforts at internal reforms. He accepted a new constitution for the Ottoman Empire and he continued to emphasize primary education and secularization of the law. A few girls were allowed to attend girls' secondary schools by the beginning of the 20th century.

However, fearful of any "seditious" reform, the sultan and the central government maintained tight control over the empire. Abdulhamid eventually drove the advocates for reform, known as "Young Turks" into exile. Further, his government whipped up anger against minority groups, particularly Armenians and Assyrian Christians. Between 1894 and 1896, between 100,000 and 250,000 Armenians were killed throughout several provinces in what has become known as the Hamidian massacres. For this bloodshed, he received the nickname the Red Sultan.

Reform Efforts in China

Like other powers, China under the Qing Dynasty felt pressure to modernize. Its major reform effort of the late 19th century was known as the **Self-Strengthening Movement**. It developed as a way for the government to face the internal and external problems confronting China. Government officials hoped to strengthen China in its competition with foreign powers by advancing its military technology and readiness and by training Chinese artisans in the manufacture of items for shipyards and arsenals. French and British advisors helped Chinese reform efforts. A stable government capable of collecting revenue allowed China to repay debts and participate in trade. For the Chinese, their existence as an independent state depended upon economic solvency. Reform in the name of modernization seemed inevitable.

As another step toward reform, the Chinese government set up its own diplomatic corps and a customs service to help collect taxes on imports and exports. The government's strategy was to graft some modern ideas and technology onto Chinese tradition rather than to create major change.

Demand for reform increased after China's defeat in the Sino-Japanese War (1894–1895). People formed clubs to call for change. One club, led by a civil servant named Kang Youwei, was able to meet with **Emperor Guangxu**. Kang convinced the ruler to support a set of sweeping reforms known as the **Hundred Days of Reform**. The reforms included the abolition of the outdated civil service exam, the elimination of corruption, and the establishment of Western-style industrial, commercial, and medical systems.

Cixi's Initial Conservatism However, the emperor's aunt and adopted mother and the most powerful political figure in the country, **Empress**

Dowager Cixi, was a conservative. At first, she opposed the reforms and wanted to protect traditional social and governmental systems. In a coup d'état, Cixi imprisoned the emperor and immediately repealed his reform edicts. She feared the influence of foreigners, so she resisted any new technology that would extend their reach into her country. For example, she stopped the extension of railroad lines and telegraph networks into the Chinese interior.

Reform of the Civil Service However, toward the end of Cixi's rule, she came to recognize the problems with the civil service system. It was designed according to Confucian ideals of respect for rank and hierarchy as well as values of civic participation and action. By the 19th century, though, the wealthy were using the civil servants to get favors. Revenue dropped off for the government as a result of bribes going into the pockets of corrupt civil servants. Moreover, non-qualified persons were purchasing civil service posts. China abandoned nearly 2,500 years of tradition, one that had yielded an educated bureaucracy of scholar-gentry. In spite of this concession, the empress's overall conservatism caused her to fail to cope with demands of modernity in China.

China and Foreign Powers Unlike Turkey, where Europeans had little to gain from either passage or opposition to progressive reforms, in China, Europeans encouraged change. When reforms were met with the conservatism of Empress Cixi and the 1900 Boxer Rebellion against foreign influence (see Topic 6.2), the Chinese government, including its provincial governors, continued to modernize, with some help from American and European advisors. Weakened by internal rebellion and fearing encroachment from Japan, China had to accept territorial "protection" from Western powers, who in return demanded trade concessions.

In 1911, the Chinese chose to become a republic. (See Topic 7.1.) In addition, they resisted being swallowed up by their external enemies. China's attempts to preserve its territorial integrity benefited from the efforts of the United States to maintain stability in Asia by preventing Japan from encroaching farther on its territory after the Russo-Japanese War of 1905. U.S. efforts were exemplified by the Treaty of Portsmouth, which settled the war and was negotiated with the help of President Theodore Roosevelt.

Resistance to Reform in Japan

Just as China ended its long-standing civil service system, the Japanese also ended a traditional system of exercising authority. In 1871, Japan gave samurai a final lump-sum payment and legally dissolved their position. They were no longer fighting men and were not allowed to carry their swords. The **bushido**, their code of conduct, was now a personal matter, no longer officially condoned by the government.

Some samurai adjusted to the change by serving the government as **genros**, or elder statesmen. Others, particularly those from the provinces of Satsuma and Choshu, resisted the change. They defended their right to dress and wear their hair in traditional ways and to enjoy relative autonomy from the centralized government. The last battle between the samurai shogunate forces and those loyal to the emperor occurred in the 1870s. Dismayed by defeat, the samurai became the main victims of Japan's rapid modernization. Ironically, some of their leaders were the same people who had supported the Meiji Restoration in the 1860s.

Rise and Decline of Liberalization Some reforms in Japan worked better than others. The new schools quickly improved literacy rates, the economy rapidly industrialized, and the country began to develop traits of democracy such as a free press, strong labor unions, and respect for individual liberties. However, by the 1920s, army officers again began to dominate the government.

Source: Wikimedia Commons

Samurai from southern Japan led the reaction against the rapid changes in Japanese society in the 1860s and 1870s.

Limits to Reform

Turkey, China, and Japan each followed its own path in responding to industrialization in the 19th century. Of the three, Turkey began to make changes earliest. However, Sultan Abdulhamid, though he supported reforms at first, became more conservative during his time as ruler. China began to make changes only later in the century. In contrast to Abdulhamid, China's Cixi started as skeptical of reform but became more liberal during her reign. Japan responded to industrialization with dramatic, rapid changes beginning with the Meiji Restoration in 1868. However, the speed and depth of its reforms prompted a backlash from conservative members of society.

KEY TERMS BY THEME

ECONOMICS: Communists
socialism
Karl Marx
Friedrich Engels
Communist Manifesto
means of production
communism

ECONOMICS: Theory
John Stuart Mill
utilitarianism

SOCIETY: Workers
labor unions
proletariat
bourgeoisie

CULTURE: Japan
bushido
genros

GOVERNMENT: Ottomans
Mahmud II
Tanzimat
Hatt-i Humayan
millets

GOVERNMENT: China
Self-Strengthening
    Movement
Emperor Guangxu
Hundred Days of Reform
Empress Dowager Cixi

MULTIPLE-CHOICE QUESTIONS

Questions 1 to 3 refer to the passage below.

"We have now received Her Majesty's decree to devote ourselves fully to China's revitalization, to suppress vigorously the use of the terms *new* and *old*, and to blend together the best of what is Chinese and what is foreign. The root of China's weakness lies in harmful habits too firmly entrenched, in rules and regulations too minutely drawn, in the overabundance of inept and mediocre officials and in the paucity of truly outstanding ones, in petty bureaucrats who hide behind the written word and in clerks and yamen runners [administrative clerks] who use the written word as talismans [an object that brings good luck] to acquire personal fortunes, in the mountains of correspondence between government offices that have no relationship to reality, and in the seniority system and associated practices that block the way of men of real talent."

Qing Reform Edict, January 29, 1901

1. Which segment of Chinese society seems to be the focus of this excerpt from the Reform Edict?

   (A) The military

   (B) The emperor

   (C) Civil servants

   (D) Peasants

2. Which of the following was most similar to the ideas in the source?

   (A) The concept of concessions

   (B) The principle of extraterritoriality

   (C) The Open Door Policy

   (D) The Self-Strengthening Movement

3. How did the Boxer Rebellion lead to the Reform Edict?

(A) The failure of the Boxer Rebellion persuaded many members of the Chinese government to support more extensive reforms.

(B) The Boxers were the "inept and mediocre officials" that the edict was trying to remove.

(C) The success of the Boxer Rebellion against the Qing opened the way for more significant reforms to be enacted.

(D) The Boxers shifted their efforts from trying to drive foreigners out of China to serving as efficient government officials.

SHORT-ANSWER QUESTIONS

1. Use the poster below to answer all parts of the question that follows.

American Federation of Labor, Library of Congress

(A) Identify ONE way in which the poster reflects the intellectual ideas of the period 1750–1900.

(B) Explain ONE way in which the development of industrialization contributed to the development of trade unions in the period 1750–1900.

(C) Explain ONE historical situation in the period 1750–1900, other than the one illustrated in the poster, in which groups of people influenced changes in industrial societies.

2. **Answer all parts of the question that follows.**

   (A) Identify ONE way in which Western European influenced reform in China in the period 1750–1900.

   (B) Explain ONE way in which reactions to Ottoman reform is similar to reactions to Japanese reform in the period 1750–1900.

   (C) Explain ONE way in which the ideas of Karl Marx compare to the ideas of John Stuart Mill.

 THINK AS A HISTORIAN: EXPLAIN THE HISTORICAL SITUATION OF A SOURCE

Knowing the historical situation of a source—including the other contemporaneous opinions swirling about a topic—helps situate the source in a spectrum of viewpoints.

In 1844, Samuel Laing, a British politician, wrote a paper called "National Distress; its Causes and Remedies" in reaction to evidence "that as wealth increases, poverty increases in a faster ratio." He proposed systematic, government-sponsored emigration as one solution to the problem.

Read the excerpts below from Laing's paper and then answer the questions that follow to help explain its historical situation.

"The truth appears to be, that while emigration is advocated simply as a matter of profit and loss, and regarded as a cheap and convenient mode of shoving misery out of sight, it is not calculated to answer the selfish ends of its promoters. But if it were taken up in a spirit of charity, and as part and parcel of a comprehensive scheme for raising the condition of the poorer classes, and prosecuted by the government and society from a sense of duty rather than of self-interest, there seems every ground for hoping that emigration might become an instrument of great good, not only to the colonies, but to the mother country. If the owners of estates, for instance, where the agricultural population is clearly redundant, were, with a disinterested view to the good of their dependants, to assist them in emigrating, and if the government was, under proper guarantees, and with proper discrimination, to cooperate in the enterprise, there seems no doubt that much practical good might be accomplished. Colonies . . . might be planted in the North American settlements with every prospect of success; indeed with the certainty that those who, if they had remained at home, would have been squalid paupers, will, in a few years, become a body of respectable freeholders, and an important acquisition to their adopted country. By the same process the condition of those at home might be greatly ameliorated, provided active steps were taken by the landlord to eradicate the evils which had led to the multiplication of a pauper population. A great writer has said, "Do the duty that lies nearest to thee, and already, in so doing, thy next duty will have become clearer." . . . Every step taken in advance with a good motive and in a right direction, clears away a thousand difficulties. When it is clearly seen that a measure will benefit human beings, and injure nothing but abstract theories, let the government strike boldly in, and the theories will soon veer round and prove that what has been done is right. . . . Do not let the government risk the certain good that is effected under the present system by any hazardous experiment unsanctioned by experience; but, on the other hand, do not let them sink spellbound under the influence of theories of *laissez faire*, and omit opportunities of doing practical good where it is in their power. Let them leave the principle of self-interest to do all the good it can, but remember that it can never be a substitute for the higher principles of duty and charity, and that emigration, like any other expedient for the relief of society, must be conducted in a disinterested spirit of enlightened benevolence, in order to accomplish its object."

Source: Samuel Liang, "National Distress; its Causes and Remedies," 1844

1. In what context does Laing use the term "self-interest"?

2. What does his use of that term suggest about the opinions of those who would disagree with his plan? How would they argue against his plan?

3. To what does Laing refer when he writes that the plan will "injure nothing but abstract theories"?

4. How would Laing respond to the idea that the "invisible hand" will do a better job than his proposal in addressing problems of poverty?

REFLECT ON THE TOPIC ESSENTIAL QUESTION

1. In one to three paragraphs, explain the conditions that led to calls for change in industrial societies and the results of those efforts.

5.9

Society and the Industrial Age

*Bleak, dark, and piercing cold, it was a night for the well-housed and fed
to draw round the bright fire and thank God they were at home; and for
the homeless, starving wretch to lay him down and die.*

—Charles Dickens, *Oliver Twist*, 1839

Essential Question: How did industrialization cause change in existing
social hierarchies and standards of living?

Industrialization affected not only governments and economies but also
people's everyday lives. Dickens illustrated the sharp contrasts in the industrial
age between the emerging middle class, who enjoyed the benefits of the new
prosperity, and the urban poor, who were ill-treated. Young children worked
in factories. Women experienced substantial changes in their lifestyle. Poor
women took jobs in domestic service and the textile industries, spending less
time at home. Middle-class women, with no economic responsibilities, felt
limited by household roles. The middle classes also started spending their free
time seeking entertainment in theaters, concert halls, and sports facilities.

Effects on Urban Areas

For the first half of the 19th century, urban areas grew rapidly and with little
planning by governments. This development left a damaging ecological
footprint and created inhumane living conditions for the cities' poorest
residents, members of the working class. Working families crowded into
shoddily constructed **tenement** apartment buildings, often owned by factory
owners themselves. Tenements were often located in urban **slums** (areas
of cities where low-income families were forced to live), where industrial
by-products such as polluted water supplies and open sewers were common.

In conditions like these, disease, including the much-feared cholera,
spread quickly. So did other public health menaces, such as fire and crime
and violence. Over time, municipalities created police and fire departments,
and several public health acts were passed to implement sanitation reform
by creating better drainage and sewage systems, supplying cleaner water,
removing rubbish, and building standards to reduce accidents and fire.

Eventually, industrialization led to increased living standards for many.
While life could be very hard for poor and working class people, the growing
middle class had increased access to goods, housing, culture, and education.

The wealth and opportunities of the middle class were among the reasons people continued to stream into cities from rural areas. People living in poverty on farms or in villages hoped to find a better life in an urban center. Many did.

Effects on Class Structure As industrialization spread, new classes of society emerged in Britain. At the bottom rungs of the social hierarchy were those who labored in factories and coal mines. They were known as the **working class**. Though they helped construct goods rapidly, the technology of interchangeable parts and the factory system's division of labor had deprived workers of the experience of crafting a complete product. In comparison to the artisans of earlier generations, workers needed fewer skills, so managers viewed them as easily replaceable. Competition for jobs kept wages low. (Connect: Examine the changes in class structure from 17th-century Europe to the second industrial revolution. See Topic 4.7.)

Source: Thinkstock

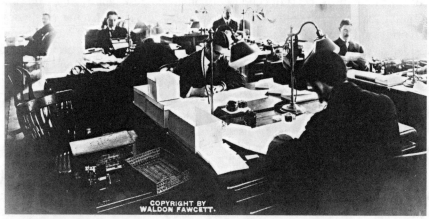

Source: Library of Congress

Industrialization created new jobs in factories (upper) and offices (lower) that pulled people from rural areas into urban areas, a process that continues around the world today.

While industrialization created low-skilled jobs, it also required those who managed the production of goods to have education and sophisticated skills. A new middle class emerged, consisting of factory and office managers, small business owners, and professionals. They were **white-collar** workers, those held by office workers. Most were literate and considered middle class.

At the top of the new class hierarchy were the industrialists and owners of large corporations. These so-called captains of industry soon overshadowed the landed aristocracy as the power brokers and leaders of modern society.

Farm Work Versus Factory Work Before industrialization, family members worked in close proximity to one another. Whether women spun fabric in their own homes or landless workers farmed the fields of a landlord, parents and children usually spent their working hours close to each other. Industrialization disrupted this pattern. Industrial machinery was used in large factories, making it impossible to work from home. Thus, individuals had to leave their families and neighborhoods for a long workday in order to earn enough money to survive.

In a factory, work schedules were nothing like they were on a farm or in a cottage industry. The shrill sounds of the factory whistle told workers when they could take a break, which was obviously a culture shock to former-farmers who had previously completed tasks according to their own needs and schedules. Considering that workers commonly spent 14 hours a day, six days a week in a factory, exhaustion was common. Some of these exhausted workers operated dangerous heavy machinery. Injuries and death were common.

Effects on Children The low wages of factory workers forced them to send their children to work also. In the early decades of industrialization, children as young as five worked in textile mills. Because of their small size and nimble fingers, children could climb into equipment to make repairs or into tight spots in mines. However, the dust from the textile machinery damaged their lungs just as much as it did to adults' lungs.

Children who worked in coal mines faced even more dangerous conditions than those in mills:

- They labored in oppressive heat, carting heavy loads of coal.
- Coal dust was even more unhealthy to breathe than factory dust.
- Mine collapses and floods loomed as constant threats to life.

Effect on Women's Lives The Industrial Revolution affected women in different ways, depending on their class position. Because their families needed the money, working-class women worked in coal mines (until the practice of hiring women for coal mining was declared illegal in Britain in the 1840s) and were the primary laborers in textile factories. Factory owners preferred to hire women because they could pay them half of what they paid men.

Middle-class women were spared factory work, yet in many ways they lived more limited lives than working-class women. Middle-class men had to leave the house and work at an office to provide for their families. If a wife stayed at home, it was an indication that her husband was capable of being the family's sole provider. Being a housewife thus became a status symbol.

By the late 1800s, advertising and consumer culture contributed to a **"cult of domesticity"** that idealized the female homemaker. Advertising encouraged women to buy household products that would supposedly make the home a husband's place of respite from a harsh modern world. Pamphlets instructed middle-class women on how to care for the home, raise children, and behave in polite society and urged them to be pious, submissive, pure, and domestic. For working-class women the cult of domesticity was even more taxing, as they had to manage the household, care for their children, and work full time.

Industrialization also spurred feminism. When men left a community to take a job, their absence opened up new opportunities for the women who remained home. One political sign of this feminism came in 1848 at Seneca Falls, New York, when 300 people met to call for equality for women.

Effects on the Environment The Industrial Revolution was powered by fossil fuels such as coal, petroleum, and natural gas. Although burning coal produced more energy than burning wood, the effects were extremely harmful. Industrial towns during the late 19th century were choked by toxic air pollution produced by coal-burning factories. Smog (smoke and fog) from factories led to deadly respiratory problems. Water became polluted, also, as the new industries dumped their waste into streams, rivers, and lakes. Cholera, typhoid, and other diseases ravaged neighborhoods.

FATHER THAMES INTRODUCING HIS OFFSPRING TO THE FAIR CITY OF LONDON.

Source: John Leech, *Punch*, July 3, 1858.

Before London built a system of public sanitation, the Thames River, the source of the city's drinking water, was filled with sewage and industrial pollution. The river spread deadly diseases throughout the city.

Industrial Revolution's Legacy

The Industrial Revolution brought about profound changes. **Mass production** made goods cheaper, more abundant, and more easily accessible to a greater number of people than ever before. Growth of factories attracted people to move, both from rural areas to cities and from agrarian countries to industrial ones. Both low-skilled workers and high-skilled professionals moved to take advantage of new opportunities provided by industrialization.

However, the natural by-products of industrial production polluted air and water supplies. Industry forever changed the nature of work and the lives of workers. Working populations became concentrated in urban centers, as opposed to being spread among rural areas. The workplace shifted from homes to factories, dramatically altering family life. The Industrial Revolution created a new—and many said unequal—working relationship between workers and owners. More crowding and more poverty brought more crime.

Global inequalities also increased because of industrialization. States that industrialized early desired more raw materials to power their production. They searched the world for items such as cotton and rubber. By exploiting overseas natural resources, they undercut early industrialization in Egypt, China, and India, and ushered in a second wave of colonization.

KEY TERMS BY THEME		
ECONOMICS: Industrialization mass production	**CULTURE:** City Life tenement slums	**SOCIETY:** Hierarchy working class white-collar "cult of domesticity"

MULTIPLE-CHOICE QUESTIONS

Questions 1 to 3 refer to the passage below.

"The invalid workman is saved from starvation by the measure we now advocate. . . .Whosoever has looked closely into the state of the poor in large towns, or into the arrangements made for paupers in country communes, and has seen for himself how—even in the best-managed villages—a poor wretch is sometimes treated when weakly and crippled, must admit that any healthy operative, contemplating that spectacle, is fully justified in exclaiming: 'It is simply horrible that a human being should be treated worse than a dog in his own house!' I say, therefore, our first object in bringing forward this bill is to ensure kindlier treatment to this class of the poor; and next year I will do my best to give Deputy Richter full satisfaction as to the extent of the provision proposed to be made by the state for the better usage of the unemployed. For the present this measure must be regarded as an experiment—an attempt to find out the depth of the financial water into which we ask the country to plunge."

Otto von Bismarck, speech, 1881

1. Which statement provides the best context for understanding the passage?
   (A) Germany lagged behind Britain in enacting reforms to improve the lives of industrial workers and the unemployed.
   (B) The problems of urban industrial workers and the unemployed were much worse in Germany than in Britain.
   (C) The United States led the way in enacting reforms to improve the lives of industrial workers and the unemployed.
   (D) Industrialization caused greater economic insecurity in the lives of many urban workers.

2. Bismarck made the proposal in the passage because he believed that
   (A) the end of capitalism would create an era of equality and justice for industrial workers
   (B) if the government did not address worker problems associated with industrialization, socialists and other radicals might incite a revolt
   (C) he had to appeal to socialists and other radicals in order to get them to join his government and provide their input
   (D) the government needed to step in to reverse the environmental effects created by industrialization and urbanization

3. Which reform was instituted by another government in response to the problems of industrialization?

(A) Britain expanded voting by reducing property-owning qualifications.

(B) The U.S. government encouraged the growth of labor unions.

(C) Russia adopted a form of utopian socialism.

(D) The United States allowed a women's rights movement to emerge.

SHORT-ANSWER QUESTIONS

1. Use the passage below to answer all parts of the question that follows.

"Five Points was the most notorious neighborhood in nineteenth-century America. Beginning in about 1820, overlapping waves of Irish, Italian, and Chinese immigrants flooded this district in what is now New York's Chinatown. Significant numbers of Germans, African Americans, and Eastern European Jews settled there as well. All but forgotten today, the densely populated enclave was once renowned for jam-packed, filthy tenements, garbage-covered streets, prostitution, gambling, violence, drunkenness, and abject poverty. . . .

Few historians devoted much attention to Five Points in the early years of the twentieth century. Academic historians concerned themselves primarily with politics and law. Slums, immigrants, and crime—none of these subjects seemed important enough to merit scholarly analysis."

Tyler Anbinder, *Five Points: The Nineteenth Century New York City Neighborhood*, 2001

(A) Identify ONE way Anbinder's description relates to the development of a consumer society in the period 1750–1900.

(B) Explain ONE way in which the global nature of trade influenced the population of urban areas in the period 1750–1900.

(C) Explain ONE historical situation in the period 1750–1900, other than the one illustrated in the passage, in which the development of industrial capitalism affected economic or societal structures.

2. Answer all parts of the question that follows.

(A) Identify ONE point that supports the claim that mass production benefited consumers.

(B) Identify ONE point that supports the claim that mass production was difficult for workers.

(C) Explain ONE way difference in how wealthy and poor people might have been affected by mass production.

THINK AS A HISTORIAN: SITUATE A HISTORICAL PROCESS
IN CONTEXT

Throughout this book you have read about the ways in which the roles and status of women have developed in specific contexts: Confucian attitudes toward women in China (Topic 1.1), the states of different classes of women within the Ottoman Empire (Topic 4.7), the push for suffrage in the context of Enlightenment ideals (Topic 5.1).

Explain the process of change in women's status and roles in the context of industrialization and urbanization in the period 1750–1900.

REFLECT ON THE TOPIC ESSENTIAL QUESTION

1. In one to three paragraphs, explain how industrialization caused changes in existing social hierarchies and standards of living.

Source: Getty Images

Women were expected to manage the household and care for the children, as this 19th-century illustration shows, even if they worked outside of the home.

5.10

Continuity and Change in the Industrial Age

Capital is, therefore, not a personal, it is a social power.
—Friedrich Engels and Karl Marx, *Communist Manifesto,*1848

Essential Question: How did the Industrial Revolution demonstrate both continuity and change?

The Industrial Revolution, an era that began in the late 18th century, produced economic, social, cultural, political, and environmental changes not seen since the first Agricultural Revolution, more than 10,000 years before. The Industrial Revolution changed how goods were produced, how people earned their living, and how businesses were structured. The Industrial Revolution also caused sweeping social changes.

An expansion of the middle class in industrial economies occurred. A working class, dependent on factory jobs, emerged. The role of women was transformed, as they made up a significant portion of the factory work force. Politically, the Enlightenment proved to be a long-lasting and influential intellectual movement that influenced events during the Industrial Revolution. The effects of the Industrial Revolution inspired the works of economic and political philosophers like Adam Smith and Karl Marx. The Industrial Revolution altered life locally as well as globally. Rivalries among nations, which had existed previously, continued into and throughout this era leading to political and economic conflict. Additionally, rigid social orders, based on economic or ethnic status, continued within industrial economies.

Economic Continuities and Changes

The Industrial Revolution transformed the production and consumption of goods. In Western Europe, access to abundant natural resources, transoceanic trade routes, and financial capital combined with an increasing population resulted in a leadership role in industrialization. The Scientific Revolution, begun in the previous era and influenced by scientific knowledge transferred to the West from the Islamic world, helped to bring about inventions that would lead to the establishment of the factory system and the mass production of goods. However, the invention of the machines used to mass produce goods meant a change from the era of skilled artisans working at their own pace to craft unique and well-built products. With automation, many factory jobs required only unskilled labor working on an assembly line doing repetitive tasks to produce identical goods. As a result, many consumer goods were now more readily available, more affordable, and in greater variety than ever before.

Industrialization Around the World New methods of industrial production associated with the Industrial Revolutions spread and changed the economies of other areas of the world outside of Western Europe. As a result, the United States, Russia, and Japan experienced increased industrial production and built more railroads. In the cases of Japan and Egypt, industrialization was encouraged through state sponsored efforts to modernize their economies with varying degrees of success. However, the industrial economies of Western Europe and the United States continued to dominate the global economy while the manufacturing output of Middle Eastern and Asian economies declined.

Share of Total World Manufacturing Output (Percentage)					
	1750	**1800**	**1860**	**1880**	**1900**
Europe	23.2	28.1	53.2	61.3	62.0
United States	0.1	0.8	7.2	14.7	23.6
Japan	3.8	3.5	2.6	2.4	2.4
The Rest of the World	73.0	67.7	36.6	20.9	11.0

Source: Paul Kennedy. *The Rise and Fall of the Great Powers*

Sources of Raw Materials Some regions of the world continued to produce minerals, crops, and other resources as they had done in previous eras. Latin America and Africa were important sources of minerals and metals used in industrial processes. Cotton from Egypt, South Asia, and the Caribbean was grown and exported to Great Britain and other European countries. Southeast Asian areas continued to be sources for spices but also for rubber, tin, and timber.

New sources of raw materials were also made possible by the invention of the steam ship and steam locomotive. Maritime trade was made faster and cheaper due to steam power, and railroads built in interior regions helped to access and exploit previously untapped natural resources. Other inventions such as the telegraph helped to improve communication across these far flung and sometimes remote areas. These and other technological innovations made the movement of goods and people easier and cheaper and led to an increase in global trade.

Western Europe Western Europe began to change from a mercantilist economic system designed to make a country wealthy through tightly regulated trade to a capitalist system in which private companies were freer to pursue their own profits. Philosopher and political economist Adam Smith believed that the private pursuit of profit would result in general prosperity.

While industrialization and capitalism produced great wealth overall, many people had hard, short lives. In response to this suffering, many reformers argued for changes. One of these was the German philosopher Karl Marx. He argued that the working class, whom he called the proletariat, were being exploited by the capital class, or bourgeoisie. He called for workers to unite and take control of the means of production, a change that would revolutionize society.

Social Continuities and Changes

Industrialization caused significant changes to social structures of Western Europe and, later, the United States. Prior to industrialization, the population of Western Europe was primarily rural and involved in farming. As factories were built in urban centers in greater numbers, mainly due to a new steam engine design invented by James Watt, agricultural workers soon migrated to find employment in these industrial cities.

Physical Labor As the Industrial Revolution spread, the need for factory labor increased. An industrial working class emerged. Members of this class were paid low wages, worked long hours in poor conditions, lived in squalid housing, and resided in crowded and polluted parts of the new industrial cities. Much of their daily lives revolved around their jobs in the factories. This was a change from the agricultural economy of the previous era, when farmers and farm laborers could more or less set their own work schedule based on the seasons. In response to their working and living conditions, the working class formed worker associations, or labor unions, that used labor strikes and collective bargaining to win concessions on wages, working conditions, and hours from the factory owners.

Office Labor Along with the emergence of the industrial working class, the Industrial Revolution also changed the size and make-up of the middle class. In pre-industrial society, the middle class was often made up of professionals such as doctors and lawyers as well as local merchants or shopkeepers. As industrialization occurred, while these pre-industrial occupations continued to be part of the middle class, other occupations were added to it, including the middle-management of factories, banks, insurance companies, shipping agents, and, of course, trading companies.

Non-Agricultural Workers as a Percentage of the Workforce			
Country	1800	1850	1900
England	68	78	84
France	41	57	69
Italy	42	56	67
Poland	44	53	58

Source: Adapted from World Bank data.

The Wealthy The Industrial Revolution also transformed social hierarchies in the period from 1750 to 1900. Wealthy owners of industrial companies who made money from investments rather than from land overtook the aristocracy in wealth and prestige. These capitalists soon made up the highest of the upper class in industrial societies.

Gender and Industrialization The role of women changed significantly during the Industrial Revolution. In an agricultural economy, women provided labor at critical times during the planting and harvesting season but were rarely paid for their labor. In a proto-industrial system, women were able to earn some extra money in the manufacturing of textiles.

Despite these activities, women were still mainly supported by the labor and income of their male family members. This pattern began to change with the Industrial Revolution. Due to the low wages paid by the factories, all family needed to work. Hence, a woman's income was just as important to the welfare of the family as a man's. Despite the importance of female labor, women were often paid less than men for the same work and denied high-wage jobs.

Political Continuities and Changes

As during the Enlightenment, philosophers living through the Industrial Revolution era developed new political ideas about the individual and government. During the Industrial Revolution, most people had little to no formal voice in government such as the right to vote, but they demanded the ability to exercise their "natural rights." Among these were the rights to petition, protest, and rebel against their governments. Sometimes these protests were based on nationalism and the right of people to choose their own governments.

However, political movements of the Industrial Revolution were almost always connected to the interests of the growing middle and working classes. For example, labor leaders advocated formation of international unions so that workers in various countries could unite to demand higher wages. But the vast majority of the protests were for the right to vote and to end aristocratic privileges. A series of uprising throughout European cities in 1848, known as the Revolution of 1848, were a sign of the growing interest in more pluralistic, more democratic governments:

- In Paris, protesters called for greater freedom of the press.
- In Berlin, people wanted a parliament to check the monarch's power.
- In cities in Hungary, people demanded freedom from Austrian control.

People wanted not just general natural rights, but specific rights recognized by their government.

Voting Rights As the number of wealthy capitalists and the middle class grew, more frequent calls for greater political participation were made. As a result, some political reforms were enacted that included the extension of voting rights to city dwellers, non-landowners, and, eventually, to the working class. However, the voting franchise was extended to male voters only. Women would not gain the right to vote in Western industrial countries until the early 20th century. Sometimes voting rights were extended through the legislative process, as in Great Britain. However, in other instances, protests and revolutions forced governments to enact political reforms.

One factor in all of these political reforms was the size and influence of the middle class. In countries where the middle class was large and economically significant, democracy emerged. However, in regions where the middle class was small or insignificant, dictatorships remained in place.

Solidarity, June 30, 1917. The Hand That Will Rule the World—One Big Union.

Source: Public Domain

The economic changes of industrial capitalism countered the laborer's vision of social equality, citizenship, and independence. As two distinct classes developed, the rich and the poor, advocating for equal rights became a movement that spanned the 19th century.

Protections for Workers Reforms that began in one country often spread. For example, Otto Von Bismarck's social reforms spread throughout Europe and eventually the world. All industrializing nations grappled with the new challenges that factory life introduced. Among these nations, Germany implemented the most comprehensive set of social reforms to protect industrial workers. Under the leadership of Chancellor Otto von Bismarck, Germany started workers' accident compensation insurance, unemployment insurance, and old age pensions for employees. Bismarck was concerned that if his government did not address these problems, socialists and more radical citizens would demand stronger government action.

Another effect of the expansion of voting rights was the emergence of political parties that represented the working class. These "labor parties" advocated for minimum wages, shorter work days, paid sick and holiday leave, better working conditions, and health and unemployment insurance.

REFLECT ON THE ESSENTIAL QUESTION

1. **Continuity and Change** Create a chart showing how life remained similar and life changed because of the Industrial Revolution in four regions of the world covered in Unit 1.

2. In one to three paragraphs, explain how the Industrial Revolution demonstrated both continuity and change.

Source: geograph.org.uk, Gareth James / Welsh National Mining Memorial

The Welsh National Mining Memorial: a memorial to all miners who have lost their lives in tragedy in Wales. Rich in coal deposits, Wales was a leader in mining innovations during the Industrial Revolution that led to the use of coal rather than wood as a primary source of fuel. About 25 percent of the Welsh workforce was employed in mining by the 20th century, despite dangerous conditions and generally low pay.

UNIT 5 REVIEW

 HISTORICAL PERSPECTIVES: DID OTTOMAN REFORMS
SUCCEED?

The industrial era was a period of massive political, economic, and social upheaval. Historians have argued over how effectively the Ottomans adapted to these changes.

A Long, Slow Decline Historians in the late 19th and early 20th centuries, living in a period when Turkish power was low, generally viewed the Ottoman Empire as the "sick man of Europe." Some mark its fall as beginning with its failure to conquer Vienna in 1683. In his widely used college textbook, *A History of the Modern World* (first published in 1950), R. R. Palmer stated that the long slide of the 19th-century Ottoman Empire put the empire "behind modern industrial nations in its scientific, mechanical, material, humanitarian, and administrative achievements." Its reforms did little to stop the slide.

Strength Through Reforms Recent historians, living in a period of increasing Turkish influence in the Middle East, have seen more vigor in the Ottomans than did previous scholars. They have credited 19th-century reforms with providing a stable foundation for the success of the Republic of Turkey, established in 1923. For example, the historian Donald Quataert argued that the Ottomans stabilized the economy and gave Europeans more confidence to invest in railroads, ports, and public utilities. These projects provided a modern infrastructure for the empire, although at the loss of some autonomy for the Ottoman government.

While acknowledging the difficulties that capitulations caused, Suraiya Faroqhi emphasized that "more recent studies prove that Ottoman commerce and artisan production were more varied than they might appear at first glance." Justin McCarthy called the changes in the Ottoman system "neither small nor cosmetic," pointing to "human rights, a constitution, Christians in high office, a parliament, the middle class in charge of the state, and the power of Islam eroded" as evidence of progress on multiple fronts. McCarthy further suggested that the empire fell not because of lack of successful reforms or the failure to modernize but because of the military power of its rivals.

Develop an Argument: Evaluate the extent to which historical evidence supports one of the perspectives on Ottoman reform.

The thesis statement must 1) assert a historically defensible claim, 2) lay out a line of reasoning, and 3) directly address the topic and focus of the task.

Historically Defensible Claim A thesis, or claim, is a nonfactual statement asserted to be true. It is a statement about which people can disagree because it requires an explanation or evaluation. A historically defensible claim is one that can be supported with sound historical evidence. For example, Marx forwarded the claim that the materials and modes of production rather than philosophical ideas shape social structures. He used examples from history of the influence of changing production methods—hunter-gatherer, slavery, feudalism, capitalism, and communism—as evidence to defend his claim.

Line of Reasoning A thesis or claim also conveys a line of reasoning for the argument that will be used to explain the relationships among pieces of evidence. In Marx's thesis, for example, the line of reasoning is *causation:* the modes of production cause the structure of social relations. Other lines of reasoning include comparison and continuity/change. Each line of reasoning needs to be embedded in a strong thesis statement. Here are two examples:

Comparison thesis statement: Social relations fundamentally differed under the production methods of the feudal system and the production methods of capitalism.

Continuity/change thesis statement: While social relations changed as the purposes and modes of production changed, the resulting social structures continued to have an underprivileged class, a continuity with long-lasting effects.

Topic and Focus of Task A strong thesis or claim directly addresses the topic and focus of the task. It must be limited to the time and geography stated in the long essay question.

Part of the task will be to "evaluate the extent to which . . . . ." In this context, "extent" means degree, scale, magnitude, scope, size, or level. To determine extent, you need to carefully analyze and evaluate the similarities or differences, continuities or changes, or causes and effects, depending on the task you are given. Which were most important, significant, influential, long-lasting, or in other ways largest in scope? And, just as important, what are your reasons and evidence for evaluating the extent as you did?

Long Essay Question: Develop an argument that evaluates the extent to which the course of state-sponsored industrialization in Egypt under Muhammad Ali and in Japan under the Meiji regime between 1750 and 1900 was similar or different.

Thesis that clearly addresses the topic and task: Between 1750 and 1900, the governments of both Muhammad Ali in Egypt and the Meiji regime in Japan employed state-sponsored programs of industrialization to help them create a European-style military, but a difference in the nature and purpose of each program's products led to significantly differing courses. (Note that the word *significantly* begins to address extent.)

Application: Read the following long essay question and a thesis statement developed to address it. Evaluate the thesis statement on how well it 1) expresses a historically defensible claim, 2) embeds a line of reasoning, and 3) addresses the topic and task, including evaluating extent, and stays within the limitations of the question. Revise the thesis statement as appropriate so that it meets all three standards.

Long Essay Question: Develop an argument that explains the extent to which industrialization changed social relations between 1750 and 1900.

Thesis Statement: From 1750 to 1900, industrialization changed the way goods were produced and consumed and affected people around the globe.

For current free response question samples, visit: https://apcentral. collegeboard.org/courses/ap-world-history/exam

LONG ESSAY QUESTIONS

Directions: Write an essay in response to one of the prompts below. The suggested writing time for an essay is 40 minutes.

In your response, you should do the following:

- Respond to the prompt with a historically defensible thesis or claim that establishes a line of reasoning.
- Describe a broader historical context relevant to the prompt.
- Support an argument in response to the prompt using at least two pieces of specific and relevant evidence.
- Use historical reasoning (e.g., comparison, causation, continuity or change) to frame or structure an argument that addresses the prompt.
- Demonstrate a complex understanding of a historical development related to the prompt through sophisticated argumentation and/or effective use of evidence.

Source: *AP® World History Course and Exam Description*

1. In the 1800s and early 1900s, industrialization transformed societies in Africa and Asia, but the process of industrialization varied from country to country.

   Develop an argument that evaluates the extent to which the process of industrialization in Egypt under Muhammad Ali and in Japan during the Meiji Era were similar or different.

2. Enlightenment ideals and the concept of nationalism swept the Atlantic world from 1750 to 1900 as people developed new standards of freedom and self-determination.

   Develop an argument that evaluates the extent to which intellectual and ideological causes influenced the revolutions that occurred in the Atlantic world during that era.

3. New inventions contributed greatly to industrialization from 1750 to 1900 in Eurasia, Africa, and the Americas, but agricultural productivity and natural resources also played a part.

   Develop an argument that evaluates the extent to which environmental factors contributed to industrialization from 1750 to 1900.

4. In the period from 1750 to 1900, businesses in Eurasia, the Americas, and Africa developed new technologies and new types of business organizations.

   Develop an argument that evaluates the extent to which the technologies and types of business organizations in Russia, the United States, and China were similar or different from 1750 to 1900.

DOCUMENT-BASED QUESTION

Directions: Question 1 is based on the accompanying documents. The documents have been edited for the purpose of this exercise. You are advised to spend 15 minutes planning and 45 minutes writing your answer.

1. Evaluate the extent to which the roles of women in Japan and Argentina were different during the 1800s.

In your response, you should do the following:

- Respond to the prompt with a historically defensible thesis or claim that establishes a line of reasoning.
- Describe a broader historical context relevant to the prompt.
- Support an argument in response to the prompt using at least four documents.
- Use at least one additional piece of specific historical evidence (beyond that found in the documents) relevant to an argument about the prompt.
- For at least two documents, explain how or why the document's point of view, purpose, historical situation, and/or audience is relevant to an argument.
- Demonstrate a complex understanding of a historical development related to the prompt through a sophisticated argument and/or effective use of evidence.

Source: *AP® World History Course and Exam Description*

Document 1

Source: Philipp von Siebold, German doctor and traveler, *Manners and Customs of the Japanese in the Nineteenth Century*, 1841.

The position of women in Japan is apparently unlike that of the sex in all other parts of the East, and approaches more nearly their European condition. The Japanese women are subjected to no jealous seclusion, hold a fair station in society, and share in all the innocent recreations of their fathers and husbands. The minds of the women are cultivated with as much care as those of men; and amongst the most admired Japanese historians, moralists, and poets are found several female names.

But, though permitted thus to enjoy and adorn society, they are, on the other hand kept in complete dependence on their husbands, sons, or other relatives. They have no legal rights, and their evidence is not admitted in a court. At home, the wife is the mistress of the family; but in other respects she is treated rather as a toy for her husband's amusement, than as the rational, confidential partner of his life.

Document 2

Source: Josefina Pelliza de Sagasta, Argentine poet and journalist, "Women Dedicated to Miss Maria   Eugenia Echenique," letter written in response to an essay by Maria Eugenia Echenique which advocated women's emancipation, 1876.

Women should be educated; give them a solid education, based on wholesome principles, cemented with moral and sensible beliefs; they should have a general knowledge of everything that awakens ingenuity and determines ideas.

But it is not for them the calculation and egotism with which they instruct English women, not for them the ridiculous ideas of North American women who pretend in their pride to be equal to men, to be legislators and obtain a seat in Congress or be university professors, as if it were not enough to be a mother, a wife, a housewife, as if her rights as a woman were not enough to be happy and to make others happy, as if it were not enough to carry out her sacred mission on earth: educating her family, cultivating the tender hearts of her children making them useful citizens, laborers of intelligence and progress, with her words and acts, cultivating love in her children and the sentiments that most enhance women: virtue, modesty and humility.

Girls, women someday, be tender and loving wives, able to work for the happiness of your life's partner instead of bringing about his disgrace with dreams and aspirations beyond your sphere.

Document 3

Source: Maria Eugenia Echenique, Argentinian feminist, written in response to a letter from Josefina Pelliza de Sagasta, 1876.

Every day we see men with unscrewed-on heads who have no love for order nor true affection for their families, who spend their lives on gambling and rambling around; cold-bloodedly, they leave their children on the street, because their wives, whose sphere of action is reduced only to love and suffering, do not know how to oppose forcefully the squandering nor how to stop in time the abuses from their husbands nor save in this way the interests of their children.

Emancipation protects women from this catastrophe. A woman, educated in the management of business, even if she does not make a profession of it, knows how to prevent or remedy the problem once it has occurred. She does not go through the pain of seeing her children begging for bread from door to door, because she has a thousand resources to satisfy their needs honorably. She goes to work, and thus she raises her children without the need for others' support that could lead her to corruption and to spend a miserable and humiliating life. Love can dry tears and sweeten the bitterness of life, but it cannot satisfy hunger nor cover nakedness. Love cannot be developed on a sublime and heroic level unless one is prepared to work, to put sentiment into practice. Emancipation, conceding to women great rights, instills in them a great heart that takes them closer to the true perfection to which men can aspire here on earth.

Document 4

Source: Lina Beck-Bernard, Swiss Romantic writer and traveler, *Five Years of Travel in the Republic of Argentina*, 1857-1862.

[In the pampas of Argentina] the privileged space that White creole [people of European and Black descent] Argentinian women held as the vessels of the future White citizens, and as creators of a European space in exile, is presented in contrast to the native women whose precarious situation is equated to their feminization. The Indians are the inhabitants of the desert, whereas White women are the "queens of the interior":

With few exceptions women are queens of the interior, and do not exercise this power in a very constitutional way. This led an Italian man married to a Creole woman to say, "One's opinion of the interior of this country could be what Machiavelli wrote about a Republican [self-governed] city-state in Italy: 'It's a paradise for women, a Purgatory [place of suffering] for men, a hell for beasts.'"

Document 5

Source: Japanese reformist journalist, newspaper article describing the lives of female silk workers in Japan, 1898.

When I encountered silk workers I was even more shocked than I had been by the situation of weaving workers. . . . At busy times they go straight to work on rising in the morning, and not infrequently work through until 12:00 at night. The food is six parts barley to four parts rice. The sleeping quarters resemble pig-sties, so squalid are they. What I found especially shocking is that in some districts, when business is slack, the workers are sent out into service for a fixed period, with the employer taking all their earnings.

Many of the girls coming to the silk districts pass through the hands of recruiting agents. In some cases they may be there for two to three years and never even know the name of the neighboring town. The local residents think of those who have entered the ranks of the factory girls in the same manner as tea house girls, bordering on degradation. If one had to take pity on just one group among all these workers, it must be first and foremost the silk workers.

Document 6

Source: Juan Bialet-Massé, Argentinian Professor of Labor Law appointed by the Argentinian President to examine working conditions in factories, "The State of the Argentine Working Classes," 1904.

The mission of women, since each sex has its role in the perpetuation of the species, is maternity, nurturing and education children. . . . For married women factory life is incompatible with these functions, as it is in general for the single woman. . .

Work for women is unacceptable, except for the misfortune of destiny: for the widow without the means of support, and for the unmarried woman who has no family to care for her, . . .

Document 7

Source: Brian Platt, U.S. historian, "Educational Reform in Japan (19th century)," *Children and Youth in History*, published 2010.

Enrollment in Japanese Primary Schools				
Date	Number of Schools	Percentage of Boys Enrolled	Percentage of Girls Enrolled	Percentage of All Children Enrolled
1873	12,597	40	15	28
1880	28,410	59	22	41
1890	26,017	65	31	49
1900	26,857	90	72	81

UNIT 6: Consequences of Industrialization from c. 1750 to c. 1900

Understand the Context

Technological change provided the framework for the historical changes between 1750 and 1900. Industrial growth fostered a wider exchange of commodities, the expansion of overseas empires, and new patterns of migration.

Imperialism Competition among industrializing states increased the desire for colonies. Some states strengthened control over existing colonies, as the British did in India. Empires expanded into new regions, evident in the rapid European colonization of Africa. Economic imperialism emerged in parts of Latin American and Asia. Europeans used Social Darwinism and religious ideologies to justify their control of others. In general, the Portuguese and Spanish declined, the British and French and Russia expanded, and the United States and Japan emerged as new empires.

Resistance to Imperialism In response to imperialism, anticolonial movements developed as part of a larger trend of emerging nationalism. Resistance to imperialism took many forms, including rebellion, the establishment of peripheral states, and religiously influenced responses. These movements set the stage for decolonization in the 20th century.

Migration New means of transportation and the pull of economic opportunity spurred long-distance migration and a larger trend of global urbanization. Although many people chose to migrate, coerced migration was also common, as slavery and indentured servitude continued to play a significant role in the global economy. Increased migration changed the demographics and cultures of both sending and receiving societies.

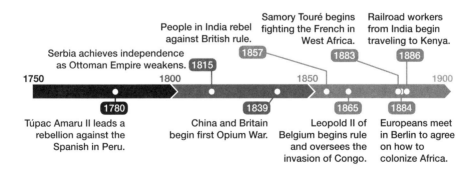

Samory Touré begins fighting the French in West Africa.

People in India rebel against British rule.

Railroad workers from India begin traveling to Kenya.

Serbia achieves independence as Ottoman Empire weakens. **1815**

1857   1883   1886

1750   1800   1850   1900

1780   **1839**   **1865**   **1884**

Túpac Amaru II leads a rebellion against the Spanish in Peru.

China and Britain begin first Opium War.

Leopold II of Belgium begins rule and oversees the invasion of Congo.

Europeans meet in Berlin to agree on how to colonize Africa.

Topics and Learning Objectives

Topic 6.1: Rationales for Imperialism pages 367–374

  A: Explain how ideologies contributed to the development of imperialism from 1750 to 1900.

Topic 6.2: State Expansion pages 375–387

  B: Compare processes by which state power shifted in various parts of the world from 1750 to 1900.

Topic 6.3: Indigenous Responses to State Expansion
pages 388–398

  C: Explain how and why internal and external factors have influenced the process of state building from 1750 to 1900.

Topic 6.4: Global Economic Development pages 399–406

  D: Explain how various environmental factors contributed to the development of the global economy from 1750 to 1900.

Topic 6.5: Economic Imperialism pages 407–416

  E: Explain how various economic factors contributed to the development of the global economy from 1750 to 1900.

Topic 6.6: Causes of Migration in an Interconnected World
pages 417–428

  F: Explain how various environmental factors contributed to the development of varied patterns of migration from 1750 to 1900.

  G: Explain how various economic factors contributed to the development of varied patterns of migration from 1750 to 1900.

Topic 6.7: Effects of Migration pages 429–438

  H: Explain how and why new patterns of migration affected society from 1750 to 1900.

Topic 6.8: Causation in the Imperial Age pages 439–442

  I: Explain the relative significance of the effects of imperialism from 1750 to 1900.

6.1

Rationales for Imperialism

Take up the White Man's Burden—
Send forth the best ye breed—
Go bind your sons to exile
To serve your captives' need;
To wait in heavy harness,
On fluttered folk and wild—
Your new-caught, sullen peoples,
Half-devil and half-child.

—Rudyard Kipling, "The White Man's Burden," 1899

Essential Question: What ideologies contributed to the development of imperialism between 1750 and 1900?

Rudyard Kipling was an English writer who spent his youth in British colonial India. The speaker in his poem urged the whites of Western countries to establish colonies for the good of the "inferior" people of the word. Whether Kipling actually supported this idea is not clear, but his poem was used to justify it. Proponents justified European colonization using a variety of explanations, from a belief in **nationalism**, a desire for economic wealth, a sense of religious duty, and a belief they were biologically superior. These various motives for establishing overseas empires—a policy called **imperialism**—would lead to conflicts in Asia and a scramble to colonize Africa. (See Topic 6.2.)

Nationalist Motives for Imperialism

In Western Europe, revolutions, the rise of nationalism, and the creation of nation-states characterized much of the 1800s. With a strong sense of identity and loyalty to a state, many world powers boldly asserted authority over other territories. Building an empire in Asia or Africa was one way for a country to assert its national identity in the global arena. Britain, France, Spain, Portugal, and the Netherlands would long possess overseas colonies.

European Nationalism After losing its American colonies, Britain looked for new lands to open to settlement. In 1788 the first British settlers arrived in the colony of New South Wales on the east coast of the island continent of New

Holland—today's Australia. (See Topic 6.2.) Britain was also expanding its influence in South Asia, gradually taking control of India from the East India Company. By 1857 Britain controlled the entire Indian subcontinent. Ceylon (Sri Lanka), Burma (Myanmar), the Malay States (which included Singapore), and parts of Borneo in Southeast Asia were also under British control.

France compensated for its humiliating defeat by Prussia in the Franco-Prussian War (1870–1871) by expanding its overseas territories. It had already occupied Algeria in Northern Africa, New Caledonia and other islands in the South Pacific, Senegal in Western Africa, and Indochina in Southeast Asia.

Italy and Germany were newly unified states in the late-19th century. Each wanted colonies not only for economic and strategic reasons but also for prestige. However, neither began acquiring an empire until the mid-1880s.

While Spain had led the quest for colonies in the first wave of imperialism during the 16th and 17th centuries, its power was greatly diminished by the 19th century. It did not play a dominant role in this second wave of imperialism.

Japan in East Asia Japan asserted its nationalist pride through incursions into Korea. This irritated China, a country that had exerted a strong presence in Korea for centuries. The conflict grew into the **Sino-Japanese War** (1894–1895). Japan's victory gave it control of Korea. Japan also seized Taiwan, which was known as **Formosa** from the time of Portuguese colonization in the 16th century until the end of World War II. (Connect: Identify three events of the late 19th and early 20th centuries that encouraged the growth of Japanese nationalism. See Topic 5.8.)

Cultural and Religious Motives for Imperialism

The Kipling quotation that opens this topic epitomized the condescending attitudes shared by imperialism's proponents. Referring to colonized peoples as children reflected how colonizers saw themselves as benevolent protectors on a "civilizing mission" rather than invaders.

Racial Ideologies and the Misuse of Science The attitudes of whites toward others were a form of racism. Colonial powers generally believed that they were inherently superior to those they subjugated. Pseudoscientists, people who present theories as science that are actually incompatible with the scientific method, strengthened these attitudes. They claimed to have proof of the intellectual and physical inferiority of nonwhite races. **Phrenologists**, people who studied skull sizes and shapes, believed that a smaller skull size proved the mental feebleness of Africans, indigenous Americans, and Asians. These ideas have been proven false.

Legitimate science was also subverted to support imperialism. British scientist **Charles Darwin's** 19th-century theory of evolution by natural selection stated that over millions of years, biological competition had "weeded out" the weaker species in nature and that the "fittest" species were the ones that survived. Some thinkers adapted Darwin's theory of biological evolution to society, creating the theory known as **Social Darwinism.** While Darwin

Source: *The Boy Travelers in Australasia: Adventures of Two Youths in a Journey to the Sandwich, Marquesas, Society, Samoan and Feejee Islands, and Through the Colonies of New Zealand, New South Wales* (1889).

The image of a New Zealand village reflects how Europeans viewed native village people as simple.

himself was not a Social Darwinist, advocates used the "survival of the fittest" theory to argue that the spread of European and U.S. power proved the biological superiority of whites. Writers and politicians then used Social Darwinism to justify further imperialism by powerful countries.

Cultural Ideologies Based on technological superiority over indigenous societies, colonial powers felt justified in superimposing aspects of their own cultures on their colonies. For administrative purposes, many colonies combined into a single colony peoples from several cultures who often spoke different languages and had different customs. Colonizers introduced their own language, which helped to unify these often diverse colonies. They also introduced their political, educational, and religious institutions and exerted other cultural influences on architecture and recreational activities. Expressing the belief of many, Congregationalist minister Josiah Strong wrote in 1885, "Is there room for reasonable doubt that [the Anglo-Saxon] race . . . is destined to dispossess many weaker races, assimilate others, and mold the remainder, until, in a very true and important sense, it has Anglo-Saxonized mankind?"

Religious Motives Missionaries were among the most tireless "civilizing" influences. Like the Spanish and Portuguese Catholic missionaries who combined conquest and evangelism during the Age of Discovery, British

Protestant missionaries of the 18th and 19th centuries also participated in colonization. Critics charged that missionaries supported imperialism by persuading people to give up their traditional beliefs, such as ancestor veneration, and adopt the faith of most Europeans, Christianity. This change in religion could pave the way for others who were more focused on economic gain. In response, missionaries pointed out that they commonly combined religious and humanitarian efforts:

- Missionaries often set up schools for instruction in religion that also taught secular subjects, which prepared students to become teachers, lawyers, and other professionals.

- Many missionaries provided improved medicines and medical care.

- Some missionaries, most famously **David Livingstone** from Scotland, worked in Sub-Saharan Africa to end the illegal slave trade.

Economic Motives for Imperialism

Some people believe the ideological motivations were more accurately justifications for pursuing economic motives. Seeking ways to maximize profits, companies chartered by the British, French, and Dutch governments signed commercial treaties with local rulers in India, East Africa, and the East Indies. These treaties gave the Europeans the right to establish trading posts and forts to protect their interests. Originally, these companies formed primarily for the spice trade. Many companies had quasi-governmental powers, raising armies and conquering territory to form colonies.

As the Industrial Revolution transformed European economies, the desire for the sources for raw materials and markets for manufactured goods provided by colonies enticed imperial powers to increase their expansion. Imperial powers often competed with one another over the best potential resources, markets, and trade as demands for low-wage labor, access to markets, and control of natural resources increased.

East India Company The English monarch granted the **East India Company (EIC)** a royal charter in 1600 giving it a monopoly on England's trade with India. After driving the Portuguese out of India, the company traded primarily in cotton and silk, indigo, and spices.

Eventually, the EIC expanded its activities from the Persian Gulf to East Asia. By the beginning of the 18th century, it had become the major agent of British imperialism in India, and after 1834 it became the British government's managing agency in India. Starting in 1620, the EIC engaged in the slave trade, and during the 19th century it illegally exported opium to China in exchange for tea. The East India Company is often referred to as the English East India Company or, after 1707, the British East India Company to distinguish it from the Dutch East India Company.

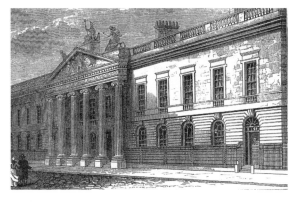

Source: Getty Images

The London office of the East India Company was the headquarters for ruling British India until the British government took charge of the colony in 1858.

Dutch East India Company In 1602 the Dutch government gave the **Dutch East India Company** (Vereenigde Oost-Indische Compagnie, or **VOC**) a monopoly on trade between the Cape of Good Hope at the southern tip of Africa and the Straits of Magellan at the southern tip of South America. The VOC concentrated on the islands around Java, replacing the Portuguese who had controlled the region. Corruption and debt led the government to take control of the company's possessions in 1799, creating the Dutch East Indies (today's Indonesia).

The "New Imperialism" After the Industrial Revolution and the Napoleonic Wars, Britain was the leading economic power throughout the first half of the 19th century and already had a sizable colonial empire. Its colonies provided raw materials such as cotton, wool, jute, vegetable oils, and rubber for its factories, as well as foodstuffs such as wheat, tea, coffee, cocoa, meat, and butter for its growing cities. Its colonies—especially settler colonies such as Australia, New Zealand, and South Africa—also provided markets for British manufactured goods.

As the Second Industrial Revolution progressed, other nations began to challenge Britain's economic lead. They looked to Asia, Africa, and the Pacific to expand their markets, provide raw materials for their factories, and food for their growing urban populations.

KEY TERMS BY THEME

GOVERNMENT: Ideas
nationalism
imperialism

GOVERNMENT: Wars
Sino-Japanese War

GOVERNMENT: Countries
Formosa

CULTURE: Ideas
phrenologists
Charles Darwin
Social Darwinism

CULTURE: Religion
David Livingstone

ECONOMICS: Companies
East India Company (EIC)
Dutch East India Company
(VOC)

Questions 1 to 3 refer to the passage below.

"The English in India had always been somewhat more detached from the indigenous environment than the Dutch in Indonesia. After the 1780s, their isolation gradually intensified and became obvious with the decline in status of Eurasian Anglo-Indians. . . . The club became the center of British social life in India and the other Asian colonies during the Victorian era. In clubs, one could feel like a gentleman among other gentlemen while being served by a native staff. . . . The large clubs of Calcutta remained closed to Indians until 1946. This type of color bar was especially disturbing because it excluded from social recognition the very people who had carried their self-Anglicizing [becoming more like the British] the furthest and loyally supported British rule. . . .

In most regions of Africa . . . the Europeans saw themselves as foreign rulers separated from the African cultures by an abyss. . . . A process of great symptomatic significance was the rejection of the highly educated West Africans who had worked with the early mission. They had envisioned the colonial takeover as an opportunity for a joint European-African effort to modernize and civilize Africa. Instead, they were now, as 'white Negroes,' despised by all."

Jurgen Osterhammel, Colonialism, 1997

1. Which theory did Europeans use most directly to justify the social patterns described in the passage?

   (A) Social Darwinism

   (B) Pan-Africanism

   (C) Popular sovereignty

   (D) Laissez-faire capitalism

2. Which statement best provides the context for the racial policies described in the passage that shaped imperialism in India and Africa?

   (A) In both places, the English did not encourage highly educated native people to prepare for self-rule.

   (B) In both places, a smooth transition of power helped the highly educated native people gain political power.

   (C) In both places, social clubs were the meeting places for native people planning to fight for self-rule.

   (D) In both places, the colonizers finally began to respect educated natives, thus weakening their own colonial rule.

3. The context for the European attitudes noted in the passage was that

(A) most Americans told the British that "all men are created equal"

(B) some scientists claimed Europeans were a biologically superior race

(C) most Indians and Africans preferred to create non-British clubs

(D) some Europeans wanted native people to leave India and Africa

SHORT-ANSWER QUESTIONS

1. Use the passage below to answer all parts of the question that follows.

"Gentlemen, we must speak more loudly and more honestly! We must say openly that indeed the higher races have a right over the lower races. . . .

I repeat, that the superior races have a right because they have a duty. They have the duty to civilize the inferior races. . . . In the history of earlier centuries these duties, gentlemen, have often been misunderstood; and certainly when the Spanish soldiers and explorers introduced slavery into Central America, they did not fulfill their duty as men of a higher race. . . . But, in our time, I maintain that European nations acquit themselves with generosity, with grandeur, and with sincerity of this superior civilizing duty. I say that French colonial policy, the policy of colonial expansion, the policy that has taken us under the Empire [the Second Empire, of Napoleon III], to Saigon, to Indochina [French Southeast Asia], that has led us to Tunisia, to Madagascar–I say that this policy of colonial expansion was inspired by . . . the fact that a navy such as ours cannot do without safe harbors, defenses, supply centers on the high seas . . . . Are you unaware of this? Look at a map of the world."

Jules Ferry, speech on French colonial expansion, 1884

(A) Identify ONE motive Ferry offers for imperial expansion in the period 1750–1900 other than an economic motive.

(B) Explain ONE way in which Ferry's argument is similar to other arguments of the period 1750–1900.

(C) Explain ONE way in which the French Revolution influenced French imperialism in the period 1750–1900.

2. Answer all parts of the question that follows.

(A) Identify ONE economic motivation behind European imperialism in the 19th century.

(B) Explain ONE reason, besides religious conversion, missionaries believed they were helping the colonized lands.

(C) Explain ONE effect imperialism had on the culture of colonized people.

In 1884–1885, in response to Germany's arrival as a competitive force
in Africa, ambassadors from throughout Europe met at the Berlin
Conference to develop some guidelines and agreements for colonizing
Africa. (See Topic 6.2.)

*Read the following excerpt from the General Act of the Berlin Con-
ference. Then explain how it articulates the political, economic, and
ideological contexts for the development of European cooperation
on colonizing and partitioning Africa.*

"WISHING, in a spirit of good and mutual accord, to regulate the
conditions most [favorable] to the development of trade and civilization
in certain regions of Africa, and to assure to all nations the advantages
of free navigation on the two chief rivers of Africa flowing into the
Atlantic Ocean; BEING DESIROUS, on the other hand, to obviate
[remove] the misunderstanding and disputes which might in the future
arise from new acts of occupation on the coast of Africa; and concerned,
at the same time, as to the means of furthering the moral and material
well-being of the native populations; HAVE RESOLVED, on the
invitation addressed to them by the Imperial Government of Germany,
in agreement with the Government of the French Republic, to meet for
those purposes in Conference at Berlin . . ."

General Act of the Conference at Berlin, 1885

REFLECT ON THE TOPIC ESSENTIAL QUESTION

1. In one to three paragraphs, explain the part ideologies played in the
development of imperialism between 1750 and 1900.

6.2

State Expansion

You must singularly insist on their total submission and obedience, avoid developing the spirits in the schools, teach students to read and not to reason.

—King Leopold II (1835–1909), letter to Christian missionaries, 1883

Essential Question: By what processes did state power shift in various parts of the world between 1750 and 1900?

King Leopold II of Belgium wanted the Belgian government to conquer colonies in a large swath of central Africa—the Congo Basin. The government was ambivalent, so Leopold established a private colony himself. However, the Belgian Parliament found the king's rule so abusive that in 1908 it took control of the region away from him. Similarly, the Dutch government revoked the charter of the Dutch East India Company for abusing its power to make treaties, build forts, and maintain armed forces in Southeast Asia. While these unusual shifts of power were taking place, other European governments, as well as the United States, Russia, and Japan, continued territorial expansion through conquest and settlement.

Imperialism in Africa

Europe had a long-standing relationship with Africa because of the slave trade. Although most European countries had declared the importation of Africans as slave labor illegal by the early 1800s, Europeans continued to export guns, alcohol, and other manufactured goods to Africa and import African natural resources, such as palm oil, gold, and ivory. England desired palm oil in particular because it kept the machinery in its textile factories from becoming rusty. In the last part of the 19th century, European tastes for African diamonds and ivory kept European empires thriving throughout the African continent. (Connect: Write a paragraph connecting late 19th century imperialism with the African slave trade. See Topic 4.4.)

Expanding Beyond Trading Posts For most of the 1800s, European presence in Africa was restricted to trading posts, with a few exceptions. The French seized Algeria in 1830, declaring they wanted to prevent pirate attacks. Dutch immigrants had lived in South Africa since the 1600s and British colonists became more numerous starting in the early 1800s. In the second half of the 1800s, European nations expanded their presence in Africa with the help of better military technology. For example, the discovery of **quinine,** a medicine that treats the tropical disease malaria, reduced the danger of living in warm, humid regions. The steamship assisted the early trips of individual explorers and business owners.

British Control of Egypt Europeans had long dreamed of dramatically shortening the water route to Asia by building a canal connecting the Red Sea with the Mediterranean Sea. A 100-mile-long canal could save a trip around the entire continent of Africa. This feat was finally accomplished in 1869 when the **Suez Canal** was completed. A French company managed the project, but most of the labor was performed by as many as 1.5 million Egyptians. Many of them were **corvée laborers,** unpaid workers who were forced to work on the project as a form of taxation. Thousands died in the course of ten years. When unrest in the region threatened British commercial interests and the operation of the canal in 1882, Britain seized control of Egypt away from the Ottoman Empire.

British West Africa Great Britain established several colonies in West Africa before the mid-19th century. In these colonies, Britain spread Western education, the English language, and Christianity:

- **Sierra Leone** was established in 1787. It was a home for freed people from throughout the British Empire who had been enslaved.

- Gambia was established in 1816. It, and Sierra Leone, were used as bases to try to stop the export of enslaved people from the region.

- Lagos became a crown colony in 1861 and served as a base for the annexation of much of the rest of what is now Nigeria.

- Britain acquired parts of what is now Ghana in stages. For example, the **Gold Coast** became a crown colony in 1874, but the Asante Empire to the north did not come under British control until 1901.

Britain used both diplomacy and warfare to expand its empire. For example, in 1873, Britain signed a treaty with King Jaja of Opobo in present-day Nigeria—an area rich in palm oil—recognizing him as ruler and agreeing to trade terms favorable to both sides. Other African rulers agreed to similar diplomatic treaties with foreign powers, believing they were protecting their sovereignty and trade rights. However, as European competition increased for control of African lands, the treaties came to be meaningless and warfare was the inevitable result as Africans resisted takeover but met with overpowering military strength.

The French in Africa France drove the Ottomans out of Algeria in 1830. By 1870 Algeria had become a **settler colony**, attracting Spanish, Italian, and Maltese as well as French immigrants. In the 1870s the French also established trading posts in Guinea, the Ivory Coast, and Niger to compete with British West African colonies.

The European Scramble for Africa

Tensions mounted among industrialized European nations as they competed for natural resources in Africa. Leaders feared that the **"Scramble for Africa,"** the competing efforts of Europeans to colonize Africa, would lead to war.

Berlin Conference Unlike many German leaders who had imperial ambitions, Otto von Bismarck had little interest in colonies. However, he did want to keep peace in Europe. So in 1884–1885, he hosted the **Berlin Conference,** a meeting of European powers to provide for the orderly colonization of Africa. No Africans were invited to the conference. European powers peaceably agreed to colonial boundaries and to the free movement of goods on Africa's major rivers such as the Niger River and the Congo River.

In most of the continent, Europeans established colonial borders that were merely artificial lines that meant little to the people who lived within them. These borders divided long-unified societies into different colonies and united longtime rival groups into the same colonies. When these colonies became independent states in the later 20th century, these borders became the cause of extensive warfare by making national unity very difficult.

South Africa and the Boer Wars During the Napoleonic Wars (1799–1815), the British replaced the Dutch in the **Cape Colony** in the southern tip of Africa. The British introduced the use of English but allowed people to use the Dutch language as well. Many of the Dutch-speaking **Afrikaners**, the descendants of 17th-century Dutch settlers, moved east of the Cape Colony, where they came into conflict with indigenous groups, including the Zulus, with whom they fought several wars.

Throughout the 19th century, the British and Afrikaners continued to fight over land. This conflict came to a boil in the **Boer Wars** (1880–1881, 1899–1902). These conflicts were bloody and brutal. In the end, the British army drove the Afrikaners and the Africans from their lands, forcing many into refugee camps. These settlements, which were segregated by race, came to be known as **concentration camps**. Medical care and sanitation were very poor, and food rations were so meager that many of the interned died of starvation. Once news arrived in Britain about the wretched conditions of the camps, activists tried to improve the lives of displaced refugees. However, while white camps received some attention, conditions in black camps remained terrible. Of the 100,000 blacks interned in concentration camps, nearly 15,000 perished.

By the end of the Boer Wars, the British had absorbed the settler colonies of British and Afrikaner peoples and the black Africans in the southern tip of Africa into its empire. Millions of Afrikaner and black African farmers had been displaced onto poor land, making it hard for them to earn a decent living.

Congo By 1875, Western European nations were poised to penetrate Africa's interior. **King Leopold II** of Belgium (ruled 1865–1909) oversaw the invasion and pacification of the Congo in central Africa in order to persuade the Belgian government to support colonial expansion. Unlike other European rulers, King Leopold owned the colony personally, using colonial officials against indigenous Congolese and a ruthless system of economic exploitation that allowed him to keep the profits made by the **Congo Free State**, which totaled some 220 million francs ($1.1 billion in today's dollars).

Visitors to the colony reported on the brutal conditions for the laborers who were forced to harvest ivory and rubber. For example, Leopold's agents severed the hands of Congolese workers in order to terrorize others into submission. Workers who could not meet their quotas were beaten or killed, while others were worked to death. Although the term *slavery* was not commonly used when describing imperial activities, laborers in the Congo often received no payment for their backbreaking work, and their spouses were held captive so that the workers would not run away. As many as 8 million people perished under King Leopold's reign of terror in the Congo. In 1908, Belgium took over control of the Congo as a regular colony, and conditions improved. (Connect: Create an outline comparing conditions in the Congo with conditions in European colonies in South America. See Topic 4.5.)

AFRICA IN 1914

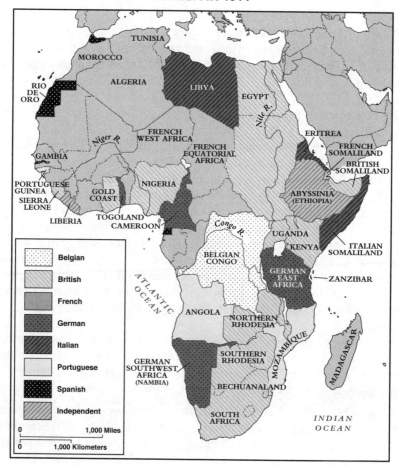

Independent Countries By 1900, the only African countries unclaimed by Europeans were **Abyssinia** (modern-day Ethiopia) and **Liberia,** a country founded by formerly enslaved people from the United States. Because Liberia had a dependent relationship with the United States, it was not fully independent. Italy attempted to conquer Abyssinia in 1895, but the native forces were too strong for the Italians.

Imperialism in South Asia

Portugal, France, and England competed for control of India's spices, gems, and trade with regions to the east. Portugal established a coastal trading port on the southwestern coast, in Goa, in the early 16th century. However, it never extended its control inland. France established trading ports in the 17th century. However, its loss to Britain in the global conflict known as the **Seven Years' War** (1756–1763) drove the French out of India.

England's **East India Company** (**EIC**), steadily encroached on the land of the weak Mughal Empire. Eventually, Britain controlled the entire Indian subcontinent, from Pakistan in the west to Kashmir in the north to Bengal in the east to the island of **Ceylon** (Sri Lanka) in the south. At first, the EIC's small forces of British soldiers protected the firm's employees. As the British crept into India's interior, they began recruiting native Indian soldiers, called sepoys, to join the British colonial army. However, as explained in the next topic, the sepoys ignited an unsuccessful rebellion against the British in 1857.

Imperialism in East Asia

China did not experience imperialism in the same way that South Asia or Africa did. It maintained its own government throughout a period of European economic domination. As a result of superior military strength, European nations carved out **spheres of influence** within China over which they had exclusive trading rights and access to natural resources. (See Topic 6.5.) Internal problems within the Qing government, such as the **Taiping Rebellion**, made it easier for foreign countries to dominate the economic affairs of China. During the Taiping Rebellion, which began in 1850, failed civil servant applicant Hong Xiuquan and starving peasants, workers, and miners attempted to overthrow the Qing Dynasty. With the help of some warlords along with French and British intervention, the Qings prevailed in 1864.

In the midst of the war, adding to China's internal problems, the Yellow River (Huang He) changed course, flooding farmland in some areas and leaving others open to drought. With agricultural lands devastated, famine followed during which many Chinese starved to death. Adding to the troubles, the bubonic plague broke out at this time. By the end of the fighting, the rebellion was probably responsible for the deaths of more than 20 million people, more than half of whom were civilians.

Between 1899 and 1901, an anti-imperialist group called the Boxers— named because many of their members practiced martial arts, which were known as Chinese boxing—was attacking Chinese Christians and Western missionaries. The Empress Dowager **Cixi** (see Topic 5.8) encouraged the Boxers and in 1900 ordered that all foreigners be killed. However, most of the estimated 100,000 people who were killed were Chinese Christians. Only about 200–250 foreigners died during the **Boxer Rebellion**. The empress and the Qing court suffered a humiliating defeat that undermined their legitimacy. Western powers and influence continued to erode Chinese sovereignty in subsequent years.

Japan Industrialized countries outside of Europe also desired colonies. Japan had sharply limited its contact with other countries since the early 1600s. In 1853, United States Commodore Matthew Perry came to Japan in large warships to secure a treaty that opened Japanese ports to trade. In the following decade, Japan overthrew its traditional government in an uprising called the Meiji Restoration and began to rapidly industrialize, hoping it could become strong enough to protect its distinctive culture. As part of this change, Japan began to look outward for territorial gains. An island nation with few natural resources and little arable land, it sought lands and natural resources to fuel its own growth.

Partly to relieve population pressures in rural areas and partly to gain knowledge of foreign places, Japan's government began to encourage agricultural workers to take seasonal contract work on Hawaii, Guam, and other locations. Through a **Colonization Society** established in 1893, leaders began plans to establish colonies in Mexico and Latin America. Japan set up an empire in East Asia that included parts of China, Korea, Southeast Asia, and Pacific islands that lasted from the 1890s until the end of World War II.

Imperialism in Southeast Asia

Portugal and Spain originally controlled European trade with Southeast Asia. After 1600, the power shifted and the English and Dutch supplanted them.

The Dutch in Southeast Asia Dutch imperialism in Southeast Asia began with a private company, just as English imperialism in South Asia had. In 1641 the Dutch seized control of the Spice Islands (now part of Indonesia), so called because they produced spices such as cloves and nutmeg that were in great demand in Europe. The **Dutch East India Company** (**VOC**) took over the spice trade from the Portuguese, setting up several trading posts on the archipelago. Although the trade was very profitable for the VOC, corruption caused the company to go bankrupt by 1800. Once the VOC folded, the Dutch government itself took control of the **Dutch East Indies**. By the mid-19th century, the islands were producing cash crops to support the Dutch economy.

Plantations produced tea, rubber, and sugar for export purposes, a situation that limited rice cultivation and eventually created enormous hardships for Indonesian farmers who relied on rice to survive. Although criticism of this agricultural policy forced the Dutch government to implement humanitarian reforms, the reforms failed to meet the needs of the Indonesian people.

The French in Southeast Asia The French government also wanted an imperial presence in Asia. After it defeated China in the Sino-French War of 1883–1885, France gained control of northern Vietnam. France later pressured Siam to cede control of the territory of modern-day Laos to the French. By the 1890s, France controlled Cambodia, Laos, and all of modern-day Vietnam. Together, these nations became known as French **Indochina**. French motives for imperialism were like those of the Dutch—a desire for cash crops. Soon rubber plantations dotted the landscape of Cambodia and Vietnam.

The British in Southeast Asia British influence in Southeast Asia began when the East India Company acquired the island of Penang off the northwest coast of the Malay Peninsula in 1786. In 1824, the British founded the port of Singapore. Chinese immigrants soon made it the most important seaport in Southeast Asia. Eventually, Britain controlled all of the Malay Peninsula, Burma (Myanmar), and northern Borneo. British investors were originally attracted by the region's mineral wealth, especially tin and gold. In addition, Britain promoted the planting of cash crops such as pepper, tobacco, palm oil, and rubber. By the end of the 19th century, **Malaya** was the world's greatest producer of natural rubber.

Siam Only one Southeast Asian nation, **Siam**—modern-day Thailand— managed to escape the clutches of 19th-century European imperialism. Siam's monarchs deftly handled diplomatic relations with the British and French, whose colonies bordered Siam. The Siamese government also instituted a series of modernizing reforms, similar to Japan's Meiji reforms. The government began to industrialize by building railroads, and it set up Western-style schools in order to create an educated populace who could fill the ranks of an efficient government bureaucracy.

Australia and New Zealand

After the loss of its American colonies, Britain began to consider the possibility of establishing various kinds of settlements in **Australia**, finally deciding to locate a **penal colony** there. In 1788 the first convicts, along with some free settlers, arrived in Australia, and the east coast became known as New South Wales. In the 1820s,

Source: His Highness Prince Pravij Jumsai, from Wikimedia Commons

On the royal coat of arms for Siam, the kingdom was represented by a three-headed elephant.

Britain took possession of the entire continent. For decades, the chief economic activity of the colony was to house convicts. The discovery that Australia was well-suited to producing fine wool provided a new industry, and in the 1830s larger numbers of free settlers began to arrive. The discovery of copper in 1842 and gold in 1851 helped spur growth.

When Britain annexed the settler colony of **New Zealand** in 1839, it was made a part of New South Wales. Two years later, after the **Treaty of Waitangi** guaranteeing that the rights of the original **Maori** inhabitants would be protected by the British crown, it became a separate colony. Nevertheless, open war broke out as European settlers encroached on Maori lands. The Australian gold rushes provided a market for foodstuffs raised by New Zealand farmers, both European and Maori. For many years, sheep grazing and dairy farming provided the base for the colony's economy.

U.S. Imperialism in Latin America and the Pacific

During the 19th century, the United States continued taking land from indigenous peoples, as Europeans had done since Columbus arrived. One notorious episode was the forced relocation of Eastern Woodlands peoples from the Southeast to a new **Indian Territory** in what is now Oklahoma. So many Native Americans died from exposure, malnutrition, disease, and exhaustion that this forced migration became known as the **Trail of Tears**.

In 1823, President James Monroe issued the **Monroe Doctrine**, which stated that European nations should not intervene in the affairs of the countries in the Western Hemisphere. Implied in the doctrine was a desire to be an imperial power in the Americas. This desire played out in the U.S. war with Mexico (1845–1848), through which the United States gained vast territories in the Southwest from Mexico.

Expansion on Land White Americans believed that they had a **Manifest Destiny**—a natural and inevitable right to expand to the Pacific Ocean. The United States bought Alaska from Russia in 1867. Two years later, in 1869, the completion of a transcontinental railway spurred development of the American West. As white settlers moved westward to take advantage of offers of free land, Native Americans were forced onto reservations. By 1893, the U.S. Bureau of the Census declared that the western frontier was now closed.

Expansion Overseas The United States turned its focus to lands overseas. The United States was not a global power for most of the 19th century. The Second Industrial Revolution brought newfound prosperity to the young republic. Economic considerations, as well as feelings of nationalism and cultural superiority, drove Americans' desire for territorial conquest. A group of American planters overthrew Hawaii's constitutional monarchy in 1895, but the islands did not become a U.S. territory until 1900. In the meantime, the U.S. victory in the **Spanish-American War** in 1898 brought Guam, Cuba, Puerto Rico, and the Philippines under U.S. control. President Theodore Roosevelt, a proponent of Social Darwinism, was especially eager to expand U.S. influence throughout the Western Hemisphere. The 1904 **Roosevelt Corollary** to the Monroe Doctrine stated that if countries in Latin America demonstrated "instability," the United States would intervene. It did several times. For example, in 1904 Roosevelt sent U.S. troops to occupy a Caribbean island nation, the Dominican Republic, until it repaid its foreign debts.

Comparing Three Types of Imperialism		
Type and Examples	**Features**	**Outcomes**
State-Run Colony • British West Africa • Belgian Congo	• Western institutions slowly replace the local culture • Often defended by claims of helping the indigenous population	• Exploitation of indigenous labor • Loss of indigenous culture • Creation of non-native elite and mixed native and non-native middle class • Imperialist countries rule by corporations or states guided by Western policy
Settler Colony • British South Africa, Australia, and New Zealand • French Algeria	• Focus on control and use of land • Settlers remove or dominate the indigenous population • Most common in sparsely populated lands	• Loss of indigenous culture • Genocide • Spread of disease • Forced conversion to Western business, political, and religious ideas • Exploitation of indigenous labor • Indigenous populations forced into extreme poverty and addiction
Economic Domination • British in China • French in China • United States in Latin America	• Commonly based on exploiting raw materials and hiring low-wage labor • Local government remains in control but becomes weak	• Social destabilization based on economic exploitation • Monoculture and lack of agricultural diversity • Soil depletion and environmental damage

Russian Expansion

Empress Catherine II ("the Great") set out to expand the Russian Empire in all directions during her reign (1762–1796), annexing about half of Poland as well as territory won from the Ottoman Empire. Her grandson, Alexander I, annexed Finland, Moldova, Georgia, Azerbaijan, and part of Armenia during his reign (1815–1825).

Beginning in the 1740s, Russian merchants sponsored voyages to Alaska. In 1808 the Russian-American Company, which was similar to the British and Dutch East India companies, established permanent headquarters in Novo-Arkhangelsk (modern-day Sitka). From there they explored the west coast of

North America. In 1811, they selected the site for a settlement at Fort Ross in California. They abandoned Fort Ross in 1839 and in 1867 sold Alaska to the United States, ending Russian plans to make the North Pacific a Russian sea.

Russia continued to push into Central Asia during the 19th century, leading to an intense rivalry between the Russian and British empires as they competed unsuccessfully for dominance in Afghanistan—a rivalry that came to be known as the **Great Game**. Russia also succeeded in annexing lands from China, most notably a large portion of Manchuria.

"SAVE ME FROM MY FRIENDS!"

Source: Wikimedia Commons

"The Great Game: The Afghan Emir Sher Ali Khan with his 'friends' Russia and Great Britain" (1878) reveals the confrontation between the British Empire and the Russian Empire over Afghanistan. The political cartoon illustrates an atmosphere of tension and distrust that existed between the two empires.

KEY TERMS BY THEME

GOVERNMENT: Rulers
King Leopold II
Cixi

GOVERNMENT: Countries
Sierra Leone
Gold Coast
Cape Colony
Congo Free State
Abyssinia
Liberia
Ceylon
Dutch East Indies
Indochina
Malaya
Siam
Australia
New Zealand

GOVERNMENT: Treaties
Berlin Conference
Treaty of Waitangi

GOVERNMENT: Ideas
Scramble for Africa
Monroe Doctrine
Manifest Destiny
Roosevelt Corollary
Great Game

GOVERNMENT: Systems
concentration camps
penal colony

GOVERNMENT: Wars and Rebellions
Boer Wars
Seven Years' War
Taiping Rebellion
Boxer Rebellion
Spanish-American War

ECONOMICS: Systems
corvée laborer
spheres of influence
settler colony

ECONOMICS: Companies
East India Company (EIC)
Dutch East India Company (VOC)

SOCIETY: Peoples
Afrikaners
Maori

SOCIETY: Organization
Colonization Society
Indian Territory
Trail of Tears

ENVIRONMENT: Tropics
quinine
Suez Canal

Questions 1 to 3 refer to the passage below.

"The American continents, by the free and independent condition which they have assumed and maintain, are henceforth not to be considered as subjects for future colonization by any European powers. . . .

We should consider any attempt on their [Europeans'] part to extend their system to any portion of this hemisphere as dangerous to our peace and safety. With the existing colonies or dependencies of any European power we have not interfered and shall not interfere. But with the Governments who have declared their independence and maintain it, and whose independence we have, on great consideration and on just principles, acknowledged, we could not view any interposition for the purpose of oppressing them, or controlling in any other manner their destiny, by any European power in any other light than as the manifestation of an unfriendly disposition toward the United States."

James Monroe, annual presidential message to Congress, 1823

1. Which statement summarizes the main idea stated in the passage?

    (A) Many former colonies of European nations in the Western Hemisphere desired a return to colonial status.

    (B) The United States intended to interfere in the administration of existing European colonies.

    (C) The European powers must respect the sovereignty of independent nations in the Western Hemisphere.

    (D) The United States must remain neutral in any attempt of a European nation to claim land in the Western Hemisphere.

2. Which event indicates that the Monroe Doctrine might have included a desire of U.S. leaders to engage in economic imperialism?

    (A) The War of 1812

    (B) The Spanish-American War

    (C) The Civil War

    (D) The Seven Years' War

3. Which aspect of the Spanish-American War most directly demonstrated that the United States wanted to become an imperial power?

    (A) Declaring war against a country in Europe

    (B) Seizing territories from Mexico

    (C) Helping Cuba become independent of Spain

    (D) Taking control of the Philippines

1. **Use the cartoon below to answer all parts of the question that follows.**

Source: Wikipedia Commons

The characters represented are (left to right in the foreground) Queen Victoria of England, William II of German, Nicholas II of Russia, Marianne (the symbol of France), and a Japanese samurai. Behind them, a Qing official throws up his hands but cannot stop them.

(A) Identify ONE reason imperial powers had an interest in China.

(B) Explain ONE response by Chinese people to the actions of people from imperial countries represented in the cartoon.

(C) Explain ONE reason why China was unable to withstand the development represented in the cartoon.

2. **Answer all parts of the question that follows.**

(A) Identify ONE way in which imperialism in Africa was similar to imperialism in East Asia in the period 1750–1900.

(B) Identify ONE way in which imperialism in Africa and imperialism in Southeast Asia differed in the period 1750–1900.

(C) Explain ONE way in which imperialism in state-run colonies was similar to imperialism in settler colonies in the period 1750–1900.

THINK AS A HISTORIAN: SITUATE THE MONROE DOCTRINE
IN CONTEXT

Following on the heels of the American and French revolutions, Argentina declared its independence from Spain in 1816 and Mexico declared its independence in 1821.

Use the information above as well as your knowledge of state expansion to describe the context in which President Monroe issued his doctrine on Latin American countries. In two or three sentences, explain why he may have issued the proclamation at the time he did.

REFLECT ON THE TOPIC ESSENTIAL QUESTION

1. In one to three paragraphs, describe the processes by which state power shifted in various parts of the world between 1750 and 1900.

Source: watchingamerica.com

Newspaper cartoon from 1912

6.3

Indigenous Responses to State Expansion

There have been repeated outcries directed to me by the indigenous peoples of this and surrounding provinces, outcries against the abuses committed by European-born crown officials. . . . Justified outcries that have produced no remedy from the royal courts.

—Túpac Amaru II, c. 1780

Essential Question: How and why did internal and external factors influence state building between 1750 and 1900?

In response to European imperialism, nationalist movements emerged throughout South America, Africa, and Asia. Often the movements' leaders, such as Túpac Amaru II in Peru, had European style educations. Many had developed a deep understanding of such Enlightenment ideals as natural rights, sovereignty, and nationalism. Some worked in official posts in colonial government. Some colonial elites used the education that imperialism provided them to drive out their conquerors in the 20th century. Anti-imperial resistance often created new states.

Nationalist Movements in the Balkans

At its most powerful, the Ottoman Empire stretched deep into Europe. However, by the early 19th century, it was losing its hold on its remaining European territories in the **Balkan Peninsula**. Inspired by the French Revolution, ethnic nationalism emerged as the peoples of the Balkans sought independence. The growing ethnic tensions in the region set the stage for World War I.

Serbia (1815) and Greece (1832) won independence only after long wars. Bosnia and Herzegovina, Montenegro, and Bulgaria all rebelled against Ottoman rule. In 1877, Serbia and Russia came to their aid in what was to be the last and most important Russo-Turkish War. After the war ended in 1878, the Treaty of Berlin freed Bulgaria, Romania, and Montenegro but placed Bosnia and Herzegovina under the control of Austria-Hungary.

Resistance and Rebellion in the Americas

In North America, following the British victory over the French in the French and Indian War, the British issued the **Proclamation of 1763**. This act reserved all the land between the Appalachian Mountains and the Mississippi River for Native Americans—the first time a European government had recognized the territorial rights of indigenous peoples. However, the British colonists resented this interference in colonial affairs. After winning independence, citizens of the new United States soon overran the Ohio and Illinois river valleys, displacing Native Americans.

Cherokee Nation After 1800, the Cherokee assimilated to white settler culture, adopting colonial methods of farming, weaving, and building. They developed a syllabic alphabet for writing their language. Within a short time, almost the entire tribe was literate, and the *Cherokee Phoenix* became the first Native American newspaper in the United States. The **Cherokee nation** adopted a constitution based on the U.S. Constitution.

But assimilation did not save the Cherokee from white Americans' greed. After the discovery of gold in 1829 on Cherokee land in Georgia, attempts began to force the Cherokee off their land. After Congress passed the **Indian Removal Act** of 1830, the Cherokee and other Southeast Native American tribes were forced to relocate to what is now Oklahoma. U.S. expansionism continued, affecting many Native American peoples.

Ghost Dance In the northwestern United States around 1869, prophet-dreamers among the Northern Paiute Indians announced that the dead would soon come back and drive out the whites, restoring the lands and traditions of Native Americans. The **Ghost Dance** rituals of dances and songs were meant to hasten this event. The Ghost Dance spread from the Sierra Nevada to the Missouri River and from northern Texas to the Canadian border. It reached the Sioux by 1890, coinciding with the Sioux revolts. Sioux warriors wore "ghost shirts." However, the Ghost Dance resistance movement fell at the Wounded Knee Massacre in 1890, marking the end of the Indian Wars.

Túpac Amaru II José Gabriel Condorcanqui was a *cacique* (hereditary chief) in southern Peru. He was descended from the last Inca ruler, Túpac Amaru, and took the name **Túpac Amaru II**. Born around 1740, he continued to identify with his Inca heritage in spite of having received a formal Jesuit education. In 1780 he arrested and executed a colonial administrator, charging him with cruelty. This action led to the last general Indian revolt against Spain, which at first was supported by some *criollos* (Spaniards born in America). The revolt spread throughout southern Peru and into Bolivia and Argentina before Túpac Amaru II and his family were captured in March 1781. They were taken to Cuzco, the former capital of the Inca empire. There Túpac Amaru II was forced to watch as his wife and sons were executed before he was tortured and executed himself.

French Intervention in Mexico In 1863 a group of Mexican conservatives conspired with Emperor Napoleon III of France to overthrow the liberal government of **Benito Juárez**, a full-blooded Zapotec. Mexico owned France money, and Napoleon III wanted to further his imperialist ambitions. He offered to make a European noble, Archduke Maximilian, the emperor of Mexico. Maximilian was crowned on June 10, 1864. After three more years of war, Mexicans forced the French to withdraw from Mexico. Maximilian was executed on June 19, 1867, and Juárez resumed the presidency.

South Asian Movements

By the mid-19th century, **sepoys,** Indian soldiers under British employ, made up the majority of the British armed forces in colonial India. Most were Hindus or Muslims. In 1857, the British began using rifle cartridges that had been greased with a mixture of the fat of cows and pigs. Hindus, who view the cow as sacred, and Muslims, who refuse to slaughter pigs, were both furious. Both were convinced that the British were trying to convert them to Christianity. Their violent uprising, known as the **Indian Rebellion of 1857** or the Sepoy Mutiny, spread throughout cities in northern India. The British crushed the rebellion, killing thousands, but the event marked the emergence of Indian nationalism.

After the Indian Rebellion, Britain also exiled the Mughal emperor for his involvement in the rebellion and ended the Mughal Empire. In its place, the British government took a more active role in ruling India. From 1858 until India won independence in 1947, the British **Raj**, the colonial government, took its orders directly from the British government in London.

Under the Raj, many Indians attended British universities. In 1885, several British-educated Indians established the **Indian National Congress.** Though begun as a forum for airing grievances to the colonial government, it quickly began to call for self-rule. (Connect: Compare the motives and outcomes of the Haitian Revolution with those of the Indian Rebellion of 1857. See Topic 5.2.)

Source: Wikimedia Commons

The first meeting of the Indian National Congress in 1885 was dominated by Hindu representatives. As a result, many Indian Muslims were suspicious of it.

Southeast Asian Resistance

By the 1880s, the only independent country remaining in Southeast Asia was Siam (Thailand). The rest of the region was under the control of the Spanish, Dutch, British, and French.

Vietnam From the beginning of French colonialism in the region, many Vietnamese resisted. By 1884, when 12-year-old Ham Nghi became emperor, his top advisers were vocal critics of the French. The French soon tried to assert their control by raiding the royal palace, but the young emperor had been removed for safety. Ham Nghi's supporters continued to resist French rule until he was captured in 1888 and exiled to Algeria. The resistance continued until 1895 under Phan Dinh Phung, who became a hero to future revolutionaries in the Vietnamese resistance movement.

Philippine Resistance The **Philippines** came under Spanish control in the 16th century, but there was no public education there until 1863. However, wealthy Filipinos sent their sons to Europe to study. One of those young men, **José Rizal**, started a reform movement called Liga Filipina (Philippine League) in 1892. Though the Liga was loyal to Spain, the Spanish feared it. They promptly arrested and executed Rizal, an action that shocked many Filipinos.

There had been numerous rebellions throughout the history of Spanish rule, but now, for the first time, Filipinos had nationalist ambitions and the education needed to carry them out. In 1896 several revolts broke out in provinces around Manila, marking the beginning of the **Philippine Revolution**. The **Spanish-American War** broke out in 1898, and after a decisive American victory in the Battle of Manila Bay, exiled Filipino revolutionaries returned. Based on U.S. sympathy for Philippine independence, the rebels expected freedom.

However, the **Treaty of Paris** ending the war merely transferred control of the Philippines from Spain to the United States. By the time the treaty was ratified in February 1899, hostilities had broken out in what was to be known as the **Philippine-American War**. The war ended in a U.S. victory in 1902. An estimated 20,000 Filipino troops were killed, and more than 200,000 civilians died as a result of the war. Of the 4,300 Americans who lost their lives, nearly two-thirds of them died of disease. Organized resistance continued until 1906, but the Philippines remained a U.S. possession until 1946.

Resistance in Australia and New Zealand

The **Aboriginal** people have been in Australia for an estimated 50,000 years and have the oldest continuous culture on Earth. At the time of European settlement, there may have been as many as 1 million people in 500 clans, speaking 700 languages.

Australia In 1788, the British began sending convicts and soldiers to establish colonies in New South Wales. The government instructed the settlers to treat the indigenous inhabitants kindly. However, the colonial government did not recognize indigenous land ownership. Further, because the indigenous inhabitants were not considered British subjects, they were not protected by law. Thousands of Aboriginal people were killed as they tried to defend their territory and resources from European settlers.

New Zealand Compared to the Aboriginals in Australia, New Zealand's **Maori** were newcomers, having arrived from Polynesia in the 14th century. Under the 1840 **Treaty of Waitangi**, Britain had promised to protect the property rights of the Maori. Within a short time, the Maori became alarmed by British settlement patterns, and the first of a series of **Maori Wars** broke out. The British were eventually able to overcome the Maori in 1846. Relations deteriorated again in the 1850s as the Maori became reluctant to sell more land to settlers, fearing for their future. Ignoring the promise of the Treaty of Waitangi, the government attempted to pressure the Maori to sell land, sending troops in 1861 to dislodge the Maori from the property in question. Another decade of fighting ensued. The war ended in an uneasy peace in 1872, but by 1900 the Maori had lost most of their land.

African Resistance

Organized African resistance to imperialism developed later than Indian resistance. One reason for this difference in timing is that European powers had been in India much longer than they had been in Africa. In addition, British colonial governments in India were partially run by Indians, while colonial governments in Africa were largely run by military officials from Europe. However, by the end of the World War I (1914–1918), Western-educated Africans had a shared identity and nationalism known as **Pan-Africanism**.

Sokoto Caliphate In West Africa in the 18th century, rulers often mixed Islamic and traditional religious practices. In 1804, a group of Muslim intellectuals led by **Usman dan Fodio** (1754–1817) started a drive to purify Islam among the Hausa tribes of the region. He created a caliphate with its seat at the new town of Sokoto. The **Sokoto Caliphate** established the slave trade as a means of economic growth at a time when the British were trying to stop it. The British navy attempted to intercept the ships of the Sokoto Caliphate, free the enslaved people, and relocate them in their colony Sierra Leone. The Sokoto Caliphate was the largest African empire since the 16th century. It was finally subdued in 1903 when the British made it part of their colony of Nigeria.

South Africa From 1811 to 1858, the British fought the native **Xhosa** people, who did not want to be ruled by Europeans, whether Dutch or English. In 1856–1857, in the region east of the Cape Colony, some of the cattle of the local Xhosa were getting sick and dying, perhaps from diseases caught from the cattle of the British settlers. The Xhosa began to kill their cattle and destroy their crops in the belief that these actions would cause spirits to remove the British settlers from their lands. Some 400,000 head of Xhosa cattle may have been killed. The immediate result of the **Xhosa Cattle Killing Movement** was famine and the deaths of thousands of people. However, the British were not driven out of the area.

In the 1870s, the British fought the **Zulu** Kingdom, located on the South African coast of the Indian Ocean, which had become a well-organized and centralized state. At first, this **Anglo-Zulu War** went in favor of the Zulus, but eventually the British defeated them, and their lands became part of the British colony of South Africa.

Samory Touré's War In West Africa in 1868, Mande chieftain **Samory Touré** (1830–1900) led a group of warriors to establish a powerful kingdom in Guinea, extending it until the early 1880s. He opposed French attempts to annex West Africa, first fighting them in 1883. The French finally succeeded but offered Samory their protection. When he was unable to extend his kingdom to the east, he again went to war with the French in 1891. After his forces were ejected, he tried to reestablish his kingdom in the upper Ivory Coast. The French finally captured him in 1898 and sent him into exile.

Source: Archieves Bordeaux Métropole

Samory Touré after his capture by the Friench, September 1898.

Mahdist Revolt In East Africa in 1881, a Sudanese Islamic cleric, **Muhammad Ahmad** (1844–1885), declared himself the **Mahdi**, or "guided one," who would restore the glory of Islam. The Sudanese had resented Egyptian rule for decades, and the arrival of the British in 1873 only fueled their resentment. Ahmad turned the political movement into a religious one, forming an army to fight against Egypt. By 1882, the Mahdist army had taken control of the area around the capital, Khartoum. The next year, a joint British-Egyptian military expedition launched a counterattack against the Mahdists. The Mahdists finally overran the British-Egyptian forces in January 1885. After Ahmad's death in June of that year, the Mahdist movement disintegrated, weakened by infighting among rival leaders. The British returned to **Sudan** in 1896, and finally defeated the Mahdists in September 1898.

Yaa Asantewaa War Beginning in 1823, the British made several attempts to subjugate the **Asante Empire** in present-day Ghana in West Africa. The first four were unsuccessful. The fifth and final war is known as the Yaa Asantewaa War or the War of the Golden Stool. It began in March 1900, when the British governor of the Gold Coast demanded the Golden Stool, a symbol of national unity. **Yaa Asantewaa** (1840–1921), a mighty warrior queen, led a rebellion against the British. It was the last African war led by a woman, and it resulted in the deaths of 2,000 Asante and 1,000 British. The death toll was higher than in the first four wars combined. The war ended in September 1900 with a British victory. Yaa Asantewaa was exiled, and Asante (as Ashanti) became part of the Gold Coast colony.

KEY TERMS BY THEME		
GOVERNMENT: Rebel Leaders Túpac Amaru II Benito Juárez José Rizal Usman dan Fodio Samory Touré Muhammad Ahmad Yaa Asantewaa **GOVERNMENT: States** Balkan Peninsula Vietnam Philippines Sokoto Caliphate Sudan Asante Empire	**GOVERNMENT: Wars and Rebellions** Ghost Dance Indian Rebellion of 1857 Philippine Revolution Spanish-American War Philippine-American War Maori Wars Xhosa Cattle Killing Movement Anglo-Zulu War **GOVERNMENT: Treaties** Treaty of Paris Treaty of Waitangi **GOVERNMENT: Relations with Indigenous Peoples** Proclamation of 1763 Indian Removal Act	**GOVERNMENT: Organizations** Indian National Congress **CULTURE: Peoples** Cherokee nation Aboriginal Maori Xhosa Zulu **CULTURE: Ideas** Mahdi Pan-Africanism **SOCIETY: British in India** sepoys Raj

MULTIPLE-CHOICE QUESTIONS

Questions 1 to 3 refer to the passage below.

"I have warned you again and again not to dally in those villages, where there is nothing to do—but you continue to saunter, ignoring the fact that soldiers are running short of food. They are receiving their pay, but the money will not last forever. Then they will all depart, leaving us to pay with our lives, because you must have learned by this time that they came only for reasons of self-interest, and to get all they can out of us. They are already beginning to desert. . . .Thus we will lose all the people that I have gotten together for the descent on Cuzco. . . . I gave you plenty of warnings to march immediately on Cuzco, but you took them all lightly, giving the Spaniards time to prepare as they have done, placing cannon on Picchu Mountain, and devising other measures so dangerous that you are no longer in a position to attack them. . . . God must want me to suffer my sins. Your wife.

P. S After I had finished this letter, a messenger arrived with the definite news that the enemy from Paruro is in Acos; I am going forward to attack them, even if it costs me my life."

Micaela Bastidas, letter to Túpac Amaru II, 1780

1. What does the above letter indicate about the author's point of view?

   (A) She believed the Spanish were fighting only to earn money.

   (B) She did not understand the importance of planning for rebellion.

   (C) She supported the rebellion of indigenous people in Peru against the Spanish.

   (D) She was too anxious to be a valuable contributor to the rebellion.

2. Which statement provides the most useful context in evaluating the author's argument about the Spanish?

   (A) She and her husband were able to escape the Spaniards and flee into the Andean wilderness.

   (B) She and her husband were brutally executed by the Spaniards.

   (C) She and her husband's forces defeated the Spanish conquerors.

   (D) She and her husband made peace with the Spaniards and were given a role in the colonial government.

3. How was the rebellion of Túpac Amaru II different from other Latin American rebellions?

   (A) Its leader identified as a person of European ancestry.

   (B) It was effective in changing governmental policy.

   (C) Its leader identified as an Incan.

   (D) It received support from Spain's rivals for influence.

1. **Use the passage below to answer all parts of the question that follows.**

"It is well known to all that in this age the people of Hindustan [northern India], both Hindus and Muslims, are being ruined under the tyranny and oppression of the infidel [unbeliever] and the treacherous English. It is therefore the bounden duty of all the wealthy people of India, especially of those who have any sort of connection with any of the Muslim royal families and are considered the pastors and masters of their people, to stake their lives and property for the well-being of the public. . . . I, who am the grandson of Bahadur Shah, have . . . come here to extirpate [destroy] the infidels residing in the eastern part of the country, and to liberate and protect the poor helpless people now groaning under their iron rule. . . .

Several of the Hindu and Muslim chiefs who . . . have been trying their best to root out the English in India, have presented themselves to me and taken part in the reigning Indian crusade. . . . [B]e it known to all, that the ancient works both of the Hindus and the Muslims, the writings of the miracle-workers, and the calculations of the astrologers, pundits [learned persons] and rammals [fortune-tellers], all agree, asserting that the English will no longer have any footing in India or elsewhere. Therefore, it is incumbent on all to give up the hope of the continuation of the British sway, [and to] side with me. . . ."

Firoz Shah, Proclamation in the *Delhi Gazette*, 1857

(A) Identify ONE reason for the proclamation by Firoz Shah.

(B) Explain ONE way in which the ideas in the proclamation affected political structures in India in 1857.

(C) Explain ONE political development in India that occured after 1857 as a result of the rebellion.

2. **Answer all parts of the question that follows.**

(A) Identify ONE way in which Enlightenment ideals influenced the series of revolts throughout India in 1857.

(B) Explain ONE way in which nationalist movements in Africa differed from nationalist movements in France in the period 1750–1900.

(C) Explain ONE way in which nationalist movements in Southeast Asia were similar to nationalist movements in South American states in the period 1750–1900.

THINK AS A HISTORIAN: SIGNIFICANCE OF POINT OF VIEW IN SOURCES

Perspective, or point of view, is a powerful filter of experience. Historical accounts from varying perspectives require historians to understand the significance of the point of view and use that understanding to determine how useful a source is, and for what purpose. For example, firsthand indigenous responses to state expansion between 1750 and 1900 provide historians with a perspective of the people whose lands and cultures were being taken over. At the same time, accounts of colonization solely through the lens of the colonizers would also provide a limited perspective. As the final word on what happened, each type of source has limitations. For this reason, historians are able to present a more accurate picture of the past when they examine sources with varying points of views and appreciate the significance of those perspectives.

Reread the excerpt from the proclamation by Firoz Shah on the previous page. Explain the significance of the excerpt's point of view. Then read the following General Order from the British Lord Canning to the 19th Regiment of Bengal on March 27, 1857. Compare the significance of Canning's point of view to that of Firoz Shah and explain how each source may have limitations because of its point of view.

"Neither the 19th Regiment nor any regiment in the service of the Government of India nor any Sepoy Hindoo [Hindu] or Mussulman [Muslim] has reason to pretend that the Government has shown directly or indirectly a desire to interfere with the religion of its troops. It has been the unvarying rule of the Government of India to treat the religious feelings of all its servants of every creed with careful respect and to representations or complaints put forward in a dutiful and becoming spirit whether upon this or upon any other subject it has never turned a deaf ear. But the Government of India expects to receive in return for this treatment the confidence of those who serve it. From its soldiers, of every rank and race, it will at all times and in all cases enforce obedience. They have sworn to give it and the Governor General in Council never ceases to exact it. To no men who prefer complaints with arms in their hands will he ever listen."

REFLECT ON THE TOPIC ESSENTIAL QUESTION

1. In one to three paragraphs, describe the internal and external factors that influenced state building between 1750 and 1900.

6.4

Global Economic Development

Peruvian guano [bird droppings] has become so desirable an article to the agricultural interest of the United States that it is the duty of the Government to employ all the means properly in its power for the purpose of causing that article to be imported into the country at a reasonable price.

—U.S. President Millard Fillmore, December 2, 1850

Essential Question: How did environmental factors contribute to the global economy between 1750 and 1900?

Economics was among the most influential of the several motives driving imperialism. Britain industrialized rapidly during the 1700s and 1800s. In order to feed industries' desires for raw materials, such as cotton, copper, and rubber, Europe looked to Asia and Africa. American agriculture, as noted by President Fillmore, looked to South America for fertilizer. The people of these continents were also potential consumers of European and American manufactured goods. Finally, colonial peoples provided the labor for large-scale projects, such as building railroads or telegraph lines. Colonial workers were paid meager wages for difficult and dangerous labor. In short, natural resources, new markets, and low-wage labor drove economic imperialism.

Technological Developments

The Industrial Revolution did not just take place in factories. It affected transportation and communication as well.

Railroads Before the introduction of **railroads**, transportation from the interiors of colonies to coastal ports was by water or by roads. Most colonies had few roads, and those that existed were usually poorly maintained and often unusable during rainy seasons. Transportation by water was limited to coastal areas and river basins. The introduction of railroads lowered the cost of transporting raw materials for shipment to Europe. At the same time, railroads helped open up colonial markets for manufactured goods.

Europeans often pointed to their railroad projects as evidence that imperialism helped the peoples of Asia and Africa. However, providing new transportation technology to the colonies primarily served the interests of the colonizers. In India, the British built a complex railway network that stretched from the interior to the coasts in order to ship raw materials out of the country easily.

British-born **Cecil Rhodes** (1853–1902), founder of De Beers Diamonds, was an especially enthusiastic investor in a railroad project that was to stretch from Cape Town, in the Cape Colony of South Africa, to Cairo, Egypt. Connecting all of the British-held colonies with a transportation network could make governance easier and aid in mobilizing for war, if necessary. The project was never completed because Britain never gained control over all the land on which it was to be built. The overwhelming majority of railway workers in Africa were natives who were paid far lower wages than their European counterparts. Thus, railroad technology was a means of extracting as many resources as possible from subject lands while paying colonial laborers as little as possible.

Steamships Because they required huge quantities of coal as fuel, early **steamships** could travel only limited distances. However, steamboats could transport people, mail, and goods on navigable rivers such as the Ganges in South Asia and the Congo in Africa. After the development of more efficient steam engines in 1870, steamships became practical for long distances. In the 1870s, the development of compression refrigeration equipment made it possible to ship perishables such as meat and dairy products across oceans.

Telegraph Invented in 1832, the electric **telegraph** transformed communications. Instead of taking days, weeks, or even months, news could travel instantaneously. Telegraph service was introduced in India in 1850, just five years after it started in Britain. Telegraph lines often followed railroad routes. Submarine (underwater) telegraph cables soon crossed oceans. In 1866 the first permanent transatlantic cable was laid between the United States and England. Telegraph service between England and Australia was introduced in 1872, and in 1874 service between Portugal and Brazil allowed instant communication between Europe and South America.

Agricultural Products

When Europeans arrived in Asia and Africa, they found mainly agricultural economies, with most people raising enough food to live on—subsistence farming—with perhaps a little left over to sell. Subsistence farming is still common throughout Sub-Saharan Africa, Southeast Asia, and parts of Latin America. Under control of imperialist powers, subsistence farmers abandoned their traditional ways and grew **cash crops** instead. These were crops such as tea, cotton, sugar, oil palms, rubber, and coffee that were grown for their commercial value rather than for use by those who grew them. Imperial demands for cash crops had a damaging effect on subject nations. As cash crops replaced food crops, food prices rose.

The growing European middle classes created a demand for meat. Cattle ranches in Argentina, Brazil, and Uruguay produced beef for export. Sheep herders in Australia and New Zealand exported lamb and mutton. New technology allowed meat to be shipped over long distances. Meat could be processed and canned in packing plants or shipped fresh or frozen in refrigerated steamships.

Guano, bat and seabird excrement, is rich in nitrates and phosphates. These make it an excellent natural fertilizer. Because of the dry climate in Peru and Chile, vast quantities of guano had accumulated before people began mining it in the 19th century. Between 1840 and 1880, millions of tons of guano were dug by hand and loaded onto ships for export, often by indentured Chinese or Polynesian laborers.

Source: American Museum of Natural History

Guano mining in the central Chincha Islands, off the coast of Peru, c. 1860.

Raw Materials

The demand for raw materials that could be processed into manufactured goods and shipped away—often back to the providers of raw materials—turned colonies into **export economies.** Imperial attention focused on the tropical climates that were conducive to the presence of raw materials, unlike some imperial countries.

Cotton Britain's Parliament banned Indian **cotton** textiles in 1721 because they competed with the native wool industry. Soon after, cotton from Britain's southern colonies in America shifted production. The colonies would provide the raw materials, and England would manufacture textiles. During the Industrial Revolution, Britain's great textile mills got 80 percent of their cotton from the United States.

When the American Civil War erupted, northern warships blockaded Confederate ports, cutting off the supply of cotton. As a result, farmers all over the world, from Australia to the West Indies, replaced food production with cotton to make up for the shortage. Cotton farmers in India were able to benefit from the shortages caused by the Civil War, but Egypt benefited most. Egypt had already developed a fine long-staple variety of cotton and ramped up production. By the end of the 19th century, 93 percent of Egypt's export revenue came from cotton. Raw cotton production from Egypt and India supported the manufacturing of textiles that Britain exported all over the world.

Rubber Natural **rubber** is made from the latex sap of trees or vines. It softens when warm and hardens when cold. In 1839, Charles Goodyear developed a process known as vulcanization that eliminated these problems and helped create the modern rubber industry. Rubber was used to produce tires for bicycles (and eventually automobiles), hoses, gaskets, waterproof clothing, and shoe soles, among other items.

Rubber trees are native to the Amazon rainforest of South America, where they grew wild but widely dispersed. Latex could also be extracted from vines native to Central Africa, though they were destroyed in the process. Each source provided about half the world's rubber supply, but they soon were inadequate to meet the demand as rubber became an important industrial material. In both sources, "rubber barons" forced indigenous people into virtual slavery. In some cases, companies mutilated or killed workers who failed to meet their quotas.

In 1876, the British India Office obtained rubber tree seeds from Brazil. After being propagated in England, the seedlings were sent to Ceylon (Sri Lanka) and Singapore. Before long, thousands of acres of forest were cleared to make room for rubber plantations in Malaya, Indochina, the Dutch East Indies, and elsewhere in Southeast Asia.

Palm Oil The machinery in Europe's factories required constant lubrication to keep it working, creating a demand for **palm oil**, which was also used for candle making. The oil palm originated in West Africa, where it was used as a staple food product for 5,000 years. Palm oil was so valued that it was used in place of money in many African cultures. Palm oil became an important cash crop in West Africa, where prisoners of tribal war were often enslaved to help with the palm oil crops. European colonists established oil palm plantations in Malaya and the Dutch East Indies.

Ivory The tusks of elephants provide the product **ivory**. Most of the ivory trade was with Africa, since both male and female African elephants have large tusks, which average six feet in length. Ivory was prized for its beauty and durability. It was used primarily for piano keys, billiard balls, knife handles, and ornamental carvings. In the mid-19th century, the European scramble for ivory preceded the scramble for colonies. The Ivory Coast (Côte d'Ivoire) got its name from the fact that the French originally set up trading posts there for the acquisition of ivory and the purchase of enslaved people.

Minerals Some of the most valuable products were mineral ores used in manufacturing. They came from around the world:

- Mexico produced silver.
- Chile produced **copper**, which was used for telegraph cables and electrical power lines.
- Northern Rhodesia (now Zambia) and the Belgian Congo produced copper.
- Bolivia, Nigeria, Malaya, and the Dutch East Indies produced **tin**, which helped meet the growing demand for food products in tin cans.
- Australia and South Africa, as well as parts of West Africa and Alaska, produced large deposits of **gold**.

Diamonds Because of his frail health, Cecil Rhodes was sent to South Africa in 1870 to join a brother on a cotton farm. In 1871 the brothers joined the **diamond** rush and went to Kimberley, the center of mining activity. After completing a degree at Oxford University, Rhodes acquired some of the De Beers mining claims and formed the **De Beers Mining Company** in 1880. By 1891, De Beers accounted for 90 percent of the world's diamond production. Rhodes also had a large stake in the world's largest gold fields, which were discovered in 1886 on South Africa's Witwatersrand. (Connect: Analyze Africa's changes in trade from the trans-Saharan trade, including the effects of the slave trade, through the industrial era. See Topics 2.4 and 4.4.)

By the age of 29, when Rhodes was elected to the Cape Parliament, he was the most powerful man in Southern Africa. He sought to expand to the north, into Bechuanaland (Botswana) and what became known as Rhodesia and is now Zimbabwe and Zambia, with the dream of building a railroad from Cape Town to Cairo—and claiming all the land along the route for the British Empire. In 1890, Rhodes became the prime minister of the Cape Colony where his racist policies paved the way for the **apartheid**, or racial segregation, that plagued South Africa during the 20th century.

Global Consequences

Industrialization was accompanied by the need to find raw materials that could be turned into finished products to be sold globally—often bought with the profits from raw materials. As urban populations grew, the demand for food was increasingly met by imports made possible by new technology such as refrigeration. As the industrialized nations grew wealthier, stock exchanges developed, allowing more people to invest their capital, and the need to protect global markets and investments grew rapidly.

Consequences of Commercial Extraction Farmers were allowed to raise only cash crops, such as sugar, cocoa, or groundnuts, at the expense of other agricultural products. This use of land led to **monocultures,** or a lack of agricultural diversity, particularly in developing nations. Large areas were often cleared of forests to make room for farming, which took its toll on both biodiversity and the climate. Cash crops such as cotton rapidly depleted the soul's natural fertility. Moreover, crop diseases and pests spread more easily when there was only one crop planted in an area.

Today, many former colonies have been unable to rediversify their land use because the development of monocultures has badly damaged croplands. As a result, they often must import basic agricultural goods in order to feed their people.

KEY TERMS BY THEME		
ENVIRONMENT: Natural Resources guano cotton rubber palm oil ivory copper tin gold diamond	**ECONOMICS:** People Cecil Rhodes **ECONOMICS:** Companies De Beers Mining Company **ECONOMICS:** Activities cash crops export economies monocultures	**TECHNOLOGY:** Inventions railroads steamships telegraph **SOCIETY:** Hierarchy apartheid

Questions 1 to 3 refer to the passage below.

"Fermented drinks such as alcohol also have the benefits of killing parasites and bringing liquid calories to the diet, but by the start of the 18th century beer production was eating up nearly half of the wheat harvest in Britain. There was no possible way for Britain's domestic agriculture to feed the rapidly expanding population and keep them in beer, too. There just wasn't enough farmland for every new mouth in the industrial era. Calories had to come from an outside source, one beyond the boundaries of the British Isles, from the wider shores of the empire. The pursuit of food has always shaped the development of society, and in the days of the Victorian empire, the very start of our modern industrialized global food-chain, tea with milk and sugar became the answer to Britain's growing need for cheap nutrition."

Sarah Rose, *For All the Tea in China: Espionage, Empire and the Secret Formula for the World's Favourite [Favorite] Drink*, 2009

1. The example in the passage highlights which common imperial pattern?
   (A) The importation of cash crops from the colonies
   (B) The development of new transportation technologies
   (C) The export of foodstuffs to colonial holdings
   (D) The transfer of industrial developments to colonies

2. How does Britain's answer to the "growing need for cheap nutrition" relate to the Western Hemisphere?
   (A) The Americas provided dairy products for Britain.
   (B) The Americas provided tea for Britain.
   (C) The Americas provided indentured servants for Britain.
   (D) The Americas provided sugar for Britain.

3. What impact did the Industrial Revolution have upon nonindustrial countries?
   (A) They became export countries.
   (B) The Industrial Revolution spread to these areas.
   (C) The colonial economy became self-sufficient.
   (D) Profits earned by these nonindustrial countries were used to create a growing middle class.

1. **Use the passage below to answer all parts of the question that follows.**

"Around the middle of the 19th century, Uruguay was dominated by the latifundium [a large landed estate or ranch, typically worked by enslaved people], with its ill-defined boundaries and enormous herds of native cattle, from which only the hides were exported to Great Britain and part of the meat, as jerky, to Brazil and Cuba. There was a shifting rural population that worked on the large estates and lived largely on the parts of beef carcasses that could not be marketed abroad. Often the landowners were also the caudillos [military or political leaders] of the Blanco or Colorado political parties, the protagonists of civil wars that a weak government was unable to prevent (Barrán and Nahum, 1984, 655). This picture still holds, even if it has been excessively stylized, neglecting the importance of subsistence [the act of supporting oneself] or domestic-market oriented peasant production."

Luis Bértola, *An Overview of the Economic History of Uruguay since the 1870s*, 2008

(A) Identify ONE way in which Uruguay's resource export economy was similar to the economy in Argentina.

(B) Explain ONE way in which the outcomes described by Bértola were caused by developments in Uruguay in the period 1750–1900.

(C) Explain ONE historical situation in the period 1750–1900, other than the one illustrated in the passage, in which resource export economies impacted the political structures of other states.

2. **Answer all parts of the question that follows.**

(A) Identify ONE way that urbanization affected the growth of export economies in the period 1750–1900.

(B) Explain ONE way in which the profits from raw materials affected global economies in the period 1750–1900.

(C) Explain ONE way in which commercial extraction of raw materials in Egypt was different from the commercial extraction of raw materials in the Amazon in the period 1750–1900.

THINK AS A HISTORIAN: EXPLAIN PURPOSE AND AUDIENCE OF SOURCES

Secondary sources, like primary sources, are created for a variety of purposes and audiences. Being able to explain those purposes and audiences is a key step in understanding the usefulness and reliability of a source. For example, some books are written for a popular audience to entertain as well as inform; some are written for a scholarly audience to further understanding in an academic discipline; some are written as propaganda to sway people's opinions.

Reread the two sources associated with the questions on pages 404 and 405. Based on the excerpts and information provided, what do you think each source's purpose and audience are? Give reasons for your answer based on details from the excerpts. Then research the works and their authors to confirm your answers.

REFLECT ON THE TOPIC ESSENTIAL QUESTION

1. In one to three paragraphs, explain how environmental factors contributed to the global economy between 1750 and 1900.

Source: Getty Images
Cattle in Uruguay

Economic Imperialism

Let us ask, where is your conscience? I have heard that the smoking of opium is very strictly forbidden by your country; that is because the harm caused by opium is clearly understood. Since it is not permitted to do harm to your own country, then even less should you let it be passed on to the harm of other countries – how much less to China!

—Lin Zexu, Chinese Commissioner in Canton,
letter to British Queen Victoria, January 15, 1840

Essential Question: What economic factors contributed to the imperialism in the global economy between 1750 and 1900?

For centuries, India was the world's leading supplier of finished cotton textiles. By the late 18th century, the Industrial Revolution and a new source of cotton from America had allowed Britain to flood the market with inexpensive textiles, pushing independent Indian textile artisans out of business. By the late 19th century, India was producing only raw cotton for Britain, not cotton textiles. After Britain's textile factories processed India's cotton, the colonial government sold some of its factory-made or "finished" textiles back to the Indian subcontinent at inflated prices.

Another critical raw material for Britain was the drug opium. The poppies from which it is obtained grew easily on South Asia's fertile lands, and selling it to the Chinese became very profitable for Britain. The Chinese, as Lin Zexu expressed in the letter to Queen Victoria, objected to the export of opium to their country, and the conflict resulted in the first Opium War. The Chinese paid a heavy price for their attempt to curtail the opium trade and ended up losing much trading independence.

The Rise of Economic Imperialism

The agricultural influence and power of raw materials shifted away from Asia and Latin America to industrialized states such as Britain, the United States, France, Japan, and Germany between the late 19th century and the beginning of the 20th century. **Economic imperialism**, a situation in which foreign business interests have great economic power or influence, developed as businesses took advantage of natural resources beyond their borders. People, raw materials, and refined materials were the main resources exploited. Cash crops and mineral resources were produced on a large scale. As in the colonial era of the 15th to the 18th centuries, colonial powers served their own economic interests by turning colonies into export economies that produced goods not for domestic use but to be sent to colonial powers to sell for profit.

Economic Imperialism in Asia

England's defeat of the Spanish Armada in 1588 created an opening for the British and Dutch to take over the spice trade in Asia from the Spanish and Portuguese, who formerly had a monopoly on it.

India The English **East India Company** formed in 1600 to engage in the lucrative spice trade. However, the company soon ran into opposition from the Dutch. By the mid-1600s cotton and silk textiles from India had replaced spices as the East India Company's major import, and by the 1700s the company dominated the world textile trade. Indian weavers learned to create fabrics with patterns that would appeal to European tastes. With the Industrial Revolution, India began supplying raw cotton to the textile mills of Britain, and the demand for finished Indian textiles decreased.

Dutch East Indies The **Dutch East India Company** had a monopoly on trade with the Dutch East Indies in present-day Indonesia, where the **Spice Islands** were located. By the second half of the 18th century, it had switched its focus from shipping to agricultural production. The Dutch government revoked the company's charter in 1799 and took direct control of the Dutch East Indies. In 1830, the Dutch government introduced the **Culture System**, which forced farmers to choose between growing cash crops for export or performing **corvée labor**, compulsory unpaid work. Under this system, villagers either had to set aside one-fifth of their rice fields for such export crops as sugar, coffee, or indigo, or work in a government field for 66 days if they had no land. If the crops failed, the villagers were held responsible for the loss. The practice was finally abolished in 1870.

China Chinese goods such as porcelain, silk, and tea were in great demand in Great Britain. However, the Chinese were not interested in British goods, and in this trade imbalance, British silver reserves became very low. To make up for this shortfall, the East India Company began forcing farmers in India to grow **opium**, an addictive drug that also relieves pain and reduces stress. The company then sold it for silver in China, where millions of people became addicted to the illegal drug. The company then used its profits to buy tea and other goods.

The Chinese emperor criminalized the use of opium in 1729. However, the ban had little effect. The Chinese objection to the importation of this drug led to the first **Opium War** (1839–1842). The Chinese government seized the British opium warehoused in the port of Canton (Guangzhou). War broke out when British warships destroyed a Chinese blockade keeping ships from Canton, the only port China allowed to trade with foreigners. The British attacked and occupied Canton and engaged in several other successful battles, finally capturing Nanking (Nanjing).

The conflict between Britain and China revealed the fate of nonindustrialized nations. China had not anticipated the power that industrialized nations were gaining or the shift in the balance of power that was taking place. Industrialized nations in Europe would begin to dominate and defeat states that lacked the military technology needed to stand against British steamships and weaponry.

The resulting **Treaty of Nanking** required China to open up four additional ports to foreigners, cede the island of Hong Kong to Britain, and pay damages. It also forced the Chinese to allow free trade, which the British took to include trade in opium.

Neither Britain nor China was completely satisfied with the Treaty of Nanking. The British wanted the use of opium legalized, while the Chinese were unhappy about the concessions they had been forced to make. Hostilities erupted in October 1856 after Chinese officers boarded a British trading ship, searched it, lowered the flag, and arrested some Chinese sailors. The French joined the British in what came to be known as the second Opium War (1856–1860). The Treaty of Tientsin (Tianjin) following that war allowed foreign envoys to reside in Beijing, opened several new ports to Western trade and residence, and allowed freedom of movement for Christian missionaries. After additional negotiations, opium was legalized, and China ceded to Britain the southern portion of Kowloon Peninsula, which was adjacent to Hong Kong. (Connect: Compare how Western states and the Qing Dynasty treated the Chinese population. See Topic 4.7.)

Spheres of Influence Japan, France, Germany, Russia, and the United States sought the same trading privileges that Britain attained after winning the Opium Wars. By the end of the century, these nations began forcing China to give them exclusive trading rights in areas known as **spheres of influence**. It was at this time that the Open Door policy, proposed by the United States, allowed for a system of trade in China to be open to all countries equally in order to keep any one power from total control of China. (See the map on the next page.)

Economic Imperialism in Africa

Before colonization, most farming in Africa was to raise food crops. After colonization, land that had been devoted to growing food was converted to cash crop production to provide raw materials for European industries and goods for European markets. In exchange, the Africans received cotton textiles, canned food, and alcoholic beverages. This unequal trade structure made the colonies economically dependent on the imperial powers.

Reliance on a single **cash crop,** one grown to be sold, in a country or region left many Africans vulnerable during periods of drought, economic decline, or falling world prices. Food production declined as farmers chose to plant cash crops such as cotton, which would increase the value of their land. Food shortages, even famines, could arise because the most arable land was devoted to growing crops for export.

SPHERES OF COLONIAL INFLUENCE IN ASIA

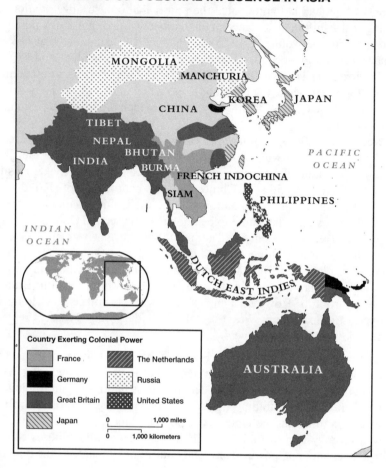

Egypt had embraced cotton as a cash crop before the American Civil War and more than doubled production between 1861 and 1863. By the end of the century, cotton accounted for 93 percent of Egypt's exports. It was also the leading cash crop in **Sudan**, where the Plantation Syndicate, a group of British weaving companies, dictated land use to farmers. When the British colonized **Uganda**, they encouraged cotton as a cash crop there as well, and it soon replaced enslaved people and ivory as the chief export.

In **Kenya**, most native peoples were herders. Groups like the Kikuyu were moved to reserves with poor soil and bad climates. In the fertile Rift Valley, the colonial government gave the land to white settlers, forcing most Africans to relocate. Those who remained were forced to provide cheap labor for white farmers. African farmers were also forbidden to participate in export of any cash crops, and prohibited from growing some cash crops, such as coffee and tea.

After missionaries introduced it to the area in the 1880s, cocoa became the major cash crop on the **Gold Coast.** This region soon became the largest cocoa producer in the world. Cocoa was also an important cash crop in the Ivory Coast, Nigeria, and the Portuguese colonies of São Tomé and Angola.

Palm oil, palm kernels, and peanuts (also called groundnuts) were already major exports from West Africa before colonization. It was a valuable raw material because it was used as a lubricant for the machines of the industrial revolution in Europe.

Slavery in Africa Slavery was outlawed in British colonies in 1833, but it persisted elsewhere in Africa. The French army often used enslaved people as payment for its African soldiers, and French colonial administrators relied on enslaved people for many of their staff. It was not until 1912 that slave raiding and trading was suppressed in most of Africa. Slavery was not abolished by law throughout Africa until the first quarter of the 20th century.

Slave labor was used to produce many of the cash crops, especially oil palms (which produced palm kernels as well as palm oil), coffee, and cocoa. Some companies felt a moral responsibility to oppose the use of enslaved people in the production of the raw materials they used. For example, cash crop production in French-ruled colonies in Africa came about as a result of the end of the slave trade in the French Empire in 1848, along with the economic transformations brought about in France by the Industrial Revolution. Quaker-owned Cadbury's, for example, stopped buying slave-grown cocoa from Portuguese African colonies in 1908 after the slave trade was exposed.

Imperial Exploitation of Colonial Crops			
Commodity	**Imperial States**	**Origin of Commodity**	**Consequences**
Opium	Great Britain	Middle East or South Asia	• Opium addiction weakened many people in China. • China's economy weakened as massive amounts of silver went to Britain to pay for opium.
Cotton	Great Britain and other European countries	South Asia, Egypt, Sudan	• Cotton became central to the global slave economy. • Food supplies declined as farmers switched to growing only cotton.
Palm Oil	All industrialized countries in Europe	Sub-Saharan Africa	• European states created and controlled a monocrop economy, while local populations did not profit from the industry. • European powers met native resistance with brutal retaliation. • Imperial states created railroads and pathways to transport goods back to Europe.

Economic Imperialism in Latin America

In the second half of the 19th century, Latin America was subjected to imperialist aggression from both Europe and the United States. The "new imperialism" was concerned with a world capitalist economy as the industrialized nations of Europe and the United States sought raw materials, low-wage labor, and new markets for their goods. The emerging middle classes of Latin America were hungry for the latest European news and fashions.

Britain replaced Spain as Latin America's major trading partner. Companies based in Britain became the largest investors in Latin America, followed by ones from France and Germany. Europeans invested over $10 billion in Latin America between 1870 and 1919, primarily in Argentina, Mexico, and Brazil.

Role of the United States The United States was not yet as established a world power as Britain or France. However, the Second Industrial Revolution brought newfound prosperity to the young republic. U.S. corporate investments came later and were concentrated at first in Mexico and Cuba. These investments supported infrastructure and industry, especially railways, shipping, and the emerging banking and financial sectors. They also financed mining, guano, and meat processing and packing plants. In 1823, the Monroe Doctrine, the U.S. policy of opposing European colonialism in the Americas, told the world that Latin America was in the U.S. sphere of influence.

Investments in Argentina In the late 19th century, Britain had invested more in **Argentina** than in its own colony of India. As much as 10 percent of British foreign investment was in Argentina. British investors, entrepreneurs, and business leaders helped turn Argentina into the richest country in Latin America and one of the dozen richest in the world by the outbreak of World War I. They improved breeding stock and developed large-scale farming throughout the grassy plains, known as the **Pampas**. They also financed infrastructure and building projects, such as the railroad and telegraph systems. Because of its location on the shallow Rio de la Plata, Buenos Aires needed to build a new port to facilitate passenger service and the massive import and export of goods and services. The British financed and designed the new port, Puerto Madera.

Mining in Chile Spain colonized the region of present-day Chile between 1540 and 1818. Chile's economic development was initially dependent on the export of agricultural produce. The wealth of these raw materials brought dependency on Spain and tension among neighboring states. Copper would come to dominate Chile's exports. The mining sector in Chile would come to be one of the pillars of the Chilean economy, making up for more than one-third of government income.

Rubber Industry in Brazil Brazil once had a booming rubber industry. However, it declined after people began growing rubber in Malaysia at a lower cost. The shift of rubber production demonstrated how trade was organized to the advantage of companies based in Europe and the United States. Economic competition brought prosperity to some regions, but it was always fragile.

Central America and the Caribbean Foreign investors often used their governments to act as "strong men" to help them achieve the ends they wanted. The United Fruit Company was an American corporation that traded in tropical fruit, primarily bananas, grown on Latin American plantations and sold in the United States and in Europe. The United Fruit Company allied itself with large landowners to pressure governments to maintain conditions that would be favorable for the U.S. company. In a short story, the writer O. Henry coined the term **"banana republics"** to describe small Central American countries under the economic power of foreign-based corporations. The banana republics were politically unstable states with an economy dependent upon the exportation of a limited-resource product, such as bananas or minerals.

Patterns of imperial control over territories and transportation networks in Central America, the Caribbean coast of Colombia, Ecuador, and the West Indies continued as companies sought political dominance to gain monopolies over natural resources.

Economic Imperialism in Hawaii

The power of investments to transform and dominate small or weak states could also be seen in the Pacific islands. A group of American businesses and sugar planters in Hawaii went so far as to overthrow the constitutional monarchy in 1893, hoping that the islands would be annexed by the United States. In 1898, Hawaii became a territory of the United States.

Contextualizing Economic Imperialism

The Industrial Revolution developed the demand for raw materials and the technological ability through steamships, railroads, and military weapons to control other territories. These set the stage for economic imperialism.

KEY TERMS BY THEME		
GOVERNMENT: Colonial Holdings Spice Islands Egypt Sudan Uganda Kenya Gold Coast Argentina	**GOVERNMENT:** Treaties Treaty of Nanking **GOVERNMENT:** Wars and Rebellions Opium War **ENVIRONMENT:** Natural Resources opium Pampas	**ECONOMICS:** Companies East India Company Dutch East India Company **ECONOMICS:** Systems economic imperialism Culture System corvée labor spheres of influence cash crop banana republics

Questions 1 to 3 refer to the passage below.

"It appeared that the Laws of the Chinese Empire forbid the importation of opium into China and declare that all Opium which may be brought into the country is liable to confiscation. The Queen of England desires that Her Subjects who may go into foreign countries should obey the Laws of those countries; and Her Majesty does not wish to protect them from the just consequences of any offenses which they may commit in foreign parts. But, on the other hand, Her Majesty cannot permit that Her Subjects residing abroad should be treated with violence, and be exposed to insult and injustice; and when wrong is done to them, Her Majesty will see that they obtain redress."

British Foreign Secretary Lord Palmerston, letter to the
minister of the Emperor of China, 1840

1. What is the context of the letter above?
   (A) Britain is seeking to gain permission for Christian missionaries to enter China.
   (B) Britain is upset that the Chinese government has denied British ships free trade privileges.
   (C) Britain has just defeated the China in the first Opium War.
   (D) There is a civil war going on in China.

2. How did the Chinese government react to this letter?
   (A) They continued to prevent the importation of opium.
   (B) They acquiesced and agreed to all its demands.
   (C) They allowed only Dutch and French ships to enter their ports.
   (D) They declared all European ships quarantined.

3. Which of the following is an accurate reflection of the relationship between China and Britain at the time of the passage?
   (A) Britain knew China was a first-rate military power.
   (B) Britain viewed China as an economic super power.
   (C) China and England both sought the support of Japan.
   (D) China was unaware of Britain's military power.

1. **Use the passage below to answer all parts of the question that follows.**

"It was at this moment that the East India Company (EIC) ceased to be a conventional corporation, trading and silks and spices, and became something much more unusual. Within a few years, 250 company clerks backed by the military force of 20,000 locally recruited Indian soldiers had become the effective rulers of Bengal. An international corporation was transforming itself into an aggressive colonial power. . . .

We still talk about the British conquering India, but that phrase disguises a more sinister reality. It was not the British government that seized India at the end of the 18th century, but a dangerously unregulated private company headquartered in one small office, five windows wide, in London, and managed in India by an unstable sociopath—[Robert] Clive.

In many ways the EIC was a model of corporate efficiency: 100 years into its history, it had only 35 permanent employees in its head office. Nevertheless, that skeleton staff executed a corporate coup unparalleled in history: the military conquest, subjugation and plunder of vast tracts of southern Asia. It almost certainly remains the supreme act of corporate violence in world history. For all the power wielded today by the world's largest corporations—whether ExxonMobil, Walmart or Google—they are tame beasts compared with the ravaging territorial appetites of the [militarized] East India Company. Yet if history shows anything, it is that in the intimate dance between the power of the state and that of the corporation, while the latter can be regulated, it will use all the resources in its power to resist."

William Dalrymple, "The East India Company: The Original
Corporate Raiders," The Guardian, 2015

(A) Identify Dalrymple's main point about British presence in India in the period 1750–1900.

(B) Explain ONE way in which the East India Company affected global economies in the period 1750–1900.

(C) Explain what Dalrymple meant when he said that the East India Company committed a "supreme act of corporate violence" in India in the period 1750–1900.

2. **Answer the following questions.**

(A) Identify ONE way in which economic imperialism in the period 1750–1900 contributed to native resistance.

(B) Explain ONE way in which the relationship between companies and industrialized states impacted colonized states.

(C) Explain ONE reason for the shift in agricultural influence in Asia or Latin America to industrialized states.

The passage on the previous page provides an incisive description of the historical development of economic imperialism. Like all historical developments, it did not occur in a vacuum but rather developed within a broader historical context.

Explain how the development of economic imperialism is situated within a broader historical context. To do so, explain what conditions made it possible and what consequences it had.

REFLECT ON THE TOPIC ESSENTIAL QUESTION

1. In one to three paragraphs, describe the economic factors that contributed to imperialism in the global economy between 1750 and 1900.

Source: Wikimedia Commons

Portrait of an East India Company official, c. 1760–c.1764

Causes of Migration in an Interconnected World

I would advise all my friends to quit Ireland—the country most dear to me;
as long as they remain in it they will be in bondage and misery.

—An Irish settler who had lived in Wisconsin for a year,
in a letter to *The Times* of London, May 14, 1850

Essential Question: How did environmental and economic factors
contribute to patterns of migration between
1750 and 1900?

An increasingly global economy characterized by economic imperialism and the availability of different modes of transportation promoted a new era in migrations. As industrialization grew, populations moved to urban centers. Some workers who left their homelands, such as the Lebanese merchants in the United States or the Italian laborers in Argentina, could travel back to their native country for visits or to retire. Others, like the Irish settler quoted above, chose a permanent resettlement as relief from economic and political difficulties. Other movements of people were coerced. To meet the demands for workers, coerced and semi-coerced migration of people resulted in slavery, indentured servitude, and convict labor.

Migration through Labor Systems

The desire for low-wage labor was linked to the exploitation of natural resources in the system of economic imperialism. Even though slavery was gradually being abolished in imperial territories in the 19th century, the demand for the agricultural goods that enslaved workers had produced was still increasing. European states recruited new laborers to work on plantations, where they produced enormous wealth that fueled industrial growth at home:

- Indian laborers migrated to British colonies in the Caribbean, South Africa, East Africa, and Fiji.
- Chinese laborers migrated to California and British Malaya to build railroads and serve as farmhands, gardeners, and domestics.
- Japanese laborers migrated to Hawaii, Peru, and Cuba to work on sugar plantations.

Source: Hawaii State Archives

Chinese contract workers on a sugar plantation in 19th-century Hawaii.

Slavery Most countries in the Americas abolished the African slave trade in the early 19th century. **Slavery** itself continued, but without a fresh supply of enslaved people, the institution declined. Only in the United States did the number of enslaved people increase after the abolition of the slave trade. The last countries to abolish slavery in the Americas were the United States (1865), Cuba (1886), and Brazil (1888).

In spite of prohibitions, Africans continued enslaving one another well into the 20th century. As slavery was being abolished, labor was still desired, so imperial countries turned to other forms of coerced labor.

Indentured Servitude People who worked for a set number of years before becoming free were **indentured servants.** Many people became indentured as a way to pay for their transportation from a desperately poor community to one with more opportunity. Others were forced to do so to pay off a debt.

Some of these servants intended to work temporarily, earning money for their family, and then return home. But many stayed in their new country. As a result, indentured laborers brought their home cultures to their new lands and altered the demographics of these lands. For example, the cultures of Mauritius (in the Indian Ocean off Southeast Africa), Fiji (in the South Pacific), and Trinidad (in the Caribbean) added a strong Indian influence.

Asian Contract Laborers Many Chinese and Indian workers were an early substitute for the slave trade. They were forced or tricked into servitude. Britain first tried this form of labor after ending the slave trade in 1806. They imported 200 Chinese to Trinidad. Between 1847 and 1874, the British, French, Dutch, and Spanish had imported between 250,000 and 500,000 Chinese workers to their colonies in Southeast Asia, Africa, and the Caribbean. About 125,000 Chinese were sent to Cuba alone, where 80 percent worked the sugar plantations.

The life of Asian **contract laborers** was riddled with difficulty and unjust treatment. While they were not property, they were unskilled laborers or porters who were exploited as substitutes for slave labor, often working for subsistence wages. The media of the time brought the treatment of them to the attention of the public by criticizing the system as a new form of slavery. In 1855, Britain stopped its trade. In 1862 Congress banned the contract Asia labor trade in the United States, and in 1874, under international pressure, Portugal ended it. A treaty between China and Spain in 1877 terminated the contracts of Chinese workers still in Cuba.

British Penal Colonies In the late 1700s, Great Britain established a **penal colony** in Australia after losing its original one in Georgia as a result of the American Revolution. The British government shipped **convicts** from England, Scotland, and Ireland as well as British colonies such as India, to Australia. There, they performed hard labor and suffered harsh treatment. Actual imprisonment of the convicts was rare. Most performed labor for free settlers, worked for the government in record keeping, or worked on government projects such as road and railway building. The majority of convicts earned their freedom after a prescribed number of years of service.

Some people sent to penal colonies were never allowed to return to Great Britain. In addition, because transportation back home was expensive, the majority decided to stay in Australia. By 1850, the British government ended the transportation of convicts to Australia, largely because a stay in Australia was not considered much of a punishment.

Australia also attracted free settlers, especially after gold was discovered there in 1851. Some 50,000 Chinese came during this gold rush. Eventually Australia became one of Britain's most successful settler colonies.

French Penal Colonies The French also had penal colonies in Africa, New Caledonia, and French Guiana. New Caledonia, an island part of an archipelago in the southwest Pacific Ocean 750 miles from Australia, served as a penal colony from 1864 to 1897 for both convicts and political prisoners. The penal colony in French Guiana, which included Devil's Island, was notorious for its harsh treatment of convicts. Prisoners were underfed and forced to do hard labor. Although the French stopped transporting convicts in 1938, Devil's Island continued to hold prisoners until 1953. (Connect: Describe the changes in the supply and demand for labor from the Spanish encomienda system to that of European nations in the 19th century. See Topic 4.4.)

Migration in the Face of Challenges

The word **diaspora** is often applied to mass emigrations from a country or region that may take place over a period of many years. The African slave trade was responsible for one of the biggest diasporas in history, the involuntary emigration of millions of people between the 16th and 19th centuries. Most diasporas, however, were the result of poverty, political conditions, or famine.

India Poverty was the principal reason that drove Indians to leave the subcontinent. In 1833, the British began sending Indians to Mauritius as indentured laborers to replace enslaved workers on the sugar plantations. By 1878, Indians were working on plantations in British Guiana (Guyana), Dutch Guiana (Surinam), Natal (South Africa), Fiji, and British and French islands in the Caribbean. Most Indian laborers signed five-year contracts. Many renewed their contracts, and some decided to stay permanently, accepting a piece of land or a lump sum rather than their passage back to India. Over 1.5 million Indians were shipped to colonies in Asia, Africa, the Caribbean, and Oceania before Britain abolished the indenture system in 1916. Between 1880 and 1938, two systems recruited labor in Southeast Asia.

- The *kangani* (foreman who oversees workers) system in Ceylon and Malaya recruited from their own extended family.

- The *maistry* (supervisors) system in Burma recruited laborers within a structured system with defined hierarchies and sent them to plantations, usually in Southeast Asia. Conditions were highly exploitative.

China The Chinese diaspora did not begin in earnest until the middle of the 19th century, with the gold rushes in California, South Australia, and western Canada. However, most Chinese migrants were not engaged in mining. Despite prejudices toward Chinese immigrants, the Chinese were instrumental in the development of the U.S. Transcontinental Railroad. Some Chinese paid their own way, but many more left China as indentured laborers. The vast majority of Chinese emigrants were males who planned to return to China after their time abroad.

People left China for many reasons, some to escape poverty or famine, others for better opportunities. Beginning in the late 18th century, a population explosion in coastal cities and contacts through foreign trade led large numbers of Chinese to **emigrate** to Southeast Asia. Most of them were illiterate, landless peasants looking for opportunities abroad. However, most of the Chinese did not arrive in Southeast Asia until the mid-19th century, after the first Opium War made it easier for them to leave. Many people left as a result of the poverty and disorder brought on by the **Taiping Rebellion** (1850–1864). (See Topic 6.2.) After the middle of the century, most Chinese emigrated to the Americas, Europe, Australia, or New Zealand.

Ireland People emigrated from Ireland for many reasons. Some left for political reasons. Britain abolished the Irish Parliament in 1801 when Ireland became part of the United Kingdom of Great Britain and Ireland. Roman Catholics and Protestant dissenters faced religious discrimination from their British rulers. Evictions of tenant farmers increased after the 1846 repeal of the Corn Laws, which had regulated the import and export of grain. During the **Great Famine** (1845–1849) that destroyed the potato crop for four years, as many as 3 million people emigrated from Ireland. Most went to the United States, but many others went to England, Scotland, Canada, or Australia.

Emigration continued even after the famine ended; as many people left Ireland in the first four years after the famine was over as left during the height of the famine. The Irish had been going to Great Britain and the United States to build canals since the 18th century, and they continued to leave to help build railroads. During the 18th and 19th centuries, 300,000 free Irish emigrated to Australia, and 45,000 Irish convicts were transported there. In the second half of the 19th century, about 45,000 Irish went to Argentina, although only about 20,000 remained there. The rest moved on to the United States.

Source: Wikimedia Commons

This illustration by Irish artist James Mahoney (1810–1879) portrays people suffering in southwest Ireland during the Irish Great Famine.

Italy The first wave of Italian emigration began with the unification of Italy in 1861 and continued until 1900. More than 7 million people left Italy during those four decades. More than half of them went to other countries in Europe, with most of the rest going to North and South America, Australia, and New Zealand. The main reason for the Italian diaspora was poverty. Two-thirds of the emigrants during this period were men with traditional skills. Farmers had an increasingly difficult time making a living in harsh conditions, especially in a society where land was subdivided over generations. Some left for political reasons, while others left for economic reasons related to organized crime, especially in South Italy. Those who left often sent money back to family members, encouraging further emigration.

Migration to Settler Colonies

Large numbers of British citizens lived in all the colonies of the British Empire. Most who moved abroad permanently went to settler colonies such as Canada, South Africa, Australia, or New Zealand. Those who went to other colonies such as India, Malaya, or Kenya, usually did so with no intention of staying permanently. Many went as officers or soldiers in the British army, as government officials in the **Colonial Service**, or as managers for plantations or other colonial enterprises.

Technical Experts Engineers and geologists migrated to South Asia and Africa. One was Andrew Geddes Bain, who emigrated to Cape Town, South Africa, in 1816. Bain initially worked on eight major roads and passes but moved on to a career in geological studies. Bain prepared the first comprehensive geological map of South Africa in 1852. In 1854, he reported back to the British government about the copper mines in Namaqualand.

British engineers were so numerous in the colonies that they formed a type of diaspora. They spread Western science and technology through the world. However, as they did, they blended their knowledge with the experience of engineers from the colonial lands. Together, people from Europe and the colonies collaborated on both public works and private industrial projects.

Argentina During the 19th century, Argentina was part of Britain's "informal" empire. Britain invested more in Argentina than it did in India, the so-called "Jewel in the Crown" of the British Empire. Unlike most of the people who emigrated to make a new life for themselves, the British who settled in Argentina during the 19th century were not trying to escape poverty or persecution. They were primarily businessmen, traders, bankers, and engineers. They founded banks, developed the export trade in agricultural products, built railroads and other infrastructure, and imported luxuries that appealed to the growing Argentine middle class.

Japan Before 1868, Japan was closed to the rest of the world. However, by 1893, the Japanese government had decided that Japan should acquire an overseas empire and established the **Colonization Society**. Its aim was to export Japan's surplus population as well as commercial goods. In 1892 the

Society made an unsuccessful attempt to start an agricultural settler colony in Mexico. The failure of that attempt did not deter the society from sending 790 Japanese to Peru in 1899 for contract work. At the same time, many young Japanese men were leaving Japan to study in the United States, congregating mostly in such cities as San Francisco, Portland, and Seattle on the West Coast.

Tensions and anti-immigrant sentiment toward Japanese people intensified as immigrants assimilated to life in America. In 1907, the Gentlemen's Agreement between the United States and Japan was an informal agreement that the U.S. would not impose restrictions on Japanese immigration, and Japan would not allow further emigration to the U.S. The agreement was never ratified and was ultimately ended by the Immigration Act of 1924.

Migration, Transportation, and Urbanization

Improvements in transportation technology allowed some who migrated for work reasons to return to their home societies, either for a period of time or permanently. For example, in 1885, an agreement between the governments of Japan and Hawaii allowed Japanese laborers to go to Hawaii to work on the sugar plantations under three-year contracts. Approximately 29,000 Japanese went to Hawaii over the next nine years. During that time, thousands more Japanese went to other destinations in the South Pacific, including Australia, New Caledonia, and Fiji, under similar contracts. Most planned to return home after a few years.

Source: Wikimedia Commons

Italian immigrants were so important to the economic and cultural development of Argentina that the city of Mendoza erected a monument to them in what is known as the Plaza Italia.

Industrial workers from Italy had similar arrangements for working in Argentina and then returning home, though many Italians settled permanently in Argentina. Since most industry was located in urban areas, both internal and external migrants often settled in cities, which increased in size and influence around the globe.

Voluntary Migration Patterns in the 19th Century			
Years	Home Country	Destination	Reasons for Migrating
1880–1914	Italy	• Argentina	• Argentina had pro-immigration policies. • Argentina offered better wages.
1868–1907	Japan	•Hawaii	• Japanese sought financial opportunities on sugar cane and pineapple plantations.
1850–1880	China	• United States	• The Chinese first sought work in gold mines, then agricultural and factory work. • There were opportunities to work on Transcontinental Railroad.
1820–1910	Ireland	• United States	• Irish were escaping the Irish Great Famine. • Irish sought labor opportunities in canal building, lumbering, and civil construction.
Coerced or Semi-Coerced Migration Patterns in the 19th Century			
1500s–1800s	Africa	• Americas • Europe	• Forced slavery administered through triangular trade system. • Europeans needed enslaved workers on plantations along the southern coast, in the Caribbean, and elsewhere, cultivating cash crops like cotton, rice, and tobacco.
1788–1868	Britain (convicts)	• Australia	• Britain transported convicts to penal colonies.
1806–1877s	China and India	•Caribbean • Southeast Asia • Africa • Americas	• The slave trade had been abolished (1806). • The contract labor system was instituted to replace slavery.
1834–1916	India (indentured servants)	• Africa • Asia • Caribbean region	• Slavery was abolished in the British Empire (1833). • The indentured servant system was instituted to replace slavery.

KEY TERMS BY THEME

GOVERNMENT: Systems
Colonial Service

GOVERNMENT: Wars and
    Rebellions
Taiping Rebellion

ECONOMICS: Systems
slavery
indentured servants
contract laborers
Colonization Society

SOCIETY: Organization
penal colony
convicts

SOCIETY: Movement
diaspora
emigrate
Great Famine

Source: archive.org
A Chinese laborer in the Philippines, 1899

Questions 1 to 3 refer to the map below.

MOVEMENTS OF FREE AND ENSLAVED PEOPLE, 1750–1900

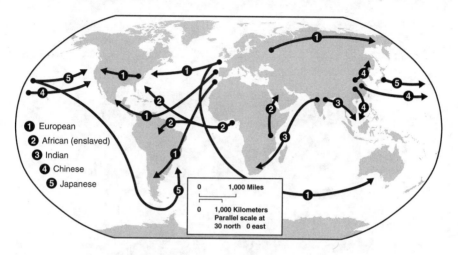

1. Which movement included forced migrants before about 1850?

   (A) 1: British to Australia

   (B) 3: Indians to Southeast Asia

   (C) 4: Chinese to Southeast Asia

   (D) 5: Japanese to North America

2. Indian migrations to places such as Mauritius (Migration 3) and islands in the Caribbean led most directly to which long-term effect?

   (A) The abolition movement and eventual ending of the slave trade network across the Atlantic Ocean

   (B) The infusion of Indian cultural expressions, such as methods of food preparation, into local traditions

   (C) The development of nationalism and movements for self-determination in places that received the Indian immigrants

   (D) The intensification of Indian efforts to create multinational corporations by establishing sugar plantations in these areas

3. Which best describes a global change between 1750 and 1900 that resulted from the movements shown on the map?

(A) Many countries became more ethnically diverse.

(B) The percentage of people who died in the same country where they were born increased.

(C) The influence of Europeans overseas decreased.

(D) The percentage of people enslaved increased.

SHORT-ANSWER QUESTIONS

1. Use the passage below to answer all parts of the question that follows.

"Due to its structural weakness, the local silk industry could not withstand foreign competition from the silk of Japan and China and later on the introduction of artificial fabrics. It is also argued by many historians that the decision of many Christians to emigrate from the mountain was also stirred by increasing urbanization, the emergence of a middle class, and the fear of conscription in the Ottoman army.

Commenting on the post-1860 generation of peasants, Akram Khater [wrote]:

'Having grown in relative prosperity, these peasants were facing limitations that threatened to send them economically a few steps backward. At the end of the 1880s silk was no longer the golden crop it had been ten or twenty years before. At the same time, rising land prices and shrinking inheritance combined to make the economic future bleak. So it was that many peasants arrived at the year 1887 with a sense of malaise [uneasiness]. They did not have much land, and what little they had did not promise to make them a 'good' living. . . . Although some villagers did migrate seasonally to neighboring cities (like Aleppo and Bursa), these areas provided limited opportunities as they were experiencing their own economic crises. . . . These drawbacks made a number of peasants look for other ways out of their dilemma—namely, how to make enough money quickly to guarantee their status as landowners and not slip back into the ranks of the landless laborers. About the only option that appeared on the economic horizons was emigration.' "

Paul Tabar, *Immigration and Human Development:*
Evidence from Lebanon, 2009

(A) Identify ONE way that interregional trade affected Lebanese emigrants in the period 1750–1900.

(B) Explain Akram Khater's argument about Lebanese emigrants.

(C) Explain ONE way in which urbanization influenced Lebanese migration in the period 1750–1900.

2. **Answer all parts of the question that follows.**

(A) Identify ONE historical situation in the period 1750–1900 in which individuals freely chose to migrate.

(B) Explain ONE historical situation in the period 1750–1900 in which individuals were coerced or semi-coerced to migrate.

(C) Explain ONE way in which a global capitalist economy affected social structures in the period 1750–1900.

 THINK AS A HISTORIAN: CONNECT MIGRATION TO OTHER DEVELOPMENTS

The Industrial Revolution was the foundation for the rapid and profound changes experienced around the world from 1750 to 1900. It spawned a number of historical developments that in turn influenced later developments. In particular, the Industrial Revolution led to:

- improvements in transportation
- fundamental changes in the way goods were produced
- the move from mercantilism to capitalism
- imperialism
- changes in land used for agricultural purposes

Choose three of the developments above and explain the connection between them and the migration of free and enslaved or coerced people between 1750 and 1900.

REFLECT ON THE TOPIC ESSENTIAL QUESTION

1. In one to three paragraphs, explain how environmental and economic factors contributed to patterns of migration between 1750 and 1900.

6.7

Effects of Migration

It shall not be lawful for any Chinese laborer to come, or having so come after the expiration of said ninety days to remain within the United States.

—Chinese Exclusion Act of 1882

Essential Question: How and why did patterns of migration affect society between 1750 and 1900?

Migration in the 19th century—whether undertaken freely to escape poverty or seek opportunity or coerced as part of an imperialist labor system—led to demographic changes with long-lasting results. Laborers tended to be male and from particular ethnic groups, such as the Indian indentured servants brought to work on sugar plantations in the Caribbean or the Chinese laborers recruited to complete the transcontinental railroad in the United States. These migrants often formed ethnic enclaves and created cultural groups that maintained elements of their native culture and religion while absorbing the influences of their new locations. For example, many Indians in Trinidad and Tobago practiced Hinduism and contributed to Caribbean musical traditions. These migrants also left behind women who sometimes took on the roles formerly filled by men and thus brought about change in migrants' home societies.

Migrant groups often experienced racial and ethnic prejudice. The Chinese Exclusion Act, noted above, was the first major U.S. federal legislation that specifically suspended immigration of a specific ethnic group.

Changes in Home Societies

The experiences of migrants and the families they left behind varied widely depending on the norms of their home cultures. Migrant laborers were more often male than female, so in some places their migration—whether internal or external—brought a shift in demographics and gender roles in the societies they left. In some societies, males waited to emigrate until a male relative was available to live with and help support the women and children who did not emigrate with the males. In these places, women's roles were much the same as before their husbands left. However, in other places, women gained some autonomy and authority as they took on responsibilities once filled by their husbands and took a meaningful place in society outside the bounds of family responsibilities. If they later followed their husbands to another country, they often participated more fully, though far from equally, in family decision-making than women who had not been on their own. If their husbands returned, women who had taken up their husbands' responsibilities sometimes continued to play a role outside of domestic life, while those who had been put in the care of male relatives remained in traditional gender roles.

Most male migrants sent **remittances**, funds from their foreign earnings, back home. If the remittance were large enough, women often reduced their hours working outside the home and spent more time with family responsibilities while also exercising considerable decision-making power over how the money was spent. In some places, the receipt of remittances correlates to girls' longer school attendance; in other places boys seem to have been the greater beneficiaries of remittance-supported education.

Effects of Migration on Receiving Societies

Immigrants were interested in a new economic start but intent on carrying with them their own traditions and culture. **Ethnic enclaves**, clusters or neighborhoods of people from the same foreign country, formed in many major cities of the world. In these areas inhabitants spoke the language of their home country, ate the foods they were familiar with from home, and pursued a way of life similar to that they had known in their home countries. At the same time, they influenced the culture of their new homes which absorbed some of the migrants' cultural traditions.

Chinese Enclaves

Many Chinese emigrated in search of work during the latter half of the 19th century—some to work on sugar plantations or for other agricultural endeavors, others to work in industry and transportation. Together, they spread Chinese culture around the world.

Southeast Asia The Chinese who migrated to Southeast Asia thrived under colonial rule. In Indochina, the French encouraged them to engage in commerce. In Malaya, they managed opium farms and controlled opium distribution for the British. In the Dutch East Indies, some Chinese held posts with the colonial government. As time went on, many Chinese throughout the region became business owners and traders, often founding family businesses. Some Chinese acquired great wealth as moneylenders or through international trade. By the end of the 19th century, the Chinese controlled trade throughout Southeast Asia and were a significant presence in the region.

The Americas Chinese immigrants first came to the United States in large numbers during the height of the California **gold rush**. Many worked in mines, but others found work on farms or in San Francisco's garment industry. Chinese laborers became indispensable during the construction of the first transcontinental railroad.

Source: Mitchell Library, State Library of New South Wales

William A. Sac's Chinese Boarding House in the gold mining town of Gulgong, New South Wales, 1871–1875.

Between 1847 and 1874, some 225,000 Chinese laborers were sent to Cuba and Peru on eight-year contracts. Almost all of them were male, and 80 percent of them were sent to work on sugar plantations alongside enslaved Africans in Cuba and replacing enlaved workers in Peru, where slavery had been abolished. Other Chinese in Cuba were employed as servants, in cigarette factories, and in public works projects. Several thousand contract laborers in Peru helped build the Andean railroad and worked in the guano mines. In the 1870s, some Chinese built settlements in the Peruvian Amazon, where they were active as merchants and grew rice, beans, sugar, and other crops.

In each area they lived, Chinese immigrants left their cultural stamp. Some Peruvian cuisine is a fusion of Chinese foods and ingredients and cooking styles of Peru. As in other areas, Chinese immigrants sometimes married local people and thus contributed to the multicultural diversity of populations.

Indian Enclaves

The British Empire abolished slavery in 1833. However, it was replaced with a system that was little better, indentured servitude. Indians were among the first indentured servants sent to work in British colonies.

Indians in Africa Many Indians went to **Mauritius,** islands off the southeast coast of Africa, and **Natal**, a colony that is today part of South Africa, as indentured servants on sugar plantations. In Natal and British East Africa, they built railways. Nearly 32,000 indentured Indian workers went to Kenya to work on railroad construction between 1886 and 1901, but only about 7,000 chose to stay. Today, Indians continue to make up significant parts of the population of these regions.

Both Hindus and Muslims emigrated from India to South Africa. The Hindus brought with them their caste system and the social laws that stem from it, but they soon abandoned the caste system. In contrast, many kept up Hindu traditions and had alters in their homes to honor deities.

The Hindu and Muslim Indian population of South Africa was divided by class, language, and religion. However, Indians in South Africa shared the injustice of discrimination, which became central to the work of a young Indian named **Mohandas Gandhi**. He arrived in Pretoria, South Africa, in 1893, where he intended to practice law. After suffering repeatedly from racial discrimination, Gandhi became an activist. He founded the **Natal Indian Congress** and worked to expose to the world the rampant discrimination against Indians in South Africa. In 1914 Gandhi returned to India, where he became a leader in the Indian nationalist movement against British rule.

Indians in Southeast Asia Between 1834 and 1937 India was the major source of labor for the British Southeast Asian colonies of Ceylon, Burma, and Malaya. Many Indians went to Malaya as indentured laborers. Indentured servitude was eventually replaced by the **kangani system**, under which entire families were recruited to work on tea, coffee, and rubber plantations in Ceylon, Burma, and Malaya. Their lives were less restricted than those of indentured laborers, and they had the advantage of having their families with them. It is estimated that about 6 million Indians migrated to Southeast Asia before the kangani system was abolished. Because Southeast Asia was relatively close, Indian workers there often kept close ties with India.

Indian traders settled in many countries where there were indentured laborers. They also looked for business opportunities throughout the British Empire, such as British East Africa.

Indians in the Caribbean Region So many Indians were sent to work on the sugar plantations in and around the Caribbean that today they comprise the largest ethnic group in **Guyana** and **Trinidad and Tobago**, and the second largest group in Suriname, Jamaica, Grenada, Saint Vincent and the Grenadines, Saint Lucia, Martinique and Guadeloupe. In many of the other Caribbean nations Indians constitute a sizable proportion of the population. In addition, they have blended ethnically with migrants from other parts of the world, creating a unique culture, affecting national cuisines, film, and music. Many of the countries in the region celebrate the arrival of the Indians with annual holidays or festivals.

Irish Enclaves in North America

Before the American Revolution, most Irish who came to North America were Protestant descendants of Scots who had previously migrated to Ireland. They are often referred to as **Scots-Irish**. Most came as indentured servants. Those who paid their own passage often went west to the frontier.

After the American Revolution, most new Irish immigrants who came to the United States settled in northern cities. Many others went to British North America (Canada), where they were able to get cheap land grants. By the 1830s, most new Irish immigrants were poorer than earlier settlers, and Catholic. Most of those who settled in cities worked in factories. Many of the men who came to the United States helped construct the **canal system**. In Canada as well as the United States, many Irish farmed. Most Irish immigrants were able to create decent lives for themselves and their children.

Half of the 3 million Irish who fled Ireland during the Great Famine came to North America. Most of this huge wave of Irish immigrants faced many hardships, not the least of them anti-immigrant nativist and anti-Catholic sentiments in the United States. Nevertheless, immigration from Ireland continued strong after the Great Famine ended until the 1880s, when it gradually slowed. Many of these new immigrants were single women who came to the United States looking for work and husbands. More than half became domestic servants. Many of the men who came during this period were unskilled laborers.

Wherever they settled, the Irish in the United States spread their culture—their lively dance music and holiday traditions such as the celebration of St. Patrick's Day. They also had a strong influence on the conditions of laborers through their efforts at promoting labor unions, and their great numbers ensured the spread of Catholicism in the United States.

Second-generation Irish were often either **white-collar** or skilled **blue-collar** workers. Many became "stars" of the new **popular culture** that was taking root at the end of the century as boxers, baseball players, and vaudeville performers. Many second-and third-generation Irish, such as the Fitzgeralds and the Kennedys, became very wealthy and powerful.

Italians in Argentina

During the 18th and 19th centuries only the United States surpassed **Argentina** in the number of immigrants it attracted. The 1853 Argentine Constitution not only encouraged European immigration, but it also guaranteed to foreigners the same civil rights enjoyed by Argentine citizens.

In the late 19th and early 20th centuries, Italians made up almost half of the European immigrants to Argentina. Today people of Italian descent make up more than 55 percent of the Argentine population. As a result, Italians have had an enormous influence on all aspects of Argentine culture and language. Argentine Spanish has absorbed many Italian words, and Italian is still widely spoken in Buenos Aires.

Argentina was underpopulated and had an enormous amount of fertile land, which appealed to Italian immigrants. Most of them were farmers, artisans, and day laborers. Wages in Argentina were much higher than in Italy. Agricultural workers, for example, could earn five to ten times as much in Argentina as in Italy. In addition, the cost of living, even in Buenos Aires, was much lower than that of many rural Italian provinces. Both of these factors allowed most immigrants to raise their standard of living greatly in a very short time. By 1909, Italian immigrants owned nearly 40 percent of Buenos Aires' commercial establishments.

Prejudice and Regulation of Immigration

In the United States and Australia, native-born residents resented immigrants from China who were willing to work for lower wages. In response to these resentments, governments institutionalized discrimination against the Chinese.

Regulation in the United States

Nativists were powerful enough in California that a revised constitution ratified in 1879 included several provisions that targeted people from China:

- It prohibited the state, counties, municipalities, and public works from hiring Chinese workers.
- It prevented individuals from China, and any others who were not considered white, from becoming citizens on the grounds that they were "dangerous to the well-being of the State."
- It encouraged cities and towns either to remove Chinese residents from within their limits or to segregate them in certain areas.

With many thousands of Chinese living in the United States by 1882, Congress banned further Chinese immigration by passage of the **Chinese Exclusion Act**. Initially limited to a ten year period, the policy was extended periodically and made permanent in 1902. This act, which was finally repealed in 1943, showed the discrimination in the United States.

After the U.S. Congress excluded Chinese immigrants, some of them began to move to Mexico. Mexican President **Porfirio Díaz** promoted immigration as well as development, especially in the northern area bordering the United States. Rather than working as laborers in the mines or railroads, most worked as truck farmers, shopkeepers, or manufacturers.

White Australia

Before the Australian gold rushes of the 1850s and 1860s, most of the Chinese in Australia were indentured laborers, convicts, or traders. During the gold rushes, the Chinese population grew to around 50,000. In response to the influx of Chinese miners, the parliament of the province of Victoria passed a **Chinese Immigration Act** in 1855 that limited the number of Chinese who could come ashore from each ship. Many Chinese got around this law by landing instead in South Australia.

In December 1860, white miners in the goldfields of New South Wales attacked the area where Chinese miners were quartered, killing several and wounding many others. Several other attacks followed. One of the worst occurred on June 30, 1861, when several thousand white miners attacked the Chinese and plundered their dwellings.

In response to this violence, the New South Wales Legislative Council passed the **Chinese Immigration Regulation and Restriction Act** in November of that year. The act, eventually repealed in 1867, was an attempt to restrict the number of Chinese immigrants from entering the colony. By the end of the gold rushes in 1881, New South Wales passed the **Influx of Chinese Restriction Act**, which attempted to restrict Chinese immigration by means of an entrance tax.

After the gold rushes, the Chinese in Australia turned to other sources of income, such as gardening, trade, furniture making, fishing, and pearl diving. While **Chinatowns** (Chinese enclaves) developed in cities across Australia, the Chinese made their biggest economic contributions in the Northern Territory and north Queensland regions. Eventually, however, anti-Chinese sentiment grew. Because the Chinese artisans and laborers would work for less than white Australians, resentment increased. Anti-Chinese leagues also began to develop.

Although the number of Chinese in Australia was declining, they were becoming more concentrated in Melbourne and Sydney and thus more visible. After six separate British self-governing colonies in Australia united under a single centralized government in 1901, the new parliament took action to limit non-British immigration. The new attorney general stated that the government's policy was to preserve a "white Australia." The **White Australia Policy**, as it was known, remained in effect until the mid-1970s.(Connect: Compare the experiences in Australia of Chinese and Japanese immigrants. See Topic 6.6.)

KEY TERMS BY THEME

GOVERNMENT: Leaders	**GOVERNMENT: Laws**	**TECHNOLOGY:**
Mohandas Gandhi	Chinese Exclusion Act	Transportation
Porfirio Díaz	Chinese Immigration Act	canal system
	Chinese Immigration Regu-	
GOVERNMENT: Countries	lation and Restriction Act	**CULTURE: Classifications**
Trinidad and Tobago	Influx of Chinese Restric-	Scots-Irish
Mauritius	tion Act	popular culture
Natal	White Australia Policy	
Guyana		**SOCIETY: Organization**
Argentina	**ECONOMICS: Activities**	ethnic enclaves
	remittances	Natal Indian Congress
	gold rush	kangani system
	white-collar	Chinatowns
	blue-collar	

Questions 1 to 3 refer to the cartoon below.

1. An American who agreed with the above cartoon would most disagree with
   (A) the installation of the Statue of Liberty in New York Harbor
   (B) the elevation of the territory of Hawaii to statehood status
   (C) the admission of Puerto Rico as an American territory
   (D) the Chinese Exclusion Act

2. The point of view of this cartoonist was that he
   (A) recognized the contributions East Asians made to industrial development in the United States
   (B) was promoting the ideals of the nativist movement
   (C) saw East Asians as political radicals and criminals
   (D) wanted to discourage Irish and Italian immigration to the United States

3. By the end of the 19th century, the United States had passed laws that

(A) restricted most immigration from all countries

(B) prevented Chinese from entering the United States

(C) discriminated only against Japanese immigrants

(D) deported American citizens with Asian ancestry

SHORT-ANSWER QUESTIONS

1. Use the map below to answer all parts of the question that follows.

CHINESE EMIGRATION IN THE 19TH CENTURY

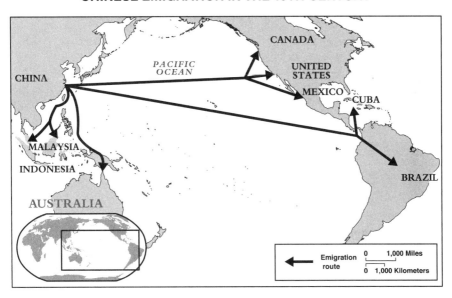

(A) Identify ONE cause of Chinese migration during the 19th century.

(B) Identify ONE effect of Chinese migration on a country other than China during the 19th century.

(C) Explain ONE effect of migration during the 19th century on the families of people who remained at home.

2. Answer all parts of the following question.

(A) Identify ONE way in which migrations in the period 1750–1900 impacted social structures.

(B) Explain ONE way in which migrants incorporated their cultures into new environments in the period 1750–1900.

(C) Explain ONE reason why states regulated the increased flow of immigrants in the period 1750–1900.

THINK AS A HISTORIAN: CONNECT MIGRATION AND
SYSTEMATIZED DISCRIMINATION

Review Topics 6.6 and 6.7, and on separate paper, complete a chart like the one below.

Causes of Emigration	Effects of Migration
	On Home Country
	On Receiving Country
	On Emigrants

Use the information in the chart to connect the historical develop-ment of emigration with the historical development of systematized discrimination (sanctioned by businesses or governments). Explain the connections regarding both causes and effects of emigration.

REFLECT ON THE TOPIC ESSENTIAL QUESTION

1. In one to three paragraphs, explain how and why patterns of migration affected society between 1750 and 1900.

6.8

Causation in the Imperial Age

The conquest of the earth, which mostly means the taking it away from those who have a different complexion or who have slightly flatter noses than ourselves, is not a pretty thing when you look into it too much.

—Joseph Conrad, *Heart of Darkness*, 1899

Essential Question: What was the relative significance of the effects of imperialism from 1750 to 1900?

Industrial capitalism caused significant developments between 1750 to 1900. The manufacturing capacity of industrialized nations caused an increase in the availability, affordability, and variety of both capital (financial assets) and consumer goods. However, this increased industrial capacity also led to an increased demand for natural resources—"the conquest of the earth"—to use in manufacturing these goods. Additionally, domestic markets soon became saturated, leading industrialized nations to seek out foreign markets to soak up the excess production. Competition for these markets increased among industrialized economies, especially those in the West. To reduce competition and increase profits, Western nations continued to look to empire-building, begun in the previous era, as a solution to these challenges.

Imperialism in the 19th century also caused significant effects, including increased migration, the rise of independence movements within the colonies, and increased political and economic rivalry among Western European nations that would lead to catastrophic events in the early 20th century.

Changes in Standards of Living

Due to increased automation, the use of interchangeable parts, the division and specialization of labor, and the assembly line, the efficiency of industrial production increased. This efficiency led to greater output, especially of such consumer goods as textiles, home furnishings, clothing, and porcelain. As the supply of consumer goods increased, the availability of goods rose and the prices fell. In addition, increased global industrial production led to greater competition and variety of both consumer and capital goods. For some people, standards of living improved with the proliferation of consumer goods.

One way economists measure standard of living is by tracing patterns in real wages—those adjusted for inflation. Real wages signify the amount of goods or services that can be bought. In the early years of the Industrial Revolution, some studies show that real wages grew slowly, but after 1819 the pace of growth accelerated, and between 1819 and 1852 they doubled. The growth of real wages paralleled the rise in consumption. By these measures, standards of living increased for people of all income groups.

At the same time, however, the distribution of income (the wealth gap) became more pronounced. Additionally, some of the rise in income was offset by the growing problems in an industrialized society—pollution, crowded cities, and the costs of wars. With these taken into consideration, standards of living may not have risen for many people.

Overseas Expansion

As more countries industrialized and the capacity to produce goods increased, overproduction became a serious economic issue. Domestic markets could no longer consume the amount of goods being produced. As a result, international trade transformed industrial economies from mercantilist to capitalist systems. Industrialized economies looked to increase exports of their products. The desire to increase exports, however, caused both economic and political rivalries among industrialized countries as businesses sought out new international customers and enlisted their government's assistance to help open previously closed or inaccessible markets.

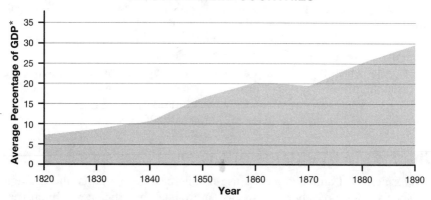

EXPORTS AS A PERCENTAGE OF THE OUTPUT OF INDUSTRIALIZED COUNTRIES

*GDP, or gross domestic product, is one measure of the total amount of goods and services produced by a country.
Source: Adapted from Federico, Giovanni and Antonio Tena-Junguito (2016 b). 'Atale of two globalizations: gains from trade and opennes 1800-2010'. London, Centre for Ecomomic Policy Reasearch. (CEPR WP.11128).

As production increased, new and greater amounts of natural resources were required by industrial economies. In addition, such common industrial resources as coal and iron, tin, bauxite, rubber, and copper were also imported from sources in Africa, Southeast Asia, and Latin America. A key effect of industrial capitalism, therefore, was the expansion of imperialism in the 19th century. Industrialized countries, especially those in Western Europe, the U.S., and Japan, saw the benefits of controlling trade and resources of other areas of the world. This trend was a continuation from the previous era during which European countries created colonies in the Western Hemisphere and in the Indian Ocean.

In contrast, the dependent colonial economies that provided raw material to and markets for the imperial powers often saw little economic development from participation in the world economy. Reliance on the cash crops introduced by imperial powers often left them vulnerable to natural disasters and volatile markets.

In this era, however, states and people in regions that had previously been able to resist European colonization found themselves increasingly dominated by Western powers. Most areas of Africa came under the direct control of European colonizers. Large portions of South Asia and Southeast Asia were colonized, mainly by Great Britain and France, respectively. Even China, the most dynamic civilization in previous eras, succumbed to the domination of Western and Japanese imperialists. Western powers were able to achieve this level of dominance because of the technological advances associated with the Industrial Revolution. Advances in military technology, ship building, and medicine helped Western European nations assert control over these other regions.

Seeds of Revolution and Rebellion

In the late 1700s, the former North American colonies of Great Britain revolted against its colonial rule and declared themselves the independent nation of the United States of America. Shortly after, France threw off the yoke of the monarchy and established a republic. In the early 1800s, former Spanish and Portuguese colonies in South America also became independent states.

As western imperialism took hold in other parts of the world, the seeds of resistance and rebellion that would, in time, lead to new nation-states took root. Westernization (assimilation of Western culture) was often resisted in colonized or dominated areas. In South Asia, for example, Indian soldiers known as sepoys rose up in rebellion against the British East India Company. While the rebellion was brutally suppressed by British soldiers, the effect was the disbandment of the British East India Company and the direct rule of India by the British government, commencing a period now known as the British Raj. Similarly, westernization was opposed in China by the Boxers who attempted to rid China of Western influence, especially from Christian missionaries. These nascent independence movements would lead to the more widespread and successful nationalism of the post-World War II period.

Migration and Discrimination

One of the more significant effects of modern imperialism was the migration from dependent or less industrial areas of the world to the dominant industrial economies. People emigrated from rural areas to urban areas within countries and from less developed areas of Europe to more developed areas of Europe.

Immigrants looking for economic opportunity left many European countries and settled in the United States and Canada, often making up a large proportion of the industrial workforce. Some immigrants signed contracts to travel to areas to work for a prescribed period of time, pay back the cost of their transport, and then either settle in these areas or return to their homelands. These indentured laborers, as they were called, came from China, Japan, South Asia, and Europe and found themselves working and living in the Americas, Southeast Asia, Africa, or Australia. If they chose to settle in their host country, they often formed enclaves, or communities, with others from their home country. Often, these immigrants were faced with discrimination based on race, religion, or other factors. The spread of global capitalism resulted in the accumulation of wealth by the middle and upper classes, while the working classes in the industrial economies, already exploited by the profit motive, found themselves in direct competition for jobs with immigrants from nonindustrial countries.

REFLECT ON THE ESSENTIAL QUESTION

1. **Causation** There are many ways to determine the relative significance of the effects of a historical development. These are some of the criteria for ranking the relative impact of effects:
   - The depth of change it brought about in people
   - The number of people it affected
   - How long the effect lasted
   - The importance of the change it represented

   Choose one of the effects of imperialism and evaluate it based on these criteria for determining significance.

2. In one to three paragraphs, explain the relative significance of the effects of imperialism from 1750 to 1900.

UNIT 6 REVIEW

HISTORICAL PERSPECTIVES: HOW DID COLONIZATION PROMOTE EUROPEAN ECONOMIC GROWTH?

In the 19th century, the European powers believed that building a modern economy required establishing colonies. They focused on the economic and political benefits of imperialism.

Problems with Imperialism By the early 20th century, as the struggles of the workers and the burden of imperialist wars began to take a toll, some historians focused on the costs of imperialism. British writer J. A. Hobson argued in his book *Imperialism: A Study* (1904) imperialist competition for new resources and markets was a flaw in capitalism. The accumulation of capital in the hands of a few profit-seeking capitalists pressured governments to take over underdeveloped nations and to protect access to them. Hobson then explained how this was justified, based on the needs of a growing population or hopes for quick profits, but that those supporting this greed for territorial acquisition did not consider the associated political and economic costs.

Hobson believed that the system could be improved through greater global cooperation and planning. In contrast, Russian revolutionary Vladimir Lenin wrote in *Imperialism, The Highest Stage of Capital Development* (1917) that imperialist conflicts would cause capitalist states to destroy each other and usher in the era of communism.

Benefits to Some In the late 20th century, historians living in an age of increasing globalization re-studied the roots of the world economy. Immanuel Wallerstein, an American social scientist, popularized world-systems theory. He described a dynamic system of two main regions:

- The core included highly developed nations that accumulated capital and demanded resources and markets from under- or less-developed regions

- The periphery consisted of regions that provided resources and markets as well as labor needed by the core

Wallerstein traced the roots of this world-system to the mid-16th century. Colonialism became the means by which peripheral states became incorporated into the world economy. However, Wallerstein noted that politics and culture vary within the world economy, so nations could be semi-peripheral at some point and possibly move to the core—or the other way around. He cited Spain as an example. Although this world-system caused inequalities, its dynamic nature insured its durability.

Develop an Argument: Evaluate the extent to which historical evidence supports the role of colonization as a factor in European economic growth.

After you analyze the task, gather and organize evidence, and develop an effective thesis statement, much of the hard work in writing a long essay is behind you. The most challenging task still remaining is to write an introduction that 1) serves as a blueprint for the rest of the essay and 2) casts the topic in a broader historical perspective.

The Introduction as Blueprint In generic terms, a good introduction conveys the framework or limits of the topic as well as a clear debatable and defensible claim. The claim should be expressed in one or more sentences in the same location—ideally the introduction. The introduction also suggests the organizational pattern and reasoning process that will unfold in the rest of the essay. In other words, it conveys (without saying), "Here's what I'm going to argue. Here's the reasoning process I am going to use to convince you. Here's the order I will use to present my ideas." The reasoning process may be causation, continuity and change, or comparison. Each reasoning process suggests a unique organization. (See Write as a Historian in Topic 7.9.)

Historical Perspective A good introduction also relates the topic of the prompt to broader historical events, developments, or processes that occur before, during, or that continue after the time frame of the question. In other words, it conveys (without saying), "Here's how this topic relates to what came before it/what came after it/what else was going on in other parts of the world or other aspects of society, and any number of broader historical patterns and trends." The introduction is a good place to point out the historical perspective, but it will need further development later in the essay. A simple reference to a historical perspective is not sufficient to earn points on the exam.

Application Find both the blueprint and historical perspective in the following introduction. How does the introduction answer these questions:

- What is the author's argument?

- What reasoning process will the author use?

- What order will the author likely use?

- How does the topic relate to broader historical events, developments, or processes?

The new global capitalist economy that developed between 1750 and 1900 brought many obvious changes as smokestacks and ships laden with raw materials for industry became commonplace. One of the most dramatic changes, however, was the effect of industrialization on patterns of migration, from the countryside to the city and from one country to another. These changes in turn brought about significantly different social conditions that laid the foundation for challenges many countries continue to face today.

For current free response question samples, visit: https://apcentral. collegeboard.org/courses/ap-world-history/exam

LONG ESSAY QUESTIONS

Directions: Write an essay in response to one of the prompts below. The suggested writing time for an essay is 40 minutes.

In your response, you should do the following:

- Respond to the prompt with a historically defensible thesis or claim that establishes a line of reasoning.
- Describe a broader historical context relevant to the prompt.
- Support an argument in response to the prompt using at least two pieces of specific and relevant evidence.
- Use historical reasoning (e.g., comparison, causation, continuity or change) to frame or structure an argument that addresses the prompt.
- Demonstrate a complex understanding of a historical development related to the prompt through sophisticated argumentation and/or effective use of evidence.

Source: *AP® World History Course and Exam Description*

1. In the period 1750 to 1900, some European powers suffered a decrease in influence, and new empires emerged—one in the Americas and one in Asia.
   Develop an argument that evaluates the extent to which the global balance of power shifted during that era.

2. From 1750 to 1900, nationalist movements emerged throughout South America, Africa, and Asia as resistance to imperialist powers increased. Develop an argument that evaluates the extent to which internal factors influenced the process of state building during that era.

3. European powers divided up much of Africa and India from 1750 to 1900, but indigenous peoples had their own opinions about imperialism.
   Develop an argument that evaluates the extent to which the responses of native people to imperialism were similar in India and Sub-Saharan Africa between 1750 and 1900.

4. As the economy grew increasingly global from 1750 to 1900, working people in Eurasia, the Americas, Australia, and Africa began moving into urban centers and across borders, but many had the same motivations their ancestors had.
   Develop an argument that evaluates the extent to which the migration patterns from 1750 to 1900 show changes or continuities over time.

DOCUMENT-BASED QUESTION

Directions: Question 1 is based on the accompanying documents. The documents have been edited for the purpose of this exercise. You are advised to spend 15 minutes planning and 45 minutes writing your answer.

1. Evaluate the extent to which imperialism affected state development around the world during the period 1750 to 1900.

In your response, you should do the following:

- Respond to the prompt with a historically defensible thesis or claim that establishes a line of reasoning.

- Describe a broader historical context relevant to the prompt.

- Support an argument in response to the prompt using at least four documents.

- Use at least one additional piece of specific historical evidence (beyond that found in the documents) relevant to an argument about the prompt.

- For at least two documents, explain how or why the document's point of view, purpose, historical situation, and/or audience is relevant to an argument.

- Demonstrate a complex understanding of a historical development related to the prompt through a sophisticated argument and/or effective use of evidence.

Source: *AP® World History Course and Exam Description*

Document 1

> **Source:** Andrew Jackson, U.S. President, proposal to U.S. Congress to remove members of the Cherokee nation and other Native American tribes from their traditional lands and relocate them westward to Oklahoma, then known as Indian Territory (this became known as the Trail of Tears), 1835.
>
> The plan of removing the aboriginal people who yet remain within the settled portions of the United States to the country west of the Mississippi River approaches its completion. All preceding experiments for the improvement of the Indians have failed. It seems now to be an established fact that they cannot live in contact with a civilized community and prosper.
>
> No one can doubt the moral duty of the Government of the United States to protect and if possible to preserve and perpetuate the scattered remnants of this race which are left within our borders. In the discharge of this duty an extensive region in the West has been assigned for their permanent residence. A territory exceeding in extent that relinquished has been granted to each tribe.

Document 2

Source: Treaty of Nanking (Nanjing)* ending the Opium War of 1839–1842 between Great Britain and the Qing Dynasty of China which gave favorable terms to the British, 1842.

Article III

It being obviously necessary and desirable, that British Subjects should have some port where they may careen [turn a ship on its side for repair] and refit their Ships, when required, and keep Stores [supplies] for that purpose, His Majesty the Emperor of China cedes to Her Majesty the Queen of Great Britain, the island of Hong-Kong, to be possessed in perpetuity [forever] by her Britannic Majesty, Her heirs and successors, and to be governed by such laws and regulations as Her Majesty the Queen of Great Britain. shall see fit to direct.

The Qing emperor was forced to sign this treaty.

Document 3

Source: Proclamation by Firoz Shah, grandson of the last and largely powerless Mughal emperor Bahadur Shah, during a revolt by Indian soldiers (known as *sepoys*) employed by the British East India Company, published in the *Delhi Gazette,* 1857.

It is well known to all that in this age the people of Hindustan [northern India], both Hindus and Muslims, are being ruined under the tyranny and oppression of the infidel and the treacherous English. It is therefore the bounden duty of all the wealthy people of India to stake their lives and property for the well-being of the public.

I, who am the grandson of Bahadur Shah . . . have come here to extirpate [root out and destroy completely] the infidels residing in the eastern part of the country, and to liberate and protect the poor helpless people now groaning under their iron rule. Several of the Hindu and Muslim chiefs who . . . have been trying their best to root out the English in India, have presented themselves to me and taken part in the reigning Indian crusade.

All agree, asserting that the English should no longer have any footing in India or elsewhere. Therefore, it is necessary for all Indians to give up the hope of the continuation of British power, and to side with me.

Document 4

Source: Moshweshewe, Chief of the Basutos, a large and powerful tribe located in British Cape Colony, present-day South Africa and Lesotho, excerpts from a letter to Sir George Grey, Governor of Cape Colony, 1858.

About sixteen years ago, Governor of the Colony, Sir George Napier, marked down my limits on a treaty he made with me. I was to be the ruler within those limits. The Boers [Dutch settlers in South Africa] then began to talk of their right to places I had then lent to them.

Then came Governor Sir Harry Smith . . . and that he was to keep the Boers in my land under proper control, and that I should hear no more of their claiming the places they lived on as their exclusive property. But instead of this, I then heard that the Boers consider all those farms as their own. Governor Smith sent a deputy to govern in the territory claimed by the Boers. He listened to the Boers, and he proposed that all the land in which those Boers' farms were should be taken from me.

I was at that time in trouble, for other tribes living in the Cape Colony were tormenting me and my people by stealing and killing; they said openly the British gave them orders to do so, and I have proof he did so. One day Governor Smith sent me a map and said, sign that, and I will tell those people to leave off fighting: if you do not sign the map, I cannot help you in any way. . . . I begged Queen Victoria [the British monarch] to investigate my case and remove "the line," as it was called, by which my land was ruined.

Document 5

Source: "The Dogs of War," political cartoon about events leading to the 1877–1878 Russo-Turkish War, from the British magazine *Punch*, 1876.

PUNCH, OR THE LONDON CHARIVARI.—June 17, 1876.

THE DOGS OF WAR.

Bull A 1. "TAKE CARE, MY MAN! IT MIGHT BE AWK'ARD IF YOU WAS TO LET 'EM LOOSE!"

Document 6

Source: Fukuzawa Yukichi, Japanese author and son of a lower samurai family, describing the spread of Western civilization in Japan in his essay "Good-bye Asia," 1885.

The opening to the modern civilization of the West began in the reign of Jaapanese Emperor Kaei (1848-1858). Our people began to discover its utility and gradually and yet actively moved toward its acceptance. However, there was an old- fashioned and bloated government that stood in the way of progress. It was a problem impossible to solve. If the government were allowed to continue, the new civilization could not enter.

The modern civilization and Japan's old conventions were mutually exclusive. If we were to discard our old conventions, that government also had to be abolished. We could have prevented the entry of this civilization, but it would have meant loss of our national independence. . . . Not only were we able to cast aside Japan's old conventions, but we also succeeded in creating a new model of progress in Asia.

Document 7

Source: Treaty of Shimonoseki between the Empire of Japan and the Qing Dynasty of China, ending the First Sino-Japanese War which was largely fought over control of the Korean Peninsula, 1895.

Article 1

China recognizes definitively the full and complete independence and autonomy of Korea, and, in consequence, the payment of tribute and the performance of ceremonies and formalities by Korea to China, in derogation [repeal] of such independence and autonomy, shall wholly cease for the future.

Article 2

China cedes to Japan in perpetuity and full sovereignty the following territories, together with all fortifications, arsenals, and public property thereon:—

(a) The southern portion of the province of Fengtien. . . .

(b) The island of Formosa, together with all islands appertaining or belonging to the said island of Formosa

(c) The Pescadores Group [islands located in the South China Sea near the island of Formosa]. . . .

UNIT 7: Global Conflict After 1900

Understand the Context

The 20th century was a time of great social and political change, much of which resulted in tension and division. People and states challenged existing political and social orders, while new technologies and scientific advancements both advanced understanding of the universe and enabled the two world wars to be increasingly destructive.

Shifting Powers Challenges to existing states and political establishments set the stage for shifting powers throughout the 20th century. Long-established states such as the Ottoman Empire dissolved, while new political experiments such as communism emerged in Russia, China, and elsewhere. The ongoing power of nationalism and traditional rivalries, combined with economic instability, soon embroiled most of Europe and its colonies, the United States, Russia, and to a lesser extent, East Asia in the First World War. Though dubbed "the war to end all wars," it was not. World War II was far larger and bloodier. Additional conflicts occurred as colonized regions fought for independence.

A Changing World Rapid advances in technology altered the understanding of the universe and the natural world in the 20th century. Advancements in communication, transportation, industry, agriculture, and medicine brought people longer lives, greater opportunities to find meaningful work, and better access to information. However, emerging military technologies also made war more deadly. World War I featured advancements such as the aircraft, while World War II enabled the development of the atomic bomb. Mass atrocities were also brought about by the intentional destruction of entire ethnic or religious groups of people, including the Holocaust during World War II. Totalitarian governments, such as the one under Joseph Stalin in the Soviet Union, adopted repressive policies that resulted in the deaths of many millions of people.

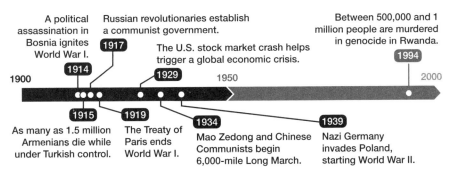

A political assassination in Bosnia ignites World War I. **1914**

Russian revolutionaries establish a communist government. **1917**

The U.S. stock market crash helps trigger a global economic crisis. **1929**

Between 500,000 and 1 million people are murdered in genocide in Rwanda. **1994**

1900

1950

2000

As many as 1.5 million Armenians die while under Turkish control. **1915**

The Treaty of Paris ends World War I. **1919**

Mao Zedong and Chinese Communists begin 6,000-mile Long March. **1934**

Nazi Germany invades Poland, starting World War II. **1939**

Topics and Learning Objectives

Topic 7.1: Shifting Power pages 453–460

A: Explain how internal and external factors contributed to change in various states after 1900.

Topic 7.2: Causes of World War I pages 461–468

B: Explain the causes and consequences of World War I.

Topic 7.3: Conducting World War I pages 469–479

C: Explain how governments used a variety of methods to conduct war.

Topic 7.4: Economy in the Interwar Period pages 480–492

D: Explain how different governments responded to economic crises after 1900.

Topic 7.5: Unresolved Tensions After World War I pages 493–502

E: Explain the continuities and changes in territorial holdings from 1900 to the present.

Topic 7.6: Causes of World War II pages 502–510

F: Explain the causes and consequences of World War II.

Topic 7.7: Conducting World War II pages 511–520

G: Explain similarities and differences in how governments used a variety of methods to conduct war.

Topic 7.8: Mass Atrocities pages 520–530

H: Explain the various causes and consequences of mass atrocities in the period from 1900 to the present.

Topic 7.9: Causation in Global Conflict pages 531–535

I: Explain the relative significance of the causes of global conflict in the period from 1900 to the present.

7.1

Shifting Power

I shall never, under any circumstances, agree to a representative form of government because I consider it harmful to the people whom God has entrusted to my care.

—Russian Tsar Nicholas II (1905)

Essential Question: How did internal and external factors contribute to change in various states after 1900?

An intense period of rebellion continued into the early 1900s. Nicholas II, the last Russian tsar, clearly did not understand the force of the political opposition to his rule that resulted in his assassination in 1918. In the 20th century's first two decades, rebellions erupted against long-standing authoritarian governments in Russia, China, and Mexico. Revolutionaries unseated ruling governments in each country, challenging the existing political and social order and instituting their own political philosophies and practices. Established land-based and maritime empires collapsed under pressure from internal and external forces. By the end of the century, a new global order had emerged.

Revolution in Russia

By the early 20th century, Russia was falling behind most of Europe, the United States, and Japan in wealth in power. Russia's most obvious challenges were internal. While governments in other industrializing states in the 19th century were actively promoting economic growth, Russia was not. It was slow to expand education for peasants, build roads and other parts of its transportation networks, and support entrepreneurs with loans and contracts. Further, the tsarist government resisted calls for political reform. It was reluctant to recognize civil liberties and to allow more citizens to participate in government.

These internal problems led to external ones. Without a strong economic base to support a military, Russia then became weaker in international affairs:

- It lost the Crimean War (1853–1856) against the Ottoman Empire, which was supported by Great Britain and France.

- It lost the Russo-Japanese War (1904–1905) in a battle for power in East Asia.

In the fall of 1917, the **Bolsheviks**, an organization representing the revolutionary working class of Russia under the leadership of Vladimir Lenin, seized power and set up a communist government with Lenin at its head. The **communists** believed that workers eventually should own the means of production and that collective ownership would lead to collective prosperity and a just society. Toward that long-term goal, the Soviet government abolished private trade, distributed peasants' crops to feed urban workers, and took over ownership of the country's factories and heavy industries (see Topic 7.4)

Key Events Leading to Revolution in Russia	
Internal	• **Bloody Sunday, January 22, 1905:** Thousands of workers marched peacefully to petition the tsar asking for better working conditions, higher wages, and universal suffrage. The tsar's troops and police began shooting. About 1,300 marchers were killed. • **The Revolution of 1905:** In strikes responding to Bloody Sunday, 400,000 workers refused to work. The tsar tried to appease the protesters. However, by the end, thousands of workers had been killed, injured, or exiled.
External	• **Russo-Japanese War (1904–1905):** Russia and Japan both wanted to expand their influence in Korea and Manchuria. Japan won easily, the first time in modern history that an East Asian state had defeated a European power. • **World War I:** Germany declared war on Russia in 1914. Russians quickly realized how poorly trained and armed their troops were. Civilians suffered from extreme food shortages.

The success of the Bolsheviks in taking power shook the world. They were the first example of communists running a large country. Throughout the capitalist world, from Europe to the United States to Japan, people worried that communists were a danger to their governments as well. The conflict between communism and capitalism would become an important issue shaping world affairs in the rest of the 20th century.

Upheaval in China

China was another land-based empire that collapsed in this period from problems it faced at home and from other countries. The Qing Dynasty had come to power in China in 1644. Finally, a revolution overthrew it in 1911, creating a republic led first by Dr. **Sun Yat-sen**. However, his rule was short.

Internal Challenges China faced daunting domestic concerns in the 19th century, each of which weakened support for the government. One of these was ethnic tension. China consisted of dozens of ethnic groups. The largest group was the Han. The rulers of the Qing Dynasty were Manchus, from a region northeast of China. Many Chinese, particularly the Han, never fully accepted the Qing as legitimate rulers of China. By the late 19th century, the Qing had ruled China for over two centuries, but they had remained ethnically distinct.

A second problem was the constant danger of famine. China experienced rapid population growth between the mid-1700s and mid-1800s, but could not expand the amount of farmland or productivity rapidly enough to provide a stable food supply. Any natural disaster, such as a drought or a flood, could result in the early deaths of thousands of people.

Third, government revenues were very low. The imperial government had not updated the tax system to adjust to changes in the economy. As a result, compared to Europe or the United States, taxes in China were low. This meant that the government did not have the resources to maintain roads, bridges, and irrigation canals.

External Challenges China had been one of the wealthiest, most powerful, most innovative states in the world for much of its recorded history. However, starting in the late 18th century, it faced growing threats to its position by industrialization in Europe. In the late 18th century, Europeans interested in the Chinese market could trade only in the city of Canton (Guangzhou). Europeans commonly bought tea, rhubarb, porcelain, and silk. In Europe, Chinese fashions, table settings, and art objects were very popular. The Chinese received European silver in exchange for they sold. However, the Chinese did not desire the products Europeans produced, and they looked down on Europeans as violent and less civilized. In response to growing European influence in China, many Chinese did rally behind the empress in the 1890s.

Chinese Republic However the desire to support the empress against foreign pressure was not enough to save the Qing Dynasty. In 1911, the last Chinese dynasty was overthrown by a revolutionary movement led by Sun Yat-sen. Though a Christian, Sun believed that China should continued to follow such Confucian principles as loyalty, respect for ancestors, and efforts to promote social harmony. He combined these traditions with ideas he later elaborated upon in his book *The Three People's Principles:*

- **Democracy:** Sun believed in sovereignty, not for all the people but for those Chinese who were "able." In Confucian terms, this meant a country governed by active and pragmatic experts in the name of the people. He felt that expelling foreign capitalists from China would enable China to redistribute revenues from land taxes more fairly, since the revenues would not have to be used to pay debts to foreigners.

- **Nationalism:** Sun advocated patriotism and loyalty, primarily to central authority.

- **Livelihood:** Sun wanted to end the extreme unequal distribution of wealth in China and the harsh economic exploitation.

Sun Yat-sen's Legacy Sun never had enough military strength to rule all of China. Various warlords controlled the majority of the country. Sun recognized the weakness of his position. After two months in office, he gave up his position to a military leader.

The party Sun led, the Chinese Nationalist Party, or Kuomintang, would later regain power. It would rule China for two decades before losing a civil war with Chinese Communists (see Topic 7.5).While both the Kuomintang and the Communists would honor Sun as the founder of the Chinese republic, neither would fully implement his principles.

Self-Determination in the Ottoman Collapse

By the beginning of the 20th century, the once-mighty Ottoman Empire—now "the sick man of Europe"—had relatively few exports and a waning agricultural economy. The empire relied mostly upon its position as a trade center. Egypt, by contrast, continued to make profits from cotton.

The Young Turks As Ottoman prosperity declined, a group of reformers known as the **Young Turks** emerged. They advocated for a constitution like those of the European states. They also advocated **Turkification,** an effort to make all citizens of the multiethnic empire identify with Turkish culture, which was heavily Islamic. For the millions of Armenians in the empire, who were mostly Christians, this was difficult. In response, some Young Turks scapegoated, or unfairly blamed, Armenians for the empire's economic problems. (Connect: Compare the cultural assimilation forced on Armenians to that forced on American Indians. See Topic 6.3.)

Fight Against Foreign Influence Turks resented many Europeans, particularly the British and the French, for their economic policies. Foreign investments had given Europeans undue power in the empire. Further, Europeans had imposed trade privileges that were unprofitable for the Ottomans. Because of these resentments, the Ottoman Empire secretly allied with Germany in World War I. (See Topic 7.2.) After Germany's defeat in World War I, the Ottoman Empire was dismantled by the victorious powers. It was replaced by a smaller nation-state, the Republic of Turkey, and several independent countries.

Victorious Allied forces immediately sent troops to occupy Anatolia (most of modern-day Turkey). Although the sultan of the Ottoman Empire remained on his throne, he had little power. He served as a mere puppet for British forces that hoped to control the lands of the former empire.

The Rise of Atatürk During the war, a group called the Turkish National Movement organized an army to fight for self-determination. Led by **Mustafa Kemal,** the Turkish Nationalists defeated British and other forces in 1921. The Republic of Turkey was established in 1923, with Kemal as the first president. The new national assembly awarded him the surname **Atatürk** ("father of the Turks") in recognition of his role in establishing the new republic.

Atatürk's policies focused on reforming Turkey to make it more like the Western democracies. He was determined to create a secular nation, not one with strong Islamic influences. He implemented several reforms: establishing public education for boys and girls, abolishing polygyny, and expanding suffrage to include women. As a symbolic gesture, he wore mainly Western suits and hats and encouraged others to do the same. Despite his reforms, he ruled as a dictator for 15 years. He did not give up power before his death in 1938.

Power Shifts in Mexico

Mexico entered the 20th century as an independent nation firmly under the control of a dictator, **Porfirio Díaz**. He oversaw a period of stability and some economic progress. However, he had allowed foreign investors, particularly those from the United States, control over many of the country's resources. Additionally, the wealthiest 1 percent of the population controlled 97 percent of the land. Typical Mexican peasants were landless.

Revolution In 1910, Díaz jailed **Francisco Madero**, the opposition candidate for president. This act, combined with the growing opposition to Díaz's strong-armed policies, accommodation to foreign powers, and opposition to land reform, ignited the **Mexican Revolution.** Madero escaped and set up revolutionary offices in El Paso, Texas. Then, in 1911, Madero's troops, under the command of **Francisco "Pancho" Villa,** defeated Mexican troops, sending Díaz into exile. One revolutionary leader, **Emiliano Zapata**, began the actual process of redistributing land to impoverished peasants.

Until 1920, Mexico suffered from political instability and devastating violence. Between 1910 and 1920, conflict resulted in around 2 million deaths, out of a population of around 15 million people. Political violence continued for another decade. However, two results came out of conflicts between 1910 and 1930 that provided Mexico with stability for the rest of the century:

- Mexico adopted a new constitution in 1917. It included the goals of land redistribution, universal suffrage, and public education. These principles continued to guide Mexico's government.

- The **Institutional Revolutionary Party**, or **PRI,** was formed in 1929. Though widely criticized as corrupt, the PRI dominated Mexican politics. Until 2000, all presidents were PRI members.

KEY TERMS BY THEME		
CULTURE: Ethnic Conflict Turkification **GOVERNMENT: Politics** Bolsheviks communists	Young Turks Mexican Revolution Institutional Revolutionary Party (PRI)	**GOVERNMENT: Leaders** Sun Yat-sen Kemal Atatürk Porfirio Díaz Francisco Madero Francisco "Pancho" Villa Emiliano Zapata

MULTIPLE-CHOICE QUESTIONS

1. Questions 1 to 3 refer to the passage below.

"China is now suffering from poverty, not from unequal distribution of wealth. Where there are inequalities of wealth, the methods of Marx can, of course, be used; a class war can be advocated to destroy the inequalities. But in China, where industry is not yet developed, Marx's class war and dictatorship of the proletariat are impracticable."

Sun Yat-sen, *Capital and State,* 1924

1. Which leader would be most likely to argue that his country faced the same problems Sun identified in China?

(A) King Leopold II of Belgium

(B) Cecil Rhodes of Rhodesia

(C) Vladimir Lenin of Russia

(D) Emiliano Zapata of Mexico

2. How did Sun Yat-sen's ideas compare to those of Karl Marx?

(A) They agreed that the dictatorship of the proletariat was practical in all countries.

(B) They agreed that class war was the most effective path to economic progress.

(C) They disagreed on whether countries should industrialize.

(D) They disagreed on whether the unequal distribution of wealth was a problem.

3. Sun's relationship with Confucianism is best summarized by which of the following statements?

(A) Sun was less concerned about economic inequality than Confucius was.

(B) Sun was less supportive of democracy than Confucius was.

(C) Sun thought that the Chinese should continue to study the teachings of Confucius.

(D) Sun thought that the Chinese should reject the teachings of Confucius.

1. **Use the passages below to answer all parts of the question that follows.**

> "Take up the White Man's burden—Send forth the best ye breed—
> Go bind your sons to exile, to serve your captives' need;
> To wait in heavy harness, On fluttered folk and wild—
> Your new-caught, sullen peoples, Half-devil and half-child."
>
> Rudyard Kipling, "The White Man's Burden," 1899

> "The African has resisted, and persisted. . . . But what the partial occupation of his soil by the white man has failed to do; what the mapping out of European political 'spheres of influence' has failed to do; what the maxim [a type of gun] and the rifle, the slave gang, labor in the bowels of the earth and the lash, have failed to do; what imported measles, smallpox, and syphilis have failed to do; what even the oversea[s] slave trade failed to do, the power of modern capitalistic exploitation, assisted by modern engines of destruction, may yet succeed in accomplishing.
>
> For from the evils of the latter, scientifically applied and enforced, there is no escape for the African. . . . It kills not the body merely, but the soul. . . . It wrecks his polity, uproots him from the land, invades his family life, destroys his natural pursuits and occupations, claims his whole time, enslaves him in his own home."
>
> Edward D. Morel, *The Black Man's Burden*, 1920

(A) Identify ONE way in which the viewpoints of the authors of these passage differ.

(B) Explain how ONE important thinker or leader from Latin America from the 18th century through the 20th century would have responded to Morel's view of capitalism.

(C) Explain how ONE important thinker or leader from Eurasia from the 18th century through the 20th century would have responded to Morel's view of capitalism.

2. **Answer all parts of the question that follows.**

(A) Identify ONE historical situation in the period after 1900 in which a new, less diverse state replaced an old, more diverse empire.

(B) Explain ONE long-term effect of the Russian Empire's collapse after 1900.

(C) Explain ONE example of states challenging existing social order in the period after 1900.

THINK AS A HISTORIAN: SITUATE THE POWER SHIFTS
IN CONTEXT

On the surface, modern revolutions appear to follow a similar pattern. In *The Anatomy of Revolution* (1938), Crane Brinton described the similarities of four political revolutions: the English Revolution of the 1640s, the American Revolution of 1776, the French Revolution of 1789, and the Russian Revolution of 1917. Brinton thought that all four revolutions went through four stages.

1. Citizens become dissatisfied with government.

2. Moderates gain more power.

3. Radicals take over in a "terror" phase.

4. The process culminates in a period of relative calm and acceptance.

Within this pattern, each revolution had unique revolutionary circumstances and outcomes. For example, Brinton acknowledged that the American Revolution, unlike the other three, lacked a "terror" phase. He concluded his study by noting that some top-down reforms imposed by government or elite leaders brought more lasting social change than the political revolutions he described.

Choose one of the revolutions covered in this topic and explain how it fits into the broader historical context of revolutionary patterns. Describe each stage or explain why the revolution did not follow the pattern Brinton described.

REFLECT ON THE TOPIC ESSENTIAL QUESTION

1. In one to three paragraphs, explain how internal and external factors contributed to change in various states after 1900.

7.2

Causes of World War I

The next great European war will probably come out of some damned foolish thing in the Balkans.

—German Chancellor Otto von Bismarck (1888)

Essential Question: What were the causes and consequences of World War I?

In the years before World War I, social and political developments, including shifting powers, contributed to the escalation of tensions that resulted in global conflict. European nations, expanding their empires, competed for raw material resources in Africa and Asia. A series of mutual alliances created entanglements that committed nations to defense systems that would draw them into war. Arms races involving Germany, Great Britain, and Russia gave military establishments great influence.

The immediate cause of the war's outbreak had its roots in yet another cause of conflict—a rising wave of nationalism. As Bismarck predicted, this clash erupted in the Balkans when Serbian nationalists, protesting Austria-Hungary's control over the territory of Bosnia-Herzegovina, assassinated Austro-Hungarian Archduke Franz Ferdinand. Thus World War I began.

Immediate Causes of the Great War

World War I, which lasted from 1914 to 1918, was known as the **Great War**—not because of its positive nature, but because of the immense scale of the fighting. No previous war had involved as many nations from different parts of the world or killed as many soldiers *and* civilians. However, World War I did more than create an enormous body count. It fundamentally weakened the Western European powers, thus encouraging the growth of nationalism and appeals for self-rule within European colonies in Asia and Africa. Treaties signed at the end of this war helped set the stage for World War II. World War I was one of the most significant events of the 20th century.

A long series of events led up to World War I. The immediate cause was the assassination by **Gavrilo Princip** of **Archduke Franz Ferdinand,** the heir to the Austro-Hungarian throne, and his wife, Sophie, on June 28, 1914. Princip, a Serbian, was a member of the **Black Hand**, a nationalist

Source: Wikimedia Commons

The arrest of Gavrilo Princip after the assassination of Archduke Franz Ferdinand and his wife in Sarajevo, Bosnia, June 28, 1914.

organization devoted to ending Austro-Hungarian presence in the Balkans. From the Austro-Hungarian perspective, however, the Black Hand was a terrorist group.

Immediately after the assassinations, Austria-Hungary sent an ultimatum to the Serbian government, demanding that it end all anti-Austrian agitation in Serbia. When the Serbian government rejected the ultimatum, Austria-Hungary declared war on Serbia on July 28, 1914. Austria-Hungary looked to its ally Germany, a stronger nation with more firepower, for military assistance to punish Serbia. Serbia, populated by ethnic Slavs, looked to other Slavic countries, particularly Russia, for help. On August 1, Germany declared war on Russia, and two days later on France. The following day, Britain declared war on Germany, and on August 6 Austria declared war on Russia. By the end of August 1914, Japan's entrance into the conflict changed a relatively minor incident into a true world war.

Long-Term Causes of the Great War

Princip's actions were not the sole cause of World War I. Tensions in Europe had been simmering for decades. One way to remember the sources of these tensions is with the acronym MAIN: Militarism, Alliances, Imperialism, and Nationalism.

Militarism Defined as aggressive military preparedness, **militarism** celebrates war and the armed forces. European powers had been competing for dominance; one way to prove their strength was to invest in the military. Great

Britain and Germany in particular spent a great deal of money on building up their armies and navies, heavily recruiting young men to join their armed forces and building more ships and amassing other military hardware. Because of the Industrial Revolution, it was possible to mass-produce weapons and supplies. A nation's militaristic attitude influenced its public to view war as a festive competition, more like a game than a gravely serious matter. "Everybody said, 'It'll be over by Christmas,'" a British soldier named Bill Haine recalled.

Alliances In their quest for power, European nations also formed **secret alliances**—groups whose members secretly agree to protect and help one another when attacked. When one member of an alliance was attacked in any way, the other members were expected to stand up for that particular member. This system explains why Russia and Germany were ready to jump into the conflict between Serbia and Austria-Hungary.

Furthermore, countries that were allied with other countries were also sworn enemies of members of other alliances. For example, Britain and France were allies with Russia in the alliance called the **Triple Entente**, and all three viewed Germany as a rival—for different reasons. France was bitter about its defeat in the Franco-Prussian War (1870–1871) and the loss to Germany of Alsace-Lorraine, a major industrial region with rich deposits of iron ore. Both Britain and France competed with Germany for colonies in Africa. After the war began, the Triple Entente became known as the **Allies** as they were joined by Italy, Japan, China, the United States, and other countries. By the end of the war, there were a total of 27 Allies and "Associated Powers."

The Allies' rival alliance before the war was known as the **Triple Alliance**, composed of Germany, Austria-Hungary, and Italy. However, when the war began, Italy remained neutral until 1915, when it switched its allegiance and joined the Allies. At the outbreak of the war, the Ottoman Empire and Bulgaria joined the former Triple Alliance, which was now called the **Central Powers**.

World War I Alliances		
Allied Powers	**Central Powers**	**Neutral States**
• France	• Germany	• Spain
• Great Britain	• Austria-Hungary	• Norway
• Russia	• Ottoman Empire	• Sweden
• Italy	• Bulgaria	• Denmark
• Portugal		• Netherlands
• Romania		• Switzerland
• Serbia		• Albania
• Greece		

Imperialism The alliance system developed largely because Western European countries became bitter rivals for global domination. One of the most important ways these nations could assert their power and generate wealth was to own overseas colonies. During the latter half of the 19th century, for example, Western European countries scrambled for any available land in Africa to add to the colonies they already owned in Asia, the Americas, and the Pacific. Once European powers had claimed nearly all the land in Africa, they began fighting with one another over colonies. Thus, imperialism was a driving force behind tensions in Europe leading up to the archduke's assassination. (Connect: Describe the development of imperialism and how it could have led to the tensions of the early 20th century. See Topic 6.2.)

Nationalism The assassination of the archduke in June 1914, the immediate cause of war, illustrates the growth of nationalism, the final long-term cause of the Great War. On a basic level, nationalism originates from a feeling of pride in one's national identity. Multinational empires such as the Ottoman Empire and the Austro-Hungarian Empire had to contend with different nationalist movements among their subject peoples. Serbs like Princip wanted to rid their land of Austro-Hungarian domination, and Arabs were tired of the limitations the Ottoman Empire imposed on them. Both groups sought **self-determination**—the idea that peoples of the same ethnicity, language, culture, and political ideals should be united and should have the right to form an independent nation-state. Militant nationalists among Serbs and Arabs fought for the Allies, thus extending the boundaries of the Great War.

Consequences of the Great War

As the 20th century began, most Europeans looked forward to a bright future. They expected a century of peace guaranteed by alliances, prosperity as a result of their colonial empires, and continued progress. All of that optimism was shattered on one fateful day in 1914.

Virtually every major event during the remainder of the 20th century was a direct or indirect result of World War I. The war led to the downfalls of four monarchies: Russia, Austria-Hungary, Germany, and the Ottoman Empire. It redrew the maps of Europe and the Middle East with the disintegration of Austro-Hungarian and Ottoman empires. Germany lost all its overseas colonies to various Allied nations, and the former Ottoman provinces of Iraq, Palestine, Syria, and Lebanon came under the control of Britain and France. But the war also led to the beginning of the end of colonialism.

New technologies made World War I the deadliest and most destructive war in human history. It disrupted European economies and had profound social consequences, including the rise of communism and fascism, colonial revolts, and genocide. There was a massive shift of power from Europe to the United States.

Source: National Library of New Zealand

New Zealand Rifle Brigade, fighting with the Allies, near the front during World War I. Helmeted soldiers prepare meals in cramped conditions. Much of World War I was fought in trenches, where soldiers could take cover from enemy fire. Photo taken near Gommecourt, France, July 25, 1918.

Germany was furious about the terms of the peace treaty. Germany was forced to take full blame for the war—although Austria-Hungary started it—and forced to agree to make reparations, impossibly large payments to its opponents to make up for their losses. The war that was to make the world safe for democracy instead gave rise to authoritarian regimes and an even greater world war.

KEY TERMS BY THEME

GOVERNMENT: Wars and Rebellions
Great War
Gavrilo Princip

GOVERNMENT: Leaders
Archduke Franz Ferdinand

GOVERNMENT: Alliances
Triple Entente
Allies
Triple Alliance
Central Powers

SOCIETY: Ideologies and Organizations
Black Hand
militarism
secret alliances
self-determination

Questions 1 to 3 refer to the image below.

Source: Getty Images

The image depicts soldiers from India who fought for the British during World War I.

1. Which of the following causes of World War I BEST explains the image and caption shown above?

   (A) Militarism

   (B) Alliances

   (C) Imperialism

   (D) Nationalism

2. As a result of colonization, these soldiers fought for which group?

   (A) The Allies

   (B) The Triple Alliance

   (C) The Black Hand

   (D) The neutral states

3. The photo reflects that one advantage Great Britain and France had over Germany in World War I was that they

   (A) had more colonial subjects to recruit as soldiers

   (B) had a stronger sense of nationalism

   (C) were more unified by shared religious beliefs

   (D) were more willing to make alliances

1. Use the passage to answer all parts of the question that follows.

"Germany's military culture developed a constellation of mutually reinforcing characteristics that enhanced tactical efficacy. Unleashed in war, however, these characteristics propelled the army to ever greater, and in the end, dysfunctional extremes of violence. . . . These interactive and self-generating characteristics . . . include:

• risk-taking;

• the dogmatic conviction that annihilation was the sole goal of war;

• resulting prescriptions for correct fighting (the offensive, concentration of force, use of reserves, hectic speed) that all greatly increased casualties;

• minutely technical planning;

• focus on the tactical and operative rather than the strategic;

• disregard of logistics and thus growing unrealism;

• the conviction (indeed requirement) of one's qualitative superiority over one's enemies;

• a romantic ruthlessness and actionism (exaggerated drive for action) on the part of officers in order to bridge the gap between risk and reality;

• and finally the acceptance of self-destruction (and thus willingness to destroy everyone else, as well).

Some of these qualities were expressed as doctrine, but many more were buried inside organizational routines and the unexamined expectations of the officer corps."

> Isabel V. Hull, *Absolute Destruction: Military Culture and*
> *the Practices of War in Imperial Germany*, 2005

(A) Identify ONE way in which imperialism influenced social structures after 1900.

(B) Explain ONE way that the German state influenced German culture in the period after 1900.

(C) Explain ONE historical situation after 1900 in which the German state reflected the characteristics listed by Hull.

2. Answer all parts of the question that follows.

(A) Identify ONE way that territorial or regional conflicts caused World War I.

(B) Explain ONE way that imperial competition for resources caused World War I.

(C) Explain ONE way that alliances after 1900 escalated global conflict.

THINK AS A HISTORIAN: EXPLAIN THE CONCEPT OF ALLIANCE

Studies have shown that alliances are honored somewhere between 50 and 80 percent of the time. If there is so much room for noncompliance, what exactly is an alliance?

Read the following portions of the December 5, 1912, amended version of the Triple Alliance. First, rewrite the articles in your own words, simplifying the language. Then generalize from the specific articles to explain the concept of alliance.

"ARTICLE 1. The High Contracting Parties mutually promise peace and friendship, and will enter into no alliance or engagement directed against any one of their States.

They engage to proceed to an exchange of ideas on political and economic questions of a general nature which may arise, and they further promise one another mutual support within the limits of their own interests. . . .

ARTICLE 4. In case a Great Power non-signatory to the present Treaty should threaten the security of the states of one of the High Contracting Parties, and the threatened Party should find itself forced on that account to make war against it, the two others bind themselves to observe towards their Ally a benevolent neutrality. Each of them reserves to itself, in this case, the right to take part in the war, if it should see fit, to make common cause with its Ally.

ARTICLE 5. If the peace of any of the High Contracting Parties should chance to be threatened under the circumstances foreseen by the preceding Articles, the High Contracting Parties shall take counsel together in ample time as to the military measures to be taken with a view to eventual cooperation.

They engage henceforward, in all cases of common participation in a war, to conclude neither armistice, nor peace, nor treaty, except by common agreement among themselves."

REFLECT ON THE TOPIC ESSENTIAL QUESTION

1. In one to three paragraphs, explain the causes and consequences of World War I.

7.3

Conducting World War I

If you could hear, at every jolt, the blood
Come gargling from the froth-corrupted lungs,
Obscene as cancer, bitter as the cud
Of vile, incurable sores on innocent tongues —
My friend, you would not tell with such high zest
To children ardent for some desperate glory,
The old Lie: Dulce et decorum est
Pro patria mori.

—Wilfred Owen, from "Dulce et Decorum Est" (1920)

Essential Question: What were some of the methods governments used to fight World War I?

British poet Wilfred Owen's "Dulce et Decorum Est" is one of the most famous war poems of the 20th century. Most of the poem describes the horrors of modern warfare, and the final lines of the excerpt, translated as "It is sweet and noble to die for one's country," he labels "The old Lie." No previous war had involved as many nations from different parts of the world and none had killed as many soldiers and civilians.

At the outbreak of World War I, Britain was the only major power going into the war without universal **conscription**, compulsory enlistment in the armed forces. Realizing that patriotism could be contagious, the British Army began to recruit "Pals Battalions" made up of men who already knew each other. The first of these was made up of a group of stockbrokers from the City of London. Other Pals Battalions were recruited in cities throughout Britain, such as Liverpool and Manchester. Because the men who volunteered were friends or associates, these battalions were especially close knit. By the end of the war, one out of four British men had served in the military.

Changes in Warfare

Many modern films such as *Saving Private Ryan,* set during World War II, and *Platoon*, set during the Vietnam War, show that war is *not* a glorious experience, but most Europeans saw warfare differently during the first few months of World War I. "Everybody said, 'It'll be over by Christmas,'" a British soldier named Bill Haine recalled. The war began in June 1914.

Hundreds of thousands of teenage boys enthusiastically enlisted in the military, dreaming of heroism. Wartime assemblies sounded more like high school pep rallies, in which speakers naively predicted swift and easy victories in battles against supposedly inferior enemies. Leaders of some of the socialist parties were among the few Europeans who spoke out against the war. Even socialists were divided on the issue, however, as many supported the war efforts of their nation.

At the time, few people actually understood how brutal 20th-century warfare could be. As the war dragged on, the world became aware of the horrific effects of new advances in war technology and tactics, such as trench warfare, poison gas, machine guns, submarines, airplanes, and tanks.

- The defining experience for most soldiers in this war was the time spent in the trenches, long ditches dug in the ground with the excavated earth banked in front in order to defend against enemy fire. **Trench warfare** was not a glorious way to fight a war. Combatant nations dug hundreds of miles of trenches facing one another, and soldiers slept, ate, and fought in the trenches for months at a time. Trenches were often cold, muddy, and rat-infested. Many soldiers died from diseases caused by unhygienic conditions. Erich Maria Remarque's 1929 novel, *All Quiet on the Western Front,* and the 1930 film based on it give a vivid sense of a soldier's life in the trenches. Remarque was a young German soldier during World War I.

- **Poison gas** was one of the most insidious weapons of the new style of warfare. Chlorine, phosgene, and mustard gas were used during World War I. Soldiers were soon equipped with gas masks, which were effective when used immediately. Although fatalities were limited, the effects of a gas attack could be extremely painful and long lasting. Many veterans suffered permanent damage to their lungs. After the war, international treaties outlawed the use of poison gas.

- Developed in the late 1800s, **machine guns** could fire more than 500 rounds of ammunition per minute, increasing the deadly impact of warfare. The weapon made it difficult for either side in a battle to gain new territory.

- Although primitive **submarines** had been used briefly in the American Civil War, they played a much larger part in World War I, wreaking havoc on the shipping lanes of the Atlantic Ocean.

- **Airplanes** in 1914 were still light, small, and unable to carry many weapons. Therefore, they did not present much of a threat to troops, vehicles, or ships. At first, airplanes were used mainly to carry on reconnaissance (observation) of enemy lines. By 1915 they were being fitted with machine guns and aerial combat began. Individual "air aces" would engage in "dog fights" with enemy aircraft.

- The British developed **tanks** to protect troops as they moved across vast areas of difficult terrain, even over trenches, with the ability to fire at the enemy. They were developed by the Royal Navy, and originally referred to as *landships*. They got their name from the fact that during their development, they were disguised as water tanks.

With both the Central Powers and the Allies using brutal weapons and tactics, neither side could defeat the other. The result was a bloody four-year **stalemate** in which the death toll and suffering rose ever higher.

The United States Enters the War

Economic ties between the United States and the Allies were one underlying reasons for U.S. entry into the war in 1917. In addition, many Americans believed that the Allied nations were more democratic than the Central Powers were. A third reason was growing resentment against the Germans, especially for **U-boat** (submarine) attacks on ships carrying civilians, including Americans. On May 7, 1915, a German submarine attacked and sank the *Lusitania*, an ocean liner carrying more than 100 U.S. citizens among its passengers.

The event that finally pushed the United States into the war was the interception of the **Zimmermann Telegram** in January 1917. In this document, the German government offered to help Mexico reclaim territory it had lost to the United States in 1848 if Mexico allied itself with Germany in the war.

Total War

Combatant nations intensified the conflict in World War I by committing all their resources to the war effort. This strategy, known as **total war**, meant that a nation's domestic population, in addition to its military, was committed to winning the war. Thus, millions of civilians, including women, worked in factories producing war materials. Workers imported from China helped make up for labor shortages in Britain, France, and Russia. Entire economies were centered on winning the war. Governments set up planning boards that set production quotas, price and wage controls, and the rationing of food and other supplies. They censored the media and imprisoned many who spoke out against the war effort.

Propaganda was another component of total war. **Propaganda** is communication meant to influence the attitudes and opinions of a community around a particular subject by spreading inaccurate or slanted information. Governments invested heavily in army and navy recruitment campaigns and other wartime propaganda. Posters and articles in newspapers and magazines often depicted the enemy crudely or misrepresented the facts of the war completely. For example, American and British propaganda demonized the German army, exaggerating reports of atrocities against civilians. Likewise, German propaganda demonized the Americans and the British.

The use of highly emotional and often misleading information fomented hatred and bitterness across borders, among civilians as well as soldiers. Other propaganda was more subtle. For example, the U.S. government sent artists to the front lines in Europe to illustrate scenes of battle and glorify Allied soldiers.

Source: Library of Congress

Source: Library of Congress

Posters recruiting sailors and soldiers for World War I in the United States and Great Britain reflected how governments used art and media to appeal to nationalist feelings in the early 20th century.

A Global War

World War I was fought in Europe, Asia, Africa, and the Pacific and Atlantic Oceans. Not since the Seven Years' War of the late 18th century had there been such a **global war**. Most of the major combatants in World War I ruled colonies in Asia, Africa, the Americas, and the Pacific. Competition for these colonies was one major reason for war. Imperialism extended the boundaries of the war, and major battles were fought in North Africa and the Middle East. Japan entered the war on the side of the Allies so that it could take control of German colonies in the Pacific—the Marshall Islands, the Mariana Islands, Palau, and the Carolines. Japan also occupied Tsingtao (Qingdao), a German-held port in China.

The British seized most of Germany's colonies in Africa. However, the Germans held on to German East Africa, later called Tanzania. The British also defended the Suez Canal from an attack by the Ottoman Empire.

Colonial troops reinforced their home countries' forces in several battles. About half a million Australians and New Zealanders enlisted to fight the war. These troops formed a special corps known as **ANZAC** and fought in a bloody year-long campaign at **Gallipoli**, a peninsula in northwestern Turkey, that resulted in heavy Allied losses with little to show for the effort. Canadian troops fought in several European battles. Britain drafted Africans and Indians for combat roles in Europe. Some 90,000 Gurkha soldiers from Nepal fought in the Indian Army. Approximately 1.3 million soldiers served in the Indian Army during the war, in Europe and Southwest Asia. The French Army included 450,000 Africans, mostly from West Africa and Algeria, as well as another 110,000 Europeans from North Africa. Some 44,000 Indochinese soldiers fought in the French army, with nearly 50,000 more working in support roles behind the lines. Some colonial troops fought in hopes that their efforts would gain them recognition from their colonizers, who often promised the colonies self-rule after the war ended.

Arabs, long under the rule of the Turkish-led Ottoman Empire, fought with the Allies because the British promised self-rule after the war if they were victorious. Arab troops attacked Ottoman forts in Arabia and present-day Israel and helped the British take over the cities of Baghdad, Damascus, and Jerusalem.

Source: Library of Congress

Source: Library of Congress

Source: Library of Congress

Source: Library of Congress

World War I armies included soldiers from Senegal in West Africa (upper left), France in Western Europe (upper right), India in South Asia (lower left), and Japan in Eastern Asia (lower right).

Women and the War In the early 20th century, most countries did not allow women to vote or to be soldiers. However, the sheer numbers of men enlisting meant that women's lives changed significantly. They began replacing those men on farms and in factories. Thousands of women served on the front lines as nurses, ambulance drivers, and switchboard operators.

Most countries forebade women from serving in combat, but Russia, Serbia, Romania, and Bulgaria allowed it. In 1917, the Russian government created an all-female battalion (military unit) as propaganda to shame men into continuing to fight. The commander Maria Bochkareva led the First Russian Women's Battalion of Death.

The Paris Peace Conference

The war itself greatly damaged Europe. However, the peace conference held in its wake would have even more profound effects on the entire world. The leaders of the victorious countries at the **Paris Peace Conference** became known as the **Big Four: Woodrow Wilson** (United States), **David Lloyd George** (Great Britain), **Georges Clemenceau** (France), and **Vittorio Orlando** (Italy). The Italians walked out of the peace conference in a rage because Italy would not get Dalmatia and other territories that they had been promised for joining the Allies, including the city of Fiume on the Adriatic Sea. Russia was not invited to the conference because it had undergone a communist revolution. Russia's Bolshevik leaders refused to honor Russia's financial debts to the Allies, who in return refused to recognize the Bolshevik government.

The Big Four had different visions of how to settle the peace. President Wilson's pledge to establish "peace without victory" reflected his belief that no one country should be severely punished or greatly rewarded. France's Clemenceau rejected this view. He believed that France, out of all the Allies represented at the conference, had suffered the most and thus deserved special considerations to be protected from Germany. He also argued that the victorious powers should seek some sort of revenge on the Central Powers for starting the war. Clemenceau complained that Wilson was an unrealistic idealist who was naive about European relations, even though Wilson had a Ph.D. in history. David Lloyd George tended to support Clemenceau's ideas, but he often acted as an intermediary between the two differing points of view.

Fourteen Points Despite Clemenceau's protests, Wilson pushed for his principles, which he outlined in a document called the **Fourteen Points**. He particularly wanted to create a **League of Nations**, an organization in which all nations of the world would convene to discuss conflicts openly, as a way to avoid the simmering tensions that had caused World War I. Although the other nations agreed to establish the League, the U.S. Senate voted against joining it and against ratifying the **Treaty of Versailles**, the 1919 peace treaty with Germany.

Wilson also believed that conquered peoples under the defeated Central Powers deserved the right to **self-determination**, to decide their own political futures. Instead of the colonies and territories of the Central Powers being snatched up by the Allies, conquered peoples should have the right to decide their own political fate. A number of new nations were created or resurrected in Europe as the Austro-Hungarian and Ottoman empires were broken up: Finland, Estonia, Latvia, Lithuania, Poland, Czechoslovakia, and Yugoslavia. The last three of these were home to Slavic peoples.

The Treaty of Versailles Because Wilson failed to convince France and Britain not to punish Germany, the Treaty of Versailles treated Germany harshly. Most notably, Germany had to pay billions of dollars in **reparations** for damage caused by the war, give up all of its colonies, and restrict the size of its armed forces. Germans took the entire blame for the war. Signing the treaty was humiliating for German leaders. Moreover, the terms of the treaty caused tremendous hardship to the nation during the decade following World War I. The German economy suffered from sky-high inflation, partly due to the reparations the country was forced to pay. The German people were bitter in the immediate aftermath of the Paris Peace Conference. Resentment toward the **Weimar Republic**, which had agreed to the terms of the Treaty of Versailles, set the stage for an extreme and militaristic political party known as the Nazis to take power barely 15 years later. (Connect: Compare the forces that led to creation of the Treaty of Versailles and the Peace of Westphalia. See Topic 3.3.)

KEY TERMS BY THEME		
GOVERNMENT: Policies	**GOVERNMENT: Leaders**	**TECHNOLOGY: Warfare**
conscription	Big Four	trench warfare
stalemate	Woodrow Wilson	poison gas
propaganda	David Lloyd George	machine guns
global war	Georges Clemenceau	submarines
self-determination	Vittorio Orlando	airplanes
reparations		tanks
	GOVERNMENT: Treaties	U-boat
GOVERNMENT: Wars and Rebellions	Fourteen Points	
Lusitania	League of Nations	**CULTURE: Popular**
Zimmermann Telegram	Treaty of Versailles	*All Quiet on the Western Front*
total war	**GOVERNMENT: Countries**	
ANZAC	Weimar Republic	
Gallipoli		
Paris Peace Conference		

Questions 1 to 3 refer to the images below.

Source: Library of Congress

The British Parliamentary Recruiting Committee published this poster in 1915, soon after the war began.

Source: Library of Congress

This photograph of an Allied trench during World War I is titled "Removing the Dead from the Trenches." It was not published until September 1919, after the war was over.

1. Comparing the World War I poster from Great Britain and the photo of the trenches supports the interpretation that the British government wanted

    (A) to persuade civilians of the seriousness of the war

    (B) to recruit soldiers by appealing to their fear of the enemy

    (C) to emphasize the positive side of military service

    (D) to portray military service as realistically as possible

2. Images such as the photo above supported the claim that World War I was a war that was

    (A) made more deadly by new technology

    (B) decided by a handful of victories in large battles

    (C) caused by the economic rather than political forces

    (D) fought on behalf of the princple of self-determination

3. Taken together, the two images demonstrated which of the following trends that occurred during World War I?

(A) Britain's powerful role on the global stage declined.

(B) People became more realistic about the costs of war.

(C) The mass casualties from the conflict broke down class barriers.

(D) The role of women changed during the war.

SHORT-ANSWER QUESTIONS

1. **Use the passage below to answer all parts of the question that follows.**

> "If you could hear at every jolt, the blood
> Come gargling from the froth-corrupted lungs,
> Obscene as cancer, bitter as the cud
> Of vile, incurable sores on innocent tongues,—
> My friend, you would not tell with such high zest
> To children ardent for some desperate glory,
> The old Lie: Dulce et decorum est
> Pro patria mori."
> ["It is sweet and noble to die for one's country."]
>
> Wilfred Owen, "Dulce et Decorum Est," 1920

(A) Identify Owen's point of view in the poem.

(B) Explain ONE reason the British would object to Owen's point of view in the poem.

(C) Explain ONE aspect of the context of World War I that explains why many soldiers fought on behalf of the political state or empire they lived in even though it was not the cultural nation they identified with.

2. **Answer all parts of the question that follows.**

(A) Identify ONE way that advances in war technologies affected the development of World War I.

(B) Explain ONE way that the development of propaganda or media influenced European society during World War I.

(C) Explain ONE way the Paris Peace Conference left problems for Europe to confront.

THINK AS A HISTORIAN: IDENTIFY SUPPORTING EVIDENCE

In 1914, on hearing of German atrocities toward Belgians, the British government undertook its own investigation headed up by Viscount James Bryce, a widely respected scholar, a former ambassador to the United States, and a friend of President Wilson. His committee reviewed the depositions of 1200 witnesses, though they did not do the actual interviewing of the witnesses. Nor were the depositions given under oath. In order to make the report as credible as possible, the committee decided to leave out the most sensational accounts. The final report used 500 of the 1200 reports. It was translated into 30 languages and was reprinted in the *New York Times*. Even though the most violent and lurid reports were eliminated, the report still detailed many gruesome acts and presented the following conclusions:

"It is proved:

(i) That there were in many parts of Belgium deliberate and systematically organized massacres of the civil population, accompanied by many isolated murders and other outrages.

(ii) That in the conduct of the war generally innocent civilians, both men and women, were murdered in large numbers, women violated, and children murdered.

(iii) That looting, house burning, and the wanton destruction of property were ordered and countenanced by the officers of the German Army, that elaborate provisions had been made for systematic incendiarism at the very outbreak of the war, and that the burnings and destruction were frequent where no military necessity could be alleged, being indeed part of a system of general terrorization.

(iv) That the rules and usages of war were frequently broken, particularly by the using of civilians, including women and children, as a shield for advancing forces exposed to fire, to a less degree by killing the wounded and prisoners, and in the frequent abuse of the Red Cross and the White Flag.

Sensible as they are of the gravity of these conclusions, the Committee conceive that they would be doing less than their duty if they failed to record them as fully established by the evidence. Murder, lust, and pillage prevailed over many parts of Belgium on a scale unparalleled in any war between civilised nations during the last three centuries.

Our function is ended when we have stated what the evidence establishes, but we may be permitted to express our belief that these disclosures will not have been made in vain if they touch and rouse the conscience of mankind, and we venture to hope that as soon as the present war is over, the nations of the world in council will consider what means can be provided and sanctions devised to prevent the recurrence of such horrors as our generation is now witnessing."

Answer the following questions about the evidence in the Bryce report.

1. On what evidence was the Bryce report based?

2. The report states that the accounts were "fully established by the evidence." Do you agree? Why or why not?

3. What effect, if any, does the final paragraph have on the report's credibility?

4. Research the impact of the report and the views of historians on its accuracy. What is their overall conclusion?

REFLECT ON THE TOPIC ESSENTIAL QUESTION

1. In one to three paragraphs, explain how governments used a variety of methods to conduct war.

Source: Wikimedia Commons

Belgium WWI war memorial

7.4

Economy in the Interwar Period

We had to struggle with the old enemies of peace—business and financial monopoly, speculation, reckless banking, class antagonism, sectionalism, war profiteering.

—U.S. President Franklin Delano Roosevelt (1936)

Essential Question: How did different governments respond to economic crises after 1900?

Not long after the global trauma of World War I, a global economic crisis resulted in the Great Depression of the 1930s and eventually led to World War II. It undermined faith in the market-based economics that had delivered such wealth as imperialism spread. As unemployment, hunger, and homelessness increased, people turned to their governments for help. Governments had long been essential to capitalism—building roads, providing schools, and regulating trade—but across the world in the 1930s, government intervention in the economy increased. The United States became more liberal as President Roosevelt identified inequities and activities that undermined the economy and could lead to war. Countries such as Germany, Italy, and Japan, however, turned radically to the right. In Russia, government economic control was instituted through the implementation of often repressive Five-Year Plans based on production quotas.

The Great Depression

From today's perspective, the effects of World War I can look small compared to the even greater destruction caused by World War II. However, the effects were massive. Many Western Europeans felt bewildered. World War I brought anxiety to the people who suffered through it. The Allied nations, though victorious, had lost millions of citizens, both soldiers and civilians, and had spent tremendous amounts of money on the international conflict. The defeated Central Powers, particularly Germany and the countries that emerged from the breakup of Austria-Hungary, suffered even greater losses.

The Treaty of Versailles forced Germany to pay billions of dollars in reparations to the war's victors. War-ravaged Germany could not make these payments, so its government printed more paper money in the 1920s.

Source: German Federal Archive. Wikimedia Commons

During the 1920s, German currency became worth so little that this man used it as wallpaper.

This action caused inflation, a general rise in prices. Inflation meant that the value of German money decreased drastically. To add to the sluggish postwar economy, France and Britain had difficulty repaying wartime loans from the United States, partly because Germany was having trouble paying reparations to them. In addition, the Soviet government refused to pay Russia's prerevolutionary debts.

Global Downturn Although the 1920s brought modest economic gains for most of Europe, the subsequent **Great Depression** ended the tentative stability. Agricultural overproduction and the United States' stock market crash in 1929 were two major causes of the global economic downturn. American investors who had been putting money into German banks removed it when the American stock market crashed. In addition to its skyrocketing inflation, Germany then had to grapple with bank failures. Germany thus suffered more than any other Western nation during the Great Depression. The economies of Africa, Asia, and Latin America suffered because they depended on the imperial nations that were experiencing this enormous economic downturn. Japan also suffered during the Depression because its economy depended on foreign trade. With the economic decline in the rest of the world, Japan's exports were cut in half between 1929 and 1931.

The Global Economy, 1929 to 1938		
Year	Total Global Production	Total Global Trade
1929	100	100
1930	86	89
1931	77	81
1932	70	74
1933	79	76
1934	95	79
1935	98	82
1936	110	86
1937	120	98
1938	111	89

Source: Adapted from data in Barry Eichengreen and Douglas Irwin, "The Protectionist Temptation: Lessons from the Great Depression for Today," March 17, 2009.

In this chart, the levels of production and trade for 1929 are represented by 100. The other numbers reflect changes from the 1929 level.

Keynesian Economics The Great Depression inspired new insights into economics. British economist **John Maynard Keynes** rejected the laissez-faire ideal. He concluded that intentional government action could improve the economy. During a depression, he said, governments should use **deficit spending** (spending more than the government takes in) to stimulate economic activity. By cutting taxes and increasing spending, governments would spur economic growth. People would return to work, and the depression would end.

New Deal The administration of President **Franklin Delano Roosevelt** used Keynes's ideas to address the Great Depression in the United States. Roosevelt and his backers created a group of policies and programs known collectively as the **New Deal**. Its goal was to bring the country relief, recovery, and reform: **relief** for citizens who were suffering, including the poor, the unemployed, farmers, minorities, and women; **recovery** to bring the nation out of the Depression, in part through government spending; and **reform** to change government policies in the hopes of avoiding such disasters in the future.

By 1937, unemployment was declining and production was rising. Keynesian economics seemed to be working. However, Roosevelt feared that government deficits were growing too large, so he reversed course. Unemployment began to grow again. The Great Depression finally ended after the United States entered World War II in 1941 and ran up deficits for military spending that dwarfed those of the New Deal programs.

Impact on Trade The Great Depression was a global event. Though it started in the industrialized countries of the United States and Europe, it spread to Latin America, Africa, and Asia. By 1932, more than 30 million people worldwide were out of work. People everywhere turned to their governments for help. As unemployment increased, international trade declined, a decline made worse as nations then imposed strict tariffs, or taxes on imports, in an effort to protect the domestic jobs they still had.

In contrast to most countries, Japan dug itself out of the Depression relatively rapidly. Japan devalued its currency; that is, the government lowered the value of its money in relation to foreign currencies. Thus, Japanese-made products became less expensive than imports. Japan's overseas expansionism also increased Japan's need for military goods and stimulated the economy.

Political Revolutions in Russia and Mexico

In the century's first two decades, rebellions erupted against long-standing authoritarian governments in Mexico, China, and Russia. (See Topic 7.1.) Revolutionaries unseated the ruling governments in each country, instituting their own political philosophies and practices. The revolutions influenced subsequent events in the Soviet Union, Mexico, and China in the interwar years. Each country took a different approach to managing their national economy.

Continuing Revolution in Russia Although Lenin and the Bolshevik Party had promised "peace, land, and bread" during World War I, they instead presided over a populace that faced starvation during the widespread **Russian Civil War** (1918–1921). Hundreds of thousands of Russians, Ukrainians, and others revolted against the Russian government's actions. Urban factory workers and sailors went on strike, and peasants began to hoard their food stocks. Industrial and agricultural production dropped sharply.

By 1921, Lenin realized that the Russian economy was near complete collapse. In an attempt to remedy this, he instituted a temporary retreat from communist economic policies. Under his **New Economic Plan** (**NEP**), he reintroduced private trade, allowing farmers to sell their products on a small scale. Although the government permitted some economic liberties, it maintained strict political control. The NEP enjoyed modest successes, but it came to an end when Lenin died in 1924.

Joseph Stalin Several years after Lenin's death, Joseph Stalin took control of the **Politburo**, the Communist Party's central organization, setting himself up as a dictator. He remained in power for almost 30 years. Once in power, Stalin abandoned Lenin's NEP and instituted the first **Five-Year Plan**, which was meant to transform the **Union of Soviet Socialist Republics** (also called the **USSR** or the **Soviet Union**) into an industrial power. He wanted his largely agricultural nation to "catch up" to the industrial nations of the West. At the same time, Stalin **collectivized** agriculture, a process in which farmland was taken from private owners and given to collectives to manage. In theory, a collective, or **kolkhoz**, was a group of peasants who freely joined together to farm a certain portion of land. In practice, however, peasants were forced by the state to work on a specific collective and were expected to follow detailed plans and to reach specific goals set by the government.

This elimination of private land ownership and the forced redistribution of land, livestock, and tools enraged farmers. Each year, the government seized food to send to the cities. The farmers retaliated against collectivization by burning crops and killing livestock. Many moved to the cities for a better life.

A series of five-year plans had mixed results. The collectivization of agriculture was a huge failure. Millions of peasants starved to death, especially in the Ukraine. However, heavy industry grew tremendously in the 1930s. Although consumer goods were in short supply, there were plenty of factory jobs available, and the cost of living was low.

Stalin's brutal regime is widely condemned today. He punished his political opponents by executing them or sentencing them to life terms in **gulags**, or labor camps, where many died. In addition, his agricultural policies led to the deaths of many millions of Soviet citizens. Because Stalin kept tight control of the press, details of his atrocities went largely unreported. Nonetheless, in the 1930s, an economically depressed world viewed the U.S.S.R. with a mix of horror and wonder. The USSR was rapidly industrializing and increasing its military power. It presented a challenge to countries with capitalist economies whose people were experiencing high levels of unemployment. (Connect: Write a paragraph connecting the USSR with the ideology of Marxism. See Topic 5.8.)

Party Rule in Mexico The economy took a different direction in Mexico. The Mexican revolution saw the emergence of one strong political party, the **Institutional Revolutionary Party**, or **PRI**. This party dominated Mexican politics for most of the 20th century. The Mexican political system has often been called corporatist since the ruling PRI party claimed favors, such as access to primary education and jobs created through improvements to infrastructure, for its constituents.

During PRI's rule, there was a vast improvement in the economy, especially in the period from 1930 to the 1970s. In the 1930s, efforts at land reform were successful under **Lázaro Cárdenas**. In 1938, for example, his regime nationalized the country's mostly foreign-owned oil industry, angering foreign investors. This company, Petróleos Mexicanos or **PEMEX**, became the second largest state-owned company in the world. Despite these reforms, however, the interwar period did not see dramatic changes in Mexico's social hierarchy.

Rise of Right-Wing Governments

In some countries, the turn to the right was radical. A new political system known as **fascism** arose that appealed to extreme nationalism, glorified the military and armed struggle, and blamed problems on ethnic minorities. Fascist regimes suppressed other political parties, protests, and independent trade unions. They justified violence to achieve their goals and were strongly anticommunist. Germany turned to fascism (see Topic 7.6), and some other countries did as well.

Rise of Fascism in Italy Benito Mussolini coined the term *fascism,* which comes from the term *fasces*, a bundle of sticks tied around an axe, which was an ancient Roman symbol for authority. This symbol helped characterize Italy's Fascist government, which glorified militarism and brute force.

The Italian fascist state was based on a concept known as **corporatism**, a theory based on the notion that the sectors of the economy—the employers, the trade unions, and state officials—are seen as separate organs of the same body. Each sector, or organ, was supposedly free to organize itself as it wished as long as it supported the whole. In practice, the fascist state imposed its will upon all sectors of society, creating a **totalitarian state**—a state in which the government controls all aspects of society.

Mussolini Takes Control Even though Italy had been considered one of the victors at the 1919 Paris Peace Conference—along with Britain, France, and the United States—Italy received very little territory from the Treaty of Versailles. This failure to gain from the war caused discontent in Italy. Amid the general bitterness of the 1920s, Mussolini and his allies in the Fascist Party managed to take control of the parliament. Mussolini became a dictator, repressing any possible opposition to his rule. Militaristic propaganda infiltrated every part of the Fascist government. For example, schoolchildren were taught constantly about the glory of their nation and their fearless leader, "*Il Duce.*"

Part of Mussolini's fascist philosophy was the need to conquer what he considered an inferior nation. During the imperialist "Scramble for Africa" in the 19th century, Italy seized **Libya** and colonized **Italian Somaliland**, now part of Somalia. However, the Italian army was pushed back by Abyssinia, modern-day Ethiopia, in the 1890s. In 1934, Mussolini called for the complete conquest of Abyssinia. In 1935, 100,000 Italian troops crossed the border from Somaliland to Abyssinia, defying sanctions from the League of Nations. This time, the Italian army overpowered Abyssinia's while the global community did little to stop the conquest. Many historians believe the Abyssinian crisis destroyed the League of Nations' credibility. In 1936, Mussolini and Germany's Adolf Hitler formed an alliance they hoped would dominate Europe.

Fascism and Civil War in Spain After the economic decline in the early 1930s, two opposing ideologies, or systems of ideas, battled for control of Spain. The **Spanish Civil War** that resulted soon took on global significance as a struggle between the forces of democracy and the forces of fascism.

The **Spanish Republic** formed in 1931 after King Alfonso VIII abdicated. In 1936, the Spanish people elected the **Popular Front**, a coalition of left-wing parties, to lead the government. A key aspect of the Front's platform was land reform, a prospect that energized the nation's peasants and radicals. Conservative forces in Spain, such as the Catholic Church and high-ranking members of the military, were violently opposed to the changes that the Popular Front promised. In July of the same year, Spanish troops stationed in Morocco conducted a military uprising against the Popular Front. This action marked the beginning of the Spanish Civil War, which soon spread to Spain itself. General

Francisco Franco led the insurgents, who called themselves **Nationalists**. On the other side were the **Republicans** or **Loyalists**, the defenders of the newly elected Spanish Republic.

Foreign Involvement Although the nations of Europe had signed a nonintervention agreement, Hitler of Germany, Mussolini of Italy, and Antonio Salazar of Portugal contributed armaments to the Nationalists. Civilian volunteers from the Soviet Union, Britain, the United States, and France contributed their efforts to the Loyalists. Many historians believe that without the help of Germany, Italy, and Portugal, the Nationalist side probably would not have prevailed against the Republic of Spain.

Guernica The foreign involvement in Spain's struggle also escalated the violence of the war. One massacre in particular garnered international attention. The German and Italian bombing of the town of **Guernica** in northern Spain's **Basque region** was one of the first times in history an aerial bombing targeted civilians. Many historians believe that the bombing of Guernica was a military exercise for Germany's air force, the **Luftwaffe**.

The tragedy of Guernica was immortalized in Pablo Picasso's painting of that name, commissioned by the Republic of Spain and completed in 1938. Although abstract, the painting brilliantly depicts the horrific violence of modern warfare and is one of the most significant works of 20th-century art.

Source: Museo Reina Sofía
Pablo Picasso, *Guernica* (1937)

Franco's Victory The Spanish Civil War (1936–1939) ended when Franco's forces defeated the Loyalist army. He ruled Spain as a dictator until his death in 1975. Spain did not officially enter World War II (1939–1945), but the government offered some help to Germany, Italy, and Japan.

Rise of a Repressive Regime in Brazil As in Europe, parts of Latin America also became more conservative. During the interwar years, Brazil was considered Latin America's "sleeping giant" because of its slow shift from an agricultural to an industrial economy. Large landowners dominated the nation's economy, which frustrated members of the urban middle class. Compounding their frustration was the workers' suffering caused by the Great Depression. Discontent led to a bloodless 1930 coup, or illegal seizure of power, which installed Getulio Vargas as president.

Vargas's pro-industrial policies won him support from Brazil's urban middle class. They believed he would promote democracy. However, his actions paralleled those of Italy's corporate state under Mussolini. While Brazil's industrial sector grew rapidly, Vargas began to strip away individual political freedoms. His *Estado Novo* ("New State") program instituted government censorship of the press, abolition of political parties, imprisonment of political opponents, and **hypernationalism**, a belief in the superiority of one's nation over all others and the single-minded promotion of national interests. While these policies were similar to those of European fascists, the Brazilian government did not praise or rely on violence to achieve and maintain control.

Moreover, even though Brazil had close economic ties with the United States and Germany in the late 1930s, Brazil finally sided with the Allies in World War II. This political alignment against the Axis powers made Brazil look less like a dictatorship and more liberal than it actually was. World War II prompted the people of Brazil to push for a more democratic nation later. They came to see the contradiction between fighting fascism and repression abroad and maintaining a dictatorship at home.

Three Approaches to Modern Industrial Society			
Policy Area	**Communism**	**Capitalism**	**Fascism**
Economics	Believed that businesses should be owned or managed by the government	Believed that businesses should be owned privately and compete with each other	Believed that businesses should be owned privately and government should restrict competition
Internationalism and Nationalism	Supported internationalism by opposing colonialism and calling for global worker solidarity	Supported a mixture of nationalism and internationalism	Supported nationalism strongly by urging each nation to pursue its unique interests
War and Peace	Believed that international peace would follow the defeat of capitalism	Expressed mixed attitudes toward war and peace	Opposed peace on the belief that it weakened society
Equality	Supported both political and economic equality	Supported political equality but not economic equality	Opposed both political and economic equality
Religion	Advocated atheism	Allowed individual religious liberty	Use religion to build nationalism

KEY TERMS BY THEME

ECONOMICS: Concepts
inflation
deficit spending
relief
recovery
reform
collectivize
kolkhoz
corporatism

ECONOMICS: Events and Policies
Great Depression
New Deal
New Economic Plan (NEP)
Five-Year Plan

ECONOMICS: Economists
John Maynard Keynes

GOVERNMENT: Wars and Rebellions
Russian Civil War
Spanish Civil War
Guernica

GOVERNMENT: Politics
Politburo
Institutional Revolutionary Party (PRI)
fascism
totalitarian state
Popular Front
Nationalists
Republicans
Loyalists
Luftwaffe

GOVERNMENT: Countries and Regions
Union of Soviet Socialist Republics (U.S.S.R.)
Soviet Union
Libya
Italian Somaliland
Spanish Republic
Basque region
hypernationalism

GOVERNMENT: Leaders
Franklin Delano Roosevelt
Lázaro Cárdenas
Francisco Franco

GOVERNMENT: Institutions
gulag
PEMEX

MULTIPLE-CHOICE QUESTIONS

Questions 1 to 3 refer to the passage below.

"It has been repeated ad nauseam [to a sickening degree] that the oil industry has brought additional capital for the development and progress of the country. This assertion is an exaggeration. For many years throughout the major period of their existence, oil companies have enjoyed great privileges for development and expansion, including customs and tax exemptions and innumerable prerogatives. . . . Potential wealth of the Nation; miserably underpaid native labor; tax exemptions; economic privileges; governmental tolerance—these are the factors of the boom of the Mexican oil industry. . . . These organizations, whether authorized by the Government or not, are charged with innumerable outrages, abuses, and murders, always on behalf of the companies that employ them. . . .

It was therefore necessary to adopt a definite and legal measure to end this permanent state of affairs in which the country sees its industrial progress held back by those who hold in their hands the power to erect obstacles. . . . It is necessary that all groups of the population be imbued with a full optimism and that each citizen, whether in agricultural, industrial, commercial, transportation, or other pursuits, develop a greater activity from this moment on, in order to create new resources which will reveal that the spirit of our people is capable of saving the nation's economy by the efforts of its own citizens."

President Lázaro Cárdenas of Mexico, speech announcing
state control of the Mexican oil industry, 1938

1. According to Cárdenas's description in the first paragraph, which of the following contributed MOST directly to the activities of foreign oil companies in Mexico?

   (A) Foreign economic imperialism in Latin America

   (B) A combination of inflation and deficit spending

   (C) The spread of laissez faire economic policies

   (D) Spain's colonial policies in Latin America

2. Based on the passage, which of the following most strongly influenced Cárdenas's views?

   (A) Free-market capitalism

   (B) The Green Revolution

   (C) Social Darwinism

   (D) Socialism

3. The speech best illustrates which of the following developments in the 1930s?

   (A) Economic crises contributed to the rise of fascist and totalitarian regimes.

   (B) States played a more active role in their economies after the Great Depression.

   (C) Increased exploitation of fossil fuels led to debates about climate change.

   (D) Government used political propaganda to mobilize civilians for total war.

1. **Use the passage to answer all parts of the question that follows.**

"To Comrades Kuraev, Bosh,
Minkin and other Penza communists

Comrades! The revolt by the five kulak [derogatory term referring to the class of prosperous peasants] volosts [a territorial/administrative unit consisting of a few villages and surrounding land] must be suppressed without mercy. The interest of the entire revolution demands this, because we have now before us our final decisive battle "with the kulaks." We need to set an example.

1. You need to hang (hang without fail, so that the public sees) at least 100 notorious kulaks, the rich, and the bloodsuckers.

2. Publish their names.

3. Take away all of their grain.

4. Execute the hostages—in accordance with yesterday's telegram.

This needs to be accomplished in such a way, that people for hundreds of miles around will see, tremble, know and scream out: let's choke and strangle those blood-sucking kulaks.

Telegraph us acknowledging receipt and execution of this.

Yours, Lenin

P.S. Use your toughest people for this."

Telegram, August 11, 1918

(A) Identify ONE historical development after 1900 that reflects the Soviet hanging order from Vladimir Lenin.

(B) Explain ONE way in which government economic intervention in Russia is similar to government economic intervention in the United States after 1900.

(C) Explain ONE way in which government economic intervention in Russia differs from that in Italy after 1900.

2. **Answer all parts of the question that follows.**

(A) Identify ONE way in which colonized states were affected by the Great Depression.

(B) Explain ONE way that the ideas of John Maynard Keynes differ from the ideas of Adam Smith.

(C) Explain ONE way in which Japan responded to the economic crisis after 1900 differently from United States.

THINK AS A HISTORIAN: SIGNIFICANCE OF HISTORICAL
SITUATION

When Mexico nationalized the oil industry, some foreign countries whose oil companies were taken over boycotted Mexican oil and urged consumers to boycott other Mexican products. As a result, Nazi Germany became Mexico's biggest customer for oil. The United States, however, had a "Good Neighbor" policy with Mexico and took a softer approach.

Read the following excerpt from a 1938 letter from U.S. Secretary of State Cordell Hull to the Mexican ambassador in Washington, D.C. Then answer the questions that follow.

"The Government of the United States . . . notes that the applicable precedents and recognized authorities on international law support its declaration that, under every rule of law and equity, no government is entitled to expropriate private property, for whatever purpose, without provision for prompt, adequate, and effective payment therefor. . . .

My Government considers that its own practice has amply demonstrated that it is the consistent friend of reform, that it has every sympathy with misfortune and need, and that it recognizes fully the necessities of the under-privileged. It cannot, however, accept the idea that these high objectives justify, or for that matter require, infringement on the law of nations or the upsetting of constitutionally recognized guarantees. . . .

Every sovereign nation is in possession of powers to regulate its internal affairs, to reorganize, when needful, its entire economic, financial, and industrial structure, and to achieve social ends by methods conforming with law.

Instead of using these recognized and orderly methods, the Government of Mexico in effect suggests that whenever special conditions or circumstances obtain in any one country, that country is entitled to expect all the other nations of the world to accept a change in the settled rules and principles of law, which are domestic quite as much as international, solely in order to assist the country in question to extricate itself from difficulties for which it is itself entirely responsible. Specifically, it is proposed to replace the rule of just compensation by rule of confiscation. Adoption by the nations of the world of any such theory as that would result in the immediate breakdown of confidence and trust between nations, and in such progressive deterioration of international economic and commercial relations as would imperil the very foundations of modern civilization. Human progress would be fatally set back. . . .

The vital interest of all governments and of all peoples in this question and the imperative need of all countries to maintain unimpaired the structure of common justice embodied in international as well as in basic national law, lead me, particularly in view of the warm friendship existing between the two countries, to appeal most earnestly to the Mexican Government to refrain from persisting in a policy and example which, if generally pursued, will seriously jeopardize the interests of all peoples throughout the world."

1. In Secretary Hull's view, what would allow for the expropriation of private property?

2. What is Secretary Hull asking the Mexican government to do?

3. Why, in this historical situation especially, would the United States be interested in preserving good relations with Mexico?

REFLECT ON THE TOPIC ESSENTIAL QUESTION

1. In one to three paragraphs, explain how different governments responded to economic crises after 1900.

Unresolved Tensions After World War I

The British Government in India has not only deprived the Indian people of their freedom, but has debased it economically, politically, culturally, and spiritually.

—Indian National Congress, Declaration of Purna Swaraj
(Independence Day Resolution, January 26, 1930)

Essential Question: How did continuities and changes in territorial holdings create tensions after World War I?

As economic crises beset countries after World War I, unresolved disputes over the control of land continued to fester. The victors in the war, European powers and Japan, generally kept or expanded control over colonial territories. However, anti-imperial resistance was growing throughout Asia and Africa. In a larger context, the spread of nationalism in these regions was part of the same global trend that included the breakup of empires in Europe, the success of communism in Russia, and the spread of anti-immigrant sentiments in the United States. The example of Turkey's push for self-determination was already discussed in Topic 7.1. Similarly, events such as the May 4th Movement in China and groups such as the Indian National Congress demonstrated how nationalism was spreading throughout the world.

Effects of the War

The effects of World War I varied around the world. The United States prospered because of all the war materials and agricultural products it sold to Britain and the other Allies. By contrast, the European countries that suffered the greatest damage in the war were economically devastated.

Effects on Colonial Lands While nationalist movements had been brewing for decades in colonies in South Asia and West Africa, the war renewed the hopes of people in these regions for independence. African and Asian colonial troops contributed thousands of soldiers to the Allied war effort. In addition, this disastrous war showed colonial peoples that imperial powers such as Britain and France were not invincible.

German propaganda during the war had predicted that colonial soldiers' experience in the war would lead to a great uprising against colonial rule.

This did not materialize, although there were several local rebellions. Between November 1915 and September 1916, a large group of villages in French West Africa, between the Volta and Bani rivers in what later became Burkina Faso, united in an effort to drive out the French. It was only with a great effort and loss of life on both sides that the French managed to put down the revolt. The rebellion forced the French to recognize that they had an obligation to the people they colonized. After World War I, many war veterans from the French colonies assisted in colonial administration after they returned home.

Colonized people's war experiences raised their expectations. They thought that the principle of self-determination, as expressed in Wilson's Fourteen Points, would get them closer to self-rule. Nationalists in Africa and Asia hoped that the blood they had shed for their "home countries" would earn them some respect from Western Europe and thus begin a **decolonization** process.

However, the peace conference's **Big Three**—David Lloyd George, Woodrow Wilson, and Georges Clemenceau (after Italy left)—were not interested in freeing the colonies. After World War I, European powers granted self-determination only to white countries in Eastern Europe. Middle Eastern lands that had been a part of the Ottoman Empire came under the control of France and Britain in the League of Nations mandate system. Former German colonies in Africa had the same fate. German territories and spheres of influence in East Asia and the Pacific were transferred to various victorious nations of World War I. India and nearly every nation in Africa—as well as most of the Middle East—continued to be controlled by European nations.

Wilson even refused to meet with a group of Vietnamese nationalists, including a young Ho Chi Minh, who asked to speak with him about self-determination for Vietnam. This rejection fueled stronger nationalist movements in colonies scattered across the southern rim of Asia and in parts of Africa. The seeds of African, Arab, and Asian nationalism were sown largely in the aftermath of World War I, although they did not come to fruition until much later.

The Mandate System

Arab rebels of the former Ottoman Empire were especially insulted by the results of the peace conference. They had been promised self-rule if they fought with the Allies. Instead, the Allies forgot all of their promises and, through the League of Nations, established a **mandate system** to rule the colonies and territories of the Central Powers. Article 22 of the League of Nations charter stated that colonized people in Africa and Asia required "tutelage" from more "advanced" nations in order to survive. Thus, the Allied countries—including France, Great Britain, and Japan—were able to increase their imperial holdings through a new form of colonization. For example, Cameroon, which had been a German colony, was divided and transferred to France and Britain as separate mandates. Japan seized the German-held islands of the Western Pacific.

The Middle East experienced enormous upheaval because of the fall of the Ottoman Empire. Palestine, Transjordan, Lebanon, Syria, and Iraq all became League of Nations mandates. These Arab states were not yet sovereign lands but virtual colonies of Great Britain and France. This infuriated the Arabs who lived in these lands and set the stage for a nationalist movement known as **Pan-Arabism**—an ideology that called for the unification of all lands in North Africa and the Middle East.

Another source of conflict arose in 1917, when the British government issued the **Balfour Declaration**, which stated that **Palestine** should become a permanent home for the Jews of Europe. Those who supported a Jewish homeland were known as **Zionists**. After the Allied victory in the Great War, European Jews moved in droves to Palestine, which Britain controlled.

MANDATES IN THE MIDDLE EAST AFTER WORLD WAR I

Anti-Colonialism in South Asia

The setback presented by the Paris Conference inspired anticolonial activists to redouble their efforts. In South Asia, the **Indian National Congress** formed in the late 19th century to air grievances against the colonial government. By the end of World War I in 1918, it had become a strong voice for independence.

Massacre at Amritsar In the spring of 1919, a group of Indian nationalists gathered in a public garden in Amritsar, Punjab, to protest the arrest of two freedom fighters. The protest took place during a Sikh festival, which had attracted thousands of villagers to the city, which Sikhs considered holy. Although the throngs were peaceful, the British colonial government had recently made such public gatherings illegal. Armed colonial forces fired hundreds of shots into the unarmed crowd, killing an estimated 379 people and wounding 1,200 more.

The Amritsar massacre radicalized many Indians. It convinced moderate members of the Indian National Congress that independence from Britain was the only way forward.

Gandhi By the 1920s, **Mohandas Gandhi** had brought the congress's cause to the Indian masses and caught the attention of the world. His **satyagraha** ("devotion-to-truth") **movement** embarked on a campaign of **civil disobedience** that encouraged Indians to break unjust laws and serve jail time. These actions, he believed, would stir the consciousness of the empire and the international community and expose the injustice of Britain's imperial system.

Gandhi, who came to be known by Indians as **Mahatma**, or "the great soul," led a boycott against British goods. After returning to India from South Africa, Gandhi wore the traditional cotton Hindu *dhoti* rather than the Western-style suits he had worn as a lawyer in Natal. Wearing homespun clothes was a form of protest against British fabrics made from Indian cotton and sold to Indians at inflated prices.

One of Gandhi's first campaigns became known as the **Salt March**. British authorities had made it illegal for Indians to produce their own sea salt. The commodity was easy to make in the tropical country, but Britain wanted a monopoly on salt. In 1930, Gandhi led thousands of Indians to the Arabian Sea and simply picked up a few grains of salt, in defiance of Britain's unjust edict.

Source: GandhiServe Foundation. Wikimedia Commons

Gandhi (shirtless) and his followers during the Salt March of 1930

The Two-State Solution While anticolonial sentiment was building, leaders of the independence movement disagreed about how India should define its national identity. Muslim leader **Muhammad Ali Jinnah**, a member of the Muslim minority in the largely Hindu Indian National Congress, originally favored Muslim-Hindu unity but later proposed a two-state plan for South Asian independence. He was concerned that Muslim interests would be overwhelmed by Hindu concerns in an independent India. He proposed creating a separate state, **Pakistan**, that would include the heavily Muslim western and eastern parts of South Asia. This proposal made several leaders, including Gandhi and **Jawaharlal Nehru**, who eventually became India's first prime minister, anxious about the region's future. Although independence did not come for India and Pakistan until after World War II, the interwar years were critical times for the anticolonial movement. (Connect: Write a paragraph connecting 20th century tensions between Hindus and Muslims in India with India's earlier religious history. See Topic 1.3.)

Nationalism in East Asia

Korea, China, and Japan had not been formally colonized by Europe, but they did suffer from European domination. These countries also demonstrated the spread of the desire for self-determination.

The March First Movement in Korea The small country of Korea had suffered under increasing Japanese influence since the 1890s. In 1910, Japan took control of Korea. After World War I, Japan expected to expand its role in East Asia, just as European states did in the Middle East. The prospect of European support for a stronger Japan, and the mysterious death of the Korean emperor, caused Korean resentment to explode. On March 1, 1919, Koreans began a series of protests that involved as many as 2 million Koreans out of a population of 17 million. The occupying Japanese forces cracked down harshly, killing several thousand Koreans. But the **March First Movement** demonstrated the power of Korean nationalism.

The May Fourth Movement in China During World War I, China supported the Allies. Britain and France hired nearly 150,000 Chinese to work in factories, dig trenches and do other support work. China hoped that the victorious Allies would support China's desire to reclaim German-controlled land on the Shandong Peninsula in northeast China. However, Japan wanted the same land. At the Paris Peace Conference in 1919, Great Britain and France sided with Japan. Infuriated, Chinese intellectuals and workers staged anti-Japanese demonstrations beginning on May 4, 1919. The **May Fourth Movement** symbolized China's growing nationalism and demand for democracy. Angered by Europe's support for Japan, many Chinese rejected Western-style government. They turned toward the Marxist model of the Soviet Union. Several May Fourth leaders joined the Chinese Communist Party. In the years after the May Fourth protests, two main groups fought for power: the communists and the nationalists.

- The **Chinese Communist Party (CCP)** was founded in 1921. It was eventually led by **Mao Zedong** (or Mao Tse-tung), the son of a prosperous peasant, who was inspired by the communist revolution in Russia. Instead of energizing the working classes of Chinese cities, however, Mao believed that China's communist revolution could be based on the revolt of peasants, who made up the vast majority of China's population.

- The Chinese Nationalist Party, or **Kuomintang**, was led by Sun Yat-sen. He was devoted to full independence and industrialization, and he allied with Mao's forces to free China from foreign domination and overthrow the warlords. Following Sun's death in 1925, **Chiang Kai-shek** took control of the Nationalist Party. Chiang was a conservative and had a deep-seated distrust of communism. In 1927, Chiang's forces attacked and nearly annihilated Mao's forces, initiating the Chinese Civil War.

The Long March Mao and remnants of the Chinese Communist Party retreated into China's interior, where for several years they trained in hiding. In 1934, Chiang's forces again attacked Mao's army in the rural areas of Jiangxi. After the attack, Mao's forces began the **Long March,** a year-long, 6,000-mile long retreat. It traversed treacherous mountains, deep marshes, and extremely dry deserts. Of the 80,000 or more who began the Long March, only 10,000 remained to assemble in 1935 in northern China.

The Chinese Communist Party was weak after the Long March. However, peasants admired Mao and his army's tremendous stamina and their commitment to their ideals. This support among peasants would later be important for the success of the Communists in winning control of the country.

While the Communists were retreating on the Long March, the Nationalist Kuomintang continued to rule much of China during the 1930s. Chiang, however, had alienated many. Old traditions were losing support, but he advocated Confucianism. When opponents criticized him, he suppressed free speech. When people accused the Nationalists of corruption, he did not stop it.

China, Japan, and Manchukuo In 1935, the Nationalists and Communists in China suspended their civil war to unite against a more pressing danger: Japan. Seeking access to natural resources on the Asian mainland, Japan had invaded Manchuria in northern China in September 1931. Tensions increased when someone, either Chinese dissidents or Japanese soldiers, attacked a railway owned by Japan near Mukden. When the League of Nations condemned Japan's actions in Manchuria, Japan gave up its membership in the League and seized more land. In 1932, the Japanese set up a puppet state called **Manchukuo.** To make Manchukuo seem like an independent Chinese state, it selected the last Chinese emperor to sit on its throne. (Connect: Create a timeline showing the steps Japan took as it moved from isolation to imperialism. See Topic 5.6.)

Japan continued to expand its empire until 1945, the year World War II ended. It seized the Philippines (under partial U.S. control at the time), the Dutch East Indies, British Malaya, Burma, and numerous Pacific islands. Japan termed these territories the **Greater East Asia Co-Prosperity Sphere**. Although Japan claimed to be liberating people from Western imperialism, people in the region experienced Japan as a conqueror.

Resistance to French Rule in West Africa

As in South Asia, people all over Africa were disappointed that their colonies did not achieve independence after World War I. Pro-independence movements in Africa began with European-educated intellectuals. For example, the future leader of Kenya, **Jomo Kenyatta,** studied in London. **Léopold Senghor,** the future leader of Senegal, studied in Paris. In Europe, African intellectuals learned to recognize the racial discrimination taking place in their homelands. Most members of the educated elite worked for the colonial government, if they were not self-employed attorneys or doctors.

Africans under colonial rule resisted the colonizers. Black workers in French West Africa staged a series of strikes, including a strike of railway workers in 1917 and a general strike in 1946. Some of these actions spread throughout French West Africa (Senegal, Benin, Ivory Coast, and Guinea). Strikers protested discriminatory wage and benefit policies and in some cases won a number of their demands through a compromise settlement.

KEY TERMS BY THEME

GOVERNMENT: Policies	**GOVERNMENT:** Movements	**GOVERNMENT:** Countries
decolonization	Pan-Arabism	Palestine
mandate system	Indian National Congress	Pakistan
Balfour Declaration	satyagraha (devotion-to-	
civil disobedience	truth) movement	**GOVERNMENT:** Imperialism
	Salt March	Amritsar
GOVERNMENT: Leaders	March First Movement	Manchukuo
Big Three	May Fourth Movement	Greater East Asia Co-
Mohandas Gandhi	Chinese Communist Party	Prosperity Sphere
Muhammad Ali Jinnah	(CCP)	
Jawaharlal Nehru	Kuomintang	**CULTURE:** People
Mao Zedong	Long March	Zionists
Chiang Kai-shek		Mahatma
		Jomo Kenyatta
		Léopold Sédar Senghor

Questions 1 to 3 refer to the passage below.

"After [World War I], the world was divided into two camps: one is the revolutionary camp which includes the oppressed colonial peoples and the exploited working class throughout the world. Its vanguard is the Soviet Union. The other is the counter-revolutionary camp of international capitalism and imperialism, whose general staff is the League of Nations.

That war resulted in untold loss of life and property. . . . French imperialism was the hardest hit. Therefore, in order to restore the forces of capitalism in France, the French imperialists have . . . built new factories to exploit the workers by paying them starvation wages. They have plundered the peasants' land to establish plantations and drive them to destitution. They have levied new heavy taxes. They have forced our people to buy government bonds. In short, they have driven our people to utter misery. They have increased their military forces, firstly to strangle the Vietnamese revolution; secondly to prepare for a new imperialist war in the Pacific aimed at conquering new colonies; thirdly to suppress the Chinese revolution; and fourthly to attack the Soviet Union because she helps the oppressed nations and the exploited working class to wage revolution.

World War Two will break out. When it does the French imperialists will certainly drive our people to an even more horrible slaughter."

Ho Chi Minh, speech in Hong Kong at the founding of the
Indo-Chinese Communist Party, 1930

1. Which statement best reflects the relationship between conditions before and after World War I as described by Ho Chi Minh?

   (A) They changed significantly.

   (B) They were remarkably similar.

   (C) They became slightly worse.

   (D) They became slightly better.

2. Which statement most accurately corresponds to the claim in the first paragraph that World War I divided the world into two camps?

   (A) The world was divided into those camps, with the Soviet Union standing for one and the League of Nations for the other.

   (B) The war divided colonized people between those allied with capitalism and those allied with imperialism.

   (C) The "oppressed colonial peoples" and "exploited working class" were not united enough to represent one camp.

   (D) The Soviet Union actually reintroduced private property and capitalism.

3. Because of Ho Chi Minh's point of view, which is the best way to evaluate the accuracy of his account?

(A) Because he was a revolutionary, assume that he used exaggerations

(B) Because he was educated, trust that he reported events accurately

(C) Because imperialism was common, see what others wrote about revolutions in their lands

(D) Because many people wrote about these events, compare his statements theirs

SHORT-ANSWER QUESTIONS

1. Use the passage below to answer all parts of the question that follows.

"We hereby declare that Korea is an independent state and that Koreans are a self-governing people. We proclaim it to the nations of the world in affirmation of the principle of the equality of all nations, and we proclaim it to our posterity, preserving in perpetuity the right of national survival. We make this declaration on the strength of five thousand years of history as an expression of the devotion and loyalty of twenty million people. . . ."

Korean Declaration of Independence, March 1, 1919

"We, having been living in one corner of the world for several decades, must ask ourselves what is the level of our national strength and our civilization. This is the final awakening of which I speak. To put it another way, if we open our eyes and take a hard look at the situation within our country and abroad, what place does our country and our people occupy, and what actions should we take?"

Chen Duxiu, Chinese Communist Party leader, *Our Final Awakening*, 1916

(A) Identify ONE way World War I influenced colonized states.

(B) Explain ONE way that the ideas from the Korean declaration are similar to the ideas in Duxiu's statement.

(C) Explain ONE historical result after 1900 of League of Nations mandates.

2. Answer all parts of the question that follows.

(A) Identify ONE example of new forms of nationalism after World War I.

(B) Explain ONE example of an imperial state that gained territory through conquest after World War I.

(C) Explain ONE example of an imperial state that gained territory through a treaty settlement after World War I.

THINK AS A HISTORIAN: SIGNIFICANCE OF PURPOSE AND AUDIENCE

Ho Chi Minh began his speech announcing the formation of the Indo-Chinese Communist Party (excerpted before the Multiple-Choice Questions) by addressing the audience:

"Workers, peasants, soldiers, youth and school students!
Oppressed and exploited fellow-countrymen!
Sisters and brothers! Comrades!"

Identify Vietnamese leader Ho Chi Minh's purpose and audience. Given those, explain the possible limitations of his account as a historical source. Describe two ways the potential limitations of this source might be overcome.

REFLECT ON THE TOPIC ESSENTIAL QUESTION

1. In one to three paragraphs, explain the continuities and changes in territorial holdings from 1900 to the present.

7.6

Causes of World War II

It is blood which moves the wheels of history.

—Benito Mussolini (1914, before he became *Il Duce*, the Leader)

Essential Question: What were the causes and consequences of World War II?

The causes of World War II lay in the unresolved issues in the aftermath of World War I. Economic instability in the postwar economies of Europe led to civil unrest in Italy and Germany. In Italy, the rise of fascism was directly related to the downturn of the Italian economy that occurred after World War I. Benito Mussolini and his National Fascist Party came to power in 1922 because of their promises to renew the Italian economy and create another Italian empire in the Mediterranean and beyond. The peace settlement after World War I also placed unsustainable economic and political terms on Germany and instituted territorial distributions that took away resources and created resentment among the German population. Thus, the ideology associated with Italian fascism and militarism—as seen in the quotation above—spread to Germany, where Hitler and the Nazis adopted it.

The Path to War

Out of the context of the broad economic and political trends emerged **Adolf Hitler**. His extreme views on the superiority of the Aryan race and his vision of a great German civilization led him to persecute Jews and other minorities and to systematically seize land.

Rise of Nazism Following Germany's defeat in 1918, the democratically elected **Weimar Republic** replaced the monarchical rule of the kaiser. Under the terms of the Treaty of Versailles, the new German government not only had to pay billions in war reparations, but it also was not allowed to have an army. The Weimar Republic, appearing weak to the demoralized German people, became especially unpopular during the Great Depression.

The rolls of the unemployed swelled due to the weak German economy. Large numbers of young men, including many World War I veterans, found themselves with few job prospects. Such an environment fostered alienation and bitterness. Many Germans perceived the Weimar Republic to be too weak to solve the country's problems, so they looked to right-wing political parties that promised strong action.

Hitler had declared his extreme anti-Semitic views in his book *Mein Kampf* ("My Struggle"), which he began writing in 1924 while in a Bavarian prison after a failed coup attempt. The National Socialist German Worker's Party, or the **Nazis**, came to power legally after the party did well in the 1932 parliamentary elections. In early 1933, the president of Germany, Paul von Hindenburg, invited Adolf Hitler to form a government as chancellor, which he did. Hindenburg died in 1934, giving Hitler the opening he needed to declare himself president.

Through manipulation, the Nazi Party instilled fear and panic in the German people, making them believe that they were in a state of emergency. For example, the Nazis staged a burning of the **Reichstag**, the German parliament building, and blamed radical extremists for the act. Using domestic security as justification, Hitler outlawed all other political parties and all forms of resistance to his rule.

Hitler openly promoted ultranationalism and **scientific racism**, a pseudoscientific theory that claimed that certain races were genetically superior to others. He also advanced an extreme form of **anti-Semitism**, or hostility toward Jews. He filled his speeches with accusations against German Jews, whom Hitler claimed were responsible for the nation's domestic problems. Nazi propaganda emphasized a need for a "pure" German nation of "**Aryans**," purged of "outsiders"—not only Jews, but also Slavs, communists, Roma (also known as Gypsies), and gay men and women. Hitler suggested that the only way for Germany to live up to its potential was to eliminate the corrupting influence of these groups, particularly the Jews.

Nuremberg Laws Hitler's anti-Jewish campaign began with laws designed to disenfranchise and discriminate against them. The **Nuremberg Laws**, passed in 1935, forbade marriage between Jews and gentiles (people who are not Jewish), stripped Jews of their citizenship, and unleashed a series of subsequent decrees that effectively pushed Jews to the margins of German society. German Jews, many of whom were successful in their careers and felt assimilated into German society, were shocked by the way they were being treated. Some Eastern European nations, such as Romania and Bulgaria, also passed laws discriminating against their Jewish citizens.

The Axis Powers Hitler then sought new allies to help him acquire *Lebensraum* (living space) for the new German empire. He did not try to hide his ambition to conquer the entire continent. Hitler's lust for land eventually brought the international community to the brink of war. He first formed a military pact with Fascist Italy, the **Rome-Berlin Axis**, in October 1936. In addition to their need for military support, the two countries shared a political ideology and economic interests. Germany then created a military alliance with Japan based on mutual distrust of communism, known as the **Anti-Comintern Pact**. The alliances among these three nations created the **Axis Powers**.

Kristallnacht Hitler's campaign to rid Germany of Jews predated his aggressive land grabs in Europe. His propaganda and the Nuremberg Laws successfully created an atmosphere of hostility, hatred, and distrust within

Germany. This tension erupted one night in early November 1938. **Kristallnacht**, the "Night of the Broken Glass," produced anti-Jewish riots that ostensibly occurred in response to the assassination of a German diplomat by a Jewish teenager. Although it appeared to be a spontaneous burst of outrage on the part of the German citizenry, Nazi leaders had actually engineered the entire operation. The riots resulted in the deaths of more than 90 German Jews and the destruction of nearly every synagogue in Germany and some 7,000 Jewish shops. More than 30,000 Jews were dragged from their homes, arrested, and sent to concentration camps. Most of these prisoners were eventually released on orders to leave Germany, an option not given to later concentration camp prisoners.

Source: Center for Jewish History, New York City

Interior of a Berlin synagogue after it was set on fire during Kristallnacht, November 9, 1938.

Nazi Germany's Aggressive Militarism

The terms of the Treaty of Versailles severely limited the German military after World War I. Yet Hitler wanted a stronger military to acquire more land. In March 1935, he broke the treaty when he announced the creation of a German air force and a policy of conscription to enlarge the size of the army.

The Treaty of Versailles Under the treaty, a strip of land in the Rhineland 31 miles wide was set up as a buffer zone between Germany and France. Germany was not allowed to station troops there. Hitler broke the agreement, sending German troops into the Rhineland on March 7, 1936. Both France and Britain protested this move, but they took no other action.

Some British believed that Hitler was the strong anticommunist leader that central Europe needed to keep order. Others were simply reluctant to return to war. So Britain followed a policy of **appeasement**, giving in to Germany's demands in hopes of keeping the peace. However, Germany's military expansion and its support of the fascist Spanish Nationalist government during the Spanish Civil War (1936–1939) indicated that Hitler was increasing his power. (Connect: Describe the connection between the militarism that led up to World War I and World War II. See Topic 7.2.)

German-Austrian Unification With his military revived and alliances in hand, Hitler felt confident about taking his next step in the creation of a new German empire, the **Third Reich**. His plan was to bring Austria, where he was born, under German rule. Hitler used the threat of invasion to pressure the Austrian chancellor into giving more power to the Austrian Nazi Party. As Hitler had planned, the Austrian Nazis then opened the door for German troops to occupy Austria with no resistance. With the **Anschluss** (political union), Austria officially became part of the Third Reich in March 1938.

Czechoslovakia The annexation of Austria was only the first step for Hitler. He wanted more. In September 1938, he issued a demand to Czechoslovakia for the border territory of the **Sudetenland**. Most of the people who lived in this region spoke German; Hitler argued that the area was a natural extension of his Aryan empire. The German leader met with the leaders of Britain, France, and Italy in Munich to discuss his demands. **Neville Chamberlain**, the British prime minister, again argued that a policy of appeasement would keep the peace and put an end to Hitler's demands for more land. The **Munich Agreement** allowed Hitler to annex the Sudetenland in return for a promise that Germany would not take over any more Czech territory. This was a fateful miscalculation. Hitler saw that the British were not willing to stand up to his illegal land grabs, emboldening him to seize control of all of Czechoslovakia with an armed invasion in 1939.

The Conflict over Poland Hitler next set his sights on the Polish port of **Danzig**. Although Germany did have some historical claims to the port, in reality, Hitler was merely looking for an excuse to invade Poland. Britain, in the meantime, had reached the end of its policy of appeasement and agreed to protect Poland from a German attack. Britain and France also reached out to the Soviet Union to form a stronger alliance against Germany.

Germany, however, was already in negotiations with the Soviets. With the signing of the **German-Soviet Nonaggression Pact** on August 23, 1939, the two nations pledged not to attack one another. During the negotiations for the pact, Hitler secretly offered Stalin control of eastern Poland and the Baltic States if Stalin would stand by during a German invasion of western Poland. With this assurance in hand, Germany invaded Poland on September 1, 1939, claiming that Poland had attacked first. Britain and France honored their agreement to protect Poland and declared war on Germany. These actions marked the official start of World War II in Europe.

Causes of World War II	
Diplomatic	• The imbalance of the Treaty of Versailles
	• Failure of appeasement
	• Failure of the League of Nations
Economic	• Global depression
	• The Treaty of Versailles
Political	• Japan's militarism
	• Germany's militarism and the rise of Hitler

Japan's Expansion in Asia

By the time Germany invaded Poland in 1939, Japan had already been moving aggressively against Korea and China for almost 50 years. In 1931, Japan had invaded Manchuria. After several months of fighting, it successfully created the state of Manchukuo under its control. Then, in 1937, a small incident in this region between Japanese troops and Chinese troops quickly escalated. Soon, Japan had launched a full-scale invasion of China. This marked the start of World War II in Asia.

KEY TERMS BY THEME

GOVERNMENT: People
Adolf Hitler
Neville Chamberlain

GOVERNMENT: Geography
Weimar Republic
Sudetenland
Danzig

GOVERNMENT: Policies
Nuremberg Laws
Kristallnacht
Lebensraum
Anschluss
Munich Agreement

GOVERNMENT: Alliances
Rome-Berlin Axis
Anti-Comintern Pact
Axis Powers
German-Soviet
  Nonaggression Pact

GOVERNMENT: Organizations
Nazis
Reichstag
Third Reich

CULTURE: Beliefs and Ideas
Mein Kampf
scientific racism
anti-Semitism
Aryans
appeasement

Questions 1 to 3 refer to the passage below.

"Perception of danger, danger to our institutions, may come slowly or it may come with a rush and a shock as it has to the people of the United States in the past few months. This perception of danger, danger in a world-wide area—it has come to us clearly and overwhelmingly—we perceive the peril in a world-wide arena, an arena that may become so narrowed that only the Americas will retain the ancient faiths. Some indeed still hold to the now somewhat obvious delusion that we of the United States can safely permit the United States to become a lone island, a lone island in a world dominated by the philosophy of force."

Franklin D. Roosevelt, address delivered at
Charlottesville, Virginia, June 10, 1940

1. What position is best supported by Roosevelt's words in this passage?
   (A) The United States should follow a strategy of appeasement toward Hitler.
   (B) The United States should avoid war with Hitler at all costs.
   (C) The United States should join the fight against Hitler.
   (D) The United States alone could stop Hitler.

2. Based on the passage, Roosevelt would have most strongly supported
   (A) the Monroe Doctrine
   (B) the League of Nations
   (C) the mandate system
   (D) the Munich Agreement

3. Which statement accurately provides the context needed to understand the passage?
   (A) Hitler's forces were overrunning Europe, and Britain asked the United States for help in spite of the strength of U.S. isolationism.
   (B) Hitler's forces were overrunning the Soviet Union, which asked the U.S. for help in spite of U.S. anticommunist sentiments.
   (C) Japan's forces were taking over communist China, which asked the U.S. for help in spite of U.S. anticommunist sentiments.
   (D) Japan had attacked the U.S. naval base at Pearl Harbor, yet many in the United States still supported isolationism.

1. **Use the passage below to answer all parts of the question that follows.**

Reich Citizenship Law of September 1935

"Article 1

1. A subject of the state is a person who enjoys the protection of the German Reich and who in consequence has specific obligations toward it. . . .

Article 2

1. A Reich citizen is a subject of the state who is of German or related blood, and proves by his conduct that he is willing and fit to faithfully serve the German people and Reich. . . .

3. The Reich citizen is the sole bearer of full political rights in accordance with the law."

Law for the Protection of German Blood and German Honor of September 1935

"Moved by the understanding that purity of German blood is the essential condition for the continued existence of the German people, and inspired by the inflexible determination to ensure the existence of the German nation for all time, the Reichstag has unanimously adopted the following law, which is promulgated herewith:

Article 1

1. Marriages between Jews and subjects of the state of Germany or related blood are forbidden. Marriages nevertheless concluded are invalid, even if concluded abroad to circumvent this law. . . .

Article 4

1. Jews are forbidden to fly the Reich or national flag or display Reich colors.

2. They are, on the other hand, permitted to display the Jewish colors. The exercise of this right is protected by the state."

> Nuremberg, September 15, 1935
> At the Reich Party Congress of Freedom

(A) Identify ONE way that German society changed after 1900.

(B) Explain ONE way in which these documents demonstrated Adolf Hitler's view of Jews.

(C) Explain ONE way in which the German state's political and social actions reflected Germany's aggressive militarism after 1900.

2. **Answer all parts of the question that follows.**

   (A) Identify ONE act of German aggression that went unchallenged by other countries leading up to World War II.

   (B) Explain ONE way in which state policies contributed to World War II.

   (C) Explain ONE way that imperial aspirations contributed to World War II.

 THINK AS A HISTORIAN: IDENTIFY ASSUMPTIONS SHAPING POINT OF VIEW

The point of view of a source is often shaped by underlying assumptions. For example, the Korean Declaration of Independence states: "We proclaim [our independence] to the nations of the world in affirmation of the principle of the equality of all nations." The underlying assumption that shapes the point of view in this statement is that all nations are equal, a position with which reasonable people agree. That sound assumption establishes a legitimacy to other aspects of the declaration. If it had instead said, ". . . in affirmation of the principle of the superiority of Koreans," the point of view would be sufficiently narrowed that its legitimacy would be questioned, since enlightened opinion recognizes equality of people and nations.

Identify the underlying assumptions in the German laws on the previous page. Explain how the assumptions shape the point of view of the authors of the laws and how that point of view might affect a reader's response.

REFLECT ON THE TOPIC ESSENTIAL QUESTION

1. In one to three paragraphs, explain the causes and consequences of World War II.

7.7

Conducting World War II

We shall not flag nor fail. We shall go on to the end. We shall fight in France and on the seas and oceans; we shall fight with growing confidence and growing strength in the air. We shall defend our island whatever the cost may be; we shall fight on beaches, landing grounds, in fields, in streets and on the hills. We shall never surrender.

—British Prime Minister Winston Churchill (June 4, 1940)

Essential Question: What similarities and differences were there in the methods governments used to conduct war?

During World War II, governments rallied all their resources in the war effort. The call to intense nationalism, as illustrated in Winston Churchill's speech in the British House of Commons, was part of concerted policies that used all forms of communication to mobilize the population. Appeal to ideological beliefs, including fascism and communism, dominated daily life during the conflict and minimized resistance to militarism.

Governments also used new military technology and tactics, including the atomic bomb and "total war," disregarding previously accepted laws of war. These policies increased the level of wartime casualties.

Japan and Imperialist Policies

With the military in control of the government, Japan harbored imperialist ambitions that would lead to a world war in the Pacific. The Mukden Incident and the takeover of land in Manchuria in a state called Manchukuo (see Topic 7.5) were early efforts in this drive.

New Order in East Asia The occupation of parts of China was but one step in Japan's overall strategy, which was to create a "New Order in East Asia." The Japanese had looked to expand into Soviet Siberia, but when Germany and the Soviets signed the **Nonaggression Pact** of 1939, Japan had to look elsewhere for new territory. Nearby Southeast Asia, which had been under the control of imperial powers in Western Europe and the United States, was the most obvious target. However, Japan faced obstacles. Its occupation of China led to economic sanctions by the United States. Because Japan's economy relied on oil and scrap iron from the United States, sanctions threatened to strangle its economy and undercut its military expansion. Therefore, Japan began to plan to retaliate against the United States with military force in the hope that by doing so, the Western powers would submit to Japan's imperial ambitions.

Germany's Early Victories and Challenges

Once war broke out in Europe, Hitler moved swiftly to acquire territory. He embarked on a strategy called **blitzkrieg**, or lightning war, to quickly subdue Poland. Germany used rapidly moving tank divisions supported by the air force in its four-week campaign. At the end of September 1939, Germany and the Soviets divided the country as they had planned when they signed the German-Soviet Nonaggression Pact.

Germany's rapid success in Poland encouraged Hitler to attack and conquer Denmark and Norway in April 1940 and the Netherlands, Belgium, and France in the following month. Germany then proceeded to bring the government and resources of the conquered nations under its control. As the Germans approached Paris, the French government fled to Bordeaux, in southern France. Germany took direct control of the northern two-thirds of the country. The French set up a new pro-Nazi regime based in **Vichy** under Marshal Henri-Philippe Pétain, an aged World War I hero. (Connect: Create a table comparing the conquests of Hitler and Genghis Khan. See Topic 2.2.)

MAJOR BATTLES OF WORLD WAR II

British-American Relations Fearing that it would be the next victim in Germany's relentless and rapid campaign, Britain asked the United States for support. Despite a long history of isolationism from European troubles, President Roosevelt believed the United States should help the British.

In 1940, the two powers signed the **Destroyers-for-Bases Agreement**, in which the United States promised delivery of 50 destroyers in exchange for eight British air and naval bases in the Western Hemisphere. In the 1941

Lend-Lease Act, the United States gave up all pretensions of neutrality by lending war materials to Britain. Also in 1941, Britain and the United States forged a policy statement known as the **Atlantic Charter**, which set down basic goals for the post-war world. The charter included such provisions as the restoration of self-government to those deprived of it, the abandonment of the use of force, and the disarmament of aggressor nations.

The Battle of Britain In Europe, Britain was the last major holdout against Nazi power. In July 1940, Hitler ordered a large campaign against the small island nation by the **Luftwaffe**, the German air force. He believed that bombardment from the air would sufficiently weaken the country so that German sea and land forces could mount a successful invasion. Initially targeting military bases in this **Battle of Britain**, the Germans turned to bombing British cities after the British Royal Air Force conducted a raid on Berlin. **Winston Churchill** termed this Britain's "finest hour" as the civilian population in London and other cities withstood months of relentless bombing.

The targeting of cities did provide one advantage for Britain: the British military was able to rebuild after the earlier raids on its bases. Ultimately, Britain's superior planes and radar system allowed it to destroy German planes faster than they could be replaced. By May 1941, Hitler was forced to postpone indefinitely any attempted invasion of Britain.

War on the Soviet Union After failing to invade Britain, Hitler turned east. He attacked the Soviet Union to eliminate Bolshevism and to create *Lebensraum*—land for settlement and development—for the German people. Germany's turning its focus to the east took pressure off Britain. Germany began its invasion of the Soviet Union in June 1941. Initially the Nazis experienced rapid success as they had in Western Europe, capturing large amounts of territory and two million Soviet troops. However, the German forces soon found themselves at the mercy of the harsh Russian winter. The Soviets defended the city of Leningrad in the **Siege of Leningrad**, which lasted three years and led to the deaths of a million Soviet men, women, and children.

Japan Overreaches

Japan experienced rapid victories in the Pacific. It launched a surprise air attack on the U.S. naval base at **Pearl Harbor** in Hawaii on December 7, 1941, destroying much of the U.S. Pacific fleet. Japan then seized the Philippines, the Dutch East Indies, British Malaya, Burma, and numerous Pacific islands.

Japan believed that the surprise attack and the damage to the U.S. Pacific Fleet would prompt the United States to negotiate a settlement favorable to Japan immediately. Instead, U.S. isolationism disappeared overnight; public opinion demanded retaliation against Japan. Great Britain and China joined the United States in the fight against Japanese aggression. The war truly became global when, within days, Hitler responded to the U.S. declaration of war against Japan with his own declaration of war against the United States.

Colonial Armies As the Axis powers expanded into new territory, Western colonies began to join the Allies in the war effort. For example, the Indian Army, which had started the war with only 200,000 men, ended the war as the largest volunteer army in history with more than 2.5 million men. Although the Indian Army sent troops to North Africa, the bulk of its troops fought against the Japanese in Southeast Asia.

Home Fronts

Like World War I, World War II was a total war. Most countries mobilized all their resources, including the civilian population, to achieve victory. The United States started with the strongest industrial sector of any country in the world and it added stringent government planning to provide factories what they needed. In addition, unlike anywhere in Europe, U.S. industry operated without threat of military attack. The United States ramped up production of the resources required for war, including ships, tanks, planes, landing craft, radar equipment, guns, and ammunition. With the enlistment of large numbers of men in the armed forces, women found far more opportunities to work in factories and offices. The U.S. government promoted art of "Rosie the Riveter" to encourage women to succeed at jobs that were once thought to be for men.

Instead of mobilizing all available citizens in the war effort, German leaders relied on forced labor, some of it in concentration camps. At its peak, 20 percent of the wartime workforce was forced labor, with 600,000 French citizens working in German war plants and 1.5 million French soldiers working in prisoner-of-war (POW) camps. The solution was counterproductive, however. The workers were treated so poorly that productivity was low.

In Japan, efforts on the home front were confused. The government presented an optimistic view of the war instead of trying to mobilize resources. The government took pride in not using women in the war effort, claiming that the enemy is "drafting women but in Japan, out of consideration for the family system, we will not." The government was able to systematically remove children from cities to the countryside when bombing of cities started late in the war. It was also successful in rationing food throughout the war. (Connect: Write a paragraph comparing and contrasting warfare during World War I with the warfare before and during World War II. See Topic 7.3.)

The Tide Turns in the European Theater

With its entry into the war in December 1941, the United States joined the other Allied powers, Great Britain and the Soviet Union. In spite of political differences, the three nations were united in their determination to achieve a military victory and agreed that Axis surrender must be unconditional.

In early 1942, the Allies were struggling in Europe and North Africa. General **Erwin Rommel**, the "Desert Fox," led German troops in Egypt and threatened to take the northern city of Alexandria. But in the second half of 1942, the tide turned. The British defeated Rommel at the **Battle of El**

Alamein. And after months of fighting, a Soviet counteroffensive successfully defeated the pride of Hitler's military, the German Sixth Army, in the **Battle of Stalingrad**. Although the Germans remained in control of most of Western Europe, the momentum of the war in Europe had turned against the Nazis.

The Tide Turns in the Pacific Theater

The year 1942 was also crucial in the war against Japan. The first Allied victory occurred in May in the **Battle of the Coral Sea,** when the U.S. Navy stopped a Japanese fleet set to invade New Guinea and the Solomon Islands, thus helping to prevent a future invasion of Australia. The following month, with the destruction of four Japanese aircraft carriers at the **Battle of Midway Island**, Allied naval forces demonstrated their superiority in the Pacific. These battles stopped the advance of the Japanese. The first major Allied offensive was on the island of **Guadalcanal**, which ended in early 1943 with an Allied victory.

The Allied forces in the Pacific under U.S. General **Douglas MacArthur** used a strategy called **island-hopping**. The Allies attacked islands where Japan was weak and skipped those where Japan was strong. The Allies slowly, and at great human cost, moved through the Philippines, getting closer to Japan itself.

Technology was critical to Allied success. The development of fleets of **aircraft carriers**, ships that allowed planes to take off from and land on their decks at sea, provided air support for battleships and increased the range and flexibility of naval forces. Aircraft were used for raids on enemy ships and bases and for intelligence gathering. Submarines sank about 55 percent of the Japanese merchant fleet, severely damaging Japan's supply lines.

The Last Years of the War

The Allied successes of 1942 put the Axis powers on the defensive in 1943. The Allies identified Italy as the weakest point under Axis control in Europe. In spite of German forces sent to aid Italy, the Allies gained control of the island of Sicily in July 1943, leading to the fall of Mussolini. After the Allies invaded southern Italy in September 1943, Italy turned against its former ally. After months of slow and costly progress, the Allies finally recaptured Rome on June 4, 1944.

June 6, 1944, has become known as **D-Day**, when about 150,000 Allied forces under the command of U.S. General Dwight Eisenhower launched an amphibious invasion from England, landing on the beaches of Normandy in northern France. Allied casualties were high. Eventually, however, the Allies established a base to begin the march toward Paris, which was liberated in August. With control of Western Europe slipping away, Germany's defeat was drawing closer.

The Germans made one final push against the Allies during the winter of 1944. The **Battle of the Bulge** was fought in the Ardennes Forest across parts of France, Belgium, and Luxembourg. An Allied victory left Germany with no realistic expectation of winning the war, yet Hitler refused to give up. Allied air raids began to systematically destroy Germany's infrastructure and Allied troops crossed the Rhine River into Germany in March 1945. One month later they were approaching Germany's capital city of Berlin.

On the Eastern Front, Soviet troops were also moving rapidly toward Germany. In July 1943, the largest tank battle of the war, the **Battle of Kursk**, was fought about 300 miles south of Moscow. The Soviets challenged this instance of German blitzkrieg by successfully holding their defensive position and then counterattacking. The Soviets then made rapid progress through the Ukraine and the Baltic States in 1944. After taking control of Warsaw, Poland, in January 1945, the Soviets moved on to Hungary, Romania, and Bulgaria. In April 1945, they advanced on Berlin.

Victory in Europe Hitler spent the war's final days hiding in a bunker, a fortified underground shelter, in Berlin. Although the country was falling apart, he continued to live under the delusion that somehow Germany would triumph. The end came on April 30, 1945, when Hitler committed suicide. His ally Mussolini had been killed by members of the Italian resistance two days before. After Hitler's death, members of Germany's High Command acknowledged that continuing the war would be futile. In the first days of May, Germany surrendered to the Allies. May 8, 1945, marked the official end of the war in Europe and was designated as Victory in Europe Day or **V-E Day**.

Victory over Japan In early 1945, U.S. forces captured the islands of Okinawa and Iwo Jima and prepared to attack the Japanese mainland. In March 1945, U.S. troops fire-bombed Tokyo, killing about 100,000 people and leaving about a million others homeless. Although the island-hopping campaign had weakened Japan's hold on the Pacific, the emperor was not ready to surrender. The United States was beginning to consider the costs of invading the Japanese homeland, which it feared might lead to enormous Allied casualties. Despite initial hesitations about using nuclear weapons, President Truman ordered the U.S. Army Air Force to drop the first atomic bomb on the Japanese city of **Hiroshima** on August 6, 1945. The nuclear age had begun. Three days later, a second bomb was dropped on **Nagasaki**, resulting in an estimated total of 140,000 Japanese civilian deaths. The months of Allied victories, combined with these devastating nuclear attacks, caused Japan to surrender unconditionally on August 14. Truman designated September 2, the day of the formal surrender ceremonies, as Victory over Japan Day or **V-J Day**.

Consequences of World War II

World War II was the bloodiest war in human history. It resulted in the deaths of around 75 million people, two-thirds of whom were civilians. As later topics explain, it changed how people thought about racism, colonial empires, and international relations. Further, it provided the context for a fierce ideological battle between the United States and the Soviet Union that would shape global affairs for the following five decades.

KEY TERMS BY THEME

GOVERNMENT: War
Vichy
Lend-Lease Act
Battle of Britain
Siege of Leningrad
Pearl Harbor
Battle of El Alamein
Battle of Stalingrad
Battle of the Coral Sea
Battle of Midway Island
Guadalcanal

island-hopping
D-Day
Battle of the Bulge
Battle of Kursk
V-E Day
Hiroshima
Nagasaki
V-J Day

GOVERNMENT: Treaties
Nonaggression Pact

Destroyers-for-Bases
  Agreement
Atlantic Charter

GOVERNMENT: Leaders
Winston Churchill
Erwin Rommel
Douglas MacArthur

TECHNOLOGY: Warfare
blitzkrieg
Luftwaffe
aircraft carriers

MULTIPLE-CHOICE QUESTIONS

Questions 1 to 3 refer to the cartoon below.

Source: Willard Wetmore Combes / Library of Congress

1. Which of the following set the stage for the event represented in the cartoon?

   (A) The creation of the Nonaggression Pact in 1939

   (B) The formation of the pro-Nazi Vichy government in 1940

   (C) The signing of the Destroyers-for-Bases Agreement in 1940

   (D) The acceptance of the Atlantic Charter in 1941

2. What development during World War II does the cartoon represent?

   (A) The alliance between Hitler and the Soviet Union

   (B) The surprise Nazi invasion of the Soviet Union

   (C) The successful Soviet defense of Stalingrad

   (D) The rise of Soviet communism during the war

3. The importance of the event depicted in the cartoon was that it was

   (A) a direct response to Germany's invasion of Poland

   (B) the battle that caused Britain and France to enter the war

   (C) the last Allied victory in Europe, ending the European part of the war

   (D) an Allied victory that was crucial in defeating Germany

SHORT-ANSWER QUESTIONS

1. **Use the passage below to answer all parts of the question that follows.**

   "Nearly 350,000 American women served in uniform, both at home and abroad. . . . . General Eisenhower felt that he could not win the war without the aid of the women in uniform. 'The contribution of the women of America, whether on the farm or in the factory or in uniform, to D-Day was a sine qua non of the invasion effort.'

   Women in uniform took office and clerical jobs in the armed forces in order to free men to fight. They also drove trucks, repaired airplanes, worked as laboratory technicians, rigged parachutes, served as radio operators, analyzed photographs, flew military aircraft across the country, test-flew newly repaired planes, and even trained anti-aircraft artillery gunners by acting as flying targets. Some women served near the front lines in the Army Nurse Corps, where 16 were killed as a result of direct enemy fire. Sixty-eight American service women were captured as POWs in the Philippines. More than 1,600 nurses were decorated for bravery under fire and meritorious service, and 565 WACs in the Pacific Theater won combat decorations. Nurses were in Normandy on D-plus-four."

   "American Women in World War II: On the Home Front and Beyond," The National World War II Museum, New Orleans

(A) Identify ONE short-term result from the service of women during World War II.

(B) Identify ONE long-term result from the service of women during World War II.

(C) Explain ONE way in which social structures changed or stayed the same during World War II.

2. **Answer all parts of the question that follows.**

(A) Identify ONE piece of historical evidence that supports the argument that World War I caused World War II.

(B) Explain ONE continuity in the types of warfare used in World War I and World War II.

(C) Explain ONE change in the types of warfare used in World War I and World War II.

 THINK AS A HISTORIAN: EVIDENCE TO SUPPORT, MODIFY, OR REFUTE

In the years following the use of atomic bombs on Hiroshima and Nagasaki, historians have considered, from almost every angle, the question of whether or not the bombs were needed to end the war. Each position has offered evidence to support it. That same evidence might *modify* someone else's argument—change it somewhat or add a complexity—or it might *refute* or disprove it entirely.

The following excerpt is from an article that appeared in *The Atlantic* in December 1946. It states a clear position on the question.

> "The facts are these. On July 26, 1945, the Potsdam Ultimatum [issued by the United States, Great Britain, and China] called on Japan to surrender unconditionally. On July 29 Premier Suzuki issued a statement, purportedly at a cabinet press conference, scorning as unworthy of official notice the surrender ultimatum, and emphasizing the increasing rate of Japanese aircraft production. Eight days later, on August 6, the first atomic bomb was dropped on Hiroshima; the second was dropped on August 9 on Nagasaki; on the following day, August 10, Japan declared its intention to surrender, and on August 14 accepted the Potsdam terms."

> On the basis of these facts, I cannot believe that, without the atomic bomb, the surrender would have come without a great deal more of costly struggle and bloodshed."

> Karl T. Compton, "What If the Atomic Bomb Had Not Been Used?"

Read the following statements and determine whether each supports, modifies, or refutes Compton's position.

1. "A [2005] Harvard University Press volume by Professor Tsuyoshi Hasegawa of the University of California, Santa Barbara, is the most comprehensive study yet undertaken of Japanese documentary sources. The highly praised study argues that the atomic bomb played only a secondary role in Japan's decision to surrender. By far the most important factor, Hasegawa finds, was the entry of the Soviet Union into the war against Japan on Aug. 8, 1945, two days after the Hiroshima bombing."—Gar Aperovitz, "From the Archives: Atomic Bombing of Japan Was Unnecessary," July, 2005

2. "My reading of the history of World War II has convinced me that Japan would not have surrendered if the bombs had not been dropped; even after that some in the military tried to prevent the Emperor from surrendering. American military leaders predicted that an invasion of Japan would have produced 1 million Americans killed or wounded. The Japanese had fought fiercely in Okinawa in the spring of 1945; 100,000 Americans and Japanese died in this one small island."—Michael Barone, *Washington Examiner*, August 2013

3. "The charge that Harry Truman was willing to condemn tens of thousands of people (including Allied servicemen and prisoners of war) to die by prolonging the war, and tens of thousands more Japanese by using the bombs merely to impress the Soviets, is one that ought not be made without substantial proof. Tweaking mangled documents, especially in a volume [Hasegawa's book] published by a prestigious academic press (Harvard), utterly fails to meet this criterion and does a profound disservice to unsuspecting readers."—Robert James Maddox, "Disputing Truman's Use of Nuclear Weapons—Again," *American Thinker*, April 2006

REFLECT ON THE TOPIC ESSENTIAL QUESTION

1. In one to three paragraphs, explain similarities and differences in how governments used a variety of methods to conduct war.

7.8

Mass Atrocities

Who, after all, speaks today of the annihilation of the Armenians?
—German Führer Adolf Hitler, August 22, 1939

Essential Question: What were the causes and consequences of mass atrocities from 1900 to the present?

The deaths of fighting forces in the two world wars were only part of the total casualties. Genocide, ethnic violence, and other atrocities took place as extremist groups rose to power. During and after World War I, the Ottoman Empire, ruled by a clique of "Young Turks" who were disturbed by the continuing decline of Ottoman power, perpetrated the Armenian genocide in which some 1.5 million Armenians died. As Adolf Hitler implemented the Holocaust, he referred to the Armenian annihilation as a reminder of how little the Nazis need fear for the systematic murder of six million Jews.

Ethnic atrocities did not end after World War II. Dictator Pol Pot wanted to "purify" Cambodian society along racial, social, and political lines, resulting in the deaths of 1.6 to 1.8 million Cambodians. (See Topic 8.6.) And in Rwanda, the majority Hutu government directed mass slaughter of the Tutsi minority.

Atrocities in Europe and the Middle East

After three years of a bloody stalemate, the United States entered World War I in 1917, despite considerable popular protests in the United States against American involvement. By the summer of 1918, when U.S. forces were in place in Europe, U.S. actions helped push the war in the Allies' favor. Allied advances against the Central Powers forced Germany to surrender on November 11, 1918, which became known as **Armistice Day**.

Between 8 million and 9 million soldiers died in the war, with more than 21 million wounded. In France, Germany, Russia, and Austria-Hungary, fewer than half of all young men who fought for their countries returned physically unharmed. Soldiers who did return often bore emotional scars.

Civilian casualties were harder to record, but estimates range anywhere from 6 million to 13 million. This was one of the first modern wars where civilians were considered legitimate targets. Although the Allies' propaganda often exaggerated accounts of atrocities, reports of German soldiers raping women and killing families during their march through Belgium were common.

World War I Casualties				
Country	Alliance	Dead (in millions)	Wounded (in millions)	Imprisoned (in millions)
Germany	Central Powers	1.8	4.2	0.6
Russia	Allies	1.7	5.0	0.5
France	Allies	1.4	3.0	0.5
Austria-Hungary	Central Powers	1.2	3.6	0.2
Great Britain	Allies	0.9	2.1	0.2
Italy	Allies	0.5	1.0	0.5
Turkey	Central Powers	0.3	0.4	Not known
United States	Allies	0.1	0.2	Fewer than 0.05

Armenian Genocide The most shocking example of such atrocities were the deaths of between 600,000 and 1.5 million **Armenians** in Turkey. This action has been called the 20th century's first **genocide**, the attempted killing of a group of people based on their race, religion, or ethnicity. The Ottoman government alleged that the Christian Armenians, a minority within the Ottoman Empire, were cooperating with the Russian army, an Ottoman enemy during World War I. As punishment for this cooperation, the Ottoman government deported Armenians from their homes between 1915 and 1917 and into camps in Syria and what is today Iraq. Many Armenians died from starvation, disease, or exposure to the elements. Turkish troops executed others. Armenians have argued that the deaths were genocide. The Turkish government has said the deaths were the result of actions of war, ethnic conflicts, and disease, not genocide. (Connect: Create a graphic organizer comparing the Armenian genocide with the Nazis' extermination of millions of Jews. See Topic 7.6.)

Pandemic Disease

War-related deaths continued past Armistice Day in the form of an **influenza epidemic**. Under peacetime circumstances, a virulent disease might devastate a concentrated group of people in a particular region. However, in 1918, millions of soldiers were returning home as the war ended. As they did, they had contact with loved ones and friends, thereby spreading the flu. In 1919, the epidemic became a **pandemic**, a disease prevalent over a large area or the entire world, killing 20 million people in Europe, the United States, and elsewhere. India alone may have lost 7 million people to the disease.

The worldwide spread of the disease was another sign that while nationalism remained a powerful political force, improvements in transportation were creating a global culture that would create global challenges. Whether people could create effective international responses was unclear.

Suffering and Famine

A more intangible casualty of the war was the loss of a sense of security and hopefulness. The term **Lost Generation**, first used to describe American expatriate writers living in Paris after the war, came to be used more broadly to describe those suffering from the shock of the war. World War I was the bloodiest war thus far in history. It resulted in tremendous suffering and death for both military personnel and civilians.

Famine in the Ukraine In the Soviet Union, peasants strongly resisted Stalin's collectivization of agriculture. They hid or destroyed their crops and killed their livestock rather than turning them over to state control. This led to famines from human action rather than by weather or crop failures. The famines in 1932 and 1933 were especially devastating in the Ukraine, one of the Soviet Union's most fertile farming regions. An estimated 7 million to 10 million peasants died as a result of these famines. The government took much of the crops that were grown to feed industrial workers or to use for industry. Although peasants starved, industry grew.

Casualties of World War II

Because of the widespread fighting, advances in the technology of destruction, and its impact on the economies and civilian life of so many nations, the effects of World War II were unprecedented. Although exact casualty figures have been impossible to determine, total deaths probably numbered 40 million to 50 million. Maybe half of those were citizens of the Soviet Union, and millions of others were from Germany, Poland, China, and Japan. Losses among U.S. troops were fewer, but still considerable: about 290,000 soldiers killed and more than 600,000 wounded. Civilian casualties from attacks on land, air, and sea; from government executions based on political rationales, including genocide; and from disease and starvation caused by the war likely exceeded military casualties.

The Nazis During the war, the world gradually learned about Nazi brutality. In its pursuit of territory, Germany forcefully removed many Slavic peoples, including one million Poles, and Roma, also known as Gypsies, from their homes. **Heinrich Himmler**, the leader of the Nazi special police, the SS, oversaw these policies. In addition, more than 7 million residents of conquered territories were forced to work in labor camps or in jobs that supported the German war effort. The Nazis sent political opponents, people with disabilities, and gay people to the camps. But the largest single group the Nazis targeted were the Jews. When Hitler became chancellor, he instituted many policies that reflected these extreme anti-Semitic views, such as the **Nuremberg Laws** of 1935 that banned Jews from certain professions and certain schools. Jews were forced to live in sections of cities called **ghettos**.

In 1942, the Nazi persecution of Jews turned into mass murder. They began a campaign led by the SS to kill all Jews in Europe, a plan they called the "**Final Solution**." Initially, Nazi killing units moved from place to place, shooting Jews and burying them in mass graves. Later the SS began rounding up Jews and shipping them to death camps, where Nazis gassed them. Auschwitz and Treblinka in Poland and Dachau in Germany were some of the largest camps. By the end of the war, the Nazis had killed about six million Jews, an act of genocide known as the **Holocaust**. The Nazis killed another five million people who belonged to other persecuted groups or were Soviet prisoners of war. The Nazis worked many to death in labor camps and massacred others.

One shocking aspect of the Holocaust was how the Nazis used technology—trains, poisonous gas, and ovens for cremation (shown here)—to make their attempt at genocide more efficient and more deadly.

The Japanese During the Second Sino-Japanese War in 1937, Japanese soldiers killed at least 100,000 Chinese soldiers and civilians in what was called the Rape of Nanking. During World War II, although the Japanese did not carry out a dedicated policy of genocide that paralleled the Holocaust, millions of people died as a result of their policies. Under the program "**Asia for Asiatics**," Japan forced people they had conquered into labor programs. These included service in the military, on public works projects, and on farms to reduce the food shortage in Japan. The Japanese army forced women in Korea, China, and other occupied countries to become "comfort women," prostitutes for Japanese soldiers. Because of these harsh programs, more than a million civilians died in Vietnam alone. Perhaps an equal number of Allied prisoners of war and local workers perished while doing forced labor for Japan.

The Allies Air warfare carried out by the United States and the other Allies brought a new type of deadly combat to civilians. The Allies' **firebombing** of German cities, particularly **Hamburg** in 1943 and **Dresden** in 1945, caused large casualties. The number of deaths in Hamburg was about 50,000. Dresden had fewer casualties, maybe 25,000 deaths, as 15 square miles of its historic city center were destroyed. The United States also used firebombing in **Tokyo**.

The final two air attacks in the war, Hiroshima and Nagasaki, produced not only high casualties, but tremendous fear about the destructiveness of a future war fought with nuclear weapons. These weapons had been developed by an international group of scientists working in the United States. The scientific achievement was impressive, but it also required developments in other areas to have military use. For example, to deliver the nuclear weapons required improvements in airplane design to allow long flights carrying heavy loads. There is a great difference between the planes used in World War II and those used in World War I. In addition, the widespread use of the aircraft carrier by several powers extended the airplanes' reach. Using these developments in planes and ships, countries could carry out air attacks anywhere in the world.

Genocide and Human Rights

The global community said "never again" to genocide after the horrors of the Holocaust. However, genocides continued to occur.

Bosnia Ethnic conflict drove the genocide in **Bosnia**. The end of World War I brought with it the creation of several new nations in Eastern Europe, including Yugoslavia. That country was home to Serbians, who were Eastern Orthodox Christians; Croats and Slovenes, who were Catholic; and Muslims in the regions of Bosnia and Kosovo. Marshal Josip Broz Tito led communist Yugoslavia from the end of World War II until his death in 1980. As dictator, Tito tried to suppress separatist tendencies among the peoples of Yugoslavia by keeping Serbia and Croatia, the two largest republics, from dominating the smaller ones.

After the Soviet Union collapsed, so did Yugoslavia. When Slovenia, Croatia, and Montenegro declared independence, they each defined citizenship in terms of ethnic background and religion. Serbian nationalists led by the demagogue **Slobodan Miloševicć** were particularly emphatic about ethnic purity. Serb forces, in attempts to dominate states such as Bosnia-Herzegovina and Kosovo, committed horrific acts of **ethnic cleansing** against Muslims from Bosnia and Kosovo, killing or driving people who were not part of the main ethnic group from their homes. Bosniaks, Kosovars, and Croats fought back, causing more casualties. Serb soldiers raped untold numbers of Muslim women. In total, more than 300,000 people in the region perished over the course of Yugoslavia's **balkanization**, or disintegration into separate states.

Rwanda One of the smallest countries in Africa, **Rwanda** was the site of one of the worst genocides in modern history. Ethnic and tribal hatred going back to the colonial era was behind the slaughter. Belgian colonizers had treated the minority **Tutsis** better than the majority **Hutus**. The latter group resented all the power that the Tutsis enjoyed. When Rwanda won independence from Belgium in 1962, the Hutu majority easily won control of the government and took revenge on the Tutsis by discriminating against them. In response, tens of thousands of Tutsis fled the country and formed a rebel army.

In 1993, Tutsi and Hutu forces in Rwanda began negotiations for a coalition government in which both ethnic groups would share power. The negotiations were cut short in 1994 when Rwanda's president, a Hutu, was killed in an airplane crash, supposedly shot down by rebel forces. This incident lit the flames of genocide. Over the next three months or so, between 500,000 and 1 million civilians—mostly Tutsis and some moderate Hutus—were killed. Some sources estimate that casualties were even higher.

International responses ranged from insufficient to callous. United Nations peacekeepers were instructed *not* to use force to restore order. There were also too few peacekeepers to protect all Rwandans. Individual countries, including the United States, evacuated their personnel from the country after Belgian peacekeepers were killed. UN peacekeepers and individual nations failed to evacuate any Rwandans. The Rwandan genocide focused attention on the lack of leadership in the international community. It became clear that the United Nations needed to think seriously about its role in violent conflicts if it wanted to effectively protect human lives and human rights.

Source: Wikimedia Commons

A school building in Rwanda has space set aside for a display of skulls, bones, and mummified bodies to remind people of the genocide of hundreds of thousands of people in 1994.

Sudan Another genocide erupted in 2003 in **Darfur**, a region located in western Sudan. Most of the people involved were Muslim, but some were nomadic pastoralists of Arab descent, while others were non-Arab farmers. The government of Sudan was controlled by Arab Muslims. Two Darfur rebel groups composed of non-Arabs took up arms against the Sudanese government in response to attacks from nomads. In response, the government unleashed Arab militants known as the **Janjaweed** (translation: "evil men on horseback") on the region. Together with Sudanese forces, the Janjaweed attacked and destroyed hundreds of villages throughout Darfur, slaughtering more than 200,000 people, mostly non-Arab Muslim Africans. More than one million people were displaced, creating a refugee crisis that spilled into neighboring Chad. Despite negotiations, appeals, and the **International Criminal Court** charging Sudan's President **Omar al-Bashir** with war crimes, the genocide continued.

The genocides in Bosnia, Rwanda, and Sudan became stains on the conscience of the world. International organizations and the broad global community were supposed to defend human rights after the Jewish Holocaust. Considering the millions of lives lost and human dignity shattered, the failure of the international community appeared obvious. (Connect: Write a paragraph comparing genocides in Africa during the last three decades with the Holocaust.)

KEY TERMS BY THEME

GOVERNMENT: War	**GOVERNMENT:** Countries	**TECHNOLOGY:** Warfare
Armistice Day	Bosnia	firebombing
Hamburg	Rwanda	**ENVIRONMENT:** Disease
Dresden	Darfur	influenza epidemic
Tokyo	**GOVERNMENT:** Leaders	pandemic
GOVERNMENT: Policies	Heinrich Himmler	**SOCIETY:** Discrimination
genocide	Slobodan Milošević	Nuremberg Laws
Final Solution	Omar al-Bashir	ghettos
Holocaust	**CULTURE:** Movements	Janjaweed
Asia for Asiatics	Lost Generation	
ethnic cleansing	**CULTURE:** Ethnic Groups	
balkanization	Armenians	
GOVERNMENT: Organizations	Tutsis	
International Criminal Court	Hutus	

Questions 1 to 3 refer to the passage below.

"The Holocaust was the systematic, bureaucratic, state-sponsored persecution and murder of six million Jews by the Nazi regime and its collaborators. . . . The Nazis, who came to power in Germany in January 1933, believed that Germans were 'racially superior' and that the Jews, deemed 'inferior,' were an alien threat to the so-called German racial community. . . .

To concentrate and monitor the Jewish population as well as to facilitate later deportation of the Jews, the Germans and their collaborators created ghettos, transit camps, and forced-labor camps for Jews during the war years. . . .

Between 1941 and 1944, Nazi German authorities deported millions of Jews from Germany, from occupied territories, and from the countries of many of its Axis allies to ghettos and to killing centers, often called extermination camps, where they were murdered in specially developed gassing facilities."

Holocaust Encyclopedia,
United States Holocaust Memorial Museum

1. Which best helps explain the passage in its broader historical context?

    (A) Several European countries reached an agreement in Munich, in 1938, that allowed Germany to seize the Sudetenland.

    (B) World War II included the first use of atomic weapons in human history.

    (C) Political conflicts before and during World War II led to acts of genocide and other large-scale ethnic violence.

    (D) During *Kristallnacht* in 1938, Jews throughout Germany and Austria were beaten and killed.

2. The policy of the Japanese that most closely paralleled the conditions described in the passage was

    (A) forcing conquered peoples into deadly forced labor programs

    (B) engaging in surprise military attacks, such as the one on Pearl Harbor

    (C) attempting to liberate the people of Asia from Western imperialism

    (D) invading Manchuria after an attack on a Japanese railway station there

3. The campaign of genocide represented in the passage is most similar to which of the following examples?

(A) The killing of 26 Republicans between August and September 1936 by fascists belonging to Franco's regime

(B) The massacre of a band of Lakota people on their way to the Pine Ridge Reservation for shelter from the winter by the U.S. 7th Cavalry in December 1890

(C) The deportation and execution of 1.5 million Armenians by the Ottoman Empire

(D) The assassination of Archduke Franz Ferdinand

SHORT-ANSWER QUESTIONS

1. Use the passage to answer all parts of the question that follows.

"Japan used a highly developed military machine and a master-race mentality to set about establishing its right to rule its neighbors. . . .

If one event can be held up as an example of the unmitigated evil lying just below the surface of unbridled military adventurism, that moment is the Rape of Nanking. . . .

When the city fell on December 13, 1937, Japanese soldiers began an orgy of cruelty seldom if ever matched in world history. . . . Years later experts at the International Military Tribunal of the Far East (IMTFE) estimated that more than 260,000 noncombatants died at the hands of Japanese soldiers in Nanking in late 1937 and early 1938, though some experts have placed the figure at well over 350,000."

> Iris Chang, *The Rape of Nanking:*
> *The Forgotten Holocaust of World War II* (1997)

(A) Identify ONE historical development of the mid-20th century that might explain why Japan acted as described in the passage.

(B) Explain ONE way in which the actions of Japan described in the passage are similar to the actions of Nazi Germany.

(C) Explain what the title of Chang's book indicates about her point of view about events she describes.

2. Answer all parts of the question that follows.

(A) Identify ONE historical development that contributed to the context for rise of extremist groups prior to World War II.

(B) Explain ONE way in which the mass destruction of specific populations impacted societies after World War II.

(C) Explain the difference between genocide and ethnic violence.

THINK AS A HISTORIAN: RELATE HISTORICAL DEVELOPMENTS

Gerda Weissmann Klein, Polish-American Holocaust survivor, questioned why the Jews in Germany did not fight back.

> "Why did we walk like meek sheep to the slaughterhouse? . . . Why did we not run away and hide? We might have had a chance to survive. Why did we walk deliberately and obediently into their clutches? I know why. Because we had faith in humanity. Because we did not really think that human beings were capable of committing such crimes."

All But My Life: A Memoir (1957)

What *does* it take to make people "capable of committing such crimes" as genocide? Historians have looked for answers to this question by relating genocide to other historical developments, such as the following:

- War—has an influence on people's psyche that makes them more likely to kill members of an "outgroup" which is perceived to be a threat

- Economic crisis—fosters a need to scapegoat others as being responsible for the economic problems, softening a resistance to killing them

- Enlightenment thinking— focuses on the perceived perfectibility of society, sometimes in terms of removing biological threats. Jews were referred to as a "virus"; Armenians were called disease-carrying "microbes."

Draw a relationship between genocide and the historical development of imperialism. Use one or more examples from Topic 7.8.

REFLECT ON THE TOPIC ESSENTIAL QUESTION

1. In one to three paragraphs, explain the various causes and consequences of mass atrocities in the period from 1900 to the present.

7.9

Causation in Global Conflict

As long as there are sovereign nations possessing great power, war is inevitable.

—German-American Physicist Albert Einstein (1945)

Essential Question: What was the relative significance of the causes of global conflict from 1900 to the present?

The 20th century saw significant changes to the global order. At the beginning of the century, the West dominated the global political order. However, the First and Second World Wars resulted in a power shift within the Western political sphere from Western Europe to the United States. These global conflicts also resulted in the emergence of new states around the world as independence movements ended the colonial relationships that existed in the previous century.

The Ottoman, Russian, and Qing empires that had existed at the beginning of the century all collapsed due to internal decay and political revolutions. Other areas of the world also saw political upheaval as nations struggled with both economic depression and calls for greater democracy. Often, though, totalitarian governments emerged out of these political and economic crises.

Political Causes of Global Conflict in the 20th Century

Many historians refer to World War I as the first "total war." The war was fought on an industrial scale by soldiers from around the world, including soldiers from colonial areas. The combatants discovered more, and deadlier, methods of killing each other. Long-range artillery, poison gas, flamethrowers, and machine guns led to the deaths of millions of soldiers on both sides. The roots of this conflict lie in several main causes. A balance of power in Europe had been established during the 19th century through a constantly shifting system of alliances. However, these alliances proved instrumental in escalating the scope of the war as European nations jumped into the conflict to honor their commitments.

Nationalism was a growing force for political change in Europe. As such, Serbian nationalism was the main spark that created conflict in the Balkans, known as the "powder keg of Europe," which led to the expansion of the war throughout Europe. An arms race among the great powers of Europe helped to increase the possibility of war as well. Lastly, the imperial rivalry among Western nations, as well as Japan and Russia, helped to increase tensions over commerce and access to resources.

Colonial Soldiers Serving with the British Army in World War I	
Colony or Dominion	Number of Soldiers Who Served (1914–1918)
India	1,500,000
Canada	418,218
Australia	331,814
New Zealand	112,223
South and East Africa	76,164
West Indies	16,000

Source: Statistics of the Military Effort of the British Empire During the Great War 1914-1920

Some of the same issues that brought about World War I also led to World War II. Fascism was nationalism in an extreme form. The fascist governments of Germany and Italy defied international pressure and treaties when they invaded neighboring territories. The alliance of Germany, Italy, and, eventually, Japan was opposed by the Western democracies of Great Britain and France. However, it was the inability of the Western democracies to offer a strong response to Germany's aggressive militarism that launched Europe and the rest of the world into war. Additionally, Japan's imperial ambitions in Asia were the main cause for war to break out in the Pacific between Japan and the United States. (Connect: Compare the motivating factors for wars fought in the 20th century with wars fought in the 19th century. See Topic 6.3.)

Economic Causes of Global Conflict in the 20th Century

The primary economic cause of global conflict in the early 20th century was the acquisition and control of markets and resources. In the 19th century, Western European governments, followed by the United States, Russia, and Japan, began policies to take control of trade, territory, or both in Asia and Africa. In previous centuries, armed conflict would often erupt over the rivalry to control the natural resources of these areas. However, as the Industrial Revolution spread from Great Britain to the rest of Western Europe, and then to the United States, Russia, and Japan, control over markets to sell consumer goods was a primary motive of imperialistic policies. Attempts were made, particularly in the late 19th century, to prevent wars over trade but these attempts had mixed success.

The Opium Wars, the First and Second Sino-Japanese War, the Crimean War, and eventually the First and Second World Wars had these economic factors as some of their root causes. For example, the desire of Imperial Japan to take over territory in Asia to obtain sources of oil, rice, rubber, and other raw materials led to the decision of the United States (and other countries) to place an embargo on Japan that cut off oil and steel exports from the United States to Japan. The result was the Japanese decision to attack the U.S. Pacific Fleet in Pearl Harbor, Hawaii, causing the United States to enter World War II. Economic crisis also helped lead to global conflict. The severe economic effects of the Great Depression (1929–1939), including high unemployment and low wages, led to the rise of populist leaders like Adolf Hitler who promised to rebuild the economies of their states.

Effects of Global Conflict in the 20th Century

Rapid advances in science and technology led to a better understanding of the natural world and brought about advances in many areas, including communication, transportation, industry, agriculture, and medicine. States also improved their war-making capabilities. As a result, one of the most significant effects of the global conflicts of the 20th century was the immense loss of life as warfare became deadlier to both combatants and civilians alike. Large-scale aerial bombing that targeted populated areas, deadly policies that targeted specific minority groups such as European Jews, and the use of new military technology such as the atomic bomb all meant that global conflict would cause unprecedented deaths among the civilian population. In addition, mass starvation and crimes against humanity were also responsible for millions of civilian deaths during the 20th century.

CIVILIAN DEATHS IN THE FIRST WORLD WAR

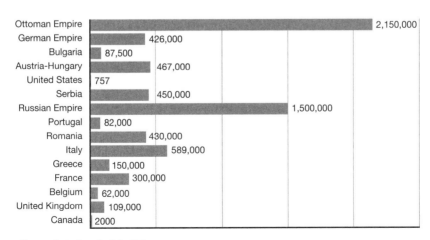

Ottoman Empire	2,150,000
German Empire	426,000
Bulgaria	87,500
Austria-Hungary	467,000
United States	757
Serbia	450,000
Russian Empire	1,500,000
Portugal	82,000
Romania	430,000
Italy	589,000
Greece	150,000
France	300,000
Belgium	62,000
United Kingdom	109,000
Canada	2000

Source: Centre Européen Robert Schuman

CIVILIAN DEATHS IN THE SECOND WORLD WAR

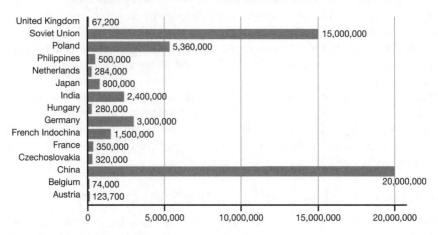

United Kingdom	67,200
Soviet Union	15,000,000
Poland	5,360,000
Philippines	500,000
Netherlands	284,000
Japan	800,000
India	2,400,000
Hungary	280,000
Germany	3,000,000
French Indochina	1,500,000
France	350,000
Czechoslovakia	320,000
China	20,000,000
Belgium	74,000
Austria	123,700

Source: Centre Européen Robert Schuman

Global conflict in the 20th century also brought about notable political changes in the world. In the beginning of the century, the Mexican Revolution took place because many Mexicans wanted political and economic reforms. Populist movements formed and, eventually, Mexico created a new constitution with more political and economic rights for the majority of Mexicans. However, true democratic institutions in Mexico emerged and evolved slowly. As a result of World War I, regime change occurred in both the Ottoman Empire and the Russian Empire. In addition to the effect of the First World War, ineffective or corrupt leadership was also instrumental in bringing about the political revolutions that toppled the monarchies of these states. While the Ottoman government was replaced by a Western-style democracy, the Russian Revolution instituted a totalitarian government headed by the Communist Party.

Resentment of the Treaty of Versailles, the peace agreement that ended World War I, also helped to bring about totalitarian regimes in Germany and Italy. These fascist governments appealed to people's nationalism and desire to restore the country's glory and standing in the world, leading their nations toward war.

World War I weakened the colonial powers, and after the war, U.S. President Woodrow Wilson advocated for the self-determination of people to choose their government or nation-state. This was seen as a sign that colonies had the right to demand independence. Many people in the colonies also felt that their support of or active participation in the war meant that they were owed some form of self-government. When those in power did not meet these demands, organized independence movements formed or grew.

The desire for independence continued to grow after World War II, as the colonial powers were further weakened by the war and unable to afford the cost and labor power to rebuild and maintain their empires. Many new states formed during this time. Former colonies that had a small foreign settler population gained their independence relatively peacefully, while colonies that had a sizeable foreign settler population often experienced a more violent process towards independence.

Perhaps the largest independence movement, in terms of the number of people involved, took place in India. Relying on passive resistance and civil disobedience, the people of the British colony of India achieved independence in 1947. However, due to religious and ideological differences, the Indian subcontinent was partitioned into a Muslim-dominated Pakistan (which originally included East Pakistan, now Bangladesh) and a Hindu-dominated India. (See Topic 8.6.) The tensions between Muslims and Hindus living in British India did not disappear with independence. These tensions have led to several military conflicts between the two countries since partition.

Another significant effect of the global conflicts of the 20th century was a repositioning of power in the Western countries—away from Western Europe and to the United States. Because of the participation of the United States in both the First and Second World Wars, as well as the smaller scale of destruction the U.S. experienced compared to Western European countries, the United States became a world power, playing the dominant role in the transatlantic relationship. However, the Soviet Union soon emerged as a second superpower in opposition to the United States.

REFLECT ON THE ESSENTIAL QUESTION

1. **Causation: Relative Significance of Causes** How can you determine which causes were more significant than others? First, recognize that a cause must be an event or set of conditions that make it more likely an outcome will occur. Then ask yourself these questions to rank the relative significance of causes—that is, which causes were most important in bringing about an outcome.

   - Is it an underlying cause or one closer to the surface? (Either can be more important.)
   - Was it one of several causes that had about an equal effect?
   - Was it part of a chain of cause and effect in which the effect became a cause for another effect before the final effect was achieved?

   Choose one of the causes of global conflict and evaluate its relative significance in generating or producing conflict.

2. In one to three paragraphs, explain the relative significance of the causes of global conflict from 1900 to the present.

UNIT 7 REVIEW

 HISTORICAL PERSPECTIVES: WHAT CAUSED TOTALITARIANISM?

Scholars disagree about why so many totalitarian states, states with complete control over every aspect of public and private life, emerged in the 20th century. While many countries moved toward democracy, Russia, Germany, Italy, and Spain became dictatorships between the two world wars. Scholars often explain the rise of totalitarianism from their own discipline's viewpoint.

An Economist's View An Austrian economist, Friedrich Hayek, argued that totalitarianism had developed gradually and was based on decisions about economic policy. In his 1944 book *The Road to Serfdom,* Hayek concluded that totalitarianism grew in Western democracies because they had "progressively abandoned that freedom in economic affairs without which personal and political freedom has never existed in the past." He viewed socialism and fascism as two sides of the same coin, since centralized government planning and state power characterized both.

Political Scientists' View In contrast, the American political scientists Carl Friedrich and Zbigniew Brzezinski focused on political and ethnic issues, not economic ones. They contended that the totalitarian regimes in Germany, Italy, and the Soviet Union had their origins in the upheaval brought about by World War I. The forces of nationalism unleashed by the war, combined with the need to respond politically to the global depression that followed World War I, created fertile ground for strong nationalistic rulers who could rise to political power and address ethnic conflict.

A Historian's View American historian and journalist William Shirer identified the origins of Nazism in Germany's distant and distinctive past. He concluded that Germanic nationalism, authoritarianism, and militarism dated back to the Middle Ages. "The course of German history . . . ," he wrote, "made blind obedience to temporal rulers the highest virtue of Germanic man, and put a premium on servility." No other country developed the same sort of Nazism because no country had Germany's past.

A Sociologist's View American sociologist Barrington Moore looked to the past to explain totalitarianism. However, rather than focus on what made each country unique, he searched for patterns in the social structures of groups of countries. In his book *Social Origins of Dictatorship and Democracy* (1966), Moore looked at why Great Britain, France, and the United States evolved into democracies, while Japan, China, Russia, and Germany evolved into dictatorships. For Moore, two vital steps in creating a democracy were developing a middle class and breaking the power of the landed aristocracy. Countries that failed to do these things were more likely to become dictatorships.

Develop an Argument: Evaluate the extent to which historical evidence supports one of the perspectives on totalitarianism.

The supporting paragraphs in your long essay will demonstrate your skill in using evidence. They will also demonstrate your ability to follow a reasoning process and develop a complex interpretation of the prompt.

Use of Evidence Suppose your thesis is that imperialism and militarism are the two most significant causes of global conflict in the period 1900 to the present. To earn any points, you need to provide two examples of evidence relevant to your thesis—that is, directly connected to your topic. For example, you might point out that imperialism caused conflict not only between competing empires but also between the imperialists and the native peoples whose land they colonized. You might also note that militarism fed nationalist competition and reduced the gravity of warfare in the eyes of the public. For both points of evidence, you would include specific examples.

However, to earn the maximum number of points, you need to show how your evidence *supports* your argument. For example, you would need to point out that because imperialism touched nearly every part of the globe and disrupted so many native peoples, it was a far more significant cause of global conflict than other causes, such as European alliances. You would use examples to show the breadth of imperialist reach and the smaller sphere of European alliances. You might explain in a second paragraph that militarism was such a significant cause of global conflict because it was the force that made imperialism possible. You might also provide examples of the increasing power of military technology to inflict harm. Using such terms as *because* and *for this reason* will help you link your evidence to your argument.

Historical Reasoning and Complexity Your supporting paragraphs also need to show that you have framed your argument with historical reasoning—causation, continuity and change, or comparison. You can show this framing in your choice of key words as well as in the organization you use. For example, if you are comparing imperialism in Africa with imperialism in South America, you could organize your material so that you cover imperialism in Africa in one or more paragraphs and then move on to cover imperialism in South America, noting similarities and differences as you go. Or you might subdivide the topic of imperialism into such categories as its effect on social structures and its effect on economic matters and discuss both regions in each category.

To earn the most points, however, your supporting paragraphs must demonstrate a complex understanding of the historical development that is the focus of the prompt. You can show your complex understanding in many ways. You can explain both similarities and differences or address multiple causes and effects. You could make insightful connections across geographic areas and time periods. You could also use evidence from other sources to corroborate (verify), qualify (set limitations), or modify (revise) an argument that addresses the question. (See Write as a Historian in Topic 8.9 for more on these uses of evidence.)

continued

Application: Review the sample scored essays on the College Board website. Explain why each received the score it did for the use of evidence, historical reasoning, and complexity.

For current free response question samples, visit: https://apcentral. collegeboard.org/courses/ap-world-history/exam

LONG ESSAY QUESTIONS

Directions: Write an essay in response to one of the prompts below. The suggested writing time for an essay is 40 minutes.

In your response, you should do the following:

- Respond to the prompt with a historically defensible thesis or claim that establishes a line of reasoning.

- Describe a broader historical context relevant to the prompt.

- Support an argument in response to the prompt using at least two pieces of specific and relevant evidence.

- Use historical reasoning (e.g., comparison, causation, continuity or change) to frame or structure an argument that addresses the prompt.

- Demonstrate a complex understanding of a historical development related to the prompt through sophisticated argumentation and/or effective use of evidence.

Source: *AP® World History Course and Exam Description*

1. From 1900 to the present, political and economic events have triggered global conflicts.
Develop an argument that evaluates the extent to which different causes of global conflict are significant in the period 1900 to the present.

2. The Paris Peace Conference after World War I had even more profound effects on the world than the war did.
Develop an argument that evaluates the extent to which the 1919 Paris Peace Conference after World War I was a success or a failure.

3. Adolf Hitler's campaign of terror against Jews in the 1930s and 1940s had its roots in earlier discrimination against Jews in Europe.
Develop an argument that evaluates the extent to which the nature of anti-Semitism in Europe from the Middle Ages through World War II shows continuities or changes over time.

4. Conflicts over territory helped cause two world wars in the 20th century, but they also led to self-rule for many peoples worldwide in the 20th and 21st centuries.
Develop an argument that evaluates the extent to which territorial holdings from 1900 to present show continuity or change over time.

DOCUMENT-BASED QUESTION

Directions: Question 1 is based on the accompanying documents. The documents have been edited for the purpose of this exercise. You are advised to spend 15 minutes planning and 45 minutes writing your answer.

1. Evaluate whether challenges to existing political and social order around the world, during the period 1900 to 1922, were due primarily to the actions of states, or due primarily to the actions of various people groups.

In your response, you should do the following:

- Respond to the prompt with a historically defensible thesis or claim that establishes a line of reasoning.
- Describe a broader historical context relevant to the prompt.
- Support an argument in response to the prompt using at least four documents.
- Use at least one additional piece of specific historical evidence (beyond that found in the documents) relevant to an argument about the prompt.
- For at least two documents, explain how or why the document's point of view, purpose, historical situation, and/or audience is relevant to an argument.
- Demonstrate a complex understanding of a historical development related to the prompt through a sophisticated argument and/or effective use of evidence.

Source: *AP® World History Course and Exam Description*

Document 1

Source: Józef Pilsudski*, Polish political activist in Russian occupied Poland, and later leader of independent Poland 1918-1922, memorandum to the Japanese government during the Russo-Japanese War, 1904-05.

Poland's strength and importance among the constituent parts of the Russian state embolden us to set ourselves the political goal of breaking up the Russian state into its main parts and freeing the countries that have been forcibly incorporated into that empire. We regard this not only as the fulfilment of our country's cultural strivings for independent existence, but also as a guarantee of that existence, since a Russia divested of her conquests will be sufficiently weakened that she will cease to be a formidable and dangerous neighbor.

Pilsudski commanded the Polish army from 1919-1920, and repelled the invading Soviet Russians at the Battle of Warsaw in 1920.

Document 2

Source: The Black Hand, Serbian nationalist secret society committed to the unification of all Serbs into a Great Serbia, organization bylaws, 1911.

Article 1: This organization is created for the purpose of realizing the national ideal: the union of all Serbs. Membership is open to every Serb, without distinction of sex, religion, or place of birth, and to all those who are sincerely devoted to this cause.

Article 2: This organization prefers terrorist action to intellectual propaganda, and for this reason, it must remain absolutely secret.

Article 3: The organization bears the name Ujedinjenje ili Smirt [Union or Death].

Article 4: To fulfill its purpose, the organization will do the following: 1. Exercise influence on government circles, on the various social classes, and on the entire social life of the kingdom of Serbia, which is considered the Piedmont [the Italian state that served as the nucleus for the unification of Italy] of the Serbian nation; 2. Organize revolutionary action in all territories inhabited by Serbs; 3. Beyond the frontiers of Serbia, fight with all means the enemies of the Serbian national idea; 4. Maintain amicable relations with all states, peoples, organizations, and individuals who support Serbia and the Serbia element; 5. Assist those nations and organizations that are fighting for their own national liberation and unification. . . .

Document 3

Source: First Arab Congress, a meeting in Paris of Arabs who were still part of the Ottoman Empire to discuss their growing interest in nationalist ideas, the Congress's resolutions, 1913.

• Radical and urgent reforms are needed in the Ottoman Empire.

• It is important to guarantee Ottoman Arabs the exercise of their political rights by giving them meaningful roles in the administration of the Ottoman Empire.

• It is important to establish decentralized governments in each of the Arab and Syrian administrative districts [giving them more autonomy within the Ottoman Empire] according to their needs and abilities. . . .

• The Arabic language must be recognized by the Ottoman Parliament and considered the official language in Syrian and Arab regions.

• These resolutions will be communicated to the Imperial Ottoman Government.

• These same resolutions will also be communicated to those powers friendly to the Ottoman Empire. . . .

Document 4

Source: German King Wilhelm II, notes in the margins of a telegram from the German Ambassador in St. Petersburg, Russia, following the assassination of the Austrian Archduke Franz Ferdinand and the prospect of a world war, July 1914.

England must have the mask of Christian peaceableness torn publicly off her face. Our Ambassadors in Turkey and India, our agents, and others must inflame the whole Islamic world to wild revolt against this hateful, lying, conscienceless people of hagglers [the English]; for if we [Germany] are to be bled to death, at least England shall lose India.

Document 5

Source: Walter Trier, German cartoonist, a cartoon map showing the political landscape of Europe from a German perspective, 1914.

Credit: Europeana/Berlin State Library

Document 6

Source: W.B Yeats; Irish poet during British occupation of Ireland; *Easter, 1916* poem following the Easter Rising by Irish Nationalists in Dublin, Ireland, which resulted in the execution of 16 of the leaders of the revolt by the British; 1916.

I write it out in a verse—

MacDonagh and MacBride

And Connolly and Pearse

Now and in time to be,

Wherever green is worn,

Are changed, changed utterly:

A terrible beauty is born.

(Note: the names are some of the leaders; green is the national color of Ireland; a terrible beauty is the birth of Irish demands for independence following the deaths)

Document 7

Source: Mahatma Gandhi, Indian nationalist, speech at his trial for sedition after his non-cooperation movement (1919-1922) to overthrow British rule in India, 1922.

[I]n India when a special appeal was made at the [first world] war conference for recruits, I struggled at the cost of my health to raise a corps . . . the response was being made when the hostilities ceased and orders were received that no more recruits were wanted. In all these efforts at service, I was actuated [motivated] by the belief that it was possible by such services to gain a status of full equality in the Empire for my countrymen. . . . I . . . hoped that the Prime Minister would redeem his promise . . . [that India's] wounds would be healed, and that the reforms, inadequate and unsatisfactory though they were, marked a new era of hope in the life of India.

But all that hope was shattered . . . the promise was not to be redeemed. I saw too that not only did the reforms not mark a change of heart, but they were only a method of further raining India of her wealth and of prolonging her servitude.

I came reluctantly to the conclusion that the British connection had made India more helpless than she ever was before, politically and economically. A disarmed India has no power of resistance against any aggressor if she wanted to engage, in an armed conflict with him. So much is this the case that some of our best men consider that India must take generations, before she can achieve Dominion Status [independence].

But I hold it to be a virtue to be disaffected towards a Government which in its totality has done more harm to India than any previous system. . . . Holding such a belief, I consider it to be a sin to have affection for the system. And it has been a precious privilege for me to be able to write what I have in the various articles tendered in evidence against me.

In fact, I believe that I have rendered a service to India and England by showing in non-co-operation the way out of the unnatural state in which both are living. In my opinion, non-co-operation with evil is as much a duty as is co-operation with good. . . . I am endeavoring to show to my countrymen that violent non-co-operation only multiples evil, and that as evil can only be sustained by violence, withdrawal of support of evil requires complete abstention from violence.

UNIT 8: Cold War and Decolonization After 1900

Understand the Context

The aftermath of the world wars provided the context for two developments in the late 20th century: the decline of colonial empires and the rise of a tense conflict between capitalist and communist states known as the Cold War. These conflicts became intertwined, resulting in numerous wars.

Decolonization Against the backdrop of the world wars, nationalist movements in African and Asian colonies intensified. In the decades following World War II, colonies achieved independence through negotiation, and in some cases, armed struggle. The creation of independent states often resulted in population resettlements and challenges to inherited colonial boundaries.

In newly independent states, as in more established states, governments actively promoted economic development. Movements to redistribute land and wealth gained support in Africa, Latin America, and Asia. Some of these movements, such as the one in China, embraced a form of communism. Even after independence, connections between postcolonial states and former colonial empires continued through migration and economic relationships.

The Cold War After World War II, with Europe weakened, the United States and the Soviet Union (USSR) emerged as competing superpowers. The resulting Cold War was a power struggle between capitalism and communism, expressed through competing military alliances, a nuclear arms race, and proxy wars in postcolonial states in Latin America, Asia, and Africa.

While the Cold War heightened global tensions, movements advocating nonviolence and alternatives to the established order, such as the Non-Aligned Movement, also became influential. By the late 1900s, Soviet economic and military stagnation and public discontent contributed to the collapse of communist governments in Eastern Europe and the end of the Cold War.

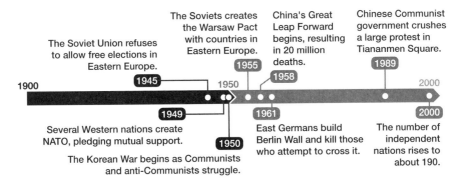

The Soviet Union refuses to allow free elections in Eastern Europe. **1945**

The Soviets creates the Warsaw Pact with countries in Eastern Europe. **1955**

China's Great Leap Forward begins, resulting in 20 million deaths. **1958**

Chinese Communist government crushes a large protest in Tiananmen Square. **1989**

1900   1950   2000

Several Western nations create NATO, pledging mutual support. **1949**

The Korean War begins as Communists and anti-Communists struggle. **1950**

East Germans build Berlin Wall and kill those who attempt to cross it. **1961**

The number of independent nations rises to about 190. **2000**

Topics and Learning Objectives

Topic 8.1: Setting the Stage for the Cold War and Decolonization

A: Explain the historical context of the Cold War after 1945.

Topic 8.2: The Cold War

B: Explain the causes and effects of the ideological struggle of the Cold War.

Topic 8.3: Effects of the Cold War

C: Compare the ways in which the United States and the Soviet Union sought to maintain influence over the course of the Cold War.

Topic 8.4: Spread of Communism after 1900

D: Explain the causes and consequences of China's adoption of communism.

E: Explain the causes and effects of movements to redistribute economic resources.

Topic 8.5: Decolonization after 1900

F: Compare the processes by which various peoples pursued independence after 1900.

Topic 8.6: Newly Independent States

G: Explain how political changes in the period c. 1900 to the present led to territorial, demographic, and nationalist developments.

H: Explain the economic changes and continuities resulting from the process of decolonization.

Topic 8.7: Global Resistance to Established Power Structures

I: Explain various reactions to existing power structures in the period after 1900.

Topic 8.8: End of the Cold War

J: Explain the causes of the end of the Cold War.

Topic 8.9: Causation in the Age of the Cold War and Decolonization

K: Explain the extent to which the effects of the Cold War were similar in the Eastern and Western Hemispheres.

Setting the Stage for the Cold War and Decolonization

We would consider it our moral duty to lend all support to the ending of colonialism and imperialism so that people everywhere are free to mould their own destiny.

—Lal Bahadur Shastri, Indian independence movement leader in the 1920s

Essential Question: What was the historical context for the Cold War after World War II?

After the global conflict of World War II, the largely unfulfilled hopes for greater colonial self-government after World War I were revived. Shastri's anti-imperialist sentiments helped explain how global affairs changed after the war ended in 1945. Colonies' desire for independence became intertwined with a global ideological conflict between capitalist countries (led by the United States) and communist countries (led by the Soviet Union).

Bringing the War to an End

During World War II, the leaders of Great Britain, the United States, and the Soviet Union, known as the **Big Three**, held several meetings to plan for the post-war world. Three of these were particularly important.

The Tehran Conference During the **Tehran Conference** in Iran in November 1943, the Allies agreed that the Soviet Union would focus on freeing Eastern Europe, while Britain and the United States would concentrate on Western Europe. In addition, Britain and the United States agreed to a Soviet demand to shift some Polish territory to the Soviet Union, which would be offset by Poland gaining territory elsewhere, mostly from Germany.

The Yalta Conference By February 1945, the Allies knew that Germany was near defeat, but they disagreed about what should happen after Germany's surrender. At the **Yalta Conference,** at a resort on the Black Sea, the leaders focused on plans for reconstructing Eastern Europe and for defeating Japan.

- Franklin Roosevelt wanted free, democratic elections in Eastern Europe. He also wanted the Soviets to join the war against Japan.

- Stalin demanded influence over Eastern Europe. Fearful that another Napoleon or Hitler would invade Russia from the West, he wanted Eastern Europe as a buffer zone. In return for Soviet help against Japan, he wanted control of islands claimed by Japan, ports ruled by China, and part ownership of a Manchurian railroad.

Roosevelt thought that after years of overseas war, the American public was unlikely to support a war against the Soviets over the fate of democracy in Eastern Europe. The conference ended with a Soviet pledge to fight Japan, but the Soviets offered only vague assurances on free elections in Eastern Europe.

The Potsdam Conference The final meeting among leaders of the Big Three, the **Potsdam Conference,** began in July 1945 in Germany. **Harry Truman**, who had become president after Roosevelt died on April 12, represented the United States. Churchill started the conference but lost his position as prime minister in mid-July and was replaced by Clement Atlee.

Truman insisted on free elections in Eastern Europe. However, by then Soviet troops had occupied the region. Stalin refused Truman's demand. With the backing of Soviet power, communists eventually gained control of East Germany, Poland, Czechoslovakia, Hungary, Bulgaria, and Romania.

By 1945, the United States and the Soviet Union lacked trust in one another and had begun the aggressive rhetoric that would become standard for four decades following World War II. Potsdam and the earlier conferences failed to settle important issues between the world's major powers. As a result, the stage was set for a cold war between countries still devastated by a hot war.

Shifting Balance of Power

When the war ended in 1945, parts of Europe and Asia had been devastated. The war resulted in 40 million to 60 million deaths. It destroyed factories, roads, bridges, and other structures needed for industrial production. It forced millions of people to move. Many were fleeing communism or searching for safety and opportunity.

Massive Destruction in Europe Wartime losses were not evenly distributed throughout Europe. In general, East and Central Europe suffered greater losses than did Western Europe. Worst hit were the Soviet Union, Poland, and Germany. Each lost between 10 and 20 percent of its population.

Countries such as Great Britain and France, despite their losses, maintained strong traditions of democracy and the rule of law. They still had strong educational systems, including outstanding universities. They remained home to large, innovative corporations. These advantages provided the foundation for Western Europe to become a global leader after the war. However, because of the massive physical destruction and population loss in victorious and defeated nations, Europe became less influential and powerful in the rest of the world, while the United States and the Soviet Union became more powerful. (Connect: Write a paragraph comparing the destruction caused by World War I and World War II. See Topic 7.8.)

The U.S.-Soviet Rivalry In 1945, then, the United States was poised to become the most powerful country in the world. Of all the major countries involved in the war, the United States suffered the least. Heavy fighting occurred on U.S. soil, in the Philippines, but the U.S. mainland was untouched by attacks. Its industrial base and infrastructure not only remained intact but also grew stronger through government-funded military contracts. Further, the loss of life in the United States was far lower than in Europe. The relative prosperity of the United States allowed it to provide financial aid to European countries after the war. This aid program, called the Marshall Plan, is described in Topic 8.2.

The United States also had developed atomic weapons and used them during the war, making the country even more formidable. The Soviets successfully tested an atomic bomb of their own in 1949. By the end of the 1940s, only the Soviet Union could challenge the United States in military might and political influence.

Advances During the War Military research at universities and in private companies, often funded by government, resulted in tremendous technological developments during World War II. Among the items that were developed for, improved, or used more widely by the military were air pressure systems for airplane cabins, refrigeration for food, stronger plywood for construction, and a variety of plastics for many uses. One of the most important advances was the spread of the use of penicillin, which saved the lives of thousands of wounded soldiers. Each of these advances would be adapted for civilian use, thereby improving the lives of millions of people.

The Start of the Cold War

The U.S.-Soviet tensions evident at Tehran, Yalta, and Potsdam made conflict likely. However, the high costs of the war meant that neither superpower wanted a full-scale war with the other. Rather, they settled into a cold war, a conflict does not involve direct military confrontation between two or more rival states. The **Cold War** between the superpowers played out in propaganda campaigns, secret operations, and an arms race.

The deadliest results of the Cold War occurred outside the lands of the two superpowers. The U.S.-Soviet rivalry led both countries to arm opposing sides in conflicts around the world, thereby transforming small civil wars and regional conflicts into much larger events. This increased the death tolls and level of destruction in these wars.

In the early 1950s, the United States and Soviet Union each developed a **hydrogen bomb** that was much more powerful than the atomic bombs dropped on Japan at the end of World War II. The arms race fostered close ties between the military and the industries that developed weapons. Before he left office in 1961, President **Dwight Eisenhower** expressed his concerns about the U.S.-Soviet competition for supremacy in nuclear armaments. He warned against allowing the **military-industrial complex,** the informal alliance between the government and the large defense contractors, to gain too much power. In later decades, citizens in many countries expressed similar worries. They began to protest the stockpiling of nuclear weapons.

Breakdown of Empires

After World War II, efforts resumed to undermine colonialism. The start of World War I had marked the high point of colonial empires. The British, the French, and other Europeans had colonized almost all of Africa, India, and Southeast Asia, and they dominated China. Empires based in Austria, Turkey, and Russia were multiethnic states, but each was dominated by one group, leaving others feeling discriminated against. After World War I, the demand for **self-determination**, the idea that each country should choose its own form of government and leaders, was spreading. The Austro-Hungary Empire and the Ottoman Empire crumbled, restructured into multiple new countries. However, in China, India, and throughout Africa, Europeans generally maintained their power, even expanding it over territories that had been part of the Ottoman Empire.

During World War II, the leading colonial powers focused on stopping Hitler. As a result, the anti-colonial movements probably grew stronger, but actual independence made little progress. However, after World War II, the foundation was set for the dismantling of colonial empires:

- In the colonized world, movements for self-determination grew. Often, they included both advocates of greater self-rule and proponents of full independence.

- World War II had so weakened Great Britain, France, and the other colonial powers that they had fewer resources to resist independence.

- The Cold War between the United States and the Soviet Union gave anti-colonial activists two superpowers to recruit as supporters.

The successful efforts of people to undermine colonial empires are described in Topics 8.5 and 8.6.

KEY TERMS BY THEME

GOVERNMENT: Europe	GOVERNMENT: United States	TECHNOLOGY: Armaments
Big Three	Harry Truman	hydrogen bomb
Tehran Conference	Cold War	military-industrial complex
Yalta Conference	Dwight Eisenhower	
Potsdam Conference		
	SOCIETY: Anti-Colonial Movements	
	self-determination	

MULTIPLE-CHOICE QUESTIONS

Questions 1 to 3 refer to the table below.

Nuclear Weapons Stockpiles, 1945 to 2015								
	1945	1955	1965	1975	1985	1995	2005	2015
United States	6	3,057	31,982	27,826	24,237	12,144	10,295	7,100
Soviet Union	0	200	6,129	19,055	39,197	27,000	17,000	7,700

Source: Hans M. Kristensen and Robert S. Norris, "Global Nuclear Stockpiles, 1945–2006," *Bulletin of the Atomic Scientists*, July 1, 2006 (data for 2015 from Arms Control Association, armscontrol.org.)

1. The data in the chart best supports which of the following claims?
   (A) The Soviet Union was primarily responsible for the escalation of the arms race in the 1950s and 1960.
   (B) The Soviet Union and the United States usually had about the same number of nuclear weapons.
   (C) The Soviet Union was behind in stockpiling weapons until about 1980, when it overtook the United State in the number of weapons.
   (D) The Soviet Union conceded defeat in the arms race when the United States had a large enough lead in the number of weapons.

2. Who predicted that increases in weapons stockpiles in the Soviet Union and the United States would have significant political and economic consequences?
   (A) President Franklin Roosevelt at the Yalta Conference
   (B) Several leaders of anti-colonial movements after World War II
   (C) President Dwight Eisenhower, who described a military-industrial complex
   (D) President Harry Truman, who insisted on free elections for Eastern European countries

3. Which accurately describes an effect of the changes shown in the table?
   (A) Both countries saw little change in their leadership as a result of the increase in the number of nuclear weapons during this period.
   (B) People around the world supported the buildup of nuclear weapons and agreed it was the best way to ensure peace.
   (C) The stockpiling of nuclear weapons actually strengthened the economies of both the United States and the Soviet Union.
   (D) The arms race was distressing to many around the world, and a strong antinuclear movement was established.

1. **Use the passage below to answer all parts of the question that follows.**

"On November 1, 1952, the United States successfully detonated "Mike," the world's first hydrogen bomb, on the Elugelab Atoll in the Pacific Marshall Islands. The 10.4-megaton thermonuclear device, built upon the Teller-Ulam principles of staged radiation implosion, instantly vaporized an entire island and left behind a crater more than a mile wide. The incredible explosive force of Mike was also apparent from the sheer magnitude of its mushroom cloud. . . . Half an hour after the test, the mushroom stretched 60 miles across, with the base of the head joining the stem at 45,000 feet.

Three years later, on November 22, 1955, the Soviet Union detonated its first hydrogen bomb on the same principle of radiation implosion. Both superpowers were now in possession of the 'hell bomb,' as it was known by many Americans, and the world lived under the threat of thermonuclear war for the first time in history."

History.com, *United States Tests First Hydrogen Bomb*, 2018

(A) Identify ONE way in which the hydrogen bomb shifted the global balance of power.

(B) Explain ONE reason why the development of atomic weapons was important to the United States and the Soviet Union.

(C) Explain ONE way the hydrogen bomb contributed to Cold War tensions after 1945.

2. **Answer all parts of the question that follows.**

(A) Identify ONE way in which hopes for self-government after World War I differed from hopes for self-government after World War II.

(B) Explain ONE historical development that contributed to the dissolution of empires after World War II.

(C) Explain ONE way in which economic gains contributed to a shift in the global balance of power after World War II.

THINK AS A HISTORIAN: SITUATE THE COLD WAR IN CONTEXT

How could two nations—the United States and the Soviet Union—fight so fiercely together as allies in World War II and then part ways so dramatically after the war that they created a Cold War that set the world on edge? Studying the context from which the Cold War arose and tracing continuity and change will help answer that question.

On separate paper, make a chart like the one below to situate the Cold War in context. Identify in what areas there was continuity and in what areas there was change.

Areas of Difference	United States	Soviet Union
Political Ideology Before World War II		
Economic Ideology Before World War II		
Foreign Goals After World War II		
Fears After World War II		

REFLECT ON THE TOPIC ESSENTIAL QUESTION

1. In one to three paragraphs, describe the historical context for the Cold War after World War II.

8.2

The Cold War

Let us not be deceived—we are today in the midst of a cold war.
—Bernard Baruch, banker and presidential advisor, 1947

Essential Question: What were the causes and effects of the ideological struggle of the Cold War?

After World War II, the democratic United States and the authoritarian Soviet Union emerged as the strongest countries in the world. Both countries had expanded their territorial control and influence after the war. After the Potsdam Conference in Germany in 1945, Truman and Stalin soon recognized their rivalry for dominance over Europe and Asia. The ideological conflict noted by Baruch, the power struggle between capitalism (led by the United States) and communism (led by the Soviet Union), was the central global conflict over the next 40 years.

Cooperation Despite Conflict: The United Nations

Despite ideological differences, the Allies shared a commitment to building a new organization to promote peace and prosperity to replace the League of Nations. The League had failed for two significant reasons:

- It lacked the support of all the world's powerful countries, particularly the United States.

- It lacked a mechanism to act quickly to stop small conflicts from escalating into large ones.

In 1943, leaders of the United States, Great Britain, the Soviet Union, and China discussed the idea of the **United Nations (UN)**. The UN was established in 1945. (Connect: Write a paragraph comparing the United Nations with the League of Nations. See Topics 7.3 and 7.5.)

Rivalry in Economics and Politics

The existence of the United Nations did not prevent tensions from growing worse between the Soviet Union and the West. Winston Churchill's March 1946 speech symbolized the Cold War. Churchill said that "an iron curtain has descended across the continent" of Europe. The metaphor of the **Iron Curtain** described the split between Eastern and Western Europe.

Capitalism and Communism One difference between the United States and the Soviet Union was how they organized their economies.

- In the United States, Western Europe, and other capitalist countries, economic assets, such as farms and factories, were mostly owned privately. Hence, private interests determined economic decisions. People had the freedom to act in their self-interest.

- In the Soviet Union, Eastern Europe, and other communist countries, economic assets were owned by the government. The system emphasized equality and fairness.

Democracy and Authoritarianism A second difference was how the rivals organized their political systems. In the United States, people chose their elected leaders through free elections. Further, they relied on an independent press to provide accurate information about the government and political parties to compete for votes. In the Soviet Union, elections were not significant, the press was operated by the government, and a single party dominated politics.

Criticisms and Similarities Each side pointed to what it saw as flaws in the other. In the United States, people attacked the Soviet system for restricting the rights of people to speak and worship freely, to elect their own representatives, and to allow businesses to operate efficiently. Soviets accused the United States of giving poor people the "freedom to starve" and for discriminating against African Americans and other minorities. The Soviet Union also stressed its emphasis on women's equality as a difference between its system and that of the United States.

Despite the difference in the U.S. and Soviet models, some analysts emphasized their similarities. For example, in both, control of big economic decisions was in the hands of groups, either the government or millions of corporate shareholders. Further, both countries often acted out of fear of the other, which made the military a powerful force in each.

Conflicts in International Affairs

Each side wanted to expand its system of thought throughout the world. This competition resulted in a long-running battle for influence over the opinions of people and alliance with governments.

The USSR and Its Satellite Countries The Soviets were determined to make the governments of Eastern Europe as much like the Soviet government as possible. They therefore directed the countries of Bulgaria, East Germany, Hungary, Poland, and Romania to develop five-year economic plans focused on developing industry and collective agriculture at the expense of consumer products. All political parties other than the Communists were outlawed.

These actions allowed the USSR (Union of Soviet Socialist Republics) to exploit the Eastern European nations to benefit the Soviets rather than to help those countries grow. The **satellite countries**—small states that are economically or politically dependent on a larger, more powerful state—were forced to import only Soviet goods and to export only to the Soviet Union. Moreover, the governments of these countries were just as dictatorial as the Soviet government. (Connect: Create a graphic comparing Communist and earlier Western imperialism. See Topic 6.2.)

World Revolution Beginning with the October Revolution of 1917, the Soviet Union viewed capitalism as a threat to its power. This view was enhanced with the concept of **world revolution,** a belief that organized workers would overthrow capitalism in all countries. The Soviets supported revolutions and uprisings between 1919 and 1923 in Germany, Bavaria, Hungary, northern Italy, and Bulgaria. Soviet interference elevated Western suspicions about Soviet intentions. After World War II, growing revolutionary feelings became a serious threat to Western powers and to governments in Central and Southern Europe.

Containment U.S. diplomat George Kennan worked in the U.S. Embassy in Moscow during the 1930s and in 1946. Kennan believed that the Soviet Union would continue to expand its borders and its influence abroad if it could. He advocated a policy of **containment**—not letting communism spread farther. Some politicians criticized Kennan for accepting the status quo. They argued for a more aggressive policy of overthrowing existing regimes in order to "roll back" the spread of communism.

Truman Doctrine Kennan's reports influenced President Harry Truman. A speech in 1947 outlined the **Truman Doctrine**, a strong statement that the United States would do what it had to do to stop the spread of communist influence, specifically in Greece and Turkey. The Soviet Union wanted to put military bases in Turkey so it could control the Dardanelles, the strait between the Black Sea and the Mediterranean Sea. In Greece, left-wing groups controlled by Communists were close to gaining control of the government. Truman pledged U.S. economic and military support to help the two countries resist this communist domination.

The Marshall Plan After World War II, the United States was deeply concerned about rebuilding Europe. The United States provided assistance to those countries soon after the war ended. However, many U.S. leaders thought more was needed to get European allies back on their feet economically. Based on the belief that a communist revolution could happen in economically unstable nations, the new goal was to rebuild Europe into a prosperous and stable region. The **Marshall Plan,** enacted in June 1947, was designed to offer $12 billion in aid to all nations of Europe, including Germany. This money would be used to modernize industry, reduce trade barriers, and rebuild Europe's damaged infrastructure. The plan worked. Economic output in the countries aided was 35 percent higher in 1951 than it had been in 1938.

The Soviet Union and its Eastern European satellites refused to participate in the plan. Instead, in 1949, the Soviets developed their own plan to help rebuild Eastern Europe—the **Council for Mutual Economic Assistance (COMECON)**. The scope of the organization was narrower than that of the Marshall Plan. It was limited primarily to trade and credit agreements among the six members. Its impact was modest compared to the Marshall Plan.

The Space Race and the Arms Race

The competition between the United States and the Soviet Union to be the dominant power was evident in the efforts of both countries to get into space first and to create more powerful weapons.

Space Race In 1957, the Soviet Union launched the first artificial satellite, called *Sputnik*, into orbit around Earth, inaugurating what become known as the *Space Race*. The United States launched its first satellite in January 1958. The two nations competed to become the first with a manned satellite orbiting Earth and, later, the first to land a human on the moon.

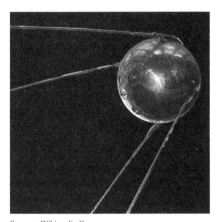

Source: Wikimedia Commons

Replica of Sputnik 1 stored in the National Air and Space Museum.

Source: Wikimedia Commons

Launch of first U.S. satellite, Explorer 1, on January 31, 1958.

Mutual Assured Destruction (MAD) Early in 1959, the Soviets tested the first intercontinental ballistic missile (ICBM) capable of delivering a nuclear warhead into U.S. territory. The United States tested a similar missile later that same year. Both countries realized that they had become so powerful that they had reached a point of **mutual assured destruction**. That is, regardless of who started a war, both would be obliterated by the end of it. Since neither side could win a nuclear war, neither side had an incentive to start one. As long as both sides kept improving their technology, the balance of terror between them would keep the peace—everyone hoped.

The Non-Aligned Movement

Many new African and Asian countries wanted to stay out of the U.S.-Soviet Cold War. They wanted an alternative framework for international economic, political, and social order—one not dominated by the two superpowers. In 1955, Indonesia hosted a conference, known as the Bandung Conference after the city where it was held, for representatives of these countries. Delegates from China, India, and 27 other countries—representing more than half the world's population—passed resolutions condemning colonialism. The impulse that prompted the Bandung Conference led countries to formally organize the **Non-Aligned Movement** in 1961. However, non-aligned countries faced challenges:

- Member states tried to combine support for stronger international institutions with efforts to advance their own interests. For example, Indian leader Jawaharlal Nehru supported a stronger UN, but he opposed its efforts to intervene in the conflict between India and Pakistan over control of the region of Kashmir.

- Member states often became more closely allied with one superpower or the other. When war broke out between Somalia and Ethiopia in 1977, the Soviet Union supplied aid to Ethiopia, prompting the United States to supply aid to Somalia.

Leaders of the Non-Aligned Movement		
Name	**Country**	**Role**
Jawaharlal Nehru	India	• Served as prime minister of India from 1947 to 1964 • Viewed as one of the most important leaders at the Bandung Conference
Kwame Nkrumah	Ghana	• Led Ghana to independence from Great Britain in 1957 • Advocated unity among Africans across country boundaries through the Organization of African Unity • Became one of the most respected African leaders of the postwar period
Gamal Abdel Nasser	Egypt	• Served three terms as president of Egypt between 1954 and 1970 • Helped negotiate compromises among people attending the Bandung Conference • Supported the Pan-Arab movement
Sukarno	Indonesia	• Became the first president of Indonesia in 1945 • Organized and hosted the Bandung Conference • Criticized both the United States and the USSR but accepted large amounts of aid from each

KEY TERMS BY THEME

GOVERNMENT: Global

United Nations (UN)

Iron Curtain

satellite countries

world revolution

containment

Truman Doctrine

Non-Aligned Movement

TECHNOLOGY: Space

mutal assured destruction

Sputnik

ECONOMICS: International

Marshall Plan

Council for Mutual Economic Assistance (COMECON)

MULTIPLE-CHOICE QUESTIONS

Questions 1 to 3 refer to the following passage.

"When forces of liberation entered Greece, they found that the retreating Germans had destroyed virtually all the railways, roads, port facilities, communications, and merchant marine. More than a thousand villages had been burned. . . . Livestock, poultry, and draft animals had almost disappeared. Inflation had wiped out practically all savings. . . . Greece must have assistance if it is to become a self-supporting and self-respecting democracy.

The United States must supply that assistance. . . . There is no other country to which democratic Greece can turn. No other nation is willing and able to provide the necessary support for a democratic Greek government . . . . If we falter in our leadership, we may endanger the peace of the world— and we shall surely endanger the welfare of our own Nation."

> President Harry Truman, address to joint session of Congress,
> March 12, 1947

1. What was the context in the United States in which Truman issued the statement included in the passage?

    (A) People were increasingly supportive of a policy of open imperialism.

    (B) People feared the spread of Soviet communism in Europe.

    (C) People argued for a return to isolationism after the loss of so many lives in World War II.

    (D) People were calling for the United States to actively overthrow undemocratic governments.

2. Which individual most clearly showed through thoughts or actions that he held ideas similar to those expressed by Truman in the passage?

    (A) U.S. diplomat George Kennan

    (B) U.S. Secretary of State George Marshall

    (C) UN Secretary General Trygve Lie

    (D) U.S. General Douglas MacArthur

3. What was the most important similarity between the comments of Truman and the Marshall Plan?

(A) Both emphasized military aid to prevent the spread of communism.

(B) Both created coalitions to finance rebuilding European infrastructure.

(C) Both provided economic aid to rebuild nations after World War II.

(D) Both required the implementation of democratic elections in order for a nation to obtain aid.

SHORT-ANSWER QUESTIONS

1. Use the passage below to answer all parts of the question that follow.

"Imperialism is weakening. Colonial empires and other forms of foreign oppression of peoples in Asia, Africa and Latin America are gradually disappearing from the stage of history. Great successes have been achieved in the struggle of many peoples for national independence and equality . . . .

The Governments of countries participating in the Conference resolutely reject the view that war, including the 'cold war,' is inevitable as this view reflects a sense both of helplessness and hopelessness and is contrary to the progress of the world. They affirm their unwavering faith that the international community is able to organize its life without resorting to means which actually belong to a past epoch of human history."

Belgrade Declaration; the first Non-Aligned Movement
Conference; Belgrade, Yugoslavia; 1961

(A) Identify ONE way in which this passage reflected the context regarding self-determination in which the Non-Aligned Movement was formed.

(B) Identify ONE way in which this passage reflected the context regarding the superpowers in which the Non-Aligned Movement was formed.

(C) Explain ONE way in which the Non-Aligned Movement was an example of other trends in international relations in the 20th century.

2. Answer all parts of the question that follow.

(A) Identify the response of the Soviet Union to the Marshall Plan.

(B) Explain the policy of containment advocated by the United States after World War II.

(C) Explain how the arms race and the space race were similar.

THINK AS A HISTORIAN: EXPLAIN THE HISTORICAL SITUATION
OF THE "RED SCARE"

Communists are sometimes called "reds." A "red scare" is a period during which non-Communists are especially fearful and suspicious that Communists are plotting a takeover, often through infiltrating government institutions. A red scare happened in the United States in the years after World War II. Senator Joseph R. McCarthy of Wisconsin became the leading voice for hunting down Communist spies and infiltrators. He made unfounded allegations against politicians and hundreds of civilians, suspecting them of being Communists and Soviet spies. In Wheeling, West Virginia, on February 9, 1950, Senator McCarthy gave an infamous speech proclaiming that he had a list of members of the Communist Party who were in the U.S. State Department.

> "The reason why we find ourselves in a position of impotency is not because our only powerful potential enemy has sent men to invade our shores, but rather because of the traitorous actions of those who have been treated so well by this Nation. It has not been the less fortunate, or members of minority groups who have been traitorous to this Nation, but rather those who have had all the benefits that the wealthiest Nation on earth has had to offer . . . the finest homes, the finest college education and the finest jobs in government we can give.
>
> This is glaringly true in the State Department. There the bright young men who are born with silver spoons in their mouths are the ones who have been most traitorous. . . . I have here in my hand a list of 205 . . . names that were made known to the Secretary of State as being members of the Communist Party and who nevertheless are still working and shaping policy in the State Department . . ."

> Senator Joseph McCarthy; speech in Wheeling, West
> Virginia; February 9, 1950

Research the historical situation in which McCarthy made his accusations. Identify three or four events that help explain the beliefs he expresses in this speech. Also explain why the historical situation limits the usefulness of this source as a factual representation of Communists in the U.S. government.

REFLECT ON THE TOPIC ESSENTIAL QUESTION

1. In one to three paragraphs, explain the causes and effects of the ideological struggle of the Cold War.

Effects of the Cold War

The only thing that kept the Cold War cold was the mutual deterrence afforded by nuclear weapons.

—Chung Mong-joon, South Korean politician and business leader, 2013

Essential Question: In what ways did both the Soviet Union and the United States seek to maintain influence during the Cold War?

With the start of the Cold War, new military alliances for mutual protection formed in different parts of the world. The threat of nuclear war, as noted above by Chung Mong-joon, kept the United States and the Soviet Union from starting a war that could end in unprecedented global destruction. But **proxy wars**, such as the ones in Korea and Vietnam, resulted in millions of deaths. In a proxy war, a major power helps bring about a conflict between other nations but does not always fight directly. These conflicts underlined the political and philosophical divide between the superpowers.

The superpowers faced off in Cuba and several other Central American countries as well as in the African country of Angola. The combination of military, economic, and nuclear influence across the globe made the world a tense place for decades after World War II—the war the two superpowers had worked together to end.

Allied Occupation of Germany

The conflict among the Allies after World War II was exemplified by the debate over how to occupy the defeated country of Germany. The Allies agreed to partition the country among France, Great Britain, the United States, and the Soviet Union. The three Western Allies wanted to combine their zones into one state under democratic principles.

Berlin Blockade The Allies also decided to divide Germany's capital, Berlin, into four zones. The three Western zones would become a free city that was located within the Soviet zone of Germany. The Soviets wanted to stop these Western plans and control all of Berlin. They set up a blockade of the Western zones in Berlin to prevent the West from moving supplies into the area by land. The Western Allies did not want to risk a military confrontation with the Soviets and ultimately began the **Berlin Airlift**. Through this operation, the Allies flew supplies into Western zones between February 1948 and May

1949, when the Soviets lifted the blockade.

Two Germanys After the blockade ended, Germany split into two states. West Germany became the Federal Republic of Germany. East Germany became the German Democratic Republic. The division of Europe into East and West was complete.

Berlin Wall As citizens of East Germany saw the prosperity and democratic lifestyle of West Germany, many wanted to move to the West. Between 1949 and 1961, about 2.5 million East Germans fled.

However, the East German and Soviet governments were determined to keep people in East Germany. They knew that the exodus to the West reflected poorly on the communist system, and it was hard on their economy. They first set up barbed-wire fences patrolled by guards along the perimeter of East Germany and between East and West Berlin. In August 1961, they began replacing the fences in Berlin with a wall, which became known as the **Berlin Wall**. Between 1961 and 1989, when the Berlin Wall fell, soldiers killed about 150 people as they tried to escape over it.

NATO, the Warsaw Pact, and Other Alliances

Only a few years after World War II ended, the Soviet Union dominated the Eastern European countries they had occupied during the war. Communist governments in those countries—buoyed by support and the direct influence of Stalin—subjected their people to the same suppression and economic system as the Soviet Union. Many Western European countries feared such a dominant communist presence on their doorstep.

Out of a desire to coordinate their defenses in case of a conflict with the Soviets, several Western nations created the **North Atlantic Treaty Organization (NATO)** in April 1949. The treaty pledged mutual support and cooperation within the alliance against conflicts and wars. Its original members were Belgium, Canada, Denmark, France, Great Britain, Iceland, Italy, Luxembourg, the Netherlands, Norway, Portugal, and the United States. Membership in this Brussels-based organization expanded considerably in the decades after its founding.

The Soviet Union's response to NATO was the **Warsaw Pact**, created in 1955. Albania, Bulgaria, Czechoslovakia, East Germany, Hungary, Poland, Romania, and the Soviet Union were the original members. Warsaw Pact nations combined their armed forces and based their army leaders in Moscow, the capital of the Soviet Union. These nations were known as the **communist bloc**.

Two countries with communist political systems successfully resisted Soviet control. Albania, located next to Greece, joined the Warsaw Pact but withdrew in 1968. It became more closely tied to China. Yugoslavia, under the authoritarian leadership of Marshall Josip Broz Tito, never joined the Warsaw Pact. In the 1990s, ethnic divisions caused Yugoslavia to break apart into several countries, including Slovenia, Serbia, and Croatia.

Other treaty organizations formed in an attempt to halt the spread of communism in other regions:

- In 1954, Australia, France, Great Britain, New Zealand, Pakistan, the Philippines, Thailand, and the United States formed the **Southeast Asia Treaty Organization (SEATO)**.
- The **Central Treaty Organization (CENTO)** was an anti-Soviet treaty organization formed by Great Britain, Iran, Iraq, Pakistan, and Turkey to prevent the spread of Communism in the Middle East. The United States was not a full member, but it joined CENTO'S military committee.

During the Cold War, the United States formed alliances with more than 40 states. It was sometimes easier for the United States to influence and negotiate through these smaller alliances than through the United Nations.

Proxy Wars

The ideological Cold War was accompanied by hot wars in Asia, Africa, Latin America, and the Caribbean. They were called proxy wars because the armies of smaller countries were proxies, or stand-ins, for the two superpowers. These wars often combined specific local issues, such as a battle against colonialism or for land reform (see Topic 8.4), with the international conflict over the spread of communism. Though proxy wars occurred in small countries, some resulted in millions of deaths.

Two of the biggest confrontations were the Korean War and Vietnam War in Asia. In both instances, the countries were split into northern and southern sections. In both countries, a communist government ruled the northern section.

Korean War Just as the victorious powers divided Germany after World War II, they also divided the Korean Peninsula. The Soviets occupied the north while the United States and its allies occupied the south. The **Korean War** (1950–1953) began when North Korea invaded South Korea in an attempt to reunite the country under its leadership. In response, the UN voted to defend South Korea militarily. The Soviet Union could have vetoed the resolution, but its representative was absent during the vote because the Soviet Union was boycotting all Security Council meetings in protest over a disagreement about China's seat on the Security Council.

UN military forces supporting the South Koreans came from 16 member countries, but the United States provided the largest number and the overall commander, General **Douglas MacArthur**. The Soviet Union did not send troops, but it sent money and weapons to North Korea. The UN forces pushed back the North Koreans across the inter-Korean border and drove toward North Korea's border with China. The Chinese, allies of North Korea and concerned that the UN forces would try to invade China as well, sent Chinese troops across the border and entered the war against the United States and its allies. After three years of fighting and some four million civilian and military casualties, the war ended in a stalemate. The two parts of Korea remained divided, with a demilitarized zone in between.

Vietnam War U.S. President Dwight D. Eisenhower, following the Truman policy of containment, sent military advisers to South Vietnam to train the South Vietnamese army and to prevent a communist takeover by North Vietnam. Eisenhower's successor, President John F. Kennedy, increased the number of advisers from 1,000 to 16,000. Some U.S. citizens believed America could not afford to lose a confrontation in Vietnam. They thought a communist victory would weaken U.S. prestige around the world.

However, the United States was supporting an undemocratic and unpopular South Vietnamese ruler, Ngo Dinh Diem. In 1963, Buddhist monk Thich Quang Duc publicly set himself on fire in Saigon to protest the South Vietnamese government's favoring of Catholics over Buddhists. His protests inspired others. A military coup, with U.S. support, soon overthrew Diem.

In 1964, President **Lyndon Johnson** sent more U.S. troops to South Vietnam. Johnson believed in the **domino theory**—the idea that if one country in the region became communist, other countries would soon follow. Johnson feared that China and the Soviet Union would bring all of Southeast Asia under communist rule. (Connect: Trace foreign intervention in Southeast Asian affairs through the Vietnam War. See Topic 6.2.)

Angola The Portuguese colony of **Angola** in southwest Africa won its independence in 1975, after 14 years of armed struggle. Like the Vietnamese, the Angolans had to fight a war to end their colonial status.

However, Angola faced greater ethnic conflict than did Vietnam. The borders of Angola, like those of many newly independent African countries, had been set by European colonial powers with little regard for traditional regions. Rival ethnic groups were thrown together under one government. Angola was more a multiethnic empire consisting of three distinct cultural groups than a nation-state in which everyone shared a common culture. Each group had fought for independence. Each wanted to control the country's lucrative diamond mines. And each was supported by other countries:

- The USSR and Cuba backed the Mbundu tribe.
- South Africa backed the Ovimbundu tribe.
- The United States backed the Bankongo tribe.

Upon independence, civil war broke out. In 2002, after 27 years of fighting, the rivals agreed on a cease-fire. However, threats of violence from militant separatist groups remained.

Contra War In Nicaragua in 1979, the 43-year dictatorship by the Somoza family was ended by the rebel Sandinistas, who called themselves socialists. Two years later, conservative opponents of the Sandinistas, known as Contras, tried to overthrow them. From 1981 to 1988, the **Contra War** gripped the country. Wanting to isolate the Sandinistas, the United States heavily backed the Contras with covert support. The Contra War took the lives of tens of thousands of Nicaraguans. The war ended after the signing of the Tela Accord in 1989 and the demobilization of the Contra and Sandinista armies.

Cold War in Cuba

Fidel Castro and other communist revolutionaries overthrew the Cuban dictator Fulgencio Batista in 1959. Castro soon set up a dictatorship in Cuba less than 100 miles off the coast of Florida. Many people in the United States were concerned about how Cuba's new leader would interact with the country's neighbor to the north.

The Bay of Pigs Crisis On August 6, 1960, the new government started to nationalize foreign-owned industries, which was a common communist strategy. Cuba nationalized businesses and properties of the national telephone and electricity companies; Texaco, Esso, and Sinclair oil companies; and 36 sugar mills owned by U.S. firms. As a result of these economic losses for its citizens, the United States broke off trade with Cuba and cut diplomatic ties. Castro in turn accepted Soviet aid and aligned Cuba's foreign policy with that of the Soviet Union.

In 1961, newly elected U.S. President **John F. Kennedy** had grave concerns about the presence of a communist country located only 90 miles from the coast of Florida. Before Kennedy took office, a group of Cuban exiles who opposed Castro had asked for U.S. government backing to invade Cuba and overthrow Castro. Kennedy gave his support. The resulting **Bay of Pigs** invasion was a total failure. Even worse for the United States, it cemented the Cuba-Soviet alliance.

The Cuban Missile Crisis In response to the Bay of Pigs, the Soviets began to support Cuba with arms and military advisors. Soviet Premier **Nikita Khrushchev**, who came to power after Stalin, saw an opportunity in Cuba. In 1962 he shipped nuclear missiles to Cuba. Khrushchev felt justified in his actions because in the summer of 1961 the United States had placed nuclear missiles in Turkey, a U.S. ally that shared a border with the Soviet Union.

Source: CIA (1962)

During the Cuban Missile Crisis, U.S. planes photographed evidence of Soviet missiles and sites in San Cristobal, Cuba. The image is a U-2 reconnaissance photograph, showing Soviet nuclear missiles, their transports and tents for fueling and maintenance.

In October 1962, U.S. intelligence learned that more missiles were on their way to Cuba. Kennedy ordered the U.S. Navy to prevent the missiles from reaching Cuba. He called his action a "quarantine" because a blockade was technically an act of war. Regardless of the term, the two superpowers were on a collision course that threatened nuclear war.

Ultimately, the two leaders pulled back from the brink. Khrushchev called back the Soviet ships and removed the missiles that had been delivered to Cuba. In return, the United States pledged to quietly remove its missiles from Turkey. After this incident, leaders of both countries realized that better communication between their countries was needed. In 1963, the two countries set up a **Hot Line**, a direct telegraph/teleprinter link between the U.S. and Soviet leaders' offices.

Antinuclear Weapon Movement

The nuclear arms race spawned a reaction known as the **antinuclear weapons movement**. One of the first such movements developed in Japan in 1954 in opposition to U.S. testing of nuclear weapons in the Pacific Ocean. In 1955, more than one-third of Japan's population signed a petition against nuclear weapons. In the late 1970s and early 1980s, the antinuclear weapons movement expanded to other countries, particularly to the United States and Western Europe. On June 6, 1982, some one million people demonstrated in New York City against the creation, buildup, and possible use of nuclear weapons.

Limiting Nuclear Power People worldwide worried about deaths and environmental harm from nuclear war or nuclear testing. In 1963, the Soviet Union, the United States, and more than 100 other states signed the **Nuclear Test-Ban Treaty**. France and China did not sign it. This agreement outlawed testing nuclear weapons above ground, underwater, and in space. The goal was to cut down the amount of radiation that people would be exposed to as a result of weapons testing. Underground testing remained legal. In 1968, the **Nuclear Non-Proliferation Treaty** called on nuclear powers to prevent the spread of military nuclear technology and materials to non-nuclear countries.

KEY TERMS BY THEME		
GOVERNMENT: International Conflicts	**GOVERNMENT:** Treaties	**TECHNOLOGY:** Military
proxy war	North Atlantic Treaty Organization (NATO)	Hot Line
Berlin Airlift	Warsaw Pact	**SOCIETY:** Activism
Berlin Wall	communist bloc	antinuclear weapons movement
Korean War	Southeast Asia Treaty Organization (SEATO)	
Vietnam War		**GOVERNMENT:** Leaders
domino theory	Central Treaty Organization (CENTO)	Douglas MacArthur
Angola		Lyndon Johnson
Contra War	Nuclear Test-Ban Treaty	Fidel Castro
Bay of Pigs	Nuclear Non-Proliferation Treaty	John F. Kennedy
Cuban Missile Crisis		Nikita Khrushchev

Questions 1 to 3 refer to the map below.

NATO AND THE WARSAW PACT, 1956

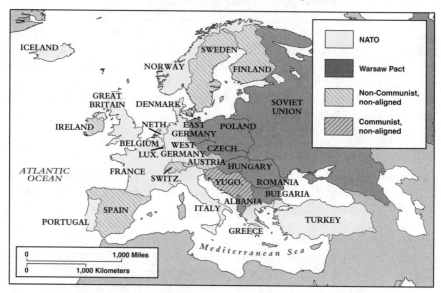

1. The map above most clearly reflects the context of the ongoing efforts of
   (A) the Marshall Plan to stimulate global economic growth
   (B) the United States to contain communism
   (C) the European Economic Union to unify the European economy
   (D) the United States to improve relations with the Soviet Union

2. Which best describes the Warsaw Pact bloc shown on the map?
   (A) A Soviet-led government based in Warsaw, the capital of Poland
   (B) A military alliance created in response to NATO by the Soviet Union and other communist nations
   (C) An economic union among Soviet-bloc countries created to counter the economic power of the European Economic Community
   (D) A military alliance of non-aligned nations of Europe, Asia, and Africa

3. Which countries most closely represented the declared position of Jawaharlal Nehru, Kwame Nkrumah, and Gamal Abdel-Nasser?
   (A) NATO
   (B) Warsaw Pact
   (C) Non-Communist, non-aligned
   (D) Communist, non-aligned

1. **Use the passage below to answer all parts of the question that follows.**

   "The epitaph for the disastrous April 17–19, 1961, attempt to overthrow communist dictator Fidel Castro by invading Cuba with 1,500 amateur soldiers and a handful of piston-engined B-26 ground-attack bombers was spoken soon afterward by President John F. Kennedy. 'How could I have been so stupid?' he asked an aide.

   A better question might have been, How could the Central Intelligence Agency have bungled things so badly? The answer is that the CIA—which planned the operation, trained its participants and helped execute its amphibious landings and air strikes—performed more amateurishly than the Cuban invaders. But the agency's senior leaders were so enamored of the plan they ignored its obvious flaws. Worse, two presidential administrations, numerous legislators, and plenty of smart generals and admirals also signed off on the scheme.

   Rebel troops and tanks began landing early on April 17. By the evening of April 19 the invasion brigade had been crushed by Castro's armor, heavy artillery and small but unopposed air force, which included four Lockheed T-33 jet trainers that, much to the CIA's surprise, were fitted with weapons.

   The end result of the ill-fated expedition included 114 men of Brigade 2506 killed and more than 1,200 captured. In those years before Vietnam some observers called the Bay of Pigs the worst defeat suffered by the United States since the War of 1812."

   > Stephan Wilkinson, "What We Learned from the Bay of Pigs,
   > 1961," *Military History Magazine*

   (A) Identify ONE immediate consequence of the failed invasion.

   (B) Explain ONE piece of historical evidence for the failure of the invasion.

   (C) Explain ONE way in which the events described in the passage reflected the relationship between Cuba and the United States prior to 1961.

2. **Answer all parts of the question that follows.**

   (A) Identify ONE way in which policies to maintain global influence in the United States were similar to the policies to maintain global influence in the Soviet Union during the Cold War.

   (B) Identify ONE way in which policies to maintain global influence in the United States were different from the policies to maintain global influence in the Soviet Union during the Cold War.

   (C) Explain ONE historical development in Latin America that contributed to furthering tensions between the United States and the Soviet Union during the Cold War.

THINK AS A HISTORIAN: EXPLAIN RELATIONSHIPS THROUGH COMPARISON

One way to explain relationships among historical developments is to use the reasoning skill of comparison. To practice this skill, complete the following activity.

Choose two of the proxy wars covered in this topic. Explain how they are related by looking at how and why they are similar and how and why they are different. Consider such factors as ethnic groups, natural resources, superpowers involved, and outcome. Organize your ideas using a chart like the one below. Then write a few sentences explaining the relationship of the proxy wars you chose.

Similarities	Differences
Explanation:	

REFLECT ON THE TOPIC ESSENTIAL QUESTION

1. In one to three paragraphs, compare how the Soviet Union and the United States sought to maintain influence during the Cold War.

8.4

Spread of Communism after 1900

The road after the revolution will be longer, the work greater and more arduous.
—Mao Zedong, 1949

Essential Question: How did communism and land reform affect China and other countries?

The Cold War provided the context in which many countries wrestled with the legacies of their past. The combined heritage of feudalism, capitalism, and colonialism often resulted in societies with a small class of powerful landowners and a large class of peasants who owned little or no land. When socialists or communists sought to make more people into landowners, they got caught up in the U.S.-Soviet ideological battle. **Land reform** was a vital issue in China, Iran, Vietnam, Ethiopia, India, and a number of Latin American countries, including Mexico, Bolivia, and Venezuela.

Communism in China

In China, the Communists and the Nationalists began fighting for control of the country in 1927. However, after the Japanese invaded, the two sides agreed to focus on fighting them instead of each other. (See Topic 7.5.)

Victory by the Communists After the defeat of the Japanese in 1945, the Chinese Civil War resumed. The Communists, led by **Mao Zedong**, won popular support because they redistributed land to peasants, opened schools and hospitals, and punished soldiers who mistreated civilians. Peasants saw the Communists as more nationalist and less corrupt than the Nationalists. In 1949, the Communists defeated the Nationalists and set up the People's Republic of China. Mao ordered the nationalization of Chinese industries and created five-year plans based on the Soviet model. Like the Soviets, the Chinese plans emphasized heavy industry instead of consumer goods.

Great Leap Forward In 1958, China went through more land reform as part of the policy called the **Great Leap Forward**. Peasant lands were organized into **communes**, large agricultural communities where the state held the land, not private owners. Those who protested this policy could be sent to "reeducation camps" or killed.

Even though failing harvests caused severe food shortages, China continued to export grain to Africa and Cuba. Mao sought to convince the outside world of the success of his economic plans. Some 20 million Chinese died from starvation. By 1960, the Great Leap Forward was abandoned.

Source: Wikimedia Commons.

During the Great Leap Forward, China set up small-scale backyard steel furnaces. However, they produced steel of very poor quality, and the effort was dropped.

Cultural Revolution In 1966, Mao attempted to reinvigorate China's commitment to communism, an effort called the **Cultural Revolution**. In practice, the Cultural Revolution silenced critics of Mao and solidified his hold on power. Its impact on China was similar to the impact of Stalin's purges in the Soviet Union. Mao ordered the **Red Guards**, groups of revolutionary students, to seize government officials, teachers, and others and send them to the countryside for reeducation. Reeducation involved performing hard physical labor and attending group meetings where Red Guards pressured them to admit they had not been revolutionary enough.

Relations with the Soviets Although China and the Soviet Union were both communist states, they were often hostile to each other. From 1961 onward, the two countries skirmished over their border. They also competed for influence around the world. For example, Albania, a Soviet satellite, took advantage of the split by allying with China against the Soviet Union, thereby receiving more autonomy and additional financial aid from China.

Turmoil in Iran

The modern country of Iran fell under foreign domination in the late 19th century. Britain and Russia fought to control the area. The competition grew even keener when oil was discovered in Iran in the early 20th century.

Foreign Influence Early in World War II, the leader of Iran considered supporting Hitler's Nazi regime. Determined not to let that happen, Russia and Britain invaded Iran. They forced the leader to abdicate power to his young son, Shah **Muhammad Reza Pahlavi**. They kept their forces in Iran until the end of the war.

Iranian nationalists objected to the new shah as a puppet of Western powers. In 1951, they forced him to flee the country. Two years later, Iran selected **Mohammad Mosaddegh** as prime minister. He vowed to nationalize the oil companies. The United States and Great Britain engineered an overthrow of the democratically chosen Mosaddegh and returned the shah to power. The shah ran an authoritarian regime that relied on a ruthless secret police force.

Land Reform in the White Revolution Despite his harsh rule, the shah instituted several progressive reforms, known as the **White Revolution** because they came without bloodshed. They included recognizing women's right to vote, creating a social welfare system, and funding literacy programs in villages.

The most important reform dealt with land ownership. The shah wanted to undercut the power of traditional landowners and increase his popularity among peasants. Under his plan, the government bought land from landlords and resold it at a lower price to peasants. The program helped many peasants become first-time landowners, but it failed to reach a majority of peasants.

Many Iranians—both landowners who had been forced to sell their land and frustrated peasants who received nothing—opposed the land reforms. Religious conservatives opposed modernizing the country, particularly changing the relationship between men and women. Advocates for greater democracy opposed the shah's harsh rule.

The Iranian Revolution In 1979, a revolution toppled the shah. Many Iranians supported the revolution because they vividly remembered the overthrow of the Mosaddegh government in 1953. The leaders to emerge from the revolution, though, were ones who rejected the shah's secular worldview for one that viewed Islam as a key part of the individual-state relationship. The new government was a **theocracy**, a form of government in which religion is the supreme authority. The new government was headed by a cleric and a Guardian Council, a body of civil and religious legal experts who were responsible for interpreting the constitution and making sure all laws complied with shariah (Islamic law). The clergy had the right to approve or disapprove anyone who ran for office. Iran opposed Western policies in the Middle East and the state of Israel.

Land Reform in Latin America

Throughout Latin America, leaders saw the concentration of land ownership as a barrier to progress. Hence, as countries freed themselves from colonialism, they considered land reform. Mexico's effort dates back to the 1930s, but much of the land reform in Latin America took place in the 1960s or later.

Venezuela In Venezuela, for example, the government redistributed some five million acres of land. Some of the land was state-owned and not previously under cultivation, while other pieces of land were seized from large landowners. The land reform, begun with a 2001 law, was not popular with the landowners who claimed that the state seized their property while it was under cultivation. Additional problems arose from illegal squatters who moved in to settle on lands that were not scheduled for land reform. Land reform efforts had political repercussions as well; those who benefitted were more willing to vote for the government instituting the reforms, while those from whom land was confiscated tended not to support the states that seized it. Land reform in Latin America varied in its details in each country, shaped partly by environmental factors, partly by a legacy from colonialism, and partly by the ideology of the rulers instituting the reforms.

Guatemala A democratically elected government under Jacob Arbenz in the Central American country of Guatemala began efforts at land reform. Feeling threatened, the United Fruit Company lobbied the U.S. government to remove the Arbenz. In 1954, he was overthrown.

Source: Pushkin Museum of Fine Arts, Moscow, Russia/Wikimedia Commons

The U.S. Secretary of State John Foster Dulles called the overthrow of Guatemala's government a "glorious victory for democracy." Diego Rivera's *Glorious Victory* (1954) portrayed Dulles holding a bomb that featured the face of U.S. President Dwight Eisenhower. Rivera used this phrase ironically for the title of his mural condemning the action.

Land Reform in Asia and Africa

Throughout Latin America, leaders saw the concentration of land ownership as a barrier to progress. Hence, as countries freed themselves from colonialism, they considered land reform. Mexico's effort dates back to the 1930s, but much of the land reform in Latin America took place in the 1960s or later.

Vietnam During World War II, Japan occupied Vietnam, which France still claimed as a colony. At the end of the war in 1945, Vietnam declared independence from Japanese and French control. Vietnam was an agricultural society. A few people controlled most of the land. Communists vowed to seize land from the large landowners and redistribute it among the peasants. This pledge won them great support among peasants. When Communists took power in the north, they carried out their policies—sometimes violently. In South Vietnam, the government was slow to implement land reform, which was one reason it remained unpopular.

Ethiopia Other than a short period from 1936 to 1941 when it was under Italian occupation, Ethiopia had remained an independent country, but it suffered problems similar to those of many colonies. During World War II, exiled Ethiopian leader **Haile Selassie** returned to power. He aligned the country with the western powers after the war, and Ethiopia enjoyed economic success based largely on its coffee trade. This led to western-style political and cultural reforms. Selassie was unable to effectively implement land reforms in Ethiopia. By the 1960s, the country was souring on his leadership. Many people saw him as a pawn of U.S. imperialism.

In 1974, a group of military and civilian leaders deposed Selassie. One of the primary figures was **Mengistu Haile Mariam**, an Ethiopian native and major in the military. He ordered the assassination of 60 former regime officials. The new government declared itself socialist and received aid and weapons from the Soviet Union and other communist countries. Famine, failed economic policies, and rebellion marred Mengistu's leadership. By 1991, he had resigned and fled to Zimbabwe.

India Southern Asia had been under British rule since 1858. That changed in 1947. Mahatma Gandhi had led the independence movement against England since the 1920s, but it wasn't until after World War II that India became independent. India was partitioned in 1947, creating two countries: Pakistan and India. Pakistan was overwhelmingly Muslim, and India was largely Hindu.

Both countries struggled to establish their new relationship and economies. India undertook economic reforms. It instituted land reforms and tried to redistribute some land to the landless, abolish the overwhelming power of rent collectors, protect land renters, and promote cooperative farming. The results were mixed. However, in Kerala, a series of policies had some success:

- 1960: The state passed land reform, but they were overturned by courts.
- 1963: Tenant won the right to purchase land from landowners.
- 1969: New laws allow tenants to become full owners of land.
- 1974: Laws provide for fixed hours of work and minimum wages.

Despite the popularity of the land reform program, the Indian central government took direct rule of Kerala in order to slow down or reverse the program.

KEY TERMS BY THEME		
SOCIETY: Global	**GOVERNMENT: Asia**	**GOVERNMENT: Middle East**
land reform	Mao Zedong	Muhammad Reza Pahlavi
communes	Great Leap Forward	Mohammad Mosaddegh
theocracy	Cultural Revolution	Haile Selassie
	Red Guards	Mengistu Haile Mariam
	White Revolution	

MULTIPLE-CHOICE QUESTIONS

Questions 1 to 3 refer to the table below.

China's Economy During Its First Five-Year Plan				
Economic Sector	Value of Output in 1952 (in Chinese currency)	Percentage of Economy in 1952	Value of Output in 1957 (in Chinese currency)	Percentage of Economy in 1957
Agriculture, Forestry, and Fishing	43 billion	58%	48 billion	48%
Industry and Construction	11 billion	16%	24 billion	24%
Government	4 billion	6%	4 billion	4%
Other	14 billion	20%	23 billion	24%

Source: "Comparison of the First Five-Year Plans of Communist China and the USSR," Central Intelligence Agency, June 1959

1. Which row in this table most clearly supports the argument that China's Five-Year Plan from 1952 to 1957 was successful?

   (A) Agriculture, Forestry, and Fishing

   (B) Industry and Construction

   (C) Government

   (D) Other

2. Which of the following statements best describes the changes in the Chinese government between 1952 and 1957?

   (A) It remained the same size, but it became a larger part of the economy.

   (B) It remained the same size, but it became a smaller part of the economy.

   (C) It grew in size and became a larger part of the economy.

   (D) It shrank in size and bacame a smaller part of the economy.

3. Which statement provides the context for understanding this table?

   (A) China was following the path of Soviet economic development.

   (B) China viewed the United States as an economic model to follow.

   (C) China wanted consumer spending to lead economic growth.

   (D) China believed that it would soon move away from communism.

1. **Use the passage below to answer all parts of the question that follows.**

   "Comrade Stalin: Concerning the telegram Comrade Mao Zedong sent to me on October 13 and your reply telegram of [October] 14, I would like to ask the following questions. Please give your instructions:

   1. After the dispatch of the 16 regiments of jet planes, can the Soviet Volunteer Air Force dispatch bombers to North Korea to support the Chinese armies' military operations?

   2. Besides dispatching the Volunteer Air Force to participate in military operations in North Korea, can the Soviet government also dispatch protective air forces to be stationed near all large Chinese coastal cities?

   3. To accelerate the building of airports . . . the Chinese government requests the Soviet government to supply steel plates to be laid at 4 airports.

   4. Can the Soviet government provide us in half a year with 15,000 vehicles of all types, but, first of all, with 5,000 load-carrying vehicles?

   5. When [the Chinese People's Liberation Army] undertakes military operations in cooperation with the North Korean People's Army, how should [the question of] the mutual command relationship be decided?

   6. When the Soviet Volunteer Air Force participates in North Korean military operations, how should [the question of] the command relationship with the Chinese Volunteer Army be decided?

   Attached is the Chinese government's requisition list for the first batch of artillery of all types . . . . Please give approval. Bolshevik Greetings!"

   Zhou Enlai, letter to Joseph Stalin, October 14, 1950

   (A) Identify ONE historical development that contributed to the Soviet Union's ability to maintain its status as a global power after 1945.

   (B) Explain ONE way the Soviet Union maintained influence in Korea based on the passage.

   (C) Explain ONE aspect of the Chinese alliance with the Soviet Union after 1945 that is reflected in the passage.

2. **Answer all parts of the question that follows.**

   (A) Identify ONE political or economic policies of Vladimir Lenin that differed from those of Joseph Stalin.

   (B) Explain ONE way in which Vladimir Lenin's view of the proletarian class differed from Mao Zedong's view of the proletarian class.

   (C) Explain ONE way in which Vladimir Lenin's view of the proletarian class was similar to Mao Zedong's view of the proletarian class.

THINK AS A HISTORIAN: EXPLAIN THE SIGNIFICANCE OF
PURPOSE IN A SOURCE

People write for a variety of purposes. Journalist Edgar Ansel Mowrer, for example, lived in Berlin in the 1930s and wrote Pulitzer-prize winning analyses on the rise of Hitler to inform the world that the transformation of Germany was far from democratic and to sound the alarm about renewed militarism. Mowrer, however, like other journalists, also wrote to express opinions. Increasingly frustrated at defeats by Communists, Mowrer expressed his opinion on why they seemed to be winning.

Explain the significance of knowing the following is an opinion piece in evaluating its usefulness as a source on the spread of communism. Identify some sentences that show it is an opinion piece.

1. "The Reds are not afraid of an atomic war. . . . Although they would prefer to conquer without a major shooting (and H-bombing) war, they presumably will start an atomic war if and when they see an opportunity to do so without danger of defeat or severe damage at home.

2. The Communists are without moral restraints. . . . At home they rule by naked terror . . . crushing discontent silently before it becomes rebellion. . . . They burn villages, shoot hostages, torture and 'brain-wash' prisoners, and rely upon fear to break further resistance."

3. The Communists promise something to everybody. . . . They call war, peace; tyranny, freedom; unrestrained exploitation, social justice. . . . No matter what you think you want—more food, a better job, personal revenge or, particularly, a whole new world order—the Red Pipers are ready with the promise, if not for today, then surely for tomorrow.

4. Communists everywhere are united. . . . They are held together by a common goal—world conquest. They think, talk, work and fight under a common symbol—the hammer and the sickle.

5. Communists put guns before butter. . . . They coldly sacrifice the living standards of their respective peoples to their political aims."

"The Reds Hold Five Big Cards—But We Can
Trump Them," *Collier's,* October 29, 1954

REFLECT ON THE TOPIC ESSENTIAL QUESTION

1. In one to three paragraphs, describe how communism and land reform affected China and other nations.

8.5

Decolonization after 1900

From its inception, South Vietnam was only considered to be an outpost in the war against communism.

—Nguyen Cao Ky, prime minister of South Vietnam, 1965–1967

Essential Question: How did people pursue independence after 1900?

In the 20th century, nationalist groups and leaders challenged colonial rule not only through land reform but also through political negotiation, as in India, and armed struggle, as in Angola (See Topic 8.3.) Struggles for independence after World War I and the failure of many independence movements added to anticolonial sentiments during World War II. Empires became politically unacceptable. European powers struggled to hold onto their colonies. Notions of freedom born of World War II rhetoric helped speed up decolonization. That process coincided with the Cold War and the development of the United Nations. Nguyen Cao Ky, a South Vietnamese military and political leader, noted (above) that his country's war was part of the Cold War.

Movements for Autonomy: India and Pakistan

The drive for Indian self-rule began in the 19th century with the foundation of the Indian National Congress. Its leader in 1920 was Mohandas Gandhi. Hindu and Muslim groups, united by their desire to get rid of the British, supported the independence movement in South Asia. The National Congress's tactics included mass civil disobedience, and it remained a powerful governmental force after Indian independence. The **Muslim League**, founded in 1906, advocated a separate nation for Indian Muslims.

Not all Indian leaders agreed with Gandhi's nonviolent, noncooperation movement or his call for unity between Muslims and Hindus. However, they put aside their differences until after World War II. Then leaders again demanded independence.

After the war, Britain grew weaker as India's fighting abilities grew stronger. When Britain failed to follow through on promises for more rights for Indians, Indian people increased their protests for full independence from British rule. The Royal Indian Navy Revolt in 1946 was instrumental in bringing Britain to the realization it could no longer rule India. As a result of economic pressures from India and from its own sluggish postwar recovery, Britain was ready to negotiate independence in South Asia.

Division and Conflict Muslims feared living in an independent India dominated by Hindus. Distrust between Muslims and Hindus dated back centuries to the 8th century, when Muslims invaded Hindu kingdoms in northern India. Muslims campaigned for an independent Muslim country—Pakistan. India and Pakistan both gained independence in 1947.

SOUTH ASIA, 1950

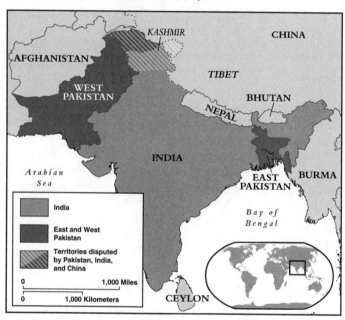

Decolonization in Ghana and Algeria

Britain agreed to negotiate independence for its West African colony of the Gold Coast, just as it had for its colonies in South Asia. The Gold Coast combined with the former British Togoland to form Ghana, the first sub-Saharan African country to gain independence in the 20th century. (The new country of Ghana was smaller in area than the historic kingdom of the same name.) Negotiations led by the United Nations helped bring about Ghana's independence in 1957. Its first president, **Kwame Nkrumah**, took office in 1960.

Ideas from modern nation-states influenced Ghanaian nationalism. Nkrumah emulated nationalistic traditions he learned during his time in the United States and Britain. For example, Nkrumah constructed a national narrative that centered on having a historical past of glory and rich tradition, founding fathers, a currency, a flag, an anthem, museums, and monuments. He was responsible for numerous public works and development projects, such as hydroelectric plants. However, some critics accused him of running the country into debt and allowing widespread corruption—an economic pattern that often happened in later African dictatorships. In 1964, Nkrumah claimed dictatorial powers when the voters agreed to a **one-party state**, with him as party leader.

Nkrumah strongly advocated Pan-Africanism, a term with multiple meanings. In the 19th century, American and British abolitionists called their plans to return freed men and women to their homes in Africa Pan-Africanism or Africa for Africans. The country of Liberia was founded on this vision. In the second half of the 20th century, for some Africans, the term Pan-Africanism meant a celebration of unity of culture and ideas throughout the continent. These Pan-Africanists rejected intervention by former colonial powers.

In keeping with his vision of Pan-Africanism, Nkrumah founded the **Organization of African Unity (OAU)** in 1963. However, three years later, a military coup overthrew Nkrumah's government and expelled many foreigners from the country. Not until 2000 would Ghana witness a peaceful transfer of civilian power from one elected president to another.

Algeria In northern Africa, the French colony of Algeria endured far more violence than Ghana before becoming independent. Mounting social, political, and economic crises in Algeria resulted in political protests. The French government responded with restrictive laws and violence.

Many Algerians, driven by feelings of nationalism, campaigned for independence after World War II. The **Algerian War for Independence** began in 1954, and it involved many groups. Because so many French people lived in Algeria as settlers, the French government considered Algeria a part of France and was adamant that it could not become a separate country. The FLN (National Liberation Front) led the Algerian movement for independence. The FLN sought self-determination through guerrilla techniques against half a million French forces sent to Algeria. While French military casualties were relatively low, hundreds of thousands of Algerians died in the war, often in violent street-by-street battles. French historian Pierre Vidal-Naquet confessed that there were "hundreds of thousands of instances of torture" by the French military in Algeria.

The Algerian conflict caused sharp divisions in France. The French Communist Party, powerful at the time, favored Algerian independence. Violence broke out in cities throughout France. In 1958, French President **Charles de Gaulle** had a new mandate for expanded presidential power under the constitution of the new Fifth Republic. De Gaulle planned the steps through which Algeria would gain independence. He then went straight to the people of France and Algeria to gain approval of his plan in a referendum, thereby bypassing the French National Assembly.

However, with the coming of independence in 1962, war broke out again in Algeria. Thousands of pro-French Algerians and settlers fled the country. The influx of these refugees into France created housing and employment problems as well as increased anti-immigration sentiment. Violence in Algeria left between 50,000 and 150,000 dead at the hands of FLN and lynch mobs.

The first president of the new Algerian Republic was overthrown in 1965 in a military coup led by his former ally. The National Liberation Front continued in power under different leadership, making Algeria a single-party state for a number of years. The FLN maintained a socialist authoritarian government that did not tolerate dissent. Meanwhile, the government led a drive for modernization of industry and collectivization of agriculture.

Algerian Civil War In 1991, violence again surfaced in Algeria, this time in reaction to one-party rule. The Islamic Salvation Front won the first round in an election that was then canceled. A bloody **Algerian Civil War** followed (1991–2002), during which the FLN continued in control. The army chose President Abdelaziz Bouteflika in 1999. In his second term, he attempted to be more inclusive of insurgents, although suicide bombings continued. In 2011, the military state of emergency, in place since 1992, was finally lifted in response to protests in the wake of major uprisings in nearby states, including Tunisia, Egypt, and Libya.

Comparing Ghana and Algeria Both Ghana and Algeria experienced growing pains under military rule. The main struggles were between those who favored multiparty states and those who favored single-party socialism. Ghana created a new constitution in 1992, easing the transfer of power between elected governments. One point of national pride was that a Ghanaian leader, Kofi Annan, became UN Secretary General in 1997. In Algeria, by contrast, religious tensions grew worse. As in other countries in North Africa and the Middle East, a growing right-wing Islamist movement that was willing to use violence challenged the power of mainstream Muslims. In 1992, an Islamist assassinated Algeria's president. As in Egypt and Turkey, the military responded by repressing Islamic fundamentalists. In 1997, Algeria banned political parties that were based on religion.

Negotiated Independence in French West Africa

As Britain negotiated independence with its African colonies, France did the same with its colonies in French West Africa. These included Senegal, the Ivory Coast, Niger, Upper Volta, and other territories. France had controlled them since the late 1800s with small military forces. France used indirect rule, which relied on local chiefs, existing governments, and other African leaders to maintain stability.

Over the years, France invested in West Africa, building railroads, advancing agricultural development, and benefitting in trade revenue that grew substantially. But by the mid-1950s, various African political parties (democratic, socialist, and communist) and leaders arose in French West Africa. By 1959, many of the French West African countries had negotiated their independence from France.

Nationalism and Division in Vietnam

World War II interrupted France's long colonial rule in Indochina, but France reoccupied the southern portion of Vietnam when the war ended. A bloody struggle began against the forces of **Ho Chi Minh**, the communist leader of North Vietnam. He appealed to nationalist feelings to unite the country under a single communist government.

France responded by attempting to reestablish its colonial rule, sparking a Vietnamese war of independence that lasted until 1954. The peace treaty split the country into North and South Vietnam, with elections planned for 1956 that would reunite the country. However, many in South Vietnam, along with the United States, opposed the Communists and feared Ho would win the election. No election took place.

War broke out between the communist North and the South. U.S. military troops supported the South. South Vietnamese who supported the Communists, known as **Viet Cong**, fought a guerrilla war against U.S. troops.

As the Vietnam War worsened, American military involvement and casualties grew. In response, the antiwar movement became more vocal. President Richard Nixon began to withdraw U.S. troops in 1971; the last troops left in 1975. North Vietnam quickly gained control of South Vietnam. It is estimated that the Vietnam War resulted in between one million and two million deaths, including about 58,000 Americans. It also destabilized Southeast Asia. Communists soon won control of Laos and Cambodia, but the spread of communism stopped there.

Beginning in the 1980s, Vietnam introduced some market-based economic reforms. In following years, Vietnam and the United States reestablished trade and diplomatic relations. (Connect: Write an outline connecting Vietnam's fight for independence with the Vietnam War. See Topics 6.2 and 8.4.)

Struggles and Compromise in Egypt

Having long been under the sovereignty of the Ottoman Empire, Egypt became a nominally independent kingdom in 1922. However, the British retained some of the same treaty rights there that they had held under their mandate following World War I. A 1936 Anglo-Egyptian treaty allowed more Egyptian autonomy. Still, it also allowed the British to keep soldiers in Egypt to protect the Suez Canal. The British army continued to influence Egyptian internal affairs.

Gamal Abdel Nasser Following World War II, Egypt became one of six founding members of the Arab League, which grew to 22 member states. In 1952, General **Gamal Abdel Nasser**, along with Muhammad Naguib, overthrew the king and established the Republic of Egypt. Naguib became its first president; Nasser its second. Nasser was a great proponent of Pan-Arabism, a movement promoting the cultural and political unity of Arab nations. Similar transnational movements would attempt to unite all Africans (Pan-Africanism) and all working people (communism).

Nasser's domestic policies blended Islam and socialism. He instituted land reform, transforming private farms into socialist cooperatives that would maintain the existing irrigation and drainage systems and share profits from crops. He nationalized some industries and businesses, including foreign-owned banks, taking them over and running them as state enterprises. However, Nasser touched off an international crisis when he nationalized the Suez Canal.

The Suez Crisis Built by Egyptian laborers—thousands of whom died while working on the project—with money from French investment between 1859 and 1869, the Suez Canal had been under lease to the French for 99 years. To the Egyptians, this lease symbolized colonial exploitation, which Nasser pledged to fight. In addition, the British owned interests in the canal, which they administered jointly with the French. In 1956, Nasser seized the canal, and Israel invaded Egypt at the behest of Britain and France. The two European countries then occupied the area around the canal, claiming they were enforcing a UN cease-fire. However, the United States and the Soviet Union opposed British and French actions and used the United Nations to broker a resolution to the **Suez Crisis**.

The removal of foreign troops was followed by an agreement for the canal to become an international waterway open to traffic of all nations under the sovereignty of Egypt. The UN deployed peacekeepers to the Sinai Peninsula in Egypt. Britain, France, and Israel were not happy with the interference of the United States in the Suez Crisis, but U.S. efforts led to a peaceful compromise. The incident also was an example of a nation maintaining a non-aligned position between the United States and the Soviet Union—the two superpowers in the Cold War.

Independence and Civil War in Nigeria

The western African country of Nigeria, the most populous state on the continent, gained independence from Britain in 1960. The **Biafran Civil War** began in 1967 when the Igbos, a Westernized, predominantly Christian tribe in the southeastern oil-rich Niger River Delta area, tried to secede from the northern-dominated government. The Igbos sought autonomy because of targeted attacks against them by the Hausa-Fulani Islamic group in the north. They declared themselves an independent nation called Biafra.

The Igbos' secession movement failed, and Biafra ceased to exist when the war ended, in 1970. Nigeria granted amnesty to a majority of Igbo generals, but civilian government did not return. A series of military coups with generals in command of the government continued until the 1999 election of Olusegun Obasanjo, who presided over a democratic civilian government called the Fourth Republic of Nigeria.

In an effort to prevent tribalism from destroying the country, the government established a federation of 36 states with borders that cut across ethnic and religious lines. However, friction continued between Christian Yoruba, Igbo groups in the south, and Islamic groups in the northern states.

The constitution of Nigeria permitted states to vote for a dual legal system of secular law and shariah. Eleven states voted for this option. In an additional effort to discourage ethnic strife, the constitution encouraged intermarriage among the ethnic groups.

Problems remained in the Niger River Delta, which had rich oil deposits. Citizens complained that the national government exploited oil resources without returning wealth to the region. Also, they contended that the oil companies had polluted their lands and rivers. Militants set fire to oil wells and pipelines in protest.

Canada and the "Silent Revolution" in Quebec

Quebec is the largest of Canada's provinces, and its history is deeply rooted in French culture. France's North American colonial territory in the early 1700s spanned from Quebec to the Gulf of Mexico. By the late 1700s, England controlled what was called New France, beginning a cultural and political divide in Quebec. People in New France were mainly Catholic, while the English-speaking parts of Britain's Canadian colony were mainly Protestant.

The Quebecois historically aligned themselves with France rather than England. Over the centuries, efforts to create a separate independent state have flared up—sometimes with violent results. The **Quiet Revolution** of the 1960s involved much political and social change in Quebec, with the Liberal Party gaining power and reforming economic policies that led to further desires for separation from the rest of British-controlled Canada. French Canadian nationalism expanded, and splinter groups adopted extreme tactics, including terrorist bombings that began in 1963. Canadian Prime Minister Pierre Trudeau, a native of Quebec, was able to preserve the country's unity. Later, in 1995, a referendum to make Quebec an independent nation failed by a narrow margin.

KEY TERMS BY THEME

GOVERNMENT: Leaders	**GOVERNMENT:** Wars, Conflicts, and Compromises	**SOCIETY:** Pro-Independence Organizations
Kwame Nkrumah		Muslim League
Charles de Gaulle	Algerian War for Independence	Organization of African Unity (OAU)
Ho Chi Minh	Algerian Civil War	
Gamal Abdel Nasser	Suez Crisis	
GOVERNMENT: Structures	Biafran Civil War	**SOCIETY:** Military-Political Organizations
one-party state	Quiet Revolution	Viet Cong

MULTIPLE-CHOICE QUESTIONS

Questions 1 to 3 refer to the passage below.

"For more than 80 years, the French imperialists, abusing the standard of Liberty, Equality, and Fraternity, have violated our Fatherland and oppressed our fellow-citizens. They have acted contrary to the ideals of humanity and justice. In the field of politics, they have deprived our people of every democratic liberty.

They have enforced inhuman laws; they have set up three distinct political regimes in the North, the Center, and the South of Vietnam in order to wreck our national unity and prevent our people from being united.

They have built more prisons than schools . . . To weaken our race they have forced us to use opium and alcohol.

In the fields of economics, they have fleeced us to the backbone, impoverished our people, and devastated our land."

Ho Chi Minh, Vietnamese Declaration of Independence, 1945

1. Which words in the passage most directly reflect Marx's fundamental criticism of capitalism?
   - (A) "They set up three distinct political regimes."
   - (B) "They have built more prisons than schools."
   - (C) "They have forced us to use opium and alcohol."
   - (D) "They have fleeced us to the backbone, impoverished our people."

2. Which movement would have most likely influenced Ho Chi Minh's sentiments expressed in the passage?
   - (A) The Enlightenment
   - (B) Abolitionism
   - (C) Mercantilism
   - (D) Social Darwinism

3. Ho Chi Minh's eventual declaration of Vietnam's independence most directly resulted in
   - (A) his decision to abandon communism and form an alliance with the United States
   - (B) an election in France in which the majority of the people voted for Vietnam to be granted independence
   - (C) a war between South Vietnam and the United States, after which France granted independence to North Vietnam only
   - (D) a war for independence from France, followed by an armed conflict involving the United States

1. Use the table below to answer all parts of the question that follows.

Ten Countries with the Largest Number of Muslims			
Country	Total Muslim Population	Percentage of Population That Is Muslim	Percentage of World Muslim Population
Indonesia	221,147,000	87	13
Pakistan	189,111,000	96	11
India	165,624,000	13	11
Bangladesh	148,821,000	90	8
Nigeria	88,577,000	50	5
Egypt	86,895,000	99	5
Turkey	81,619,000	99	5
Iran	80,032,000	99	5
Algeria	38,424,000	99	2
Morocco	32,657,000	99	2

Source: World Factbook, CIA

(A) Identify ONE region with large Muslim populations based on the information in the table.

(B) Explain ONE reason for the global distribution of Islam in the countries listed in the table.

(C) Explain ONE example that supports the argument that Islam is stronger outside the Middle East than it is in the Middle East.

2. Answer all parts of the question that follows.

(A) Identify ONE example of a colony that achieved independence through armed struggle after 1900.

(B) Explain ONE way in which nationalist leaders in Asia sought independence differently from the ways nationalist leaders in Africa sought independence after 1900.

(C) Explain ONE example of a regional, religious, or ethnic movement that challenged colonial rule and imperial boundaries after 1900.

THINK AS A HISTORIAN: MAKE CONNECTIONS THROUGH COMPARISONS

People in the United States are accustomed to recognize a wall of separation between church and state. However, in some emerging nations during decolonization, especially in Africa and South Asia, religion became a major force in determining a new government that was acceptable to the people.

Compare the process of decolonization in two countries in which religion played a prominent role. How were the resulting governments similar, and how were they different?

REFLECT ON THE TOPIC ESSENTIAL QUESTION

1. In one to three paragraphs, explain how various peoples pursued independence after 1900.

Source: Centers for Disease Control and Prevention's Public Health Image Library

This 1968 photo shows a corn soya mix that was made into a breadlike food to help feed the 500,000 children who suffered from malnutrition during the Biafran Civil War.

8.6

Newly Independent States

India is free but she has not achieved unity, only a fissured and broken freedom.
—Indian nationalist and philosopher, Sri Aurobindo, 1947

Essential Question: What political changes led to territorial, demographic, and nationalist developments and the economic shifts that resulted?

As imperialistic powers handed over governmental control to their former colonies, they often created new states. Between 1945 and 2000, the number of independent states in the world more than doubled, from approximately 75 to around 190. The boundaries of the new states often led to conflicts, population displacement, and resettlement. In India, as lamented by Sri Aurobindo, an Indian nationalist and philosopher, the country was partitioned into Hindu India and Muslim Pakistan. Later, Pakistan divided again, creating Bangladesh. In the Middle East, the newly created Israel displaced Palestinian residents.

Newly independent countries often instituted strong policies to promote economic development. At the same time, migrants from the newly independent countries kept alive cultural and economic ties as they migrated to the colonizing countries, usually to the large cities.

Israel's Founding and Foreign Relations

The **Zionist movement** originated in the 1890s from reaction to the Dreyfus Affair. (See Topic 5.1.) Theodore Herzl, a Hungarian Jewish intellectual and journalist, used the affair as evidence that assimilation of Jews into European society was failing to provide safety and equal opportunity. At the First Zionist Congress in 1897, he urged the creation of a separate Jewish state.

Birth of Israel Zionists hoped that the new state could be established in Palestine because that was where their ancestors had lived. In modern times, Palestine was part of the Ottoman Empire, and most of its inhabitants were Arabs who practiced Islam. In a new state, Zionists argued, Jews could be free of persecution. In 1917, during World War I, the British government issued the Balfour Declaration, which favored the establishment in Palestine of a "national home" for the Jewish people. However, British Foreign Secretary Arthur James Balfour wrote that "nothing shall be done which may prejudice the civil and religious rights of existing non-Jewish communities in Palestine."

The situation was complicated because British officer T. E. Lawrence, known as "Lawrence of Arabia," promised certain Arabs an independent state as well. The British Foreign Office hoped that Arabs would rise up against the Ottoman Empire, which would make it easier to defeat during World War I. The Balfour Declaration promised civil and religious rights to non-Jews in Palestine, but the supporters of the Arabs did not trust the British.

In 1918, after World War I, Britain was given a mandate over former Ottoman lands in the Middle East. Soon Zionists began to immigrate to Palestine from Europe and from other Middle Eastern areas. As immigration increased, the Arabs in the area protested their loss of land and traditional Islamic way of life.

World War II and the deaths of six million Jews in the Holocaust provided another impetus for Jewish immigration. The fate of the European Jews brought worldwide sympathy for the survivors. Britain, trying to hold the line on Jewish immigration in the face of Arab opposition, turned the matter over to the United Nations. As in India, leaders hoped that partition would bring peace and stability. In 1948, after the UN divided Palestine into Jewish and Arab sections, the Jewish section declared itself to be a new country: Israel.

Multiple Wars War broke out immediately between Israel, which had support from the United States, and the Palestinians, who had support from neighboring Arab countries. Arab forces from Syria, Jordan (then called Transjordan), Lebanon, and Iraq invaded Israel. After several cease-fires, the Israeli army won, and an armed truce was declared. Immediately after the truce, about 400,000 Palestinians became refugees, living in camps near the Israeli border. Three other Israeli-Palestinian wars followed:

- In 1956, Israel, with support from France and Great Britain, invaded Egypt's Sinai Peninsula, in part to liberate the Suez Canal, which the Egyptian government had nationalized under Gamal Abdel Nasser's economic programs (See Topic 8.5.) Following international protests, Israel and its allied forces were ordered to withdraw from Egypt.

- In the **Six-Day War** of 1967, Israel fought on three fronts at once. Israel gained the Gaza Strip from Egypt, the West Bank and East Jerusalem from Jordan, and the Golan Heights from Syria.

- In the **Yom Kippur War** of 1973, Israel repelled a surprise invasion by Egypt and Syria.

Israeli-Egyptian Peace After 30 years of conflict between Israel and its Arab neighbors, U.S. President Jimmy Carter mediated the **Camp David Accords**, a peace agreement between Prime Minister Menachem Begin of Israel and President Anwar Sadat of Egypt. However, the Palestinians and several Arab states rejected the 1979 peace treaty. The **Palestinian Liberation Organization (PLO)** and its longtime leader Yasser Arafat wanted the return of occupied lands and the creation of an independent nation of Palestine.

Ongoing Violence In the 21st century, the peace process became more complicated when the Palestinians split into two factions. The **Fatah** faction controlled the West Bank. The **Hamas** faction controlled Gaza. Security concerns led the Israeli government to implement tighter border controls on the West Bank and on Gaza. These controls, amounting to economic sanctions, severely restricted normal activity for hundreds of thousands of Palestinians and fomented anger. Israel further angered Palestinians by approving new settlements on lands it had occupied during previous wars, lands Palestinians considered theirs.

Without a peace process, violence continued. Between 2000 and 2014, over 7,000 Palestinian and over 1,000 Israelis were killed. Many countries in the Middle East remained hostile to United States over its support of Israel.

1947
UN PLAN OF DIVISION FOR PALESTINE

2018
ISRAELI AND PALESTINIAN LANDS

Cambodia Gains Independence and Survives Wars

After World War II, Vietnam's neighbor Cambodia pressured France to grant it independence in 1953. Cambodia's royal family continued to head the government and tried to maintain its status as a non-aligned nation during the first two decades of the Cold War. However, Cambodia was eventually drawn into the Vietnam War.

Following the Vietnam War, a communist guerrilla organization called the **Khmer Rouge**, under the leadership of Pol Pot, overthrew the right-wing government of Cambodia. Once in power, Pol Pot and the Khmer Rouge imposed a ruthless form of communism, following the Chinese model of "cultural revolution" that targeted intellectuals and dissenters. The slaughter and famine that followed took more than two million lives—about one-quarter of the country's population. Mass graves of victims from the "killing fields" of Cambodia continued to be discovered in the countryside and jungles for decades afterward. (Connect: Create a graphic organizer comparing the tactics of the Khmer Rouge under Pol Pot with that of Joseph Stalin. See Topic 7.4.)

In 1977, Vietnamese troops invaded Cambodia to support opponents of Pol Pot and the Khmer Rouge. At the end of the ensuing war, the Vietnamese took control of the government in Cambodia and helped the country to regain some stability, even as some fighting continued and hundreds of thousands of refugees fled the country. In 1989, Vietnamese forces completed their withdrawal from Cambodia. A peace agreement reached in 1991 allowed free elections, monitored by the United Nations. Prince Norodom Sihanouk became a constitutional monarch, and the country developed a democratic government with multiple political parties and aspects of a market economy.

India and Pakistan Become Separate Countries

In 1947, the British divided colonial India into two independent countries—a mostly Hindu India and a mostly Muslim Pakistan. India's population was about 10 times larger than Pakistan's. In both countries, women had the right to vote.

The partition of the colony was chaotic, and violence broke out along religious lines. At least 10 million people moved: Hindus and Sikhs fled their homes in Pakistan to resettle in India, and Muslims fled India for Pakistan. In the political turmoil, between 500,000 and one million people died.

Source: Wikimedia Commons

This Buddhist shrine at Choeng Ek, Cambodia, houses remains of victims of the Khmer Rouge in the "killing fields."

After partition, Pakistani-India distrust grew. While India became the world's largest democracy, Pakistan had both elected leaders and authoritarian military rulers. Moderates in both countries confronted powerful conservative religious movements that opposed compromise with the other country.

Kashmir Conflict One persistent tension between India and Pakistan was over **Kashmir**, a border region in the mountainous north. At the time of partition, most people in Kashmir were Muslims, but its leader was a Hindu. Therefore, both Pakistan and India claimed Kashmir. At times the rivalry there broke out into armed conflict. The tension between the two countries became more significant after each began developing nuclear weapons. Eventually, India controlled about 45 percent of the Kashmir region, Pakistan controlled about 35 percent, and China controlled about 20 percent.

Women Gain Power in South Asia

In some newly emerging countries, women became heads of state. Often, they replaced their fathers or husbands. In India and Pakistan, women won the right to vote in 1947.

Sri Lanka The world's first female prime minister was **Sirimavo Bandaranaike.** She won that position in 1960 in Ceylon (later Sri Lanka). Her husband was assassinated in office in 1959, and Bandaranaike ran for office to fill his seat. She continued her husband's socialist economic policies. But in 1965, with a sagging economy, she was voted out of office. Five years later, she returned to power and instituted much more radical policies, including land reforms, restrictions on free enterprise, and a new constitution that changed the country's name to Sri Lanka. While some of her reforms succeeded, the economy stalled again, and in 1977, she was again voted out of office.

Bandaranaike remained active in Sri Lankan politics. Her children became leaders as well. When her daughter Chandrika became the country's first female president in 1994, she appointed her mother again to the role of prime minister.

India In 1966, two years after the death of India's first prime minister, Jawaharlal Nehru, his only child, **Indira Gandhi,** became India's leader. (She was not related to Mohandas Gandhi.) She was underestimated at first but proved to be effective, distancing herself in some ways from her father's old-guard advisors and making political and economic moves to strengthen India's economy. War with Pakistan took a toll on the economy, though India won the conflict with the help of military support from the Soviet Union.

Indira Gandhi became a revered leader in India, though further economic strife would undermine her popularity in the ensuing years. High inflation and growing poverty threatened her rule. She declared a national emergency in 1975 and jailed many opposition leaders. Her 20-point economic program proved successful, alleviating inflation, reforming corrupt laws, and increasing national production. But some of her policies were unpopular with the people of India despite the economic gains. In 1977, Gandhi lost in the elections. She returned to power as prime minister in 1980 but was assassinated in 1984.

Pakistan Pakistan elected **Benazir Bhutto** prime minister in 1988. Her father had also served as prime minister. She was the first elected female leader of a majority Muslim country. Bhutto struggled to improve Pakistan's economy and reduce its poverty. Corruption charges dogged her and her husband. Bhutto won election to two nonconsecutive terms and then went into exile from 1999 until 2007. Shortly after she returned to Pakistan, an assassin killed her.

Tanzania Modernizes

Tanganyika gained its independence from Britain in 1961, later becoming the United Republic of Tanzania. Its first president, **Julius Nyerere**, instituted African socialist political and economic ideas—summarized in the Arusha Declaration of 1967. It was an egalitarian approach based on cooperative agriculture. Literacy campaigns, free education, and collective farming were key components of what Nyerere called *ujamaa* (Swahili for "familyhood"). He also advanced the country's economic independence away from foreign aid. Economic hardships challenged Nyerere's leadership for years, as did conflicts with Uganda and its leader Idi Amin. Though personally popular, Nyerere could not pull Tanzania out of poverty. He resigned the presidency in 1985 but remained an important social leader until his death in 1999.

Emigration from Newer Countries to Older Ones

People from these newly independent countries sometimes moved to the former colonial powers. For example, large numbers of refugees and immigrants from Pakistan, India, and Bangladesh moved to London after the chaos of World War II and other conflicts. London was a **metropole**—a large city of a former colonial ruler. Similarly, Vietnamese, Algerians, and West Africans migrated to Paris and other cities in France, and Filipinos migrated to the United States. Many migrants found jobs in the medical field. Others worked on railroads, in foundries, and in airports. In this way, economic and cultural ties between the colonial power and newly independent countries remained strong.

KEY TERMS BY THEME

GOVERNMENT: The Middle East	**GOVERNMENT: Asia**	**GOVERNMENT: Africa**
Zionist movement	Khmer Rouge	Julius Nyerere
Six-Day War	Kashmir	**ENVIRONMENT: Emigration**
Yom Kippur War	Sirimavo Bandaranaike	metropole
Camp David Accords	Indira Gandhi	
Palestinian Liberation Organization (PLO)	Benazir Bhutto	
Fatah		
Hamas		

Questions 1 to 3 refer to the passage below.

"After four wars during 30 years, despite intensive human efforts, the Middle East, which is the cradle of civilization and the birthplace of three great religions, does not enjoy the blessings of peace. The people of the Middle East yearn for peace so that the vast human and natural resources of the region can be turned to the pursuits of peace and so that this area can become a model for coexistence and cooperation among nations. . . .

Peace requires respect for the sovereignty, territorial integrity and political independence of every state in the area and their right to live in peace within secure and recognized boundaries free from threats or acts of force. Progress toward that goal can accelerate movement toward a new era of reconciliation in the Middle East marked by cooperation in promoting economic development, in maintaining stability and in assuring security."

Camp David Accords, 1978

1. According to the above passage, what basic element is required for peace in the Middle East?

    (A) More natural resources

    (B) Secure borders

    (C) Economic cooperation

    (D) Territorial fluidity

2. Who rejected the proposed peace treaty?

    (A) Anwar Sadat of Egypt

    (B) Menachem Begin of Israel

    (C) Yasser Arafat of the Palestinian Liberation Organization (PLO)

    (D) U.S. President Jimmy Carter

3. Which was the intended consequence of the Camp David accords?

    (A) An election defeat for Menachem Begin

    (B) An alliance between Egypt and Iran

    (C) A peace agreement between Israel and Egypt

    (D) An invasion of Gaza by the PLO

1. **Use the passage below to answer all parts of the question that follows.**

   "At the turn of the 1960s . . . a state-sponsored agency that recruited workers from the French Antilles, and the lack of economic opportunities throughout sub-Saharan African nations spurred a large-scale working class labor migration to Paris. However, this postwar labor migration occurred in the midst of changing *mentalité* (attitudes). The attributes of colonialism had recently been challenged . . . .

   However, when Antilleans [people from an archipelago in the Caribbean] and sub-Saharan Africans migrated to France in the 1960s, their former colonial status still determined their social conditions, especially in the labor and housing markets. As the Antillean writer Françoise Ega who lived in France during the period observes, 'the French government and society perceive all Polish people as agricultural workers, all Algerians as unskilled construction workers, and all Antillean women as maids.' Although race, gender, and ethnicity structure the labor landscape, only offering people of African descent menial worker, household employee, or lower rank tertiary worker positions, Antilleans and sub-Saharan Africans had migrated to France with clear-cut professional goals; they desired decent wages, congenial and respectful treatment, and the possibility of receiving a job promotion related to their hard work."

   Wendy Pojmann, *Migration and Activism in Europe Since 1945*, 2008

   (A) Identify ONE imperialist idea that continued in Europe after 1945.

   (B) Explain ONE way in which one European state developed migration policies after 1945.

   (C) Explain ONE piece of historical evidence that supports the writer's claim that "the attributes of colonialism had recently been challenged" in Europe by 1960.

2. **Answer all parts of the question that follows.**

   (A) Identify ONE event that caused a significant change in the movement to support the creation of Israel.

   (B) Explain ONE event that caused a significant change in Israeli-Arab relations.

   (C) Explain ONE example of a religion- or culture-based conflict in a former colony outside of the Middle East during the 20th century.

THINK AS A HISTORIAN: USE EVIDENCE TO SUPPORT, MODIFY, OR REFUTE A CLAIM

Historical evidence can support, modify, or refute an argument or claim. In fact, evidence that can be used to support one argument might also be used to refute another. That flexibility of the historical record is partly why history is so reliant on interpretation. To appreciate the ways in which historical evidence relates to claims, complete the following activity on the partition of India into two states: India and Pakistan.

Carefully read each of the following statements. Then, for each one, develop a claim or argument that the statement supports. Develop a second claim that the same statement either modifies or refutes.

1. "We are not two nations. Every [Muslim] will have a Hindu name if he goes back far enough in his family history. Every Muslim is merely a Hindu who has accepted Islam. That does not create nationality . . . We in India have a common culture. . . . When communal riots take place, they are always provoked by incidents over cows and by religious processions. That means that it is our superstitions that create the trouble and not our separate nationalities . . . We must not cease to aspire, in spite of [the] wild talk, to befriend all Muslims and hold them fast as prisoners of our love."

Writings and words of Mahatma Gandhi in *The Essential Gandhi: An Anthology*, edited by Louis Fischer, 1962 (reprinted by permission of the Navajivan Trust)

2. "I know there are people who do not quite agree with the division of India and the partition of the Punjab and Bengal. Much has been said against it, but now that it has been accepted, it is the duty of every one of us to loyally abide by it and [honorably] act according to the agreement."

Muhammad Ali Jinnah's first presidential address to the Constituent Assembly of Pakistan, August 11, 1947

3. "Jinnah felt eclipsed by the rise of Gandhi and Nehru, after the First World War. In December, 1920, he was booed off a Congress Party stage when he insisted on calling his rival "Mr. Gandhi" rather than referring to him by his spiritual title, Mahatma—Great Soul. Throughout the nineteen-twenties and thirties, the mutual dislike grew, and by 1940 Jinnah had steered the Muslim League toward demanding a separate homeland for the Muslim minority of South Asia. This was a position that he had previously opposed. . . . Even after his demands for the creation of Pakistan were met, he

insisted that his new country would guarantee freedom of religious expression. In August, 1947, in his first address to the Constituent Assembly of Pakistan, he said, "You may belong to any religion, or caste, or creed—that has nothing to do with the business of the State." But it was too late: by the time the speech was delivered, violence between Hindus and Muslims had spiralled beyond anyone's ability to control it."

William Dalrymple, "The Great Divide:
The Violent Legacy of Indian Partition,"
The New Yorker, June 22, 2015

REFLECT ON THE TOPIC ESSENTIAL QUESTION

1. In one to three paragraphs, explain the political changes that led to territorial, demographic, and nationalist developments and the economic shifts that resulted.

8.7

Global Resistance to Established Power Structures

What difference does it make to the dead, the orphans, and the homeless, whether the mad destruction is wrought under the name of totalitarianism or the holy name of liberty and democracy?

—Mohandas Gandhi, *Non-Violence in Peace and War: Vol. 1*, 1948

Essential Question: What were differing reactions to existing power structures after 1900?

The conflicts of the 20th century affected newly independent states and long-established ones. Some of the most successful challenges to existing order, such as the one led by Mohandas Gandhi, used nonviolence. Other movements, such as Shining Path in Peru, used violence against civilians to achieve political results. Some leaders, such as Francisco Franco in Spain, used the military to crush resistance. The military-industrial complex that President Eisenhower warned about took hold in other countries, as governments increased arms supplies and traded weapons with one another.

Nonviolent Resistance as a Path to Change

Despite the frequent wars and violent protests of the 20th century, movements around the world also used nonviolence to bring about political change. Three of these movements were particularly large and effective, in part because of their visionary leaders.

Mohandas Gandhi Topic 7.5 described how Mohandas Gandhi led nonviolent marches, boycotts, and fasts to oppose British colonial rule in India. In 1947, India became independent.

Martin Luther King Jr. The most prominent of African American civil rights leaders in the United States in the 1950s and 1960s was a Baptist minister, the Reverend **Martin Luther King Jr**. The civil rights movement used various tactics to achieve its goals:

- Court decisions, such as *Brown v. Board of Education of Topeka, Kansas*, that banned forced racial segregation of schools in the United States

- A year-long boycott of public buses in Montgomery, Alabama (1955–1956), which ended segregation in public transit
- Massive marches, such as the 250,000-person March on Washington for Jobs and Freedom in 1964

These efforts provided the foundation for the movement's biggest successes, such as the Civil Rights Act of 1965, which is covered in Topic 9.5.

Nelson Mandela In South Africa, the white-minority government codified a system of racial segregation, called apartheid, into law in the 20th century. Leading the black resistance to apartheid was a socialist lawyer, **Nelson Mandela** (1918–2013). Though early in his life he sometimes supported sabotage and other forms of violence, he was known for leading nonviolent protests. The victory over apartheid is described in Topic 9.5.

Challenges to Soviet Power in Eastern Europe

In the 1950s and 1960s, reformers in Eastern European satellites of the Soviet Union sought to become less dominated by the Soviets. In most cases, the Soviets clamped down hard against dissent.

Poland In 1956, Polish workers demonstrated against Soviet domination and demanded better living conditions. As a result, a new secretary of the Polish Communist Party, **Wladyslaw Gomulka**, came to power. He decided to pursue an independent domestic policy in Poland but continued to be loyal to the Soviet Union, allowing the continued presence of Soviet troops in Poland. The Soviet-established forced collectivization of farms ended at this time.

Hungary In that same year, Hungarian protesters convinced the country's political leader **Imre Nagy** to declare Hungary's freedom from Soviet control and demand the withdrawal of Soviet troops from the country. Nagy vowed to support free elections in which non-Communist parties would participate. He announced Hungary's neutrality in the Cold War and the withdrawal from the Warsaw Pact. Soviet leaders responded by invading Hungary, gaining control of Budapest in 1956. The Soviets captured Nagy and executed him. Many Hungarians fled to the West as refugees.

Czechoslovakia The reform movement in Czechoslovakia reached a peak in the **Prague Spring** of 1968. **Alexander Dubcek**, first secretary of the Communist Party, acceded to the demands of the Czech people by increasing freedom of speech and the press and allowing greater freedom to travel. He also agreed to make the political system more democratic.

As with Hungary, Soviet leaders feared the Prague Spring's independence. Soon the armies of four Warsaw Pact nations crushed it. In 1968, the Soviet Union used the **Brezhnev Doctrine**, named for then-Soviet leader Leonid Brezhnev, to justify its actions. This doctrine stated that the Soviet Union and its allies would intervene if an action by one member threatened other socialist countries. (Connect: Explain the continuity or change between the Eastern European resistance movements in the 19th and 20th centuries. See Topic 6.3.)

1968: The Year of Revolt

Events in Czechoslovakia were just one of many upheavals in 1968:

- In Yugoslavia, students marched against authoritarian government.
- In Poland and Northern Ireland, people protested over religious issues.
- In Brazil, marchers demanded improvements in public education and fairer treatment of workers.
- In Japan, students protested both university financial policies and government support for the United States in the war in Vietnam.

In many countries, protests took place on university campuses. Tensions started building up after World War II, when higher education had opened up for more people in Western society and facilities were crowded. As a result, discontent was high among the student population by the 1960s, resulting in a call for university reforms. Student grievances mounted as civil rights, women's rights, workers' rights, and the war in Vietnam commanded attention.

Source: Wikimedia Commons

The student movement in Mexico was met by military resistance. Two months before the 1968 Olympics began in Mexico City, armored vehicles entered the city to suppress the social movement.

France In 1968, the student movement reached epic proportions in Paris, France. Hundreds of thousands of students took to the streets, resulting in violence when police forces moved in. In sympathy, some 10 million French workers went on strike. It was the largest general strike in French history. President Charles de Gaulle called new elections in France and was able to remain in office when his party won.

The United States In the United States, students and others demonstrated for rights for women and African Americans. However, the largest and most heated protests were against the country's involvement in the war in Vietnam. After members of the Ohio National Guard killed four unarmed students during an antiwar demonstration at **Kent State University** on May 4, 1970, students and faculty at hundreds of U.S. colleges and universities went on strike.

An Age of Terrorism

In the post-Cold War period, large-scale open conflict between sovereign states was rare. Instead, individuals unaffiliated with any government committed terrorist acts in Western Europe, South America, the Islamic world, and the United States that intimidated and murdered civilians.

Conflict in Northern Ireland Most of Ireland, the portion dominated by Roman Catholics, gained independence from the United Kingdom in 1922. However, Northern Ireland, which was dominated by Protestants, remained part of the United Kingdom. Northern Ireland Catholics suffered discrimination, and many wanted their region to join the rest of the Irish Republic. Northern Ireland Protestants fiercely refused.

The Catholic-Protestant conflict in Northern Ireland became more violent in the 1960s, with Catholics fighting as part of the **Irish Republican Army (IRA)** and Protestants with the **Ulster Defence Association**. Between 1969 and 1994, some 3,500 people died in the conflict. Some members of the IRA took their independence campaign to England by engaging in acts of terrorism, the use of violence to achieve political ends. These acts included setting off bombs in London and other cities. In 1994, the two sides reached a cease-fire. Later the IRA renounced violence and turned to politics to achieve its goals.

Separatists in Spain Another group that used terrorist tactics to advance a political agenda was the **Basque Homeland and Freedom (ETA)** organization, founded in 1959, which wanted independence for the Basque region in northern Spain. ETA actions killed more than 800 people and injured many others. In 1973, members of ETA killed the hand-picked successor to longtime dictator Francisco Franco. (See Topic 7.4.) Over the years, ETA announced several cease-fires. In 2011 it declared an end to violent actions and promised to work within the political system to achieve Basque independence.

Peru's Shining Path During the 1970s, former philosophy professor **Abimael Guzmán** built a revolutionary organization called **Shining Path** based on the ideas of Mao Zedong and Cambodia's Khmer Rouge. In 1980, the Shining Path began decades of bombings and assassinations in Peru in order to overthrow the existing government and replace it with a communist one. Shining Path's 20 years of terrorism caused an estimated 37,000 deaths. Guzmán was arrested and sentenced to life in prison in 1992, though the Shining Path continued its attacks through the late 1990s. In 2011 one of the group's top leaders admitted defeat and began negotiations with the Peruvian government.

Islamic Terrorism Several small groups used a fundamentalist interpretation of Islam, one widely condemned by mainstream Muslims, to justify terrorism. Among these groups were the Boko Haram in West Africa, al-Shabaab in East Africa, the Islamic State of Iraq, the Levant (ISIL) in the Middle East, and the Taliban in Afghanistan. Most victims were Muslims. Some high-profile attacks occurred in European cities such as Madrid, London, and Paris.

One of the deadliest groups was al-Qaeda. Financed by Saudi billionaire Osama bin Laden, al-Qaeda carried out attacks in many countries, including one in the United States on September 11, 2001. In this attack, terrorists killed themselves and more than 3,000 people when they hijacked and crashed planes in New York City, near Washington, D.C., and in rural Pennsylvania. Most of the world, even bitter foes of the United States such as Iran, rallied to support the United States. Focused efforts by the United States and its allies severely weakened al-Qaeda. Bin Laden was killed in a raid on his home in 2011.

Terrorism in the United States While the September 11 attack was the deadliest act of terrorism in the United States, it was not the only one. Acts of terrorism in the United States come from different sources and groups, including domestic groups, some of which are associated with white-nationalist or extreme right-wing views. One of the largest of these occurred when two anti-government extremists bombed a federal building in Oklahoma City in 1995, killing 168 people. Other attacks targeted Muslims, Jews, and blacks.

Response of Militarized States

States in which military dictators ran the government tended to respond to internal conflicts in ways that made the conflicts even worse. Spain under Franco and Uganda under Idi Amin are two prominent examples.

The Franco Dictatorship in Spain The dictator Francisco Franco ruled Spain from 1939 to 1975. (See Topic 7.4.) He had come to power by overthrowing a popularly elected government that included many leftists. Franco's fervent anti-communism made him an ally of the United States. It also led his government to execute, imprison, or send to labor camps hundreds of thousands of political dissenters. However, opposition to his authoritarianism remained. When Franco died, Spain took the opportunity to move toward democracy.

Intensified Conflict in Uganda under Idi Amin Few countries in the 1970s suffered as much as Uganda, a small country in eastern Africa ruled from 1971 to 1979 by Idi Amin, a military dictator so brutal he was known as the "Butcher of Uganda." Although he was aligned with Western democracies early on, he was later backed by the Soviet Union and East Germany. He declared himself president for life and set policies that worsened ethnic tensions, denied people basic human rights, and undermined economic stability. Amin was unpredictable. He was for a time the chairman of the

Organization of African Unity and even a member of the United Nations Commission on Human Rights. But in 1972 he forcefully expelled 60,000 Asians from Uganda, most of whom were of Indian descent, and turned over their businesses to his supporters. He is believed to be responsible for up to 500,000 deaths among targeted ethnic groups during his reign. When he threatened neighboring Tanzania with attack, Ugandan nationalists joined forces with Tanzanian troops and forced Amin into exile.

The Military-Industrial Complex

Conflicts around the world intensified because of fear and economic pressure. Countries that felt threatened, including the United States and the Soviet Union, built strong militaries to defend themselves. These military forces required large factories to build planes, tanks, and other goods. Since many countries lacked facilities to make their own weapons, the international weapons trade expanded greatly.

As the defense industries expanded, so did the number of people who relied on them for jobs. Cutting back on defense spending, then, became very difficult. In 1961, U.S. President Dwight Eisenhower, a highly decorated general in World War II, called this combination of government defense departments and private businesses supplying their demands the military-industrial complex. He warned that it could grow powerful enough to threaten the country's democracy.

KEY TERMS BY THEME

GOVERNMENT: Europe
Wladyslaw Gomulka
Imre Nagy
Prague Spring
Alexander Dubček
Brezhnev Doctrine
Irish Republican Army (IRA)

Ulster Defence Association
Basque Homeland and Freedom (ETA)

GOVERNMENT: South America
Abimael Guzmán
Shining Path

SOCIETY: Protests
Martin Luther King Jr.
Nelson Mandela
Kent State University

Questions 1 to 3 refer to the passage below.

"I am a political prisoner. I am a political prisoner because I am a casualty of a perennial war that is being fought between the oppressed Irish people and an alien, oppressive, unwanted regime that refuses to withdraw from our land. . . . I believe and stand by the God-given right of the Irish nation to sovereign independence, and the right of any Irishman or woman to assert this right in armed revolution. That is why I am incarcerated, naked and tortured. . . . Foremost in my tortured mind is the thought that there can never be peace in Ireland until the foreign, oppressive British presence is removed, leaving all the Irish people as a unit to control their own affairs and determine their own destinies as a sovereign people, free in mind and body, separate and distinct physically, culturally and economically."

Bobby Sands, who died in a prison hunger strike in Belfast
in 1981

1. The author of the above passage view himself as a

   (A) terrorist

   (B) freedom fighter

   (C) victim of terrorism

   (D) political theorist

2. What organization was the author most likely affiliated with?

   (A) Ulster Defence Association

   (B) Basque Homeland and Freedom (ETA)

   (C) Irish Republican Army (IRA)

   (D) Royal Irish Constabulary Special Reserve

3. Was the conflict in Northern Ireland ever resolved?

   (A) A cease fire was reached, and the IRA renounced violence.

   (B) The British withdrew from Northern Ireland.

   (C) The violence continues but less intensely.

   (D) A wall was built between Northern Ireland and the Irish Republic.

1. **Use the passage below to answer all parts of the question that follows.**

   1. We demand the immediate evacuation of all Soviet troops, in conformity with the provisions of the Peace Treaty.

   2. We demand the election by secret ballot of all Party members . . . and of new officers for the lower, middle and upper echelons of the Hungarian Workers Party . . .

   3. A new Government must be constituted under the direction of Imre Nagy: all criminal leaders of the Stalin-Rákosi era must be immediately dismissed.

   4. We demand general elections by universal, secret ballot . . . to elect a new National Assembly. We demand that the right of workers to strike be recognized.

   5. We demand revision and re-adjustment of Hungarian-Soviet and Hungarian-Yugoslav relations in the fields of politics, economics and cultural affairs . . .

   6. We demand the complete reorganization of Hungary's economic life under the direction of specialists . . .

   7. We demand complete revision of [industry operations] and an immediate and radical adjustment of salaries [including] a minimum living wage for workers.

   8. We demand that . . . agricultural products be utilized in a rational manner. We demand equality of treatment for individual farms.

   9. We demand complete recognition of freedom of opinion and of expression, of freedom of the press and of radio, as well as the creation of a daily newspaper . . .

   10. We demand that the statue of Stalin, symbol of Stalinist tyranny and political oppression, be removed as quickly as possible and be replaced by a monument in memory of the martyred freedom fighters of 1848–49.

   Excerpts from The 16 Points, Hungarian Students National
Policy Demands, October 22, 1956

   (A) Identify ONE element of the historical context in which the passage was written.

   (B) Explain ONE way in which the 1956 Hungarian Revolution was similar to uprisings in Czechoslovakia during the Cold War era.

   (C) Explain ONE way in which the 1956 Hungarian Revolution differed from the conflict in Northern Ireland during the Cold War era.

2. **Answer all parts of the question that follows.**

(A) Identify ONE individual or group that intensified state conflicts in South America after 1900.

(B) Explain ONE way in which militaries responded to conflicts in ways that further intensified conflict after 1900.

(C) Explain ONE way in which the Brezhnev Doctrine impacted power structures in Eastern Europe after 1900.

 THINK AS A HISTORIAN: POINT OF VIEW AND THE LIMITS OF SOURCES

The year 2018 marked the 50th anniversary of the year—1968—that stands out most in the decade of the 1960s. At their annual meeting that year, members of the American Historical Association considered what made that year so remarkable and how historians answer questions like that. Dr. Alan Shane Dillingham spoke about using first-hand primary sources: "I think the limitations of historical narratives dominated by participants tell a kind of romantic story—obstacles overcome, that kind of stuff. That's important, but it can also simplify these moments and prevent you from seeing important connections."

Following are excerpts from an interview with a young guerrilla officer in the Peruvian terrorist group Shining Path. Explain how the point of view of this source could both illuminate and limit a historian's understanding of Shining Path's rise to power.

- "All popular war is violent. . . . We use selective annihilation of mayors and government officials, for example, to destroy the presence of the state and create a vacuum. Then we fill that vacuum."

- "We are all prepared to die, and we fear nothing because the armed popular struggle will advance and triumph."

- "We are fighting against a neofeudal society where the state has almost no presence in many areas and the masses have long been exploited."

> " 'More War Will Bring Peace,' Say Peru's Maoists
> after 15,000 Die," *Chicago Tribune*, July 9, 1989, "

REFLECT ON THE TOPIC ESSENTIAL QUESTION

1. In one to three paragraphs, explain the differing reactions to existing power structures after 1900.

End of the Cold War

Mr. Gorbachev, tear down this wall!

—Ronald Reagan; speech in West Berlin, Germany; June 12, 1987

Essential Question: What caused the end of the Cold War?

Power structures continued to change in the 1980s and 1990s. President **Ronald Reagan's** appeal to Soviet leader **Mikhail Gorbachev** came two years before the Berlin Wall fell in 1989. Two years after the fall, a coup ousted Gorbachev from power. The Soviet Union collapsed and the Cold War was over. The U.S.-Soviet Union rivalry that had dominated the world stage for nearly five decades ended. Governments in only a few countries, such as China, North Korea, Cuba, and Vietnam, still called themselves communists, Political alliances changed, and economic interactions among nations expanded.

The Final Decades of the Cold War Era

Despite the persistent mistrust between the two countries, diplomatic relations between the United States and the Soviet Union were maintained—albeit inconsistently at times—during the last decades of the conflict. Proxy wars and support of opposing sides in international conflicts remained standard for both nations. These conflicts reinforced the fundamental disagreement between the capitalist United States and the communist Soviet Union. Agreements between the superpowers to limit nuclear weapons played a key role in ending the Cold War. However, the path to a thaw was not always steady. (Connect: Describe the similarities in the competition between world powers in the Cold War and during the imperial era. See Topics 4.4 and 4.5.)

Détente and a Colder War After resolving the crises of the 1960s, which included the Bay of Pigs and the Cuban Missile Crisis, the relationship between the superpowers improved in the following decade. This period of time was called **détente**, a relaxation of strained relations between nations.

One symbol of détente was the visit of President Richard Nixon to the Soviet Union in 1972. Nixon and Soviet leader Leonid Brezhnev signed the **Strategic Arms Limitation Treaty (SALT)**, designed to freeze the number of intercontinental ballistic missiles that each power could keep. To play one power against the other, Nixon also visited China that year. It was the first visit by an American president in the existence of communist China.

Détente served both the U.S. and Soviet needs at the time. The Soviet Union faced challenges during the late 1960s and the 1970s.

- Economically, the USSR was in a crisis. It was no longer growing. Central governmental controls prevented farmers and manufacturers from deciding what to grow or make and what to charge for it. Foreign trade was extremely limited.

- Eastern European Soviet bloc countries were bucking for reforms and freedom from Moscow's direct control. The Soviet military violently put down the Prague Spring, a liberation movement in Czechoslovakia.

- Russia faced skirmishes with China along their shared border—a reflection of the troubled relationship between the two communist countries.

The United States also faced difficulties. President Nixon was mired in the Vietnam War, a costly and unpopular conflict. The American economy was suffering as well. The possibility of establishing relations with China would, Nixon knew, open potential new markets to the United States and at the same time press a bit on the strained Soviet-Chinese relationship. Détente could help the United States maintain its containment policy and might ease tensions between the superpowers.

As a result of détente, the United States started to sell excess stores of American grain to the Soviet Union, where drought had created a shortage. This benefitted American farmers, who now had access to a new, large market for goods, and the struggling people of the Soviet Union. However, after the Soviets invaded Afghanistan in 1979, U.S. President Jimmy Carter halted the grain shipments. This action marked the end of détente.

Soviet-Afghan War The Soviets invaded Afghanistan to prop up that country's communist government against Muslim fighters. Estimates of Afghan civilian deaths vary from 562,000 to two million. Millions of Afghans fled to Pakistan and Iran, and many within the country became homeless. Ultimately, the Soviet army could not conquer the guerrilla groups in the rough terrain of Afghanistan. Soviet legitimacy was undermined and new forms of political participation in Afghanistan developed. As the Soviet Army withdrew in 1989, a civil war continued in Afghanistan. While the collapse of the Soviet Union would not occur until 12 years after the Afghan War began, the war put immense stress on the Soviet Union's centralized economic system and left Soviet leadership vulnerable to reform.

Reagan and Gorbachev During the presidency of Ronald Reagan (1981–1989), tensions between the Americans and the Soviets increased even further. Reagan referred to the Soviet Union as the "evil empire" and sent military aid, including weapons, to support the Afghans. The Soviet Union resented this overtly militaristic move.

In addition, by the early 1980s, the United States and the Soviet Union had more than 12,000 nuclear missiles, each one pointed at the other side. Not only would the superpowers destroy each other with a nuclear exchange, but the rest of the world would also be destroyed—seven times over.

In light of this growing tension, Reagan declared that the United States would create a missile defense program he called the **Strategic Defense Initiative**, or **SDI**. Dubbed "Star Wars" (after the internationally popular 1977 film) by critics, the system would supposedly destroy any Soviet nuclear missiles that targeted the United States or its allies. Lacking such a system, the Soviets would be unable to keep U.S. missiles from hitting targets in the Soviet Union. The Soviets saw this move as the beginning of an arms race in space. While it was not an immediate threat that required a quick response, it worried liberal and moderate Soviets who wanted reforms. They saw it as a long-term economic concern and one that strengthened the hand of Soviet conservatives. The Soviets objected loudly to Reagan's plan.

The Thaw The increase in tensions during the 1980s led to other nations believing that they must choose sides between the superpowers. Non-aligned nations hoped they would not experience a nuclear holocaust that the two nations caused.

In this tense atmosphere, Mikhail Gorbachev, a more progressive Communist than previous Soviet leaders, came to power in 1985. He favored **perestroika**, attempts to restructure the Soviet economy to allow elements of free enterprise, and **glasnost**, the policy of opening up Soviet society and the political process by granting greater freedom. Reagan and Gorbachev met three times in two years. The two men liked each other and, despite tough negotiations, created a working relationship that ultimately delivered results.

In 1987, the Soviet Union and the United States agreed on a new nuclear arms treaty. The **Intermediate-Range Nuclear Forces Treaty (INF)** restricted intermediate-range nuclear weapons. Around the world, people could breathe a cautious sigh of relief as the world's two superpowers reduced the risk of nuclear war. The INF and other U.S.-Soviet agreements quieted some of the more bellicose Cold War supporters in both countries. With less pressure from Soviet conservatives, Gorbachev could more easily implement political and economic reforms in the Soviet Union.

Source: Edmund S. Valtman / Library of Congress

The man is Mikhail Gorbachev, who looks on sadly at a symbol of the Soviet Union, the hammer and sickle, broken into pieces.

The End of the Soviet Union

One aspect of Gorbachev's reform program was an end to economic support for the Soviet satellites in Eastern Europe. He also implied that the Soviet Army would no longer come to the rescue of communist regimes in Eastern Europe. In effect, economic reform in the Soviet Union provided greater freedom to other communist countries. Once people in these countries got a small taste of freedom, they wanted more. As a result, democratic reform movements swept through Eastern European nations in 1989. The Berlin Wall was torn down. In October 1990, East and West Germany reunited as one country.

The Spread of Reforms With most of the Eastern European nations caught up in democratic reforms, it was not long before the Soviet Union was also swept into the movement. Lithuania, Georgia, and other Soviet republics began to overthrow their rulers and declare independence. The Warsaw Pact dissolved. Gorbachev's reforms ultimately led to his political downfall and the end of the Soviet Union in December 1991. Among the former Soviet republics that became independent countries, Russia emerged as the strongest. The Cold War had ended.

New Challenges The decline of a superpower presented opportunities and several challenges. Political alliances changed, and economic interactions among nations expanded. With this new openness, particularly with regard to trade, the world became more interconnected than ever before. This interconnectedness produced greater wealth for some but hardships for others. The post-Cold War world had to grapple with new democracies, vast economic inequality, ethnic conflict and genocide, terrorism, environmental degradation, and global epidemics.

KEY TERMS BY THEME

GOVERNMENT: Global	perestroika	TECHNOLOGY: Military
Ronald Reagan	glasnost	Strategic Defense Initiative
Mikhail Gorbachev	Intermediate-Range Nuclear	(SDI)
détente	Forces Treaty (INF)	
Strategic Arms Limitation		
Treaty (SALT)		

MULTIPLE-CHOICE QUESTIONS

Questions 1 to 3 refer to the passage below.

"Egalitarian Marxism, a more human form of communism without terror or Russians, continued to have broad appeal. But the [crushing of] anti-Stalinist uprisings of 1956 in Hungary and 1968 in Czechoslovakia left [people] feeling bewildered, if not betrayed. What they got was 'vegetarian' communism . . . more goods, some travel abroad, less repression, but only the most muted voice in politics.

Early '70s [communist] regimes looked stable, relatively prosperous and likely to endure. But the command economy couldn't uphold the social contract: [Soviet bloc countries] borrowed heavily from the West to maintain an aging industrial base and a standard of living comfortable enough to keep populations relatively quiescent. [Foreign debt] and a cycle of falling productivity and growing discontent accelerated."

Ronald Grigor Suny, "Empire Falls: The Revolutions of 1989," *The Nation,* 2009

1. Based on the passage, it can be inferred that Suny might also support which of the following assertions?

   (A) Had the socialist economies performed better, communist governments might have stayed in power longer.

   (B) The use of terror and abuse of human rights worsened as communist governments faced internal challenges.

   (C) The public's distaste for socialism doomed the communist governments from their beginnings.

   (D) The communist regimes were purposefully undermined by Western interference in their economies.

2. Which of the following additional factors contributed most to the collapse of the Soviet Union?

   (A) Pro-democracy protests during the Prague Spring

   (B) An increase in the standard of living for most people

   (C) The success of NATO-led military operations

   (D) The establishment of the Non-Aligned Movement

3. The events described in the passage contributed most directly to which of the following developments in the late 20th century?

   (A) The spread of free market capitalism and economic liberalism

   (B) The expansion of social welfare states and socialist economies

   (C) A rejection of Western European culture and consumer products

   (D) Increased Cold War tensions between the U.S. and the Soviet Union

1. **Use the passage below to answer all parts of the question that follows.**

   "Behind me stands a wall that encircles the free sectors of this city, part of a vast system of barriers that divides the entire continent of Europe . . . . Standing before the Brandenburg Gate, every man is a German, separated from his fellow men. Every man is a Berliner, forced to look upon a scar. . . . . As long as this gate is closed, as long as this scar of a wall is permitted to stand, it is not the German question alone that remains open, but the question of freedom for all mankind . . . .

   General Secretary Gorbachev, if you seek peace, if you seek prosperity for the Soviet Union and Eastern Europe, if you seek liberalization, come here to this gate.

   Mr. Gorbachev, open this gate!

   Mr. Gorbachev, tear down this wall!"

   Ronald Reagan, address at the Brandenburg Gate, June 12, 1987

   (A) Identify President Reagan's argument in the passage above.

   (B) Explain how ONE historical situation that supports Reagan's argument.

   (C) Explain ONE way in which the resolution of Cold War tensions between the United States and the Soviet Union impacted other states.

2. **Answer all parts of the question that follows.**

   (A) Identify ONE military and technological development of the United States that contributed to the end of the Cold War.

   (B) Explain ONE way in which the Soviet Union contributed to its own collapse in 1991.

   (C) Explain ONE way in which the economic structures in communist countries led to the end of the Cold War.

Read the following summary of the beginnings of a process set in motion by the introduction of perestroika. Then, in a paragraph, explain how the process continued, leading to the breakup of the Soviet Union.

"From modest beginnings at the Twenty-Seventh Party Congress in 1986, perestroika, Mikhail Gorbachev's program of economic, political, and social restructuring, became the unintended catalyst for dismantling what had taken nearly three-quarters of a century to erect: the Marxist-Leninist-Stalinist totalitarian state.

The world watched in disbelief but with growing admiration as Soviet forces withdrew from Afghanistan, democratic governments overturned Communist regimes in Eastern Europe, Germany was reunited, the Warsaw Pact withered away, and the Cold War came to an abrupt end.

In the Soviet Union itself, however, reactions to the new policies were mixed. Reform policies rocked the foundation of entrenched traditional power bases in the party, economy, and society but did not replace them entirely. Newfound freedoms of assembly, speech, and religion, the right to strike, and multicandidate elections undermined not only the Soviet Union's authoritarian structures, but also the familiar sense of order and predictability. Long-suppressed, bitter inter-ethnic, economic, and social grievances led to clashes, strikes, and growing crime rates.

Gorbachev introduced policies designed to begin establishing a market economy by encouraging limited private ownership and profitability in Soviet industry and agriculture. But the Communist control system and over-centralization of power and privilege were maintained and new policies produced no economic miracles. Instead, lines got longer for scarce goods in the stores, civic unrest mounted, and bloody crackdowns claimed lives, particularly in the restive nationalist populations of the outlying Caucasus and Baltic states.

. . . Boris Yeltsin, who had become Russia's first popularly elected president in June 1991, . . . embarked on even more far-reaching reforms as the Soviet Union broke up into its constituent republics and formed the Commonwealth of Independent States."

"Perestroika," Library of Congress Archives

REFLECT ON THE TOPIC ESSENTIAL QUESTION

1. In one to three paragraphs, explain what caused the end of the Cold War.

8.9

Causation in the Age of the Cold War and Decolonization

Walls in the mind often stand longer than those built of concrete blocks.

— Willy Brandt, December 1991

Essential Question: Why and to what extent were the effects of the Cold War similar in the Eastern and Western Hemispheres?

The end of World War II marked the beginning of a new world order as the nations of Western Europe no longer dominated the world stage. The United States and the Soviet Union took over as the superpowers. In Western Europe, however, countries were free from domination by a superpower and retained their political independence and democratic governments. The Marshall Plan had helped them rebuild and achieve a level of economic prosperity that was unknown among the countries of Eastern Europe.

However, during this time, Western European colonial empires began to crumble as anti-imperialist sentiment fueled independence movements in Africa and Asia. Resentment of European and American economic imperialism also rose in Latin American countries, leading to revolutionary movements that aimed to overturn the political and social status quo in these countries. The United States and the Soviet Union regularly supported opposing sides in these clashes, projecting their own differences onto regional conflicts.

The Cold War also influenced economic, social, and cultural aspects of global events, providing further evidence that this conflict had far-reaching effects that affected the latter half of the 20th century.

Challenges to Existing Social Orders

The years following World War II were a time of unprecedented conflict as people and states challenged the established order. How they carried out their challenges, how the existing powers responded, and how the challenges were (or were not) resolved depended in part on the position of the challenging people or states in the geopolitical balance of power.

Toward the end of World War II, a serious ideological and economic rift emerged among the "Big Three" Allied powers—the Soviet Union, the United States, and Great Britain. The United States and Great Britain, along with France (which had recently been liberated from German occupation), occupied the western half of Germany. The Soviets occupied the eastern half. Agreements made at Yalta and Potsdam were supposed to have settled the future status of Western and Eastern European countries affected by the war. However, after the war officially ended, it became apparent that the Soviet Union was not going to relinquish control over the Eastern European territories it occupied during the war. The Soviets viewed these states as a buffer against future aggression from the West. Even though the countries of Eastern Europe were officially independent, the Soviet Union had immense influence over their governments and internal affairs. The so-called Soviet bloc was made up of East Germany and these satellite nations of the USSR. The United States distrusted the motives of the Soviet Union and believed the Soviets were intent on bringing about a global communist revolution.

After China became a communist state in 1949 and the United States recognized it could not free Eastern Europe from Soviet influence, the United States established a policy of containment. The policy used military, economic, and political means to stop the spread of communism outside of the areas where it was currently practiced. Containment drove the direction of U.S. foreign policy throughout the Cold War.

Three Alignments The Cold War thus caused a division of the world into three alignments. The "First World" was the United States and its allies. The "Second World" was the Soviet Union, the Soviet bloc countries of Eastern Europe, and other communist nations around the world. The third alignment was often called the "Third World" but was more accurately described as the non-aligned countries that did not have close military or ideological ties with any of the First or Second World countries.

COLD WAR BLOCS AND HOTSPOTS

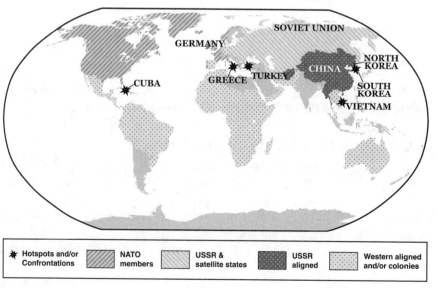

As the map on the previous page shows, the United States was the First World superpower situated in the Western Hemisphere. The dominant superpower in the Second World, the Soviet Union, was in the Eastern Hemisphere. These superpowers represented a geopolitical balance of power. Third World countries were mainly those with colonial pasts; they were in Asia, Africa, and Oceania in the Eastern Hemisphere and Latin America in the Western Hemisphere.

Superpower Rivalries

One result of the superpower rivalry was the division of Europe. The western portion had, for the most part, democratic and free-market societies, while the eastern portion was autocratic and communist. The dividing line ran through Germany, which was divided into the two independent countries of West and East Germany. The capital city of Berlin was similarly divided. The Iron Curtain, as it was termed, reflected the Western democratic view that the Soviet-bloc countries were a threat to the individual freedoms and liberty of the people living on both sides of the border. The Soviets believed, based on their historical perspective, that the Western democracies were intent on invading the Soviet Union. Mistrust on both sides led to a nuclear arms race that was an existential threat to Europe and the world.

The Arms Race The United States developed an atomic bomb at the end of World War II. It used the bomb to end the conflict with Japan by dropping two of them—one on the city of Hiroshima and the other on Nagasaki. The devastation to the two cities shocked the world. The Soviet Union soon developed its own nuclear weapon, and the nuclear arms race was on. The number of nuclear weapons and the means to use them increased for both states. Relations between the superpowers grew tense, and the fear in Europe, and elsewhere, was that any provocation could lead to nuclear annihilation. Both the United States and the Soviet Union took defensive actions that resulted in Europe becoming what was effectively an armed camp with millions of troops and weapons, both conventional and nuclear, facing off against each other.

During this time, two international military alliances formed. The United States and its allies formed the North Atlantic Treaty Organization (NATO). The Soviet Union and its allies created the Warsaw Pact. Both groups sought to ensure collective security through military cooperation. Part of the "cold" factor in the Cold War is that there never was direct, "hot" military conflict between the two superpowers. But the brinkmanship and proxy battles that characterized this war put most people on Earth on edge whenever the United States and the Soviets appeared poised to launch a nuclear attack.

Hopes for Greater Self-Government

The high point of empires and colonization was World War I. The British, the French, and other Europeans had colonized almost all of Africa, India, and Southeast Asia, and they dominated China. The Turkish Ottoman Empire controlled the Middle East. But the desire for self-government that had fueled colonial rebellions throughout the Americas in the 18th and 19th centuries as well as national independence movements in Europe in the 19th century spread throughout the world in the 20th century. The two world wars crystallized the opposition to the empires. Although most hopes for independence remained unfulfilled after World War I, the war did result in the breakup of two large multiethnic empires, Austria-Hungary and Ottoman Turkey.

World War II, however, accelerated the dismantling of global colonial empires. Between the end of World War II in 1945 and the year 2000, the number of independent states more than doubled, going from around 75 to around 190.

As the Cold War established new alignments among both newer and established states, it extended far beyond its ideological roots and exerted political, economic, social, and cultural influence on nearly all parts of the globe.

Comparing Political Effects of the Cold War

The Cold War affected the Eastern and Western Hemispheres in similar ways, since each was dominated by a superpower and also had former colonies and emerging new nations. However, most countries in the Western Hemisphere had become independent long before the Cold War. The Eastern Hemisphere paid an especially heavy price as a result of the Cold War, since several key proxy conflicts were located in Asia and Africa. Nonetheless, rivalries between the superpowers played out in both hemispheres.

Many transitions to independence were largely peaceful and nonviolent; others involved open armed rebellions. In some cases, these insurgent movements were led by communist groups and supported by the Soviet Union, such as in Vietnam and Angola. As a result, the United States would either support the colonial power against the communist insurgency or would support opposition groups that would establish a non-communist government. Often these Western-backed governments proved to be unpopular with the majority of the people, which only heightened anti-imperialist feelings.

Political Effects in Asia The Cold War brought armed conflict and played a part in internal revolts and crises in some countries of Asia. The U.S. policy of containment led to wars in Korea and Vietnam. Communist revolutions overtook Cambodia and Laos. The Soviets invaded Afghanistan to prop up the communist government in that country. Anti-communist crackdowns occurred in Indonesia and the Philippines. Communist China had a falling-out with the Soviet Union and began to seek better relations with the United States.

Political Effects in Africa As with Asia, the Cold War brought conflict and turmoil to Africa. Communist insurrections supported by the Soviet Union were often met by government resistance supported with arms supplied by the United States. Communist governments came to power in Ethiopia and Angola. In the case of Angola's war for independence from Portugal, the Soviet Union and the United States fought a proxy war. The Soviets supported the use of Cuban soldiers and provided arms and military training to help establish a communist-style government in the country. The United States provided arms and supported anti-communist groups.

Political Effects in the Western Hemisphere Latin America also experienced the results of the Cold War conflict between the superpowers. Communist revolutions were successful in Cuba and Nicaragua. Communist insurrections, sometimes backed by the Soviet Union or Cuba, occurred in El Salvador, Columbia, Peru, and Guatemala. The United States would support the government in power—often a dictatorship made up of military officers or right-wing politicians—to try to stop the spread of communism.

Comparing Economic Effects of the Cold War

The Cold War divided Europe in economics as well as politics. The Western countries, aided by the United States' Marshall Plan, rebuilt their economies after the destruction of World War II with a mixture of free-market principles and state-sponsored economic development. The Eastern bloc nations struggled in a transition away from communism to free-market economies. Developing countries—those in the "Third World"—faced unique challenges.

State Response to Economic Challenges in the West To promote economic security, many Western European governments created public health systems, built public housing, provided unemployment insurance, and developed state-backed pension plans. The creation of the welfare state, as it became known, was to counteract the attraction of the communist system that promised to provide many of these benefits. As a result, the Western European nations' economies boomed while the Eastern European economies, under a communist system, struggled to recover from the costs and effects of the war.

Health Care Insurance Coverage by Country			
Country	Percentage Covered by a Government Program	Percentage Covered by Private Insurance	Total Percentage of Population Covered
Denmark	100	0	100
Greece	100	0	100
Australia	100	0	100
South Africa	84	16	100
Germany	89	11	100
United Kingdom	100	0	100
United States	36	55	91
India	22	5	27

Source: Organization for Economic Cooperation and Development (data for 2016)

State Response to Economic Challenges in the Eastern Bloc The Soviet government quickly transitioned its economy after the war to peacetime endeavors. Yet the military-industrial complex was so large in the Soviet Union that it employed about 20 percent of the workers, many of whom became unemployed during the transition. The Soviet-bloc countries faced a serious economic crisis as the government instituted economic reforms to encourage free-market practices and move away from a state-controlled economy.

However, moving from a state-controlled to a free-market economy proved to be an extremely complex endeavor. Debates swirled about whether to institute reforms gradually or all at once, and party officials resisted the loss of their control over the economy. In the end, reformers have succeeded in removing state controls over prices, and formerly state-owned businesses have been privatized. After a period of decline, the Russian economy is improving.

China made a more gradual transition to a free-market economy and has become a global economic powerhouse.

State Response to Economic Challenges in Developing Countries Many former colonies still had close economic ties to the countries that had colonized them and remained dependent on the extraction and exporting of natural resources. The perspective of many people in the former colonies was that the industrial countries were using this relationship to exploit and undermine the economies of these developing countries. Getting control of their resources was a top priority of developing nations. Oil-rich Angola, for example, left in disarray after years of civil war, has a government-controlled oil conglomerate that accounts for about 70 percent of government revenue and has helped the nation rebuild and update infrastructure.

Comparing Social and Cultural Effects

The tension and turmoil of the Cold War era created social effects for all sides involved. For example, the proxy wars cost millions of people their lives, especially in Southeast Asia. In the Vietnam war alone, two million soldiers and two million civilians died over 20 years of conflict. Bombs destroyed villages, and chemical defoliants killed anything growing on farmlands. Families were separated and displaced. Many rural villagers left for the city, where they thought they could find safety. Saigon, the capital city, tripled in size as refugees from the countryside flooded in. Most of the fighting took place in South Vietnam, so it sustained the most damage, but North Vietnam was also bombed—especially such infrastructure as railroads and highways.

Social Tensions The Cold War created suspicions as well. Americans were afraid of communist infiltration, and some people's careers were ruined when they were unjustly accused of being communists. In the Soviet Union, people were afraid to express their beliefs openly if they disagreed with the government. They knew they could be sent away to a political prison camp. People everywhere lived under the threat of a nuclear attack. Some people built bomb shelters where they hoped they could safely weather an atomic attack.

Cultural Effects With greater personal freedom, and with help from the United States, Western Europeans experienced a cultural rebirth after World War II. Scientific research, music, art, and architecture flourished. Eastern Europe, in contrast, lacked freedom of expression. Because of the Cold War, governments actively blocked the spread of Western culture. The people of Eastern Europe did not see much in the way of cultural achievements beyond those that were government-sponsored or approved.

During the Cold War, many people from former colonies moved to the metropole (see Topic 8.6), furthering the blending of cultures. At the same time, the imperial powers left a legacy of culture in their former colonies, including the languages spoken, as the chart below shows.

European-Based Languages Spoken Widely in Sub-Saharan Africa		
Language	Number of Native Speakers	Countries Where the Language is Common
French	120 million	• Senegal • Democratic Republic of the Congo
Portuguese	14 million	• Angola • Mozambique
Dutch (Afrikaans)	7 million	• South Africa
English	7 million	• South Africa
Spanish	1 million	• Equatorial Guinea

In places where a Cold War superpower had maintained order, such as Afghanistan and Yugoslavia, violent culture clashes occurred when the superpower retreated. In Yugoslavia, for example, which had been stitched together and annexed to Serbia after World War I, ethnic tensions flared as Serbia's ultra-nationalist president, Slobodan Milosevic, pitted one group against another to strengthen his own position after the fall of the Soviet Union left a power vacuum. Wars in the region took tens of thousands of lives and created hundreds of thousands of refugees.(Connect: Analyze the changing goals for both superpowers during the Cold War. See Topics 8.1, 8.3, and 8.8.)

Development of Global Institutions

The end of the Cold War and the growth of globalization has reset the geopolitical framework. The idea of a balance of power has yielded to a more cooperative approach as countries recognize global interdependence. To further cooperation, global organizations such as the United Nations and the World Trade Association have been established. Others address such transnational issues as environmental degradation and global warming, human rights, and epidemic diseases.

1. **Causation and Comparison: Varying Effects of the Cold War** On separate paper, make a chart like the one below to compare the effects of the Cold War on the Eastern and Western Hemispheres.

Effects of the Cold War		
	Western Hemisphere	Eastern Hemisphere
Political Effects		
Economic Effects		
Social Effects		
Cultural Effects		

2. In one to three paragraphs, explain why and to what extent the effects of the Cold War were similar in the Eastern and Western Hemispheres.

Source: Deutsche Fotothek

Playgrounds around the world featured space-themed play equipment during the Cold War and the space race. This rocket slide was in East Germany.

UNIT 8 REVIEW

 HISTORICAL PERSPECTIVES: WHY ARE SOME COUNTRIES
WEALTHY?

In 1776, Adam Smith published the first modern, in-depth look at why some countries are wealthier than others, *The Wealth of Nations*. Smith recognized a need for government, but emphasized the benefits of trade.

Modernization After World War II, Western Europe and the United States grew wealthier rapidly. Scholars in these regions, such as American political scientist David Apter, developed *modernization theory*. The problems of poor, newly emerging countries were seen as the natural by-products of the transition from a traditional, agrarian society to a modern, developed society. Developed countries could provide economic and technological assistance to help in this transition.

Self-Reliance In the 1970s, a new generation of scholars saw developed countries as the problem, not the solution. They rejected modernization theory, arguing that it placed the blame for poverty on poor countries, not on the former colonial powers. According to *dependency theory*, former colonies were victims of the international marketplace. In this theory, the way out of poverty was self-reliance.

Globalization Recent writers, such as journalist Thomas Friedman, focused not on self-reliance but on *globalization*. Friedman saw the increasing interconnectedness of economies around the world as an opportunity for countries to prosper. His "flat world" referred to relatively inexpensive technologies that allowed developing nations to compete with developed ones for jobs and the creation of innovative products. In response, Canadian journalist Linda McQuaig attacked Friedman as an "apologist of globalization." Friedman's critics charged that he looked at the benefits of increased trade and investments without seeing the costs incurred in poor countries through these actions.

Trade Ha-Joon Chang, a British economist who was born and raised in South Korea, took a historical view. In *Kicking Away the Ladder: Development Strategies in Historical Perspective* (2002), he evaluated the path to prosperity for today's wealthy countries in Western Europe and the United States. All once had high tariffs and other trade barriers to protect their growing industries from foreign competition. Only after they became wealthy did they advocate for free trade. However, today wealthy countries press poor ones to open their borders economically. The lesson of history, he argued, was to let poor countries use the same protectionist methods that led to prosperity for other countries.

Develop an Argument: Evaluate the extent to which historical evidence supports one of the perspectives on nations' wealth after 1900.

A strong conclusion helps create unity by circling back to the ideas in your introduction and thesis statement. The conclusion is also a good opportunity to extend and refine the complex understanding you have developed and woven throughout your essay.

Providing Unity While wrapping up your essay with a return to the ideas in your introduction helps provide unity, simply restating your thesis is not a strong way to end the essay. Suppose your thesis is that the main causes of the end of the Cold War were the decline in communist ideology and the weakness of the Soviet economy. Avoid simply restating it ("Thus we can see that the decline of communist ideology and the weakness of the Soviet economy were the main causes of the end of the Cold War"). Instead, you might say, "Although many factors led to the end of the Cold War, including Gorbachev's efforts at reform and the development of communication technologies that allowed for the rapid spread of liberal ideas, most served to feed the two main causes—declining support for communism and a faltering Soviet economy." This change extends the thesis statement rather than simply repeating it.

Demonstrating Complexity An extension of your thesis statement such as the one above also helps demonstrate a complex understanding of the topic by referring to multiple causes. The College Board identifies the following ways to demonstrate a complex understanding: "Corroborate, qualify, or modify an argument using diverse and alternative evidence in order to develop a complex argument." You might, for example, analyze multiple variables to arrive at a nuanced conclusion: "Economic, ideological, political, social, and religious factors all played a role in the fall of the Soviet Union and the end of the Cold War." You might make a connection within or across regions: "A democracy movement was building in China as well, but China used military force to put it down, while Gorbachev decided not to use military force."

Other ways you can demonstrate a complex understanding are to consider the significance of a source's credibility and limitations and explain why a historical argument is or is not effective. Most of the development of your complex understanding must be done within the body of your essay for you to earn the point for complexity, but you can use the conclusion to summarize or extend that understanding.

Application: Review the sample scored essays on the College Board website. Evaluate the conclusion of each sample. For any that lack a conclusion, draft one that would provide unity to the essay and summarize a complex understanding of the historical development that is the focus of the prompt.

For current free response question samples, visit https://apcentral. collegeboard.org/courses/ap-world-history/exam

LONG ESSAY QUESTIONS

Directions: Write an essay in response to one of the prompts below. The suggested writing time for an essay is 40 minutes.

In your response, you should do the following:

- Respond to the prompt with a historically defensible thesis or claim that establishes a line of reasoning.
- Describe a broader historical context relevant to the prompt.
- Support an argument in response to the prompt using at least two pieces of specific and relevant evidence.
- Use historical reasoning (e.g., comparison, causation, continuity or change) to frame or structure an argument that addresses the prompt.
- Demonstrate a complex understanding of a historical development related to the prompt through sophisticated argumentation and/or effective use of evidence.

Source: *AP® World History Course and Exam Description*

1. After World War II, Europe weakened and the Soviet Union and the United States emerged as superpowers, creating policies that affected postcolonial states.
   Develop an argument evaluating the extent to which the effects of the Cold War were similar or different in the Eastern and Western Hemispheres.

2. During the Cold War, the United States and the Soviet Union used technology, military might, and economic power to promote their competing ideologies.
   Develop an argument that evaluates the extent to which the ways the United States and the Soviet Union sought to maintain influence over the course of the Cold War were similar or different.

3. After 1900, countries in Eurasia, Africa, and Latin America experienced communist revolutions or insurrections, many of which involved land reform.
   Develop an argument that evaluates the extent to which various causes and effects of movements to redistribute economic resources were significant.

4. From 1900 to the present, colonies in Africa, Latin America, and Asia developed nationalist movements and became independent states.
   Develop an argument evaluating the extent to which the process of decolonization resulted in economic change or continuity over time.

DOCUMENT-BASED QUESTION

Directions: Question 1 is based on the accompanying documents. The documents have been edited for the purpose of this exercise. You are advised to spend 15 minutes planning and 45 minutes writing your answer.

1. Evaluate the extent to which decolonization had an impact on the actions of newly independent states during the period 1945-2000.

In your response, you should do the following:

- Respond to the prompt with a historically defensible thesis or claim that establishes a line of reasoning.
- Describe a broader historical context relevant to the prompt.
- Support an argument in response to the prompt using at least four documents.
- Use at least one additional piece of specific historical evidence (beyond that found in the documents) relevant to an argument about the prompt.
- For at least two documents, explain how or why the document's point of view, purpose, historical situation, and/or audience is relevant to an argument.
- Demonstrate a complex understanding of a historical development related to the prompt through a sophisticated argument and/or effective use of evidence.

Source: *AP® World History Course and Exam Description*

Document 1

Source: President of Indonesia, Sukarno, speech at the opening of the Bandung Conference which promoted Afro-Asian cooperation and opposition to colonialism, 1955.

Perhaps now more than at any other moment in the history of the world, society, government, and statesmanship need to be based upon the highest code of morality and ethics. And in political terms, what is the highest code of morality? It is the subordination of everything to the well-being of mankind. But today we are faced with a situation where the well-being of mankind is not always the primary consideration. Many who are in places of high power think, rather, of controlling the world. Yes, we are living in a world of fear. The life of man today is corroded and made bitter by fear. Fear of the future, fear of the hydrogen bomb, fear of ideologies such as communism or capitalism. Perhaps this fear is a greater danger than the danger itself, because it is fear which drives men to act foolishly, to act thoughtlessly, to act dangerously.

All of us, I am certain, are united by more important things than those which superficially divide us. We are united, for instance, by a common detestation of colonialism in whatever form it appears. We are united by a common detestation of racialism. And we are united by a common determination to preserve and stabilize peace in the world.

Document 2

> **Source:** Prime Minister of India, Jawaharlal Nehru, speech to the Bandung Conference Political Committee, 1955.
>
> My country has made mistakes. Every country makes mistakes. I have no doubt we will make mistakes; we will stumble and fall and get up. The mistakes of my country and perhaps the mistakes of other countries here do not make a difference; but the mistakes the Great Powers make do make a difference to the world and may well bring about a terrible catastrophe.
>
> I speak with the greatest respect of these Great Powers because they are not only great in military might but in development, in culture, in civilization. But I do submit that greatness sometimes brings quite false values, false standards. When they begin to think in terms of military strength—whether it be the United Kingdom, the Soviet Union or the U.S.A.—then they are going away from the right track and the result of that will be that the overwhelming might of one country will conquer the world . . . If I join any of these big groups I lose my identity . . . If all the world were to be divided up between these two big blocs what would be the result? The inevitable result would be war.

Document 3

> **Source:** Leaders of the five key non-aligned (neutral) nations at the Headquarters of the Yugoslav Delegation to the United Nations Associated Press, 1959. From left to right: Indian Prime Minister Nehru, President Nkrumah of Ghana, President Nasser of the United Arab Republic (Egypt), President Sukarno of Indonesia, and President Tito of Yugoslavia.
>
>

Document 4

Source: Resolution on Imperialism and Colonialism created by the All-African People's Conference, Ghana, 1959.

Whereas the great bulk of the African continent has been carved out arbitrarily [randomly] to the detriment of the indigenous African peoples by European Imperialists, namely: Britain, France, Belgium, Spain, Italy, and Portugal . . .

Whereas all African peoples everywhere strongly deplore the economic exploitation of African peoples by imperialist countries thus reducing Africans to poverty in the midst of plenty . . .

Whereas imperialists are now coordinating their activities by forming military and economic pacts such as NATO, European Common Market Free Trade Area (the EU), Organization for European Economic Co-operation, and the Common Organization in Sahara for the purpose of strengthening their imperialist activities in Africa and elsewhere . . .

That the political and economic exploitation of Africans by imperialist Europeans should cease forthwith. That the use of African manpower in the extremely wicked game of power politics by imperialists should be a thing of the past.

Document 5

Source: Office of the Historian, Bureau of Public Affairs, United States Department of State, "Decolonization of Asia and Africa, 1945–1960."

As the Cold War competition with the Soviet Union came to dominate U.S. foreign policy concerns in the late 1940s and 1950s, the Truman and Eisenhower Administrations grew increasingly concerned that as the European powers lost their colonies or granted them independence, Soviet-supported communist parties might achieve power in the new states. This might serve to shift the international balance of power in favor of the Soviet Union and remove access to economic resources from U.S. allies.

Events such as the Indonesian struggle for independence from the Netherlands (1945–50), the Vietnamese war against France (1945–54), and the nationalist and professed socialist takeovers of Egypt (1952) and Iran (1951) served to reinforce such fears, even if new governments did not directly link themselves to the Soviet Union. Thus, the United States used aid packages, technical assistance, and sometimes even military intervention to encourage newly independent nations in the Third World to adopt governments that aligned with the West. The Soviet Union deployed similar tactics in an effort to encourage new nations to join the communist bloc. . . . Many of the new nations resisted the pressure to be drawn into the Cold War, joined in the "non-aligned movement."

Document 6

Source: Egyptian President Gamal Abdel Nasser, resignation radio broadcast after Egypt had been defeated by Israel in the Six Day War, 1967.

We cannot hide from ourselves the fact that we have met with a grave setback in the last few days, but I am confident that we all can and, in a short time, will overcome our difficult situation, although this calls for much patience and wisdom as well as moral courage on our part. . . .

. . . There is clear evidence of imperialist collusion with the enemy [Israel] — an imperialist collusion, trying to benefit from the lesson of the open collusion of 1956*, by resorting this time to abject and wicked concealment. Nevertheless, what is now established is that American and British aircraft carriers were off the shores of the enemy helping his war effort.

The forces of imperialism imagine that Gamal Abdel Nasser is their enemy. I want it to be clear to them that their enemy is the entire Arab nation, not just Gamal Abdel Nasser. The forces hostile to the Arab national movement try to portray this movement as an empire of Abdel Nasser. This is not true, because the aspiration for Arab unity began before Abdel Nasser and will remain after Abdel Nasser. I always used to tell you that the nation remains, and that the individual (Nasser)—whatever his role and however great his contribution to the causes of his homeland is only a tool of the popular will, and not its creator.

The 1956 Suez Crisis when Israel, Britain and France re-occupied the Suez Canal.

Document 7

Source: Tanzania's former President (and the first President of independent Tanzania in 1961) Julius Nyerere, speech on African unity in the 21st century, Ghana, 1997.

For centuries, we had been oppressed and humiliated as Africans. We were hunted and enslaved as Africans, and we were colonized as Africans. The humiliation of Africans became the glorification of others. This is how we experienced our *Africanness*. We knew that we were one people, and that we had one destiny regardless of the artificial boundaries which colonialists had invented.

With our success in the liberation struggle, Africa today has 53 independent states. . . . Africa would be the strongest continent in the world, for it occupies more seats in the UN General Assembly than any other continent. Yet the reality is that ours is the poorest and weakest continent in the world. . . . Unity will not end our weakness, but until we unite, we cannot even begin to end that weakness.

The future of Africa, the modernization of Africa that has a place in the 21st century is linked with its decolonization and detribalization. Reject the nonsense of dividing the African peoples into English speakers, French speakers and Portuguese speakers. This attempt to divide our peoples according to the language of their former colonial masters must be rejected with the firmness and utter contempt that it richly deserves. . . . A new generation of self-respecting Africans should spit in the face of anybody who suggests that our continent should remain divided and living in the shadow of colonialism, in order to satisfy the national pride of our former colonial masters.

My generation led Africa to political freedom. The current generation of leaders and peoples of Africa must pick up the flickering torch of African freedom, refuel it with their enthusiasm and determination, and carry it forward.

UNIT 9: Globalization After 1900

Understand the Context

Unprecedented advancements in science and technology, from airplanes to the internet, increased globalization in the 20th century. These changes provided the setting for vast political and social change, including the spread of democracy and increased international trade.

Innovation by Necessity Science and technology exploration changed the way people in the 20th century viewed the universe and the natural world. Advancements were often a reaction to some sort of large, global problem. An increase in diseases that threatened human populations throughout the world necessitated medical advancements such as vaccines. Deforestation and a decline in the fresh water supply meant that humans had to compete over natural resources and develop environmentally friendly practices. Other conditions necessitated advancements in communication, transportation, and other global industries.

Reaction to Globalization Many states employed free-market economic policies that paved the way for emerging multinational organizations. Access to education and the political process improved as disseminating knowledge and information became easy with technology. Classrooms and political movements came to include more diverse participants, including those from various races, classes, and religions. Communication innovations also led to discussions about human rights that challenged previous forms of discrimination.

The globalization of the 20th century also led to changes in the arts and humanities, especially in the second half of the century. Arts and entertainment increasingly reflected a new, globalized world and consumer culture began to transcend borders. Countries also had to learn to work together as they never had before. The United Nations formed with stated goals not only to maintain world peace but also to facilitate international cooperation.

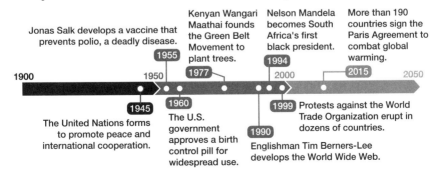

Jonas Salk develops a vaccine that prevents polio, a deadly disease.

1955

Kenyan Wangari Maathai founds the Green Belt Movement to plant trees.

1977

Nelson Mandela becomes South Africa's first black president.

1994

More than 190 countries sign the Paris Agreement to combat global warming.

2015

1900   1950   2000   2050

1945

The United Nations forms to promote peace and international cooperation.

1960

The U.S. government approves a birth control pill for widespread use.

1990

Englishman Tim Berners-Lee develops the World Wide Web.

1999 Protests against the World Trade Organization erupt in dozens of countries.

Topics and Learning Objectives

9.1

Advances in Technology and Exchange

Technology made large populations possible; large populations now make technology indispensable.

—Joseph Krutch, writer and naturalist (1893–1970)

Essential Question: How has the development of new technology changed the world since 1900?

While the population of the world grew, globalization made the world feel smaller, as did advances in telecommunications technology. Starting in the early 1900s, **radio** brought news, music, and cultural events to a wide range of people. Later in the century, air travel and **shipping containers,** large standard-sized units that could be carried on a truck or train or stacked on ship, promoted the widespread movement of people and goods. Energy technologies, such as the use of oil and nuclear power, made it possible to transport goods faster and more cheaply than ever. The internet, first developed for the U.S. Defense Department during the Cold War, emerged as a regular tool of communication for much of the public by the late 1990s. Knowledge economies, based on developing or sharing information, took root in cities around the world.

Communication and Transportation

Decades before the introduction of the **internet**, communication technologies were connecting people around the world. Television and radio ads encouraged people to "reach out and touch someone" by making a long-distance phone call. By the 1990s, mobile technologies such as cellphones put the tools of information creation and dissemination into the hands of individuals around the world. Twitter, Facebook, and other social networking sites made the media accessible to anyone anywhere.

The impact of this revolution became apparent quickly. Videos taken on phones of police actions in the United States and other countries led to inquiries into racial profiling and sparked outrage. Social media also played a role in the "Arab Spring," a series of antigovernment protests that spread from country to country in North Africa and the Middle East in the 2010s as people shared their protest experiences on social media.

While communication technologies put people in virtual touch, transportation advancements move people and goods into actual proximity. Every day, about 2 million people fly on an airplane. Cargo planes transport commercial shipments around the clock. Giant tankers—up to one-quarter mile in length—loaded with thousands of shipping containers ply the seas in increasing numbers, some of them too big to fit through the Panama Canal.

The Green Revolution

In the mid-20th century, the **Green Revolution** emerged as a possible long-term response to hunger. Scientists developed new varieties of wheat, rice, and other grains that had higher yields and greater resistance to pests, diseases, and drought. The new varieties were first developed by **crossbreeding**—breeding two varieties of a plant to create a hybrid. More recently, scientists have used **genetic engineering**—manipulating a cell or organism to change its basic characteristics. Farmers also used more irrigation, fertilizers, and pesticides. In Brazil and elsewhere, people burned down forests and plowed the land for agriculture. Acreage devoted to crops, especially grains, increased dramatically worldwide.

The Green Revolution solutions were not free of problems. Many small farmers could not afford the new fertilizers or pesticides. For this reason, they were often unable to compete with large landowners. Many small farmers were forced to sell their land, increasing the holdings of large landowners even more. Also, since some of the techniques developed in the Green Revolution involved the use of mechanized equipment, fewer jobs were available for farm laborers. Finally, the heavy applications of chemicals damaged the soil and the environment.

TOTAL GRAIN PRODUCTION IN CHINA 1945–2010

Source: National Bureau of Statistics of China, 2009.

Genetic engineering created its own set of concerns as well. Some argued that a genetic modification designed to give a plant resistance to insects might inadvertently cause a decline in the population of pollinating insects, such as bees. Another problem was the loss of old seed varieties as new genetically engineered plants were adopted.

Energy Technologies

In 1900, coal accounted for about half of the global energy consumed. As extraction, refinement, and transportation technologies allowed for widespread use, petroleum, also known as crude oil, and natural gas joined coal in fueling industrial output and helped increase productivity. Research in the 1930s and 1940s that led to the atomic bomb also led to the first use of nuclear power plants to generate electricity for factories and homes.

Fossil fuels—coal, petroleum, and natural gas—are nonrenewable resources. Once they have been used up, the supply is permanently depleted. Fossil fuels have contributed to air pollution and to the cloak of greenhouse gases, especially carbon dioxide, that allow sunlight through the Earth's atmosphere but block the escape of Earth's heat. Nuclear power, while considered a clean energy, has its own dangers. Accidents at nuclear plants have caused serious problems with leaked radiation, and storing nuclear waste has hazardous consequences.

Technologies continue to be developed to combat the emission of carbon dioxide and other greenhouse gases as well as minimize harm from nuclear power. The building of nuclear power plants declined starting in the 1980s, and nuclear power accounts for only about 5 percent of global energy consumption. Renewable resources, such as wind and solar power, are beginning to supply energy to both industries and homes, but they too represent only 5 percent of global energy output. (Connect: Analyze the role of various energy sources in the first and second industrial revolutions and in the 21st century. See Topic 5.5.)

Medical Innovations

A number of advances in medicine have had a dramatic effect on the survival and longevity of humans. Medical research and advancement benefit from, and also inspire, new technologies.

Antibiotics In 1928, Scottish biologist Alexander Fleming was working in his lab in London when he accidentally discovered that a particular fungus produced a substance that killed bacteria. He had discovered penicillin. Penicillin became the first **antibiotic,** a useful agent in curing bacterial infections. During World War II, antibiotics saved the lives of soldiers who would have died in any previous war from a minor wound that became infected. After the war, antibiotics spread to civilian use, where they fought a range of illnesses.

"I would like to sound one warning," Fleming said in a speech as he accepted the Nobel Prize. He pointed out that the extensive use of antibiotics carried a risk. By killing off certain strains of a disease, antibiotics allowed the evolution of strains of the disease unaffected by them. These antibiotic-resistant strains could be untreatable. This prospect raised fears of renewed epidemics of diseases once under control.

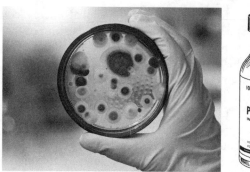 

Source: Getty Images

Penicillium fungi are the source of penicillin, which people can take orally or by injection. Penicillin works by interfering with bacteria cell walls. Scientists began to treat humans with the drug in 1941.

Reliable Birth Control Another groundbreaking medical advance was in **birth control**. In the early 1950s, scientist Gregory Pincus developed a birth control pill, a more reliable method than the barrier methods then in use. Scientists tested the pill on women in the 1950s, and the U.S. government approved it for widespread use in 1960.

As a result of the pill and other forms of birth control, **fertility rates** declined in much of the world. In other words, the average woman began having fewer babies than her mother or grandmother had. Birth control transformed sexual practices and played a part in reshaping gender roles. By 2018, more than 300 million women worldwide were using modern forms of contraception, including the pill.

Vaccines Vaccines have existed since 1796, but governments and nonprofit organizations did not begin developing and widely distributing **vaccines** to prevent deadly diseases until after 1900. Thanks to vaccines, polio and measles became rare, and smallpox was eradicated by the 1980s. Vaccines are also available to prevent mumps, measles, tetanus, diphtheria, and whooping cough, all potentially serious diseases. As of 2019, a malaria vaccine is in the trial stage.

According to the World Health Organization (WHO), vaccines were preventing as many as 3 million deaths each year in the 21st century. However, the WHO also said that better vaccination coverage would save another 1.5 million people annually. Some people were unable to get vaccinated because they lived in hard-to-reach areas.

KEY TERMS BY THEME		
SOCIETY: Communication radio internet **ENVIRONMENT:** Ecology Green Revolution	crossbreeding genetic engineering **TECHNOLOGY:** Travel shipping containers	**TECHNOLOGY:** Medicine antibiotic birth control fertility rates vaccines

MULTIPLE-CHOICE QUESTIONS

Questions 1 to 3 refer to the passage below.

"For the underprivileged billions in the forgotten world, hunger has been a constant companion, and starvation has all too often lurked in the nearby shadows. To millions of these unfortunates, who have long lived in despair, the Green Revolution seems like a miracle that has generated new hope for the future. . . .

The Green Revolution has won a temporary success in man's war against hunger and deprivation; it has given man a breathing space. If fully implemented, the revolution can provide sufficient food for sustenance during the next three decades. But the frightening power of human reproduction must also be curbed; otherwise the success of the Green Revolution will be ephemeral [temporary] only."

Norman Borlaug, agricultural scientist, 1970

1. According to this excerpt from his Nobel lecture, Dr. Borlaug feared that
   (A) the Green Revolution had not succeeded in reducing world hunger
   (B) scientists had gone too far in altering plant species
   (C) the world's population would begin to decline due to efforts to curb hunger
   (D) global population could once again overtake the available food supply

2. One criticism of the process discussed in this passage is that
   (A) engineering cannot change a grain's genetic characteristics
   (B) it ignores new techniques of irrigating and fertilizing farmlands
   (C) it could increase the number of pollinating insects, such as bees and beetles
   (D) its costs make small farmers unable to compete with large-scale farming

3. Which most directly led to the increase in food supply as part of the Green Revolution?

(A) The colonization of Africa by several European powers and resulting control over food production

(B) The crossbreeding and genetic engineering of crops, such as wheat, rice, and other grains

(C) The decolonization of Africa and subsequent repurposing of arable farmlands for the production of cereal grains

(D) The domestication of new types of beasts of burden to help farm laborers cultivate land

Source: Getty Images

Contraceptive use is a factor in how long women stay in school.

1. Use the passage below to answer all parts of the question that follows.

"Gender equity is defined by the World Health Organization as, 'the fairness and justice in the distribution of benefits and responsibilities between women and men,' (Euro.who.int., 2002). When women can have control over their fertility, they have control of their lives which creates a society where gender equity can occur with all genders benefiting from the same resources. Contraceptive use promotes gender equality by improving the accessibility of education, employment and health care to women. If women are using contraception to postpone or prevent a pregnancy from occurring, they are able to stay in school and seek gainful employment upon completion.

Family planning is deeply influenced by inequality because the caliber of medical care between men and women is just not the same across the board. These gender differences are greater where women have relatively lower socioeconomic status than that of men (WHO, 2011; Nelson, 2011). It stands to reason that gender inequality intersects with other social determinants of health, such as race, ethnicity and socioeconomic status, to produce health disparities between men and women that are similar to social divisions within society (WHO, 2008)."

Linda Hanes, *The Birth of Development: The Social,
Economic and Environmental Advantages to Contraceptive
Use on a Global Scale*, 2016

(A) Identify ONE way Hanes claims that contraceptive use promotes gender equality.

(B) Explain ONE historical development that supports Hanes's argument.

(C) Explain ONE way in which practices described by Hanes changed the world from 1900 to present.

2. Answer all parts of the question that follows.

(A) Identify ONE medical innovation that increased the ability of humans to live longer lives from 1900 to the present.

(B) Explain ONE way in which energy technologies changed the world from 1900 to the present.

(C) Explain ONE way in which new types of communication affected how people obtained information from 1900 to the present.

THINK AS A HISTORIAN: IDENTIFY AND CONNECT PATTERNS

Line graphs visually represent changes over time. Historians examine graphs and charts to identify patterns or trends. They often compare one pattern or trend with another to see relationships. Critical decisions in history were often based on the graphs that military or other government agencies created.

Between 1917 and 1997, the percentage of women in the workforce rose from about 20 percent to 45 percent. Identify and explain the birth rate pattern represented in the graph below. Explain a connection between the information in the graph and women in the workforce.

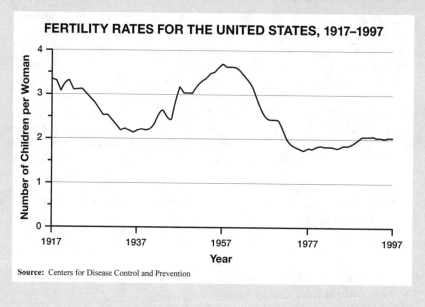

FERTILITY RATES FOR THE UNITED STATES, 1917–1997

Source: Centers for Disease Control and Prevention

REFLECT ON THE TOPIC ESSENTIAL QUESTION

1. In one to three paragraphs, explain how the development of new technology changed the world since 1900.

Technological Advancements and Limitations — Disease

We live in a world fraught with risk from new pandemics. Fortunately, we also now live in an era with the tools to build a global immune system.

— Nathan Wolfe, virologist (born 1970)

> **Essential Question:** How have environmental factors affected human populations since 1900?

As virus specialist Nathan Wolfe pointed out, progress in science and medicine, combined with government-run public health measures, drastically reduced illnesses and deaths from many diseases after 1900. These included **pandemics**, epidemic diseases that spread across national borders. The disease **smallpox**, for example, had plagued the ancient Egyptians and devastated the native population of the Americas and Australia. As recently as the 1960s, it killed millions of people each year. However, the World Health Organization (WHO) conducted a global vaccination campaign to wipe out the disease. In 1979, scientists declared success. Smallpox had been eliminated from the planet, except for the culture kept alive at the Centers for Disease Control in the United States.

Other diseases persisted, especially those related to poverty, including malaria, tuberculosis, and cholera. New epidemics also emerged, such as deadly strains of flu, HIV/AIDS, and Ebola. Other conditions, such as heart disease and Alzheimers, became more common as people began living longer. Each medical problem spurred even more technological and medical advances to try to combat it.

Disease and Poverty

Even when cures exist, some diseases persist because the conditions of poverty are contributing factors. Poor housing or working conditions, contaminated water, and lack of access to health care are commonplace among populations with low incomes, and they all contribute to the spread of disease.

Malaria A parasitic disease spread by mosquitoes in tropical areas, **malaria** killed more than 600,000 people each year in the early 21st century. Most of these were young African children. The international non-governmental organization (NGO) **Doctors Without Borders** treated about 1.7 million people annually. Experts developed preventive approaches, such as distributing mosquito nets treated with insecticide as cover during sleep. However, people can still become infected during waking hours. A vaccine for malaria has been in development for many years, but one that is effective in most cases is still in trials. Nonetheless, progress has been made. In 2019, the World Health Organization certified Algeria and Argentina as malaria-free. The organization cautioned, however, that some types of mosquitoes were becoming resistant to insecticides.

Tuberculosis Another disease associated with poverty is **tuberculosis (TB),** an airborne infection that spreads through coughs and sneezes and affects the lungs. Before 1946, no effective drug treatment was available for this deadly disease. Then a cure was developed involving antibiotics and a long period of rest. In countries where TB is common, vaccines are administered to children. In the early 21st century, a strain of tuberculosis resistant to the usual antibiotics appeared. The number of infected patients increased, especially in prisons, where people live in close quarters. The WHO began a worldwide campaign against tuberculosis in the 2010s.

Cholera A bacterial disease that spreads through contaminated water, **cholera** causes about 95,000 deaths per year. Like tuberculosis and malaria, cholera affects mainly poor people in developing countries. Methods to counter cholera include boiling or chlorinating drinking water and washing hands. Although cholera vaccines are available, they do not reduce the need to follow these preventive measures. A severe cholera infection can kill within a few hours, but quickly rehydrating an exposed person can effectively eliminate the risk of death.

TOP 10 CAUSES OF DEATHS IN LOW-INCOME COUNTRIES IN 2016

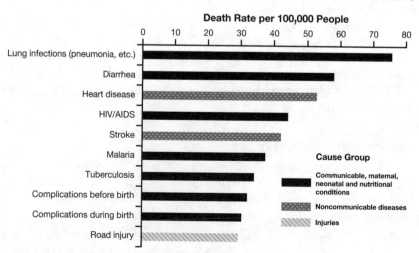

Source: Global Health Estimates 2016: Deaths by Cause, Age, Sex, by Country and by Region, 2000-2016. Geneva, World Health Organization; 2018. World Bank list of economics (June 2017). Washington, DC: The World Bank Group; 2017 (https://datahelpdesk.worldbank.org/knowledgebase/articles/905319-wtorld-bank-country-and-lending-groups).

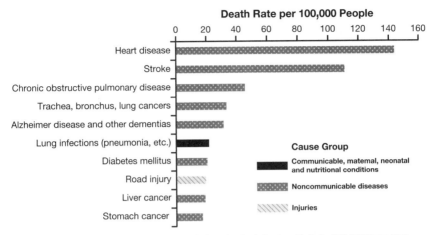

TOP 10 CAUSES OF DEATHS IN UPPER-MIDDLE-INCOME COUNTRIES IN 2016

Death Rate per 100,000 People

Source: Adapted from Global Health Estimates 2016: Deaths by Cause, Age, Sex, by Country and by Region, 2000-2016. Geneva, World Health Organization; 2018. World Bank list of economies (June 2017). Washington, DC: The World Bank Group; 2017 (https://datahelp-desk.worldbank.org/knowledgebase/articles/905319-world-bank-country-and-lending-groups).

Polio Another disease caused by water contaminated by a virus transmitted in fecal matter, **polio** once infected 100,000 new people per year. It could result in paralysis and sometimes death. The world cheered when an American researcher, **Jonas Salk**, announced on April 12, 1955, that an injectable vaccine against polio had proven effective. Six years later, an oral vaccine, developed by **Albert Sabin**, became available.

Vaccines became the centerpiece of a global public health campaign to eliminate polio. A joint effort by governments, private organizations, and United Nations agencies began in 1988. In less than 30 years, polio was eliminated in all but a few countries. In places where it still exists, such as Pakistan and Afghanistan, war makes administering the vaccine difficult. Political unrest and religious fundamentalism make people fearful of programs advocated by outsiders. Still, the success of the campaign showed that coordinated global efforts could help solve global problems. (Connect: Compare the effects of diseases during the Age of Exploration to those in the 20th century. See Topic 4.3.)

Emerging Epidemics

Some diseases have emerged that caused major social disruption. In the fall of 1918, as World War I was drawing to a close, a new fight erupted. The issue of the *Journal of the American Medical Association* published on December 12, 1918, described the battle this way: "Medical science for four and one-half years devoted itself to putting men on the firing line and keeping them there. Now it must turn with its whole might to combating the greatest enemy of all—infectious disease." In fact, more soldiers died from the flu than from battle. One quarter of all Americans and one-fifth of the world's population became infected with this particularly virulent strain of the flu, which killed 20 million people worldwide. Its victims tended to be between the ages of 20 and 40. The effects of the flu were so disastrous that longevity in the United States fell by 10 years. More people died from the flu in 1918–1919 than had died in four years of the Bubonic Plague (1347–1351). Like the plague, the flu spread along trade routes and with military troops.

HIV/AIDS Another disease outbreak causing social disruption occurred between 1981 and 2014. **Acquired immunodeficiency syndrome (AIDS)**, which is caused by the **human immunodeficiency virus (HIV)**, killed more than 25 million people around the world. HIV weakens the immune system, so people more easily succumb to other illnesses. The virus is contracted through the exchange of bodily fluids, usually through unprotected sex, blood transfusions, or sharing intravenous needles. Funding for the research on the disease, which was associated in its early days with homosexual men and drug addicts, was difficult to come by, and a high percentage of its first victims died.

By the mid-1990s, however, medical researchers had developed ways to treat the disease but not to cure it. **Antiretroviral drugs** could stop HIV from weakening the immune system, thus allowing a patient to live with the virus for many years. However, the drugs were very expensive, so access to treatment was difficult, particularly for patients in poor countries. Brazil is a notable exception. In 1996 it established a policy of providing free antiretroviral drugs to any person who needed them. Deaths have declined dramatically, and the program has actually saved the government money by lowering the number of hospitalizations, medical leaves, and early retirements.

After 2000, the WHO, the United States government, and private groups increased funding for AIDS prevention and treatment, but the disease remains a serious problem. In 2018, about 40 million people globally were living with HIV, the majority in developing countries or low-income neighborhoods of developed countries. Each week, more than 600 young women between the ages of 15 and 24 become infected with HIV, and many lack access to healthcare.

Ebola Another recent and frightening epidemic is Ebola. Discovered in the Congo in 1976, **Ebola** is a deadly disease caused by a virus that infects the African fruit bat, humans, and other primates. Humans get the virus from exposure to fluids of infected people or animals. The disease causes extensive bleeding, organ failure, and, for the majority of infected people, death. In 2014, a massive outbreak in West Africa caused fear around the world. However, a coordinated, intensive public health effort contained and then ended the outbreak. As with polio, countries demonstrated their ability to work together to confront a danger. The WHO took a leading role in this public health response, issuing emergency warnings and implementing a "road map" for handling the outbreaks.

Diseases Associated with Longevity

As longevity increases, diseases that typically do not develop until later in life began to assert themselves. These diseases are more common in countries where peoples' incomes are higher.

Heart Disease The most common cause of death in developed countries is **heart disease**. This disease is associated with lifestyle, genetics, and increased longevity. One of the major discoveries in fighting heart disease was the **heart transplant**, first performed by the South African **Christiaan Barnard** in 1967. **Robert Jarvik** led a team that designed an **artificial heart**, used as a temporary device while the patient waited for a compatible human heart. Other researchers developed less invasive procedures: replacing valves, installing stents in arteries, replacing the vessels leading to the heart, and developing medications to reduce blood conditions that led to heart disease. In the 2000s, people with heart disease lived longer than similarly affected people did in the 1970s.

Alzheimer's Disease As people lived longer, a form of dementia known as **Alzheimer's disease** that affects elderly and some middle-aged people also became an increasing concern. Alzheimer's patients progressively lose their memory, eventually leading to a stage in which they do not recognize their loved ones. Since the disease undermines bodily functions, it leads to death. Researchers continue to search for a cure.

KEY TERMS BY THEME

ENVIRONMENT:		TECHNOLOGY: Medical
Epidemics	Albert Sabin	Advances
pandemics	polio	antiretroviral drugs
smallpox	acquired immunodeficiency	heart transplant
malaria	syndrome (AIDS)	Christiaan Barnard
Doctors Without Borders	human immunodeficiency	Robert Jarvik
tuberculosis (TB)	virus (HIV)	artificial heart
cholera	Ebola	
Jonas Salk		
	SOCIETY: Disease	
	heart disease	
	Alzheimer's disease	

Questions 1 to 3 refer to the map below.

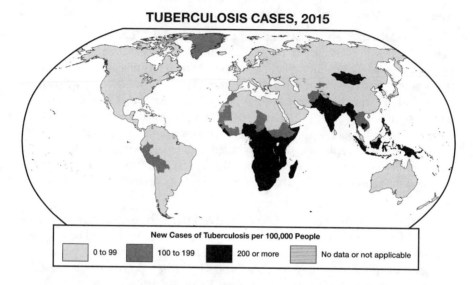

TUBERCULOSIS CASES, 2015

New Cases of Tuberculosis per 100,000 People

| 0 to 99 | 100 to 199 | 200 or more | No data or not applicable |

Tuberculosis is an infectious bacterial disease that spreads through the air.

1. Which of the following best explains the overall trend of tuberculosis cases shown on the map?

   (A) The role of trade routes in spreading disease

   (B) The lack of a global agency to coordinate public health campaigns

   (C) The spread of diseases in countries with rising birth rates

   (D) The persistence of diseases associated with poverty

2. Which of the following is the most reasonable inference about countries with the lowest rates of tuberculosis infection?

   (A) Climate conditions kill off the tuberculosis bacteria.

   (B) Medical workers control the spread of tuberculosis with antibiotics.

   (C) Scientific advances have ended the threat of new epidemic diseases.

   (D) These countries receive the lowest numbers of immigrants.

3. Which differences shown on the map most directly reflected which more general development in the late 20th century?

   (A) Longer life expectancy

   (B) Deforestation and desertification

   (C) Neocolonialism

   (D) The uneven expansion of Internet access

1. Use the passage below to answer all parts of the question that follows.

"The health problems faced by the world's poorest populations are not caused by a lack of drugs specifically related to their problems and diseases. The real problem is ensuring that these populations can actually access vital medicines. Many governments fail their populations in this respect by imposing punitive tariffs and taxes on medicines, and by skewing their spending priorities in favour of defense over health. The governments of poor countries hinder the creation of wealth, imposing obstacles in the way of owning and transferring property, imposing unnecessary regulatory barriers on entrepreneurs and businesses, and restricting trade through extortionate tariffs . . . [leaving] poor populations without the necessary resources to access the medicines that could so easily transform their quality of life.

Emerging health threats, ranging from drug-resistant strains of AIDS and tuberculosis to avian flu, remind us of the importance of ensuring that the pharmaceutical industry continues to discover and develop new drugs. Innovation is a fragile process, and it can be weakened or thwarted by poor public policies."

> Phillip Stevens, Director of Health Projects, *Diseases of Poverty and the 10/90 Gap*, 2004

(A) Identify ONE action governments take, in Stevens's view, that keep people in need from accessing medications.

(B) Explain ONE historical example that supports Stevens's argument.

(C) Explain ONE way in which environments have shaped societies between 1900 and the present.

2. Answer all parts of the question that follows.

(A) Identify ONE example of a medical development that affected populations around the world between 1900 and the present.

(B) Identify ONE example of a disease that affected populations around the world between 1900 and the present.

(C) Explain ONE example of a scientific development that affected populations around the world between 1900 and the present.

THINK AS A HISTORIAN: CONNECT WORLD WAR I AND THE
FLU EPIDEMIC

Although they occupy different realms—one geopolitical and one medical—World War I and the flu epidemic of 1918 were closely related. What connections can you find between the two developments? Think about these factors as you try to answer that question:

- how the pathogen originated and mutated

- the conditions in which the pathogen might thrive

- the methods by which the pathogen might spread

You can explore the connections between the war and the flu by exploring content at the Centers or Disease Control and Prevention (CDC) website.

Explain how World War I relates to the flu epidemic of 1918–1919. Locate the simulator by searching online for "The 'Spanish' Influenza pandemic and its relation to World War I."

REFLECT ON THE TOPIC ESSENTIAL QUESTION

1. In one to three paragraphs, explain how environmental factors have affected human populations since 1900.

9.3

Technology and the Environment

Climate change does not respect border; it does not respect who you are—rich and poor, small and big. Therefore this is what we call global challenges which require global solidarity.

—Ban Ki-moon, UN Secretary General, 2007–2016

Essential Question: What were the causes and effects of environmental changes from 1900 to the present?

During the 20th and 21st centuries, human agricultural, industrial, and other commercial activity contributed to many environmental changes that led to increased competition for increasingly scarce resources. These problems include:

- **Deforestation**—the loss of Earth's trees as a result of cutting down trees so the land could be used for agriculture

- **Desertification**—the removal of the natural vegetation cover through expansion and intensive use of agricultural lands in arid and semi-arid lands

- A decline in **air quality** as a result of increased pollutants in the air

- Increased consumption of the world's supply of fresh water

Scientists observed that, along with these changes, Earth was getting warmer. Ban Ki-moon, a South Korean politician and diplomat, and many other world leaders concluded that climate change was a global problem and debated the best ways to approach it through global action.

Causes of Environmental Changes

A number of interconnected factors contributed to the environmental changes that have taken place since 1900.

Population Growth In 1900, the world population was 1.6 billion. By 1950 it had risen to 2.55 billion, and by 2000 the population was 6.12 billion. All of the billions more people that lived on the planet since 1900 needed to be fed. Growing populations led to a demand for more croplands. This increase in land used for agricultural purposes resulted in deforestation, soil erosion, and smaller habitats for many species of plants and animals.

Growing populations affected not only land resources but also water resources. Overfishing in the oceans has led to the near disappearance of cod. Although fresh water is a renewable resource, growing populations consume increasing amounts of it.

Urbanization Another cause of environmental change is the increasing size and number of cities. By some estimates, by 2025, 5.1 billion people will live in cities, which will pressure those who grow food to use intensive farming methods that deplete the soil and cause erosion or to clear more forests for agricultural use. City dwellers also produce vast amounts of waste, some of which pollutes the water they depend on.

Globalization and Industrialization The global reach of industrialization has also affected the environment. As industry spread to developing countries, energy and other natural resources used in manufacturing were in demand, drawing further on the reserves of resources. Workers in industry in these developing countries are creating a new middle class that increases the market for such products as cars that require metals and other resources and that also contribute to pollution.

Effects of Environmental Changes

While humans have always competed for raw materials and natural resources, this competition became more intense as industrialization spread. With an ever-growing population, humans grappled with hunger, environmental damage, and global epidemics.

Resource Depletion Since the mid-1800s, when petroleum extraction began in earnest and oil pumped energy into the Industrial Revolution, about half of the earth's finite resources of this vital resource have been used up. With the rapidly growing urban and industrial population, some experts predict the remaining half could be used up at a much faster rate, within the next 30 to 40 years. While supplies of coal will last longer, if coal is used to make up for the loss of petroleum, coal reserves could also be depleted in 60 years. (Connect: Evaluate the claim that the Industrial Revolutions have created dependency on natural resources that will soon lead to their depletion. See Topic 5.5.)

Inequality and Scarce Resources According to the United Nations, 31 countries are facing **water scarcity** and more than 1 billion people lack clean, accessible drinking water. As water consumption continues to increase, some corporate interests are depleting, polluting, and exploiting water sources. The World Health Organization predicts that by 2025, half of the world's population will lack clean and safe drinking water.

Water scarcity is also linked to other inequalities. Surveys from 45 developing countries show that women and children bear the primary responsibility for water collection in most households. This is time not spent working at an income-generating job or attending school. A study in Ghana found that a 15-minute reduction in water collection time increases the proportion of girls attending school by 8 percent to 12 percent.

In 2015, world leaders agreed to 17 goals for a better world by 2030. Many of these global goals address the environmental problems the world faced after 1900 that relate to extreme poverty, inequalities and injustice, and climate change.

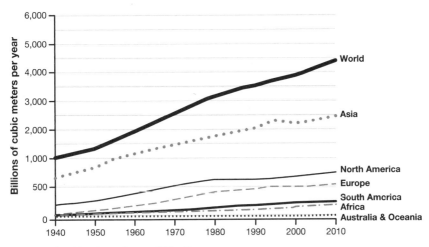

GLOBAL WATER CONSUMPTION, 1900–2025

Source: Adapted from Sampa, Commons.Wikimedia.org

Changes in the Atmosphere Factories, automobiles, airplanes, and many other products and processes of industrialization have emitted huge amounts of pollutants, including carbon dioxide and other **greenhouse gases**—those that build up in the atmosphere and let the heat of the sun reach Earth but trap it from escaping Earth. At the same time, some of Earth's natural carbon trapping resources, including forests and ground cover for unused farmlands, are shrinking.

Development of Renewable Energy Sources Concerned about unsustainable demands for energy through **fossil fuels** (coal, oil, petroleum, and natural gas), companies and nations began to invest in **renewable energy,** energy derived from resources that are continuously replenished, such as wind, solar, tidal, and geothermal power. At first, high costs slowed development of such sources. However, as new techniques and technologies reduced costs, these sources became increasingly attractive options. Renewable energy provides only about 7 percent of the world's energy needs. However, a 2018 study predicted that by 2050, half the world's electricity will come from wind power and solar power.

Increasing Environmental Awareness In 1968, the "Club of Rome"— an organization of scientists, industrialists, diplomats, and others—formed in Europe to promote solutions to global challenges facing humanity. It called attention to concerns that resource depletion would limit economic growth. In many countries, people joined a **Green Party** that focused on environmental issues. Some supported the **Green Belt Movement** to protect wilderness areas from urban growth. (See Topic 9.5.) By the 21st century, the Green Belt

Movement had planted more than 51 million trees in Kenya. The trees help to preserve ecosystems and lessen the effects of greenhouse gases. Planting trees also created employment and the improved soil quality.

Debates About Global Warming

Air pollutants and greenhouse gases prompted debates about rising temperatures. Scientists, including those on the United Nations' Intergovernmental Panel on Climate Change, cited data showing that the emissions of carbon dioxide and other greenhouse gases caused by the burning of fossil fuels were causing **global warming**. This is an increase in the average temperature of the world. Experts advised governments to reduce their countries' **carbon footprint**—the amount of carbon dioxide that each person produces. Without a reduced carbon footprint, global warming would contribute to catastrophes: more powerful hurricanes, more severe droughts, and rising sea levels that could flood islands and coastal areas. Some activists argued that the term "global warming" was too mild to express the urgency of action. They said that humanity faced a "climate emergency" or "climate crisis."

Climate-change skeptics, in contrast, questioned whether global warming was happening and whether human activities had any influence on the climate. In addition, some people in the energy industries resisted the interference of government, arguing that market forces would cause consumers to reduce their carbon footprint if that became necessary. In contrast, other leaders of energy companies began planning for a shift to renewable fuel sources.

Most government leaders, however, agree that global warming requires a global response, but countries disagree on how to reduce carbon emissions.

Debate over Reducing Carbon Emissions		
Issue	Developed Countries (including the United States and Western Europe)	Developing Countries (including China, India, Russia, and Brazil)
Reason for Reducing or Producing Carbon Dioxide	Developing countries need to reduce their rapidly increasing outputs of carbon dioxide.	Developing countries are trying to provide electricity, cars, and a path out of poverty for their citizens. (Developed countries already did this by using huge amounts of coal and oil.)
Quantity of Carbon Dioxide Produced	In 2007, China passed the United States as the world's biggest emitter of carbon dioxide.	Developing countries emit far less carbon dioxide *per person* than developed countries do. Therefore, developed countries must take the lead in restricting their use of fossil fuels.

Kyoto The first major international agreement to reduce carbon emissions was the **Kyoto Protocol**, signed in 1997. Developed nations in Western Europe, along with the United States, argued that developing countries, such as China, India, Russia, and Brazil, needed to curb their rapidly increasing output of carbon dioxide. However, the United States refused to ratify it, and China and India were not required to agree to the strictest terms of the protocol.

Global Action at Paris In 2015, 195 countries signed a deal, the **Paris Agreement**, that gave new hope for progress against global warming. Leaders of both the United States and China supported this new deal. However, in 2017, President Donald Trump announced that the United States would withdraw from the Paris Agreement.

Climate Activism Increasing global temperatures led to calls to action. "You say you love your children above all else, and yet you are stealing their future in front of their very eyes," 15-year-old climate activist Greta Thunberg raged in a speech at a United Nations climate conference in 2018. Beginning with a solo protest in her native Sweden, Thunberg eventually led a global climate strike with more than 1.6 million participants in more than 125 countries.

Extinction Rebellion, a climate activist group formed in 2018, engaged in civil disobedience in London, blocking a main bridge and key intersections for more than a week, chaining themselves to the headquarters of big companies, and interrupting "business as usual" in other ways. About a thousand people were arrested, but the group succeeded in having Members of Parliament call a citizens' assembly to discuss ideas for addressing the climate emergency. Many other citizen groups are pressuring lawmakers in many countries to take necessary steps to avert the worst consequences of continued warming predicted in reports from the UN's Intergovernmental Panel on Climate Change.

A New Age?

What should people call the time period we live in? Traditionally, geologists have called the current period the Holocene epoch. *Holocene* means "entirely recent." This time period started about 11,700 years ago, at the end of the last significant ice age.

However, some scientists believed humans have left the Holocene. They wanted to call the present time the **Anthropocene**. This term means "new man." These scientists wanted to change the name because humans now affect almost the entire planet. In 2019, a panel of scientists voted to approve the name. *Anthropocene* reflects the idea that humans are the strongest influence on Earth's climate and environment—for better and for worse.

KEY TERMS BY THEME

CULTURE: Movements and Organizations	**ENVIRONMENT:** Scientific Studies	renewable energy
Green Party	deforestation	global warming
Green Belt Movement	desertification	carbon footprint
	air quality	Anthropocene
	greenhouse gases	**GOVERNMENT:** International Agreements
	fossil fuels	Kyoto Protocol
	water scarcity	Paris Agreement

Questions 1 to 3 refer to the image below.

1. Which of the following best describes the point of view of the creator of the image?

   (A) Scientists have the primary responsibility to analyze global environmental issues.

   (B) People from around the world need to work together to protect the earth from environmental damage.

   (C) The impacts of climate change cannot be reversed by human action.

   (D) People competing for scare resources are causing conflicts among countries.

2. Which of the following best explains the relationship of developed and developing countries in regard to climate change?

   (A) Developing countries in Africa emit more greenhouse gases per person than developed countries because they are more agriculural.

   (B) Developing countries are more vulnerable to climate change than developed countries because they have fewer resources to fight it.

   (C) Developing countries have more influence in international affairs to combat climate change than developed countries have.

   (D) Developing and developed countries have agreed to allow China and the United States to continue emissions at current levels.

3. Which of the following developments accelerated global awareness of climate change in the late 20th century?

(A) The increasing population of developing countries

(B) The use of pesticides during the Green Revolution

(C) The development of nuclear power plants to produce electricity

(D) The growth of the information sector of the global economy

SHORT-ANSWER QUESTIONS

1. Use the passage below to answer all parts of the question that follows.

Excerpts from key articles of the Paris Agreement are set out below:

- "Long-term temperature goal (Art. 2) – The Paris Agreement, in seeking to strengthen the global response to climate change, reaffirms the goal of limiting global temperature increase to well below 2 degrees Celsius, while pursuing efforts to limit the increase to 1.5 degrees."

- Global peaking (Art. 4) – . . . Parties aim to reach global peaking of greenhouse gas emissions (GHGs) as soon as possible, recognizing peaking will take longer for developing country Parties, so as to achieve a balance between . . . emissions . . . and removals . . . in the second half of the century.

- Sinks and reservoirs (Art. 5) – The Paris Agreement also encourages Parties to conserve and enhance, as appropriate, sinks and reservoirs of GHGs . . . including forests.

- Climate change education, training, public awareness, public participation, and public access to information (Art. 12) is also to be enhanced under the Agreement."

United Nations, Paris Agreement, December 2015

(A) Identify ONE environmental change that influenced the Paris Agreement.

(B) Explain the context in which the Paris Agreement was developed.

(C) Explain the significance of the Paris Agreement in light of the environmental debates after 1900.

2. Answer all parts of the question that follows.

(A) Identify ONE position in the debate about the nature and causes of climate change.

(B) Explain ONE way in which human competition over resources affected global interactions from the period 1900 to the present.

(C) Explain ONE way in which population growth affected the environment after 1900.

THINK AS A HISTORIAN: ENVIRONMENTAL CHANGES IN
DIFFERENT CONTEXTS

The geopolitical context of environmental change provides one lens through which to see complex interrelationships. Economic context provides another useful lens, as Sean Mcelwee explains below:

> "Marx's ideas about overproduction led him to predict what is now called globalization—the spread of capitalism across the planet in search of new markets. 'The need of a constantly expanding market for its products chases the bourgeoisie over the entire surface of the globe,' he wrote. 'It must nestle everywhere, settle everywhere, establish connections everywhere.' While this may seem like an obvious point now, Marx wrote those words in 1848, when globalization was over a century away. And he wasn't just right about what ended up happening in the late 20th century—he was right about why it happened: The relentless search for new markets and cheap labor, as well as the incessant demand for more natural resources, are beasts that demand constant feeding."
>
> *Rolling Stone*, January 20, 2014

Considering both geopolitical and economic contexts, explain why environmental harms accelerated following the Cold War.

REFLECT ON THE TOPIC ESSENTIAL QUESTION

1. In one to three paragraphs, explain the causes and effects of environmental changes from 1900 to the present.

9.4

Economics in the Global Age

A market economy is to economics what democracy is to government:
a decent, if flawed, choice among many bad alternatives.

—Charles Wheelan, *Naked Economics: Undressing the Dismal Science* (2002)

Essential Question: How did the global economy change and remain the same from 1900 to the present?

Global trade exploded with the end of the Cold War. The new global economy was part of a renewed emphasis on market-oriented policy advocated by leaders such as **Ronald Reagan** in the United States and **Margaret Thatcher** in Great Britain. They advocated cutting taxes, regulations, and government assistance to the poor as a way to promote economic growth. As Wheeler pointed out, this was a flawed choice producing greater wealth for many but hardships for others. At the same time, revolutions in information and communications technology led to the growth of knowledge economies in some regions, while industrial production and manufacturing were increasingly situated in Asia and Latin America.

Acceleration of Free-Market Economies

Globalization is interaction among peoples, governments, and companies around the world. The Indian Ocean trade and European imperialism are both examples of globalization. However, the term usually refers to the increased integration of the global economy since the 1970s. The Eastern Bloc nations that had been under Soviet control suddenly could trade freely with capitalist democracies. India and other countries that had been nonaligned during the Cold War relaxed restrictions on trade in the 1990s. This opening up of a country's economy is called **economic liberalization**.

Ronald Reagan and Margaret Thatcher wanted **free markets**, which are economic systems based on supply and demand, with as little government control as possible. While Reagan and Thatcher were strongly nationalistic, corporations used the shift in emphasis to move jobs to countries with lower wages, lower taxes, and fewer regulations. Critics charged that globalization led to labor exploitation and environmental damage.

Economic Liberalization in Chile In Chile in 1973, **Augusto Pinochet** took power in a U.S.-backed coup against a democratically elected socialist government led by Salvador Allende. Pinochet ruled from 1974 to 1990. Then a coalition of citizens ousted him because of his violent tactics. Indicted for kidnapping, torture, money laundering, and murder, Pinochet died in 2006 before he could be convicted. "We buried our democracy, and we buried freedom," the Chilean author Isabel Allende said about his rule.

However, during his rule, the Chilean economy took a turn away from state control toward a free-market approach. Among the goals of this approach were privatizing formerly state-run businesses and taming the serious inflation Chile was experiencing. Economists known as the Chicago Boys because they studied under free-market economist Milton Friedman at the University of Chicago helped design Chile's economic reforms. The reforms were unpopular because they did not address poverty and other social concerns, and Pinochet used repression to enact them. Subsequent administrations, however, guided the economy with a balanced approach, using a combination of economic growth as a result of free trade and government programs to significantly reduce poverty. (Connect: Evaluate the success of the free-market economic approach of both Chile and the Soviet Bloc. See Topic 8.9.)

Chinese Economic Reforms Economic liberalization reached China as well. In 1981, **Deng Xiaoping** became the Chinese leader. Under him, the Communist Party backed away from its commitment to economic equality, and more actively promoted economic growth. Deng called his policy "Let some people get rich first." The government took several steps to open up the economy, even as it kept overall control:

- It replaced communes with peasant-leased plots of land where the peasants could grow their own crops and sell part of them in markets. This reform led to agricultural surpluses instead of the famines of the past.

- It allowed factories to produce more products for consumers.

- It encouraged foreign companies to set up factories in special economic zones. Foreign firms were attracted to China because of low wages and lax environmental laws.

- It reopened the Shanghai stock market and allowed private ownership of some businesses.

Some Chinese thought that these economic reforms should be accompanied by political reforms, such as freedom of speech and the press and the end of the Communist Party's monopoly on political power. Political discourse did become somewhat freer than in the past. In 1989, however, a large but peaceful student-led demonstration in **Tiananmen Square** in Beijing was met by force from the government. Soldiers using guns and tanks broke up the demonstrations, killing hundreds of people. (See Topic 9.5.)

Economic Change: New Knowledge Economies

In the late 1900s, revolutions in information and communications technology led some countries to undertake a new kind of economy—the **knowledge economy**. A knowledge economy creates, distributes, and uses knowledge and information. Designers, engineers, teachers, and many others have jobs in the knowledge economy. In the United States, the knowledge economy is evident in the vast stretch of technology companies in Silicon Valley in California, where workers use their knowledge to create ways for other people to use theirs through technology, communication, innovation, and collaboration.

Knowledge Economy in Finland In many cases, knowledge economies have evolved with the explosion of information and communication technology. In knowledge economies, governments and investors put resources into research, education, innovation, and technological infrastructure.

Finland, for example, had been an agrarian economy in the 1950s but followed other European countries in industrializing after World War II. When the Soviet Union collapsed, Finland lost one of its main customers of manufactured goods and faced an economic crisis. In the 1990s, Finland turned a corner by entering the global marketplace, encouraging competition, and establishing the Science and Technology Policy Council to set a direction of economic growth through technology and innovation. Finland experienced great economic growth in this endeavor and led the way in the development of mobile phones. By investing in education and communications technology, Finland was able to build on its success with mobile phones and establish software companies. These industries required highly educated workers, while outsourcing hardware production to countries with lower labor costs.

Japanese Economic Growth Japan followed a somewhat different path. After World War II, Japan implemented economic policies similar to 18th-century mercantilist policies that were designed to increase exports and decrease imports, as well as policies to boost competitiveness:

- To encourage exports, the government coordinated its finance and labor policies with large corporations and gave them subsidies to help them keep their costs low.

- To discourage imports, the government used high tariffs and other trade restrictions on goods made abroad.

- To prepare its citizens to be productive workers, Japan emphasized rigorous education.

These policies, aided by large investments from the United States and other countries, turned Japan into a manufacturing powerhouse.

However, Japan's impressive growth came at a high cost for its consumers. Low-wage workers producing items for foreign markets often could not afford to buy what they made. For example, Japanese-made cars were more expensive in Japan than they were in the United States. Over time, Japanese unions became strong enough to negotiate higher wages, and international pressure forced Japan to relax its trade restrictions. Japan's economy diversified, and it became a knowledge economy and an international center of banking, finance, and information technology. Although Japan's growth slowed after the 1980s, Japan remained the third-largest economy in the world in 2014, behind only the United States and China.

Closely following Japan's economic model were four states known as the **Asian Tigers**—Hong Kong, Singapore, South Korea, and Taiwan. Like Japan, these states prospered through government-business partnerships, high exports, intense education, and a low-wage workforce. The success of the Asian Tigers and China raised hundreds of millions of people from poverty.

Economic Continuities: Shifting Manufacturing

As the knowledge economy develops in some regions, industrial production and manufacturing in those regions, including in the United States, have declined. Manufacturing plants are increasingly located in Asia and Latin America rather than the United States and Europe. Countries in both Asia and Latin America have become known for their contributions to the textile and apparel industries, though they manufacture many other products. So while it has moved to different regions, manufacturing continues to play a key role in the global economy.

Vietnam and Bangladesh Importers who once purchased their manufactured goods from China have been finding other options in such Asian countries as Vietnam and Bangladesh, where labor costs tend to be significantly lower than in China (where they are already significantly lower than in the United States and Europe). Both Vietnam and Bangladesh have become known for their exports of clothing. In compounds the size of small villages in some places, garment manufacturers—often funded by foreign investors—churn out the clothes that end up on hangers in stores in developed countries. Clothing accounts for 80 percent of exports from Bangladesh. Phones are the largest export from Vietnam, worth about $45 billion in 2017, with apparel and electronic goods each bringing in $25.9 billion.

Workers in both Vietnam and Bangladesh have mounted strikes in recent years, protesting both low wages and poor working conditions. Their pay has increased slightly as a result, but not enough to keep up with rising costs of living.

Manufacturing in Mexico and Honduras In 1994, the United States, Canada, and Mexico negotiated **NAFTA**, the North American Free Trade Agreement. This agreement encouraged U.S. and Canadian industries to build *maquiladoras* (factories) in Mexico that used low-wage Mexican labor to produce tariff-free goods for foreign export. Many factories hired large numbers of young women and exposed them to harsh working conditions.

Source: Public Domain

A maquiladora [factory] in Mexico takes raw materials and assembles, manufactures, or processes the material and exports the finished product.

Labor unions in the United States complained that NAFTA led to the export of thousands of U.S. jobs to Mexico, where wages and benefits were lower and safety and environmental standards were weaker.

Honduras in Central America, the second largest exporter of textiles in the Americas, has sought to upgrade its manufacturing using principles of sustainability—recycling or treating its waste materials—and fair labor practices, including housing and education plans for workers, through business-government partnerships. As in Vietnam and Bangladesh, considerable business investment comes from enterprises in South Korea and Taiwan.

Transnational Free-Trade Organizations

Several organizations contributed to the growth of the global economy in the decades following World War II. Some countries joined regional organizations such as the European Economic Community, **Mercosur** (in South America), and the **Association of Southeast Asian Nations (ASEAN)**. Many countries signed an international accord, the **General Agreement on Tariffs and Trade (GATT)**, which lifted restrictive barriers to trade. **Protective tariffs**, which are taxes on foreign imports, had been at a world average rate of 40 percent before GATT. By lowering and eliminating many tariffs, the agreement promoted more international trade and helped restore economic prosperity to war-ravaged Europe. By the 1990s, average tariff rates had sunk below 5 percent, easing the movement of goods across national borders and lowering prices for consumers.

In 1995, the **World Trade Organization (WTO)** took over GATT's operations. The WTO made rules that governed more than 90 percent of all international trade. In part because of its power, the organization became controversial. Its meetings were closed to the public, and its board members represented mostly corporate interests. Also, the organization's rules favored trade over consideration of issues of moral concern. For example, through strict application of WTO rules, a member nation that refused to buy clothing made by sweatshop labor could suffer trade sanctions from the organization.

Multinational Corporations

A **multinational corporation** is one that is legally incorporated in one country but that makes or sells goods or services in one or more other countries. The joint-stock companies of the Commercial Revolution, such as the British East India Company and Dutch East India Company (see Topic 4.5) were the earliest examples of multinational corporations. Multinational corporations were also the business means through which imperialist nations made their wealth during the age of imperialism, exploiting the resources and labor of the colonized regions for profit in home countries.

Today's multinational corporations take advantage of both knowledge economies and more traditional manufacturing and industrial economies. They employ leading edge workers in the knowledge economy—software designers, communications specialists, and engineers—and at the same time hire low-wage workers abroad to make their products. They also have a global market in which to sell their goods and services.

To free-market supporters, multinational corporations produce the greatest gains for both developed and developing countries. For example, in the early 1990s, India opened its markets and allowed in more imports. With its highly educated, English-speaking workforce, India became a software and information technology powerhouse, drawing investments from American and European companies that wanted to outsource jobs and lower labor costs. Multinational corporations, such as **Microsoft** and **Google**, also invested in the Indian economy. The influx of corporate wealth and foreign goods created a thriving consumer culture among India's middle class, the ranks of which swelled tremendously after 2000. In 2014, the Indian middle class was estimated to be the largest of any country in the world, with more than 350 million people.

The India-based multinational corporation **Mahindra & Mahindra**, which produces cars, farm equipment, military vehicles, and electrical energy, is headquartered in Mumbai, India, but has operations not only throughout India but also in South Korea, China, Australia, the United States, South Africa, and other Africa nations. Some multinational corporations are criticized because they lack a strong national identity and therefore do not necessarily adhere to the ethical standards of their home country. They are also criticized for exploiting workers and establishing their operations in such a way that they avoid as many taxes as possible. Mahindra & Mahindra, in contrast, has received awards for its socially responsible corporate practices and is considered one of the most trusted businesses in India.

In contrast, Swiss-based multinational **Nestlé** corporation, the largest food company in the world, has been the subject of many controversies and criticisms, including purchasing cocoa for its chocolate products from suppliers who use child labor and engage in cocoa production on protected lands. It has also faced criticism for its bottled water business for its attitude toward drinking water as a product rather than a human right. At the same time, Nestlé invests in a number of research programs aimed at sustainable agriculture and training for farmers.

KEY TERMS BY THEME

ECONOMY: World Trade
economic liberalization
free markets
Asian Tigers
NAFTA
maquiladora
Mercosur
Association of Southeast
   Asian Nations (ASEAN)
General Agreement on
   Tariffs and Trade (GATT)
protective tariffs
World Trade Organization
   (WTO)

GOVERNMENT: Leaders
Ronald Reagan
Margaret Thatcher
Deng Xiaoping
Augusto Pinochet

SOCIETY: China
Tiananmen Square

ECONOMY: Globalization
knowledge economy
multinational corporation
Microsoft
Google
Mahindra & Mahindra
Nestlé

Source: Wikimedia Commons
A Mahindra plant in Mumbai, India

MULTIPLE-CHOICE QUESTIONS

Questions 1–3 refer to the passage below.

"[Google] has become famous in India for its program of Saathis—the Hindi word for friend—which it launched in 2015 to help draw more women online. Women make up a small percentage of internet users in the country. Google partnered with Tata Trusts, the philanthropic arm of India's manufacturing and retail conglomerate, and recruited about 60,000 so-called Saathis, all women, in more than 200,000 villages across India, to teach other women how to get online. Google trained the Saathis and gave them each a smartphone, while Tata pays them a stipend of about $40 a month. . . .

Google claims the Saathis have so far trained about 22 million people, mostly women, in basic skills like how to make WhatsApp calls and pay bills online. It aims to reach about 300,000 villages by the end of this year. Several Saathis and their trainees have seized the chance to start cottage industries with their new Internet skills, downloading instructional videos on YouTube on how to make homemade honey or embroider shirts, for example. . . . 'I learned how to decorate bangles with thread and stones on YouTube,' says Parveen Begum, 32, whose husband, a devout Muslim, did not permit her to work outside the house. She now sells her bangles to local clients. 'Women come to my house to learn the Internet,' she says. 'I will train about 1,200 people in the end.'"

Vivienne Walt, "Google's Hopes and Dreams in India,"
Fortune, February 20, 2019

1. Which of the following describes a likely benefit to Google of its efforts in India?

   (A) Google is looking to India's women as a source of low-cost labor.

   (B) Google is creating potential future customers by introducing technology.

   (C) Google is looking to avoid U.S. taxes by establishing a presence in India.

   (D) Google is looking for ways to extract natural resources from India for its finished products.

2. Which best states a claim about globalization that this article could be used to support?

   (A) Companies both encourage and benefit from economic growth.

   (B) The pay difference among workers around the world doing similar jobs will grow larger over time.

   (C) Google's relationship with India's middle class is mainly charitable.

   (D) One limit to economic liberalism is that companies fail to transfer skills to workers around the world.

3. In what way have Google and YouTube benefited the women in the Saathis program economically?

(A) It pays them a $40 per month stipend.

(B) It saves them money through online bill paying.

(C) It exposes them to ideas they might use to make money.

(D) It gives women more freedom to work outside the home.

SHORT-ANSWER QUESTIONS

1. Use the image below to answer all parts of the question that follows.

Credit: Thomas O'Hallorhan, *U.S. News & World Report*, Library of Congress Prints and Photographs Division

U.S. Vice President Lyndon B. Johnson in a textile mill with Vietnamese men standing in front of a large quantity of textiles with a "Texas Cotton U.S.A." banner, 1961.

(A) Identify ONE reason cotton from Texas was shipped to Vietnam, as reflected in the image.

(B) Explain ONE way in which globalization contributed to the development of foreign manufacturing in the late 20th century.

(C) Explain ONE way in which economic trends in Vietnam were similar to the economic trends in Mexico in the late 20th century.

2. Answer all parts of the question that follows.

(A) Identify ONE way in which governments encouraged economic liberalization in the late 20th century.

(B) Explain ONE way in which revolutions in information and communications technology affected knowledge economies in the late 20th century.

(C) Explain ONE way in which industrial production affected Asia or Latin America in the late 20th century.

THINK AS A HISTORIAN: POLITICAL CAMPAIGN VS. ACADEMIC
RESEARCH

A writer or speaker's purpose and audience are significant factors to consider when evaluating the usefulness and accuracy of a historical source.

Read the following two statements on free trade. First, explain their relationship to each other: Do they agree or disagree on the main points? Second, determine the purpose of the statement by looking at the source. Explain how the purpose and audience may limit the usefulness of the source, if at all.

> "I do not believe in unfettered free trade. I believe in fair trade which works for the middle class and working families, not just large multinational corporations. I was on the picket line in opposition to NAFTA. We heard people tell us how many jobs would be created. I didn't believe that for a second because I understood what the function of NAFTA [and other trade agreements] is—it's to say to American workers, hey, you are now competing against people in Vietnam who make 56 cents an hour minimum wage."
>
> Senator Bernie Sanders, MSNBC Democratic
primary debate in New Hampshire, February 4, 2016

> "To take advantage of opportunities provided by globalization, firms have become multinational, establishing worldwide supply, production, and distribution networks. Many workers at firms that have successfully adapted to globalization have benefited, but large numbers of U.S. jobs have disappeared due to foreign competition or to offshoring by domestic firms. In effect, globalization means a substantial portion of the U.S. workforce is directly or indirectly in competition with lower-wage workers around the world."
>
> Dr. Timothy Hogan, Arizona State University, *An
Overview of the Knowledge Economy, with a Focus
on Arizona*, August 2011

REFLECT ON THE TOPIC ESSENTIAL QUESTION

1. In one to three paragraphs, explain how the global economy changed and remained the same from 1900 to the present.

9.5

Calls for Reform and Responses

We pledge ourselves to liberate all our people from the continuing bondage of poverty, deprivation, suffering, gender and other discrimination.

—Nelson Mandela (1918–2013)

Essential Question: How have social categories, roles, and practices changed and stayed the same since 1900?

In the age of global economics, global transportation and communication, and global devastation from war, human rights were, for the first time, also elevated to the level of global discourse, which challenged long-held assumptions about race, class, gender, and religion. Efforts to establish and safeguard human rights opened doors of educational and professional opportunity and political participation for some who had previously been excluded. People sought liberation from the "continuing bondage," in Nelson Mandela's terms, that had kept them in poverty. People around the globe also began to protest the inequalities and environmental damage that globalization had created or reinforced.

An Era of Rights

In December of 1948, the United Nations laid the groundwork for an era of rights when it adopted a foundational document, the **Universal Declaration of Human Rights**, asserting basic rights and fundamental freedoms for all human beings. It stated that everyone is entitled to these rights without distinctions based on "race, colour [color], sex, language, religion, political or other opinion, national or social origin, property, birth or other status."

The UN and Human Rights Since its creation, the United Nations has promoted **human rights**, basic protections that are common to all people. As part of its humanitarian work, the UN created the **United Nations International Children's Emergency Fund (UNICEF)** in 1946 to provide food for children in Europe who were still suffering more than a year after the end of World War II. In 1948, the UN formalized its position on human rights in the Universal Declaration. Since that time, the UN has investigated abuses of human rights, such as genocide, war crimes, government oppression, and crimes against women.

The **International Court of Justice** is a judicial body set up by the original UN charter. It settles disputes over international law that countries bring to it. Also called the World Court, it has 15 judges, and each must be a citizen of a different country. It often deals with border disputes and treaty violations.

Another main aim of the UN is to protect **refugees**, people who have fled their home countries. In times of war, famine, and natural disasters, people often leave their country and seek refuge in a safe location. Working through sub-agencies such as NGOs (non-governmental organizations) and the agency UNHCR (United Nations High Commissioner for Refugees), the UN provides food, medicine, and temporary shelter. Among the earliest refugees the UN helped were Palestinians who fled the disorder when the UN partitioned Palestine to create the state of Israel in 1948.

Global Feminism On January 21, 2017, the day after Donald Trump's inauguration as president, the Women's March on Washington drew about 500,000 demonstrators standing up for women's rights and other concerns. However, the march drew even more power from the millions more demonstrators who took part in locations on every continent around the globe, from Antarctica to Zagreb, Croatia and from Buenos Aires, Argentina to Mumbai, India. As many as five million people stood together that day representing a global solidarity for women's rights. That march was the most dramatic sign of global feminism, but other landmark events since 1900 had done their part to solidify the movement.

Landmark Events in Global Feminism after 1900		
Date	Event	Highlight
March 1911	First International Women's Day Celebration	One million demonstrators in Austria, Denmark, Germany, and Switzerland stand for women's rights
April 1915	Meeting of First International Congress of Women	Representatives from 12 nations, including the United States, attended.
June 1975	United Nations First World Conference on Women	Representatives from 133 nations met in Mexico City and planned for the advancement of women over the next decade.
December 1979	Convention on the Elimination of All Forms of Discrimination Against Women (CEDAW)	An "international bill of rights for women" adopted by United Nations
September 1995	Meeting of Fourth International Congress of Women	Thousands of participants and activists met in Beijing, China, where then-First Lady Hillary Clinton declared that "women's rights are human rights."

The 1979 Convention on the Elimination of All Forms of Discrimination Against Women outlined many rights and protections that are cornerstones of global feminism:

- The right to vote and to hold office
- The right to freely choose a spouse
- The right to access the same education as men
- The right to access family planning resources and birth control.

Cultural and Religious Movements Discourse on rights also became part of cultural and religious movements. For example, the **Negritude Movement**, which took root primarily in French West Africa, emphasized pride in "blackness," the rejection of French colonial authority, and the right to self-determination. **Léopold Sédar Senghor** of Senegal wrote poems about the beauty and uniqueness of African culture and is now regarded as one of the 20th century's most distinguished French writers. (Senghor later served as first president of independent Senegal.) During the 1920s and 1930s, American intellectuals such as W. E. B. Du Bois, Richard Wright, and Langston Hughes wrote movingly about the multiple meanings of "blackness" in the world. What many now refer to as "black pride" of the 1960s had its roots in the Negritude Movement

Inherent rights became a focus of a religious ideology as well. **Liberation theology**, which combined socialism with Catholicism, spread through Latin America in the 1950s and 1960s. It interpreted the teachings of Jesus to include freeing people from the abuses of economic, political, and social conditions. Part of this liberation included redistributing some wealth from the rich to the poor. In many countries, military dictators persecuted and killed religious workers who embraced liberation theology.

However, advocates of liberation theology had a few notable successes. In Nicaragua, they helped a rebel movement topple a dictator and institute a socialist government. In Venezuela, President Hugo Chávez was deeply influenced by the movement. Then, in 2013, the Roman Catholic Church selected a cardinal from Argentina as pope, the first one from Latin America. The new leader, who took the name **Pope Francis**, reversed the Vatican's opposition to liberation theology.

Steps toward Gender Equality

During the 20th century, men and women made great strides toward securing some of their rights and participating more fully in professional and political life. In the first part of the century the percentage of women who could read and who attended college increased, and in country after country, women won the right to vote. However, not all the women in a country won the right to vote at the same time. In the United States, for example, white women won the right to vote in national elections in 1920. Native American and African

American women did not have full voting rights throughout the country until the Voting Rights Act of 1965. Britain granted women the right to vote in 1918, but at first only women over 30 who met a property qualification could do so. British women did not achieve the same right to vote as men until 1928. In Australia, white women gained some voting rights in 1894, but aboriginal men and women did not gain the right to vote until 1962.

When Women Won the Right to Vote	
Country	Year
New Zealand	1893
Azerbaijan	1918
Britain	1918
United States	1920
Brazil	1932
Turkey	1934
Japan	1945
India	1947
Morocco	1963
Switzerland	1971
Kuwait	2005
Saudi Arabia	2015

As of 2018, only the tiny country of Vatican City did not allow women to vote. Whether women are able to exercise their vote is another issue. In Pakistan, women gained the right to vote in 1947. However, in 2013, women cast only 10 percent of votes there.

Steps toward Racial Equality

In the United States, African Americans won major victories against discrimination and segregation. Through the 1965 **Civil Rights Act,** which outlawed discrimination based on race, color, religion, sex, or national origin, and the 1965 **Voting Rights Act**, which banned discrimination in voting, the federal government stepped in to protect the rights of all citizens. African Americans also sought equality of education through desegregation of schools.

South Africa's Colonial Legacy South Africa's system of **apartheid**, instituted in 1948, enforced the segregation of people based on race. Although white South Africans made up only 15 percent of South Africa's population, apartheid reserved good jobs and other privileges for them. So-called **pass laws** required black South Africans to carry identity documents when entering areas set aside for whites, which they often had to do when traveling to their jobs. They were banned from living in certain areas of the country. Mixed marriages were prohibited. Although South Africa had 11 major languages, classes for blacks were taught only in Afrikaans, the language of many of the white South Africans who ruled the nation. These dehumanizing decrees marginalized the 85 percent of South Africans who were black, South Asian, or mixed race.

The white-dominated South African government had its basis in European colonization of Africa in general and the Dutch and British colonization of South Africa in particular. The colonizers pushed the native people off the fertile lands and gave them no say in government. South Africans began to demand equal treatment. "I am not interested in picking up crumbs of compassion," said **Desmond Tutu**, Anglican Archbishop of Cape Town, South Africa, and human rights activist. "I want the full menu of rights."

Challenges to Apartheid In 1964, **Nelson Mandela**, a leader of the **African National Congress (ANC)**, was imprisoned for life for agitating against apartheid. The ANC's primary goals were to end white domination and create a multiracial South Africa. Mandela's imprisonment throughout the 1960s, 1970s, and 1980s inspired a global movement to end apartheid. Black protests in South Africa, which were often peaceful, were crushed violently by the government's forces. South Africa's reputation grew worse in the eyes of the global community. Musicians staged concerts calling for Mandela's release from prison, college students urged universities and corporations to divest from South Africa, and many countries voted for strict economic sanctions against the country. The United Nation expelled South Africa in 1974 because of its apartheid,

As South Africa became a **pariah state** (undesirable state) in the 1980s, its leadership began to take notice. Mandela himself began negotiations with the government in 1986 while still in prison. In 1989, **F. W. de Klerk** became the nation's acting president. He recognized the need for change. Within six months, de Klerk announced Nelson Mandela's release from prison.

Although euphoria was high in the weeks following Mandela's release, apartheid remained the law of the land. Police violence against protesters persisted, which stalled negotiations between Mandela and de Klerk. However, a series of reforms in the 1990s ended apartheid. In 1994, South Africa held its first free elections and rejoined the United Nations. The African National Congress won the majority of the seats in the Parliament. The Government of National Unity was established with ANC members in the majority. On May 10, 1994, Nelson Mandela was sworn in as president, South Africa's first black leader.

Uniting South Africa Immediately the Government of National Unity set up the **Truth and Reconciliation Commission (TRC)**. Unlike the Nuremberg Trials that sought retribution for crimes against humanity committed by Nazis during World War II, the TRC sought to restore and establish an atmosphere of trust in the new multiracial South Africa. The TRC organized a series of 19 public hearings designed to expose the truth of human rights violations that had occurred during apartheid, while at the same time granting amnesty to members of the apartheid regime who agreed to testify.

Source: Wikimedia Commons

Nelson Mandela voted for the first time in 1994, at age 76. In that
year, he was selected as president of South Africa.

Caste Reservation in India The fight for civil rights was also a global
effort as people from different races and social classes began to demand
equality. In India, the 1949 Constitution outlawed discrimination against the
Dalits, also known as untouchables. Pakistan outlawed discrimination against
Dalits in 1953. Before then, many people believed that being touched by a
Dalit required the person who was touched to undergo a cleansing ritual.
People in India and Pakistan continued to discriminate against Dalits until
well into the 21st century.

To open doors of opportunity to social groups or castes that had faced
historical discrimination, the government of India established the **caste
reservation system**. Through this system, the government guaranteed that a
certain percentage of government and public sector jobs and enrollment in
higher education would be set aside for people whose caste had conferred an
underprivileged life.

Human Rights Repression in China

After the economic reforms of the late 1980s and 1990s, China quickly became an economic powerhouse. The economic liberalization, however, was not matched by democratic reforms. The Chinese Communist Party (CCP) ruled the People's Republic with an iron fist. It censored the news industry and controlled what students were taught in primary and secondary schools. Such practices limited freedom of speech and thought. The CCP also required all nonstate organizations and groups to register with the government. International nongovernmental organizations (NGOs) were not free to operate in China unless they were willing to undergo strict regulation. Opposition political parties did not stand a chance in China's governing system, although some debate was allowed in the legislative process. Overall, however, the governing system was designed to thwart all challenges to the CCP's authority.

How could the CCP have such power? The Communists had controlled China since 1949. The government owned and controlled all industries. Government officials had killed or imprisoned those who had spoken out against previous government actions, such as the Great Leap Forward.

Tiananmen Square Chinese intellectuals and students had a history of protesting against their government based on the May Fourth Movement in 1919. In the spring of 1989, pro-democracy activists organized a public event mourning the death of a sympathetic high official. The protesters demanded a chance to speak with Chinese leaders about freedom of the press and other reforms. After the Chinese government refused to meet with the activists, citizens in more than 400 Chinese cities staged sit-ins, refused to attend classes, and began hunger strikes. Hundreds of thousands of students, professors, and urban workers staged a massive protest in Beijing's Tiananmen Square. After seven weeks of protests, the government declared martial law. It sent troops armed with tanks and assault weapons into Beijing. Citizens responded by setting up barricades to block the troops.

On June 4, 1989, the army arrived in Tiananmen Square and attacked the unarmed protesters. The Chinese government claimed that nobody died in Tiananmen Square that day. No mention of the event was included in school texts, and the government blocked all Web sites that discussed the Tiananmen Square incident and human rights abuses in China. However, estimates by Amnesty International, the International Red Cross, and the *New York Times* indicated that anywhere from several hundred to a few thousand civilians were killed. As Chinese officials continue to describe the Tiananmen event as a western conspiracy, Tiananmen mothers are prohibited from openly mourning family members who died in June 1989. The government still imprisons those who commemorate June 4. (Connect: Analyze the methods of protest at Tiananmen Square and the May 4th Movement. See Topic 7.5.)

Minority Rights in China The communist government in China has struggled with the demands of the nation's 55 ethnic minorities. Some prominent examples were calls by Tibetans for more autonomy or independence and the complaints of the Uighur people concerning religious and political discrimination in the northwest province of Xinjiang.

In 2011, some of the Mongolian people in China protested against the high number of Han Chinese who had moved into Inner Mongolia, an autonomous region of northern China, and disrupted their pastoral way of life. The Han are the largest ethnic group in China and worldwide. The Mongolians protested the environmental damage that came with settled agriculture, strip-mining of coal, building of highways, damming of rivers, and overgrazing of land.

Steps toward Environmental Repair

People realized that part of securing their rights in a globalized world is to claim their environmental rights to clean water and air and a sustainable planet with biodiversity. A number of organizations try to identify and achieve goals toward guaranteeing those rights.

Earth Day Starting in 1970, citizens in the United States designated April 22 each year as **Earth Day**, a day for people to focus on environmental awareness. Organizers hoped to highlight recycling, developing alternative energy, eating locally grown and organic foods, and passing antipollution legislation. Today, about 174 countries observe and participate in Earth Day activities with the Earth Day Network, an environmental advocacy group.

Greenpeace Founded in 1971 as an organization to advocate for the environment, **Greenpeace** grew into a multinational agency with offices in more than 55 countries. It battles deforestation, desertification, global warming, the killing of whales, and overfishing. Greenpeace has engaged in lobbying and education, but it became famous for its direct actions, such as confronting whaling boats in the ocean.

Green Belt Movement In 1977, Kenyan activist **Wangari Maathai** founded the **Green Belt Movement**, a direct response to the environmental degradation resulting from the colonial experience. Women in rural Kenya were reporting that streams were drying up and their food supply was unpredictable. The Green Belt Movement helped women work together to plant trees to improve the soil and collect rainwater. More than that, however, Dr. Maathai and the Green Belt Movement helped women see their capacity for making changes through participation in public life rather than leaving decisions to others.

Source: Wikimedia Commons

In 2004, Maathai won the Nobel Prize for Peace, becoming the first African woman to do so. "We are called to assist the Earth to heal her wounds and in the process heal our own," she said.

Steps toward Economic Fairness

To counterbalance the strictly commercial interests of the powerful World Trade Organization (see Topic 9.4), organizations from around the world combined resources to create the World Fair Trade Organization (WFTO) in 1989. Member organizations subscribe to the following 10 principles of fair trade, and the WFTO monitors its members to make sure they follow these principles.

World Fair Trade Organization Principles of Fair Trade
1. Creating Opportunities for Economically Disadvantaged Producers
2. Transparency and Accountability
3. Fair Trading Practices
4. Payment of a Fair Price
5. Ensuring no Child Labor and Forced Labor
6. Commitment to Non Discrimination, Gender Equity and Freedom of Association
7. Ensuring Good Working Conditions
8. Providing Capacity Building
9. Promoting Fair Trade
10. Respect for the Environment

KEY TERMS BY THEME

SOCIETY: Leaders and Thinkers
Nelson Mandela
Negritude Movement
Léopold Sédar Senghor
Pope Francis
Liberation Theology
W. E. B. DuBois
Desmond Tutu
F. W. de Klerk
Wangari Maathai

ENVIRONMENT: Actions
Earth Day
Greenpeace
Green Belt Movement

GOVERNMENT: United Nations
Universal Declaration of Human Rights
United Nations International Children's Emergency Fund (UNICEF)
International Court of Justice

GOVERNMENT: Power and Control
human rights
refugees
Civil Rights Act
Voting Rights Act
apartheid
pass laws
African National Congress (ANC)
pariah state
Truth and Reconciliation Commission (TRC)
Dalits
caste reservation system
Tiananmen Square

MULTIPLE-CHOICE QUESTIONS

Questions 1–3 refer to the following passage.

"To you and all the Commissioners and staff of the TRC [Truth and Reconciliation Commission] we say, on behalf of the nation: Thank you for the work you have done so far! If the pain has often been unbearable and the revelations shocking to all of us, it is because they indeed bring us the beginnings of a common understanding of what happened and a steady restoration of the nation's humanity. The TRC . . . was established by an Act of Parliament with overwhelming support. It is composed of individuals from all backgrounds and persuasions. It has put the spotlight on all of us. . . . [W]e are confident that it has contributed to the work in progress of laying the foundation of the edifice of reconciliation. . . . Reconciliation requires that we work together to defend our democracy and the humanity proclaimed by our Constitution . . . . The wounds of the period of repression and resistance are too deep to have been healed by the TRC alone, however well it has encouraged us along that path. Consequently, the Report that today becomes the property of our nation should be a call to all of us to celebrate and to strengthen what we have done as a nation as we leave our terrible past behind us forever.

Let us celebrate our rich diversity as a people, the knowledge that when the TRC in its wisdom apportions blame, it points at previous state structures; political organisations [organizations]; at institutions and individuals, but never at any community. Nor can any individual so identified claim that their brutal deeds were the result of some character inherent in any community or language group... Above all, we should remember that it was when South Africans of all backgrounds came together for the good of all that we confounded the prophets of doom by bringing an end to this terrible period of our history."

Nelson Mandela, statement on receiving the Truth and
Reconciliation Commission report, October, 1998

1. What is the "terrible past" that the author refers to in the above passage?

   (A) The system of apartheid

   (B) The imprisonment of Mandela

   (C) The Boer Wars

   (D) The Zulu massacre

2. What was the goal of the South African Truth and Reconciliation Commission?

   (A) To prevent the white South Africans from retaking political control

   (B) To establish a new system of governing South Africa

   (C) To establish an atmosphere of multiracial trust

   (D) To punish the South African Boers for implementing apartheid

3. How does the TRC differ from the Nuremberg trials?

(A) The Nuremberg trials sought retribution.

(B) The TRC forgave all apartheid implementers.

(C) The Nuremberg trials prevented future ethnic injustice.

(D) The TRC was international in scope.

SHORT-ANSWER QUESTION

1. Use the passage below to answer all parts of the question that follows.

"I think these may be my last words. My name is Chai Ling. I am twenty-three years old. My home is in Shandong Province. . . . The situation has become so dangerous. . . . If we withdraw from the square, the government will kill us anyway and purge those who supported us. If we let them win, thousands would perish, and seventy years of achievement would be wasted. Who knows how long it would be before the movement could rise again? The government has so many means of repression—execution, isolation.

. . . I believe that democracy is a natural desire. It should guarantee human rights and independence, and foster self-respect—all of which people are entitled to.

Unfortunately, the basic human instinct for independence has been greatly inhibited and degraded among the Chinese. . . . The square is our last stand. If we lose it, China will retreat into another dark age, the people will once again turn against one other, with no real feelings or communication between them. If a nation's own people don't stay and help it to grow and develop, who will? But I will not be there to protect the square because I'm different from the others: my name is on the blacklist. I don't want to die."

Chai Ling, Interview at Tiananmen Square, 1989

(A) Identify ONE historical event that affected Ling's argument in the passage.

(B) Explain how ONE historical situation that supports Ling's argument.

(C) Explain ONE way in which struggles for democracy in China are similar to the struggles for democracy in South Africa.

2. Answer all parts of the question that follows.

(A) Identify ONE way in which access to education affected social structures after 1900.

(B) Explain ONE way in which people challenged old assumptions about race, class, gender, or religion after 1900.

(C) Explain ONE way in which the development of the United Nations affected global integration after 1900.

THINK AS A HISTORIAN: HUMAN RIGHTS IN A DIGITAL AGE

This topic has explored an era of human rights in the context of a shifting world after World War II and decolonization. The Universal Declaration of Human Rights assigns responsibility to each member nation to protect and promote the human rights of its people.

In November 2018, the UN High Commissioner of Human Rights, Michelle Bachelet, addressed students at the University of Geneva in Switzerland, situating human rights in a new context, the digital landscape:

> ". . . [W]e are seeing increasing reports of the use of bots and disinformation campaigns on social media to influence the opinions and choices of individual voters.
>
> Maybe you think this doesn't apply to us: we are too clever to be affected by a bunch of bots. But I am not so sure. It appears the internet is increasingly becoming an arena for sometimes very sophisticated forces for propaganda—whether by movements of violent extremism, or by private actors or even State authorities for political purposes.
>
> In such a context, can there be any doubt that our freedom to think, to believe, to express ideas, to make our own choices and live as we wish, is under threat?
>
> If our thoughts, our ideas and our relationships can be predicted by digital tools, and even altered by the action of digital programmes, then this poses some very challenging and fundamental questions about our future."

Situate human rights in the broader context of the digital landscape. Identify three challenges to promoting and protecting human rights in this context.

REFLECT ON THE TOPIC ESSENTIAL QUESTION

1. In one to three paragraphs, explain how social categories, roles, and practices have changed and stayed the same since 1900.

Globalized Culture

What is interesting is the power and the impact of social media. . . .
So we must try to use social media in a good way.
—Malala Yousafzai, Pakistani human rights activist (born 1997)

Essential Question: How has globalization changed culture since 1900?

At the start of the 20th century, political and social developments led to new directions in the arts. Writers, painters, and musicians developed **modernism,** a rejection of tradition in favor of experimentation and uncertainty. World War I, a global depression, and World War II had focused attention on survival. After World War II, however, citizens of wealthier nations began to develop a **consumer culture**—one in which people tended to focus more on what they bought and owned than on where they lived, what they did for a living, or what they believed. As trade restrictions loosened and new technology became more widely available, people worldwide began sampling arts, popular culture, and ideas from faraway countries. However, few could predict the global connectedness made possible by social media, nor its power to do both good and ill.

Political, Social, and Artistic Changes

Change was everywhere at the start of the 20th century. In just about every main field of human endeavor, new perspectives and discoveries were redefining the way people thought about their social and physical environments. Key political changes also helped shape society.

Political Changes At the beginning of the 20th century, imperialism was creating sometimes fierce competition among nations. Two world wars raised the conflict to the level of deadly force, although allies standing together developed a good working relationship and understanding of one another. The Cold War divided much of the world into camps, stressing differences rather than commonalities. After the Cold War, however, both economic and cultural barriers fell, bringing countries closer together. In some key ways, collaboration gradually replaced competition as nations formed cooperative regional organizations such as the European Union and NAFTA as well as global associations such as the United Nations for conflict resolution and the World Trade Organization to regulate international trade.

Social Changes Along with these changes came social changes. International organizations and collaboration brought people of different cultures into closer contact with one another, just as international exchanges had done in the past. Rights movements—civil rights and women's rights especially—helped bring formerly marginalized voices into the mainstream conversation.

People were also questioning long-held beliefs about humans and their environments. Albert Einstein (1879–1955) and other scientists upended people's understanding of physical reality. Sigmund Freud (1856–1939) probed the invisible inner workings of the human psyche. Jean-Paul Sartre (1905–1980) philosophized that nothing had meaning. Technological developments in communication, transportation, and medical and other scientific knowledge brought change after change—from horses to cars, from telegraph to radio, from antibiotics to vaccines.

Artistic Changes These changes were reflected in the visual arts, literature, and music of the time. Cubism, a style Picasso used in his famous painting *Guernica*, challenged traditional perspective in the visual arts (See Topic 7.4.) Stream-of-consciousness writing by such authors as Marcel Proust (1871–1922) and James Joyce (1882–1941) rebelled against traditional narrative forms, and atonal music such as that composed by Arnold Schoenberg (1874–1951) explored musical expression outside of familiar tonalities, to name just a few examples. Many scholars suggest these expressions were a response to the mechanized, urbanized society widespread in the early 1900s.

An especially vibrant expression of 20th century perspectives was the Harlem Renaissance, a "rebirth" of African American culture as it sought to distance itself from the stereotyped portrayal of African Americans in literature and onstage. During the Harlem Renaissance, writers, poets, musicians, and social activists made Harlem a thriving center of energy for black artistic expression. Jazz emerged and became an international language.

Global Consumer and Popular Culture

In the 1920s, **popular culture**—the culture of everyday people rather than the educated elite—expressed itself through new media: radio and motion pictures. Radio, movies, and later television created a culture shared throughout a nation, and eventually throughout the world. Radio provided a variety of programs, from easy-going comedies to music hours featuring the latest in big band entertainment, and during World War II it played a vital role in national defense in most industrialized nations. Movies provided relief from the anxieties and pressures of the Great Depression while reflecting it in its themes. Charlie Chaplin's "Little Tramp" character of silent movies epitomized the down and out.

Radio and television also ushered in the consumer culture that characterized much of the developed world after World War II. The "free" programming reaching into the homes of millions of people carried with it commercials for the products of sponsors. Industry turned from wartime production to the manufacture of consumer products, and people around the world were eager to buy. In the 1990s, the internet connected people around the globe.

PRIMARY NEWS SOURCE FOR PEOPLE IN THE UNITED STATES

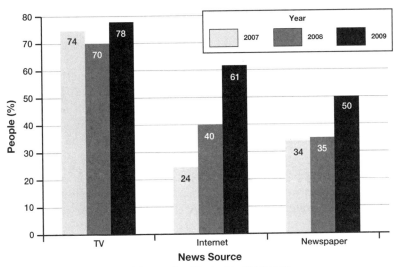

A shift toward online-only sources took place as media outlets set up large online presences.
Source: Pew Research Center for the People.

In the early 21st century, the United States remained the world's most influential culture. Through **Americanization**, people the world over learned more about the United States than Americans learned about the rest of the world. This dominance of the United States created resentment among those who felt that American popular culture diluted their unique cultural identity. In the early 21st century, many people around the world considered American consumer culture to be **throwaway culture**. They objected to the waste and pollution that was part of the focus on newer, cheaper, more disposable products.

English Spreads and Changes Through the influence of the British Empire and through American movies, corporations, and scientific research, English became a second language in much of the world. In the early 21st century, about 300 million people in China were learning English—which was about the same as the population of the United States.

Many English-speaking corporations moved their call centers to India and the Philippines, where there were large numbers of fluent English speakers who would work for relatively low wages. As more people from other countries learned English, they spoke it in new ways. For example, Indian English included the word *prepone*, which meant the opposite of *postpone*.

Global Brands and Commerce As multinational corporations advertised and distributed their products, **global brands** such as Apple, Nike, and Rolex emerged. A company called Interbrand names the top global companies each year based on financial performance, ability to influence consumer choice, and ability to command a premium price. The 2018 winners included Toyota, which sells more cars than any other brand; tech giants Apple, Google, Amazon, Microsoft, and Facebook; and the company that famously announced its desire to "buy the world a Coke" in its 1971 multicultural commercial, Coca-Cola.

Online commerce makes shopping a global affair as well. Sites such as Amazon (in more than 17 countries) and Alibaba (mostly in Asia) make a massive selection of items available. The online auction site eBay operates in 30 different countries. Although their platform is international, these online retailers must pay a variety of sales taxes according to the laws of each country or state in which they sell products. (Connect: Write a paragraph comparing Americanization in the 21st century with assimilation in the 19th century. See Topic 6.3.)

Global Influences on Popular Culture Although the United States is still the dominant culture internationally, influences from other cultures have been welcomed in the United States and elsewhere. For example, Indian musicals made in **Bollywood**, the popular name given to the film industry in Bombay (Mumbai), enjoy popularity worldwide. Bollywood itself is a blend of film styles. India makes more films than any other country.

A style of Japanese hand-drawn animation known as **anime** became hugely influential. In 2016, 60 percent of the world's animated TV shows were based on anime. Anime was introduced to American culture in the 1980s through the movie *Akira*. Television shows in the late 1990s, such as *Pokeman* and *Dragon Ball,* brought anime into the American mainstream.

Reggae music from Jamaica is global in both its origins and its popularity. It emerged in the 1960s, blending New Orleans jazz and rhythm and blues styles with mento, itself a fusion of African rhythms and European elements. It is associated with the Rastafari religion which promotes Pan-Africanism, the connectedness of all Africans whether they live in Africa or in the diaspora. It often blended with musical traditions of other countries as its popularity became global in the 1970s through the music of Bob Marley.

Another style of music that fused a variety of traditions and became a global hit was the Korean music nicknamed **K-pop**. Its artists, who sang in a mixture of Korean and English, became global stars in the early 21st century. Their popularity has also boosted the popularity of other South Korean exports. In fact they are considered so valuable that the government has invested in K-Pop concerts and tours. Internet-based **streaming video** sites such as YouTube and Vimeo helped popularize K-Pop and other musical styles with a global audience.

Social Media and Censorship Facebook, Twitter, Snapchat, and other forms of **social media** changed communication. They can inspire but also manipulate, as attested to by **Malala Yousafzai**, the Pakistani activist and the youngest Nobel Prize laureate. People debated their power for good or ill.

In some countries, such as China, the government banned social media from outside the country. However, China allowed its own forms of social media, including WeChat, Weibo, and YuKu. The government censored any criticism of the Communist Party that appeared on these platforms.

Global Culture in Sports The globalization of popular culture included sports as well. The establishment of the modern **Olympic Games** in 1896 reflected an early sense of internationalism. In 2016, the Olympics in Rio de Janeiro, Brazil, attracted about 3.6 billion viewers worldwide.

Source: Thinkstock

Since Olympic athletes represent their home nations, the games demonstrate the strength of nationalism. However, since the Olympics draws people together from nearly every country in the world, it is also an example of internationalism.

Soccer emerged as the most popular sport in the world, in part because it required so little equipment that it could be played almost anywhere. The **World Cup** soccer competition rivaled the Olympics as a global event. Basketball also became a global game, and players such as Michael Jordan and LeBron James became internationally known. In 2014, the National Basketball Association (NBA) included players from 30 countries or territories. In 2017, reporters from 35 countries covered the NBA Finals. In 2018, 27 percent of major league baseball players were foreign-born, from 21 different countries.

As sports became more popular globally, they also became more available to women. Some Muslim female athletes—including fencers, weightlifters, beach volleyball players, hockey players, and figure skaters—competed while wearing hijab, known in English as a headscarf. They adapted athletic wear so they could compete while following traditional Muslim practices regarding female modesty in clothing. Hajar Abulfazi, a soccer player from Afghanistan, explained that she wore the hijab to "show the next generation and their parents how Afghan women and girls can maintain respect for religion and culture while pursuing sports achievements."

Global Culture and Religion

Globalization promoted new religious developments. In the 1970s, former Beatles band member George Harrison released a song containing the words of a Hindu mantra, or sacred utterance. This launched the popularity of the **Hari Krishna** movement, which was based on traditional Hindu scriptures. It quickly gained popularity in the United States and Europe. In what some called **New Age** religions, forms of Buddhism, shamanism, Sufism, and other religious traditions were revived and adapted for a largely Western audience.

In China in the 1990s, **Falun Gong,** a movement based on Buddhist and Daoist traditions, gained popularity. Although the communist government allowed the movement at first, Chinese authorities began to restrict it in 1999. The suppression prompted international protests against the Chinese regime for human rights abuses.

In the early 21st century, most people around the world identified with some form of religion. However, an increasing number of younger people in many countries identified as **nonbelievers**. They were not necessarily atheists (people who do not believe in any god) or agnostics (people who believe that it may not be possible to know if God exists). Most were simply not affiliated with any religious institution.

KEY TERMS BY THEME

SOCIETY: Belief Systems
Hari Krishna
New Age
Falun Gong
nonbelievers

CULTURE: Sports
Olympic Games
World Cup

CULTURE: Arts
consumer culture
modernism
popular culture
Bollywood
anime
reggae
K-pop

SOCIETY: Influences
Americanization
Malala Yousafzai
throwaway culture

TECHNOLOGY: Commerce and Entertainment
global brands
streaming video
online commerce
social media

MULTIPLE-CHOICE QUESTIONS

Questions 1-3 refer to the following two sources:

Source A

"The world of the 20th Century, if it is to come to life in any nobility of health and vigor, must be to a significant degree an American Century. . . . Once we cease to distract ourselves with lifeless arguments about isolationism, we shall be amazed to discover that there is already an immense American internationalism. American jazz, Hollywood movies, American slang, American machines and patented products, are in fact the only things that every community in the world, from Zanzibar to Hamburg, recognizes in common."

Henry Luce, founder of *Time* and *Life* magazines, "The American Century," *Life Magazine*, February 17, 1941

Source B

McDonald's Menu Items from Countries Around the World (2013)	
Menu Item	**Country**
McFalafel	Egypt
McNoodles	Austria
Ebi Filet-O-Shrimp Burger	Japan
McCurry Pan	India
Mashed Potato Burger	China
Pineapple Oreo McFlurry	Colombia

1. In Source A, what was the historical context that caused Henry Luce to advocate for the United States to take a worldwide leadership position and bring about an "American century"?

(A) Great Britain had no powerful country as an ally in its war against Germany when Luce wrote this.

(B) America had isolated itself economically from the rest of the world since 1917.

(C) The United States had entered World War I as soon as Britain and Germany began fighting.

(D) American culture, including magazines, had little appeal outside the United States.

2. In Source B, which of the following conclusions is best supported by the evidence in the chart?

(A) McDonald's has exactly the same menu items in every restaurant around the globe.

(B) Consumers of McDonald's menu items are not familiar with typical McDonald brand names.

(C) McDonald's menu items have been globalized but reflect local tastes and preferences.

(D) People in China do not like McDonald's Quarter Pounder hamburgers.

3. Based on both sources, it can be concluded that from the mid-20th century to the early 21st century

(A) arts, entertainment, and popular culture continued to reflect the influence of a globalized society

(B) global conflict was the most significant cause of globalization

(C) localized culture was mostly ignored because of globalized culture

(D) only American culture underwent globalization during this period

SHORT-ANSWER QUESTIONS

1. Use the passage below to answer all parts of the question that follows.

"Western leaders exploited the lure of their popular culture during the Cold War. They created radio and television stations such as Radio Free Europe/Radio Liberty to broadcast as much popular culture material into the Soviet bloc as could be programmed. This programming was done to achieve the very purpose the Soviets accused it of: to westernize the values of those who watched or listened to it. . . .

In using American pop culture as a tool of the Cold War, Western policymakers were exploiting what political scientist Joseph Nye has referred to as 'soft power.' The notion of soft power refers to cultural, social, intellectual, and ideological ideas, values, attitudes, and behaviors that influence human life. Nye distinguishes these soft forms of power from 'hard power,' which is typically associated with the use of violent, coercive tools of social action like armies and economic sanctions. Soft power is a significant factor in global politics, Nye argues. . . . As such, it provides a way for one people—in the case of the Cold War, people in the political West—to change the attitudes and behaviors of other cultures without resorting to war or other forms of coercion."

Lane Crothers, *Globalization and American Popular Culture*, 2013

(A) Identify ONE historical situation, other than the one illustrated in the passage, that supports Crothers's argument.

(B) Explain how Crothers's argument in the passage affects international politics today.

(C) Explain ONE way in which globalization during the Cold War differs from globalization in the late 20th century to the present.

2. **Answer all parts of the question that follows.**

(A) Identify ONE way in which a globalized society influenced entertainment.

(B) Explain ONE way in which social changes of the 20th century led to changes in the arts.

(C) Explain ONE way in which consumer culture transcended national borders in the late 20th century.

 THINK AS A HISTORIAN: COMPARE PERIODS OF GLOBALIZATION

The globalization that began in about 1960 was actually the second wave of globalization. The first occurred between the years 1870 and 1914, engendered by the Industrial Revolution and the search for new markets and brought to a halt by the beginning of World War I.

Explain how the globalization that began in 1960 is similar to and different from that which began in about 1870 and ended in 1914. Consider the following questions as you explain the broader historical context for each.

1. How reciprocal were the exchanges?

2. Who led the way?

3. What motives drove the globalization?

4. What role do knowledge economies play?

REFLECT ON THE TOPIC ESSENTIAL QUESTION

1. In one to three paragraphs, explain how globalization has changed culture since 1900.

Resistance to Globalization

The whole of the global economy is based on supplying the cravings of two percent of the world's population.

—Bill Bryson, nonfiction writer (born 1951)

Essential Question: What were the various responses to globalization from 1900 to the present?

While globalization of culture has in many ways raised awareness and appreciation of cultural diversity, the economics of globalization have led to serious concerns. Resistance to globalization has come from non-governmental and governmental sources. A network of opponents to economic globalization promotes equal distribution of economic resources, challenging the lopsided economy described above by author Bill Bryson. Participants contend that corporations and global financial institutions, such as the **International Monetary Fund (IMF)** and the World Trade Organization (WTO) work to maximize profit and sacrifice safety and labor conditions, environmental conservation needs, and national independence.

Some countries, such as North Korea, have resisted economic and cultural globalization. Others, such as Saudi Arabia and China, have resisted cultural globalization, particularly through controlling the internet. These countries want goods and money to flow freely among nations, but they are more restrictive of how people and ideas cross borders.

The Roots of Globalization and Anti-Globalization

Globalization affected the relationships among and within nations. After World War II, several organizations contributed to the growth of a global economy. The General Agreement on Tariffs and Trade (GATT), the European Economic Union, Mercosur (in South America), and the Association of Southeast Asian Nations (ASEAN) all formed between 1947 and the early 1990s. These organizations were meant to help economies and expand prosperity. Falling tariff rates eased the movement of goods across national borders.

In 1995, the World Trade Organization (WTO) took over GATT's operations. The WTO makes rules for more than 90 percent of international trade. The rules and its closed board meetings led people to believe that the WTO did not care for their welfare. (Connect: Compare the economic practices of the 17th century to globalization in the 20th and 21st centuries. See Topic 4.5.)

The **"Battle of Seattle"** In 1999, protests erupted at a WTO conference in Seattle. The WTO had planned a round of trade negotiations for the new millennium. Then more than 40,000 protesters arrived. Special interest groups, including labor unions, family farmers, student groups, and environmentalists shut down the WTO's meeting and drew global attention to the issues of the new global economy. Anti-WTO demonstrations took place in dozens of other countries as well.

Many people consider the Seattle protests to be the beginning of the anti-globalization movement. They were also one of the first social movements to be coordinated through the internet. However, the WTO itself remained powerful. China joined in 2001, increasing the group's territorial and economic reach.

Source: WTO protestors (1999)

The "Sea Turtle" protesters outside the 1999 World Trade Organization Conference in Seattle, Washington.

Why Resist Globalization?

Why did people protest globalization when it made goods and services more freely available? Opponents had different reasons. Many of them centered on the idea that consumers who buy products and services with a few clicks often have no idea who creates those products and services and what the short-term and long-term costs really are. A series of scandals in different parts of the world showed some of the hazards of globalization. Working conditions are especially problematic

- Much of the chocolate that consumers bought in the early 21st century had its origins in **child labor** in West Africa. The largest chocolate companies missed deadlines in 2005, 2008, and 2010 to make sure their suppliers did not use child laborers. In 2015, the U.S. Department of Labor estimated that more than 2 million children took part in dangerous labor in the cocoa-growing regions of the world.

- Working conditions in Western nations could also be harsh. In 2019, employees of **Amazon**'s warehouses described such intense pressure to fulfill orders that workers risked being fired if they took a bathroom break. At the time, Amazon employed more than 600,000 people and another 100,000 at holiday time, though not all of them worked in warehouses.

- In 2013, the collapse of the **Rana Plaza factory**, an eight-story building in Dhaka, Bangladesh, shocked the world. More than 1,000 people died and another 2,500 suffered injuries. Most of the dead and injured were female garment workers who made clothing for Western companies. **Muhammad Yunus**, a Bangladeshi who won the Nobel Prize for Peace, called the disaster "a symbol of our failure as a nation." He suggested that companies worldwide set an international minimum wage.

Source: Wikimedia Commons

The Rana Plaza collapse is considered the deadliest structural failure accident in modern human history, and therefore also the deadliest garment-factory disaster in history.

Environmental Damage Critics of globalization pointed out that the fuel involved in shipping products vast distances increased the amount of greenhouse gases in the environment, thus worsening the climate emergency. Also, in the early 21st century, Brazil cut down thousands of square miles of rainforest each year to make way for cattle farms. The meat was one of the country's most valuable exports.

Proponents of globalization argue that it can help the environment. They point out that Costa Rica and other nations have developed **ecotourism** industries that make profits while showing off the country's natural wonders.

Threats to National Sovereignty Many liberal groups believe that globalization often harms children, workers, and the environment. However, many conservative groups also distrust globalization.

In 2016, 52 percent of British voters agreed to leave the European Union, an international political and economic organization of 28 countries. This British exit was nicknamed **Brexit**. Britain was a founding member of the EU in 1993, but conservative British politicians argued that the EU interfered with Britain's right to govern itself. Many Brexit proponents contended that the EU required Britain to accept too many immigrants.

Negotiations to leave the EU broke down when British prime minister **Theresa May** was unable to craft a deal that was acceptable to her own political party, let alone to the other 27 nations in the EU. May resigned in 2019. Brexit critics believed that leaving the EU would be economically disastrous for Britain, an island nation that depended on imports.

Economic Resistance

Critics of globalization believe that international agreements and institutions can destroy small local businesses. Large corporations could use the International Monetary Fund (IMF) and the WTO to achieve their goals, but local individuals and businesses could not. For example, many small businesses and individuals could not cross state lines or national borders. They could not extract the natural resources they needed or use the wide variety of labor sources that big corporations and transnational businesses used. In an attempt to combat globalization, some businesses, especially restaurants, have insisted on providing their customers locally grown or made products.

Globalization critics also distrusted the World Bank (see Topic 9.8), an international organization affiliated with the United Nations. The bank's mission is to improve the economic development of member states. In 1988, about 20,000 people protested meetings of the IMF and the World Bank in West Berlin. Protesters insisted that these agencies favored richer nations over poorer ones. In 2001 and 2002, anti-IMF and anti-World Bank protests took place in 23 countries, including many of the world's poorest nations. In 2014, the World Bank made reforms to its structure and governance, but critics maintained that the world's richest nations controlled the bank.

What Measures Do Anti-Globalists Favor? The anti-globalization movement has grown into a social movement as well. Its followers tend to focus on these issues:

- **Human rights**, which are basic freedoms that every person has, such as freedom from slavery and freedom to express opinions

- **Fair trade**, which is a system that ensures the person who provided the good or service receives a reasonable payment for it
- **Sustainable development**, which means business ventures that allow people and companies to make a profit without preventing future generations from meeting their own needs
- **Debt relief** or **debt restructuring** so that countries that owe huge sums to the IMF do not have to risk economic breakdown

Anti-Globalization and Social Media

Anti-globalization activists have used the internet to perpetuate and spread their ideas in nearly every country on Earth. However, access to global communication through social media outlets has met resistance in some countries. In 2009, more than 1,000 rioters clashed with police in the city of Urumqi, China. The unrest resulted from tensions between members of the Han ethnicity and members of the **Uighur** ethnicity, most of whom are Muslim. Chinese authorities blamed the riots on the growth of social unrest based on Twitter and Facebook and banned both platforms. The government introduced a new platform called **Weibo** as a substitute. It could stream incoming posts while tracking and blocking "sensitive" content. Weibo has become a vehicle of negotiation between the Chinese government and its citizens.

In some other countries, governments allow social media platforms but influence or control their content. For example, critics contend that Saudi Arabian officials use Twitter and Facebook to harass and intimidate citizens. "If the same tools we joined for our liberation are being used to oppress us and undermine us, and used to spread fake news and hate, I'm out of these platforms," explained **Manal al-Sharif**, a women's rights activist.

In some parts of the world, resistance to participating in an interconnected society persists. The coming together of economies and cultures threatens some people's and governments' sense of autonomy and identity.

KEY TERMS BY THEME

SOCIETY: Leaders and Thinkers
Muhammad Yunus
Theresa May
Manal al-Sharif

SOCIETY: Issues and Problems
child labor
Rana Plaza factory

ecotourism
human rights
fair trade
sustainable development
debt relief
debt restructuring

GOVERNMENT: Politics
Brexit
Uighur

TECHNOLOGY: E-Commerce and Social Media
Amazon
Weibo

MULTIPLE-CHOICE QUESTIONS

Questions 1 to 3 refer to the image below.

Source: Wikimedia Commons
Protesters at a meeting of the World Trade Organization (WTO), Seattle, Washington (1999).

1. Which of the following 20th-century developments contributed most directly to the reaction shown in the photograph?
   (A) Unprecedented population growth
   (B) Rising economic and cultural globalization
   (C) Increasing risk of nuclear war
   (D) The emergence of fascism

2. The protesters shown in the picture focused on World Trade Organization policies they said led to
   (A) greater decentralization of political power
   (B) higher levels of immigration into developed countries
   (C) weaker environmental protections
   (D) lower agricultural production in developing countries

3. A historian would most likely use the photograph as evidence of which of the following trends in the late 20th century?
   (A) Increasing public concern about human impact on the environment
   (B) The declining influence of unions and the labor movement
   (C) The global dominance of American media and popular culture
   (D) Growing acceptance of free-market policies

1. **Use the passage below to answer all parts of the question that follows.**

"Critique of, and resistance to, the spread of consumer culture is as old as the emergence of consumer culture in the 18th century. Systematic critique of the institutional bases of consumer culture have been offered by social theorists that highlight the alienating dehumanizing effects of materialism, while others have commented on the envy, possessiveness, and non-generosity . . . consumer culture sometimes entails. . . .

Religious, environmentalist, nationalist, and anti-corporate critiques have emerged with considerable vigor. Many of these forms of resistance appear to be motivated by a global sense of anxiety about the risk to life and happiness provoked by the globalization of consumer culture itself. In one global study of global brands, the authors found 'Thirteen percent of consumers are skeptical that transnational companies deliver higher quality goods. They dislike brands that preach American values and don't trust global companies to behave responsibly. Their brand preferences indicate that they try to avoid doing business with transnational firms.'"

Jagdish Sheth and Naresh Maholtra, "Global Consumer
Culture" in Encyclopedia of International Marketing

(A) Identify ONE thinker from the 18th and 19th centuries who might have views consumer culture as described in the passage.

(B) Explain ONE reason some consumers avoid transnational firms, according to the authors.

(C) Explain ONE way in which globalization increased despite growing resistance in the late 20th century.

2. **Answer all parts of the question that follows.**

(A) Identify ONE example of a state government that resisted globalization after 1900.

(B) Explain ONE social reason for resistance to globalization after 1990.

(C) Explain ONE reason for resistance to global financial institutions after 1990.

THINK AS A HISTORIAN: COMPARE POINTS OF VIEW

Attitudes toward globalization depend in large part on perspective, or point of view.

Read the following two statements on globalization. Explain in your own words what each one means. Then describe the point of view of each author and explain the significance of that point of view in evaluating the statement as a source.

1. "We are moving toward a global economy. One way of approaching that is to pull the covers over your head. Another is to say: It may be more complicated—but that's the world I am going to live in, I might as well be good at it."

   —Phil Condit, Former Chairman and CEO of
   Boeing, 1999

2. "What's going on in this country? Unions stand against those trends. We've got to somehow insulate the robust American economy from this global economy that seems to want to devour our standard of living."

   —James P. Hoffa, General President of
   the Teamsters Union, 1998

REFLECT ON THE TOPIC ESSENTIAL QUESTION

1. In one to three paragraphs, explain the various responses to globalization from 1900 to the present.

9.8

Institutions Developing in a Globalized World

We have actively sought and are actively seeking to make the United Nations an effective instrument of international cooperation.

—Dean Acheson, U.S. diplomat, (1893–1971)

Essential Question: How did globalization change international interactions between states after 1900?

In an era of increasing globalization, people formed international organizations to promote useful working relationships among nations. Dean Acheson, a U.S. secretary of state, described how the mission of the United Nations (UN) fit with this goal of maintaining world peace and making international cooperation easier. Working through agencies such as the IMF (International Monetary Fund) and the World Bank, the UN provides technical advice and loans to developing nations. Other international organizations and treaties, such as the World Trade Organization (WTO) and the General Agreement on Tariffs and Trade (GATT), promote free trade worldwide. However, the United Nations was born of the devastation of world wars and preventing conflict was its primary goal.

The United Nations: A Structure for Peace

Despite ideological differences, the Allies shared a commitment to preventing conflicts from escalating into war. In 1943, representatives of the United States, Great Britain, the Soviet Union, and China discussed the idea of the United Nations. The UN was born on October 24, 1945, a day still honored as United Nations Day. At its founding, there were 51 member states. By 2019, that number had grown to 193.

League of Nations vs. United Nations Countries had tried to create a similar international organization previously. In 1920, at the end of World War I, the Allied powers created the League of Nations. (See Topic 7.3.) Its purpose was to resolve international disputes and prevent another world war. However, the United States never joined the League. Some Americans believed that doing so would undercut U.S. authority. The League disbanded after it failed to prevent World War II. Countries hoped that a new, more powerful organization would help keep the peace. This time around, all the major powers realized they would need to belong for the organization to have any chance of success.

Assemblies of the United Nations

Within the UN, six main bodies implement its work.

- The **General Assembly** is the only UN body in which all members have representation. It decides important questions on peace and security, admission of new members, and budget. To make a decision, a two-thirds majority of those present and voting must agree. Each member nation has one vote.

- The **Security Council** acts on issues the General Assembly debates. It may even use military force against a country accused of violating UN principles. The Security Council has five permanent members, the leading Allies of World War II: the United States, France, Great Britain, Russia, and China. It elects 10 other members on a rotating basis. Each permanent members has veto power in the Security Council. Granting veto power to these five nations was controversial in 1945. Other nations resented giving them so much power. Conflicts among these five often prevented the UN from taking action to confront problems.

- The **Secretariat** is the UN's administrative arm. The secretary general leads and influences the entire organization. He or she usually comes from a small, neutral nation so one of the more powerful countries cannot have an outsize influence on what the UN does. All five permanent members of the Security Council must approve the secretary general's selection. Staffers of the Secretariat must take an oath of loyalty to the UN and are not allowed to receive instructions from their home countries.

- The **International Court of Justice** settles disputes countries bring to it about international law. The court has no power to enforce its decisions, but the Security Council may make recommendations or take action in response to a judgment. Most countries obey the court's decisions.

- The **Economic and Social Council** is the largest and most complex part of the UN. It directs economic, social, humanitarian, and cultural activities. In the early 21st century, the council promoted green energy and looked for ways to raise people's wages in poorer countries.

- The **Trusteeship Council** supervised the governments of trust territories, including land that is now Israel, Papua New Guinea, and Nauru. The council's mission was to help those areas become self-governing and independent. The last trust territory, Palau, became independent in 1994. Since then, the council has suspended its operations. Some people have suggested that the council should become trustees of the seafloor or of outer space.

The UN and Human Rights

One of the goals of the United Nations was the promotion of human rights. The UN adopted the **Universal Declaration of Human Rights** in 1948. It included several basic rights and freedoms:

- freedom from slavery, torture, and degrading punishment
- equality before the law
- the right to a nationality
- the right to own property, either individually or with others
- freedom of thought, conscience, religion, opinion, and expression
- equal pay for equal work
- the right to rest and to enjoy paid holidays
- equal rights for children born within and outside of marriage
- the right to adequate food, clothing, shelter, health care, and education

The declaration was a milestone achievement. Individuals from different countries, cultures, and legal traditions came together to draft a document that set standards for all governments and all people. People have translated the declaration into more than 500 languages. Since 1948, the UN has investigated abuses of human rights, such as genocide, war crimes, government oppression, and crimes against women.

Keeping the Peace

Since the end of World War II, the United Nations has been well known for its **peacekeeping** actions. Of primary importance is prevention through diplomacy. The UN sends special envoys to help resolve problems peacefully, mindful that it was formed to prevent "the scourge of war."

The organization has also frequently sent peacekeeping forces, consisting of civilians, police, and troops from member countries, to try to ease tensions in trouble spots. The first peacekeeping mission was related to the 1948 Arab-Israeli conflict in Palestine. After that, UN peacekeepers served in the Congo, Lebanon, East Timor, and the Balkans.

Expansion in the 1990s In 1988, the UN had only five active peacekeeping operations. By 1993, it had 28. Individual countries supplied soldiers to form UN peacekeeping forces. They came from dozens of countries—including Canada, Venezuela, Ukraine, Egypt, and Bangladesh. The soldiers were usually lightly armed and instructed to return fire only if attacked.

In the 1990s, the United Nations sent peacekeeping missions to hotspots in Africa, Central America, the Caribbean, and Southeast Asia. In Africa, UN troops kept peace while Namibia changed from a South African colony to an independent state. Peacekeeping troops helped end devastating civil wars in

Mozambique, El Salvador, and Cambodia. In Haiti, they maintained peace while a democratic government replaced a military dictatorship.

Some efforts failed. In 1994, UN peacekeepers could not prevent massacres in Rwanda. In 1995, UN forces withdrew from Somalia while a civil war raged there. The struggle to bring order to Bosnia in the former Yugoslavia took years and had mixed results. As a UN officer in Bosnia observed, "It's much easier to come in and keep peace when there's some peace around."

Source: Wikimedia Commons

UN peacekeepers at their headquarters in Kinshasa, Democratic Republic of the Congo, where violent conflicts continue to break out following a civil war (1997–2003) that killed 5 million.

Challenges for Peacekeeping Missions One problem faced by UN peacekeepers has been their slow response. By the time countries agree on the UN mission and send forces, the war might have grown and become hard to control. A second problem happens when people expect the peacekeeping troops to stop the fighting instead of simply monitoring a truce, running free elections, and providing supplies to civilian populations. By 2019, the United Nations was involved in fewer but larger peacekeeping missions. The number of missions had dropped to 15, but the number of troops involved had increased.

Number of UN Peacekeepers Deployed	
Year	Number
2000	30,000
2007	80,000
2014	95,000
2019	102,000

Source: Global Peace Operations Review.

Other UN Priorities

In addition to assemblies and peacekeeping, the UN has other missions.

Protecting Refugees The UN also protects refugees. In times of war, famine, and natural disasters, people often flee their country and seek refuge in a safer location. Working through partners such as NGOs (nongovernmental organizations) and the agency of UNHCR (United Nations High Commissioner for Refugees), the UN provides food, medicine, and temporary shelter. Among the earliest refugees the UN helped were Palestinians who fled the disorder following the UN partition of Palestine to create the state of Israel in 1948. In 2019, the UN helped refugees who fled Venezuela and Myanmar.

Feeding the Hungry In 1961, the UN established its **World Food Program (WFP)** to provide food aid. Its first missions were in Iran, Thailand, and Algeria in 1962. Since its founding, the WFP has fed more than 1.4 billion people, many of whom were affected by natural disasters or political unrest.

Supporting Education, Science, and Culture Fighting in World War II destroyed schools, libraries, and museums in many European countries. In 1945, the UN created the **United Nations Educational, Scientific, and Cultural Organization (UNESCO)**. After repairing war damage, UNESCO began to focus on developing literacy, extending free education, and protecting cultural and environmental sites by designating them World Heritage Sites. The United Kingdom, Singapore, Israel, and the United States have all left UNESCO in disputes over politics and priorities. Although the UK and Singapore rejoined the organization, as of 2019 the United States had not.

Other UN Missions The UN also created the World Health Organization, which improves human health by controlling epidemics and providing vaccines. The United Nations Children's Fund (UNICEF) was created to help children after World War II. After that, the fund provided aid to children in the developing world and at disaster sites. The UN program **Human Rights Watch (HRW)** has monitored human rights abuses in 100 countries. HRW uses the Universal Declaration of Human Rights as its guide and advocates for policies that prevent abuses.

The Global Goals In 2015, the UN General Assembly set 17 goals to accomplish by 2030. These included wiping out hunger and poverty, achieving gender equality, ensuring clean water and sanitation for all, and fighting climate change. On this project, the UN worked with NGOs, including the Bill and Melinda Gates Foundation. (Connect: Evaluate the success of the United Nations in handling political crises compared to its success in dealing with other priorities. See Topic 8.5.)

International Financial NGOs

Several NGOs have worked closely with the United Nations on economic issues. Each NGO was independent and caused controversy.

The World Bank Created in 1944, the **World Bank** fought poverty by providing loans to countries. It first focused on dams and roads. Later it expanded its mission to social projects, such as education and disease prevention. Critics charged that the World Bank often ignored how its projects damaged the environment and local culture. For example, a dam might permanently flood many farms. A highway might promote growth, but the resulting profits might all go to investors overseas rather than people living in the region.

The International Monetary Fund (IMF) Created in 1945, the **International Monetary Fund (IMF)** was designed to help a country's economy by promoting stable currency exchange rates. It focused on making short-term loans and providing economic advice to countries. Some economists argued that conditions on IMF loans failed to take into account each country's individual needs. Large, wealthy nations influenced the IMF. It acted on their behalf, critics insisted, even while it claimed to help developing nations.

The IMF and the World Bank worked together to create Pathways for Peace in 2018. This report described how countries could work together to prevent violent conflicts.

NGOs Separate from the UN

Although the UN is well funded and powerful, other NGOs also help maintain world peace and improve communication among countries during a time of globalization. For example, the **International Peace Bureau** was founded in 1891 and won the Nobel Prize for Peace in 1910. It began working for nuclear disarmament in the 1980s. It also lobbied governments to reduce military spending. By 2019, it had 300 member organizations in 70 countries. The chart on the next page lists other international organizations committed to peace and cooperation.

Source: Guinea Red Cross Volunteers
Red Cross volunteers in Guinea go door to door with information about Ebola.

International Organizations for Peace and Cooperation

Organization	Mission
Center for International Humanitarian Cooperation (established 1992)	Promotes healing and peace in countries affected by natural disasters, armed conflicts, and ethnic violence
International Committee of the Red Cross (established 1863)	Responds quickly and efficiently to help people affected by armed conflict and disasters in conflict zones
Institute of International Humanitarian Affairs (Fordham University) (established 2001)	Trains and educates current and future aid workers at local, regional, national, and international levels
International Development Association (part of World Bank) (established 1960)	Supports a range of development activities, such as primary education, basic health services, clean water and sanitation, agriculture, business climate improvements, infrastructure, and institutional reforms.
International Organization for Migration (established 1951 and became a UN-related organization in 2018)	Mandated to help European governments identify resettlement countries for the estimated 11 million people uprooted by World War II, when it arranged transport for nearly a million migrants during the 1950s. Provides service and advice to governments and migrants.
The Organization for Economic Co-operation and Development (established 1961)	Shapes policies that foster prosperity, equality, opportunity and well-being

---

KEY TERMS BY THEME

GOVERNMENT: Parts of the United Nations
General Assembly
Security Council
Secretariat
secretary-general
International Court of Justice
Economic and Social Council
Trusteeship Council

ECONOMICS: International Organizations
World Bank
International Monetary Foundation (IMF)

SOCIETY: International Cooperation
Universal Declaration of Human Rights
peacekeeping action
World Food Program (WFP)
United Nations Educational, Scientific, and Cultural Organization (UNESCO)
Human Rights Watch (HRW)
International Peace Bureau

MULTIPLE-CHOICE QUESTIONS

Questions 1 to 3 refer to the passage below.

"WE THE PEOPLES OF THE UNITED NATIONS DETERMINED

- to save succeeding generations from the scourge of war, which twice in our life-time has brought untold sorrow to mankind, and

- to reaffirm faith in fundamental human rights, in the dignity and worth of the human person, in the equal rights of men and women and of nations large and small, and

- to establish conditions under which justice and respect for the obligations arising from treaties and other sources of international law can be maintained, and

- to promote social progress and better standards of life in larger freedom,

AND FOR THESE ENDS

- to practice tolerance and live together in peace with one another as good neighbors, and

- to unite our strength to maintain international peace and security, and

- to ensure, by the acceptance of principles and the institution of methods, that armed force shall not be used, save in the common interest, and

- to employ international machinery for the promotion of the economic and social advancement of all peoples"

Preamble to the United Nations Charter, 1945

1. Which best describes the historical context in which the United Nations was founded?
   (A) The impact of trench warfare in World War I
   (B) The success of the League of Nations
   (C) The long-running U.S.-Soviet nuclear arms race
   (D) The causes and effects of both World War I and World War II

2. Which is the best example of the United Nations using its power as described in the preamble?
   (A) Negotiating an end to World War II
   (B) Sending peace-keeping missions to several different countries
   (C) Helping the United States exit the Vietnam War
   (D) Preventing the Cold War from spreading

3. Which of the following statements is best supported by the Preamble to the United Nations Charter?

(A) The United Nations should have supreme authority over all the governments of the world.

(B) The United Nations was formed to maintain world peace and facilitate international cooperation.

(C) The United Nations works to prevent war between members only and does not get involved in economic or social issues.

(D) The United Nations does not promote democracy or democratic values in the world.

SHORT-ANSWER QUESTION

1. **Use the passage below to answer all parts of the question that follows.**

"Whatever the international tensions and the UN shortcomings, the existence of the United Nations as an institution for all countries created a sense of being part of a world-wide community and helped develop a global consciousness. For developing countries, the United Nations provided a political arena and spearheaded their struggle for decolonization and political emancipation, engendering a feeling of empowerment and importance, and providing a means of participating on the world stage as equals. . . .

The norms and standards set by the United Nations specialized agencies have enriched life, both nationally and internationally. The smaller and more technical specialized agencies like the International Telecommunication Union (ITU), the World Meteorological Organization (WMO), the International Civil Aviation Organization (ICAO), the Universal Postal Union (UPU), etc. have, through their standards and regulatory regimes, helped in maintaining international order in such diverse areas as meteorology, communications, aviation, etc. Successive global conferences convened by United Nations organizations have helped to identify and focus global attention on new problems relating to such issues as environment, population, energy, science and technology, food and nutrition and women's place and role in society and social development in general."

South Centre, *For a Strong and Democratic United Nations:
A South Perspective on UN Reform*, 1997

(A) Identify ONE argument in the passage.

(B) Explain ONE limitation of the argument selected in the previous question.

(C) Explain ONE historical situation in the late 20th century in which the development of the United Nations affected global relations.

2. **Answer all parts of the question that follows.**

(A) Identify ONE way in which international interactions affected human rights issues in the late 20th century.

(B) Identify ONE way in which globalization changed international interactions in the late 20th century.

(C) Explain ONE way in which an international organization, other than the UN, furthered international cooperation in maintaining world peace in the late 20th century.

 THINK AS A HISTORIAN: COMPARE TWO ARGUMENTS ON THE UNITED NATIONS

Is the United Nations still relevant? That was the question posed in 2006 by the University of Pennsylvania Law Review as part of its Debate series. Two law professors participated in the written debate. Excerpts from their conflicting answers to that question appear below.

Read the following two statements on the United Nations. Explain in your own words the gist of each one. Then compare the arguments and write a few sentences summarizing the differences between them.

"The UN offers . . . the possibility for wide, and sometimes even universal, participation in the creation of the legal rules that regulate international affairs. Every state is represented at the UN and can be included in the processes of international lawmaking. While it is true that bilateral or regional agreements may result in deeper levels of commitment—greater synergies of interests are likely to be found amongst smaller numbers of states—the challenges and dangers the global community faces today demand the near universal participation in legal regimes made most possible through the UN. Whether international law seeks to regulate the Internet, respond to global warming, combat international terrorism, or address pandemic diseases, the exclusion or defection of only a small number of states may well render the broader enterprise of legalization worthless. A handful of serious polluters, a few safe havens for terrorists, or even one epicenter of disease outbreak may well undermine an otherwise global legal regime. The UN, with its broad reach, its all-encompassing membership, and its agenda-setting potential may well be the best (and perhaps the only) hope for developing universal legal regimes that can effectively respond to these new challenges."

William Burke-White, University of Pennsylvania Law School

"Professor Burke-White points to various global problems—WMD [weapons of mass destruction] proliferation, terrorism, infectious disease, and the like. He does not claim that perfect solutions may be found for these problems . . . He argues only that no international institution can take certain kinds of lawmaking steps regarding these issues better than the UN. He shows that the UN has taken many such lawmaking steps and that proponents hope that such steps will lead to reducing the net harm produced by these problems. He thus concludes that the UN is "urgently needed." Nowhere does he actually demonstrate that these lawmaking steps actually reduce the net harm produced by the problems. Indeed, if one looks at the actual examples cited by Professor Burke-White, it seems clear that the UN has not had a positive effect at all.

"Despite an impressive outpouring of words, the UN has done little effectively to address the problems mentioned by Professor Burke-White—like terrorism prevention, global climate change, and proliferation of weapons of mass destruction—and in some ways has even exacerbated them. The UN has done nothing to prevent North Korea from obtaining nuclear weapons, and it seems highly unlikely that the UN will do anything effective to prevent Iran from completing its plans to obtain such weapons. The UN has played a useful role in collecting some kinds of information about Al Qaeda, but has actually undermined other antiterror efforts."

Abraham Bell, Lecturer, Bar-Ilan University Faculty
of Law and Visiting Professor, Fordham Law School

REFLECT ON THE TOPIC ESSENTIAL QUESTION

1. In one to three paragraphs, explain how globalization changed interactions between states after 1900.

9.9

Continuity and Change in a Globalized World

Today, no country can ever truly cut itself off from the global media or from external sources of information; trends that start in one corner of the world are rapidly replicated thousands of miles away . . .
— Francis Fukuyama, political scientist (born 1952)

Essential Question: How did science, technology, politics, justice, transportation, communication, and the environment change and stay the same after 1900?

One perspective shared by many scholars is that the 20th and 21st centuries were periods of unprecedented change. One factor in bringing about this transformation was the pace of discovery in science and the number of technological achievements made since the turn of the 20th century. These scientific and technological advancements led to changes in society, politics, economics, culture, and the environment. While many outcomes of these advancements were positive, they also included some unintended consequences that had negative impacts. Responses to these outcomes were varied.

Advances in Science and Technology

People made significant advances in understanding the universe and the natural world. These included:

The Origin of the Universe Several scientific theories tried to determine how the universe began. One of the best-known and best-supported theories was the *Big Bang*. This theory, that the universe started with one single cosmic event, led to a better understanding of the universe as well as atomic and subatomic science.

Wave Science Discoveries extended human knowledge and use of radio, light, sound, and microwaves. These breakthroughs led to improvements in radio and cellular communications as well as faster internet service.

Medical Science Experts made discoveries about germs, viruses, diseases, and the human body. These discoveries led to cures or vaccines for common diseases such as polio, tuberculosis, and tetanus. Experts pioneered new treatments for chronic diseases such as cancer and arthritis. The discovery of antibiotics, such as penicillin, helped people recover from or prevent infections. Reliable methods of birth control allowed women to control the size of their families. These and other medical advancements meant that people could live longer and better lives.

Energy Technologies Inventors and entrepreneurs made advancements in extracting and producing oil. Nuclear power became a significant source of energy. Renewable energy sources, including wind, solar, and thermal energy, became much cheaper to produce. In 2018, the International Renewable Energy Agency predicted that renewable energy sources would be consistently cheaper than fossil fuels by 2020. The increase in sources of power led to increased productivity, greater production of material goods, and faster transportation.

Communication Technologies In the 20th century, radio and television technology was further developed and telephone coverage increased so that most people eventually had a telephone in their homes. Internet communication and cell phones then replaced the older systems of communication. As a result, the amount and extent of mass communications increased, as did the global transfer of information.

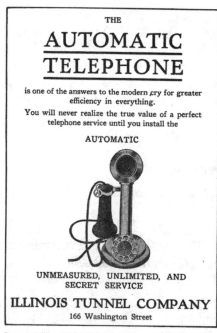

Source: Wikimedia Commons (Left), Getty Images (Right).

Technology advanced from voice communication over wires to massive amounts of data available almost anywhere.

Transportation Technologies Airplanes were invented in the first years of the 20th century. Later, jet airplanes closed the distance between regions of the world. Shipping technology improved, with faster and larger ships carrying prefabricated shipping containers. These ships and planes could transport more goods farther and faster than ever before. Improved transportation technology resulted in the expansion of the global trade network and interactions among cultures.

Agricultural Technologies Scientists produced genetically modified crops that were more resistant to drought and disease and had higher yields. The most significant effect of these advances, known as the Green Revolution, was higher population growth rates, especially within developing countries. Another effect was the decline in biodiversity, as these genetically modified crops began to be cultivated at the expense of local crop types.

Changes in a Globalized World

Partly as a result of the advances in science and technology, the world experienced a number of significant changes to societies, economies, politics, cultures, and the environment.

Social Changes During this period, the world's population grew faster than at any previous time in history. The increase in population meant increasing challenges to existing social orders. The greatest growth rate in population occurred in developing countries, while developed countries saw a slowing of their population growth. In the developing countries, the population growth rate was largest in the lower socioeconomic classes. Improvements in communication and transportation made it easier for people to migrate from less developed countries to more developed ones. That led to a "brain drain" in some countries as more highly educated and skilled people left their home countries to find jobs elsewhere.

Girls and women in this era began to experience an increase in socioeconomic status, especially in the more developed countries. Women in these societies began to enter careers traditionally reserved for men. Their right to vote in elections was finally legalized, and in some cases w omen held the highest political offices in their nations. Because birth control allowed women to make choices, fertility declined in developed countries. Some women chose to put off having children until later in life or decided to not have children at all. In some countries, though, women saw little improvement in their status as societies resisted the change that was happening elsewhere. (Connect: Analyze changes in the practice of birth control from the mid-20th century to the early 21st century. See Topic 9.5.)

Economic Changes The trend toward economic globalization that started in the 19th century intensified during the 20th and 21st centuries. More developed nations continued to exploit less developed areas of the world, harvesting their raw materials and using the less developed areas as markets for finished goods. However, significant changes to the world economic order took place. While the West, and especially the United States, was still a dominant economic force in the world economy, its superiority was being challenged by new sources of economic strength. Governments in Japan, Hong Kong, South Korea, Taiwan, and Singapore began policies that led to economic growth. These policies started the trend of Asian economies, which relied on inexpensive labor and high-quality manufacturing, competing against the Western economies to make consumer goods and high-tech products. Because of the modernization policies established after the death of Mao Zedong, which relaxed government control, China eventually became the second-largest economy in the world after the United States and a major exporter of goods to the rest of the world. India became an economic powerhouse by developing a labor force that specialized in software development and engineering.

Economic Policy Initiatives		
Program	Goal	Results
Soviet Union: Lenin's New Economic Policy (1921–1928)	Increase farm production and ease the transition to a communist economy	Peasants could own land. Small businesses were allowed. The Soviet economy began to recover from the Russian Civil War.
Soviet Union: Stalin's First Five-Year Plan (1928–1932)	Rapidly industrialize the Soviet economy	Industrial output grew. Farms were collectivized instead of having individual owners. Massive famines occurred.
China: Mao Zedong's Great Leap Forward (1958–1960)	Rapidly industrialize the Chinese economy	Peasants on collective farms were forced to produce steel using crude furnaces. Massive famines occurred.
China: Deng Xiaoping's Four Modernizations (1970s)	Attract foreign investment and move toward a market-oriented economy	China opened its economy to foreign producers. Industrial output increased, and China's economy grew rapidly.
United States: Roosevelt's New Deal (1933–1941)	Stimulate the economy and provide jobs during the Great Depression	The government hired millions to work on infrastructure projects, enacted Social Security, and regulated investments and banks.
United States: Reagan's Economic Recovery Tax Act (1981)	Stimulate the economy out of recession with supply-side economics	The economy came out of recession. Stock market and income inequality rose.
Great Britain: Expansion of the Welfare State (1945–1951)	Reduce income instability and inequality and provide a social safety net	The government provided citizens with health care, pensions, free education, and help for the poor. It also created huge bureaucracies.
Great Britain: Thatcher's Privatization of Industry (1980s)	Stimulate the British economy and reduce inflation	The economy grew and inflation was reduced, but unemployment rose to record levels.

Political Changes Mass protest movements helped bring about political and social change. Demonstrations in India showed how to effectively use nonviolent resistance and win social and political change. Activists championed civil rights in the United States, Northern Ireland, Canada, and other countries. Anti-war protests erupted in the United States and Western Europe. Women's rights movements emerged in the Western democracies and spread across the globe. Protests against the system of apartheid brought an end to racial segregation in South Africa. Democracy movements led to political protests and revolutions in North Africa and the Middle East called the "Arab Spring."

Source: Wikimedia Commons

Tahrir Square was the focal point of the 2011 Egyptian Revolution against former president Hosni Mubarak and his policies of police brutality. Over 1 million gathered in Tahrir Square on February 9, 2011, demanding the removal of the regime and for Mubarak to resign.

Governments were sometimes slow to respond to these calls for change. In some cases, they persecuted, imprisoned, or attacked the protesters.

During this time period, governments also began to play a larger role in managing or regulating their nations' economies. This increased government intervention in the economy was a change from the free-market, or laissez-faire, economics practiced in the previous era.

Cultural Changes Once information (and people) could quickly spread across the globe, the pace of cultural interactions and exchanges intensified. People all over the world consumed Western culture, particularly aspects that originated in the United States, in the form of movies, television shows, and music. Fashion styles that appeared in one area of the world quickly were imitated and adopted in other regions. A consumer culture spread.

One significant change in the process of cultural exchanges from the previous era was that these exchanges were often a two-way street. For instance, while global audiences watched Hollywood movies, cuisine from China, Japan, India, and Latin America often found its way to the plates of Americans and Europeans. Music and art from East Asia found a loyal fan base in the United States. The Internet helped increase the rate and scope of these transfers, and advances in cellular technology made even the most remote areas on Earth accessible to these cultural exchanges.

Environmental Changes In the 20th and 21st centuries, humans attempted to overcome the challenges of their environment in many new ways. With jet airplanes, travel between points on the globe was measured in hours rather than in days, months, or years. New technologies in petroleum extraction meant that sources of energy were cheaper and more abundant than previously imagined. The Space Age broke the terrestrial limits placed on humans by their environment, and space exploration became possible.

However, although humans overcame some challenges, they also harmed the environment. Airborne pollution increased as factories, automobiles, and homes got their power from carbon-based fuels. Water pollution also increased as people and companies dumped waste in rivers, lakes, and oceans. Debates about the sources and causes of climate change developed as average temperatures around the globe increased, polar ice caps began to melt, and more intense and catastrophic weather events occurred.

REFLECT ON THE ESSENTIAL QUESTION

1. **Continuity and Change** In 1919, economist John Maynard Keynes wrote:

   > "What an extraordinary episode in the progress of man that age was which came to an end in August 1914! . . . The inhabitant of London could order by telephone, sipping his morning tea in bed, the various products of the whole earth . . . he could at the same time and by the same means adventure his wealth in the natural resources and new enterprise of any quarter of the world . . . he could secure forthwith, if he wished it, cheap and comfortable means of transit to any country or climate . . . ."

   This review topic emphasizes changes. Use Keynes's description of life in 1914 as a starting point for noting continuities since 1900 as well. Consider such areas as technology, globalization, relation of developed to developing nations, status of women, and cultural exchange.

2. In one to three paragraphs, explain how science, technology, politics, justice, transportation, communication, and the environment changed and stayed the same after 1900.

UNIT 9 REVIEW

 HISTORICAL PERSPECTIVES: WHAT HAPPENS TOMORROW?

One reason people study the past is to provide insight into the future. And even though predictions are risky, people continue to make them.

Optimism After Communism Inspired by the fall of the Soviet Union, some intellectuals felt hopeful. In his provocatively titled 1992 book, *The End of History and the Last Man*, Francis Fukuyama posited that history as people knew it was over. He argued that democracy was the ideal form of government and capitalism was the best economic system, and they were spreading throughout the world. Eventually, all countries would adopt them, and the political and economic conflicts that had driven wars in the past would vanish. Critics of Fukuyama argued he was wrong, just as Karl Marx had been in the 19th century when he also argued that people were entering the final phase of history.

Cultural Conflict One of Fukuyama's former teachers, Samuel Huntington, rejected the entire end-of-history argument. In response, he wrote *The Clash of Civilizations and the Remaking of World Order* (1996). While Fukuyama was influenced by the end of the rivalry between the United States and the Soviet Union, Huntington was struck by the increasing tensions around religion and culture. He contended that people's beliefs and affiliations would draw the fault lines for conflicts in the post-Cold War world. Huntington cited several examples of cultural conflict, including Hindu and Muslim tensions in India and the rise of Islamic fundamentalism and its hostility toward Western culture.

Cultural Understanding Critics asserted that Huntington's generalizations were oversimplified and reflected a pro-Western prejudice. One of these critics is Nobel prize-winning economist Amartya Sen. In his 2006 work, *Identities and Violence: The Illusion of Destiny,* Sen rejected Huntington's suggestion that people of different beliefs and ethnic groups could not get along, pointing to the existence of peaceful diverse societies around the world. Further, as globalization spread through all parts of life, people found many ways to identify themselves in the 21st century besides by religion and ethnicity.

Hope in Technology Debates over the post-Cold War world began before the Internet and smartphones were common. By 2011, technology was connecting people around the globe. When physicist Michio Kaku published *Physics of the Future* (2011), he was optimistic that technology and trade could break down the cultural barriers. He held out hope for material abundance and greater peace.

Develop an Argument: Evaluate the extent to which historical evidence supports one of the perspectives of the future of world history.

WRITE AS A HISTORIAN: REREAD AND EVALUATE

How you use the 40 minutes allotted for the long essay depends on what you believe will work for you. However, allowing plenty of time to understand the task and gather your evidence before you start writing will likely make your writing easier and stronger. Be sure also to leave enough time at the end of the 40 minutes to reread and evaluate your essay.

As you evaluate your essay, start at the most basic level: Did you fulfill the task the prompt requires? Check the key terms of the question and the key terms you use in your response, and be sure they align.

For an easy reminder of what else you should look for as you evaluate your essay, remember this sentence: The clearest essays require care. The first letter of each word, T, C, E, R, and C, can remind you of the key elements your essay must contain:

1. **Thesis/claim.** The thesis must make a historically defensible claim that responds to the prompt and lays out a line of reasoning. It must also consist of one or more sentences located in one place, either in the introduction or the conclusion.

2. **Contextualization:** Place your thesis in historical context, relating the topic of the prompt to broader historical events, developments, or processes that occur before, during, or continue after the time frame of the question.

3. **Evidence:** Provide a number of specific and relevant pieces of evidence, and clearly show how they support your thesis.

4. **Reasoning:** Use the historical reasoning process of comparison, continuity and change, or causation to frame your argument. Use an organizational strategy appropriate to the reasoning process.

5. **Complexity:** Check that you have woven a complex understanding throughout your essay (or fully developed it in one place). Look for an explanation of multiple variables and both causes and effects, similarities and differences, and continuities and changes; connections across and within periods; the significance of a source's credibility and limitations; and the effectiveness of a historical claim.

Application: After answering one or more of the long essay questions on the next page, use the reminders in the sentence "The clearest essays require care" to evaluate your essay. Make revisions where you believe you can make your essay stronger, clearer, or more aligned with the rubric expectations.

For current free response question samples, visit: https://apcentral. collegeboard.org/courses/ap-world-history/exam

LONG ESSAY QUESTIONS

Directions: Write an essay in response to one of the prompts below. The suggested writing time for an essay is 40 minutes.

In your response, you should do the following:

- Respond to the prompt with a historically defensible thesis or claim that establishes a line of reasoning.
- Describe a broader historical context relevant to the prompt.
- Support an argument in response to the prompt using at least two pieces of specific and relevant evidence.
- Use historical reasoning (e.g., comparison, causation, continuity or change) to frame or structure an argument that addresses the prompt.
- Demonstrate a complex understanding of a historical development related to the prompt through sophisticated argumentation and/or effective use of evidence.

Source: *AP® World History Course and Exam Description*

1. From 1900 to the present, changes in transportation and communication led to a more interconnected world.
   Develop an argument that evaluates the extent to which these technological advances resulted in political and social changes in that era.

2. From 1900 to the present, increasing globalization has made transportation faster and easier, but it has also caused pandemics to become more widespread.
   Develop an argument that evaluates the extent to which the effects of the influenza pandemic of 1918–1919 were similar to, or different from, the HIV/AIDS epidemic that began in the 1980s.

3. After 1900, religious and ideological differences led to the partition of some states in Eurasia so their peoples could have independence.
   Develop an argument that evaluates the extent to which the partition of India in 1947 and the partition of Palestine in 1948 were similar or different.

4. After World War II, capitalist and communist powers divided up and heavily influenced the territories of Germany and Korea.
   Develop an argument that evaluates the extent to which the partition of Germany and the partition of Korea were similar or different between 1945 and the present.

DOCUMENT-BASED QUESTION

Directions: Question 1 is based on the accompanying documents. The documents have been edited for the purpose of this exercise. You are advised to spend 15 minutes planning and 45 minutes writing your answer.

1. Develop an argument that evaluates the extent to which human health is linked to a country's status as a developing or a developed nation.

In your response, you should do the following:

- Respond to the prompt with a historically defensible thesis or claim that establishes a line of reasoning.
- Describe a broader historical context relevant to the prompt.
- Support an argument in response to the prompt using at least four documents.
- Use at least one additional piece of specific historical evidence (beyond that found in the documents) relevant to an argument about the prompt.
- For at least two documents, explain how or why the document's point of view, purpose, historical situation, and/or audience is relevant to an argument.
- Demonstrate a complex understanding of a historical development related to the prompt through a sophisticated argument and/or effective use of evidence.

Source: *AP® World History Course and Exam Description*

Historical Background

Developing nations are generally described as countries with a less developed industrial base; low levels of safe drinking water, sanitation, and hygiene; high levels of pollution; and widespread poverty.

Developed nations are generally described as countries with advanced technological infrastructure, developed economies, better educational opportunities, greater wealth of the people, and higher living standards.

Document 1

Source: UNICEF, "Vaccines Bring 7 Diseases Under Control," 1996.

Two hundred years after the discovery of vaccine by the English physician Edward Jenner, immunization can be credited with saving approximately 9 million lives a year worldwide. . . So far only one disease, smallpox, has been eradicated by vaccines, saving approximately 5 million lives annually. . . Polio could be next. . . If the year 2000 goal of eradicating polio is achieved, the United States will be able to save the $270 million a year that is currently spent on polio vaccination. The savings for Western European countries will amount to about $200 million a year. . .In all, vaccines have brought seven major human diseases under some degree of control - smallpox, diphtheria, tetanus, yellow fever, whooping cough, polio, and measles. Most of the vaccines now in use have been available for several decades, but only in the last 15 years has protection been extended to the majority of children in the developing world. Only about a quarter were being immunized when, in the mid-1980s, UNICEF and WHO called for a new commitment to regularly reaching 80% of infants by 1990. In most nations, that goal was reached and has since been sustained - saving over 3 million young lives each year. As frequent disease is also a major cause of malnutrition, immunization is also helping to protect the normal growth of millions of children.

Document 2

Source: Locations of Ebola outbreaks, cases of Ebola and deaths, November 2014.

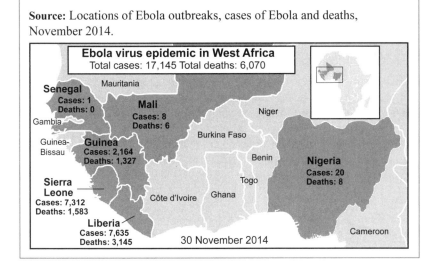

Ebola virus epidemic in West Africa
Total cases: 17,145 Total deaths: 6,070

Senegal
Cases: 1
Deaths: 0

Mauritania

Mali
Cases: 8
Deaths: 6

Niger

Gambia

Guinea-Bissau

Guinea
Cases: 2,164
Deaths: 1,327

Burkina Faso

Benin

Nigeria
Cases: 20
Deaths: 8

Sierra Leone
Cases: 7,312
Deaths: 1,583

Côte d'Ivoire

Togo

Ghana

Liberia
Cases: 7,635
Deaths: 3,145

30 November 2014

Cameroon

Document 3

Source: British website article during Black History Month, "The History of AIDS in Africa in 1990s," 2015.

Sub-Saharan Africa was the hub of the HIV epidemic of the 1990s. In 1993, there were an estimated 9 million people infected in the sub-Saharan region out of a global total of 14 million. In 1998, sub-Saharan Africa was home to 70% of people who became infected with HIV during the year, with an estimated one in seven of these new infections occurring in South Africa.

South Africa had reacted slowly to the emerging epidemic. A new government in 1994 had concentrated on unifying the country's health systems and expanding primary health care for the poor. This restructuring weakened the health systems just as the HIV/AIDS epidemic was at the peak of expansion. In 1998 the health ministry stopped trials of AZT [a drug helping with the symptoms of AIDS] to prevent mother-to-child-transmission claiming that it was too expensive and that it would focus its funds on other prevention campaigns.

This provoked the first major political action by HIV positive Africans over their own treatment. . . . in 1998 the Treatment Action Campaign (TAC) was founded. Led by Zackie Achmat, this group was to become important in the fight for treatment in South Africa.

In 1996 a new the effective combination therapy became available for those living with HIV in developed countries. The new drugs were so effective that AIDS death rates in developed countries dropped by 84% over the next four years. However . . . at a cost of $10,000-15,000 per person per year it would have cost sub-Saharan countries between 9% and 67% of their GDP to provide triple combination therapy to everybody living with HIV in their countries.

This was impossible for the majority of African nations and the disparity in treatment options angered many people for whom treatment was too expensive. South Africa began to lobby the multi-billion-dollar pharmaceutical corporations of the West to either allow local companies to manufacture HIV/AIDS drugs themselves (compulsory licensing) or import them from other countries, that were producing generic (or copied) drugs at a low cost.

Document 4

Source: Mark Fischetti, writer and researcher, "Developing Countries Are Battling Diseases of the Rich and Poor," *Scientific American*, 2016.

Life expectancy worldwide has risen for decades. But more people are living more years with debilitating ailments, according to a new study by the Institute for Health Metrics and Evaluation in Seattle. In developed countries, the trouble comes almost entirely from diseases that are not transmitted directly from one person to another, conditions such as heart and lung disease and back pain—ills typically associated with lifestyle choices such as diet and exercise.

In developing nations, however, the prevalence of these ailments is increasing rapidly, even as those countries continue to try to stamp out communicable diseases such as diarrhea and malaria that have plagued them for a long time. If developing nations are clever, though, they can create health policies that impede the new threats and keep reducing the old ones.

Document 5

Source: "Cholera: how African countries are failing to do even the basics," *The Conversation*, a U.S. academic research magazine, 2017.

Each year, 1.3 to 4.0 million cases of the illness occurs around the world, leading to between 21,000 to 143,000 deaths. About two-thirds of these are in developing countries, mostly in sub-Saharan Africa.

Cholera is . . . transmitted through contaminated water or food in areas with poor sanitation and lack of clean drinking water. Cholera is referred to as a disease of poverty because of the lack of social development in the areas in which it occurs. The constant threat of natural catastrophes such as flooding and man-made ones including civil unrest, make the management and prevention of cholera a huge challenge in most of Africa. Several conditions on the continent make it fertile ground for the emergence and rapid spread of cholera. These include: Inadequate access to clean water and sanitation facilities, especially in urban slums, where basic infrastructure isn't available, camps for internally displaced persons or refugees, where minimum requirements of clean water and sanitation have not been met . . . other humanitarian crises including flooding and earthquakes, civil unrest or war that causes disruption of water and sanitation systems.

But generally, the lack of comprehensive programs for improvement of general public health especially for vulnerable populations like refugees and informal settlement residents is a challenge. The increase in population, especially in urban settlements, has been exponential over the last two decades posing a major challenge for public health as more people flock to the cities in search of jobs. . . . On top of this a lack of political maturity in many African countries as well as greed for political power has led to civil unrest and chaos which in turn has resulted in internal displacements of huge populations.

There are recommended vaccines that can minimize the spread of cholera. But they are rarely used as for most governments this not a priority. Vaccines can prevent up to 65% of vulnerable populations from getting cholera.

Document 6

Source: United Nations Report on HIV/AIDS, Regional HIV and AIDS Statistics and Features, 2018.

Cases of HIV and AIDS, 2016			
Region	All People with HIV	New Cases of HIV	Deaths Resulting from AIDS
Latin America	1.8 million	97,000	36,000
Caribbean	0.3 million	18,000	9,400
North America and Western and Central Europe	2.1 million	73,000	18,000
Eastern Europe and Central Asia	1.6 million	190,000	40,000
North Africa and the Middle East	0.2 million	18,000	11,000
Western and Central Africa	6.1 million	370,000	310,000
Eastern and Southern Africa	19.4 million	790,000	420,000
Asia and the Pacific	5.1 million	270,000	170,000
WORLD TOTAL	36.7 million	1.8 million	1.0 million

Document 7

Source: "Why The World Ignores Diseases Of Poverty," *Huffington Post*, news and opinion website and blog, 2018.

More than 1 billion people worldwide are infected with diseases of poverty. These conditions disproportionately afflict the world's poorest, either in the developing world, or in developed countries with extreme inequality. Though well-known conditions such as HIV/AIDS and malaria are considered diseases of poverty, many of the other illnesses that primarily strike the world's poorest are lesser-known and frequently misunderstood.

The World Health Organization has designated about 20 of these conditions as "neglected tropical diseases." This diverse array of conditions—such as leprosy, dengue, Chagas, and elephantiasis, to name a few—don't attract the global media attention or funding that certain wide-ranging tropical diseases, such as malaria, have garnered in recent years. Neglected diseases cost developing economies billions of dollars annually and lock sufferers into a cycle of poverty that is nearly impossible to escape.

AP® World History Practice Exam

Section 1

PART A: MULTIPLE-CHOICE QUESTIONS

Directions: Each of the questions or incomplete statements below is followed by four suggested answers or completions. Select the one that is best in each case.

Questions 1 and 2 refer to the passage below.

"I will give you my father's words just as I received them; royal griots [storytellers] do not know what lying is. . . . Fear enters the heart of him who does not know his destiny, whereas Sundiata knew that he was striding towards a great destiny. . . . There is one that will make a great king. He forgets nobody. . . . In the same way as light preceded the sun, so the glory of Sundiata, overleaping the mountains, shed itself on all the Niger plain. . . . The arms of Sundiata had subdued all the countries of the savanna. . . . With Sundiata peace and happiness entered Niani. . . . Every king wants to have a singer to perpetuate his memory, for it is the griot who rescues the memories of kings from oblivion, as men have short memories. . . . The prophets did not write and their words have been all the more vivid as a result. . . . But whoever knows the history of a country can read its future. . . . Kings are only men, and whatever iron cannot achieve against them, words can."

Epic of Sundiata, the story of the founding of the Mali Empire

1. Which of the following best describes the most likely purpose of telling these details about Sundiata?
   (A) To persuade listeners that his rule over the Mali Empire was justified
   (B) To prove that words matter more than deeds
   (C) To compare him to the current ruler of the Mali Empire
   (D) To assess his positive qualities and his flaws

2. The best evidence to support the claim in the excerpt that Sundiata "was striving towards a great destiny" is that Mali became
   (A) the protector of pilgrimage routes to Mecca
   (B) linked to the Americas in an Atlantic system
   (C) a kingdom of prosperous Muslim farmers
   (D) wealthy from trans-Saharan trade conducted by Muslims

Questions 3 and 4 refer to the passage below.

"South-eastern China was also the chief centre [center] of porcelain production, although china [Chinese] clay is found also in North China. The use of porcelain spread more and more widely. The first translucent porcelain made its appearance, and porcelain became an important article of commerce both within the country and for export. Already the Muslim rulers of Baghdad around 800 used imported Chinese porcelain, and by the end of the fourteenth century porcelain was known in Eastern Africa. Exports to South-East Asia and Indonesia, and also to Japan gained more and more importance in later centuries. Manufacture of high-quality porcelain calls for considerable amounts of capital investment and working capital; small manufacturers produce too many second-rate pieces; thus we have here the first beginnings of an industry that developed industrial towns such as Ching-te, in which the majority of the population were workers and merchants, with some 10,000 families alone producing porcelain. Yet, for many centuries to come, the state controlled the production and even the design of porcelain and appropriated most of the production for use at court or as gifts."

Wolfram Eberhard, *A History of China*, 1969

3. Which of the following conclusions about porcelain is best supported by the passage?
   (A) People in the Middle East preferred luxury items made in Persia.
   (B) Proto-industrialization in the manufacture of luxury goods led to urbanization in China.
   (C) Much of the porcelain manufacturing industry in China was controlled by foreign merchants.
   (D) Japan was a leading consumer of Chinese porcelain in the 1300s.

4. What development most aided the growth in the labor supply needed for the increasing production of porcelain and other manufactured goods?
   (A) The use of the magnetic compass and other transportation improvements enabled peasants to travel to Chinese cities more easily.
   (B) The invention of inexpensive paper created an easier way to communicate and to advertise for job openings in the porcelain factories.
   (C) The spread of gunpowder weapons allowed landlords to force rebellious peasants to end their revolts and move into the cities to work in porcelain factories.
   (D) The changes in agriculture, including the introduction of a fast-growing variety of rice known as champa, increased food production.

Questions 5 and 6 refer to the passage below.

"2. Leaders of a religion, preachers, monks, persons who are dedicated to religious practice, the criers of mosques, physicians and those who bathe the bodies of the dead are to be freed from public charges [duties].

3. It is forbidden under penalty of death that anyone, whoever he be, shall be proclaimed emperor unless he has been elected previously by the princes, khans, officers and other Mongol nobles in a general council.

4. It is forbidden chieftains of nations and clans subject to the Mongols to hold honorary titles.

5. [It is] forbidden ever to make peace with a monarch, a prince or a people who have not submitted."

Excerpt from "Yassa", the laws of Genghis Khan, early 13th century

5. The passage most strongly supports the idea that the Mongols
   (A) promoted Islam, which was the faith of the Mongol khan
   (B) created a loose confederation of local kings, sultans, and caliphs
   (C) formed alliances with rival empires that had successfully resisted Mongol invasions of their territories
   (D) developed a decentralized government in which local rulers were chosen by Mongol khans

6. Which of the following was the most immediate political change in the Mongol Empire after the death of Genghis Khan?
   (A) Descendants of Genghis Khan each took control of part of the empire.
   (B) Trade along the Silk Roads stopped for almost a century.
   (C) Mongol rulers quickly lost control of China.
   (D) Russian rulers in Moscow became more powerful.

Questions 7 to 9 refer to the passage below.

"Apart from his navigational skills, what most set Columbus apart from other Europeans of his day were not the things that he believed, but the intensity with which he believed in them and the determination with which he acted upon those beliefs. . . . Columbus was, in most respects, merely an especially active and dramatic embodiment of the European—and especially the Mediterranean—mind and soul of his time: a religious fanatic obsessed with the conversion, conquest, or liquidation of all non-Christians; a latter-day crusader in search of personal wealth and fame, who expected the enormous and mysterious world he had found to be filled with monstrous races inhabiting wild forests, and with golden people living in Eden."

David E. Stannard, *American Holocaust: Columbus and the Conquest of the New World*, 1992

7. Which of the following best explains the ideas expressed by the author in the title and contents of the passage?

   (A) Stannard is critical of the motives and impact of Columbus.

   (B) Stannard believes Columbus was an unselfish explorer.

   (C) Stannard thinks Columbus was motivated primarily by his hopes to spread Christianity in the Americas.

   (D) Stannard respects Columbus for searching for a Northwest Passage to the East Indies.

8. Spanish goals diverged from those Stannard attributed to Columbus in the passage with the

   (A) beginning of the fur trade in the northern part of the Americas

   (B) realization that enslaved Africans could be used to raise cash crops

   (C) discovery of precious metals in the Inca and Aztec Empires

   (D) development of a profitable tobacco industry

9. European exploration at the end of the 15th century was motivated most strongly by a desire to

   (A) gain access to resources and overseas trade routes

   (B) revive the Crusades to take control of Jerusalem

   (C) sell European ship-building technology to the Arabs and Chinese

   (D) acquire natural resources such as coal and oil to support industrialization

Questions 10 and 11 refer to the timeline below.

States in South Asia

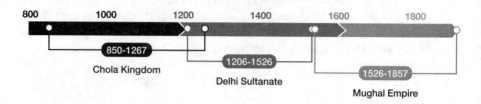

10. What factor is most responsible for the trend of increasing trade in the Indian Ocean during the period shown on the timeline?
    (A) The participation of European merchants
    (B) The growth of Dar al-Islam
    (C) The journeys of Zheng He
    (D) The advances in Chinese silk manufacturing

11. Which of the following was most responsible for the 1526 transition of power in South Asia?
    (A) Acceptance of Christianity
    (B) Development and use of gunpowder weapons
    (C) Increased wealth from porcelain trade
    (D) Collection of tributes from weaker neighboring states

Questions 12 and 13 refer to the image below.

Source: 16th-Century Benin Bronzes at the British Museum / Mike Peel / www.mikepeel.net / Wikimedia Commons

In this brass plaque, the seated figure in the middle is the king of the Benin kingdom in West Africa. Kneeling beside him are two attendants. The two smaller figures in the back represent Portuguese traders. The date of its creation is uncertain, but it was no earlier than the 15th century.

12. As shown by the Benin Bronze above, the most influential context shaping West Africa in the 16th century was the

(A) adoption of European political structures by West African rulers

(B) diffusion of European art styles to West African artists

(C) power of West African Empires to maintain authority

(D) preference of West African people for European governance

13. The Benin Bronze shown above could best be used as evidence for a historian studying

(A) hierarchy in West African society

(B) technology in Western Europe

(C) the use of monumental architecture to consolidate ruling authority

(D) the spread of Islam to West Africa

Questions 14 and 15 refer to the map below.

THREE ISLAMIC EMPIRES IN THE SIXTEENTH CENTURY

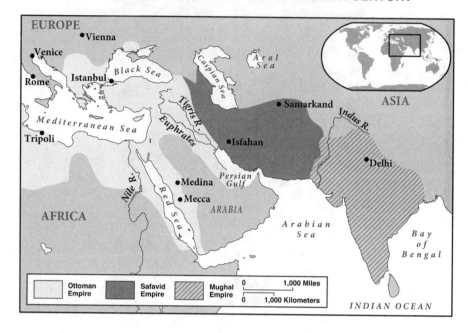

14. The empires shown on the map expanded during the 15th and 16th centuries mostly as a result of diffusion of technology of

   (A) printing

   (B) gunpowder

   (C) mapmaking

   (D) transportation

15. Which of the following arguments about empires in the 16th century is best supported by the evidence shown on this map?

   (A) Shi'a Muslims were more successful at uniting people than were Sunni Muslims.

   (B) The influence of Turkic culture was strong in southern and southwestern Asia.

   (C) Mongol khans ruled southern and southwestern Asia for over 250 years.

   (D) Political unity characterized Dar al-Islam after the Abbasid Caliphate.

Questions 16 and 17 refer to the passages below.

Source 1

"Montezuma, who with one of his sons and many other chiefs who had been captured at the beginning, was still a prisoner, asked to be carried to the roof of the fort where he could speak to the captains and the [Aztec] people, and cause the war to cease. I had him taken there, and when he reached the parapet on the top of the fort, intending to speak to the people who were fighting there, one of his own subjects struck him on the head with a stone with such force that within three days he died. I then had him taken out, dead as he was, by two of the Indian prisoners, who bore him away to his people; but I do not know what they did with him."

Hernán Cortés, letter to King Charles V of Spain, circa 1520

Source 2

"The 'Chronicle' tells us that once the Spanish had fled from Mexico [a temporary setback] and those who had remained behind had been killed, the Aztecs entered the chambers of Montezuma in order to treat him more cruelly than they had dealt with the Spaniards. There they found him dead with a chain about his feet and five dagger wounds in his chest. Near him lay many noblemen and great lords who had been held prisoner with him. All of them had been slain shortly before the Spaniards abandoned the building."

Diego Durán, Spanish Roman Catholic priest, c. 1580

16. The views expressed in Source 1 and Source 2 are best used as evidence of which of the following?

(A) Anger over the spread of European religions to North America

(B) Displeasure about European mercantilist policies to claim overseas territories

(C) Outrage by native people over Aztecs forcing religious conversion

(D) Resentment of Aztec conquests by local groups

17. An important context of the successful Spanish conquest was that

(A) the Aztec population grew after the introduction of Spanish technology

(B) the Aztec rulers viewed the Spanish as their allies against other Europeans

(C) the Aztec people shared culture inherited from earlier Mesoamerican societies

(D) the Aztec empire collected tribute from the people and regions they conquered

Questions 18 to 20 refer to the table below.

British Sugar Consumption, 1700–1770			
Year	British Population (millions of people)	Sugar Imports (millions of pounds)	Sugar Consumption (pounds per person)
1700	6.1	28.0	4.6
1710	6.4	30.1	4.7
1720	6.3	47.3	7.5
1730	6.2	68.6	11.1
1740	6.2	72.2	11.6
1750	6.3	76.2	12.1
1760	8.0	110.2	13.8
1770	8.5	137.9	16.2

18. Which of the following contributed most to the trend in British population shown in the table in the years from 1750 to 1770?

(A) The end of imperial wars with rival European nations

(B) The migration of laborers from British colonies to Britain

(C) The spread of disease pathogens along trade routes

(D) The changes in how people lived as a result of the industrial revolution in Britain

19. Which of the following statements describes developments in the Americas that contributed to the changes in British sugar imports?

(A) Sugar was an American crop that was introduced to Europeans as part of the Columbian Exchange.

(B) Europeans adopted the system of chattel slavery practiced by American societies that used it for growing sugar.

(C) Plantations in the Caribbean and Brazil produced large amounts of sugar.

(D) British primarily relied on indentured servants to work on their sugar colonies in the Caribbean.

20. Which of the following ideologies led to the British economic interactions with their American colonies that are shown in the table?

(A) free-trade

(B) mercantilism

(C) socialism

(D) laissez-faire capitalism

"As a rich man is likely to be a better customer to the industrious people in his neighborhood than a poor, so is likewise a rich nation. . . . [Trade restrictions,] by aiming at the impoverishment of all our neighbors . . . , tend to render that very commerce insignificant and contemptible. . . .

The statesmen who should attempt to direct private people in what manner they ought to employ their capital, would not only load himself with a most unnecessary attention, but assume an authority which could safely be trusted, not only to no single person, but to no council or senate whatever, and which would nowhere be so dangerous as in the hands of a man who had folly and presumption enough to fancy himself fit to exercise it."

Adam Smith, *The Wealth of Nations,* 1776

21. Which of the following was the most important broader context in which the above passage was written?

    (A) The beginning of the Industrial Revolution

    (B) The emergence of nationalism

    (C) The rise of socialism

    (D) The increase in silver production in the Americas

22. A government enacting policies based on Adam Smith's ideas would be most likely to

    (A) subsidize agricultural production

    (B) regulate membership in skilled trades

    (C) limit the amount of shoe imports

    (D) reduce tariffs on goods entering the country

23. Adam Smith disagreed with mercantilism because of his belief that good governments should

    (A) sponsor state industries to achieve regional economic development

    (B) nationalize communications and transportation infrastructures

    (C) reduce their interventions aimed at controlling trade

    (D) limit the extension of colonial rule to new territories

Questions 24 and 25 refer to the passage below.

"We find that your country is [far] from China. Yet there are barbarian ships that strive to come here for trade for the purpose of making a great profit. The wealth of China is used to profit the barbarians. That is to say, the great profit made by barbarians is all taken from the rightful share of China. By what right do they then use the poisonous drug to injure the Chinese people? Even though the barbarians may not necessarily intend to do us harm, yet in coveting profit to an extreme, they have no regard for injuring others. Let us ask, where is your conscience? I have heard that the smoking of opium is very strictly forbidden by your country; that is because the harm caused by opium is clearly understood. Since it is not permitted to do harm to your own country, then even less should you let it be passed on to the harm of other countries—how much less to China!"

Lin Zexu, Chinese official, letter to Queen Victoria, 1839

24. All of the following contributed to causing the situation described by the passage EXCEPT

   (A) The highly organized imperial bureaucracy of Qing Dynasty China

   (B) Chinese demands for European manufactured goods

   (C) The Chinese concept of China as the civilized "middle kingdom"

   (D) European demands for Chinese goods such as tea and silk

25. Which of the following developments was most immediately caused by the circumstances described in the passage?

   (A) The British switched from selling opium to selling tea in China.

   (B) The British defeated China in a war and exanded their opportunities to trade in China.

   (C) The Chinese formed an anti-British alliance with France.

   (D) Japan used the conflict between China and Great Britain to justify the Sino-Japanese War.

CAPITAL AND LABOUR.

Source: *Capital and Labour,* drawn by Robert Jacob Hamerto, who sometimes used the penname Shallaballa, seen near the lower righthand corner (12 August 1843), Vol. 5: 48-49. *Punch; or The London Charivari.*

26. The image's message indicates that the artist would most likely support
    (A) the abolition of slavery
    (B) the organization of labor unions
    (C) the policies of laissez-faire economics
    (D) the end of serfdom

27. Which group was most likely to agree with the artist in the 1840s?
    (A) socialists
    (B) land-holding nobles
    (C) colonial governors
    (D) bureaucratic elites

28. The image was most likely produced in the context of the early decades of the Western European transition from
    (A) feudalism to capitalism
    (B) artisan production to factory manufacturing
    (C) absolutism to constitutional monarchy
    (D) imperial states to those founded in ethnic nationalism

Questions 29 to 31 refer to the passages below.

Source 1

"The Communists disdain to conceal their views and aims. They openly declare that their ends can be attained only by the forcible overthrow of all existing social conditions. Let the ruling classes tremble at a Communistic revolution. The proletarians have nothing to lose but their chains. They have a world to win. Working men of all countries, unite!"

Karl Marx and Friedrich Engels, The Communist Manifesto, 1848

Source 2

"Even in interpreting the psychology of the worker of the transitional period, Marx exhibited a rationalistic bias. The worker's opposition to the capitalist order is a total opposition to its laws, its factories, and its government. But this revolutionary consciousness of the worker is to take him next to Marxist socialism, where he will accept the factory system and the state, the *only* difference being the abolition of capitalism. Why shouldn't the revolutionary protest of the worker flow into other channels: into rejection of industrialism as well as capitalism, into rejection of the socialist as well as the capitalist state?"

Adam B. Ulam, The Unfinished Revolution: Marxism Interpreted, 1960

29. The ideas expressed in Source 1 most directly emerged out of
    (A) desires to convert native peoples in colonies to Christianity
    (B) unsuccessful attempts in Russia to end rule of the tsars
    (C) appeals for equality in the ideology of the Enlightenment
    (D) popular movements for decolonization

30. The ideas expressed in Source 2 do not support which principle of Karl Marx?
    (A) The proletariat must unite to take over factories, mines, and other means of industrial production.
    (A) Capitalist societies are divided into two basic classes.
    (B) Government and societal institutions work to keep the power of the bourgeoisie.
    (C) The working class is exploited by business owners through low pay and often dangerous working conditions.

31. One similarity between Source 1 and Source 2 is that both
    (A) believe that capitalism is the final stage of economic development
    (B) recognize why workers might support a revolution
    (C) argue that industrialization was a mistake
    (D) criticize the rationalism of the Enlightenment

Questions 32 and 33 refer to the passages below.

Source 1

"It is widely stated that . . . if only the [government would] permit trade there will be no further difficulty. However, it is their practice first to seek a foothold by means of trade and then to go on to propagate Christianity and make other unreasonable demands. . . . We must never choose the policy of peace."

Tokugawa Nariaki, message to the Japanese Tokugawa Shogunate,
August 14, 1853

Source 2

"We must construct new steamships, especially powerful warships, and these we will load with goods not needed in Japan. For a time, we will have to employ Dutchmen as masters and mariners, but we will put on board with them Japanese of ability and integrity. . . . [The ships] will in fact have the secret purpose of training a navy."

Ii Naosuke, message to the Japanese Tokugawa Shogunate,
October 1, 1853

32. The ideas expressed in the Source 1 and Source 2 correspondence share the most similarity in goals to those of nineteenth-century reformers seeking modernization in the

(A) Ottoman Empire

(B) United States

(C) Mughal Empire

(D) Germany

33. Source 1 was most directly influenced by which of the following developments?

(A) The American independence movement

(B) The Haitian Revolution

(C) The Japanese colonization of the Korean peninsula

(D) The opening of foreign trade ports in China after the Opium War

Source: Battle of Port Arthur. The subtitle noted Nishiki-e of the traditional technique. (plate 41, February 1904)

The Japanese naval attack on Russian ships stationed at Port Arthur, Manchuria, marked the start of the Russo-Japanese War.

34. Which of the following best describes the results of the events depicted in the image?

(A) They exposed Japanese weakness and demonstrated the growing power of Russia.

(B) They marked the first victory in the modern era of Europeans over an Asian nation.

(C) They revealed Russian weaknesses and illustrated the growing power of Japan.

(D) They prompted both Russia and Japan to begin industrialization in their countries.

35. Which of the following statements best reflects the influence of the Meiji Restoration on the outcome of the Russo-Japanese War, as depicted in the image?

(A) Japan lost the war because of the political instability caused by the changes.

(B) Japan modernized its military as a part of the restoration, allowing for a victory.

(C) The Meiji Restoration neglected educational reforms, leaving Japan at a technological disadvantage.

(D) The Meiji Restoration elevated women to equal status, allowing them to serve in the military.

Questions 36 and 37 refer to the map below.

MANDATES IN THE MIDDLE EAST AFTER WORLD WAR I

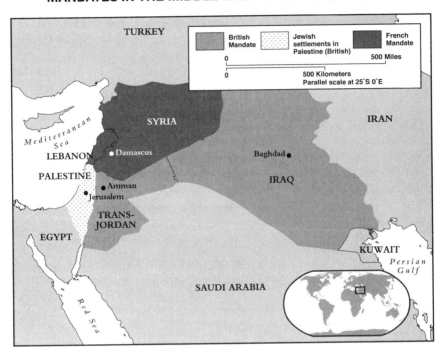

36. Which of the following most directly led to the political rule of territory shown on the map?
    (A) The victory by the Allies (Triple Entente) in World War I
    (B) The rise of nationalist movements in former colonies and territories
    (C) The enactment of United States President Wilson's principle of self-determination
    (D) The hopes for greater self-government to be established after World War I

37. Which of the following factors contributed most to changing the political rule of territory in the Middle East in the period from 1920 to 1945?
    (A) Pan-Arab ideology led to successful movements for self-rule.
    (B) Efforts by Arab states to create their own colonies in the region.
    (C) The willingness of Britain and France to return self-rule to their mandates.
    (D) International organizations such as the United Nations facilitated international cooperation.

Questions 38 to 40 refer to the passage below.

"The absolute equality of races, physical, political and social, is the founding stone of World Peace and human advancement. . . . The beginning of Wisdom in interracial contact is the establishment of political institutions among suppressed Peoples. The habit of democracy must be made to encircle the earth. . . . Surely . . . there can be found in the civilized world enough of altruism, learning and benevolence to develop native institutions for the native's good rather than continuing to allow the majority of mankind to be brutalized and enslaved. . . .

It is to the shame of the world that today the relations between the main groups of mankind and their mutual estimate and respect is determined chiefly by the degree in which one can subject the other to its service,—enslaving labor, making ignorance compulsory, uprooting ruthlessly religion and custom and destroying government so that the favored few may luxuriate in the toil of the tortured many. . . . It is shameful, irreligious, unscientific and undemocratic that the estimate that half the peoples of the earth put on the other half, depends mainly on their ability to squeeze money out of them."

Pan-African Congress, "The London Manifesto," 1921

38. The reference to a system that is "shameful, irreligious, unscientific and undemocratic" is best understood as a challenge to

(A) fascism

(B) economic nationalism

(C) socialism

(D) communism

39. The sentiments expressed in this passage contributed most strongly to which of the following developments?

(A) Civil wars in post-colonial African states that led to dictatorships

(B) Land reforms led by Europeans to divide colonial-era land titles

(C) The migration of former colonial subjects to European metropoles

(D) The beginning of decolonization and African self-rule

40. The situation described in the second paragraph was most similar to which of the following?

(A) The sixteenth-century trading-post empire of the Portuguese in the Indian Ocean basin

(B) The spread of the United States population west to the Pacific Ocean in the last half of the nineteenth century

(C) The seventeenth-century Spanish colonial empire in North America

(D) The settler colonialism of the British in Canada in the last half of the eighteenth century and the first half of the nineteenth century

Questions 41 to 43 refer to the passage below.

"We are making out a full and detailed report but it takes time to collate the enormous amount of information which we have collected. The trouble started early on the morning of the 16th and both sides were equally responsible. The Hindus started putting up barricades at Tala Bridge and Belgachia Bridge and other places to prevent Muslims processions coming into the town and Muslims goondas [gang members] went round forcing Hindus to close their shops. As previously mentioned in my D.O. [daily orders] of the 15th the air was electric and this caused crowds to gather, lathis [heavy stick used as a weapon by Indian police] were produced and in no time North Calcutta was a scene of mob riot. By 1100 hours there were brick bat fights all over North Calcutta. . . .

Soon after midnight on the 16/17th these gangs fought out the most desperate battles, murder and butchery of a worst type were carried on in the side lanes and byways of North Calcutta. Round Vivekananda Road/ Central Ave., crossing, about 50 Hindu Behari rickshaw pullers were caught in a cul-de-sac and butchered. Further up Central Ave., round the temple which stands in the middle, a party of some 30 Mohamedans [Muslims] were killed. It was during the period midnight 16/17th and 0700 hours on the 17th that most of the casualties occurred. All the roads in the affected areas were red with bricks. . . . The result of this riot has been complete mistrust between the two communities."

Excerpts from a British military report on the Calcutta riots, India, 1946

41. The events described in the passage are best understood in the context of which of the following?

(A) Inter-religious competition fueled by colonial missionary efforts

(B) The spread of fascist ideology in South Asia

(C) Resistance to the British military draft during World War II

(D) Tensions during negotiations over the British withdrawal from India

42. The conflict described in the passage resulted most directly in which of the following?

(A) The establishment of the Non-Aligned Movement

(B) The outbreak of a Communist revolution in South Asia

(C) The partition of South Asia into India and Pakistan

(D) The strengthening of British rule over the Indian subcontinent

43. The passage best illustrates which of the following causes of global conflict in the 20th century?

(A) The challenge of redrawing inherited colonial boundaries

(B) The promotion of proxy wars during the Cold War

(C) The destructiveness of total war

(D) The influence of transnational ideologies

Questions 44 to 46 refer to the passage below.

"The ruling circles of the U.S.A., striving for world supremacy, openly declared that they could achieve their aims only from 'positions of strength.' The American imperialists unleashed the so-called cold war, and sought to kindle the flames of a third world war. In 1949, the U.S.A. set up an aggressive military bloc known as the North Atlantic Treaty Organization (NATO). As early as 1946, the Western States began to pursue a policy of splitting Germany, which was essentially completed in 1949 with the creation of a West German State. Subsequently they set out to militarize West Germany. This further deepened the division of Germany and made her reunification exceptionally difficult. A dangerous hotbed of war began to form in Europe. In the Far East the United States strove to create a hotbed of war in Japan, stationing its armed forces and building military bases on her territory."

B. N. Ponomaryov et al., *History of the Communist Party of the Soviet Union*, 1962

44. NATO as described in the passage is best understood as

    (A) an economic agreement encouraging free trade among its members

    (B) a political body promoting international cooperation

    (C) a compact of nations that threatened peace in Europe and elsewhere

    (D) a transnational agreement founded to oppose extremist groups

45. Which of the following actions best shows the Soviet Union's perception of NATO as a threat?

    (A) The Soviet creation of the eight nation Warsaw Pact

    (B) The Soviet veto of the UN's decision to defend South Korea from a North Korean invasion

    (C) The Soviet installation of nuclear missiles in Cuba

    (D) The Soviet decision to sign the Nuclear Test-Ban Treaty

46. Which of the following U.S. actions best supports a counterargument to the claim that "the American imperialists unleashed the so-called cold war"?

    (A) Accepting the creation of Soviet-style Communist governments in Eastern Europe after World War II rather than deploy troops

    (B) Continuing to recognize the Nationalists as China's rulers even after they lost their war against Chinese Communists

    (C) Supporting South Korea against North Korea in the Korean War

    (D) Stockpiling hundreds of atomic weapons before other states developed similar technology

Questions 47 to 49 refer to the passage below.

"National integration shall be actively encouraged, whilst discrimination on the grounds of place of origin, sex, religion, status, ethnic or linguistic association or ties shall be prohibited. . . .

[The Constitution shall] encourage inter-marriage among persons from different places of origin, or of different religious, ethnic or linguistic association or ties. . . .

[It shall be the duty of the State to] promote or encourage the formation of associations that cut across ethnic, linguistic, religious and or other sectional barriers."

The Nigerian Constitution, 1999

47. Which of the following trends in the last half of the twentieth century most clearly led to the the writing of the passage above?

(A) The establishment of a world led by the United States and the Soviet Union

(B) The integration of economies through globalization

(C) The spread of emerging diseases from one place to another

(D) The need to settle issues caused by the drawing of colonial boundaries

48. Which of the following best explains the reason for including a statement in the Nigerian Constitution encouraging "inter-marriage among" people of diverse backgrounds?

(A) The objective of reducing the socioeconomic gap between classes

(B) The desire to promote a unified state

(C) The support for cultural pluralism

(D) The goal of countering the spread of European religions

49. The ideas of the passage are most similar to the ideas expressed by the

(A) founding document of the International Monetary Fund

(B) Universal Declaration of Human Rights of the United Nations

(C) apartheid laws of South Africa

(D) leaders of the Bolshevik Revolution in Russia

Questions 50 to 52 refer to the graph below.

WORLD POPULATION AND CEREAL CROPS, 1961-2014

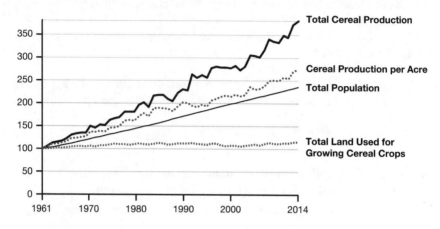

50. Which of the following best explains the overall cereal production trend shown in the graph?

(A) Mechanization of agriculture during the Industrial Revolution

(B) Expansion of women's participation in the workforce

(C) Innovations of the Green Revolution

(D) Increasing use of nuclear energy

51. Which of the following best explains the population trend shown in the graph in the period from 1961 to 2014?

(A) The expansion of social welfare programs after World War II

(B) Medical advances such as vaccines and antibiotics

(C) Improved methods of transportation and communication

(D) Rising birth rates in highly industrialized countries

52. Which of the following conclusions about cereal production is best supported by the data in this graph?

(A) It supported a growing world population.

(B) It failed to eliminate starvation and food insecurity.

(C) It led to increased deforestation and water pollution.

(D) It resulted from globalization.

Questions 53 to 55 refer to the passage below.

"The beauty of globalization is that it can free people from the tyranny of geography. Just because someone was born in France does not mean they can only aspire to speak French, eat French food, read French books, visit museums in France, and so on. . . . Globalization not only increases individual freedom, but also revitalizes cultures. . . . Thriving cultures are not set in stone. . . .

It is a myth that globalization involves the imposition of Americanized uniformity, rather than an explosion of cultural exchange. For a start, many archetypal 'American' products are not as all-American as they seem. Levi Strauss, a German immigrant, invented jeans by combining denim cloth . . . with Genes, a style of trousers worn by Genoese sailors. So Levi's jeans are in fact an American twist on a European hybrid. Even quintessentially American exports are often tailored to local tastes. MTV in Asia promotes Thai pop stars and plays rock music sung in Mandarin. CNN en Español offers a Latin American take on world news. . . . Britain's favorite takeaway is a curry, not a burger: Indian restaurants there outnumber McDonald's six to one. . . . Trendy Americans wear Gucci, Armani, Versace, Chanel. . . . Nike shoes are given a run for their money by Germany's Adidas, Britain's Reebok, and Italy's Fila."

> Philippe Legrain, "Cultural Globalization is Not Americanization,"
> *Chronicle of Higher Education,* 2003

53. The author's most likely purpose is to show that the spread of American culture is

(A) a form of imperialism spreading under the label of globalization

(B) a cause of a fundamentalist religious backlash against globalization

(C) the foundation on which globalized culture is created

(D) one influence among many leading to globalized syncretic cultures

54. Which of the following statements provides the strongest evidence to support the argument of the author in the passage?

(A) McDonald's operates restaurants in over 100 countries.

(B) Films from Hollywood dominate the global movie market.

(C) Soccer, the world's most popular sport, was spread by the British.

(D) About one billion people are fluent in English.

55. Which of the following historical developments during the second half of the 20th century is best conveyed by the passage?

(A) Popular culture increasingly reflected a globalized society.

(B) As culture became more globalized, women had more freedom.

(C) New ways to communicate reduced the role of geographic distance.

(D) New international organizations fostered international cooperation.

PART B: SHORT-ANSWER QUESTIONS

1. Use the chart below to answer all parts of the question that follows.

Transport of Enslaved Africans, 1500–1900		
Destination	**Peak Century**	**Number of People**
The Americas	18th	11,656,000
Middle East	19th	1,050,000
North Africa	19th	3,150,000
East Africa and India	19th	1,042,000
Total	18th	16,898,000

Source: Adapted from Paul Lovejoy, *Transformations in Slavery: A History of Slavery in Africa*, 1983

(A) Identify ONE way in which the transatlantic slave trade is similar to the slave trade in one of the other regions listed in the chart.

(B) Identify ONE way in which the transatlantic slave trade differed from the slave trade in one of the other regions listed in the chart.

(C) Explain ONE historical situation that contributed to the development of slavery in the 18th and 19th centuries.

2. Use the passage below to answer all parts of the question that follows.

"45. Christians are to be taught that he who sees a needy man and passes him by, yet gives his money for indulgences, does not buy papal indulgences but God's wrath.

81. This unbridled preaching of indulgences makes it difficult even for learned men to rescue the reverence which is due the pope from slander or from the shrewd questions of the laity [non-clerical members of a religion]."

Martin Luther, *The 95 Theses,* 1517

(A) Identify ONE way in which Luther believed that the selling of indulgences changed how people viewed the pope.

(B) Explain ONE way in which Luther compares what Roman Catholics were taught about indulgences and what he thinks they should have been taught.

(C) Explain ONE change that was called for by a religious reformer, other than Luther, during the Protestant Reformation.

Choose EITHER Question 3 OR Question 4.

3. **Answer all parts of the question that follows.**

   (A) Identify ONE <u>continuity</u> in the Silk Roads trade between 1200 and 1750.

   (B) Identify ONE <u>change over time</u> in Europe because of the Silk Roads trade between 1200 and 1750.

   (C) Explain ONE <u>change over time</u> in ideas and beliefs that were spread by the Silk Roads trade between 1200 and 1750.

4. **Answer all parts of the question that follows.**

   (A) Identify ONE <u>continuity</u> in international relations between the start of World War I and the start of World War II.

   (B) Identify ONE <u>change over time</u> in international relations between the start of World War I and the start of World War II.

   (C) Explain ONE way that the role of Japan in international relations showed either a <u>continuity</u> or a <u>change over time</u> between the start of World War I and the start of World War II.

Section 2

PART A: DOCUMENT-BASED QUESTION

Directions: Question 1 is based on the accompanying documents. The documents have been edited for the purpose of this exercise. You are advised to spend 15 minutes planning and 45 minutes writing your answer.

1. Evaluate the continuities or changes in the relationship between China and Great Britain between 1792 and 1864.

In your response you should do the following:

- Respond to the prompt with a historically defensible thesis or claim that establishes a line of reasoning.
- Describe a broader historical context relevant to the prompt.
- Support an argument in response to the prompt using at least four documents.
- Use at least one additional piece of specific historical evidence (beyond that found in the documents) relevant to an argument about the prompt.
- For at least two documents, explain how or why the document's point of view, purpose, historical situation, and/or audience is relevant to an argument.
- Demonstrate a complex understanding of a historical development related to the prompt through a sophisticated argument and/or effective use of evidence.

Source: *AP® World History Course and Exam Description*

Document 1

Source: British historian Arnold Toynbee, *A Study of History* (1947), depiction of Britain's first ambassador to China, Lord Macartney, during his initial meeting with the Chinese Emperor Qianlong, 1793.

Note: Lord Macartney, with a large feather in his hat, is kneeling center-right and presenting the emperor with a gift.

Document 2

Source: Chinese Emperor Qianlong, letter to Britain's King George III, 1793.

The Celestial Court of China has pacified and possessed the territory within the four seas. Its sole aim is to do its utmost to achieve good government and to manage political affairs, attaching no value to strange jewels and precious objects. The various articles presented by you, O King, this time are accepted by my special order to the office in charge of such functions in consideration of the offerings having come from a long distance with sincere good wishes.

As a matter of fact, the virtue and prestige of the Celestial Dynasty of China having spread far and wide, the kings of the myriad nations come by land and sea with all sorts of precious things. Consequently there is nothing we lack, as your principal envoy and others have themselves observed. We have never set much store on strange and ingenious objects, nor do we need any more of your country's manufactures.

Document 3

Source: Chinese Emperor Qianlong, letter to Britain's King George III, 1793.

In my travels in China, I often perceived the ground to be hollow under a vast superstructure, and in institutions of the most stately and flourishing appearance I discovered symptoms of speedy decay. In fact the volume of the empire is now grown too ponderous and disproportionate to be easily grasped by a single hand, be it ever so strong. . . . I should not be surprised if its dislocation or dismemberment were to take place in my lifetime.

A sudden transition from slavery to freedom, from dependence to authority, can seldom be borne with moderation or discretion. Every change in the state of man ought to be gentle and gradual, otherwise it is commonly dangerous to himself and intolerable to others. The Chinese, if not led to freedom from the grip of the Emperor gradually, but let loose on a burst of enthusiasm would probably fall into all the excesses of folly, suffer all the symptoms of madness, and be found as unfit for the enjoyment of freedom as the French.

Document 4

Source: Lin Zexu, Imperial Commissioner stationed in Chinese port of Canton, letter to Queen Victoria about British East Indies imports of opium into the port, 1839.

We find that your country is sixty or seventy thousand li from China. Yet there are barbarian ships that strive to come here for trade for the purpose of making a great profit. The wealth of China is used to profit the barbarians . . . . By what right do they use this poisonous drug to injure the Chinese people?

I have heard that the smoking of opium is very strictly forbidden by your country; that is because the harm caused by opium is very clearly understood. Since it is not permitted to do harm in your country, then even less should you allow it to be passed on to do harm in other countries. Of all that China exports to other countries, there is not a single thing that is not beneficial to people: they are of benefit when eaten, or of benefit when used, or of benefit when resold: all are beneficial. This is for no other reason than to share the benefits with the people of the whole world . . . . We have heard heretofore that your honorable ruler is kind and benevolent. Naturally you would not wish to give unto others what you yourself do not want.

Document 5

Source: Excerpts from The Treaty of Nanking (Nanjing) at the end of the Opium Wars between Britain and China, 1842.

Article II

His Majesty the Emperor of China agrees that British Subjects, with their families and establishments, shall be allowed to reside, for the purpose of carrying on their commercial pursuits without molestation or restraint at the Cities and Towns of Canton, Amoy, Foochow fu, Ningpo, and Shanghai.

Article III

His Majesty the Emperor of China cedes to Her Majesty the Queen of Great Britain, etc., the Island of Hong Kong, to be possessed forever by her Britannic Majesty, Her Heirs and Successors, and to be governed by such Laws and Regulations as Her Majesty the Queen of Great Britain, etc., shall see fit to direct.

Article VII

It is agreed that the Total amount of Twenty one Millions of Dollars shall be paid from China to Britain as follows: Six Millions immediately. Six Millions in 1843, Five Millions in 1844, Four Millions in 1845.

Document 6

Source: Chris Feige and Jeffrey A. Miron, "The Opium Wars, Opium Legalization, and Opium Consumption in China," *Applied Economics Letters* 15(12): 911–913.

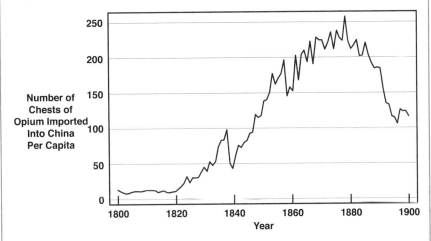

Note: In the First Opium War China fought Britain from 1837-1842. In the Second Opium War, China fought Britain, France, Russia, and the United States from 1856-1860.

Document 7

Source: Chinese Qing Dynasty Royal Decree of a Declaration of War against Foreign Powers, 1900.

For more than 200 plus years, the Royal court had always acted in deep kindness, those foreigners came from faraway, our ancestors had always treated them with respect. During the reign of Daoguang Emperor and Xianfeng Emperor, foreigners began to be allowed to trade with China [late 1700s and early 1800s]. . .

In the past, the Royal court had treated these foreigners like one would treat one's own neighbors, never did the court offend them. They call themselves educated nations, yet they do whatever they like here in China, just because they have strong army and powerful weapons - they have wanted to break off the good relationship with China.

. . . we shall not live a miserable and submissive life, be shamed in history for the next ten thousand years, we should fight this war in a big way . . . The foreigners have cunning and deceptive plans, we hold the rules from heaven, the foreigners relied on brute force, we have the support of the heart of the people. China has many loyal patriots, they are not afraid to die. We have more than 20 provinces, a huge population of 400 million, it is not difficult to put out the foreigners fierce fire, to showcase the might of our nation.

PART B: LONG ESSAY QUESTION

Directions: Answer Question 2 OR Question 3 OR Question 4. On the exam, you will be given 40 minutes to answer one question.

2. In the 13th century, various belief systems and practices infiltrated South and Southeast Asia.

   Develop an argument that evaluates the extent to which Hinduism, Islam, and Buddhism changed political or social structures in South and Southeast Asia.

3. In the 15th century, growth of interregional trade and innovation promoted the growth of new trading cities.

   Develop an argument that evaluates the extent to which Indian Ocean trading contributed to the development of new states.

4. In the 20th century, a variety of internal and external factors contributed to state decline.

   Develop an argument that evaluates the extent to which challenges to colonial rule changed South Asian society in the period between 1750 and 2001.

In your response, you should do the following:

- Respond to the prompt with a historically defensible thesis or claim that establishes a line of reasoning.
- Describe a broader historical context relevant to the prompt.
- Support an argument in response to the prompt using at least two pieces of specific and relevant evidence.
- Use historical reasoning (e.g., comparison, causation, continuity or change) to frame or structure an argument that addresses the prompt.
- Demonstrate a complex understanding of a historical development related to the prompt through sophisticated argumentation and/or effective use of evidence.

Source: *AP World History Course and Exam Description*

Index

A

Abbas I (Abbas the Great), 148
Abbasid Empire
 Abbasid caliphate, lv
 Abbasids, lv
 class and diversity in, 17
 commerce of, 17
 culture, 16–17
 economic competition of, 16
 invasions of
  Crusaders, 16
  Egyptian Mamluks, 15
  Mongols, 16
  Seljuk Turks, 15
 slavery, 17–18
 state-building, 65
 women in, 18
Abdulhamid, 336
Abelard, Peter, 53
Abolitionism, 280
Aboriginals, 391, 392
Absolute monarchy, 155
Abyssinia, 379, 486
Accords, Camp David, 590
Achaemenid Empire, xlviii
Acoma Revolt of 1599, 249
Acquired immunodeficiency syndrome (AIDS), 644
Adams, Abigail, 283
Afghanistan, 384, 603, 609, 618, 621, 643, 683
Afonso (king), 226
Africa. *See also* Sub-Saharan Africa
 Bantu-speakers in, 43–44
 christianity in, l
 Cold War and, 618
 cultural life in, 49, 212, 402
 dar al-Islam in, 19
 economic imperialism in, 409–411
 European scramble for, 377–378
 expansion of Islam, 113, lvii–lviii
 foods of, 236
 French in, 376
 Indians in, 432
 music of, 212
 political structures of, 43–44, 45–47
 Portuguese in, 200
 post-classical civilizations, lvii–lviii
 railroads in, 326, 399
 scramble for, 377
 slavery, 17–18, 48
 slave trade in, 225
 social structures of, 47–48
 trade in, 44–45
 trading posts in, 219
 visual arts in, 49

African Diaspora, 212
African National Congress (ANC), 671
African slave trade, 239, 418, 420. *See also* Atlantic
 Slave Trade.
African States, 219
Africanus, Leo, 72
Afrikaners, 377
Afro-Eurasia, 214
 cultural influences of Islam in, 29, 113
Agricultural revolution, 297, xlii
Agriculture
 cash crops, 212, 399
 collective, 555
 collectivized, 483
 effects, of exchange networks, 121–123
 Green Revolution, 634
 growing population and urbanization, 300
 in Middle Ages, 54
 in Sub-Saharan Africa, 43
 technologies and, 709
 urbanization and, 650
Ahmad, Muhammad, 394
Aircraft carriers, 515
Airplanes, 470
Air quality, 649
A'ishah al-Ba'uniyyah, 17
Akbar (the Great), 159–160, 252
Ala-ad Din Ata-Malik Juvaini, 93
al-Andalus, 19
al-Bakri, Ubaydallah, 73
Al-Bashir, Omar, 527
Al-Beruni, 30
Alcohol, 404
Algeria, 581–582
Algerian Civil War, 582
Algerian War for Independence, 581
Alighieri, Dante, 60
Ali, Muhammad, 318
Ali, Sunni, 164
Allies, 463, 525, 616
Al-Qaeda, 603
Al-Sharif, Manal, 692
Alzheimer's disease, 645
Amaru II, Túpac, 389
Amazon, 690
Americanization, 681
Americas
 Chaco and Mesa Verde, 34
 civilizations, li
 comparison with, 39
 continuities and diversity, 39
 declaration of independence, 285
 effect of migration, 430
 Europeans in, 220–222

Canada, 585
Canal system, 433
Candide (Voltaire), 276
Candomblé, 237
Cannon, 91
Cape Colony, 377
Capital, 232, 300, 313
Capitalism, 263, 277, 555
Caravansaries, lii
Caravanserai, 79
Carbon footprint, 652
Cárdenas, Lázaro, 485, 489
Caribbean region, 432
Carpa Nan, 38
Cartier, Jacques, 203
Cartography, 191
Cash crops, 211, 212, 399, 409
Castas, 256
Caste reservation system, 672–673
Castro, Fidel, 565, 569
Catherine II (Empress), 383
Catholic Reformation, 170
Centralized Bureaucracy, 179
Central Powers, 463
Central Treaty Organization (CENTO), 564
Ceylon, 379
Chamberlain, Neville, 506
Champa rice, 4, 121
Champlain, Samuel de, 203
Chang, Ha-Joon, 623
Charles V, 169
Chattel slavery, 218
Chengdong, Li, 254
Cherokee nation, 389
Child labor, 333, 345, 689
Chile
    economic liberalization in, 658
    minerals, 402
    mining in, 412
China
    agricultural productivity, 4–5
    Buddhism in, 8, 111
    bureaucracy, 3
    Civil service reform, 3–4, 337
    communism in, 571–572
    economic developments in, 4–6
    economic imperialism in, 408–409
    exploration of, 200
    external challenges, 454–455
    foreign powers and, 337
    Grand Canal, 4
    human rights repression in, 673
    imperial bureaucracy, 3
    intellectual and cultural developments, 7–8
    internal challenges, 454
    Japan and, 9–10
    Korea and, 10–11
    liberalization, Economic, 658
    manufacturing and trade, 5
    markets in, 12
    May Fourth Movement in, 497
    meritocracy, 3–4
    minority rights in, 674
    neo-confucianism, 9
    postclassical China, 4–5
    proto-industrialization, 5
    reform in, 336–337
    relations with the Soviets, 572
    Republic of, 455
    social structures in
        class structure, 6
        role of women, 7
    Song Dynasty in, 3–4, 9
    spread of Islam, 95–96
    state-building in, 65, 66
    Tang Dynasty, 8, 11
    taoism, 8
    taxes, 6
    trade, 95–96
    tributary system, 6
    Vietnam and, 11
Chinatowns (Chinese enclaves), 435
Chinese Communist Party (CCP), 498
Chinese enclaves, 430
Chinese Exclusion Act, 434
Chinese Immigration Act, 434–435
Chinese Immigration Regulation and Restriction Act, 435
Cholera, 642, 719
Christianity, xlix–l, lix, 46, 173
Churchill, Winston, 511, 513, 554
Cities and towns
    declining cities, 114–115
    effects of the Crusades, 115
    factors contributing to growth, 114
    growth of trading cities, 129
Citrus crops, 122
Civil disobedience, 496
Civilizations
    China, xliii
    early American civilizations, li
    Egypt, xlii–xliii
    Indus, xliii
    Mesopotamia
        first civilization in, xlii
    non-river valley civilizations, xliii
Civilizing mission, 368
Civil Rights Act, 670
Cixi, Dowager, 337, 380
Classical age
    early trade networks, lii
    fall of empires, liii
    government in, lii
Classical liberalism, 279
Class structure. See Social classes
Clemenceau, Georges, 474, 494
Climate activism, 653
Clough, Shepard B., 302
Coal, 310

Coaling stations, 311
Coal Revolution, 310–312
Code of chivalry, 54
Coercive labor system, 223
Cold War, 549–550, 554–558, 608
  arms race, 557, 617
  economic effects of, 619–620
  growth of globalization, 621
  political effects of, 618–619
  proxy wars, 562, 564
  social and cultural effects, 620–621
College of Manufacturers, 187
Colonial crops, 411
Colonialism
  resolution on, 630
Colonial legacy, 670
Colonial service, 422
Colonies, 224
  administration of, 236
  African, 375–376
  in the Americas, 263
  cultural changes, 237
  effects of World War I, 493–494
  Japan, 380, 422–423
  penal, 381
  political changes, 236
  resources from, 299
  settler, 376
  Spanish colonialism, challenges to, 289
  struggles for power in England, 246
Colonization Society, 380, 422
Columbian Exchange, 189, 209, 213–214
Columbus, Christopher, 196
Commercial extraction, 403
Commercial Revolution, 233, 662
Common Sense (Paine), 278
Communes, 571
Communications, 312, 633, 708
Communism, 334, 555, 571–572
  communists, 453
Communist bloc, 563
Communist Manifesto, 334
Company rule, 306
Compass, 193
Compton, Karl T., 519
Concentration camps, 377
Condit, Phil, 695
Confucianism
  Analects, xlvii
  developments in East Asia, xlvii
Congo, 377–378
Congo Free State, 378
Cong, Viet, 583
Conquistadores, 210, 223
Conscription, 469
Conservatism, 275, 278
Constantinople, l, 114
Consumer culture, 679, 694
Consumerism, 327
Containment, 556

Contra War, 567
Copper, 402
Corporations, 325, 326–327
Corporatism, 485
Cortés, Hernán, 210
Corvée labor, 308, 376
Cotton, 298, 304, 401, 407, 410, 411
Council for Mutual Economic Assistance
  (COMECON), 557
Council of Trent, 170
Counter-Reformation, 170
Cradle of civilization, 595
Creole, 212
Creole Revolutions, 288
Criollos, 255, 389
Crop rotation, 297
Crossbreeding, 634
Crothers, Lane, 686
Crusades, 58
  Crusaders, 16
Cuban Missile crisis, 565–566
Cultural ideologies, 369
Cultural Revolution, 572
Culture
  Aboriginal people, 391
  American Indians, 210
  consumer, 679
  consumerism, 327
  effects of migration, 430
  Greece, 292
  Indian, 432
  Korea, 10
  Mississippian, 33
  Mongol, 85
  nomadic, 90
  popular, 680
  Roman, xlviii
  Russian, 89
  scientific and technological innovations, 113–114
  technological effects, of interaction, 111
Czechoslovakia, 506, 600

D

Daguan, Zhou, 139
Dahomey, 236
Daimyo, 159
Dalits (untouchables), 672
Danzig, 506
Daoism, xlvii
Dar al-Islam, lv, 26, 95, 117
Darfur, 527
Darwin, Charles, 368
D-Day, 516
De Beers Mining Company, 402
Debt relief, 692. *See also* Debt restructuring
Debt restructuring, 692
de Busbecq, Ogier Ghiseline, 272
Declaration of Sentiments, 280
Declaration of the Rights of Man, 286

Liverpool, 300
Livingstone, David, 370
Locke, John, 276, 285
Lola Rodríguez de Tió, 289
Long March, 498
Lost Generation, 523
Lotzer, Sebastian, 270
Louis XIV, 156, 254
L'Ouverture, Toussaint, 287
Loyalists, 486
Luce, Henry, 685
Luftwaffe, 487, 513
Lure of Sugar, 211
Lusitania, 471
Lutheranism, 168
Luther, Martin, 168, 599–600

M

Maathai, Wangari, 674
MacArthur, Douglas, 515, 564
Machine guns, 470
Madero, Francisco, 457
Magellan, Ferdinand, 201
Magna Carta, 56
Magnetic compass, 78, 114, 193
Mahdi, 394
Mahdist Revolt, 394
Mahindra & Mahindra, 662
Mahmud II, 334
Maholtra, Naresh, 694
Maistry, 420
Maize, 211
Majapahit Kingdom, 28
Malacca, 97
Malaria, 641–642
Malaya, 381
Malaysia, 96
Mali, 46, 105–106
Mamluks, 15, 318
Mamluk Sultanate, 15
Manchester, 300
Manchu, 145
Manchukuo, 498
Mandate system, 494–495
Mandela, Nelson, 600, 671, 676
Manifest Destiny, 382
Manila, 201
Mann, Charles, 40
Manorial System, 54
Mansa, 179
Mansa Musa, 72, 106
Manufacturing, 305–306, 660–661
Maori, 382
Maori Wars, 392
Maquiladoras, 660
Maratha Empire, 245
March First Movement, 497
Marconi, Gugliemo, 313
Marco Polo, 58

Mariam, Mengistu Haile, 574
Maritime empires, 192
Maroons, 287
Maroon wars, 246
Marshall Plan, 507, 556–557
Marxist-Leninist-Stalinist totalitarian state, 614
Marx, Karl, 334
Mary II, 246
Mass culture, 327
Mass production, 347
Matamba, 243
Matrilineal society, 33
Mauritius, 432
Maximilian, 390
Mayan civilization
    government in, 34
    religion in, 34–35
    science and technology, 35
May Fourth Movement, 497
May, Theresa, 691
Mazzini, Giuseppe, 290
Mcelwee, Sean, 656
Means of production, 334
Medical innovations, 635–636
Medical science, 707–708
Mediterranean Sea, lii
Mehmed II, 252
Meiji Restoration, 319, 338
Mein Kampf (My Struggle), 504
Melaka, *See* Malacca
Mercantilism, 200, 224, 263
Mesoamerica, li
Mestizos, 256, 288
Metacom's War, 243, 246
Metropole, 594
Mexican Revolution, 457
Mexicas. *See* Aztecs
Mexico, 484–485, 660
Mexico City, 221
Microsoft, 662
Middle Kingdom, 8
Middle Passage, 226
Migrations
    China, 420
    discrimination and, 442
    effect of, 429–435
    India, 420
    Indians in Africa, 432
    Ireland, 420–421
    Italian emigration, 422
    labor systems and, 417
    out of Africa, xli
    regulation of, 434–435
    to settler colonies, 422
    slavery, 418
    voluntary patterns of, 424
Militarism, 462–463
Military
    centralized bureaucracy, 179–180
    Mughal Empires, 179

Sailendra dynasty, lv
Saint-Simon, Henri de, 279
Salk, Jonas, 643
Salt March, 496
Salt Riot in Moscow, 272
Samarkand, 79, 114
Sanders, Senator Bernie, 666
Sands, Bobby, 605
Santería, 237
Satellite countries, 556
Satyagraha ("devotion-to-truth") movement, 496
Saving Private Ryan, 469
Schappeler, Christoph, 270
Scientific racism, 504
Scientific Revolution, 173
Scots-Irish, 433
Scramble for Africa, 377
Second World, 616
Seed drill, 297
Selassie, Haile, 574
Self-determination, 464, 475, 550
Self-Strengthening Movement, 336
Seljuk Turks, 15
Senghor, Léopold Sédar, 669
Separatists, 602
Sepharad, 255
Sepoys, 390
Serfdom, 157, 280
Serfs, 54, 255
Settler colony, 376
Seven Years' War, 379
Seydi-Ali, 271
Shah, 148
Shanghai Banking Corporation, 326
Shariah, 172
Sheth, Jagdish, 694
Shining Path, 602
Shirer, William, 536
Shogunate, Tokugawa, 159
Siam, 381
Siebold, P. F., 361
Siege of Leningrad, 514
Siege weapons, 87
Sierra Leone, 376
Sikhism, 172
Silent Revolution, 585
Silk Roads, 127
    demand for luxury goods, 77
    effects of, 78–81
    growth of exchange networks, 77–78
    innovations in commerce, 81
    Kashgar, 78
    transportation technologies, improvements in, 78
Silver, 223–224
Simony, 168
Sinhala dynasties, 28
Sino-Japanese War, 336, 368
Six Day War, 590
Slavery and enslaved people
    in Africa, 411

capture and shipment, to the Americas, 225–226
chattel, 218
demographic, social, and cultural changes, 227
forced labor, 211
gender distributions, 236
Indian Ocean Slave Trade, 227–228
migration and, 417
trade, 96
transatlantic trade, 211
Slums, 343
Smallpox, 641
Smith, Adam, 277, 325, 623
Social classes
    casta system, 255–256
    caste reservation, 672
    Europe, 254–255
    India, 252
    Ottoman social system, 251–252
    in Russia, 255
    treatment of religious minorities, 252
Social contract, 276
Social Darwinism, 368
Socialism, 275, 334
Social media, 682
Soil erosion, 123
Songhai Kingdom, 106
South Africa, 377, 670–671
South Asia. S*ee specific countries*
    anti-colonialism in, 495–496
    centralization of power, 159
    cultural interactions in, 26–27
    Islam in, 25
    Northern India, political structures in, 24–25
    political structures in Southern India, 23–24
    rebellion in, 245
    social structures in, 26
    women power in, 593–594
South Asian Movements, 390
Southeast Asia. *See specific countries*
    British in, 381
    effect of migration, 430
    French in, 381
    Hinduism and Buddhism in, 113
    Islam in, 29, 113
    land-based kingdoms, 28
    sea-based kingdoms, 28
    Sufis in, 29
Southeast Asia Treaty Organization (SEATO), 564
Soviet-Afghan War, 609
Soviet Union
    Cold War and, 549
    Communism in, 555
    effects of Cold War in, 618–619
    end of Cold War in, 608–609, 611
    satellite countries, 555–556
    under Joseph Stalin, 483–484
    Warsaw Pact and, 563–564
    World War II and, 513
Space Race, 557
Spain

War/warfare
  advances during, 549
  massive destruction in Europe, 548
  start of the Cold War, 549–550
Water scarcity, 650
Water transportation, 310–311
Watt, James, 310
Wave Science, 707
Wealth of Nations, 325
Weapons, arms race, 617
Weibo, 692
Weimar Republic, 475, 503
West Africa
  empire expansion of, 105–107
  French rule in, 499
Western Eurasia, empires in, 107
Western Eurasia and Christianity
  Greece, xlviii
  Persia, xlviii
  Rome, xlviii–xlix
Western Europe, 352
Western Hemisphere, 619
White Australia Policy, 435
White-collar workers, 345, 433
White Legend, 265
White Lotus Society, 90
White Revolution, 573, 578
Whitney, Eli, 298
Wilkinson, Stephan, 569
William of Orange, 246
Wilson, Woodrow, 474, 494
Witte, Sergei, 307
Wollstonecraft, Mary, 282, 284
Women
  Industrial Revolution and, 345–346
  in Islam, 18
  in Safavid Empire, 149
  during World War I, 474
  voting rights for, 669–670
Working class, 344
World Bank, 701
World Fair Trade Organization (WFTO), 675
World Food Program (WFP), 700
World Health Organization (WHO), 636
World Revolution, 556
World Trade Organization (WTO), 662
World War I
  alliances, 463
  casualties, 522
  causes of, 461–464
  colonial soldiers in, 532
  consequences of, 464–465
  defeat of Germany, 456
  effects of, 493–494
  global war, 472–473
  Paris Peace Conference, 474–475
  reparations, 475
  total war, 471
  Treaty of Versailles, 475
  U.S. entrance, 471

  warfare during, 469–471
  women in, 474
World War II
  Axis powers, 504
  British-American relations, 513
  casualties of, 523–525
  causes of, 503–507
  colonial armies in, 514
  consequences of, 507
  early German victories in, 512
  home fronts in, 514–515
  Japanese imperialism and, 511–512
  last years of, 516
  Pearl Harbor, 514
  victory in, 516–516

X

Xhosa, 392
Xhosa Cattle Killing Movement, 393

Y

Yaa Asantewaa War, 394
Yalta Conference, 547–548
Yat-sen, Sun, 454, 455
Yom Kippur War, 590
Yousafzai, Malala, 682
Yuan Dynasty, 89
Yuanzhang, Zhu, 90
Yukichi, Fukuzawa, 449
Yunus, Muhammad, 690

Z

Zaibatsu, 321
Zambos, 256
Zamindars, 160
Zanj Rebellion, 48
Zapata, Emiliano, 457
Zechariah, 21
Zedong, Mao, 498, 571, 572, 602, 710
Zimbabwe, 46–47
Zimmermann Telegram, 471
Zionism, 281
Zionist movement, 589
Zionists, 495
Zoroastrianism, xliv
Zulu, 393